# WEALTH PLANNING STRATEGIES FOR CANADIANS 2011

Christine Van Cauwenberghe

B.Comm. (Hons), LL.B., CFP, TEP

CARSWELL®

ISBN 978-0-7798-2702-2

**A cataloguing record for this publication is available from Library and Archives Canada.**

Composition: Computer Composition of Canada Inc.

Printed in Canada by Thomson Reuters

THOMSON REUTERS

CARSWELL, A DIVISION OF THOMSON REUTERS CANADA LIMITED

One Corporate Plaza
2075 Kennedy Road
Toronto, Ontario
M1T 3V4

Customer Relations
Toronto: 1-416-609-3800
Elsewhere in Canada/U.S.: 1-800-387-5164
Fax 1-416-298-5082
www.carswell.com
E-mail www.carswell.com/email

*To Christopher*
*and Andrew*

# FOREWORD

As one may gather from Ms. Van Cauwenberghe's introductory chapter, "wealth planning" is an elusive concept. It is not unreasonable to suggest that the phrase has as many meanings as there are speakers who utter it — or, for that matter, listeners who hear it. In the author's view, it comprises financial planning, tax planning, disability planning, estate planning and insurance planning, as well as a consideration of family law issues — all of which are addressed in this book. The author makes two key observations: firstly, that the topic should be of interest not only to the affluent, but to anyone who is concerned about his or her future and the future of his or her family; and, secondly, that individuals should be concerned not only with financial well-being but with personal well-being too.

The financial advisor would be astonished — and overwhelmed — by the complex legal web forming the overlay to individual wealth planning; a web made up of firstly, the myriad of applicable statutes and, secondly, the countless court decisions arising over the decades — and, occasionally, over centuries! Pitfalls confront individuals at every turn, there to spring surprises on the unsuspecting who may be labouring under one or more misapprehensions as to the state of the law: to name just three such misconceptions, the belief that a party to a common-law relationship, if it lasts long enough, automatically acquires all of the property rights of a party to a legal marriage; the belief that a surviving spouse is entitled to inherit all of the property of the deceased spouse who dies without a will; and the belief that marital property is always split 50-50 on separation or divorce.

Ms. Van Cauwenberghe has done an admirable job of laying out, in an organized and well-thought out fashion, the categories of marital and family relationships; the multi-faceted planning issues arising from special assets – for example, vacation properties (including the "dreaded family cottage") and business interests; and the variation in the legal rules from one provincial jurisdiction to another. Readers will better appreciate the complexities that can arise from rather mundane fact situations by virtue of the case studies found at the end of most of the 25 chapters comprising this book. Equally useful are the reference materials contained in Part III of the book.

While the book's sheer size may be intimidating, lay readers should find the language quite user-friendly — a noteworthy accomplishment for any lawyer-author. That having been said, this work is not intended as a substitute for proper and timely professional advice. None the less, it does an excellent job of helping the financial advisor to identify issues that should be examined critically in the wealth planning exercise. Armed with the information this book provides, the lay person will be well prepared to follow through with his or her professional adviser(s).

Barry S. Corbin
Corbin Estates Law Professional Corporation

# ACKNOWLEDGMENTS

Writing a book, especially on a technical topic, can be a long and arduous task. Fortunately, I am surrounded by individuals who continue to support and inspire me every day. I am grateful for their help, as they encouraged me to continue my pursuit, and made the effort much more enjoyable.

First, I would like to thank my family and friends, especially my husband, Chris, who read through the entire manuscript and gave many helpful comments. It is quite amusing to hear a prosecutor talk about jurisdictional advantages as to where to die. I also thank my parents, Ray and Ria, my sister and brother-in-law, Sonia and Kyle, and my mother- and father-in-law, Anita and Armand, who encouraged me throughout the process.

I would also like to thank my work colleagues, who truly are a pleasure to work with, and from whom I learn something every day – Debbie Ammeter, Dave Ablett, Bob Allebone, Nicole Boulette, Aurele Courcelles, Jack Courtney, Tannis Dawson, Caroline Gervais, Myron Knodel, Sara Kinnear, Jack Littleton, Josee Maure, Jane Olshewski, Murray Pituley, Mark Probyn, Richard Reif, Marie-Claude Riendeau, Todd Sigurdson, Mike Turenne, Normand Verville and Larry Wozney. Special thanks to Marie-Claude Riendeau for providing her comments on the Quebec portions of the manuscript. I also appreciate all the knowledge I have acquired from the financial planners who I deal with regularly – they are very committed to their profession and their clients, and constantly motivate me to work harder to find better alternatives for the problems they and their clients face.

I have been privileged to meet a number of wealth planning practitioners and authors who were very generous with their time and comments, and I appreciate their willingness to help with my project. These individuals include Barry Corbin, a well respected estate planning lawyer and the co-author of *Best of Money and Family Law: Valuation, Division, Taxation and Succession,* who took time from his busy schedule to read the draft manuscript and write the foreword to the book; Sandy Cardy, author of *The Cottage, the Spider Brooch and the Second Wife;* Tim Cestnick, author of *Winning the Tax Game;* Jean Blacklock, author of *Food for Thought: Bringing Estate Planning to Life;* Evelyn Jacks, author of *Essential Tax Facts;* John Poyser, co-author of *Practitioner's Guide to Trusts, Estates and Trust Returns;* Joel Cuperfain, co-editor of *Canadian Taxation of Life Insurance;* and Kurt Rosentretor, author of *Wealth Building.*

I am also fortunate to have several friends and colleagues who have provided me with very useful information regarding the publishing process outside of the wealth planning industry. These individuals include Sheldon Bowles (co-author of *Gung Ho!* and *Raving Fans)*, Jill Hart (who was involved with *Reindeer Days Remembered*), Prof. Jennifer Schulz (co-author of *Alternative Dispute Resolution Practice Manual*), and Brian Mennis (author of *Average to Awesome: The 8 Keys to Make a Quantum Leap*). I would also like to thank my good friends Kingsley Bowles, Stuart Ash and Silvia de Sousa for their valued counsel regarding intellectual property law issues, and I appreciate the support of Dan Collison and Lisa Collins, two excellent wealth planners with lots of experience in teaching and providing information to financial advisors.

Last, but definitely not least, I would like to thank my publisher, Carswell, and all the people there who have assisted in the publication of this book, particularly Gail Armstrong, Elda Sherman, Ken Mathies and Andrew Lawetz as well as Catherine Leek from Green Onion Publishing. I have appreciated your advice and support, and the fact that you had confidence in the value of the book from the very beginning.

March 2010

# TABLE OF CONTENTS — OVERVIEW

# TABLE OF CONTENTS

## Part I
## Introduction

### Chapter 1 — Introduction to Wealth Planning



## Part II
## Life Scenarios

### Chapter 2 — Single

**Chapter 3 — Common-Law Couples**

**Chapter 7 — Divorced**



**Chapter 8 — Blended Families**

**Chapter 9 — Widowed**

**Chapter 13 — Elderly Parents**

**Chapter 14 — Seniors and Retirees**

**Chapter 16 — Business Owners**

# Part III
# Reference Chapters

## Chapter 17 — Family Property

**Chapter 18 — Powers of Attorney**

**Chapter 19 — Distribution of an Estate**

**Chapter 20 — Personal Representatives**

## Chapter 23 — Trusts



## Chapter 24 — Charitable Giving

**Chapter 25 — Insurance**

# Part

# INTRODUCTION

# CHAPTER 1

# INTRODUCTION TO WEALTH PLANNING



## 1.1 WHAT IS WEALTH PLANNING?

The phrase "wealth planning" has been used in many contexts. Many people believe that wealth planning is only necessary if you are "wealthy". But what does wealth really mean? The definition is different for everyone. Many people define wealth strictly based on financial assets. Therefore, they feel that if they do not have significant financial assets, no planning is necessary. This could not be farther from the truth.

This book is geared not only towards those who have a large financial portfolio. It is for anyone who is concerned about their future and their family's future, and wants to ensure that a lack of planning will not result in unnecessary hardship in the event of an unforeseen event, such as a disability or premature death. "Wealth" can be comprised of non-financial assets as well — peace of mind and a happy family are things many people want to protect. For many families, the most important assets are family heirlooms, not financial assets. In the case of families with young children, the issue of guardianship is usually paramount in their minds.

Regardless of your particular set of priorities, the only way in which you can ensure that your wishes will be carried out is by structuring a plan, usually with the assistance of an advisor. If you do not prepare a proper wealth plan, you could inadvertently disinherit family members, either due to an unforeseen tax liability, or due to the fact that you did not understand how the law would apply when distributing your estate. In a worst case scenario, a lack of planning could lead to litigation between family members, leaving a legacy of pain and resentment. Becoming the leading case in the law reports is usually not the way most people would wish to be remembered for all time.

In many ways, wealth planning is more about emotion than money. The most important part of your wealth plan is to determine what is important to you. Once you have identified your needs, you will be able to work with an advisor to ensure these needs will be satisfied. For most individuals, their priorities include securing their own financial future, securing the financial future of their family and loved ones, and, if possible, leaving a legacy for others to enjoy. The strategies used to achieve these objectives will be different for each person, and the purpose of this book is to highlight which strategies may be most appropriate for you. The overarching message of this book is that everyone, no matter what their personal circumstances, could benefit from a well thought out wealth plan.

## 1.2 THE WEALTH PLANNING PROCESS

Most people take a haphazard approach to wealth planning. They address isolated issues only, and often do not understand how the various components of their wealth plan must be consistent in order to operate properly. Here are the key components of a wealth plan that must be addressed.

### 1.2.1 Financial Planning

Financial planning involves a review of your financial situation and a determination of your goals and needs for the present and future. For example, based on projections, you and your financial advisor will determine how much you will need to achieve certain objectives (e.g. retire at age 60, send your children to university, etc.), and how much you will need to save on an annual basis in order to achieve those objectives. The amount you will need to save will be based in large part on the amount of time you have to achieve your goals, and the level of risk you are prepared to incur in order to possibly earn higher returns. The aim of this book is not to advise you as to which investments may be best for you — there are mountains of books which attempt to identify which types of investments are suited for which types of investors. The purpose of this book is only to highlight the need for financial planning in certain circumstances (e.g. Have you planned for retirement? Have you planned for your children's education?), and recommend various strategies for achieving those goals (e.g. RRSPs, RESPs, etc.).

## 1.2.2 Tax Planning

Taxation plays a significant role in the wealth of every Canadian. If less is paid in tax to the various civic, provincial and federal governments, more will be available for personal use. However, the *Income Tax Act* is extremely complicated, and almost incomprehensible to the average Canadian. This book will identify those tax planning techniques that could be most beneficial to you, and those rules that could have the most significant impact on your wealth plan. For example, many Canadians do not understand how income tax will affect their estate at the time of death, mistakenly assuming that probate fees will have the largest impact. Generally speaking, probate fees are insignificant, and the focus of your planning efforts should be directed towards saving income tax. In fact, in many cases, certain probate planning techniques will work at cross-purposes with many strategies which attempt to reduce income taxes. It is important to understand which tax planning strategies are relevant for you in order to determine how to best structure your wealth plan.

## 1.2.3 Family Law Issues

Many aspects of your wealth plan can be inadvertently hijacked by family law rules. If you do not understand what rights your common-law partner, spouse or children (and in some cases, parents, grandparents, siblings and grandchildren) have against your assets, you could be exposing yourself to financial problems. These rules may be relevant even if you do not experience a breakdown in your relationship, since many laws regarding the support of dependants and the division of property are also relevant at the time of death.

Entering or ending a relationship is a major life change which must be factored into your wealth plan. There are some basic techniques which can be used to protect your assets (or the assets of your children) from a family property claim, but in many cases, these strategies must be implemented well in advance of a relationship breakdown. Understanding how the family laws work in your jurisdiction may help you to structure your wealth plan in a manner which will provide you (or your children) with more protection.

Family laws must also be carefully examined prior to making gifts to a family member, or loaning them money. In many cases, individuals come to regret the decisions they have made, simply because they did not understand how other people could make claims against their property, or the property they gave to children or other family members. Again, many individuals feel this is an issue only for the wealthy. In reality, it is also an issue for the not so wealthy, as they have less to lose, and may therefore require more protection.

## 1.2.4 Disability Planning

No one likes to think about the possibility that some day they may become disabled. However, the reality is that many Canadians do suffer from a temporary or permanent disability at some point in their life. In fact, young Canadians are far more likely to suffer a permanent disability than die, so every adult Canadian, no matter what their age, should be prepared.

The reason for doing this type of planning is not just to make your own life easier, but also to provide some guidance to your family and caregivers in the event you are not able to communicate for a period of time. Many people are under the mistaken assumption that if something happens to them, either a spouse, common-law partner or child will automatically have the authority to make financial and health care decisions for them. However, in many cases this is not true. Therefore, disability planning can help to prevent the need for your family to go to court to ask permission to act on your behalf — given that your family will already be traumatized by your disability, having to go to court would be a waste of their energies. The main parts of your disability plan should include:

- a power of attorney for finances;
- a power of attorney for health care decisions; and
- a review of your insurance needs, including disability insurance, critical illness insurance and long-term care insurance.

Although your life could be permanently affected by the disability, ensuring you have a plan in place will help to minimize the difficulties your families may experience in caring for you, and will help to protect both your financial future and the financial future of your dependants.

### 1.2.5 Estate Planning

Estate planning is the process which involves determining what sort of inheritance you either need to leave your dependants, or want to leave for others, even if they are not financially dependent upon you. Again, many people are under the mistaken assumption that estate planning is something you only need to consider if you are "rich" or "old". In fact, every adult Canadian needs to have an estate plan in place, particularly those individuals with young children. Avoiding the subject is a selfish act. You will not be the person who will have to live with the consequences of your lack of planning — your family and friends will pay the price if your plan is not properly structured. Although there may be numerous components to your estate plan, it will be comprised primarily of:

- your last will and testament;
- any beneficiary designations you have made on registered investments (where authorized by law) and insurance products; and
- any survivorship provisions on any jointly held property (for example, if you own your home in "joint tenancy" with your spouse, and your spouse survives you, they will inherit the home regardless of the terms of your will, except in the province of Quebec).

Many individuals do not understand how the various components of their estate plan operate. For example, some individuals are under the impression that adding one of their children as a direct beneficiary of their registered assets is a good strategy because it can help save probate fees. However, they do not realize that by doing so, their estate may be divided inequitably between their children, even if their will indicates that their estate is to be divided equally. Unfortunately, if only one child is a direct beneficiary of the registered asset, the asset will generally belong to that child only (except in some cases in Quebec), and the terms of the will are irrelevant. Even if all the children are appointed as direct beneficiaries, there could still be an unequal division if one of the children predeceases the parent (since their children may be effectively disinherited). In addition, the estate will be liable for the tax, even though the proceeds were paid directly to the designated beneficiary or beneficiaries. Understanding how the various strategies work together is important to ensure that your estate plan operates as you intended.

It is also important to understand how your estate will be taxed at the time of your death. Many individuals are aware of the fact that at the time of their death the provincial government will assess what is commonly referred to as a "probate fee" against their estate. However, most individuals do not understand that this probate fee is extremely small compared to the estate as a whole, and they mistakenly structure their estate with the sole purpose of saving probate fees. Unfortunately, if you do this, you may lose the opportunity to do income tax planning, which could result in much more significant savings. The probate fees in Canada range from effectively nothing, to a maximum of 1.5% of the value of the estate. The highest income tax rates in Canada are almost 50% in some jurisdictions, and are assessed on a complex system of rules, not simply a percentage of the value of the estate. Ensure that you are saving the most tax possible, and do not assume that this will be achieved by doing probate planning. In many cases, your beneficiaries will be happy to pay the probate fees if that will result in substantial income tax savings.

Also do not assume that your estate plan will remain consistent throughout your life. Individuals in non-traditional family situations such as common-law couples and blended families need to be particularly diligent in structuring their affairs so that they do not unintentionally disinherit a common-law partner or a child. For many people, the estate plan is the most emotional part of their wealth plan, so be sure to communicate with your family about the manner in which you intend to distribute your estate. Once you have decided what your estate planning objectives are, speak to an experienced estate planning professional to determine which strategies will be most effective for you.

## 1.2.6 Insurance Planning

Understanding how insurance will factor into your wealth plan is an important part of the wealth planning process. In many instances, insurance will be the most effective strategy for protecting your financial future in the event of disability or death. However, insurance can also have tax benefits and can assist in funding other liabilities, particularly if you have dependent parents who may need expensive long-term care. Your insurance plan will usually be an adjunct of the other components of your wealth plan, but due to its complexities and potential long-term benefits, it often warrants specific attention.

# 1.3 HOW TO USE THIS BOOK

This book is essentially divided into two parts — Life Scenarios and Reference Chapters. Depending upon your situation, you may need to read only a few chapters, or potentially the entire book. Each chapter is then further divided into the various parts of the wealth planning process, and includes a section itemizing how the laws in your province are different, as well as case studies that illustrate how the rules operate together.

## 1.3.1 Life Scenarios

First, you should read the chapter or chapters that address your "Life Scenario". For example, if you are married with children, you will probably want to read the chapters entitled "Married" and "Children". If you are recently separated, you may want to read the chapters entitled "Separated" and "Single" to reflect your new life situation. Each individual will have a different life situation — the Life Scenario chapters are effectively divided into chapters addressing your marital status (e.g. single, common-law couples, engaged, married, separated, divorced, blended families, widowed), your dependants or extended family (e.g. children, grandchildren, elderly parents) and specific stages of your life or specific assets that require special consideration (e.g. disabled persons, senior and retirees, vacation properties and business owners). Depending upon your situation, you may want to read several chapters.

The purpose of the Life Scenario chapters is to try to highlight issues that are most important in your particular situation. The Life Scenario chapters attempt to narrow the focus to those issues that you should be discussing with your advisor. These chapters effectively provide a road-map for you to follow with your advisors when structuring your wealth plan.

## 1.3.2 Reference Chapters

There are many concepts and strategies that are referred to in numerous chapters. Therefore, in order to reduce repetition, general information regarding more broad areas has been compiled in the "Reference Chapters" section of the book. Generally speaking, the Life Scenario chapter that is relevant for you will direct you to the Reference Chapters as and when necessary. However, if you are interested in more in-depth information on specific issues that are not addressed in your Life Scenario chapter, the Reference Chapters may provide you with the detail you need. The Reference Chapters discuss the issues raised in the Life Scenario chapters in more detail, providing you with the information you will need to decide if a particular strategy is appropriate for you.

## 1.3.3 Jurisdiction Differences

Near the end of each chapter is a section entitled "Jurisdiction Differences". This section highlights the laws in your province or territory which are unique. Although the chapters try to highlight appropriate strategies for individuals in your situation, it is important to remember that the vast majority of laws in Canada dealing with property law, family law and estate law are governed by provincial or territorial legislation, not federal legislation. Although there are some very important federal statutes (particularly the *Income Tax Act*), most of the statutes that will impact your wealth plan will vary between the provinces. This is why it is very important to review your wealth plan each and every time you move to a new jurisdiction. The provincial statutes vary quite significantly across the country, so the strategies that work for someone who lives in British Columbia may not be at all appropriate for someone who lives in Alberta. This also underscores the importance of speaking with a qualified advisor in your jurisdiction to ensure that your wealth plan is appropriate for you. Relying on comments made in the media or by family members in other jurisdictions may prove to be detrimental, as the comments may be based on rules in a different jurisdiction.

If you are a First Nations Canadian, you should also be sure to review the chapter to determine if there are any issues relevant to having that status. These issues are not listed in the Jurisdiction Differences section, but are rather listed as a separate part of the chapters where there are unique considerations for First Nations Canadians.

One area of the law that this book does not cover is anything related to the laws outside of Canada. If you own foreign property or you are a citizen of another country (particularly the United States), then you may have tax or legal issues to consider beyond the information provided in these pages. If you own foreign property, or are a citizen of another country, you should speak to an advisor who is experienced in dealing with cross-border issues, as the strategies recommended in this book may not be appropriate for you in all cases

## 1.3.4 Case Studies

Most of the chapters include at least one case study at the end. These case studies will help to illustrate how the various strategies work together in different scenarios. For example, although you may be interested in saving both income tax for your estate and saving probate fees, it is often difficult to achieve both at the same time. Therefore, if you implement a probate savings strategy, that may render any income tax planning strategies ineffective. It is important to understand how the rules operate in conjunction, since some objectives are mutually exclusive. These case studies will help you to focus on which objectives are most important, and how to compensate for other objectives that you may not be able to achieve completely.

## 1.4 THE NEED FOR PROFESSIONAL ADVICE

The strategies discussed in this book should not be implemented without professional assistance. Even though you may feel you have a sufficient understanding of the relevant issues, there may be changes in the law, or other relevant issues which mean that the strategy is not right for you. Under no circumstances are pre-prepared legal documents such as "will kits" or "power of attorney kits" recommended. You should always review your situation with an advisor to ensure all aspects of your wealth plan have been properly addressed. Many people who feel that their situation is "simple" are surprised to learn from their advisors that there are actually a number of complexities that must be addressed. If your wealth plan is not properly customized, it will not have the desired impact.

A professional can also provide an objective and rational approach to issues which are often emotionally charged. In many families, professionals act as mediators, and are able to initiate conversations that family members themselves want to discuss, but are too intimidated to raise with their family. A professional may help you to find solutions to problems that you thought were insurmountable.

When choosing an advisor, make sure you are choosing someone with the appropriate skills and background. Here are some things to consider.

- When choosing a financial advisor, ask if he or she is a Certified Financial Planner ("CFP"). If the advisor indicates that he or she is not a CFP, ask if he or she has obtained the Registered Financial Planner ("RFP") designation. Although not as common as the CFP designation, the RFP designation does indicate that the advisor has completed a course of study and must maintain a specific level of knowledge. If the advisor is neither a CFP nor an RFP, ask what technical background he or she possesses. If he or she does not have any education or training in the area, this may indicate a lack of knowledge, although some very experienced financial advisors do not necessarily have these credentials.

- When choosing an accountant, ask if he or she has a professional designation (e.g. Chartered Accountant, Certified General Accountant, or Certified Management Accountant) and if he or she is an expert in personal tax matters, or focuses more on corporate issues. If he or she professes to having a specialty, ask what specialized training he or she has taken (for example, the "In-depth Tax Course" offered by the Canadian Institute of Chartered Accountants?). Do not assume that all accountants specialize in personal taxation or wealth planning. Confirm with your accountant in advance that he or she has the required experience.

- When choosing a lawyer, ask if he or she specializes in estate planning. Many lawyers will state that they do "wills and powers of attorney", but they will not necessarily understand tax law, trust law, estates law or family law. Law, like medicine, is a very specialized profession — for example, you would not go see an eye doctor if you were experiencing problems with your feet. Ensure your lawyer is well versed in estate planning, and is capable of assisting you in developing your wealth plan. If he or she is not an expert in the area, you may simply be given a standard form document. Although you will have an estate plan, it may not be the *optimal* estate plan for you. You want to choose someone who is not only capable of drafting the necessary documents, but is also capable of giving advice.

There are two other affiliations that may provide an indication of whether or not your advisor has the required expertise:

- Many accountants, lawyers and financial planners who specialize in the area of wealth planning are members of the Society of Trust and Estate Practitioners ("STEP"), and will have the letters "TEP" (which stands for "Trust and Estate Practitioner") after their name.

- Also, most tax lawyers and tax accountants are members of the Canadian Tax Foundation. Membership in this organization does not result in a professional designation in the same way as the TEP designation, so you would have to ask your advisor if they are a member of the Canadian Tax Foundation if you are interested in knowing this.

If you find an advisor who is a member of one or both of these organizations, it is quite likely that they do, in fact, specialize in the area of wealth planning.

If you have found a good financial planner and/or accountant, and/or lawyer, but you do not have a professional from each background, ask the professional you are dealing with to recommend the type of professional you are looking for. Financial planners, accountants and lawyers often have good working relationships, so your advisor may be able to help you find other advisors with the type of expertise you need.

By addressing all the issues raised in the chapters relevant to your life situation with your advisors, you should be able to structure your wealth plan in a manner that achieves your objectives in the most optimal manner.

# Part II

# Life Scenarios

# CHAPTER 2



# SINGLE



Wealth and succession planning is not just for people who are in relationships or who have dependants. Every individual needs to ensure that they are taken care of financially, and they are protected in the case of future disaster. This chapter will discuss some of the planning issues that should be considered by "singletons".

# 2.1 FINANCIAL PLANNING

## 2.1.1 Emergency Fund

Since self-sufficiency is crucial for single individuals, always ensure that you have liquid assets available in the amount of at least three months of income, so that you will be able to survive an unexpected life event, such as a disability or job loss. It is important to ensure that these funds are easily accessible, and not invested in a locked-in instrument, such as a non-redeemable GIC.

A tax-free savings account ("TFSA") may be a good place to invest your emergency funds, since all the income earned in a TFSA is tax free, and there is no tax upon withdrawal. However, individuals over the age of 18 may only contribute up to $5000 into a TFSA annually, which may not be a sufficient amount in case of emergency, so you also may need some money saved in non-registered investments as well.

## 2.1.2 Retirement Plan

As is the case with any individual, consideration must be given to whether you are saving sufficient amounts on a regular basis to provide you with the desired lifestyle in retirement. In the case of retirement funds, it may be advisable to invest them in a registered retirement savings plan (an "RRSP"), since any contributions made to an RRSP will result in a tax deduction on your income tax return. However, you will pay tax on any withdrawals from the plan, which is why RRSPs are usually only used for funds which you want to save for retirement, and therefore want to grow on a tax-deferred basis for as long as possible.

If you are in a low-income tax bracket, and the tax deduction will not be useful to you, it may be better to save your retirement funds in a TFSA. This is because all the income and growth in a TFSA can be withdrawn completely tax free, which may help to preserve any rights you may have to social assistance payments, including Old Age Security payments. Speak to your financial advisor to ensure that you know how much money you need to save on an annual basis to be able to afford the lifestyle you want in retirement and where best to invest it.

## 2.2 TAX PLANNING

Although there are no tax planning strategies unique to single individuals, minimizing taxes is still a key objective:

- If you have children, see section 10.2.9 of Chapter 10, "Children", for a description of how you may be able to income-split with your children, in order to reduce your tax bill;
- If you are a high income earner, and you anticipate that you may receive an inheritance in the future, see section 13.5 of Chapter 13, "Elderly Parents", for a description of how the use of testamentary trusts in a will may help you to pay less tax when you receive the inheritance; and
- If you are a senior or retired, see section 14.2 of Chapter 14, "Seniors and Retirees", for recommendations regarding strategies to keep your net income low, which will, in effect, maximize the amount of Old Age Security, and other tax and social security benefits to which you may be entitled.



## 2.3 FAMILY LAW ISSUES

Generally speaking, single individuals tend to have few, if any, concerns regarding claims against their property due to a family law dispute. However, there are some instances when family law issues may arise.

- If you have a child, whether or not you are married or in a common-law relationship, you may be required to pay child support based on the child support guidelines issued for each province. See section 10.3 of Chapter 10, "Children", for more information on child support.
- If you have an elderly parent who is unable to support himself or herself, you may be required to pay parental support for an indeterminate length of time. See section 13.3 of Chapter 13, "Elderly Parents", for more information on parental support.

# 2.4 DISABILITY PLANNING

The statistics on disability indicate that more and more Canadians are suffering from both short- and long-term disabilities. Although the reasons for this are unclear, our increasingly stressful and fast-paced lifestyle may play a part. Regardless of the reasons, single individuals must ensure that both they, and their dependants, are protected in the case of a disability, especially if their salary is their sole source of income.

## 2.4.1 Powers of Attorney

A power of attorney is an extremely important document for any individual, but particularly so if you are single. If you are incapacitated, even for a short period of time, you will want to ensure that someone has been designated to take care of your affairs in the event that you are unable to. No matter how young or old you are, you should have a power of attorney, especially if you have dependants or a business (see Chapter 16, "Business Owners", for a more complete discussion on the issues relevant to business owners). If you do not have a power of attorney, who will manage your affairs if you become involved in an accident which renders you unconscious?

If you have not designated anyone as your attorney, then your family will have to apply to court for what is known as a committeeship. The individuals who have first priority to apply for a committeeship are generally a spouse (and in some jurisdictions, a common-law partner), children, parents, and then other family members. Do you really want a separated spouse to be able to manage your affairs when you are not able to? What if you are estranged from your parents and would not have chosen them to take on this position? Even if you are comfortable with the person who has first right to become your committee, why would you put them through the expense and delay of having to go to court? Powers of attorney are generally relatively inexpensive documents that your lawyer can draft quickly. See Chapter 18, "Powers of Attorney", for a more complete discussion on this subject, including health care directives, which are a form of power of attorney for health care decisions as opposed to financial ones.

## 2.4.2 Disability Insurance

If you are single, you should ensure that your disability insurance is adequate for your needs. In many cases, individuals rely on the group insurance provided by their employers, but this may not be adequate in all circumstances, and it is not portable if you change jobs. You should review your disability insurance coverage with your financial advisor to ensure that it will be sufficient in the event of disability. In many cases, an individual policy may be a better option than a group plan, since it will continue in force even if you change employers. Also, some group policies provide that you are disabled only if you cannot complete the tasks of *any* job at the same pay level. Many individuals, especially professionals, do not want to be forced to do a different type of job. If you want to ensure that you will be covered even if you are only unable to continue in your current position, then you will need an "own occupation" clause in your coverage, which is sometimes not included in group policies. See section 25.1.1 of Chapter 25, "Insurance", for a further description of the types of features you should look for in a disability insurance policy. Disability insurance can also be purchased for the purpose of ensuring that mortgage payments continue to be paid during a disability. If you have a considerable mortgage, speak to your financial planner about whether or not this type of insurance is appropriate for you.



Keep in mind that you will not be able to insure 100% of your current salary, since insurers want to ensure that there is some motivation for you to return to the workforce. However, since disability insurance premiums are generally not tax deductible when they are paid, disability payments are generally not taxed when they are received (note that this may not be the case if your employer has paid some or all of your disability insurance premiums). Assuming your costs of living will be lower in the event of a disability (since you will not be required to pay for transportation to work, etc.) and assuming that the after-tax amount you are receiving prior to disability is in the same range as the tax free amount you will receive from a disability policy, you should be able to maintain the same standard of living. However, in many cases, there are unforeseen costs that can arise as a result of a disability, particularly if you have to renovate your home or purchase special equipment.

## 2.4.3 Critical Illness Insurance

Critical illness insurance is another form of insurance which protects against worst case scenarios. It provides a lump sum payment in the event of certain listed types of illnesses (usually cancer, stroke, heart attack, etc.). Even if you have disability insurance in place, it may not be sufficient if you experience a critical illness. Disability insurance insures your income, but even then you can only insure a portion of your income, never 100%. Individuals who suffer from a critical illness often have additional expenses, such as medical expenses, home renovations and home care costs that may be more than their income can bear. If you want to ensure that you are properly taken care of in the event of a critical illness, especially if you have no life partner or other family member to provide you with funds in the event you need them, you should consider critical illness insurance. You should review the costs and benefits of this type of coverage with your financial planner to ensure that you or your dependants will not suffer unnecessarily if you experience a critical illness. See section 25.1.2 of Chapter 25, "Insurance", for more details.

### 2.4.4 Long-Term Care Insurance

Single individuals should also consider long-term care insurance as part of their long-term planning. If they require care in their home or institutional care for an extended period of time, they may find that their assets will not be sufficient to provide them with the level of care that they desire. Many single individuals are not able to accumulate the same amount of assets that couples can, since they have to rely on only one source of income. They are also less likely to have someone in their life who is able to provide daily care to them in the way that a spouse might. Long-term care insurance provides funds in the event that you are not able to perform various daily tasks (e.g. feeding yourself, dressing yourself or bathing yourself). This ensures that if you require extensive personal care for an extended time period, you will have sufficient funds. You should speak to your financial advisor for more information on this type of insurance. Like all insurance products, you will only be able to purchase this type of insurance if you qualify, so do not wait too long to investigate whether or not it would be appropriate for you. See section 25.1.3 of Chapter 25, "Insurance", for more details.

## 2.5 ESTATE PLANNING

### 2.5.1 No Dependants

If you have no dependants, then you may not feel that it is necessary to plan for what will happen in the case of your death. However, planning in advance will make it easier for your survivors to administer your estate, and may help to ensure that your wishes are carried out. Here are some things to consider.

#### *2.5.1.1 Will Planning*

Some single individuals do not feel that it is necessary for them to write a will. However, there are numerous reasons why every single adult should have a will.

- If you do not choose a personal representative (sometimes referred to as an "executor"), the court will choose one for you, and it may not be the person you would have chosen. That person may also have to post a bond in order to administer the estate, which will be an extra expense that could have been avoided had they been named in a will. While your parents are still young, they may be an appropriate choice as personal representatives, but this decision should be reviewed as time goes by to ensure they are still capable of acting. Younger relatives, such as a cousin, niece or nephew, may be a more appropriate choice as time passes, or potentially a corporate trustee.

- If you die without a will, and you do not have any dependants, then you may prefer to have your estate given to charity as opposed to financially independent relatives (see Chapter 19, "Distribution of an Estate", for a more complete discussion about who will receive your estate if you die without a will). For example, if your parents are already financially independent, you may prefer to leave your estate to charity. Writing a will is one way to ensure that these wishes will be carried out, and in the most tax effective manner possible. (See Chapter 24, "Charitable Giving", for more information on this issue.)

Keep in mind that if you write a will while you are single, any subsequent marriage generally will render all previous wills void, except in the province of Quebec (see Chapter 5, "Married", for a further discussion of the implications of marriage). Also note that in some jurisdictions, entering into a common-law relationship will also render any previous wills void (see Chapter 3, "Common-Law Couples", for a further discussion of the implications of entering into a common-law relationship). If you are currently single, but you are contemplating marriage and you would like your will to survive your marriage, then your will must be written in contemplation of marriage.

### 2.5.1.2 Beneficiary Designations

In many cases, it is not advisable for single individuals to designate a direct beneficiary on their registered assets or insurance policies. A couple of examples follow.

- Single individuals sometimes name one of their two parents as the direct beneficiary of their RRSP or insurance policy. However, in the event your parents separate or divorce prior to the time of your death, the parent who was appointed as beneficiary may receive the entire asset, and will not be obligated to share it. This can be especially unfair in the case of RRSPs, where the beneficiary will receive the funds tax free, but the estate will be responsible for paying the tax. Only if the estate has insufficient funds to pay the tax will the beneficiary of the RRSP be required to pay any of the tax. Therefore, even if the other parent receives a part of the estate, their part of the estate will be diminished by the tax liability resulting from the payment of the RRSP to the parent who received the RRSP proceeds.

- Another problem may arise if you marry or enter into a common-law relationship at a later date. A marriage, new relationship or even the birth of a child generally will not affect a beneficiary designation, so if you change your will but forget to change your beneficiary designations, your estate may not be distributed as intended.

If you do designate a direct beneficiary, be sure to review these designations on a regular basis to ensure they are consistent with your current wishes.

Note that in the province of Quebec, beneficiary designations are not effective on all forms of registered investments.

#### *2.5.1.3 Donation of Body Tissue/Funeral Arrangements*

If you want your organs to be used for transplant purposes, or you want your body tissue available for use in scientific research, you must ensure that you make your wishes known in advance. Be sure to complete the organ donation card attached to your driver's licence, or inform your doctor of your wishes.

Also consider if there are any particular aspects of your funeral arrangements that you would like known in advance. For example, if you feel strongly about cremation, ensure that you have written your preferences down, and communicated these preferences to your personal representative.

### 2.5.2 Dependants

If you do have dependants, then in addition to the issues listed in section 2.5.1, you will want to ensure that you have addressed the needs of the people who rely upon you. (See Chapter 10, "Children", for a more complete discussion on the issues relevant to having children.) Here are some of the issues that you should consider.

### 2.5.2.1 Guardianship

If the child's other parent is still alive and able to take care of the child, then your child will not necessarily be left an orphan in the event of your death, but you still need to think about worst case scenarios. Have you appointed an alternate guardian in your will in the event the child's other parent is not capable of taking care of them? Have you discussed your wishes regarding how you would like your children raised with the child's other parent, or your chosen guardian? If the child does not have another parent alive or who is capable of caring for them, then you will need to pay particular attention to this issue, and ensure that you have nominated both a primary guardian and an alternate. See section 10.5.1 of Chapter 10, "Children", for more information on choosing a guardian.



### 2.5.2.2 Beneficiary Designations

Many single individuals choose to name their children as the direct beneficiary of their insurance policies and RRSPs in order to avoid probate. (Please see Chapter 22, "Probate", for a discussion on probate and an explanation as to why probate planning should not be the predominant goal in your estate plan.) In many jurisdictions, probate fees are minimal, and there may be income tax advantages to designating your estate as the beneficiary of your life insurance or registered assets. In the case of children, however, there may be even more reason not to name them as direct beneficiaries. If your child is a minor, and he or she receives the funds directly through a direct beneficiary designation, then the Public Trustee (or Children's Lawyer, depending upon your jurisdiction of residence), may be entitled to manage the funds until the child attains the age of majority. This may lead to unnecessary expenses and restrictions on the use of the money. It may be better to leave the money to your estate, and have it managed by your personal representative or the trustee of a trust established for your child. You will then be able to choose the person who will manage these funds, communicate with them how you would like the money spent, and put restrictions on when your child may receive the money. The Public Trustee will only be able to hold the money until your child reaches the age of majority, which may still be too young, especially if the amount in question is quite large. You may prefer to have the funds given over a period of time — for example, one-quarter of the capital at age 21, half of the remainder at age 25, and the remaining amount at age 30. See section 10.5.3 of Chapter 10, "Children", for a further discussion on the importance of using trusts where assets may be left to a minor.

Also, be careful not to make the mistake of appointing your personal representative as beneficiary of your RRSPs or life insurance on the assumption that he or she will manage those funds for the benefit of your children. There have been cases where individuals have appointed a sibling as a beneficiary of an asset, assuming that the sibling would use those funds for the benefit of their children. However, the person who receives the funds is under no obligation to use them for the benefit of anyone else, and if they have their own children or creditor issues, they may be tempted to use the money for their own purposes. Alternatively, if they suffer a marital breakdown, their former spouse may claim half of the funds as theirs. If you want your children to receive the funds, but they are too young to manage them on their own, you should designate your estate as the beneficiary, and your personal representative will then be obligated to manage the funds in the best interests of the beneficiaries of your estate. If you are very intent on saving probate, consider the use of an insurance trust for your insurance proceeds (see section 22.3.7 of Chapter 22, "Probate", for a further discussion about the use of insurance trusts). Also, as stated above, if an RRSP or RRIF is left to a direct beneficiary, the estate will be liable for the tax (unless the beneficiary is a spouse or common-law partner or, in some cases, a child). If the RRSP or RRIF is left to a sibling, the sibling will receive the gross amount of the funds, and the estate will be liable for the tax liability, leaving even less in the estate for the child.

Note that in the province of Quebec, direct beneficiary designations are not effective on all forms of registered investments.

### 2.5.2.3 *Pets*

For many single people, their pets are like their children, and they want to ensure that they are well taken care of at the time of their death. Although property cannot be bequeathed to a pet, an amount of money could be left to an individual, in return for a promise to care for the pet for the remainder of the pet's life. It is important to speak in advance with the person you would like to take on this responsibility. (See section 10.5.11 of Chapter 10, "Children", for a further discussion on this issue.)

## 2.6 INSURANCE PLANNING

In section 2.4, we discussed the need for disability insurance, critical illness insurance and long-term care insurance. For single individuals, insurance that protects them in the case of disability may be particularly important, especially if they do not have a partner to support them in the event they are no longer able to earn an income.

Single individuals must also consider whether or not they have adequate levels of life insurance, whether or not they have dependants.

### 2.6.1 No Dependants

Even if you do not have any dependants now, is it possible that you may have children or other dependants in the future? If so, then it may be advisable to consider obtaining an insurance policy now, in the event you become uninsurable later. Many individuals consider the issue of life insurance too late in life (i.e. once they begin to experience health problems), by which time the insurance is either unavailable, or extremely expensive. If possible, purchase a life insurance policy while you are young and healthy, and increase the death benefit as necessary.

For singletons who are doing well financially, life insurance also can provide certain tax advantages, and the funds accumulated in the policy may be accessed in a tax-advantaged way in order to supplement your retirement income. See section 25.2.3 of Chapter 25, "Insurance", for a discussion regarding the tax advantages of permanent insurance.

### 2.6.2 Dependants

If someone is financially dependent upon you, then you must ensure that you have adequate life insurance to take care of their needs in the event you are not able to. If you have a group policy through your place of employment, you should not assume that the death benefit paid under this policy will be sufficient. Many group policies pick an arbitrary amount to pay as a death benefit, and that amount may or may not be sufficient for your purposes. Be sure to speak with your financial planner about the amount of money it will take to raise your children in the manner to which they are accustomed. Also, do not forget about potential post-secondary education costs or other costs in the event your child becomes disabled in the future or requires special care.

# 2.7 JURISDICTION DIFFERENCES

There are no jurisdiction differences for this chapter.

# 2.8 CASE STUDIES

## 2.8.1 Single, No Children

Kim is 34, single, with no children or other dependants. She has a good income, a mortgage and no other debts. She also has an RRSP, on which she has named her father as the direct beneficiary. She thinks that her situation does not require any wealth planning, since upon her death, her parents will inherit the RRSPs directly, and simply sell her house and inherit the equity.

Kim is correct in thinking that her situation is straightforward compared to others, but that does not mean that she has no wealth planning issues. For Kim, her main concern should be not whether she dies, but whether she is unable to earn an income at some point in her life, particularly due to a disability or illness. She should review her annual income requirements with her financial advisor, and ensure that she has sufficient insurance in each of the following scenarios:

- disability,
- critical illness, and
- chronic illness, which requires long-term care.

Kim must also ensure that she has appointed someone as her power of attorney in the event she is not able to make decisions for herself, even if the period of incapacity is short. For example, what will happen if she is in a car accident, and is in a coma for a period of weeks or months? Who will be authorized to write cheques from her bank account to ensure that all of her bills are paid? Kim should choose a person who is trustworthy, responsible and preferably lives close by. Since she trusts her father, she appoints him as her attorney for the purposes of making financial decisions. However, what would happen if her father died before the power of attorney was brought into force? Kim decides to appoint her friend, Dave, as her alternate attorney. Kim discusses this issue with both her father and Dave prior to appointing them, to ensure that they are comfortable with the appointment, and that they know where to find the relevant documents when needed. Also, since Kim is quite young, and not likely to want anyone to manage her affairs until it is absolutely necessary, she signs a "springing" form of attorney, which states that it will only "spring" into force when two medical doctors certify that she is no longer capable of managing her own affairs.

Kim also considers whom she would like to have authority to make medical decisions on her behalf if she is not able to. Kim feels that her mother would be the best choice, as they have discussed health issues on many occasions. Kim appoints her father as her alternate choice, in the event her mother is not able to act as her attorney for health care at the appropriate time.

Once Kim has reviewed the implications of dealing with a disability, she should also consider whether or not she has fully considered all of the implications of death. Although she has no dependants now, it is possible that she could have some in the future. By appointing her father as the direct beneficiary of her RRSP, he will be entitled to those funds regardless of whether or not she gets married or has children (except in Quebec, where direct beneficiary designations are not effective in respect of all types of registered investments). Kim will have to remember to change the designation as her situation changes in the future. If Kim is concerned she will forget to change the designation, it may be easier to simply designate her estate as the beneficiary of her RRSP, although that may mean that her estate will have to pay probate fees. (However, probate fees in Canada are quite small — see Chapter 22, "Probate", for a discussion of the relevant fees in your province.)

Even if Kim does not have a common-law partner, spouse or dependants at the time of her death, designating her father as the beneficiary could have unintended consequences. Consider the following: What if Kim's parents separate or divorce prior to the time of her death? Kim has designated her father alone, but fully anticipates that he will share the funds with her mother in the event of her death. However, if her parents separate for some reason, then her mother will not be entitled to any of those funds. In addition, since RRSPs are fully taxable at the time of death, her estate will be liable for any taxes owing on the RRSPs, even though it is her father who has received the funds. In many cases, the probate savings from designating a beneficiary is not worth the risk of an unequal distribution of your estate. For example, let's assume that Kim lives in Manitoba. The probate fee on a $100,000 RRSP would be only $700. Kim could, of course, choose to designate both her mother and father as the beneficiaries of the RRSP plan, but that does not alleviate the problem of her needing to change the beneficiaries every time she has a new relationship or a child. In many cases, probate planning is not worth the risk. In Kim's case, she should either appoint her estate as the beneficiary of her RRSP, or if she believes that she will remember to change the beneficiary when necessary, then perhaps her mother and father together.

Kim should also consider whether or not it would be easier for her heirs to distribute her estate if she had a will. If Kim has no will, then her parents will inherit her estate equally, which is what she wants. However, who will have the authority to administer her estate? Since she has not appointed a personal representative, her parents will have to apply to the courts to be appointed as administrators, and will probably have to post a bond, which can be costly. Once they have received the proper authorization from the court, they will be able to proceed, but the court process could result in unnecessary cost and delay. If Kim writes a will and appoints her parents as her personal representatives, they will have the authority to act immediately after the time of her death, and, if they live in the same jurisdiction as Kim, they will generally not have to post a bond.

When Kim starts to consider where she would like her estate to go, she realizes that she really does not want to leave everything to her parents. Her parents are financially well-off, and do not need her money. Kim has considered giving money to charity at various times, but never seems to have sufficient funds to make a significant gift. She considers whether leaving a charitable gift through her will would allow her to make the type of gift she has been thinking about (see Chapter 24, "Charitable Giving").

Finally, Kim considers whether or not she would like to leave any instructions regarding the use of her body parts, or the type of funeral she would like. Many Canadians who state that they would like to donate organs do not complete an organ donation card. If Kim wants to donate her organs, she should complete the proper forms, and, if possible, keep an organ donation card in her wallet so that it can be easily found when required. Also, if she has any specific requests regarding the type of funeral she does or does not want (e.g. Cremation? Religious service?), she should write this information down, and also verbally communicate the information to her personal representatives (her parents), in case the written instructions are not found until it is too late.

### 2.8.2 Single, With Children

Ian is 28, and has a child, Jocelyn. Ian has sole custody of Jocelyn and is not married to Jocelyn's mother, nor are they living in a common-law relationship. Ian's primary concern is for Jocelyn's welfare. She is now 7.

Since Jocelyn is still a minor, Ian decides to appoint his sister, Silvia, as his power of attorney regarding finances, and his brother, Mike, as his power of attorney regarding health care. Ian has also reviewed his disability and critical illness coverage with his financial advisor to ensure that in the event he suffers a debilitating injury or illness, he will still have enough income to support both himself, and Jocelyn. Ian considers the same issues as Kim in Case Study 2.8.1 when planning for disability.

Since Ian has a dependant, he is much more concerned than Kim in Case Study 2.8.1 about what may happen at the time of his death. First, Ian discusses the need for life insurance with his financial advisor to determine how much he would need to leave to his estate in order to take care of Jocelyn until she is at least 18 or 19. If Ian also wants to help finance her post-secondary education, the insurance need may be even greater. When Ian purchases the policy, he designates his estate as the beneficiary of the death benefit, or the trustee of an insurance trust (see Chapter 22, "Probate", for a discussion about insurance trusts). If he designates Jocelyn, then the funds may have to be managed by the provincial trustee until Jocelyn attains the age of 18 or 19 (depending upon their jurisdiction of residence), which could result in added expense. Ian wants his personal representatives to manage the money in his estate, and he has spoken to them about the types of things he feels are important. For example, Ian has told his personal representatives that he feels very strongly about Jocelyn learning how to play the violin, and they can spend as much of his estate as they feel is necessary in order to give her private lessons.



Ian must also ensure that he has a properly drafted will in order to ensure that his estate will be well managed after he is gone, and Jocelyn is taken care of. Ian speaks with his sister Silvia and his brother Mike about acting as Jocelyn's guardian. He decides to nominate Mike as the primary guardian, with Silvia to act as alternate in the event Mike is not capable of acting. Mike is married to Kaitlyn, but Ian does not nominate Kaitlyn, as he does not want to risk a custody dispute in the event Mike and Kaitlyn separate or divorce. Ian is aware that the person he chooses as guardian may or may not be approved by the courts, but his choice will generally be respected unless the court feels it is not in the child's best interest.

Ian then decides to appoint Silvia as his personal representative (also referred to as an executor in some jurisdictions), and he appoints Mike as his alternate in the event Silvia is not able to carry out her duties. Ian leaves all of his assets in his estate to Jocelyn, but provides that the assets are to be held in trust until she attains the age of majority (18 or 19 depending upon their jurisdiction of residence). However, he gives his personal representative the power to encroach on the capital of the trust in order to provide for Jocelyn's educational, medical or other needs, using their discretion. He then provides that Jocelyn is entitled to receive all of the annual income in the trust once she reaches the age of majority. Jocelyn is entitled to one quarter of the capital at the time she turns 21, one half of the remaining capital at the time she turns 25, and all of the remaining capital at the time she turns 30. In this way, Ian knows that his personal representative will be able to control part or all of the funds until such time as Jocelyn is more likely to be mature enough to manage them.

Ian then reviews all of the beneficiary designations he has made on any of his RRSPs, insurance policies and segregated funds. Since Jocelyn is a minor, he does not want to name her as the direct beneficiary, since he does not want the provincial authorities to have the right to manage these funds until Jocelyn attains the age of majority. Instead, he appoints his estate as the beneficiary of all of these assets so that they will be managed by his personal representative in a manner which is more consistent with his intentions. This will also ensure that the funds are held in trust even past the age of majority, since under Ian's will, Jocelyn is not entitled to receive any of the capital before the age of 21 without the consent of his personal representative. Ian has heard that if he appoints Silvia (his primary representative) as the beneficiary of these assets that he may be able to save probate. Although Ian likes the idea of saving probate, if he names Silvia as the beneficiary of these assets, then the assets will belong to Silvia, and she is under no obligation to give any of the funds to Jocelyn. Although Ian trusts Silvia, Silvia has her own children, and may be tempted to keep some of the money for herself. Also, Silvia's marriage may break down, potentially resulting in half of the funds going to her former spouse. Ian does not want to risk Jocelyn's inheritance for the sake of a few hundred dollars in probate, and in any event, he has decided to establish an insurance trust, so that no probate will be paid on the insurance proceeds. Ian decides to name his estate as the beneficiary on all of his registered assets, and names the trustees of an insurance trust as the beneficiary of his insurance proceeds. He then ensures that his will creates an insurance trust, and names his personal representative as the trustee of that trust.

# CHAPTER 3

# Common-Law Couples

3 Common-Law

More and more Canadians are choosing to live in common-law relationships, whether as a temporary arrangement prior to marriage, or a permanent one. Many individuals are under the impression that their financial and legal situation will be "simpler" if they choose not to get married, but that is generally not the case. The law with respect to common-law couples is in a state of flux across Canada, and has undergone tremendous change over the past ten years. Unfortunately, many jurisdictions have implemented legislation which is inconsistent with the applicable federal statutes, which means that although common-law couples may have certain rights normally reserved for married couples, they may not have others. In fact, the legislation across the country varies quite dramatically, so common-law couples must understand the laws of their jurisdiction, and if they move, they cannot assume that the laws of their new jurisdiction will be the same. It is imperative that common-law couples understand which wealth planning strategies are appropriate for them, and how they differ from married couples.

Throughout this book, all references to common-law couples will include both opposite-sex and same-sex couples, unless otherwise specified.

## 3.1 "COMMON-LAW" STATUS

### 3.1.1 When Are You Living Common-Law?

The first issue to be determined is what is "living common-law"? The factors that the law relies on when determining if someone is living in a common-law relationship include the following:

- Shelter — do you live under the same roof?
- Sexual and personal behaviour — are you in a conjugal relationship?
- Services — who prepares the meals? Shopping? House cleaning?
- Social — do you go to social activities as a couple?
- Societal — what is the attitude of the community towards you as a couple?
- Support — what are your financial arrangements?
- Children — what is your attitude concerning children?

Simply having a child together is generally not enough to be considered to be living common-law. Even if you have a child, you must also be living together in a relationship of some permanence before you will be considered a common-law couple.

Keep in mind that even if a couple is not living together, it may still be possible for them to be considered a common-law couple. Although shared shelter is one of the primary considerations in making a determination as to whether or not a couple is living common-law, courts have been known to make a finding of common-law status even where the parties live in different residences.

Living in a common-law relationship brings with it many rights and responsibilities in Canada. However, each statute has its own requirement regarding how long you must have common-law status before you will become subject to that statute. Refer to section 3.9, "Jurisdiction Differences" to determine the tests in your province. You will note from the discussion in this chapter that in some cases it may be an advantage to be considered to be living common-law, and in some cases a disadvantage. If you are uncertain as to whether or not you are living common-law, it is imperative that you discuss the issue with your partner. If you are in fact living common law, you should sign a cohabitation agreement and a will acknowledging that and setting out your agreement regarding the division of property both at the time of separation and death.

It is also very important to determine the date on which you began to live common-law, since many rights and obligations commence after you have lived together for a specified period. Keeping a record of when you began to live common-law can help to avoid disputes, although keep in mind that a court may disagree with you as to when you became a common-law couple. Regardless of what any documentation you have prepared may say, you cannot arbitrarily choose a date and assume that a court will agree with you if all of the evidence points to the relationship having started on a different date.



### 3.1.2 Trying to Avoid Common-Law Status

Generally speaking, you either are living in a common-law relationship, or you are not. Some couples try to deny that they are living in a common-law relationship because they do not want to lose certain tax advantages, or because they believe that it will help protect their property. The best way to protect your property is to honestly acknowledge the nature of your relationship, and if you are living common-law, then enter into a cohabitation agreement which is drafted by a well trained lawyer. "Do it yourself" solutions are generally dangerous. For example, some individuals ask their partner to sign a lease prior to letting them move in, to prove there is a landlord/tenant relationship. However, if the court finds that the relationship was conjugal in nature, they are likely to ignore the lease document, leaving your property exposed to a family property claim. If you do not want your property exposed to the claims of a common-law partner, then it is best to have a cohabitation agreement in which your partner releases their right to claim part of your property. Simply denying the relationship is a dangerous approach.

Also, some couples try to deny their common-law status by refusing to file their income tax returns as a couple. Couples who do this should be aware that filing a false income tax return is a violation of the law, which could result in civil proceedings against them, including reassessment, interest and civil penalties, and, in the worst cases, it is an offence that could be criminally prosecuted, resulting in a fine and potentially imprisonment.

In addition, a tax return can be used as evidence by government authorities to deny CPP survivor benefits or other pension benefits when one of the partners dies. Although there may be some income tax disadvantages to being considered a common-law couple, there may also be some advantages, so you should consider all of the implications. It is extremely important for common-law couples to speak with a professional when entering into such a relationship so that their legal obligations can be properly documented — simply denying the relationship is not a solution.

## 3.1.3 Moving to Another Jurisdiction

Common-law couples need to be particularly cognizant of the fact that their rights could change dramatically every time they move to a new province, let alone to another country. The rules regarding common-law couples vary widely across the country — refer to section 3.9, "Jurisdiction Differences", to compare the law in your current jurisdiction of residence and the jurisdiction to which you are contemplating moving. Under Canadian law, each province has the power to enact laws respecting property, and very few of these laws are consistent across Canada. Even if you live in a province which allows you to register your relationship as a "civil union", "domestic partnership" or "adult interdependent relationship", that status will generally only be effective in the jurisdiction where registration took place.

## 3.1.4 Property in Other Jurisdictions

If you have property in more than one jurisdiction, it will be very important for you to have a properly drafted will. If a common-law partner dies without a will, then all of their personal property will be distributed according to the laws of the jurisdiction where they were domiciled when they died, and their real property will be distributed according to the jurisdiction where the property is located. Therefore, if you were domiciled in Ontario when you died, you owned property both in Ontario and British Columbia, and you did not have a will, your common-law partner would not be entitled to inherit any part of the property in Ontario, but they may be entitled to inherit part or all of the property in British Columbia. If you own real property in more than one jurisdiction, be aware of the rules in the other jurisdiction(s), and ensure that you have reviewed your situation with an experienced estate planning lawyer. See section 3.9, "Jurisdiction Differences", for more information on the jurisdictions relevant to your situation.

## 3.2 FINANCIAL PLANNING

The financial planning issues for common-law couples are essentially the same as for married couples. See section 5.1 in Chapter 5, "Married", for more information on this subject. However, if you live in a jurisdiction where you would have different family property rights or different rights at the time of death than if you were married, this may impact the way in which you structure your finances. Be sure to read the remainder of this chapter and the rules in your jurisdiction (found in section 3.9, "Jurisdiction Differences") to determine if the rules in your jurisdiction could impact your financial situation.

## 3.3 TAX PLANNING

Assuming you are living common law, how does that affect your income tax situation? Under the federal *Income Tax Act*, a common-law partner is a person who is not your spouse, and with whom you are living in a conjugal relationship, and to whom at least one of the following applies:

1. He or she has been living with you in a conjugal relationship for at least 12 continuous months; or

2. He or she either:

   a. Is the parent of your child by birth or adoption; or

   b. Has custody and control of your child (or had custody and control immediately before the child turned 19 years of age) and your child is wholly dependent on him or her for support.

Note that simply having a child together is not sufficient – you must also be living in a conjugal relationship in order to be considered a common-law couple for the purposes of item #2. You are no longer considered to be living common-law once you have been living separate and apart for 90 days.

In addition, an individual immediately becomes your common-law partner if you previously lived together in a conjugal relationship for at least 12 continuous months and you have resumed living together. However, under proposed changes, a person will be your common-law partner only after your current relationship with that person has lasted at least 12 continuous months (unless you meet either of the conditions set out in item #2 above), meaning that if you separate, you will once again have to live together for 12 continuous months before you will be considered to be living common law. Therefore, if the couple had been living together for ten years, separates for more than 90 days, and then resumes cohabitation for only six months before one of them dies, they will not be treated as a common-law couple for the purposes of the various tax provisions discussed below. If passed into law, this proposed change will apply retroactively to 2001 and later years.

If you do meet the tests for being considered a common-law couple, then you must file your income tax returns as a couple. *Filing as a common-law couple is not optional.* If you file as separate individuals and a determination is later made that you were living as a couple at the time, you could be subject to interest and penalties, and, in a worst case scenario, criminal charges. Filing a false return is a federal offence, so be sure that you are filing your returns properly and honestly. In fact, if you start to live common law with someone, you should inform the CRA as soon as you meet either test (i.e., after living together for 12 months or if you have lived together for a shorter period of time and you have a child together), especially if you are receiving any benefits like the Canada Child Tax Benefit or GIS, as your entitlement to these benefits will now be recalculated based on your new marital status. If you delay, you may have to repay some of your benefits, which may be difficult to do if you have spent the money.

What are some of the advantages of being considered a common-law couple under the *Income Tax Act*?

- *Pension Income Splitting.* The ability to reduce your taxes either by splitting the CPP credits to which both you and your partner are entitled, or by allocating part of your pension income to your common-law partner on his or her tax return. For more details on these strategies (and other income-splitting opportunities), see section 14.2.2.1 of Chapter 14, "Seniors and Retirees" and section 5.2.1 of Chapter 5, "Married".

- *Transferring Assets without Triggering Gains.* The ability to transfer assets between each other without triggering any capital gains or losses (although transferring assets to a common-law partner is generally not recommended without signing a cohabitation agreement — see the discussion on family law issues in section 3.4).

- *Spousal RRSPs.* The ability to contribute to a spousal RRSP for your partner. (However, a common-law partner may not want to make a spousal RRSP contribution for other reasons — see the discussion on family law issues in section 3.4).

- *Spousal Tax Credit.* The ability to claim a spousal credit, if your partner does not earn more than the allowed threshold of income, which is generally very low (for 2010, the spousal credit was $10,382, an amount which is indexed annually).

- *Transfer of Personal Tax Credits.* The ability to transfer certain tax credits back and forth between partners (including the age, pension income, charitable donation, disability, and Canada Child tax credits, and up to $5000 of the tuition, textbook and education amounts) so that these credits do not go unused.



However, there are many disadvantages to being considered a common-law couple for income tax purposes.

- *Loss of Eligible Dependant Credit.* If either partner was claiming an "eligible dependant" credit in respect of a minor child they were supporting, they will no longer be able to claim that credit. Although the amount of the eligible dependant credit will vary between jurisdictions, the credit can be worth as much as $2000 per child. If each partner was claiming the credit in respect of a child prior to living common-law, they could lose as much as $4000 in tax credits once they start filing as a couple.

- *Loss of Principal Residence Exemption.* Under the *Income Tax Act*, the capital gain on a principal residence is tax exempt, so if one partner owned a home and the other partner owned a cottage, the gain on both properties would have been exempt if they were not considered a couple. However, once the couple is living common-law, they will only be able to designate one home as a principle residence, and any capital gain on the property which is not exempt is taxable. For common-law couples who have been living together for a long time, since the *Income Tax Act* only recognized opposite-sex couples as the equivalent to married in 1993, and same-sex couples in 2001 (although couples could elect such treatment beginning in 1998), you will be able to each claim a principal residence for the years in which you were not allowed to file returns as a couple. For further information, see Chapter 15, "Vacation Properties".

- *Potential Loss of Benefits.* The couple must pool their income when determining eligibility for certain amounts, including the Guaranteed Income Supplement and Guaranteed Income Allowance, the GST credit and the Canada Child Tax Credit. If both partners are earning an income, the ability to receive these amounts or claim these credits will decrease more quickly.

- *Attribution Rules.* Once a couple is living common-law, they will become subject to a number of rules which will limit their ability to "income-split". Income-splitting is a technique where the higher-income partner transfers or loans income-earning assets to the lower-income earning partner so that the amount of tax paid by the couple as a whole is decreased. Unfortunately, the *Income Tax Act* will "attribute" income and capital gains earned on the transferred assets back to the higher-income partner, except in a very few scenarios (for example, where the higher-income partner has made a spousal RRSP contribution to the RRSP of the lower-income partner, and the funds are not withdrawn from the RRSP within a prescribed period of time). The attribution rules apply to a person who is the taxpayer's common-law partner at the time of the loan or transfer of the property, as well as a person who became the taxpayer's common-law partner after the loan or transfer of property was made to that person. Therefore, you cannot avoid the attribution rules by transferring the property prior to becoming a common-law couple.

- *Child Care Expense Deduction.* The Child Care Expense Deduction must generally be used by the lower-income partner. Therefore, high-income individuals who were claiming the deduction may now find that it is not as valuable if it must now be claimed by a lower-income partner who may not have the ability to use the deduction if their taxable income is too low.

Regardless of the advantages and disadvantages of being considered "common-law" under the *Income Tax Act*, the important thing to keep in mind is that you must speak with your advisors on a regular basis to ensure that you are filing your tax returns properly, and taking advantage of the benefits which are available. However, in doing so, you must not lose sight of the property law issues which are relevant to common-law partners, and which are discussed in section 3.4, especially when you are transferring assets to a common-law partner, or making spousal RRSP contributions.

There are some tax strategies which are available to married and common-law couples, and which are discussed in more detail in section 5.2 of Chapter 5, "Married". Although common-law couples can generally take advantage of these strategies to the same degree as married couples, they should keep in mind that their property rights may not be the same as a married couple (see section 3.4 for further discussion). Therefore, in the discussion on tax planning strategies in Chapter 5, where recommendations are made to shift assets from one married spouse to another, consideration should be given as to whether or not this strategy is advisable for common-law couples if there is no cohabitation agreement in place. If one common-law partner gives assets to the other common-law partner, and they do not live in a jurisdiction where they have the right to a division of family property upon relationship breakdown or the right to inherit the property at the time of death, transferring assets from one common-law partner to another solely for tax purposes may not be recommended.

## 3.4 FAMILY LAW ISSUES

Many common-law couples assume that since they are treated the same as married couples under the *Income Tax Act*, they will be treated the same as married couples for all purposes. However, that is not the case. As noted earlier, most family laws are governed by provincial legislation, and the laws across Canada are extremely inconsistent. It is important to be familiar with the laws in your province in order to understand what your rights are (see section 3.9, "Jurisdiction Differences", for the rules in your province).



### 3.4.1 Spousal Support

Almost all Canadian jurisdictions provide that common-law couples may seek support from their partner, if they can prove financial need and if they meet certain other conditions which are referred to in section 3.9, "Jurisdiction Differences". In Quebec, *de facto* couples are not entitled to support no matter how long they have lived together – only couples which register as a civil union are entitled to make a claim for spousal support in Quebec.

Keep in mind that the factors considered by a court in determining whether or not an individual is entitled to spousal support differ in each jurisdiction, and are beyond the scope of this book. If you have separated from a common-law partner and feel that you need support, you should seek the assistance of a qualified family lawyer in your jurisdiction.

## 3.4.2 Division of Family Property

### *3.4.2.1 Family Property Remedies for Common-Law Couples*

For many couples, the ability to receive support from a former common-law partner is not an important issue, since they each earn an income. However, the right to divide the assets acquired during the course of the relationship may be a much more important concern. It is important to note that unlike married couples, *common-law partners do not have any statutory right to a division of assets upon relationship breakdown in many jurisdictions.* Therefore, if all of the assets have been accumulated in the name of one partner, the other partner will not be automatically entitled to share in those assets. Going back to the provisions of the *Income Tax Act,* recall that assets may be transferred to your partner without triggering capital gains, and common-law partners may make a spousal RRSP contribution for their common-law partner. Although you are *allowed* to do this, you must seriously consider whether or not you *want* to engage in such strategies in the knowledge that you may never receive the property back. However, in some provinces, common-law partners do have a statutory right to apply for a division of property or an equalization payment, so see section 3.9, "Jurisdiction Differences", for a discussion of the rules in your province.

Even if you live in a jurisdiction which does not give you the right to apply for a division of family assets at the time of relationship breakdown, this does not mean that you will not be entitled to your partner's property under any circumstance. You may be able to file a lawsuit arguing that there has been an "unjust enrichment" on your partner's part, and therefore you should either be awarded damages or a part of the property, using the argument that your partner is holding the property for you under what lawyers call the "constructive trust" doctrine. For example, you may be able to rely on this principle if you have contributed towards the mortgage payments for a home which is in your partner's name. However, there is generally no unjust enrichment in respect of gifts given to a partner. If you provided housework, child care or personal care to a spouse, you may have a claim if your services allowed the spouse to earn income. There are also other forms of legal actions that may be launched, including a suit for payment for "services" which is referred to by lawyers as "quantum meruit" (this argument involves a situation where a promise was made for the services, but not paid).

Since litigation is a very uncertain process, relying on a future lawsuit is generally not advisable. Even if you do "win", it will generally only be after a long and expensive legal process. The better approach is to reduce your agreement to writing before a dispute arises. If you have agreed that any property acquired during the relationship is divisible, or if you have agreed that it is not, you should speak to a lawyer experienced in this area about signing a cohabitation agreement, to prevent an expensive and bitter court procedure in the future. Cohabitation agreements are discussed further in section 3.4.2.6.

### *3.4.2.2 Pensions*

Canada Pension Plan ("CPP") credits earned over the course of a common-law relationship are divisible, so long as the partners have lived together in a conjugal relationship for a period of at least 12 months. (Note that unlike the definition of common-law couple in the *Income Tax Act*, couples who are the parents of a child together will not be entitled to a division of pension credits unless they have lived together for at least 12 months.) Upon relationship breakdown, partners can apply to have the credits equally divided, so long as:

- the application is made within four years of the date of separation, or within 3 years of the death of the partner, if a former partner is deceased;
- the couple has been separated for at least one year; and
- the parties have provided a written and signed separation agreement or court order.

If your common-law partner is receiving disability benefits from the CPP, you may also be entitled to have these benefits split at the time of relationship breakdown. However, as discussed in section 3.1.2, it is possible that your federal pension benefits may be denied if you have not been filing your income tax returns as a common-law couple. Ensure that any documentation you complete indicates your accurate marital status — failure to do so could result in a denial of benefits at a later date.

In order to qualify for a division of benefits under the Quebec Pension Plan, *de facto* couples must have either lived together in a conjugal relationship for a period of at least 3 years, or for a period of at least 1 year while raising a child together.

For other pension plans, the rules will be governed by the relevant legislation. For federal pension plans (e.g., those covering the airlines, banks, and other federal industries), the rules are the same as those for the CPP, as discussed above. For provincial plans, the rules can vary quite significantly from province to province, so confirm with your pension administrator whether or not your partner would qualify for pension benefits in the event of relationship breakdown.

### *3.4.2.3 Where Treated Like a Married Couple*

You will note in section 3.9, "Jurisdiction Differences", that some jurisdictions have enacted legislation that provides that, either after a certain time period or after registration of your relationship with the provincial authorities, you will attain essentially all the same property rights as a married couple. If you live in one of these jurisdictions, consider the points outlined below.

- If your home is owned in the name of one partner, the other partner may have the right to stay in the house, and it is possible that the home cannot be mortgaged or sold without the other partner's consent, even if their name is not on title.

- If your "family property" is divisible, then it is possible that even assets acquired prior to the time of the relationship could be shareable. If you live in a jurisdiction where common-law partners have the right to apply for a division of family property, it may be advisable to enter into a cohabitation agreement setting out how your property will be divided. See Chapter 17, "Family Property", for a discussion of the rules regarding divisions of family property if you live in a jurisdiction where common-law partners are entitled to make such an application.

- In some jurisdictions, businesses are considered family property, and therefore shareable. If one partner has a business, the other partner may become entitled to a portion of that business. Even in jurisdictions where businesses are not sharable, it is possible that a common-law partner could become entitled to a portion of the business if they are found to have made a "contribution" to the business, whether direct, or indirect (which could include domestic work that enables the other partner to grow their business).

These are just some of the issues to consider if you live in a jurisdiction where common-law partners have property rights. Speak to a family lawyer for more information on your particular circumstances.

### 3.4.2.4 Jointly Held Assets

Common-law couples should also carefully consider how to hold title to their assets. In some cases, a couple may decide to take title to real property or financial investments in joint names simply because they are pre-occupied with saving probate fees at the time of death, or have not given proper consideration to the issue. However, probate fees across Canada are extremely small and should not be a major consideration in your wealth plan (see Chapter 22, "Probate", for more information on probate fees). In fact, adding a joint owner to a property can make the situation much more complicated. If you have contributed all of the funds towards the asset, will adding your partner as a joint owner make the assets shareable? If your partner can prove that the transfer was a "gift", this may in fact be the case. There have been cases where individuals have added a common-law partner to a property without giving it much thought, only to seriously regret that decision later, especially if they have to go to court to retain the right to their property.

Even if you have both contributed to the property, you should enter into a co-ownership agreement to decide what will happen in the case of relationship breakdown or death.

- Will one person have the right to buy out the other?
- If the property is sold, will each person be entitled to exactly half of the proceeds, or did one partner contribute more than the other, and therefore expects to receive more?
- Can each partner sell his or her interest in the property to anyone else, or will the other partner have the first option to buy their interest?
- Is the property considered a family home for the couple, in which case there are restrictions on selling or mortgaging even a portion of it without the other partner's consent? (See the Homestead Rights section for your province in section 3.9, "Jurisdiction Differences".)
- If the property is held as joint tenants, do the partners understand that except in Quebec, the last person to die may inherit the entire property? If one of the parties has children or other dependants to whom they want to leave something, jointly owned property should perhaps be held as "tenants in common", as opposed to "joint tenants". Where property is held as "tenants in common", there is no right of survivorship. (See Chapter 8, "Blended Families", for a discussion as to the problems that can result if

you own property in joint ownership with a partner and you have children from a previous relationship.)

Regardless of whether or not property is held as joint tenants or tenants in common, a co-ownership agreement should be entered into in order to minimize disputes in respect of the property at a future time.

### 3.4.2.5 Business Owners

You should also be careful when intermingling personal and business assets for maximum tax advantage. For example, some business owners or self-employed individuals structure their affairs so that, to the extent possible, any interest they pay on an outstanding debt is tax deductible. In order for interest to be tax deductible, it must be paid on loans taken out for the purpose of earning income. Therefore, interest on personal loans for items such as homes, cottages, cars and boats is not deductible. As a result, these individuals sometimes instead choose to shift as much of their debt as possible towards their business. However, a problem may arise where a couple then separates, and the non-business owner partner argues that they are entitled to half of the gross value of the house, since they are a joint owner of the home, and the home is free and clear of any mortgage (or the amount of the mortgage is artificially low due to the refinancing of the business). If a businessperson wants to embark on this type of planning, they should consult with their legal advisors prior to doing so.

### 3.4.2.6 Cohabitation Agreements

The above discussion illustrates the reasons why individuals in common-law relationships are well-advised to enter into cohabitation agreements with their partner to ensure that disputes are minimized in the event the relationship breaks down. Here are a few points to consider when signing a cohabitation agreement.

- Due to the uncertainty surrounding property rights for common-law couples, and the possibility that the law in your jurisdiction may change, you may wish to enter into a cohabitation agreement even if you are completely comfortable with the current law in your jurisdiction. This is because you may want to "lock-in" the current rules, and try to avoid the retroactive application of laws that may be passed in the future.

- A cohabitation agreement may also be recommended if there is any possibility that you and your partner may move to another jurisdiction in the future, which may have a different regime.

- Cohabitation agreements may also be useful in situations where a dispute has arisen over how long the couple has been living common-law. If you are relying on certain legal rights, and you must prove that you have lived in a common-law relationship for a specific period of time, a cohabitation agreement may provide the evidence you need of the length of the relationship. This may be particularly helpful in the event your partner dies, and his or her other heirs dispute any claim you may have against the estate (in jurisdictions where common-law partners have such rights).

- If you want to protect your property from becoming shareable, be sure that you and your partner not only release any rights that may be granted by statute, but also the ability to make a constructive trust or unjust enrichment claim.

- If one partner will be giving up a career or other source of income in order to raise a child, a cohabitation agreement may be recommended to give that person some financial security.

- Be aware of the fact that a cohabitation agreement cannot contemplate everything. For example, the ability of an individual to make a claim under his or her partner's insurance policies will depend upon the definition of "spouse" in the insurance policy – a private agreement will not bind an insurance company.

- You should speak to a qualified family lawyer in your jurisdiction of residence prior to entering into any type of cohabitation agreement, since a cohabitation agreement that deals with one issue may inadvertently result in the couple becoming subject to other family laws that were not intended.

- Individuals should seek the advice of a licenced professional with experience in the area, and, in all cases, each partner should receive independent legal advice.

- Cohabitation agreements should be in writing, signed by both parties and properly witnessed.

### 3.4.3 Child Support

If you have children, or intend to have children in the future, please see Chapter 10, "Children", for more information on the issues to consider.

Individuals who enter into a common-law relationship with a person who has a dependent child or dependent children must be prepared for the possibility that they may be required to provide ongoing support to that child, even if the relationship ends. If a court finds the common-law partner to be "in loco parentis", which essentially means that a person has taken on a parental role, that partner will have the same financial responsibilities as a natural or adoptive parent, although the extent of the responsibility will vary from jurisdiction to jurisdiction. Even if the child has two natural or adoptive parents who provide support to the child, it may still be possible for a former common-law partner to have a child support order registered against him or her. Common-law partners must be prepared for this responsibility, as in some cases, the obligation can extend into the child's adulthood.

Generally, parties will not be able to contract out of such an obligation, as a court is likely to overlook any contract that is not in the best interests of the child. The only way in which to potentially avoid the obligation is to avoid treating the child as yours in any way, although the courts appear to be willing to rule that a common-law partner is a parent to a partner's child even when they have almost no involvement in their life other than living common-law with the child's natural or adoptive parent. If you are attempting to avoid this type of obligation, you must be consistent in your actions — for example, if you list the child as a dependant on your insurance policies, it may be hard to argue later that the child is not in fact dependent upon you. If you are about to enter into a relationship where your partner has a child, speak with an advisor in your jurisdiction about the possible obligations you may have towards that child.

## 3.5 DISABILITY PLANNING

Individuals in common-law relationships should review their disability plan to ensure that it is consistent with their intentions.

- Have you designated your common-law partner as your power of attorney for finances and/or power of attorney for health care decisions? If you signed a power of attorney previous to entering into the relationship, that power of attorney may still be in force, meaning that someone else will have first priority to manage your affairs if you become incapacitated. If you have not appointed anyone as your power of attorney for finances or health care decisions, do not assume that your common-law partner will automatically have the right to make those decisions on your behalf. In many cases, they will have to apply to court for that right, and there could be many individuals who would have a prior right to act in that capacity — for example, separated (but not divorced) spouses, parents or children. See Chapter 18, "Powers of Attorney", for more information.

- Is your disability insurance sufficient for your needs, particularly if your common-law partner is financially dependent upon you?

Many of the disability issues relevant to common-law couples are the same as those that are relevant to married couples. See section 5.4 of Chapter 5, "Married", for more information.

## 3.6 ESTATE PLANNING

### 3.6.1 Pension Survivor Benefits

Where at the time of death, a person was living in a conjugal relationship with the deceased for a continuous period of at least one year, they will be entitled to receive survivor benefits under the Canada Pension Plan to the same extent as a married spouse. Unlike the rules in the *Income Tax Act*, living together for a shorter period of time with a child is not sufficient.

If you have been contributing to the Quebec Pension Plan, then in order to qualify for survivor benefits, *de facto* couples must have either lived together in a conjugal relationship for a period of three years, or for a period of one year while raising a child together.

A surviving common-law partner may also be entitled to survivor benefits under an employee pension plan, depending upon the rules in your jurisdiction. However, you should not assume that you will qualify for a pension – if you met the pension's definition of "common-law partner" after your partner had already started receiving the pension (and they elected to receive higher individual payments instead of choosing lower payments with a survivor pension), then your partner may no longer be able to change the payments in order to provide for a survivor pension. Speak to your financial planner about whether or not you will be entitled to receive survivor benefits under your partner's pension – if not, you will have to factor this into your financial plan when determining how much you need to save for your retirement.

## 3.6.2 Right to Inherit

Individuals in common-law relationships should ensure that they are aware of the laws in their jurisdiction regarding their rights in the event their common-law partner dies. *Individuals in common-law relationships cannot assume they will be entitled to their partner's estate at the time of death.* See section 3.9, "Jurisdiction Differences", for a further discussion of the rules in your province. If the understanding is that each partner is to leave their estate to the survivor, that should be set out in a properly drafted will. It is important that the will be drafted by a qualified professional — under no circumstances would a "will kit" be recommended. If you have other heirs whom you wish to benefit, especially children from previous relationships, the situation can be even more complex. (See Chapter 8, "Blended Families", for a further discussion where ex-spouses or children from previous relationships are involved.)

If you live in a jurisdiction where common-law partners do not have property rights at the time of death, then executing a properly drafted will may be particularly important. This could be especially true if you have children who will be entitled to inherit your property, as any unrealized capital gains or deferred taxes on registered assets will be triggered far sooner than if the assets had been left to the common-law partner. Speak with an experienced estate planning lawyer to ensure your will is consistent with your current intentions.

## 3.6.3 Inheriting Tax Effectively

See section 5.5.2 in Chapter 5, "Married", for a discussion on how spousal trusts can be an effective mechanism for leaving inheritances in a tax efficient manner. The tax advantages respecting spousal trusts are also available for couples who are considered to be living common-law under the *Income Tax Act* (see section 3.3, "Tax Planning").

## 3.6.4 Appointing Personal Representatives

It is important for individuals in common-law relationships to have properly drafted wills not only if they want to ensure that their partner is left part or all of their estate, but also if they want to appoint their partner as their personal representative. Common-law couples cannot assume that a court will name their surviving partner as their personal representative if they have not done so in their will — in some jurisdictions, common-law partners are not considered next of kin, so children or parents would have first priority to act as administrator of the estate. (The "administrator" is essentially the executor. The term administrator is used when the person has been appointed by the court, as opposed to by a will.)

### 3.6.5 Preventing Challenges from Other Family Members

Some individuals in common-law relationships, particularly same-sex relationships, do not want to leave their estate to their partner in their will for fear that their family will challenge the will. In order to prevent these types of disputes, these individuals should consider holding their property jointly, or using an alter ego trust. However, these strategies have many drawbacks, which are discussed in Chapter 22, "Probate". If you are in this situation, it will be important for you to discuss your situation with a qualified professional.



### 3.6.6 Implications of Marriage at a Later Date

Given that wills are generally rendered void at the time of marriage (except in Quebec), it may be worthwhile to put a clause in your will indicating that the will is being drafted in contemplation of marriage (if, in fact, marriage is being contemplated at some point in the future). This will negate the necessity of redoing your will after you marry (except in Prince Edward Island if the couple marries more than one month after writing the will, since a will drafted in contemplation of marriage cannot be written more than one month in advance of the marriage itself). See Chapter 5, "Married", for further information on the implications of marriage.

Note that in some jurisdictions, entering into a common-law relationship will also negate a will. See section 3.9, "Jurisdiction Differences", for details pertaining to your jurisdiction.

### 3.6.7 Dependant's Relief Applications

If you die while in a common-law relationship, and your surviving common-law partner does not feel that he or she was left a sufficient amount of the estate, it is possible that the law may allow him or her to make a claim against your estate (commonly known as a "dependant's relief application"). The rights of a surviving common-law partner to make a claim against an estate vary from jurisdiction to jurisdiction. Generally, the ability to make a dependant's relief claim will depend upon financial need, although in some cases a moral obligation will also be considered. See section 19.6 in Chapter 19, "Distribution of an Estate", for an explanation as to who is entitled to make a dependant's relief application against an estate in your jurisdiction.

### 3.6.8 RRSP and RRIF Beneficiary Designations

Individuals in common-law relationships must be particularly careful when making direct beneficiary designations on registered investments. This is because such a designation can have unintended tax consequences should you happen to be separated at the time of death. Normally, spouses can receive registered investments on a tax-deferred basis at the time of their spouse's death, and this tax-deferral is available even if the couple is separated, but not divorced. However, with common-law couples, this tax-deferral will only apply so long as the couple has not been separated for more than 90 days. This could cause significant problems in a situation where the couple has been separated for more than 90 days, but the former common-law partner is still designated as the direct beneficiary, since the former common-law couple will still receive the gross proceeds of the registered investment, but the estate will be responsible for paying the tax liability associated with that asset. If the beneficiaries of the estate are not the common-law partner, then these beneficiaries could in effect receive less of the estate because they had to pay the taxes for the registered investments received by the former common-law partner. For this reason, it may be better to name your estate as the beneficiary of your registered investments, and distribute them in your will.

### 3.6.9 Other Issues

There are also certain other estate planning issues that you should discuss with your partner.

- Do you have emergency funds so that a surviving partner can cope financially if your assets are frozen for a period of time after death?
- Have you discussed funeral arrangements? Do you want to be buried next to each other? What type of service would you like?
- If you would like to donate your organs, is your common-law partner aware of this? Do they know where you keep your organ donation card?

These types of discussions need to take place sooner rather than later in order to ensure that an already traumatic event does not become even more stressful.

## 3.7 INSURANCE PLANNING

When you enter into a common-law relationship, you should consider whether you have adequate insurance in place. As discussed in section 3.5, it is important to review the provisions of your disability insurance, to determine if it is sufficient for your purposes, and also consider whether or not critical illness and long-term care insurance are necessary.

In addition to this, you should also review your life insurance needs with your financial advisor. If you and your partner have only been able to maintain your lifestyle because your income is available, think about how your death might impact the survivor's financial well-being. If their standard of living would fall significantly, consider whether additional life insurance is necessary. Life insurance can also provide retirement planning strategies for affluent Canadians beyond their RRSPs. See section 5.6 of Chapter 5, "Married", for the types of insurance couples should consider or Chapter 25, "Insurance", for more insurance-oriented strategies.



## 3.8 FIRST NATIONS MEMBERS

Individuals who are living in a common-law relationship and are living on a reserve generally have fewer property rights than common-law partners living off reserve. Under the *Indian Act* (Canada), band members have the right to occupy reserve land, but the land is Crown land held in trust for the particular band. Occupancy of the land may be managed by the band, or registered in the Indian and Northern Affairs Canada's Reserve Land Register. The *Indian Act* (Canada) does not contain any reference as to how land is to be divided upon the breakdown of a common-law relationship. However, the courts cannot order that a certificate of possession be given to someone in particular, and they cannot order that one partner be allowed to occupy the home, or order another partner to leave the home.

See section 19.5 of Chapter 19, "Distribution of an Estate", for information as to how a First Nations Member's estate is treated at the time of death. First Nations Canadians who are in a common-law relationship (or non-First Nations Canadians who are involved in a common-law relationship where reserve land is being occupied) should speak with an experienced advisor to ensure they understand their rights and obligations, and to ensure that their wealth planning documents will operate in a manner consistent with their intentions.

# 3.9 JURISDICTION DIFFERENCES

## 3.9.1 Alberta

### *3.9.1.1 General Definition*

For the purposes of most statutes in Alberta, common-law couples will be entitled to certain rights if they meet the definition of an "adult interdependent relationship" ("AIR"). A relationship of interdependence means a relationship outside of marriage in which two persons share one another's lives, are emotionally committed to one another and function as an economic and domestic unit — it does not need to be conjugal. A person is the adult interdependent partner ("AIP") of another person if:

- the person has lived with the other person in a relationship of interdependence:
  - for a continuous period of at least three years; or
  - of some permanence, if there is a child of the relationship by birth of adoption; or
- they have entered into an AIP agreement.

Alberta legislation allows for non-conjugal relationships, so even a brother and sister could enter into an AIR, but only if they sign an AIP agreement, not simply by living together for a specific period of time. However, these couples do not have rights with respect to each other's pension, as pension plans recognizing platonic relationships cannot be registered under the *Income Tax Act.* They are also not considered to be common-law couples for the *Income Tax Act.* As AIP agreements have specific requirements in order to be enforceable (e.g. witnesses), you should speak to a family lawyer if you would like to enter into this type of agreement.

### 3.9.1.2 Support Rights

Under Alberta law, an individual who meets one of the three tests listed in section 3.9.1.1 for being an adult interdependent partner will be entitled to apply for support from their partner, although the amount ordered will vary depending upon the facts of the case.

### 3.9.1.3 Family Property Rights

In Alberta, only married couples are entitled to a division of family property under the family property legislation. Upon relationship breakdown, a common-law partner must either rely on the provisions of a cohabitation agreement (or AIP agreement), or must rely on one of the legal arguments referred to in section 3.4.2.1.

### 3.9.1.4 Homestead Rights

Common-law partners do not currently have any rights of possession to a family home that is not registered in their name, although a court may grant an adult interdependent partner a right of exclusive possession in the event of separation.



### 3.9.1.5 Rights at the Time of Death

If an adult interdependent partner (as defined in section 3.9.1.1) dies without a will, the surviving partner will be entitled to inherit in the same manner as a surviving spouse. See section 19.6 of Chapter 19, "Distribution of an Estate", for information on how an estate is distributed in Alberta.

If an adult interdependent partner dies with a will, then their surviving partner will only receive the amount provided for in the will, as they will not have the right to apply for a division of property under Alberta's family property legislation. However, they may be entitled to make a dependant's relief application to receive a portion of the estate if the amount left to them in the will is insufficient.

### *3.9.1.6 Effect on Previous Wills*

It is very important for common-law couples in Alberta to understand that a will is rendered void upon entering into an AIP agreement, although a will is not rendered void simply by living together for a period of time, whether with or without a child. Wills drafted in contemplation of entering into such an agreement are not voided at the time of the AIP agreement.

Couples who enter into AIP agreements should ensure that they re-write their wills after the date of the agreement, if their will was not written in contemplation of the relationship. Couples who have not entered into such an agreement, but are contemplating doing so, should indicate in their current wills that they are being drafted in contemplation of entering into such an agreement, so that the will is not voided because of the later agreement.

## 3.9.2 British Columbia

### *3.9.2.1 General Definition*

For the purposes of most statutes in British Columbia, common-law couples are defined as couples who have lived together in a "marriage-like" relationship for at least two years.

### *3.9.2.2 Support Rights*

Couples who meet the test referred to in section 3.9.2.1 will be entitled to apply for support, although the amount ordered will vary depending upon the facts of the case.

### *3.9.2.3 Family Property Rights*

Only married couples are entitled to a division of family property under British Columbia's family property legislation. Upon relationship breakdown, a common-law partner must either rely on the provisions of a cohabitation agreement, or must rely on one of the legal arguments referred to in section 3.4.2.1.

#### *3.9.2.4 Homestead Rights*

Common-law partners do not have any rights of possession in a family home that is not registered in their name.

#### *3.9.2.5 Rights at the Time of Death*

If one partner dies without a will, the surviving partner is entitled to the same portion of the estate as a married spouse would be if they have lived together in a marriage-like relationship for at least two years. See section 19.6 of Chapter 19, "Distribution of an Estate", for information on how an estate is distributed in British Columbia.

If one partner dies with a will, but does not leave a sufficient amount for the surviving partner in the will, the surviving partner may make an application under the *Wills Variation Act*, arguing that the deceased had a "moral obligation" to provide for him or her in the will if they have lived together in a marriage-like relationship for at least two years.

#### *3.9.2.6 Effect on Previous Wills*

Entering into a common-law relationship has no effect on previous wills, so a new will should be executed if you would like your common-law partner to inherit all or part of your estate.

### 3.9.3 Manitoba

#### *3.9.3.1 General Definition*

For the purposes of most statutes in Manitoba, common-law couples are defined as couples who have done one of the following:

- registered their relationship under *The Vital Statistics Act*;
- lived together in a conjugal relationship for a period of at least three years; or

- lived together in a conjugal relationship for a period of at least one year, and have a child together.

See below for a further discussion of which definitions must be met for which purposes.

### 3.9.3.2 Support Rights

Common-law couples who meet any of the tests listed in section 3.9.3.1 will be entitled to apply for support, although the amount ordered will vary depending upon the facts of the case.

### 3.9.3.3 Family Property Rights

Common-law couples who have registered their relationship under *The Vital Statistics Act* or who have lived together for at least three years will be entitled to apply for an equalization of family property in the event of relationship breakdown in the same manner as a married spouse. See section 17.4.3 of Chapter 17, "Family Property", for more information on how family property is divided in Manitoba.

Note that common-law couples who have only lived together for a period of one year with a child will not be entitled to this right. Separated partners from relationships which did not meet the required tests must either rely on the provisions of a cohabitation agreement, or must rely on one of the legal arguments referred to in section 3.4.2.1.

### 3.9.3.4 Homestead Rights

*The Homesteads Act* (Manitoba) applies to common-law couples, so that on the death of one of the partners, the survivor will be entitled to a life interest in the home, and a provision to the contrary in a will may not be effective, although the parties may be able to contract out of this provision. Note that this is only effective if the couple has registered their relationship under *The Vital Statistics Act* or lived together for at least three years — living together for one year with a child is not sufficient.

Common-law partners may not act as power of attorney for each other when dealing with the family home. When appointing a power of attorney, be sure to appoint an alternate who will be able to sign documents relating to the family home in the event you become incompetent to handle your affairs. See section 18.4.3.1 of Chapter 18, "Powers of Attorney".

#### *3.9.3.5 Rights at the Time of Death*

If a common-law partner dies without a will, the surviving partner will be entitled to inherit in the same manner as a surviving spouse if they meet any of the tests set out in section 3.9.3.1. See section 19.6 of Chapter 19, "Distribution of an Estate", for information on how an estate is distributed in Manitoba.

If a common-law partner dies with a will, the surviving partner can either choose to take the portion of the estate provided for in the will, or make an application for an equalization of family property if they either:

- registered their relationship under *The Vital Statistics Act*; or
- lived together in a conjugal relationship for a period of at least three years.

If the surviving common-law partner is in financial need, they may also make a claim under *The Dependant's Relief Act* if the couple was living together at the time of death or had been living together within three years of the time of death or if the surviving partner was being paid or was entitled to be paid maintenance and support by the deceased under an agreement or a court order at the time of death. For the purposes of a dependant's relief application, a person who meets any of the three tests listed in section 3.9.3.1 will be considered a common-law partner.

#### *3.9.3.6 Effect on Previous Wills*

Entering into a common-law relationship has no effect on previous wills, so a new will should be executed if you would like your common-law partner to inherit all or part of your estate.

### 3.9.4 New Brunswick

#### *3.9.4.1 General Definition*

For the purposes of most statutes in New Brunswick, common-law couples are defined as couples who have lived together in a conjugal relationship either:

- continuously for a period of not less than three years in a family relationship in which one person has been substantially dependent upon the other for support; or

- in a family relationship of some permanence where there is a child born of whom they are the natural parents.

### 3.9.4.2 Support Rights

Couples who meet either of the tests listed in section 3.9.4.1 will be entitled to apply for support, although the amount ordered will vary depending upon the facts of the case.

### 3.9.4.3 Family Property Rights

In New Brunswick, only married couples are entitled to a division of family property under the family property legislation. Upon relationship breakdown, a common-law partner must either rely on the provisions of a cohabitation agreement, or one of the legal arguments referred to in section 3.4.2.1.

### 3.9.4.4 Homestead Rights

Common-law partners do not have any rights of possession in a family home that is not registered in their name.

### 3.9.4.5 Rights at the Time of Death

If a common-law partner dies without a will, their surviving partner will not be entitled to any part of their estate under the intestacy legislation.

If a common-law partner dies with a will, their surviving partner will only be entitled to receive that portion of the estate given to them in the will, as they will have no right to apply for a division of family property.

However, if they were living together at the time of death, or had been living together within the year prior to the time of death, and they meet one of the tests listed in 3.9.4.1, the surviving common-law partner may be able to make a dependant's relief application to receive a part of the estate, whether or not the deceased died with or without a will.

#### 3.9.4.6 Effect on Previous Wills

Entering into a common-law relationship has no effect on previous wills, so a new will should be executed if you would like your common-law partner to inherit all or part of your estate.

### 3.9.5 Newfoundland

#### 3.9.5.1 General Definition

For the purposes of most statutes in Newfoundland, a common-law couple is defined as a couple who has lived together in a conjugal relationship for a period of either:

- at least two years; or
- at least one year and they are the biological or adoptive parents of a child.

#### 3.9.5.2 Support Rights

Couples who meet either of the tests listed in section 3.9.5.1 will be entitled to apply for support, although the amount ordered will vary depending upon the facts of the case.

#### 3.9.5.3 Family Property Rights

In Newfoundland, only married couples are entitled to a division of family property under the family property legislation. Upon relationship breakdown, a common-law partner must either rely on the provisions of a cohabitation agreement, or one of the legal arguments referred to in section 3.4.2.1.

#### 3.9.5.4 Homestead Rights

Common-law partners do not have any rights of possession in a family home that is not in their name.

### 3.9.5.5 Rights at the Time of Death

If a common-law partner dies without a will, their surviving partner will not be entitled to any part of their estate.

If a common-law partner dies with a will, their surviving partner will only be entitled to receive that portion of the estate given to them in the will, as they will have no right to apply for a division of family property or make a dependant's relief application.

### 3.9.5.6 Effect on Previous Wills

Entering into a common-law relationship has no effect on previous wills, so a new will should be executed if you would like your common-law partner to inherit all or part of your estate.

## 3.9.6 Northwest Territories

### 3.9.6.1 General Definition

In the Northwest Territories, common-law couples are defined as couples who have been living together in a conjugal relationship either:

- for a period of at least two years; or
- in a relationship of some permanence with a natural or adopted child.

### 3.9.6.2 Support Rights

Common-law couples who meet either of the tests listed in section 3.9.6.1 will be entitled to apply for support, although the amount ordered will vary depending upon the facts of the case.

### 3.9.6.3 Family Property Rights

Common-law couples who meet either of the tests listed in section 3.9.6.1 will be entitled to a division of family property in the event of relationship breakdown in the same manner as married spouses. See section 17.4 of Chapter 17, "Family Property", for more information how family property is divided in the Northwest Territories.

### 3.9.6.4 *Homestead Rights*

The Homesteads Act applies to common-law couples who meet either of the tests listed in section 3.9.6.1, so that on the death of one of the partners, a non-owning survivor will be entitled, for 60 days after the spouse's death, to retain possession, rent free, as against both the deceased partner's estate and a person who, at the time of the deceased spouse's death, owns an interest in the family home as a joint tenant with the deceased spouse.

### 3.9.6.5 *Rights at the Time of Death*

If a common-law partner dies without a will, the surviving partner will be entitled to inherit in the same manner as a surviving spouse. See section 19.6 of Chapter 19, "Distribution of an Estate", for information on how an estate is distributed in the Northwest Territories.

If a common-law partner dies with or without a will, the surviving partner can either choose to take the portion provided in the will or intestacy legislation, or make an application for a division of family property.

A surviving common-law partner may also make an application under the *Dependant's Relief Act* to receive part of the estate. In addition, a person who cohabited with the deceased for one year immediately before the time of the death of the deceased and was dependent on the deceased for maintenance and support may also make a dependant's relief application.

### 3.9.6.6 *Effect on Previous Wills*

Entering into a common-law relationship has no effect on previous wills, so a new will should be executed if you would like your common-law partner to inherit all or part of your estate.

## 3.9.7 Nova Scotia

### *3.9.7.1 General Definition*

In Nova Scotia, a couple can register their relationship as a "domestic partnership", which will give them many of the same rights as a married couple. In order to obtain these rights, the couple must register their relationship under Nova Scotia's *Vital Statistics Act,* and they must be living, or intend to live, in a conjugal relationship. You will be entitled to register your relationship if you and your partner are both adults, you have resided in Nova Scotia for at least three months or own property there, and you are not already married or in another registered relationship. Couples who do not register their relationship will have very few property rights, as discussed below.

### *3.9.7.2 Support Rights*

Individuals in a registered domestic partnership and couples who have been living together in a conjugal relationship for at least two years will be entitled to apply for support, although the amount ordered will vary depending upon the facts of the case.

### *3.9.7.3 Family Property Rights*

Individuals in a registered domestic partnership will be entitled to a division of family property in the event of relationship breakdown in the same manner as a married spouse. See section 17.4 of Chapter 17, "Family Property", for more information on how family property is divided in Nova Scotia.

Common-law couples who have not registered their relationship as a domestic partnership are not entitled to a division of family property under the family property legislation. Upon relationship breakdown, a common-law partner must either rely on the provisions of a cohabitation agreement, or one of the legal arguments referred to in section 3.4.2.1.

### 3.9.7.4 Homestead Rights

Domestic partners have the same rights of possession of a family home that is not registered in their name as married spouses do. Common-law partners who are not in a registered relationship generally do not have such rights.

### 3.9.7.5 Rights at the Time of Death

If a domestic partner dies without a will, the surviving partner will be entitled to inherit in the same manner as a surviving spouse. (See section 19.6 of Chapter 19, "Distribution of an Estate", for information on how an estate is distributed in Nova Scotia.) However, surviving common-law partners who have not registered their relationship do not have the right to inherit if their partner dies without a will.

If a domestic partner dies with a will, the surviving partner can either choose to take the portion provided in the will, or make an application for a division of family property. A domestic partner may also make an application under Nova Scotia's *Dependant's Relief Act* to receive part of the estate. Common-law couples who have not registered their relationship generally do not have these rights.

### 3.9.7.6 Effect on Previous Wills

Registering a domestic partnership will revoke all previous wills, unless the will was made in contemplation of that partnership. Nova Scotia's *Wills Act* does not provide for the possibility that after having written a will in contemplation of a domestic partnership with a particular person, you then marry that same person. If you later marry your domestic partner, you must either sign a new will after the date of marriage, or sign a new will prior to the date of marriage, which is drafted in contemplation of marriage.

Entering into a common-law relationship that has not been registered as a domestic partnership will have no effect on a previous will, so you will need to sign a new will if you want your common-law partner to inherit all or part of your estate.

## 3.9.8 Nunavut

The rules in Nunavut are generally the same as in the Northwest Territories. See section 3.9.6.

## 3.9.9 Ontario

### *3.9.9.1 General Definition*

For the purposes of most statutes in Ontario, common-law couples are defined as couples who have either:

- lived together in a conjugal relationship for at least three years; or
- lived together in a relationship of some permanence and they are the natural or adoptive parents of a child.

### *3.9.9.2 Support Rights*

Couples who meet either of the tests set out in section 3.9.9.1 will be entitled to apply for support, although the amount ordered will vary depending upon the facts of the case.

### *3.9.9.3 Family Property Rights*

In Ontario, only married couples are entitled to apply for an equalization of family property under the family property legislation. Upon relationship breakdown, a common-law partner must either rely on the provisions of a cohabitation agreement, or must rely on one of the legal arguments referred to in section 3.4.2.1.

### *3.9.9.4 Homestead Rights*

Common-law partners do not have any rights of possession in a family home that is not registered in their name.

### 3.9.9.5 Rights at the Time of Death

If a common-law partner dies without a will, their surviving partner will not be entitled to any part of their estate under the intestacy legislation.

If a common-law partner dies with a will, their surviving partner will only be entitled to receive that portion of the estate given to them in the will, as they will have no right to apply for an equalization of family property.

Whether the deceased died with or without a will, the surviving common-law partner may be able to make an application to receive a portion of the estate under Ontario's *Succession Law Reform Act,* if the deceased was providing support or was under a legal obligation to provide support to the common-law partner immediately before his or her death. For the purposes of the dependant's relief legislation, a person will be considered a common-law partner if they cohabited with the deceased for a period of at least three years continuously, or in a relationship of some permanence and they are the natural or adoptive parents of a child. However, this three-year period does not have to occur immediately prior to death.



### 3.9.9.6 Effect on Previous Wills

Entering into a common-law relationship has no effect on previous wills, so a new will should be executed if you would like your common-law partner to inherit all or part of your estate.

## 3.9.10 Prince Edward Island

### 3.9.10.1 General Definition

There is no general definition of common-law partner in Prince Edward Island, so please refer to the sections below for the conditions necessary in each situation.

### 3.9.10.2 Support Rights

For the purposes of support, a spouse includes either of two persons who have cohabited outside marriage:

- continuously for a period of not less than three years; or
- in a relationship of some permanence, if they are the natural or adoptive parents of a child.

However, the amount of support awarded will vary depending upon the facts of the case.

### 3.9.10.3 Family Property Rights

In Prince Edward Island, only married couples are entitled to a division of family property under the family property legislation. Upon relationship breakdown, a common-law partner must either rely on the provisions of a cohabitation agreement, or must rely on one of the legal arguments referred to in section 3.4.2.1.

### 3.9.10.4 Homestead Rights

Common-law partners do not have any rights of possession in a family home that is not registered in their name.

### 3.9.10.5 Rights at the Time of Death

If a common-law partner dies without a will, their surviving partner will not be entitled to any part of their estate under the intestacy legislation.

If a common-law partner dies with a will, their surviving partner will only be entitled to receive that portion of the estate given to them in the will, as they will have no right to apply for a division of family property.

Whether the deceased died with or without a will, an opposite-sex common-law partner who, for a period of at least three years immediately prior to the date of death of the deceased, lived and cohabited with the deceased as the spouse of the deceased, and was dependent upon the deceased for maintenance and support, may make an application under Prince Edward Island's *Dependants Relief Act* to receive a portion of the estate.

#### 3.9.10.6 Effect on Previous Wills

Entering into a common-law relationship has no effect on previous wills, so a new will should be executed if you would like your common-law partner to inherit all or part of your estate.

### 3.9.11 Quebec

#### 3.9.11.1 General Definition

Since Quebec is not a common-law province, but is instead governed by a civil code, unmarried couples are referred to as *de facto* couples. *De facto* couples generally do not have any property rights no matter how long they live together, although the *Quebec Pension Plan* considers a *de facto* partner to be a spouse if they have either lived together for at least three years, or they have lived together for at least one year and have either a natural or adopted child (both parties must be parents of the child). The one-year test may be waived in the case of death.

Unmarried couples may also choose to enter into a civil union, in which case they will be effectively treated like married couples for virtually all purposes under Quebec law.



#### 3.9.11.2 Support Rights

A partner in a civil union will be entitled to apply for support in the same manner as a married spouse, although the amount ordered will vary depending upon the facts of the case. Partners to a *de facto* couple are not entitled to make an application for support.

#### 3.9.11.3 Family Property Rights

A partner in a civil union will be entitled to a division of family property (which is known as the family patrimony) in the event of relationship breakdown in the same manner as a married spouse. See section 17.4 of Chapter 17, "Family Property", for more information on how the family patrimony is divided in Quebec. Partners to a *de facto* couple are not entitled to a division of the family patrimony.

### 3.9.11.4 Homestead Rights

A partner in a civil union has the same rights of possession to a family home that is not registered in their name as married spouses do. Partners to a *de facto* couple have no rights regarding possession of family homes that are not registered in their name.

### 3.9.11.5 Rights at the Time of Death

If a partner to a civil union dies without a will, the surviving partner will be entitled to inherit in the same manner as a surviving spouse. See section 19.6 of Chapter 19, "Distribution of an Estate", for information on how an estate is distributed in Quebec where there is no will. The surviving partner of a *de facto* couple has no right to inherit at the time of death where there is no will.

If a partner to a civil union dies with a will, the surviving partner can either choose to take the portion of the estate provided in the will, or make an application for a division of the family patrimony or support in the same manner as a married spouse. The surviving partner of a *de facto* couple has no right to apply for a division of the family patrimony or support.

It is significant that *de facto* spouses have very few property rights as against a deceased partner (other than perhaps pension rights), since in Quebec there is no right of survivorship on jointly held property and direct beneficiary designations are not allowed on many types of registered investments. Therefore, it may be particularly important for individuals involved in a *de facto* relationship to have a properly drafted will.

### 3.9.11.6 Effect on Previous Wills

Since marriage has no impact on a will in Quebec, entering into a civil union or *de facto* relationship will have no impact on a will.

## 3.9.12 Saskatchewan

### 3.9.12.1 General Definition

In Saskatchewan, the definition of common-law couple varies from statute to statute, as described below.

### 3.9.12.2 Support Rights

Common-law couples:

- who have lived together in a conjugal relationship for at least two years, or

- who are in a relationship of some permanence and have a child together,

will be entitled to apply for support, although the amount ordered will vary depending upon the facts of the case.

### 3.9.12.3 Family Property Rights

Common-law couples who have cohabited as spouses continuously for a period of at least two years will be entitled to a division of family property in the event of relationship breakdown in the same manner as a married spouse. However, the assets which are shareable will generally be only those which are acquired after the two-year time period has been met, except in the case of a family home or household goods which are generally shareable even if acquired prior to the relationship. See section 17.4 of Chapter 17, "Family Property", for more information on how family property is divided in Saskatchewan.

Only common-law couples who have lived together for a sufficient period of time will be entitled to this right. Separated partners from relationships that did not meet the required test must either rely on the provisions of a cohabitation agreement, or must rely on one of the legal arguments referred to in section 3.4.2.1.

### 3.9.12.4 Homestead Rights

A common-law partner who has been cohabiting with a common-law partner for at least two years prior to the time of death, or who cohabited with the common-law partner for a period of at least two years, and that period ended within 24 months preceding the time of death, has the same rights of possession of a family home that is not registered in their name as married spouses do.

### 3.9.12.5 Rights at the Time of Death

If a common-law partner dies without a will, the surviving partner will be entitled to inherit in the same manner as a surviving spouse, if they had lived together as spouses continuously for at least two years, and if they were either living with the deceased partner at the time of death, or had ceased living with them within two years of the time of death. See section 19.6 of Chapter 19, "Distribution of an Estate", for information on how an estate is distributed in Saskatchewan where there is no will.

If a common-law partner dies with a will, the surviving partner can either choose to take the portion of the estate provided in the will, or make an application for a division of family property, if they had been living together continuously for a period of at least two years.

A surviving common-law partner may also make an application under the *Dependant's Relief Act* to receive part of the estate. For the purposes of the *Dependant's Relief Act,* a common-law couple includes both a couple who had cohabited continuously for a period of not less than two years prior to the time of death, or a couple in a relationship of some permanence where they were the parents of a child.

### 3.9.12.6 Effect on Previous Wills

In Saskatchewan, *a will written after 2001 is rendered void after a person has been in a common-law relationship for a period of at least two years, unless it was drafted in contemplation of that relationship.* Therefore, if you drafted a will prior to entering into the relationship, or in the first two years of the relationship, and the will did not specifically state that it was drafted in contemplation of that relationship, it will become void once you have lived together for a period of two years. It should be noted that if a will contemplates a common-law relationship, and the couple then gets married, the marriage will not revoke a will (marriage generally revokes a will unless the will was written in contemplation of that marriage).

## 3.9.13 Yukon

### *3.9.13.1 General Definition*

In the Yukon, the definition of common-law couple varies from statute to statute, as described below.

### *3.9.13.2 Support Rights*

Individuals of an opposite-sex, common-law relationship who have cohabited in a relationship of some permanence, may, during cohabitation or not later than three months after the cohabitation has ceased, apply to a court for an order for support, although the amount ordered will vary depending upon the facts of the case.



### *3.9.13.3 Family Property Rights*

In the Yukon, only married couples are entitled to division of family property under the family property legislation. Upon relationship breakdown, a common-law partner must either rely on the provisions of a cohabitation agreement, or must rely on one of the legal arguments referred to in section 3.4.2.1.

### *3.9.13.4 Homestead Rights*

Common-law partners do not have any rights of possession in a family home which is not in their name.

### *3.9.13.5 Rights at the Time of Death*

If a common-law spouse has cohabited with the deceased as a couple for at least 12 months immediately before the other person's death and the other person dies without a will, the court may order that there be retained, allotted and applied for the support, maintenance, and benefit of the common-law spouse, so much of the net real or personal estate, or both, of the intestate as the court sees fit, to be payable in the manner the court directs.

If a common-law partner dies with a will, their surviving partner will only be entitled to receive that portion given to them in the will, as they will have no right to apply for a division of family property. However, a common-law partner who, for a period of at least 12 months immediately prior to the date of the death of the deceased, lived and cohabited with the deceased as the spouse of the deceased and was dependant upon the deceased for maintenance and support, may make an application under the *Dependants Relief Act* to receive a portion of the estate.

### *3.9.13.6 Effect on Previous Wills*

Entering into a common-law relationship has no effect on previous wills, so a new will should be executed if you would like your common-law partner to inherit all or part of your estate.

# 3.10 CASE STUDIES

## 3.10.1 Living Common-Law, Jurisdiction Generally Does Not Recognize Status

Jim and Liz are living common-law in Ontario, a province which generally does not recognize common-law partners. (Note that the consequences in this case would be substantially similar in New Brunswick, Newfoundland, Prince Edward Island, and the Yukon. This case study would also generally apply to couples in Nova Scotia or Quebec who have not registered their relationship, or couples in other provinces who have not lived together long enough to meet the provincial tests for being a common-law couple.) Jim and Liz have been living together as a common-law couple for more than five years.

Jim and Liz have not yet signed a cohabitation agreement, wills, powers of attorney, or any other wealth planning documents. Jim and Liz have been operating under the assumption that since they must file their income tax returns in the same manner as a married couple, that they have all the same rights as a married couple. Jim owned a home prior to the relationship, and Liz moved in with him, but the title to the home was never changed to joint ownership. Jim and Liz have a three-year-old daughter and a newborn son. Liz is currently at home raising their family, and does not anticipate returning to work in the near future. Since Jim earns all of the family income, all of their savings are in his name, which includes a $100,000 RSP. They have asked their lawyer what would happen in the event of relationship breakdown or death.

Jim and Liz's lawyer informs them that in the event of relationship breakdown, Jim would probably have to pay support to Liz and the children (if she had custody of the children), but he would not be required to make an equalization payment in accordance with the provincial family law legislation. Although Liz may be able to sue Jim using legal arguments such as unjust enrichment and quantum meruit, that could involve a lengthy and expensive process, and there is no guarantee as to what percentage of Jim's assets Liz would receive. Also, since they are not spouses, Liz would have no right of possession to their home. Liz is obviously concerned to learn that she would have limited property rights — as a result, they decide to sign a cohabitation agreement setting out their agreement regarding the division of family property, to give Liz more security.

Jim and Liz's lawyer also informs them that since they do not have wills, their children would receive their estates in the event one of them was to die. This would mean that the Public Trustee would have to manage the estate until the children reach the age of majority, at which time the estate would be paid out to the children. Therefore, if Jim died first, his home and RRSPs would go to his children, leaving Liz with nothing, and potentially triggering a large tax bill, as the RRSPs are taxable at the time of death unless they are left to a spouse or common-law partner or children who are minors.



Liz may be able to make an application to receive part of Jim's estate under the provincial dependants' relief legislation, but again, it is uncertain as to how much of the estate she would receive, as it would be up to the court to award her the amount it deemed appropriate. Both Jim and Liz are not happy with this arrangement, so they agree to sign wills designating each other as their primary beneficiaries, personal representatives and guardians of their children.

Liz and Jim also decide that they need to review the following with their lawyer, accountant and financial advisor to ensure that their wealth plan is in proper order:

- their tax situation, to see if there is any opportunity to income split in the future;
- their powers of attorney for finances and health care decisions;

- their beneficiary designations on insurance policies and registered assets; and
- their insurance needs, including disability, critical illness, long-term care and life insurance.

Jim and Liz now realize that they cannot assume that they have the same property rights as married couples, and they have agreed to review their wealth plan with their advisors on a regular basis.

## 3.10.2 Living Common-Law, Jurisdiction Generally Recognizes Status

Suzie and Siobhan are living common-law in Saskatchewan, a province which generally recognizes common-law partners (note that the consequences in this case study would be substantially similar in Alberta, British Columbia, Manitoba, the Northwest Territories, Nova Scotia, Nunavut and Quebec, if the couple has met the provincial conditions for being a common-law couple, adult interdependent relationship, registered domestic partnership or civil union, as applicable). Suzie and Siobhan have been living together as a common-law couple for just over a year.

Suzie and Siobhan have not signed a cohabitation agreement, wills, powers of attorney or any other wealth planning documents. Suzie owned a home prior to the relationship, and Siobhan moved in with her, but title to the home was never changed to joint ownership. Suzie and Siobhan each earn a substantial income, and they have no children. They have asked their lawyer what would happen in the event of relationship breakdown or death.

Suzie and Siobhan's lawyer informs them that in Saskatchewan, common-law couples who have cohabited as spouses for a period of at least two years have substantially the same rights as married couples. (Note that the time period requirement or registration requirement varies from jurisdiction to jurisdiction. See section 3.9, "Jurisdiction Differences", for the rules in your jurisdiction.) Therefore, if they continue to live together for at least one more year, they will each be entitled to apply for a division of family property in the event of relationship breakdown in the same manner as a married couple. Suzie is surprised to hear that in Saskatchewan, family homes which were acquired prior to the relationship are shareable — she had assumed that only assets acquired during the course of the relationship, or the growth in value, would be shareable. (In Saskatchewan, only the assets acquired after the two-year time period requirement has been met are shareable, except for a family home and household goods.) Suzie and Siobhan decide to sign a cohabitation agreement indicating that the value of Suzie's home as at the date on which they started living together belongs to Suzie, and only the growth in value from that date will be divisible in the event of relationship breakdown. (Note that there will be some differences in some of the jurisdictions listed at the beginning of this case study. For example, in Alberta and British Columbia, common-law couples are not subject to the family law legislation regarding the division of family property unless they specifically agree to that. Also, in most jurisdictions, the value of assets purchased prior to the time of the relationship is not shareable. See section 17.4 of Chapter 17, "Family Property", for a discussion of the family property rules in your jurisdiction.)

Suzie and Siobhan also learn that once they have lived together for a period of at least two years, the survivor will inherit part or all of the deceased's estate in the same manner as a surviving spouse (see section 19.6 of Chapter 19, "Distribution of an Estate", for a description of how an estate is distributed in your jurisdiction if there is no will). Although they are generally happy with that, Siobhan had wanted to leave some of her assets to her parents, who are not financially well off. Even if Siobhan had signed a will leaving all or part of her estate to her parents, that will would no longer be effective once they have lived together for two years, since in Saskatchewan, wills are automatically revoked after living common-law for two years. If she wants to do that, she will need to sign a new will. Suzie is also concerned that Siobhan's parents will argue that Suzie is not entitled to any part of Siobhan's estate, since they have refused to acknowledge that Suzie and Siobhan are involved in a spousal relationship. Suzie and Siobhan both decide to sign wills to ensure that everyone is aware of their wishes (which indicate that they are in contemplation of their common-law relationship and are not to be revoked at the two-year mark). They also decide to put the house in joint ownership, so that it can pass to the survivor without paying probate fees, and without potentially becoming subject to a challenge of the estate by Suzie's family. However, Siobhan pays Suzie for her half of the house prior to doing this. If Siobhan did not pay Suzie, then Suzie could lose half of the value of the home at the time of separation without any compensation.

Suzie and Siobhan also decide that they need to review the following with their lawyer, accountant and financial advisor to ensure that their wealth plan is in proper order:

- their tax situation, to see if there is any opportunity to minimize tax in the future, possibly through the use of testamentary trusts, since they are both earning a substantial income, and will be able to invest any amounts left to them should one of them die (see Case Study 5.8.2 for an example of how testamentary trusts can save tax where beneficiaries are in a high income tax bracket);

- their powers of attorney for finances and health care decisions;
- their beneficiary designations on insurance policies and registered assets; and
- their insurance needs, including disability, critical illness, long-term care and life insurance.

Suzie and Siobhan now realize that they need to customize their wealth plan as a result of their relationship, and they have agreed to review their wealth plan with their advisors on a regular basis.

# CHAPTER 4

# ENGAGED





Getting engaged can be an exciting event. The frenzy leading up to the wedding can fray the nerves of even the most well tempered individuals. However, in the hustle and bustle of preparing for your big day, there are issues you should consider to ensure that your wealth plan is in order, and your assets will be protected in the event of marriage breakdown, death or disability. The following is a discussion of some of the issues which should be discussed prior to the wedding day. For further discussion on the issues related to getting married, see Chapter 5, "Married".

## 4.1 FINANCIAL PLANNING

Prior to getting married, it is very important that you sit down with your fiancé(e) and discuss your philosophies towards finances. Disagreement over finances is one of the leading causes of marriage breakdown, so it is often best to try and avoid, or at a minimum manage, these types of disagreements from the beginning. For example, one of you may be a saver and one of you may be a spender. Try to agree on a fair distribution of your combined income, and a reasonable amount which will be saved on a monthly basis towards joint goals such as retirement or saving for a house.

Finances can be a particularly sensitive topic in blended families (e.g. families where there are children from previous relationships). In blended families, there are usually competing interests between different families, and potentially different opinions on spending and saving money. If you are in a blended family situation, see Chapter 8, "Blended Families".

Maintaining independence is often a key goal for individuals who are getting married. Although it may be a good idea to combine your finances to a certain degree, consider whether or not there will be less tension if each spouse has a separate bank account where they can keep some of their "fun" money, which they can spend at their discretion.

Also, consider whether or not you should each have a credit card. If you only have one joint credit card, then the card will be cancelled in the event the primary cardholder dies, or chooses to cancel the card due to separation. In many cases, spouses prefer to each be the primary cardholder on one credit card, so that they will continue to have credit regardless of what happens to the other spouse. Some widows and widowers experience problems obtaining credit if they have not had a credit history for many years (or decades). It is a prudent idea to divide credit facilities between each spouse so that each maintains a credit history.

## 4.2 TAX PLANNING

If the parties have not lived together prior to getting married, their marriage will mean that they will be filing their tax returns jointly for the first time. See section 5.2 in Chapter 5, "Married", for a further discussion of the implications of having to file your tax returns as a married couple, and the strategies you may be able to implement to reduce your taxes. Also see section 3.3 of Chapter 3, "Common-Law Couples", for a discussion of some of the tax advantages and disadvantages a couple may begin to experience when they start to file their income tax returns as a couple.

Couples should speak with their professional tax advisors for further information regarding the tax implications of getting married.

# 4.3 FAMILY LAW ISSUES

## 4.3.1 Family Property Rules

Many individuals who get married choose not to sign a pre-nuptial agreement, since marriage breakdown is not a topic which couples like to think about or discuss. In many cases, this is not a problem, either because the marriage stands the test of time, or because the assets are divided in an equitable manner. However, several jurisdictions have unique rules which can result in a division of property that can be very different from what the parties expected. For example, many people expect that only the assets which are acquired during the course of the marriage will be shareable. However, in some provinces, including Newfoundland, Ontario and Saskatchewan, a family home (which could include a cottage) may be shareable even if it was acquired by one spouse prior to the date of marriage. In British Columbia and Nova Scotia, many different assets may be shareable, regardless of whether or not they were acquired before or after the time of marriage. Whether or not you choose to enter into a pre-nuptial agreement, be aware of the family property laws in your jurisdiction prior to getting married so that there are no nasty surprises later. See section 17.4 of Chapter 17, "Family Property", for further discussion of the family property rules in your province, and section 17.2.5 for a discussion about the things to consider when entering into a domestic contract.

In many cases, if you and/or your fiancé(e) have significant assets, a pre-nuptial agreement should be signed regardless of whether or not you are satisfied with the division of family property set out in the current legislation, since legislation can change at any time, and it is always possible that you may move to another jurisdiction where the rules may be quite different. At a minimum, keep records of the assets which you are bringing into the marriage so that you will receive "credit" for these assets if your jurisdiction exempts assets acquired prior to the relationship.

Negotiating a marriage contract also provides both parties with an opportunity to understand more about each other's financial history, since each person has to provide complete disclosure about their assets and liabilities, and the person asking the awkward questions is usually a lawyer or other independent third party. If your partner has gone bankrupt in the past, has a bad credit rating or is not diligent in filing their tax return, this may impact your decision to get married. Arguments over finances are one of the leading causes of marital breakdown, and if there is going to be a large debt to pay off, this could severely impact your financial future.

In recent years, there has been much attention paid to the fact that some pre-nuptial agreements have been struck down or varied by the courts. Although this sometimes happens, bear in mind the circumstances outlined below.

- Many of the provisions which the courts have varied have had to do with either spousal support or child support. A court will not uphold a provision it feels to be unfair, especially if the provision will detrimentally affect a child. There are no guarantees that provisions regarding spousal or child support will be upheld, especially if your circumstances have changed since the date of the agreement.

- Provisions respecting a division of property are often viewed quite differently than provisions regarding support. If the parties have agreed in advance that their property will be divided in a certain manner, most courts will give a pre-nuptial agreement quite a bit of weight. However, to the extent there was not full disclosure at the time of the agreement, or the agreement was entered into under duress, it is possible that a court may ignore the provisions in an agreement regarding a division of property.

- For a pre-nuptial agreement to have a good chance of withstanding a court challenge, both parties *must receive independent legal advice prior to signing the agreement.* If you choose to have one lawyer represent both parties, this will drastically increase the risk that the agreement will be set aside.

- If you signed a cohabitation agreement while you were living common-law, do not assume that it will automatically become a pre-nuptial agreement or marriage contract at the time of your marriage. Confirm with your family lawyer if the agreement must be updated in order to remain in effect.

If you have significant assets, expect to inherit significant assets, or you are concerned about how the family law rules work in your jurisdiction, be sure to meet with an experienced family lawyer well in advance of the wedding. Do not wait until the last minute to sign the agreement. The agreement should be signed as far in advance of the wedding day as possible in order to avoid any future suggestion of duress. If your fiancé(e) is reticent about signing an agreement, consider an agreement which includes a "sunset" clause, meaning that it will cease to be effective if the marriage continues for a pre-determined period of time (e.g. at least five years, ten years, etc.).

### 4.3.2 Gifts from Family Members

If the parents of either spouse will be giving money to the couple to purchase a home or other item, the parents must be comfortable with the fact that the money may be shareable in the event of marriage breakdown. (See section 17.4 of Chapter 17, "Family Property", for a discussion as to how family property is divided in your jurisdiction and section 17.2.2 for a general discussion regarding making loans and gifts to children.) In fact, if their child dies, their daughter-in-law or son-in-law may inherit the asset outright. If the intent is that the money is a loan, then legal documentation must be signed to that effect, and the parties must treat the funds as a loan. However, even if legal documentation is put in place, if there is no evidence that the loan was ever meant to be repaid, it is possible that a court would still consider the amount shareable in the event of marriage breakdown.

If you receive a gift or inheritance, those assets will generally be exempt from a division of marital property (although see section 17.4 of Chapter 17, "Family Property", for a discussion of the family property rules in your jurisdiction). However, if inherited or gifted assets are then used to purchase a family asset, they will become shareable. For example, if you inherit $100,000 from your parents upon their death, you could choose to invest that sum in a separate account in your name only, and keep records to evidence that those funds are from an inheritance, and therefore not shareable. In addition, if your parent's will indicates that any growth on those assets is also not shareable, then the growth on those investments will generally be protected, although some jurisdictions will not uphold a clause of that nature. However, what if you redeem those investments to buy a cottage? If the cottage is used by your spouse and family, then it may become a family asset and become shareable. Individuals who receive gifts or inheritances should understand the implications of using these assets for family purposes. Once an asset becomes shareable, it will no longer be exempt from a division of property, so care must be taken when dealing with these assets.



## 4.4 DISABILITY PLANNING

Before you get married, review your disability insurance situation with your financial advisor. Be sure that you and your spouse will be able to maintain your standard of living if you are going to take on an obligation (such as a mortgage) which requires either or both of your incomes to sustain.

Couples should not assume that they automatically have the right to act for each other in the event one of them becomes incapacitated. Even if you are married, you need to give your spouse a power of attorney if you want them to be able to handle your financial affairs when you are not able to. In fact, in some jurisdictions, a spouse is not allowed to act as attorney for their spouse when dealing with the marital home, even when their spouse has expressly given them that right. Be sure to appoint an alternate attorney in order to ensure that someone will be able to handle your financial affairs in the event you or your spouse is not able to. See Chapter 18, "Powers of Attorney", for further discussion on this issue.

Also consider giving your spouse a power of attorney for personal care. Individuals are not automatically entitled to make medical decisions for their spouse in all jurisdictions, and many hospitals require these documents before accepting the instructions of a spouse.

## 4.5 ESTATE PLANNING

Although no one wants to think about it, you should ensure that your estate plan is in order so that there are no unpleasant surprises in the event that you or your future spouse dies. Here are a few things that you should keep in mind.

- Review your will prior to your wedding day. It is important to remember that, except in the province of Quebec, any wills signed prior to the date of marriage will be rendered void upon marriage, unless the will was drafted in contemplation of marriage. (See section 5.7 of Chapter 5, "Married", for further information on when a will is rendered void in your jurisdiction.) In order to ensure that there is no time during which you do not have a will, you should sign your new will prior to getting married, but ensure that it is drafted "in contemplation of marriage".

- If you are drafting a will in contemplation of marriage, consider wording that makes any bequests to your future spouse dependent upon the marriage actually taking place.

- If you are in a blended family situation, it becomes especially important to ensure that you balance the interests of your new spouse with those of any children from a previous relationship. It is imperative that you seek professional advice to ensure that your estate plan and financial plan are in order. (See Chapter 8, "Blended Families", for more information.) You do not want a situation where your children are inadvertently disinherited due to your marriage to your new spouse.

- When writing your will, you may want to include a provision on guardianship, even if you don't have children yet, in order to ensure your children have a guardian when they need one. Many couples are too overwhelmed at the time their children are first born to worry about changing their wills. If you are re-writing your will due to your marriage, consider if a guardianship clause would be appropriate, so that you do not need to change your will again once your children are born. See section 10.5.1 of Chapter 10, "Children", for further discussion on choosing a guardian.

- Make sure you change your beneficiary designations as required, including RRSPs, RRIFs, TFSAs and insurance policies, including supplemental insurance. Marriage does not automatically nullify any beneficiary designations made prior to the date of marriage, except in the province of Quebec. However, keep in mind that most pensions provide that a surviving spouse or common-law partner will be entitled to receive any death benefits, regardless of who is designated as beneficiary. Also keep in mind that just because you are getting married does not automatically mean you should designate your spouse as the direct beneficiary of all of your assets, particularly if you have children from a previous relationship. See section 5.5.4 of Chapter 5, "Married", and 8.5.1 of Chapter 8, "Blended Families".

## 4.6 INSURANCE PLANNING

Be sure to review your life insurance requirements before you get married. If you die prematurely, your spouse may have to sell their home or other assets if they cannot afford their current standard of living without your income. If you or your spouse could suffer a deterioration in your standard of living if one of you were to die, be sure that you have adequate insurance so that an already traumatic event does not become even more difficult due to lack of finances. Insurance can become quite expensive as you get older, so it may be a good idea to apply for insurance while you are still young and healthy.

Also review your disability insurance plan to ensure that it will provide sufficient protection in the event of disability, particularly if your spouse will be financially dependent upon you. Consider whether critical illness or long-term care insurance would be appropriate for you (see Chapter 25, "Insurance", for a discussion about these different types of insurance).

Review your medical and dental plans to ensure that your new spouse will be covered, if they do not have a medical or dental plan of their own. Compare your medical and dental plans with the plans of your spouse, and decide whether adding your spouse as a dependant is worth the additional cost. If you are covered under both your own plan and your spouse's, ensure that your dentist or other provider is aware of the fact that part of the payment may be coming from a separate insurer.

## 4.7 JURISDICTION DIFFERENCES

There are no jurisdiction differences for this chapter.

## 4.8 CASE STUDIES

### 4.8.1 Engaged, One Spouse Owns a Home

Kevin and Marie-Claude are engaged to be married in a few months. Kevin has investments worth approximately $400,000, and Marie-Claude has a home worth approximately $400,000. Kevin and Marie-Claude decide to keep Marie-Claude's home in her name alone, and Kevin will move into it after the wedding day.

If Kevin and Marie-Claude live in British Columbia, Newfoundland, Nova Scotia, Ontario or Saskatchewan, their assets will not be divided in the manner which Kevin and Marie-Claude originally anticipated. Kevin and Marie-Claude had assumed that any assets acquired prior to the date they were married would be exempt from a division of marital property. Unfortunately, in some provinces, there is a major exception to this rule — the marital home is divisible even if it was purchased prior to the date on which they were married (and in some provinces, any asset acquired prior to the date is shareable). Therefore, if Kevin and Marie-Claude live in Newfoundland, Ontario or Saskatchewan at the time they separate, their assets would be divided as follows:

Kevin's investments:

- originally worth $400,000
- currently worth $500,000

- increase of $100,000 is divisible
- original value is exempt from division

Marie-Claude's house

- originally worth $400,000
- currently worth $500,000
- entire value is divisible
- original value is not exempt in their jurisdiction

Therefore, the difference between the divisible amounts is $400,000 ($500,000 - $100,000), and Marie-Claude must transfer funds or property equalling 50% of that difference, or $200,000, even though they both brought assets of equal value into the marriage, and they both grew equally in value. In fact, Marie-Claude may have to sell her home in order to satisfy Kevin's family property claim. It would be in Marie-Claude's best interest to have a pre-nuptial agreement signed prior to their wedding date so that it is clear that the value of the home prior to the date of marriage is exempt from a division, and it is only the assets acquired after the date of marriage (or their increase in value) which are shareable.

Note that if Kevin and Marie-Claude lived in British Columbia or Nova Scotia, Marie-Claude may not have to make any payments to Kevin. Although the entire value of her home may be divisible in British Columbia and Nova Scotia, it is possible that all of Kevin's assets acquired prior to the date of marriage will also be divisible if they are considered family assets, so they would offset one another.

If Kevin and Marie-Claude lived in a province other than British Columbia, Newfoundland, Nova Scotia, Ontario or Saskatchewan, it is unlikely that either of them would have to transfer any of their property to the other, since they each brought in assets to the marriage of equal value, and their assets both grew equally in value during the marriage. Since the total growth during the marriage was experienced equally (Kevin's assets increased by $100,000 and Marie-Claude's assets grew by $100,000), and they both left the marriage with assets of equal value. However, they may still prefer to enter into a pre-nuptial agreement to "lock-in" their agreement, in case they later decide to move to another jurisdiction, where the division of assets may not be as they anticipated.

If Marie-Claude had added Kevin as a joint owner on her home, the asset would be divisible. If Marie-Clause wants to keep the asset exempt, she should keep it in her sole name alone.

## 4.8.2 Engaged, One Spouse Owns a Business

Daniel and Sara are in their early 50s and are engaged to be married. They live in a jurisdiction where businesses are shareable as family assets. (See section 17.4 of Chapter 17, "Family Property", for a description of which assets are shareable in your jurisdiction). Daniel has owned a car dealership for over 25 years, which has become extremely successful. Daniel owns the car dealership through a corporation, of which he owns 100% of the shares. Daniel would like to pass the corporation on to his children from a previous marriage (Laurie and Caroline), but he is concerned that if he marries Sara, the growth in the value of the business will be shareable. If he remains married to Sara for a significant period of time, the amount which he might have to pay her either at the time of marriage breakdown, or at the time of death, may be so significant that he may have to borrow money from a bank, or potentially sell the business and divide the proceeds. At this stage of his life, the possibility of selling the business will not impact Daniel personally to a large degree, since he may decide to retire soon in any event. What is of concern to David is the fact that he wants to pass the dealership onto Laurie and Caroline, and he is worried that he may not be able to do that given his potential obligations to Sara.

Daniel and Sara decide to speak to an experienced family lawyer well in advance of their wedding date to determine how to best address this issue. They decide to enter into a pre-nuptial agreement which provides that under no circumstances is Sara to be entitled to a portion of the business. They agree that Sara may be entitled to a larger portion of their non-business assets to compensate, as well as spousal support, as she has decided to quit her job and help out at the dealership. Daniel and Sara also prepare wills which provide that the shares in Daniel's business are to go to Laurie and Caroline in the event of his death, with Sara receiving the remainder of Daniel's estate. In addition, they prepare new powers of attorney, review their beneficiary designations on their insurance policies and registered assets, increase their insurance policies as necessary, and review their tax situation with their accountant to determine if there are any possibilities to save tax.

# CHAPTER 5

# MARRIED

There are many wealth and succession planning issues that married couples need to consider. Although in many cases these issues should be addressed prior to getting married, it is usually not too late to address them after you are married. However, married couples should not assume that if they establish a wealth plan at the time they get married that the process is complete. A wealth plan should be reviewed at least every three to five years and after any major life event to ensure that there are no changes in personal circumstances or legislation that would necessitate a change to your plan.

# 5.1 FINANCIAL PLANNING

## 5.1.1 Credit Cards

Everyone should try to maintain their own credit rating, which is assessed individually, not as a couple. Therefore, it may be a good idea to have two credit cards, where one spouse is the primary cardholder on one card, and the other spouse is the primary cardholder on the other. If a primary cardholder leaves the other spouse or dies, the secondary credit card will be cancelled, which may put the other spouse in a difficult predicament. For example, if one spouse does not earn an independent source of income, they may not qualify for their own card in the event their spouse leaves them or dies. A spouse who is considering quitting their job (perhaps to raise a family) should obtain a credit card prior to quitting work (or obtain a card using their spouse as a guarantor) while they still have a source of income, and will have an easier time qualifying for credit. Also be sure to use the card on a semi-regular basis so that it does not go dormant. Although for obvious reasons, it is best to always pay credit card balances in full before the due date to minimize interest charges and to maintain a good credit rating.

## 5.1.2 Pension Plans

If you are reliant upon one or both incomes that are currently being earned by you and your spouse, review the terms of any pension plans on which you may be relying. Some pension plans do not pay a survivor benefit, although most will pay the surviving spouse 60% of the amount to which the pension-earning spouse was entitled. If the pension will not be paying a survivor benefit, or if the benefit will not be sufficient to maintain the survivor's lifestyle, you should speak to your financial advisor about supplemental life insurance to fund any deficit. It is also possible that a surviving spouse will not be entitled to receive a survivor's pension under a pension plan if they became the spouse of the pension plan member after pension payments have started. If you are relying on a survivor's pension and you married later in life, have your spouse confirm the terms of his or her pension to confirm that you are entitled to receive a survivor's pension. If not, you may need additional insurance on the life of your spouse.

Also, speak to your financial advisor as to the most effective way to have your pension paid out. It may be possible to receive a higher pension amount if you forego the survivor benefit. In many cases, the higher benefit amount is more than that required in order to fund a life insurance policy which would provide the spouse with sufficient capital to generate an equivalent income to the survivor pension at the time of death. Another advantage to this strategy is the fact that the death benefit received from the insurance policy will be received tax free, whereas pension payments are taxable, and may affect your right to receive certain government benefits, such as Old Age Security ("OAS"). However, not all pensions will allow the spouse to waive the survivor benefit, and it is important to review the costs and benefits of doing this with a qualified professional before you waive any entitlements. You will also obviously need to be insurable at a reasonable rate in order for this strategy to be an option.

If you change your name after you get married, you will need to apply for a new Social Insurance Number if you want to receive OAS or CPP benefits. All of your records need to be in the same name with the federal government, so it is generally recommended that you apply for a new SIN as soon as possible, so that there is no delay at the time you are eligible to start to receive your benefits. You should also apply for a new passport with your new legal name.

### 5.1.3 Emergency Funds

If you do not earn an income, and if the majority of the family assets are in your spouse's name, would you be able to maintain yourself for a period of a few weeks, if not months, if your spouse predeceased you? It is important to ensure that there are some "emergency funds" in the hands of each spouse, so that you are able to maintain yourself financially in case the funds of the other spouse are inaccessible, even for a short period of time. It can sometimes take several months for an estate to be administered, so consider what your cash flow needs may be during that time. A tax-free savings account ("TFSA") may be a good place to accumulate an emergency fund. See section 5.2.1.1 for more information on TFSAs.

## 5.2 TAX PLANNING

When a couple gets married, they must file their income tax returns as a married couple, which has a number of consequences. If you were living common-law prior to getting married, then you will already have been filing as a couple, so getting married will not change your tax situation. See section 3.3 of Chapter 3, "Common-Law Couples", for more information on the advantages and disadvantages of filing income tax returns as a couple.

Married couples should arrange their financial affairs so that as a family unit, they are paying as little tax as possible. Here are some strategies to consider if you want to ensure that your tax bill is minimized.

## 5.2.1 Income Splitting

In Canada, taxation is based on income earned individually, as opposed to family income. Therefore, a couple will pay less in tax if they each earn $50,000, than if one of them earns $100,000 and the other earns nothing. This is because the higher the taxable income, the higher the tax rate. Therefore, unless both spouses are in the same tax bracket, you may save money if some of the income earned by the higher-income earner can be reported by the lower-income earner.

Unfortunately, this is not easy to do. The *Income Tax Act* contains a set of rules called the "attribution rules". If the higher-income spouse simply transfers or loans some of their income to the lower-income spouse, the *Income Tax Act* will "attribute" that income back to the original taxpayer. However, there are some strategies which allow income splitting without the attribution rules applying.

### *5.2.1.1 Tax-Free Savings Accounts*

Individuals may contribute up to $5000 annually (which amount will be indexed) to a TFSA in which none of the income, capital gains or withdrawals are taxable. Any Canadian over the age of 18 will be allowed to open a TFSA, and there will be no attribution on any of the amounts. Therefore, a higher income-earning spouse will be able to make contributions to a TFSA in the name of a lower income-earning spouse, and all the income earned on those contributions will accrue to the lower income-earning spouse tax free. TFSAs will be of benefit to high-income earners who would like to shelter the growth on their investments (although unlike RRSPs, there will be no tax deduction for the contribution, so contributions to an RRSP may still take first priority in terms of tax advantages). However, TFSAs will also be of assistance to low-income earners, since unlike RRSPs, none of the amounts withdrawn from a TFSA will be taxable, so withdrawals will not impact federal benefits such as the Old Age Security pension, the Guaranteed Income Supplement, the Age Credit, the GST credit or the Canada Child Tax Benefit. Speak to your financial advisor about the benefits of opening a TFSA both for yourself and your spouse.

### 5.2.1.2 Pension Income Splitting

Married couples are entitled to allocate a portion of certain types of their pension income to their spouse. This may result in less tax being paid if one spouse is in a higher income tax bracket than the other. Please see section 14.2.2.1 of Chapter 14, "Seniors and Retirees" for more information on pension income splitting, as well as some other types of income splitting available to older individuals, including a division of CPP benefits.

### 5.2.1.3 Spousal RRSPs

If one spouse will be earning less than the other spouse during retirement, consider whether the higher-income spouse should be making RRSP contributions to a spousal RRSP, as opposed to making RRSP contributions to an RRSP in their own name. In this manner, the spouse with the lower income will be entitled to withdraw funds from the spousal RRSP during their retirement, and pay less tax than if the funds were withdrawn by the higher-income spouse. In addition, if one spouse would not otherwise have any pension income, a spousal RRSP may allow both spouses to use the pension credit when they turn 65. To be effective, this strategy should be implemented several years before retirement to allow more money to accumulate in the spousal RRSP.

The amendments to the *Income Tax Act* allowing couples to divide their pension income in a number of instances have led many people to believe that spousal RRSPs are no longer a valuable strategy. However, spousal RRSPs may still be useful in the following situations:

- if you want to retire before age 65, since if you are under 65, eligible pension income typically only includes payments from a registered pension plan and will not generally include amounts paid from an RRSP or RRIF;

- where you would like to split more than 50% of your pension income, since you can theoretically split 100% of your RRSP income;

- if you are over 71, since you cannot contribute to your own RRSP after that time;

- when the executor of an estate wishes to make an RRSP contribution after the time of death in order to reduce the taxes payable by the estate; and

- where you would like to invest more assets in the name of the lower-income earning spouse, since assets withdrawn from a spousal RRSP can be invested in the name of the spouse, assuming the attribution rules described below don't apply.

However, there are special "attribution" rules which apply to spousal RRSPs, so it is not possible for a spouse to simply make a contribution to a spousal RRSP, and then have the other spouse immediately withdraw the funds. If you make a contribution to a spousal plan and then your spouse withdraws the funds within a short time period after, the amount withdrawn will be taxable in your hands. The attribution rules will apply if any contributions to *any spousal plan* were made in the current year or in either of the two prior years. This means that if you make a contribution in 2009, your spouse cannot withdraw the funds in any of 2009, 2010 or 2011. In addition, if you want your spouse to be able to make a withdrawal in 2009, then you cannot make a contribution to any spousal plan in his or her favour in any of 2010, 2011 or 2012. For example, if your spouse withdraws $3000 from his or her spousal RRSP in February of 2012, and you then make a $4000 contribution to a spousal RRSP in September of 2012, the $3000 withdrawal will still be taxable in your name. Be very careful when making contributions to a spousal RRSP to ensure that the attribution rules will not apply.

### 5.2.1.4 Lower-income Spouse Does the Saving; Higher-income Spouse Does the Spending

In order to minimize taxes, the higher-income spouse should pay as many of the family expenses as possible (including the tax bill for the lower-income spouse), and the lower-income spouse should try to save as much of their income as possible. In this way, the lower-income spouse can invest their savings, and any income earned on these savings will be taxed in the hands of the lower-income spouse.

### 5.2.1.5 Prescribed Rate Loans

If you have investments which are earning taxable income, and the investment income is being taxed in the hands of the higher-income spouse, consideration should be given to entering into a "prescribed rate loan". This strategy allows one spouse to lend money to the other spouse at a prescribed rate (which is released by the Canada Revenue Agency every quarter). The lower-income spouse must pay the prescribed amount of interest to the higher-income spouse by January 30th of the year following any year in which the loan was outstanding (including the year in which the money is lent). However, any income earned above that interest rate will be taxed in the hands of the lower-income spouse. If the loan is used for the purpose of earning income (i.e. it is invested in income-producing assets), then the interest paid by one spouse to the other should be tax deductible. The interest paid will be taxable in the hands of the recipient spouse.

For example, if a higher-income spouse (the "Lender") had $50,000 in non-registered investments, he or she could sell those investments (which could trigger a capital gain or loss), and then loan the $50,000 to the lower-income spouse (the "Borrower"). The Lender would enter into a loan agreement which provides that the Borrower will pay the prescribed rate of interest to the Lender no later than January 30th of each year following every year in which the loan is outstanding. Let's assume that the prescribed rate at the time the loan is entered into is 3%, and the Borrower invests the $50,000 in investments which produce an annual return of 5%. The Borrower would then be required to pay $1500 ($50,000 x 3%) to the Lender no later than January 30th following each year in which the loan is outstanding. However, if the Borrower earns $2500 on the investments ($50,000 x 5%), they will pay tax on the additional $1000 ($2500 – $1500, assuming the interest is deductible), and the Lender will only be required to pay tax on the $1500 interest payment.

The following are a few key points to keep in mind when implementing this strategy:

- The Borrower will only be able to deduct the interest payment from their taxable income if the interest was incurred for the purpose of earning income (i.e., the loan was used to purchase income-earning investments, not used for a non-income purpose, such as contributing to an RRSP).

- The prescribed rate in effect at the time the loan is entered into will continue to be the amount which the Borrower must pay to the Lender, even if interest rates rise in the future.

- If the Lender experienced a capital loss when he or she sold the assets, that capital loss will be denied if the Borrower invests in identical securities within 31 days of the Lender selling their investments. This is due to the application of the superficial loss rules.

If you believe that a prescribed rate loan would be a good strategy for you, be sure to speak to both your financial and legal advisors to ensure that the loan is properly structured and documented.

### 5.2.1.6 Borrowing for the Purpose of Investing

Instead of borrowing funds from a spouse in order to make an investment, one spouse could borrow funds from a financial institution for the purpose of investing, if they are prepared to incur the risks of utilizing this strategy, and after consulting with their financial advisor. If they do incur such a loan, the lower-income spouse could borrow money from the higher-income spouse to pay the interest on an investment loan, which may allow the borrowing spouse to create an investment portfolio faster. If the investment portfolio is established in the name of the lower-income spouse, then any income earned on those investments will be taxed in the hands of the lower-income spouse in the future. However, the higher-income spouse should not guarantee the investment loan or provide any sort of collateral for the loan, or the attribution rules could apply, resulting in the income from the investments being taxed in the hands of the higher-income spouse.

### 5.2.1.7 Paying a Salary to a Spouse

If the higher-income spouse is self-employed, consider whether it would be advisable for that spouse to hire the lower-income spouse as an employee to whom they would pay a salary. Obviously, this is an effective strategy only to the extent that the lower-income spouse is validly earning that salary, and the salary paid is reasonable. If the higher-income spouse is earning employment income, and they want to be able to hire their spouse and deduct the salary, they should speak to their employer, as the employer will have to make such arrangement a term of the contract, or the salary may not be deductible.

If the lower-income spouse is also earning some income from another employer, it is possible that there may be an overpayment of CPP. Be sure to calculate the total CPP that has been paid, and obtain a refund if necessary.

### 5.2.1.8 Issuing Shares of a Corporation to a Spouse

If you own shares of a corporation which is considered a "small business corporation" under the *Income Tax Act*, consider whether it would be possible to have some of the profits of that corporation taxed in the hands of a lower-income spouse. This strategy generally does not work with investment corporations, due to the "attribution rules", unless both spouses have contributed funds to the corporation. For more information, see section 16.2 of Chapter 16,

"Family Businesses", for a discussion about the advantages and disadvantages of having a corporation.

## 5.2.2 Maximizing the Charitable Donation Credit

When filing your income tax returns, ensure that your tax credits are being used by the spouse who will receive the most benefit from them. For example, if you are both making charitable contributions, consider claiming all of the contributions on the income tax return of one spouse or the other. This may result in a greater tax savings because the federal tax credit rate applied to the first $200 in charitable contributions is lower than the tax credit rate applied to contributions in excess of $200. Therefore, you will receive a higher tax credit if one person claims charitable contributions of $300, than if both spouses claim charitable contributions of $150. For example:

| | | |
|---|---|---|
| Each Spouse Claims $150 | | |
| Spouse 1 | $150 x 15% | = $22.50 |
| Spouse 2 | $150 x 15% | = $22.50 |
| Total tax credit | | = $45.00 |
| | | |
| One Spouse Claims $300 | | |
| Spouse 1 | $200 x 15% | = $30.00 |
| | $100 x 29% | = $29.00 |
| | | = $59.00 |
| Spouse 2 | | = $ 0 |
| Total tax credit | | = $59.00 |

This example calculates only the federal portion of the tax credit. There will also be a provincial tax credit, which is calculated in a similar manner, using provincial tax rates (although there are different thresholds in Quebec — see section 24.5 of Chapter 24, "Charitable Giving", for more information).

It is generally best to claim tax credits on the higher-income earner's return to try and save provincial surtaxes in those provinces which assess surtaxes.

## 5.2.3 Maximizing the Medical Expense Credit

There is one credit, the medical expense credit, which may be more valuable if claimed on the lower-income earner's return. This is because only medical expenses in excess of 3% of your salary, or a set threshold, which is approximately $2000, may be claimed. Therefore, the lower the salary, the smaller the threshold required before you are allowed to begin claiming these expenses. If both spouses have incurred medical expenses, consider adding the expenses together and claiming the amount by which the combined amount exceeds the threshold on the tax return of the lower-income spouse. If it initially appears that you do not have sufficient expenses to meet the threshold, keep in mind that premiums paid for medical and dental coverage are considered medical expenses.

If one spouse requires an attendant, it may be more advantageous to claim the attendant costs as a medical expense rather than using the attendant caregiver credit, if one spouse has low taxable income. See Chapter 12, "Disabled Persons", for more information on the medical expense and attendant caregiver credits.

## 5.2.4 Transferring Unused Tax Credits

There are certain personal tax credits that may be transferred between spouses if one spouse does not have sufficient taxable income to use them. These credits include:

- the age credit;
- the pension credit;
- the tuition, textbook and education tax credits; and
- the disability tax credit.

When you file your tax returns, be sure to review the tax return of your spouse to ensure that no personal credits remain unused (although there are certain rules regarding the transfer of the education, tuition and textbook tax credits from children. See section 10.2.11 of Chapter 10, "Children" for more information).

## 5.2.5 Transferring Unused Capital Losses

If you have an asset that has an unrealized capital loss that you cannot use (perhaps because capital losses may only be used against capital gains, and you do not have any assets in a gain position), consider transferring the loss to a spouse who is able to utilize it (perhaps because he or she has taxable capital gains).

- First, the spouse who wants to use the loss ("Gain Spouse") must purchase the asset from the spouse who has no need for the loss ("Loss Spouse"). This purchase must be completed for fair market value and must be properly documented. *In our example, we will assume that Loss Spouse originally acquired shares in a company for $20,000, and those shares are now worth $10,000, so Gain Spouse acquires those shares for $10,000, which is their current fair market value.*

- Then, Gain Spouse must elect that the spousal rollover provisions will *not* apply. If Gain Spouse does not make this election, the attribution rules will apply so that the loss must be claimed in Loss Spouse's name. *In our example, if Gain Spouse elects out of the spousal rollover provisions, instead of the proceeds of disposition being deemed to be $20,000, they will be $10,000, which would trigger a loss.*

- However, because Loss Spouse owned the asset within 30 days of the date on which Gain Spouse disposed of the asset, the superficial loss rules will automatically apply. The superficial loss rules are a series of rules which operate to deny losses when affiliated individuals own identical assets on the 30th day before or after the original owner disposed of the shares. These rules operate so that one married spouse cannot sell assets that are in a loss position, and then have their spouse immediately reacquire that same stock, yet still allow the original owner to claim a capital loss on their tax return. Because the superficial loss rules applied to deny the loss in the hands of Loss Spouse, Gain Spouse will automatically acquire the asset at the higher cost base. *In our example, Loss Spouse will be denied the $10,000 capital loss, so the loss will be transferred to Gain Spouse, whose cost base will now be $20,000 for the shares, even though he or she only paid $10,000 for them.*

- If Gain Spouse holds the shares for at least 31 days and then disposes of them, they will be able to claim the loss in their hands, and use the loss against capital gains. *In our example, if Gain Spouse were to sell the shares after 31 days had passed, and assuming he or she received $10,000 for the shares, he or she would have a capital loss of $10,000, since their cost base was $20,000.*

Another option may be to have Loss Spouse sell the shares on the open market, then have Gain Spouse repurchase those shares, and hold them for 31 days before reselling. Depending upon commissions and other expenses, this may or may not be an easier route to go.

When your spouse triggers the capital loss, they will be required to use that loss against any capital gains which they are reporting in that taxation year. However, if there are excess capital losses, the excess amount may be carried back three years, or carried forward indefinitely. In the year of death (and the year prior to death), capital losses may generally be used against all types of income, and are not restricted to only being used against capital gains.

### 5.2.6 Maximizing the Spousal Tax Credit

You will be able to claim a spousal tax credit in respect of your spouse, if he or she earns less than a prescribed amount (currently $10,382). However, the amount of this credit is reduced by every dollar of income earned by your spouse.

If you are not able to income split with your spouse to reduce the amount of tax you pay as a family (see section 5.2.1), then it may be better to minimize the amount of income earned by your spouse in order to maximize the amount of the spousal tax credit (although in most cases, if at all possible, it would be better to transfer more of the higher-income spouse's income to the lower-income spouse). If your spouse is earning dividends from a taxable Canadian corporation, the *Income Tax Act* allows you to elect to report all of this income on your own tax return to avoid reducing the spousal tax credit. However, no partial elections are allowed, and prior to making the election, you should calculate the difference of tax due to your higher marginal rate. In some cases, it may be better to have the lower-income spouse pay the tax and lose the spousal credit. Also note that if the lower-income spouse paid interest in order to earn dividends, this amount cannot be transferred, and the interest deduction may lose its value if the lower-income spouse has no taxable income.

## 5.3 FAMILY LAW ISSUES

Although no one wants to think about the possibility of their marriage ending, in reality, it happens far too often. Even if you do not perceive yourself to be wealthy or in need of a pre-nuptial agreement, it is important for you to be aware of the family property rules in your province, so that there are no nasty surprises later. Although raising the subject of a marriage contract may seem awkward at first, communication regarding finances is important at an early stage in the relationship, and may in fact decrease the chances of divorce at a later date. A marriage contract can also serve to protect individuality, and provide for increased communications regarding finances throughout the relationship. In particular, early discussions regarding finances may decrease tensions in the following situations:

- blended families, where children from a previous relationship are distrustful of the new spouse, and need reassurances that their parent will not be "taken to the cleaners";
- situations where one spouse has significantly more wealth than the other, or one spouse will give up their career for the sake of the relationship;
- families where one spouse has brought in an asset with significant emotional attachment, such as a cottage, business or heirlooms; and
- situations where the spouses have significantly different spending patterns and/or views towards debt.

## 5.3.1 Important Family Property Laws

It is important to understand that the rules regarding how family property will be divided are different in each jurisdiction. The family property laws in some jurisdictions work in unexpected ways, so it is important to be familiar with the rules in your jurisdiction. See Chapter 17, "Family Property", for a complete discussion of the rules in your jurisdiction. Below are some of the rules which most frequently take people by surprise.

### *5.3.1.1 Assets Acquired Prior to the Time of Marriage*

Most people assume that it is only the assets which are acquired during the course of the marriage which are shareable. However, in Newfoundland, Ontario and Saskatchewan, the marital home may be shareable, even if it was acquired by one of the spouses prior to the time of marriage. In British Columbia and Nova Scotia, all family assets may be shareable, regardless of when they were acquired, and in Manitoba and New Brunswick, assets acquired "in contemplation" of marriage may be shareable. Some jurisdictions also provide that assets acquired while living common-law are shareable.

### 5.3.1.2 Businesses

Some jurisdictions include businesses as family assets, whereas some jurisdictions do not. Even in jurisdictions where businesses are generally not shareable, they may become shareable if the spouse makes a contribution to the business, whether direct or indirect.

### 5.3.1.3 Inheritances and Gifts

Do not assume that inheritances and gifts from third parties are always exempt from a division of family property. In some jurisdictions they are not exempt, and in other jurisdictions, the inheritance or gift may only be exempt if it has been kept separate, and not used for family purposes. For example, if an inheritance is used to acquire a family asset, such as a home or cottage, it may become shareable. However, even in jurisdictions where an inheritance is not shareable, the growth may still be shareable unless certain conditions are met. If you want to increase the chances of an inheritance or gift being exempt from a division of family property, then you should attempt to keep it as separate as possible. In particular, you should avoid adding your spouse as a joint owner to any investments made with the inherited or gifted money.

### 5.3.1.4 Right to Possession of Family Home

Most individuals assume that both spouses have the right to possess the family home, and in most cases, this is true. However, the right to occupy a family home is personal as against the owning spouse — if the home is owned by your spouse's parents, and then you separate, or your spouse dies, you may be left with nothing. You should carefully consider what your needs are when entering into a relationship — if the property is owned by your spouse's parents, then you are at risk if the marriage ends. Individuals in this position must be particularly aware of their rights if they choose to leave their career in order to raise a family or engage in other pursuits.

### 5.3.1.5 Not All Debt Is Shareable

You should be careful when intermingling personal and business assets for maximum tax advantage. For example, some business owners or self-employed individuals structure their affairs so that to the extent possible, any interest they pay on outstanding debt is tax deductible. In order for interest to be tax deductible, it must be paid on loans taken out for the purpose of earning income. Therefore, interest on personal loans for items such as homes, cottages, cars and boats is not deductible. As a result, business owners sometimes choose to shift as much of their debt as possible towards their business. However, a problem can arise where a couple then separates, and the non-business-owner spouse argues that he or she is entitled to half of the gross value of the house, since it is free and clear of any mortgage (or the amount of the mortgage is artificially low due to the refinancing with the business). Since in many cases a business is not shareable, the business owner will retain the business, but will also retain all of the debt, much of which may have arisen due to family purchases. If a businessperson wants to embark on this type of planning, they should consult with their legal advisors prior to doing so.

## 5.3.2 Domestic Contracts

If you decide that you are not comfortable with the laws regarding the division of family property in your jurisdiction, and you want to sign a marriage contract, be sure to obtain independent legal advice first. In order to increase the chances of a court agreeing that you have a valid prenuptial agreement or marriage contract:

- the parties should understand the nature and consequences of the agreement or contract; and

- the parties should fully disclose all their significant assets, debts and liabilities.

The agreement may also have to meet other conditions in your jurisdiction regarding witnesses and independent legal advice, etc., so be sure to speak with an experienced family lawyer prior to entering into the agreement.

If you signed a cohabitation agreement while you were living common-law, do not assume that it will automatically become a marriage contract at the time of your marriage. Confirm with your family lawyer as to whether or not the agreement must be updated in order to remain in effect. See section 17.2.5 in Chapter 17, "Family Law", for more information on issues relevant to domestic contracts.

# 5.4 DISABILITY PLANNING

Many married couples assume that since they are married, their spouse will look after them in times of need. Although married couples are blessed with having a life partner to turn to in times of crisis, they should ensure that their affairs are organized in a way that makes their spouse's job as easy as possible. If they do suffer from a disability, their spouse will suffer from enough stress and trauma without having to worry about administrative details. Here are some of the things that married couples should consider.

## 5.4.1 Powers of Attorney

Couples should not assume that their spouse will be able to act on their behalf at any point in time. Generally speaking, no one has the ability to look after your financial affairs, unless you grant them that power, or a court grants them that power. If you do not sign a power of attorney, and you are incapacitated, your spouse will have to make a court application in order to take over the administration of your finances. Assuming a court grants your spouse the power to administer your finances, their powers will be supervised by the court, and limited to the extent provided by law. If you have assets or a business that you want your spouse to be able to administer without limits, delays, or expense, it is extremely important that you appoint him or her as your attorney. Even if you do not own a business, always make sure you have a valid power of attorney in place (whether or not you choose to appoint your spouse as your attorney). You should also not assume that your spouse will be able to act for you in every circumstance — in some jurisdictions a spouse may not act for an incapacitated spouse when dealing with a family home, so you may also need to appoint an alternate attorney to handle this type of situation. See Chapter 18, "Powers of Attorney", for further discussion on this issue.

## 5.4.2 Disability Insurance

As is the case with any individual who depends upon their income to fund their lifestyle, you should ensure that your disability insurance is adequate for your needs. In many cases, individuals rely on the group insurance provided by their employers, but this may not be adequate in all circumstances. Consider the impact that a disability may have on your family if your spouse chooses to quit his or her employment to care for you — disability insurance may be the key to preventing financial ruin or difficult choices. If you are the sole income earner, and therefore both you and your spouse are dependent upon your income in order to fund your lifestyle, obtaining adequate disability insurance is even more crucial. See section 25.1.1 of Chapter 25, "Insurance", for further information on this subject.

### 5.4.3 Critical Illness Insurance

Critical illness insurance is another form of insurance which protects against worst case scenarios. It provides a lump sum payment in the event of certain listed types of illnesses (usually cancer, stroke, heart attack, etc.). Even if you have disability insurance in place, this may not be sufficient if you experience a critical illness. Disability insurance insures your income, but even then you can only insure a portion of your income, never 100%. In addition, individuals who suffer from a critical illness often have additional expenses, such as medical expenses and living expenses (e.g. home renovations, home care costs, etc.), which may be more than their income can bear. If you want to ensure that you are properly taken care of in the event of a critical illness, you should consider critical illness insurance. See section 25.1.2 of Chapter 25, "Insurance", for a further discussion of this topic.

### 5.4.4 Long-Term Care Insurance

Long-term care insurance is another form of protection that a couple should consider. If one spouse (or possibly two) requires care in their home or an institution for an extended period of time, they may find that their assets will not be sufficient to provide them with the level of care that they desire, or they can only afford such care if the other spouse makes a substantial change to their standard of living. Long-term care insurance provides funds in the event that you are not able to perform various daily tasks (e.g. feeding yourself, dressing yourself or bathing yourself). This ensures that if you require extensive personal care for an extended time period, that you will have sufficient funds without your spouse experiencing a significant change in their lifestyle. You should speak to your financial advisor to see whether you need this type of insurance. See section 25.1.3 of Chapter 25, "Insurance", for a further discussion of this topic.

# 5.5 ESTATE PLANNING

## 5.5.1 Why You Need a Will

When you are married, it is important to review your estate plan with an estates lawyer to ensure that your affairs are in order. In all provinces and territories (other than Quebec), marriage generally voids all previous wills, although it will not impact other documents such as powers of attorney and beneficiary designations. Therefore, even if you prepared a will prior to getting married, that will is no longer enforceable, unless it was drafted "in contemplation of marriage" (see section 5.7 for the rules in your jurisdiction). Here are some of the more common reasons why married individuals need a will.

### *5.5.1.1 If You Have Children*

If you have children who are minors, you should ensure that you have a provision dealing with guardianship. Even if you do not yet have children, you may want to include a provision on guardianship, in order to ensure your children have one when they need one. Many couples are too overwhelmed at the time their children are first born to worry about changing their wills to include a guardianship provision, so it may be advisable to include such a clause even if you do not have children now, but intend to have them in the future. See section 10.5.1 of Chapter 10, "Children", for more information on choosing a guardian.

Many couples with children also unwisely assume that even if neither spouse has a will, they will receive their spouse's entire estate at the time of their spouse's death. This is a dangerous, and in most cases untrue, assumption. As with all adults, you should ensure that you have a properly drafted will. Even if you are married, this does not necessarily entitle you to all of your spouse's assets. For example, in most provinces, if you have children, they may be entitled to a portion of your spouse's estate (see section 19.6 of Chapter 19, "Distribution of an Estate", for a further explanation as to how an estate is distributed in your jurisdiction where there is no will). Having assets pass directly to children may be problematic for many reasons.

- You may need all of your spouse's estate for your own financial well-being, especially if you have been relying on two incomes in order to fund your lifestyle.

- If your children are minors, the Public Trustee, or Children's Lawyer (depending upon where you live) may have authority over your child's portion of the estate. You do not want to be burdened with seeking the consent of a government authority to deal with assets such as the family home if your child is now a part owner of that asset. The surviving parent will not have authority to manage your children's money, and the children will automatically become entitled to receive the funds upon attaining the age of majority. Since this is generally not what parents want, it is preferable to ensure that any money that may go to a child is left to them in trust in a properly drafted will (see section 10.5.3 of Chapter 10, "Children").

- If the assets have unrealized capital gains (for example, on investments or a vacation property) and they are inherited by your children, those capital gains will be taxable at that time. If an adult child is entitled to receive part or all of your RRSP or RRIF, then your estate will be liable to pay the tax on the amount they receive. Normally, especially in first marriages, spouses want their assets to go to their spouse, or to a trust for their spouse, in order to defer the taxation of the gain until the time of the death of the second spouse. (See Chapter 21, "Taxation at Death", for an explanation as to how an estate is taxed at the time of death).

The best way to avoid these problems is to have a will drafted by an experienced lawyer, who can ensure that sufficient amounts are left to the surviving spouse, as well as ensuring that proper controls are attached to any amounts left to a child. If you have step-children, then the issues can become even more complex — see Chapter 8, "Blended Families", for a discussion of the issues relevant in these situations.

### *5.5.1.2 Common Disaster Clauses*

It is important for couples to have a common disaster clause in their will, especially if they live in a province where the older spouse is deemed to die first (see section 19.6 of Chapter 19, "Distribution of an Estate", for the rules in your jurisdiction). If you live in a province where the older spouse is deemed to die first, and you die in a common disaster, then the heirs of the younger spouse will receive everything, and the heirs of the older spouse could potentially receive nothing. If you live in a province where the spouses are deemed to predecease each other, then the heirs of one spouse receive the assets of that spouse, and the heirs of the other spouse will receive his or her assets. Although this may appear to be more equitable, if the spouses have for some reason put the majority of their assets in the name of one spouse (perhaps for creditor protection if one spouse owns a business, for example), this may result in unintended consequences. Therefore, you may wish to include a provision that specifies who will receive which assets, even in the event of a common disaster, if the heirs of the spouses are different.

#### *5.5.1.3 Ability to Make Tax Elections*

Your will should give your personal representative the power to make tax elections so that the spouse has the ability to trigger gains or roll over their RRSP or RRIF. Although the Canada Revenue Agency would probably not challenge the ability of the personal representative to do so even without this power, it is best to include this type of provision in your will to avoid any potential disputes.

### 5.5.2 Spousal Trusts

Married couples should also ascertain if there are any methods by which to save tax after the time of death. One estate planning strategy which may help a surviving spouse to save tax is a "spousal trust". This type of trust is created in your will, and takes effect at the time the first spouse dies. Trusts which are created in a will are referred to as "testamentary trusts" since they are created by your last will and testament. If a deceased spouse leaves their estate to their surviving spouse in a testamentary trust, then the assets left to the trust can be invested in the name of the trust. The tax savings results from the fact that the trust will be treated as a separate taxpayer under the *Income Tax Act*, which could result in less tax overall. Case Study 5.8.2 examines a couple who use a testamentary trust in order to reduce the tax payable by the surviving spouse. Testamentary trusts and spousal trusts are also discussed in more depth in Chapter 23, "Trusts".

In order to allow the assets to rollover to the trust without triggering any gains, a spousal trust must provide that the surviving spouse is entitled to all of the income from the trust on an annual basis, and no one other than the spouse may encroach upon the capital of the trust. You may or may not decide to give your spouse the right to encroach upon the capital, but if you do not, you should ensure that they sign a waiver of their family property rights. If they do not do so, it is possible that they will attempt to "break" the trust by arguing that they did not "receive" anything from the trust (being a beneficiary of a trust is not the same as receiving the assets directly). In some situations, particularly blended families, spousal trusts should be considered very carefully (see Chapter 8, "Blended Families", for more information on the issues to be considered in that case).

Another reason why spousal trusts are often used is for control purposes. For example, if you leave your entire estate to your spouse, and then your spouse remarries after the time of your death, there is no guarantee that your children will ever receive any part of your estate. If you want to ensure that your children will be entitled to receive at least your part of the estate, then you should leave your estate to your spouse in trust. This is because the assets in the trust will be distributed to your heirs after the death of your spouse, not your spouse's heirs (which may include a new spouse).

If you believe that a spousal trust would be appropriate in your circumstance, speak to an experienced estates lawyer about the issues to consider when implementing such a strategy as part of your estate plan. For example, in order to have assets go into the trust, you must actually have assets in your estate. In the case of many married couples, they hold title to all of their assets jointly, and designate each other as the direct beneficiary of all of their registered assets and insurance policies so that all of their assets pass directly to the survivor without passing through the estate (note that in Quebec, this is generally not the case). If you want to use the spousal trust strategy, ensure that all of your estate is structured in a manner which is consistent with this objective. This may require you to separate some of your jointly held assets and designate "estate" as the beneficiary on certain plans.

## 5.5.3 Leaving Assets to Beneficiaries Other Than a Spouse

Although disinheriting a spouse is usually not what a married person would want, sometimes there is a desire to leave an estate to other individuals, particularly children from a previous relationship. The issue is also relevant for spouses who are separated, but not yet divorced.

If you are married, your spouse may be entitled to claim a portion of your estate, regardless of the terms of your will. Generally speaking, at a minimum, a spouse will be entitled to the portion of your estate that they would have been entitled to if you had separated or divorced during your lifetime. However, if you and your spouse have signed a domestic contract in which you agreed that at the time of death you would not be entitled to a portion of each others' estates, that contract may override any provincial family property rights (although this is not the case in every jurisdiction). If this situation applies to you, then it will be important that both you and your spouse execute a proper will so that it is quite clear as to whom the estate should go. If a spouse dies without a will, the survivor may be entitled to a portion of the estate under the intestacy legislation in place at the time, despite their intention that their estate pass to other beneficiaries. (See section 19.6 of Chapter 19, "Distribution of an Estate", for a description as to how much your spouse is entitled to in your jurisdiction if you die without a will.)

If you are separated, it is likely that you will not want to leave your entire estate to your separated spouse. However, unless you change your will, beneficiary designations and title to your assets, nothing will automatically change simply due to your separation (in most jurisdictions). Even if you do change your will, keep in mind that your separated spouse could continue to have a claim against your estate if you have not settled all family property matters between you. See Chapter 6, "Separated", for further discussion on the issues to be considered by separated individuals.

It is important to remember that regardless of whether or not you have arranged your affairs so that your spouse will be entitled to little or none of your estate, it is still possible that they may make a dependant's relief application against your estate if they were financially dependent upon you prior to the time of your death (and in some jurisdictions, even if the spouse was not financially dependent upon you). If the court feels that the amount left to your surviving spouse is insufficient to maintain them in their standard of living, it is possible that the court will order certain amounts to be paid from the estate in favour of the spouse. It is not possible to contract out of these rights by signing a domestic contract, although a court will likely take the domestic contract into consideration when making its order. See section 19.6 of Chapter 19, "Distribution of an Estate", for a description of the dependant's relief rights which your spouse may have after the time of your death.

Given the above, if you would like to leave some assets to individuals other than your spouse, consider the steps outlined below.

- Speak to your estate planning lawyer to determine how much of your estate your spouse would be entitled to, and then perhaps leave the remainder to your other beneficiaries.

- If you do not have sufficient assets to satisfy both the needs of your spouse and the needs of your other beneficiaries, consider the use of insurance to provide your estate with the necessary funds.

- One strategy that many blended families use to ensure that their children from a previous relationship receive a part of their estate is a spousal trust, which will allow your estate to be held in trust for your spouse during their lifetime, and then passed on to your children or other beneficiaries after the death of your spouse. For more information on spousal trusts, see section 5.5.2, Case Study 5.8.2, and Chapter 23, "Trusts". Please also see Chapter 8, "Blended Families", if relevant to your situation.

## 5.5.4 Pension Survivor Benefits

You may be entitled to receive survivor benefits under the Canada Pension Plan or Quebec Pension Plan, if your deceased spouse contributed to either of those plans. You should apply for survivor benefits as soon as possible after the time of death.

In addition, you may be entitled to survivor benefits under an employee pension plan if your deceased spouse was a member of such a plan. However, you should not assume that you will qualify for a pension. If you were married after your spouse had already started receiving the pension (and he or she elected to receive higher individual payments instead of choosing lower payments with a survivor pension), then your spouse may no longer be able to change the payments in order to provide for a survivor pension. In fact, if your spouse was married to a previous spouse at the time he or she began to receive the pension, it may be their previous spouse who is entitled to receive the survivor benefits. Speak to your financial planner about whether or not you will be entitled to receive survivor benefits under your spouse's pension – if not, you will have to factor this into your financial plan when determining how much you need to save for your retirement or whether or not you or your spouse should purchase additional life insurance.

## 5.5.5 Direct Beneficiary Designations

When you get married, and if possible even before, review all your beneficiary designations on your registered investments and insurance policies. If you have designated anyone other that your spouse or your estate as your beneficiary, your spouse may not receive the funds at the time of your death. Marriage generally does not revoke beneficiary designations made prior to the date of marriage, so you should ensure that these designations are changed as necessary. One exception to this rule relates to pensions and locked-in retirement plans, in which case a beneficiary designation in favour of anyone other than a spouse or common-law partner will be void (except in some cases where the designation is made on a plan received from a deceased spouse or common-law partner). Make sure that the designations for all supplementary insurance policies are reviewed as well, as these sometimes require separate forms.

Although many spouses automatically appoint each other as the direct beneficiary of these plans, in many cases, it would be better to appoint the estate. Prior to designating anyone as a direct beneficiary of your assets, speak with your lawyer to ensure that the designation is consistent with your estate plan. For example, if you wanted the funds to go into a spousal trust, then the assets will need to flow through your estate in order to go into the trust, so you would not want a direct beneficiary. See section 22.3.6 of Chapter 22, "Probate", for a discussion of the risks of designating direct beneficiaries on your assets, and section 22.3.7 for a discussion regarding the use of an insurance trust, which is a probate planning technique involving your insurance.

### 5.5.6 Funeral Arrangements

Consider what type of funeral arrangements you would like. Although this may seem like an awkward topic, it is important to have at least a general sense of what your spouse would like. This topic may be especially important for members of blended families, where children may want one spouse to be buried side-by-side with a deceased parent. Discussing the issue in advance can help to deflect arguments after the time of death, when emotions may be running high.

### 5.5.7 Separation and Divorce

In some jurisdictions, separation will affect the distribution of an estate, and in several jurisdictions, divorce will impact the distribution of an estate. If you are separated or divorced, or contemplating a separation or divorce, see Chapter 6, "Separation", or Chapter 7, "Divorce", for more information regarding the distribution of your estate in those situations.

## 5.6 INSURANCE PLANNING

Although it generally goes without saying that every Canadian needs to be properly insured, this may be particularly so for married individuals.

### 5.6.1 Disability and Illness Insurance

If you have a spouse or child who is relying on your income in order to maintain their standard of living, then it is important to ensure that you have sufficient insurance in place. See section 5.4, "Disability Planning", for a discussion regarding the need for disability insurance, critical illness insurance and long-term care insurance to prevent a financial disaster in the event of illness or disability.

## 5.6.2 Life Insurance

Again, if your spouse and/or children are relying upon your income in order to preserve their standard of living, it is important to review your life insurance needs on a periodic basis. Generally speaking, there are three primary uses for life insurance.

### *5.6.2.1 To Create an Estate*

If you are young or have significant liabilities or obligations, it is doubtful that you will have saved a sufficient amount to satisfy the needs of your dependants. If you have dependants, you should speak to your financial advisor to determine how much insurance you will need. Keep in mind that you will need insurance not only to pay any outstanding debts such as a mortgage, but probably also a lump sum that can be invested to replace your annual income. See section 25.2 of Chapter 25, "Insurance", to determine what type of life insurance may be appropriate for you.

### *5.6.2.2 To Preserve an Estate*

At the time of death of the second spouse, there will be a tax liability due to the deemed disposition of all assets which have an unrealized capital gain (see Chapter 21, "Taxation at Death", for an explanation as to how an estate is taxed at the time of death). Although this tax liability can be deferred until the death of the second spouse, it generally cannot be deferred when the assets are transferred to the next generation. Therefore, if you want to ensure that any assets that may have an unrealized capital gains (such as a vacation property or family business) can pass to the next generation, it may be advisable to ensure that there is sufficient insurance in place to satisfy any tax or other liabilities.

### *5.6.2.3 To Equalize an Estate*

As discussed in Chapter 15, "Vacation Properties", and Chapter 16, "Business Owners", there are some assets that are not easily divided. Therefore, in order to prevent family disputes, it may be better to give the property or business to one child only, and give the other children something else of equivalent value. Unless you have other significant assets, it may be necessary to purchase insurance in order to ensure that your other children will receive an asset of equal value.

When the liability will arise only upon the death of the second spouse, then you should consider a joint and last-to-die policy, if the premiums are less expensive. These policies payout only upon the death of the second spouse, and are generally available even if only one of the spouses is insurable. However, in many cases, it may be better to simply insure the one spouse who is insurable, and not insure the other spouse. In some cases, a joint policy may be more expensive than a single policy, and with a single policy, the proceeds will still be received by the time the second spouse dies. In fact, they may be received even prior to that if the insured spouse dies first. You should ask your advisor whether a single policy, or a joint last-to-die policy would be more economical for you.

## 5.7 JURISDICTION DIFFERENCES

### 5.7.1 Alberta

Marriage revokes any previous wills, unless the will was drafted in contemplation of the marriage.

### 5.7.2 British Columbia

Marriage revokes any previous wills, unless the will was drafted in contemplation of the marriage.

### 5.7.3 Manitoba

Marriage revokes any previous wills, unless:

- the will was drafted in contemplation of the marriage;
- the will was declared to be made in contemplation of a common-law relationship and the couple gets married; or

- the will fulfills obligations to a former spouse or common-law partner under a separation agreement or court order.

### 5.7.4 New Brunswick

Marriage revokes any previous wills, unless:

- the will was drafted in contemplation of the marriage; or
- the parties later divorce and the couple did not have any children or grandchildren.

### 5.7.5 Newfoundland

Marriage revokes any previous wills, unless the will was drafted in contemplation of the marriage.

### 5.7.6 Northwest Territories

Marriage revokes all previous wills, unless the will was made in contemplation of marriage.

### 5.7.7 Nova Scotia

Marriage revokes all previous wills, unless:

- the will was drafted in contemplation of the marriage; or
- the spouse elects to take the amount left to them under a will if they do so within one year of their spouse's death.

### 5.7.8 Nunavut

Marriage revokes all previous wills, unless the will was made in contemplation of marriage.

## 5.7.9 Ontario

Marriage revokes all previous wills, unless:

- the will was drafted in contemplation of the marriage; or
- the surviving spouse specifically elects to inherit under the will within one year of the date of death.

## 5.7.10 Prince Edward Island

Marriage revokes all previous wills, unless the will was drafted in contemplation of the marriage, and it was executed within one month of the marriage.

## 5.7.11 Quebec

Quebec is the only jurisdiction where marriage does not render a will void. In Quebec, a beneficiary designation in favour of a spouse is deemed to be irrevocable unless expressly made revocable, so the spouse's consent will be needed to change it. Everywhere else in Canada, a beneficiary designation is considered to be revocable unless it is expressly made irrevocable. Where an irrevocable designation has been made, the policy owner must obtain the consent of the beneficiary to alter or revoke the designation, assign the policy, withdraw funds, transfer ownership or change the policy coverage. Keep in mind that beneficiary designations on many forms of registered investments (such as some types of RRSPs and RRIFs) are void in Quebec.

## 5.7.12 Saskatchewan

Marriage revokes all previous wills, unless:

- the will was drafted in contemplation of the marriage; or
- the person marries a person with whom they were living common-law, and they had already signed a will in contemplation of that common-law relationship.

### 5.7.13 Yukon

Marriage revokes all previous wills, unless the will was made in contemplation of marriage

## 5.8 CASE STUDIES

### 5.8.1 Married, With Children, No Will

Jake and Jessica have been married for five years, and have no wills or powers of attorney in place. Jake and Jessica have a two-year-old daughter, Silvia. Jake and Jessica own a home worth $300,000, which is in Jessica's name only, since Jake owns a business and he does not want the home exposed to the creditors of the business. Jake has about $50,000 in RRSPs and Jessica has $60,000 in RRSPs. Jake and Jessica both have group insurance, but they have never reviewed their policies with their advisors to determine if they would be sufficient for their needs. Jake and Jessica live in Prince Edward Island, and do not feel that they need to do any estate planning at this time.

Unfortunately, Jessica becomes extremely ill, and dies at the age of 33. This leaves Jake to care for Silvia and administer Jessica's estate. Jake goes to visit his lawyer to find out how to best do this.

Jake is surprised to hear that he is not entitled to inherit all of Jessica's estate. Jake is entitled to a portion of her estate, but not all of it, because Jessica had a daughter. In PEI, Jake is entitled to one-half of Jessica's estate, and Silvia is entitled to the other half (see section 19.6, of Chapter 19, "Distribution of an Estate", for information on how estates are distributed in other jurisdictions where there is no will). Jake decides that he will take Jessica's RRSPs, since if those are given to Silvia, the income tax liability will be payable sooner than if he transfers the money to his own RRSP. Jake will then also inherit a portion of the value of the home, and Silvia will inherit the rest.

Unfortunately, since Silvia is a minor, the provincial authorities will be responsible for managing her estate. They may or may not agree that it is in her best interests to have her estate tied up in the family home. Assuming they do agree that it is best not to sell the family home, Silvia will be entitled to her portion of the estate when she reaches the age of majority, which is 18 in Prince Edward Island. At that point, she may want to sell the home and spend the money on other things. This would obviously not be a good situation for Jake.

Since Jake will now be a co-owner of the home along with Silvia, it is possible that his share of the home could be seized if he experiences creditor issues with his business. If Jessica had instead left the home to him in trust, it is possible that it could have been protected from seizure in the future. Also, Jessica could have indicated that her entire estate was to go to Jake for his lifetime, with the remainder to pass to Silvia only after Jake died, and only if Silvia had attained a more mature age, such as 25 or 30. Since Jessica did not write a will, Silvia will be receiving her portion of the estate far sooner than Jessica or Jake intended.

Jake is also surprised to hear that Jessica's group policy pays a set death benefit of $200,000. Jessica was a high-income earner, but the amount of the death benefit in her group policy was not set according to income level. Since the income earned on the $200,000 will not replace Jessica's salary, Jake will have to make some difficult decisions regarding how to scale down their standard of living.

As a result of the difficulties Jake has experienced with Jessica's estate, he instructs his lawyer to draft a will and power of attorney for him, and discusses his insurance needs with his financial planner to avoid potential problems for Silvia in the future.

## 5.8.2 Married, With a Spousal Trust

Lissette and Harry live in British Columbia, and they both earn between $80,000 and $90,000. Lissette and Harry are in their mid-50s, and they have three adult children. Lissette and Harry are in a traditional first marriage, so they do not see the need to do anything other than have a will which provides that they will inherit each other's estates, and after the death of the survivor, their estate will be divided three ways equally between their children.

However, Lissette and Harry have heard that there may be a way for the survivor to pay less tax on the amount received from the estate. They decide to speak to their financial advisor, who tells them that it may be best to create spousal trusts in their wills. This strategy could work as outlined below.

- When the first spouse dies, the survivor will receive approximately $1,000,000 in cash and insurance proceeds. The home is in joint names, so it will pass directly to the survivor, and they have named each other as direct beneficiaries on their RRSPs. Even in retirement, they will be earning about $60,000-$70,000 in pension income, and since their house is paid off, they believe that the survivor should be able to invest the amount left in the estate. If the $1,000,000 is invested in a portfolio which produces an annual income of 2% (plus capital gains which will accrue), their taxable income will increase by $20,000 per year, to $80,000-$90,000 per year.

- Alternatively, the $1,000,000 inheritance could be left to each other but through a testamentary trust (of which the survivor would be the beneficiary). Their advisor tells them that if the $20,000 of interest income was instead earned within a testamentary trust, it would be taxed at a tax rate approximately 10% lower than if earned in their personal names. This is because a testamentary trust is treated as a separate taxpayer by the Canada Revenue Agency, so it will have access to the lower rates of tax on the first dollars of income (although it is not entitled to claim personal tax exemptions). Therefore, by using a testamentary trust, they will save about $2000 in tax per year.

- In addition, their financial advisor informs them that their Old Age Security payments will begin to be "clawed back" once they start earning over approximately $67,000 per year. If they were to earn $77,000 personally, they would lose $1500 in OAS payments annually, since the clawback is 15% of your earnings over the threshold ($77,000-$67,000) x 15% = $1500.

- Therefore, by using testamentary trusts in their wills, they will be able to save $3500 per year, every year until the survivor dies. If the survivor lives ten years past the death of the first spouse, they will have saved $35,000 in taxes.

- After the death of the first spouse, they will then be able to create testamentary trusts for their children. This appeals to Lissette and Harry, because their three children are currently studying to be a dentist, an entrepreneur and a physiotherapist. By using testamentary trusts, their children may be able to save tax for another 21 years after the death of both Lissette and Harry. In addition, if their children are experiencing creditor problems or marital difficulties, the use of a trust may help them to protect their estate.

Lissette and Harry discuss the strategy with their estate planning lawyer and they decide to create testamentary trusts in their will. However, in order for the strategy to work, they must ensure that sufficient assets actually pass through their estate. As a result, they instruct their financial advisor to change all their non-registered assets from joint names, to individual names. Although they realize that this will mean that a small probate fee will be assessed on the assets which pass through probate, they understand that the tax savings will, in many cases, be far more significant.

They also change the beneficiary designation on their insurance policies as instructed by their lawyer, who has established an insurance trust in their wills. Previously, they had designated each other as the direct beneficiaries, but by doing so, they were precluding the use of an insurance trust, which is a form of testamentary trust. By using an insurance trust, the survivor will be able to take advantage of the income tax savings provided by a testamentary trust, and their estate will not have to pay probate on the insurance proceeds at the time of their death. See section 22.3.7 of Chapter 22, "Probate", for more information on insurance trusts.

### 5.8.3 Transferring an Unutilized Capital Loss to a Spouse

See Section 5.2.5 for an example of how an unutilized capital loss may be transferred to a spouse.

# CHAPTER 6

# SEPARATED

Separating from a spouse or common-law partner can be a traumatic and difficult experience. However, it is important to ensure that you understand how a separation may affect your wealth and succession plan.

This chapter will address issues which are relevant to both married couples and common-law couples who are experiencing a breakdown in their relationship. However, you should speak to a family lawyer before implementing any of the strategies discussed in this chapter.

# 6.1 FINANCIAL PLANNING

When you separate, you will need to consider several short- and long-term financial issues.

- *Ownership of Property.* It may be advisable to separate any investments or bank accounts which are in joint names into individual names, so that your partner or spouse cannot redeem the investments and leave you without sufficient funds.

- *Discontinuing Payments.* If you are making any payments in favour of your spouse or partner (for example, contributions to a spousal RRSP), consider whether these payments should be discontinued.

- *Access to Credit.* It may be advisable to inform your financial institution that you will not be liable for any charges incurred by your spouse after the date of separation, and, if possible, close all joint lines of credit and open separate ones. Also, it may be recommended that you remove your partner or spouse as an authorized user of your credit cards — if necessary, you may need to cancel your card, and obtain a new one. If you are the primary credit cardholder on a credit card, be aware of the fact that you will probably be liable for any charges made on the card by a secondary cardholder (which is usually a spouse, but which could also include a child instructed to make a purchase by a spouse). You may want to cancel any credit cards where you are the primary cardholder, and obtain new ones.

- *Canada Child Tax Benefits.* Once you are separated from your spouse or common-law partner, make an election as soon as possible to have any Canada Child Tax Benefits paid based on your income only, if your children are living with you. Although you may not have been entitled to receive any benefits when your family income included the income of your spouse, your income may now be low enough to allow you to receive these benefits. In fact, if you are in receipt of any federal benefits (such as the GST credit, etc.), you should inform Service Canada of your change in marital status, as this could impact the amount you are entitled to receive.

- *Social Assistance Payments.* If you are a low-income earner, you should inform the Canada Revenue Agency ("CRA") when you have separated for more than 90 days by filing Form RC65, as you may become entitled to receive more in social assistance (e.g. Guaranteed Income Supplement). A separation may also impact how much you may receive in the form of provincial social assistance if your income is very low.

Ending a relationship can be a major life event which requires you to adjust your personal plans. In addition to immediate financial concerns for day-to-day living, you should speak to a financial planner about your current and future financial situation, since your retirement plan was presumably based on the assumption that your common-law relationship or marriage would continue. Now that you are a single individual, you will have to work with your financial planner to ensure that your retirement or other savings objectives can be attained, possibly requiring a change in lifestyle.

## 6.2 TAX PLANNING

The settlement of your property or financial issues as a result of a relationship breakdown brings with it numerous income tax issues.

For the purposes of the *Income Tax Act,* common-law couples who have lived together in a conjugal relationship for a period of at least 12 months, or who have lived together for a shorter period of time but are raising a child together, are treated in the same manner as married spouses. Therefore, unless otherwise indicated, the term "spouse" throughout this section will include common-law partners (although this is not the case throughout the entire chapter).

Under the *Income Tax Act,* common-law couples who cease to cohabit because of a breakdown in their relationship are deemed to be cohabiting until the separation has lasted at least 90 consecutive days. If a couple had lived together for at least 12 continuous months prior to the time of separation, and then resume cohabitation after a period of separation, they will once again be considered common law. However, amendments to the *Income Tax Act* (which would be effective retroactively as of 2001) propose to change the Act so that couples must have lived together *throughout the 12-month period that ends at that time* (these amendments are not yet law). If you separate before you have lived together continuously for at least 12 months, then you will have to live together for a continuous 12-month period starting from the date you resume cohabitation before you will be considered common law again.

The *Income Tax Act* sometimes treats married couples as separate individuals immediately at the time of separation, in some cases after a 90-day period of separation, and in some cases only at the time of divorce, as discussed further below.

The following are some of the tax issues and strategies you should consider at the time of separation. Professional tax assistance should be sought for these issues as the rules are very technical, and the application of the rules may vary depending upon personal circumstances.

## 6.2.1 Transfer Assets Tax Effectively

### *6.2.1.1 Account for Tax Liabilities*

When you and your spouse are dividing your family assets, take into consideration any tax liabilities which may be attached to those assets. For example, if one spouse receives a principal residence that has no tax liability (because of the principal residence exemption), and the other spouse receives investments of equivalent face value that have an unrealized capital gain, the spouse receiving the investments will receive less on an after-tax basis. A tax professional can help you to determine the after-tax value of each of your assets to ensure a more equitable division.

### *6.2.1.2 Consider Triggering Capital Gains*

Although assets can generally be transferred between spouses without triggering capital gains, consider whether it may be beneficial from a tax perspective to trigger capital gains as part of the property settlement. If the spouse who is transferring the assets has any unused capital losses that he or she has carried forward from previous years, or unused capital gains exemption room relating to shares in a small business corporation or qualified farm property, he or she may not be opposed to triggering capital gains when transferring the property to the recipient spouse. If assets are transferred at fair market value, that may result in a lower tax bill for the recipient spouse at a later date.

If a spouse agrees to trigger capital gains when transferring an asset to another spouse, he or she must specifically elect to transfer the property at fair market value. A spouse cannot choose to trigger only a portion of the capital gain — he or she must either transfer the property at its cost base, or at fair market value (although they can choose to trigger the capital gain on some assets but not others). However, if triggering the capital gain will result in minimal tax consequences for the transferor, this strategy could be helpful in the negotiating process, as it will result in a higher after-tax value for the recipient spouse.

Keep in mind that a common-law partner is only considered a "spouse" for 90 days after the time of separation. Therefore, if one former common-law partner transfers assets to the other former common-law partner after the 90-day period has passed, the transfer will be deemed to take place at fair market value, unless the transfer is part of a property settlement as set out in a written separation agreement.

### *6.2.1.3 Consider Triggering Capital Losses*

If the property is in a loss position, the transferor spouse may prefer to transfer the asset at fair market value in order to trigger the loss. However, in order to use this strategy, the loss cannot be considered a "superficial loss" (a superficial loss arises when one spouse disposes of an asset that the other spouse owned either 30 days before or 30 days after the date of disposition). Therefore, at the time of the transfer, the spouses must either be divorced if they were married, or separated for at least 90 days due to relationship breakdown if they were living common-law.

### *6.2.1.4 Beware of the Attribution Rules*

Normally, spouses must beware of the attribution rules when transferring assets between each other. For example, if one spouse transfers an asset to the other spouse while they are still married or living common-law, then the transferor spouse will continue to be responsible for paying the tax on any taxable income that may be earned on that asset during the time when the recipient spouse owns the asset. In addition, the transferor spouse will continue to be liable to pay the tax on any capital gain realized upon the sale of that asset, even though it is the recipient spouse who will be receiving the proceeds of sale. These rules are known as the "attribution" rules, and must be kept in mind when structuring a property settlement. However, the attribution rules will cease to apply in the two situations described below.

1. *Income Attribution.* The attribution rules regarding income will cease to apply once the parties are living separate and apart as a result of relationship breakdown.

2. *Capital Gains Attribution.* The attribution rules regarding capital gains will automatically cease to apply when a married couple divorces, or when a common-law couple has lived separate and apart due to relationship breakdown for at least 90 days. If a married couple does not divorce, but they are living separate and apart due to a relationship breakdown, then they may specifically elect that the attribution rules regarding capital gains will not apply. There is no formal election form required, but both spouses must sign a document which indicates that they are making the election, and this document should be filed with the transferring spouse's personal income tax return for the taxation year in which the property is transferred. If you would like to elect that the attribution rules regarding capital gains do not apply, you should include a clause to this effect in your separation agreement.

The attribution rules need to be considered when property is transferred between spouses.

### 6.2.1.5 Obtain an Indemnity for Unpaid Taxes

Spouses can be liable for outstanding taxes owed by a spouse if they have received property from that spouse for less than fair market value. However, this liability will not apply in respect of property which is transferred on account of relationship breakdown pursuant to a court order or written agreement, and provided the parties were living separate and apart at the time the property was transferred. Therefore, if you received assets from your spouse prior to the time of your separation, you should ensure that as part of your separation agreement, your spouse certifies that they have no outstanding taxes owing, and, if he or she is assessed any taxes for previous years, they will indemnify you if you are required to pay any amounts as a result of these reassessments.

## 6.2.2 Principal Residence Exemption

Generally speaking, couples may only designate one residence as their principal residence for tax purposes. A second principal residence exemption will only become available once a married couple has been living separate and apart for at least 12 months, and they are separated pursuant to a judicial order or written separation agreement. In the case of common-law couples, they are deemed to no longer be spouses after a separation of 90 days. As part of your property settlement, it may be advisable to negotiate who will be entitled to use the principal residence exemption for the years prior to separation. For example, if one spouse receives the house and one spouse receives the cottage, and they were married for ten years, they may agree to each claim the principal residence exemption for five of these years (since they could only claim one principal residence exemption as a couple for those years). If the spouses do not come to an agreement regarding who will have the right to claim the principal residence exemption and when, then the person who sells one of the properties and claims the exemption first will effectively receive the benefit from it. However, if the couple only owned one residence during the time they were married, this should not be a concern.

## 6.2.3 Spousal Tax Credit

Spouses are entitled to claim the spousal tax credit in any year in which their spouse's income does not exceed a certain threshold, if they support their spouse. Although the threshold for 2010 is $10,382, it is indexed annually, so confirm the amount of the current threshold with your advisor. Many spouses are not able to claim this credit, as their spouse earns too much income. However, in the year of separation, only the income earned by your spouse during the period prior to separation will be relevant for determining whether or not a supporting spouse may claim a spousal tax credit. Therefore, if you separate early in the year, and you support your spouse, you may be able to take advantage of this credit.

However, if you are paying spousal support, and you are claiming a tax deduction in respect of the spousal support, you will not also be able to claim a spousal tax credit. If you are paying support to your spouse, but the amount of support is small, it may be more beneficial to claim the spousal tax credit than deduct the spousal support.

An individual is precluded from claiming both the spousal credit and the eligible dependant credit, so if a spouse is claiming a tax credit in respect of their child, they will not also be able to claim a tax credit in respect of their spouse.

## 6.2.4 Eligible Dependant Credit

If you are supporting a child or children who are under the age of 18 and not earning much income, you may be able to claim the eligible dependant credit in respect of those children. Where there is a joint custody arrangement, only one spouse will be entitled to claim the credit in respect of each child, which will be a subject for negotiation. Where there is joint custody over more than one child, the separation agreement could be structured so that one parent can claim the credit for one child while the other can claim it for a second child. It is obviously preferable to be able to claim the credit in respect of a younger child, since the credit will be available for a longer period of time.

If an individual is paying child support payments to their spouse, they will not be entitled to claim the eligible dependant credit in respect of that child.

## 6.2.5 RPPs, RRSPs and RRIFs

If you have a written separation agreement or a court order, a lump-sum amount can be transferred from your Registered Pension Plan ("RPP"), Registered Retirement Savings Plan ("RRSP") or Registered Retirement Income Fund ("RRIF") to the RPP, RRSP or RRIF of your spouse, without attracting tax. Normally, transfers cannot be made between registered plans without paying tax on the amount transferred. When transferring amounts between plans, make sure that the transfers happen directly — if the funds are first paid out to one of the spouses, the amount will be considered a taxable withdrawal.

Normally, when a spouse or common-law partner makes a contribution to a spousal RRSP, the attribution rules work such that the contributor spouse must report any withdrawals made by the annuitant spouse either in the year any contribution is made to that spousal RRSP or either of the next two calendar years. However, for the purposes of the spousal RRSP attribution rules, spouses are treated as being separate and apart effective immediately upon the time of separation such that a contributor spouse will not have to report any amounts withdrawn by an annuitant spouse, even if they are still legally married, and even if they have not been separated for at least 90 days.

## 6.2.6 Support Payments

### *6.2.6.1 Spousal Support*

If you will be paying spousal support, it is important to consult with a professional to ensure that the payments will be tax deductible. Generally speaking, in order to be deductible, the payments must be:

- periodic (as opposed to a lump sum payment);
- paid pursuant to a written separation agreement or court order; and
- represent an allowance, meaning that the recipient must be allowed to use the payments however he or she wishes.

The couple must also be living separate and apart for at least 90 days as a result of a breakdown of the relationship, and the payments must have been made in the year in which the agreement was entered into or the immediately preceding year. This is important to keep in mind if the negotiations continue into the second or third year — if a separation agreement or court order is not obtained by the end of the second year, it is possible that you will not be able to deduct some of the support payments which you have already made. Note also that the agreement must be a formal agreement in writing between the parties — a series of letters or notes between you and your spouse or your lawyers is not sufficient.

Payments to third parties (for example, private school tuition payments made directly to the school) may be deductible if they meet the following conditions:

- the payments must be periodic (as opposed to a lump sum);
- the payments must be made pursuant to a written agreement or court order; and
- the payments cannot be used for the purchase of tangible property unless they are in respect of medical or educational expenses.

There are numerous other conditions which must also be met in order for third party payments to be deductible, so it is important to speak with a well-experienced family lawyer prior to making such payments.

To the extent that support payments or third-party expense payments are deductible for the paying spouse, they will be taxable income for the recipient spouse. Given that the payments could impact the tax payable by both spouses, it is crucial that both spouses obtain independent legal advice prior to entering into any type of separation agreement regarding spousal support. In fact, in some cases, it may be preferable for the payments *not* to be deductible by one spouse and taxable to the other, depending upon their income levels. However, the parties cannot simply choose to ignore the provisions of the *Income Tax Act.* If the parties definitely do not want the *Income Tax Act* to apply, then the payments must be structured in a way which would not meet the conditions required for deductibility.

If you are required to pay child support and spousal support as part of a separation agreement, ensure that the amount paid for each is specifically indicated. If the separation agreement or court order does not specifically state that the amount being paid is in respect of spousal support, the entire amount will be treated as child support, and is therefore non-deductible. The same comment applies for third party payments, as discussed above. If it is not made clear that the third party payments are for the benefit of the spouse, they will not be deductible.

If a court order or written agreement provides for the payment of spousal support, it should be registered with the Canada Revenue Agency by filing Form T1158, "Registration of Family Support Payments".

### 6.2.6.2 Child Support

Under the current income tax rules, child support payments are neither deductible by the payor, nor taxable to the recipient. However, if you entered into an agreement regarding child support prior to May 1, 1997, it is possible that your child support payments are deductible by the payor and taxable to the recipient, provided that the agreement has not been changed such that there is a new "commencement date" after April 30, 1997. If you are making child support payments pursuant to a separation agreement signed prior to May 1, 1997, consult with an advisor prior to agreeing to any amendments to the agreement. If the amendments are sufficient to find that there is a new "commencement date" (which essentially means there is a new agreement), then the child support payments will no longer be deductible.

## 6.2.7 Deductibility of Legal Fees

You may be able to deduct some of your legal fees relating to your separation. For example, a spouse who is receiving support payments should be able to deduct legal fees relating to:

- establishing a right to spousal or child support;
- enforcing a right to spousal or child support;
- obtaining an increase in spousal or child support;
- defending an application to have spousal or child support reduced; or
- applying to have child support made non-taxable.

However, not all legal fees are deductible. For example, they are not deductible in the following instances:

- legal fees paid by the payor in negotiating the amount of support or requesting a termination of support; or
- legal fees in respect of other matters, such as child custody or a division of family property.

## 6.2.8 Child Care Expenses

Child care expenses which are deductible under the *Income Tax Act* must generally be claimed by the lower income-earning spouse, regardless of which spouse incurred the expenses. However, after the time of separation, child care expenses may be claimed by the spouse who incurred the expense, so the higher income-earning spouse may now be able to deduct child care expenses, if he or she has been paying them, and the child for whom the expenses have been made is living with the payor.

Once the parties have been living separate and apart for at least one year, both spouses may claim child care expenses incurred by each of them in respect of the same children, although the Canada Revenue Agency will review the expenses to ensure they relate to a period of time when the children are living with the parent who is claiming the expense. Child care expenses are discussed more fully in section 10.2.3 of Chapter 10, "Children".

## 6.3 FAMILY LAW ISSUES

Generally speaking, it is a good idea to speak with a family lawyer *before* you make the decision to separate, since decisions made early on in the process could affect your rights well into the future.

If you do decide to separate, you should determine the exact date on which the separation occurred, which may not be immediately obvious, especially if you continue to live in the same residence for a period of time. The date of separation may be important for various reasons. In some jurisdictions, it is the value of property at the date of separation which is relevant when dividing property, and, in many statutes, certain rights will only continue for a certain time period after the time of separation (see section 6.7, "Jurisdiction Differences", for more information). Again, it is important to speak with an advisor as soon as possible in order to ensure that you do not miss any of these important dates.

If you are moving out of the family home, you should also ensure that you have copies of all important legal and financial documents, including those stored in a safety deposit box to which your partner or spouse has access.

Here are some of the family law issues and strategies that you should consider when you separate.

### 6.3.1 Division of Property

If you are married, your "family property" will be divisible, regardless of who holds title to the asset. However, the definition of family property and the manner in which it is to be divided varies from jurisdiction to jurisdiction. Please see Chapter 17, "Family Property", for a discussion of how family property is divided, and section 17.4 in particular regarding the types of assets which are divisible in your province or territory. Note that if you have not lived in a jurisdiction for very long, you may be subject to the rules of the jurisdiction in which you and your spouse lived previously.

If you believe that your spouse has title to more of the family property than you do, speak to your lawyer about the process involved in dividing your assets. In many cases, you will not be entitled to the property itself, but you may be entitled to an "equalization payment". However, there are certain time limits by which these property claims must be made. See section 6.7, "Jurisdiction Differences", for more information regarding the limitation periods in your province.

Once you have come to an agreement with your spouse or partner as to how your property is to be divided (with the assistance of a family lawyer), be sure to change the registration on any properties as may be required, including vehicle licensing. Also be sure to notify any utilities if you will no longer be required to pay for bills incurred on a property you no longer occupy.

Common-law couples cannot assume that the family property laws of their jurisdiction will apply to them. In many cases, the family property laws do not provide for a division of family property between common-law partners. If this is the case, and one of the common-law partners wants to receive some of the property that is in the name of the other partner, they will have to sue that common-law partner, and ask the court for one of the other legal remedies that may be available to them, including a declaration of unjust enrichment, constructive trust or quantum meruit. However, these lawsuits are often difficult and expensive to pursue, and there is no guarantee as to the amount which a court will award to a former common-law partner. For more information regarding the division of family property for common-law couples, see section 3.4 of Chapter 3, "Common-Law Couples", and section 6.7, "Jurisdiction Differences".

## 6.3.2 Spousal Support

### *6.3.2.1 Right to Receive Support*

If one of the spouses or common-law partners was financially dependent upon the other, they may wish to negotiate support payments as part of their separation agreement. The factors to be considered in determining the amount of support to be paid will vary from jurisdiction to jurisdiction and from case to case, so it is imperative that you speak with an experienced family lawyer to determine whether or not you should expect to receive or pay support.

Common-law partners do not always have the right to ask for support. See section 3.9 of Chapter 3, "Common-Law Couples", to find out the criteria your jurisdiction uses when determining if a common-law partner has the right to apply for support.

#### *6.3.2.2 Tax Deductibility*

It is possible that spousal support payments may be tax deductible by the payor if the payments are structured in the correct manner. See section 6.2.6.1 for a discussion as to when spousal support payments may be tax deductible.

#### *6.3.2.3 Liability of an Estate*

Do not assume that support payments will continue after the time of death of the payor. If the recipient spouse needs the payments to continue, then consider making that a term of the separation agreement to ensure that the estate is responsible for the support obligation.

If an obligation to pay support could continue indefinitely into the future, that could delay the administration of the estate indefinitely and severely impact the amount left for the other estate beneficiaries. As well, the estate will not receive a tax deduction for the payments, which may cause further hardships for the other beneficiaries. If the obligation is to continue beyond the time of death, consider whether the agreement should provide that a lump-sum payment is to be paid at the time of death, so that the estate can make the payment, and administer the remaining funds immediately.

In many cases, it will be necessary to use insurance to fund the obligation. See section 6.6.1 for the issues to consider when purchasing insurance for this type of obligation.

### 6.3.3 Child Support

Child support payments may also be negotiated as part of the separation agreement. In most cases, child support payments are not tax deductible for the payor (although it is possible that child support payments made under a separation agreement which was entered into prior to May 1, 1997, will be tax deductible — see section 6.2.6.2 for further information).

It is important to remember that not only natural and adoptive parents are potentially liable for child support payments. Individuals who have taken on a parental role, and who have supported a child of their spouse or common-law partner may continue to be liable to support that child after the time of separation. Individuals cannot contract out of this liability, and a court may ignore any domestic contract which purports to release a step-parent from a child support obligation.

See section 6.6.1 for a discussion on the role insurance can play to ensure that there are sufficient funds in the estate of a parent who is obligated to make support payments.

## 6.3.4 Pensions

Couples who have been married or in a common-law relationship for at least one year may apply for a division of Canada Pension Plan ("CPP") benefits which accrued during the course of the marriage or common-law relationship (unmarried couples in Quebec must live together for a period of three years or one year with a child in order to make such an application for Quebec Pension Plan ("QPP") payments). The one year time period requirement is calculated from January of the year in which the couple married or began to cohabit until December 31 of the year before their marriage ended or they separated. Couples cannot choose to opt out of this division of benefits, unless their provincial legislation allows such opting out, and they specifically agree to this. Currently, only Alberta, British Columbia and Saskatchewan allow couples to opt out of a division of CPP, and Quebec allows couples to opt out of a division of QPP.

There generally is no limit on when a separated spouse may apply for a division of CPP benefits, but if your separated spouse dies, you must apply for the division of benefits within three years of the date of their death. In order to apply for a division of CPP benefits from a common-law partner, you must apply for a division of benefits within four years of the time of separation, even in the case of the death of the separated partner.

If at the time of your separation, you and your spouse are retired and have arranged to divide your CPP payments, this will cease on the twelfth month after you separate, or the month in which you divorce (although you should obviously inform HRDC of the separation if you want the pension splitting to stop).

Federal or provincial laws may also allow spouses to divide pension benefits accrued by either spouse in a pension plan administered by his or her employer. Once you have come to an agreement regarding the division of your property, be sure to file a copy of your separation agreement or court order with the pension administrator to ensure that you receive your portion of the pension payout at the appropriate time.

## 6.3.5 Separation Agreements

In most cases, the best method by which to address the issues discussed above is to sign a separation agreement. As these agreements can become quite complicated, *it is always recommended that each party obtain independent legal advice from an experienced family lawyer.* If the issues are contentious, then obviously a court order may be required. However, if the parties are able to come to an out-of-court settlement, then it is important to reduce this agreement to writing. Under no circumstances, no matter how amicable, would it be appropriate for both spouses to consult with the same advisor, or to sign an agreement without legal advice. The rules regarding family property are quite complex, and can vary between the jurisdictions.

Another reason why it may be important to have a written agreement is because the Canada Revenue Agency sometimes requires either a written agreement or court order before they will grant certain tax benefits. Examples of situations where the Canada Revenue Agency requires a written agreement include where:

- the parties are separated, but each party wants to claim the principal residence exemption while they are still legally married, as opposed to being limited to one exemption as a couple;
- the parties would like to transfer RPPs, RRSPs or RRIFs between each other without triggering any tax consequences; and
- the parties would like to elect out of the attribution of capital gains on assets sold by either spouse after the time of separation (see section 6.2.1.4).

Speak to your family lawyer about the issues below prior to finalizing the separation agreement.

- If you are liable for any joint debts (including mortgages, lines of credit, etc.), you may want to notify these creditors that you are no longer liable for debts incurred by your separated spouse (although your creditors may not be anxious to release any personal guarantees without receiving some assurances that your spouse will be able to service the debt on his or her own). You may also want your former spouse to release you from certain liabilities as part of the separation agreement.
- When dividing property, make sure that all liabilities have been accounted for. For example, if you made a withdrawal from your RRSP under the

Home Buyer's Plan when you purchased your home, then ensure that this debt is accounted for in the negotiations if you will not be receiving the home as part of the property settlement. If the home is transferred to your spouse, but you made the RRSP withdrawals, you will be required to make the repayments to your RRSP, or you will have to include taxable amounts in your annual income until the loan is accounted for, even though you no longer own the home. The same issue is relevant if you have made a withdrawal under the Lifelong Learning Program so that your spouse could attend post-secondary education. The repayment of this loan should be factored into the separation agreement, as you will be required to repay the amounts withdrawn from your RRSP over time. If you do not make these repayments, you will be required to pay tax on those amounts.

- If you will be receiving real property as part of the settlement, ensure that your lawyer searches the title to determine if there are any outstanding encumbrances which will affect its value (e.g. an unpaid mortgage). Searches should also be conducted for personal property, such as a vehicle, to ensure that the asset is free and clear of encumbrances when you receive it.

- If you had a joint last-to-die insurance policy, which was to pay out upon the death of the second spouse or common-law partner, consider who will continue to own this policy in the future, and if it is possible to change the terms of the policy or obtain a new policy, since you will no longer be planning for your future needs on a joint basis.

- If you have established an RESP for a child, consider who will continue to be the subscriber, since it will be the subscriber who will be entitled to withdraw the contributions and decide whether or not to use them to fund the child's post-secondary education.

- If you have designated your former spouse as a direct beneficiary of an RPP, RRSP, RRIF or insurance policy, and you no longer want them to receive those assets, be sure to specifically revoke those designations in the agreement. A general revocation clause will not be sufficient — the revocation clause must specifically refer to the plan (or plans) affected by the change, or the funds could still be paid to the former spouse. Even if a revocation of this kind is placed in the separation agreement, it is still always recommended that the designation in the contract itself be changed as soon as possible. See section 6.5.4 for a further discussion on this issue.

## 6.4 DISABILITY PLANNING

After the time of separation, be sure to review your disability insurance to ensure that it is sufficient for your needs. Now that you are single again, you will not be able to rely on your spouse to ensure that you are taken care of in the event of a disability. (You may also wish to consider critical illness insurance and long-term care insurance — see Chapter 2, "Single", for more information on the type of disability planning single people should consider.)

If appropriate, you may also want to amend your power of attorney to remove your separated spouse as your attorney, and replace them with someone else. If you do not change your power of attorney, your spouse may still be entitled to act on your behalf in the event of your incapacity (see section 6.7, "Jurisdiction Differences", for the rules in your province). If you do not change these documents, and your separated spouse or common-law partner chooses not to act as your attorney at the required time, another person may have to step forward and make a court application to act on your behalf if you have not appointed an alternate. Not only is this extremely expensive, but the person approved by the court may not be the person you would have chosen for that role.

You should also review any documents that give someone else authority to make medical decisions on your behalf in the event you become incapacitated. Again, separation from your spouse does not automatically nullify any such appointments in most jurisdictions (see section 6.7, "Jurisdiction Differences"). You must specifically change these documents in order to give these powers to another person.

If you do choose to change your power of attorney, either for finance or health care decisions, you should give notice to anyone who received notice of your previous power of attorney that you have terminated the prior appointment and made a new one. See Chapter 18, "Powers of Attorney", for the factors to consider when choosing an attorney.

## 6.5 ESTATE PLANNING

Although it may not be immediately obvious, your estate plan could be significantly impacted by a change in marital or relationship status. When you separate, speak to an advisor about your estate plan, and the changes that may be necessary to reflect your new life situation. Here are some of the estate planning issues and strategies you should consider when you separate.

## 6.5.1 Rewrite Your Will

The time of separation is a good time to review your estate plan to ensure that it conforms with your wishes. Depending upon the jurisdiction in which you live, a separation may or may not impact certain gifts given under your will. For example, in some jurisdictions, a separation will have no impact on a will, meaning that if you have left your estate to your separated spouse in your will, then he or she will still be entitled to that gift in the event of your death (see section 6.7, "Jurisdiction Differences", for the rules in your jurisdiction). If you have no will, in many jurisdictions a separated spouse is still entitled to receive a portion, if not all, of a deceased spouse's estate. (See section 19.6 of Chapter 19, "Distribution of an Estate", for a description as to whom will be entitled to inherit your estate in the event you die without a will).

As a result, it is generally a good idea to change your will at the time of separation to indicate that you no longer wish for your spouse to inherit all or part of your estate. However, even if you change your will, your separated spouse may continue to have a claim against your estate if you have not yet come to a settlement regarding your family property. Therefore, if your will leaves all of your estate to beneficiaries other than your spouse, your spouse may still have a claim against the estate for any amount owing under a family property settlement. Any amount remaining after the family property claim has been paid can be paid out to beneficiaries as provided in your will.

If you decide to leave your entire estate to your children, be careful in how the gift is structured. For example, if you do not indicate to the contrary, your children will be entitled to their inheritance upon attaining the age of majority, which in many cases, is still too young. Instead, it may be advisable to leave the money to them in trust. See section 10.5 of Chapter 10, "Children", for more issues to consider when leaving money to young children.

## 6.5.2 Consider Severing Jointly Held Property

When you are reviewing your estate plan, be sure to confirm with your lawyer how title to your assets is held. If you hold assets as joint tenants with your separated spouse, then your spouse will receive those assets in the event of your death, regardless of the terms of your will (except in Quebec, where there is no right of survivorship on jointly held assets). Consider changing the registration for these assets to "tenants in common" as opposed to "joint tenants" so that there is no right of survivorship. Assets will presumably be transferred into the name of one spouse or the other as part of the family property settlement, but this process could take a long time, and you do not want to risk the possibility that if you die before these matters are settled, your separated spouse could receive all the jointly held assets, leaving little or nothing for your other beneficiaries.

### 6.5.3 Consider Life Insurance to Fund Support Obligations

If you are making child or spousal support payments that are to continue past the time of your death, ensure that you have adequately provided for this obligation as part of your estate plan. Depending upon your net worth, you may need to consider purchasing insurance to ensure that there are sufficient funds available to fund this liability, as well as leave the intended amount for your other beneficiaries. If you have not anticipated this liability, estate assets may have to be sold to make the support payments, which may not be desirable. See section 6.6.1 for a further discussion of this issue.

### 6.5.4 Review Your Beneficiary Designations

It is important to note that your beneficiary designations will not be impacted by a separation. Therefore, it is important that you review any beneficiary designations on your pensions, RRSPs, RRIFs, and life insurance policies to ensure that the designations are still consistent with your intentions. Even if you have signed a separation agreement that is intended as a full release of any and all claims that either party has against the other, that may not be enough to deny someone proceeds of a life insurance policy, pension plan or registered plan if they are still designated as the direct beneficiary. You should specifically change the beneficiary on each and every contract (usually by designating "estate" as your beneficiary) so that the assets are distributed according to the terms of your will. If your spouse has been designated as the irrevocable beneficiary on an insurance policy, their consent will be necessary before any changes can be made.

Another reason to change your beneficiary designation is to ensure that there are no unintended tax consequences for your estate. If you designate your spouse or common-law partner as the beneficiary of your RRSP or RRIF, then at the time of your death, they will receive the gross amount held in your plan. However, the tax liability resulting from those registered investments will go to the estate. If you are separated but still legally married, your estate may be able to avoid this tax liability if your spouse agrees to contribute the funds to their own RRSP or RRIF, thereby deferring the taxation of those amounts until they withdraw the funds. However, they may choose not to contribute the funds to a registered plan, leaving your estate with the tax liability.

Some individuals make the error of removing their spouse or common-law partner as their beneficiary, only to add their children instead. If you have children, particularly minor children, it is generally not recommended that they be appointed as direct beneficiaries of registered assets or an insurance policy (see sections 10.5.3 and 10.6.2 of Chapter 10, "Children"). If a minor becomes entitled to receive money directly, the funds will usually have to be managed by the provincial authorities (referred to as the Public Trustee in most jurisdictions), who will charge a fee. In addition, the child will become entitled to the funds when they reach the age of majority, which is usually still too young to receive a large lump-sum of money.

It is also not recommended that you designate a guardian or personal representative as a direct beneficiary — if you appoint someone other than the person whom you wish to ultimately benefit from the gift, you run the risk that the guardian or personal representative will keep the funds as their own, and not use them for the intended purpose.

In many cases, it is best to designate your estate as the beneficiary, since your estate can provide that the funds are to be managed by a chosen individual, and held in trust until the children are mature enough to properly manage the funds. This will help to protect the funds from a family property division if your child experiences a bad marriage, or could protect the funds from other creditor exposure your child may experience. Although designating the estate as a direct beneficiary may result in probate fees (see Chapter 22, "Probate"), these fees are usually very minimal.

Another potential issue may be any creditor exposure that the estate has. In some cases, individuals prefer to designate direct beneficiaries in order to protect these assets from creditors of an estate. If you want to protect these funds from creditor exposure of the estate, then in the case of insurance consider establishing an insurance trust (see 10.6.3 of Chapter 10, "Children") to protect the insurance proceeds without leaving them directly to a minor. If you have creditor issues, speak to an advisor prior to making any beneficiary designations.

Given the complexities involved, you should always confer with an estates expert before changing a beneficiary designation.

### 6.5.5 Divorce

If you do later decide to divorce your spouse, your estate could be further impacted by that decision. See Chapter 7, "Divorced", for more information. Be sure to review your estate plan again at that time to ensure that no additional changes are required.

## 6.6 INSURANCE PLANNING

At the time of separation, you should review your insurance needs with an insurance professional to determine if any additional insurance is required. Consider the issues described below.

### 6.6.1 Obtain Insurance to Fund Support Obligations

Consideration should be given to funding any support obligations in the event of death, disability or critical illness. This may be especially important if the supporting spouse is self-employed. The cost of the policy can be factored into the amount of support to be paid.

If insurance is put in place to fund a support obligation which will continue beyond the date of death, term insurance may be the most appropriate choice, as it is cost effective, and can be cancelled once there is no longer an insurance need. If permanent insurance is purchased, and the recipient spouse is named as the irrevocable beneficiary, ensure that an agreement is put in place so that the recipient spouse will consent to the beneficiary being changed once there is no longer a support obligation. Generally, the recipient spouse will want to be designated as the irrevocable beneficiary of the policy, as well as the owner of the policy (even if it is the payor spouse who will be obligated to make the payments), so that they will receive notice of any cancellation or lapse in the policy. If insurance is purchased to fund a child support obligation, it is usually not recommended that a child or an insurance trust in their favour be listed as an irrevocable direct beneficiary of that policy, as a court would have to consent to any changes of a designation in favour of a minor.

If your spouse does not agree to pay for insurance coverage as part of the settlement, it may be advisable for you to take out a life insurance policy on your separated spouse, and pay the premiums, so that you are not left destitute in the event of his or her death. You would be the owner and beneficiary of such policy and your separated spouse would be the life insured. This may be especially important if you are still raising young children.

### 6.6.2 Review Your Medical and Dental Insurance

As part of your separation agreement, negotiate how you and your child(ren) be covered for dental and medical insurance. Even if your spouse's plan allows you to continue to be covered while separated, it may still be a good idea to obtain your own insurance, so that you will have more control. If your spouse decides to obtain "single" coverage instead of "dependant" coverage without telling you, you could have a problem.

### 6.6.3 Review Your Disability, Critical Illness and Long-Term Care Insurance

If you will now be a single-income household, review your disability, critical illness and long-term care insurance to ensure that you and your dependants will be taken care of in the event of disability or illness. See Chapter 2, "Single", for further information on the types of insurance which single individuals should consider.

### 6.6.4 Review Your Life Insurance Coverage

During the time of your marriage or common-law relationship, it is possible that you obtained a joint last-to-die insurance policy which would pay out upon the death of the second spouse or common-law partner. This type of coverage may have been obtained in order to fund a tax liability at the time of death of the second spouse on the assumption that any tax liability would have been deferred at the time of death of the first spouse. Now that you are no longer involved in the relationship, you may wish to have a life insurance policy of your own. This may be particularly important if you own an asset such as a family business, and you want to ensure that the asset is preserved for your heirs, and not sold to pay a tax liability. Speak with an insurance professional about the need for additional insurance, and ensure that the joint insurance policy is addressed in the separation agreement.

# 6.7 JURISDICTION DIFFERENCES

## 6.7.1 Alberta

### *6.7.1.1 Common-Law Couples*

- *Support.* In Alberta, common-law relationships are referred to as "adult interdependent relationships" ("AIRs"). See section 3.9 of Chapter 3, "Common-Law Couples", for the conditions required to be an AIR. The parties are referred to as "adult interdependent partners" ("AIPs"). AIPs may apply for support from their partner, and there is no time limit for doing so after the time of separation.

- *Family Property.* AIPs do not have a right to apply for a division of family property under the provincial family law legislation unless they entered into an agreement that provides for such division. However, AIPs may have other legal remedies, which are discussed in section 3.4.2.1 of Chapter 3, "Common-Law Couples".

- *Powers of Attorney.* Separation will have no impact on an AIP's power of attorney for finances or personal directive for health care decisions.

- *Estates.* Separation from an AIP will generally have no impact on an AIP's will (see section 3.9 of Chapter 3, "Common-Law Couples", for a discussion as to the rights of an AIP at the time of death). However, if an AIR is terminated, and one of the AIPs then dies *without* a will, their surviving former AIP will no longer be entitled to inherit any part of their estate (although if the AIR has terminated as a result of getting married, the survivor may be entitled to inherit as a spouse). An AIR is terminated if the AIPs:

  - enter into a written agreement;

  - live separate and apart for more than one year and either of them intends that the relationship not continue;

  - marry each other or one of them marries a third party;

  - one of them enters into an AIR with a third party (which is only possible if they themselves have not entered into an agreement); or

- one or both AIPs have obtained a declaration of irreconcilability under the legislation.

### 6.7.1.2 *Married Couples*

- *Support.* There is no time limit in which a married person must make an application for support.

- *Family Property.* A division of family property generally cannot be made until the parties have been living separate and apart for at least one year (unless the court believes that there is no possibility of reconciliation). Once the couple has met that threshold, they must make the application within two years of the time of separation. However, a spouse may also make an application within two years of receiving a judgment of divorce or a declaration of irreconcilability. If a spouse is dissipating property, then the other spouse has two years to make an application from the time of separation. If one spouse is making gifts to third parties, then the other spouse only has two years from the time of separation to make an application, or one year from the date on which the property is transferred, whichever is earlier. See section 17.4 of Chapter 17, "Family Property", for a description of the types of assets that are considered family property in Alberta.

- *Powers of Attorney.* Separation will have no impact on a spouse's power of attorney for finances or personal directive for health care decisions.

- *Estates.* Separation will generally have no impact on a spouse's will (see section 19.6 of Chapter 19, "Distribution of an Estate", for a discussion as to the rights of a spouse at the time of death). However, if a separated spouse dies *without* a will, and the surviving spouse is living in a conjugal relationship with someone else, they will not inherit any part of the estate (unless they still have an outstanding family property claim against the estate).

## 6.7.2 British Columbia

### 6.7.2.1 *Common-Law Couples*

- *Support.* Common-law couples who have been living together in a marriage-like relationship for at least two years may apply for support within one year of separation.

- *Family Property.* Common-law couples do not have the right to apply for a division of family property under the family property legislation unless they have entered into a cohabitation agreement that provides for such division. However, common-law partners may have other legal remedies, which are discussed in section 3.4.2.1 of Chapter 3, "Common-Law Couples".

- *Powers of Attorney.* Although separation will have no impact on a power of attorney, it will terminate a representation agreement, where a separated common-law partner is named as a representative. See Chapter 18, "Powers of Attorney", for more information on representation agreements in British Columbia.

- *Estates.* A separation will generally have no impact on a common-law partner's will (see section 3.9 of Chapter 3, "Common-Law Couples", for a discussion as to the rights of a common-law partner at the time of death). However, if one common-law partner dies *without* a will, and immediately before the death of that partner the couple had separated for not less than one year with the intention of living separate and apart, and had not during that period lived together with the intention of resuming cohabitation, then the surviving partner will not inherit any part of the estate, unless a court orders otherwise.

### 6.7.2.2 *Married Couples*

- *Support.* A claim for spousal support may be made by a married spouse or a formerly married spouse within two years of the making of an order:

  - for dissolution of the person's marriage;

  - for judicial separation; or

  - declaring the person's marriage to be null and void

(although there is no time limit for applying for support under the federal *Divorce Act*).

- *Family Property*. A spouse may make a claim for a division of family property within two years of receiving a judicial separation or a divorce. See section 17.4 of Chapter 17, "Family Property", for more information on which types of assets are considered family property in British Columbia.

- *Powers of Attorney*. Although separation will not impact a power of attorney, it will terminate a representation agreement where a separated spouse is named as a representative, if an order dividing family property has been made under the *Family Relations Act*. See Chapter 18, "Powers of Attorney", for more information on representation agreements in British Columbia.

- *Estates*. A separation will generally have no impact on a spouse's will (See section 19.6 of Chapter 19, "Distribution of an Estate", for a discussion as to the rights of a spouse at the time of death). However, there are two exceptions.

  1. When a spouse is named as a beneficiary or personal representative in a will drafted after marriage but prior to death, the gift or appointment will be revoked, if an order of judicial separation has been made in respect of the marriage, unless a contrary intention appears in the will.

  2. If immediately before the death of one spouse, the spouses had separated for not less than one year with the intention of living separate and apart, and had not during that period lived together with the intention of resuming cohabitation, and one spouse dies without a will, the surviving spouse will not inherit any part of the estate, unless a court orders otherwise.

  However, a surviving spouse could still have an outstanding family property claim against the estate.

  Also be aware, however, that in British Columbia, separated spouses (but not divorced) still have the ability to make an application under the *Wills Variation Act* if they feel they have not been left a sufficient amount in the will. Therefore, if you are separated, but still legally married, there is no guarantee that your estate will be divided as you intended, even if you change your will after the time of separation.

## 6.7.3 Manitoba

### 6.7.3.1 Common-Law Couples

- *Support.* Common-law couples who have registered their relationship with the Vital Statistics Agency, or who have lived together either for three years, or for one year while raising a child together, will have the ability to apply for support. There is no time limit on when a common-law partner may apply for support.

- *Family Property.* In order to make an application for a division of family property under the provincial family property laws, the couple must have registered their relationship with the Vital Statistics Agency or lived together for three years (see section 17.4 of Chapter 17, "Family Property", for a discussion as to which assets are considered family property in Manitoba). If the common-law relationship was registered, then the parties have 60 days from the date on which a dissolution of the relationship is registered to apply for a division of family property. If the relationship was not registered, then they have three years from the date on which they began living separate and apart. Common-law partners in situations that do not meet these conditions will only be entitled to a division of family property if they have signed a cohabitation agreement to that effect, or if they pursue legal arguments outside of the provincial legislation (see section 3.4.2.1 of Chapter 3, "Common-Law Couples", for further information).

- *Powers of Attorney.* Separation will have no impact on a common-law partner's power of attorney for finances or health care directive.

- *Estates.* A separation of at least three years, or the registration of the dissolution of a registered partnership, will impact the estate of a common-law partner as outlined below.

  - If the deceased partner died with a will, the surviving common-law partner will not receive any gifts or be entitled to act as personal representative, unless the will was signed after the time of separation.

  - If the deceased partner died without a will, the surviving partner will not inherit any part of the estate.

A surviving partner will also not inherit any part of an estate of a former common-law partner if the deceased partner died without a will, and the couple had already equalized their assets under *The Family Property Act.*

However, a surviving common-law partner could still have a claim against the estate if there is an outstanding family property claim. See section 3.9 of Chapter 3, "Common-Law Couples", for a general discussion as to the rights of a common-law partner at the time of death.

### 6.7.3.2 Married Couples

- *Support.* There is no time limit by which spouses must apply for spousal support.
- *Family Property.* Separated spouses may make an application for a division of family property at any time prior to the time of divorce. After the time of divorce, an application must be made within 60 days. See section 17.4 of Chapter 17, "Family Property", for a discussion as to which types of assets are considered family property in Manitoba.
- *Powers of Attorney.* Separation will not impact a power of attorney for finances or a health care directive.
- *Estates.* Separation will generally have no impact on a spouse's will (see section 19.6 of Chapter 19, "Distribution of an Estate", for a discussion as to the rights of a spouse at the time of death). However, if the deceased died without a will, and if, at the time of death, the deceased and his or her spouse were living separate and apart from one another, then the surviving spouse shall be treated as if he or she had predeceased the deceased for the purpose of determining whether or not they are entitled to any part of the estate if either or both of the following conditions are satisfied:
    - during the period of separation, one or both of the spouses made an application for divorce or an accounting or equalization of assets under *The Family Property Act* and the application was pending or had been dealt with by way of final order at the time of the intestate's death; or
    - before the time of death, the deceased and his or her spouse divided their property in a manner that was intended by them, or appears to have been intended by them, to separate and finalize their affairs in recognition of their marriage breakdown.

## 6.7.4 New Brunswick

### *6.7.4.1 Common-Law Couples*

- *Support.* Common-law partners who have lived in a common-law relationship for at least three years, or who have lived in a relationship of some permanence where there is a child born of whom they are the natural parents, may be entitled to apply for support from their former partner. An application for support must be brought within one year of the end of the relationship.

- *Family Property.* Common-law partners in New Brunswick are not entitled to a division of family property under the provincial family property legislation unless they have signed a cohabitation agreement authorizing such division. However, common-law partners may pursue other legal remedies, which are discussed in section 3.4.2.1 of Chapter 3, "Common-Law Couples".

- *Powers of Attorney.* Separation will have no impact on a common-law partner's powers of attorney for finances or personal care.

- *Estates.* Separation will have no impact on a common-law partner's will or estate plan. See section 3.9 of Chapter 3, "Common-Law Couples", for a discussion as to the rights of a common-law partner at the time of death.

### *6.7.4.2 Married Couples*

- *Support.* There is no time limit in which a spouse must make an application for an order of support.

- *Family Property.* Spouses have until 60 days from the date of divorce to make an application for a division of family property. See section 17.4 of Chapter 17, "Family Property", for a discussion as to which types of assets are considered family property in New Brunswick. Because the limitation period only runs from the date of divorce, it may be particularly important for separated couples in New Brunswick to settle their affairs, if there is no intention of divorcing, in order to ensure that a claim is not made many years into the future.

- *Powers of Attorney.* Separation will have no impact on a spouse's powers of attorney for finances or personal care.

- *Estates.* Separation will have no impact on a spouse's will or estate plan (see section 19.6 of Chapter 19, "Distribution of an Estate", for a discussion as to the rights of a spouse at the time of death).

## 6.7.5 Newfoundland

### 6.7.5.1 Common-Law Couples

- *Support.* A financially dependent common-law partner may be able to apply for support if the couple had lived together in a conjugal relationship for a period of at least two years, or for a period of at least one year and they are the biological or adoptive parents of a child. An action or application for support must be started within two years from the day of separation, or within two years of a default under a domestic contract.

- *Family Property.* Common-law partners are not entitled to a division of family property under the provincial family law legislation unless they have signed a cohabitation agreement authorizing such division. However, common-law partners may be able to pursue other legal remedies, which are discussed in section 3.4.2.1 of Chapter 3, "Common-Law Couples".

- *Powers of Attorney.* Separation will have no impact on a common-law partner's power of attorney for finances or advance health care directive.

- *Estates.* Separation will have no impact on a common-law partner's will or estate plan. See section 3.9 of Chapter 3, "Common-Law Couples", for a discussion as to the rights of a common-law partner at the time of death.

### 6.7.5.2 Married Couples

- *Support.* Spouses may make an application for an order of support under provincial legislation within two years from the date of separation, unless there is a domestic contract, in which case the application must be made within two years of the date of default. However, there is no time limit for making an application for support under the federal *Divorce Act.*

- *Family Property.* An application for a division of family property must be brought within the following time limits:

- two years after the day the marriage is terminated by divorce or judgment of nullity;
- six years after the day the spouses separate and there is no reasonable prospect that they will resume cohabitation; and
- one year after the first spouse's death.

See section 17.4 of Chapter 17, "Family Property", for a discussion as to which types of assets are considered family property in Newfoundland.

- *Powers of Attorney*. Separation will have no impact on a married person's power of attorney for finances or advance health care directive.
- *Estates*. Separation will have no impact on a spouse's will or estate plan (see section 19.6 of Chapter 19, "Distribution of an Estate", for a discussion as to the rights of a spouse at the time of death).

## 6.7.6 Northwest Territories

### *6.7.6.1 Common-Law Couples*

- *Support*. Common-law partners who have been living together in a conjugal relationship for a period of at least two years, or in a relationship of some permanence with a natural or adopted child, may make an application for support within two years of the date of separation, or within two years after default under a domestic contract.
- *Family Property*. Common-law partners who have been living together in a conjugal relationship for a period of two years, or in a relationship of some permanence with a natural or adopted child, are entitled to a division of family property. Common-law partners have two years from the date of separation to make an application for a division of family property. See section 17.4 of Chapter 17, "Family Property" for a description as to which types of assets are considered family property in the Northwest Territories.
- *Powers of Attorney*. A separation will have no impact on a common-law partner's power of attorney for finances or health care directive.

- *Estates.* A separation will generally not affect a common-law partner's will or estate plan (see section 3.9 of Chapter 3, "Common-Law Couples" for a discussion as to the rights of a common-law partner at the time of death). However, if there is no will, the surviving common-law partner will not receive any part of the estate, if

- before the death of the intestate, the spouses were separated and:

    - either spouse had made an application to determine his or her entitlement under the Family Law Act; or

    - had entered into a domestic contract respecting the division of property;

- immediately before the death of the intestate, the surviving partner was cohabiting with another person; or

- immediately before the death of the intestate, the spouses were separated and the intestate had entered into a spousal relationship with another person.

### 6.7.6.2 *Married Couples*

- *Support.* Separated spouses may make an application for support any time within two years of the date of separation, except in the case where support is paid under an agreement, in which case no proceeding may be brought more than two years after default. However, there is no time limit for bringing an application for support under the federal *Divorce Act.*

- *Family Property.* Spouses have two years from the date of divorce or separation to make an application for a division of family property. See section 17.4 of Chapter 17, "Family Property", for a discussion regarding which types of assets are considered family property in the Northwest Territories.

- *Powers of Attorney.* A separation will not impact a spouse's power of attorney for finances or health care directive.

- *Estates.* Separation will generally have no impact on a spouse's will or estate plan (see section 19.6, of Chapter 19, "Distribution of an Estate", for a discussion as to the rights of a spouse at the time of death). However, if a separated spouse dies without a will, then the surviving spouse will receive no part of the estate where:

- before the time of death, either spouse had commenced a divorce proceeding and the spouses had not reconciled;
- before the time of death, the spouses were separated and:
  - either spouse had made an application to determine his or her entitlement under the *Family Law Act*, or
  - had entered into a domestic contract respecting the division of property;
- immediately before the time of death, the surviving spouse was cohabiting with another person; or
- immediately before the time of death, the spouses were separated and the deceased had entered into a spousal relationship with another person.

## 6.7.7 Nova Scotia

### *6.7.7.1 Common-Law Couples*

- *Support.* Common-law partners who have lived in a common-law relationship for at least two years, or domestic partners in a registered domestic relationship, may apply for support at the time of separation. There is no time limit for making an application for support.
- *Family Property.* Only registered domestic partners are entitled to make a claim for a division of family property, and there is no time limit for doing so, which is why it may be particularly important for domestic partners to settle their affairs in order to ensure that a claim is not made many years into the future. However, domestic partners are not entitled to make a claim after they have dissolved their partnership. See section 17.4 of Chapter 17, "Family Property", for a description as to which types of assets are considered family property in Nova Scotia. Common-law couples who have not registered their relationship as a domestic partnership may only be entitled to a division of family property if they have signed a cohabitation agreement that allows for such division, or if they pursue one of the legal remedies discussed in section 3.4.2.1 of Chapter 3, "Common-Law Couples".
- *Powers of Attorney.* Separation will have no affect on a common-law partner's power of attorney for finances. Unless a personal directive expressly

provides otherwise, where, after making a personal directive in which the maker's spouse is appointed as delegate, the spouse is no longer a spouse, the appointment of the spouse as delegate is revoked.

- *Estates.* Separation has generally no affect on a common-law partner's will (see section 3.9 of Chapter 3, "Common-Law Couples", for a discussion as to the rights of a common-law partner at the time of death). However, if a domestic relationship is terminated, a surviving domestic partner will not be entitled to inherit any part of the estate where a former domestic partner died without a will (unless there is an outstanding family property claim). A domestic partnership is terminated if the parties live apart for one year with the intention that the relationship not continue, if one of them marries, if they register a statement of termination, or if they register an agreement with the court pursuant to the *Maintenance and Custody Act* (although if they marry each other, then they may be able to inherit as a spouse).

### 6.7.7.2 Married Couples

- *Support.* There is no time limit in which a separated spouse must make a claim for support.

- *Family Property.* A separated spouse may make a claim for family property any time after the time of separation, although where a spouse has died, the application must be made within six months of the date of death. In addition, the legislation only applies to married spouses, so an application cannot be made after the time of divorce. See section 17.4 of Chapter 17, "Family Property", for a description as to which types of assets are considered family property in Nova Scotia.

- *Powers of Attorney.* Separation has no affect on a spouse's power of attorney for finances or health care proxy.

- *Estates.* Separation will have no impact on a spouse's will or estate plan (see section 19.6 of Chapter 19, "Distribution of an Estate", for a discussion as to the rights of a spouse at the time of death).

## 6.7.8 Nunavut

See section 6.7.6, "Northwest Territories", as the rules in Nunavut are generally the same as in the Northwest Territories. However, the definition of common-law partner includes only opposite-sex partners, so a same-sex, common-law partner may not have the same rights, unless they were able to successfully challenge the legislation.

## 6.7.9 Ontario

### *6.7.9.1 Common-Law Couples*

- *Support.* If a common-law couple has been living together for at least three years, or if they are in a relationship of some permanence and raising a child together, then a separated common-law partner may be entitled to apply for support. There is no time limit by which a separated partner must make an application for support.
- *Family Property.* Common-law partners are not entitled to apply for a division of family property unless they have signed a cohabitation agreement that allows for such division, or pursue one of the legal remedies discussed in section 3.4.2.1 of Chapter 3, "Common-Law Couples".
- *Powers of Attorney.* Separation will have no impact on a common-law partner's power of attorney for finances or personal care.
- *Estates.* Separation has no affect on a common-law partner's will or estate plan. See section 3.9 of Chapter 3, "Common-Law Couples", for a discussion as to the rights of a common-law partner at the time of death.

### *6.7.9.2 Married Couples*

- *Support.* There is no time limit by which a separated spouse must make an application for support.
- *Family Property.* An application for a division of family property must be made within two years of the date of divorce, six years of the date of separation or six months of the date of death, whichever is the earliest. See section 17.4 of Chapter 17, "Family Property", for a description of the types of assets that are considered family property in Ontario.
- *Powers of Attorney.* Separation has no affect on a spouse's powers of attorney for finances or personal care.

- *Estates.* Separation will have no impact on a spouse's will or estate plan (see section 19.6, of Chapter 19, "Distribution of an Estate", for a discussion as to the rights of a spouse at the time of death).

## 6.7.10 Prince Edward Island

### *6.7.10.1 Common-Law Couples*

- *Support.* Common-law partners who have lived in a marriage-like relationship for a period of at least three years, or in a relationship of some permanence where they were raising a child together, may be entitled to make a claim for support. Common-law partners must make an application for an order for support within two years from the date of separation.

- *Family Property.* Common-law partners do not have the ability to make a claim for a division of family property, unless they have signed a cohabitation agreement that provides for such division, or they pursue one of the legal remedies discussed in section 3.4.2.1 of Chapter 3, "Common-Law Couples".

- *Powers of Attorney.* Separation will have no impact on a common-law partner's power of attorney for finances, but the appointment of a common-law partner in a health care directive will be revoked at the time of separation, unless the health care directive states to the contrary.

- *Estates.* Separation has no affect on a common-law partner's will or estate plan. See section 3.9 of Chapter 3, "Common-Law Couples", for a discussion as to the rights of a common-law partner at the time of death.

### *6.7.10.2 Married Couples*

- *Support.* A spouse who wishes to make an application for an order for support under provincial legislation must do so within two years from the day the spouses began living separate and apart. However, there is no time limit for making an application for support under the federal *Divorce Act.*

- *Family Property.* An application for a division of marital property may not be brought after the earlier of two years after the day the marriage is terminated by divorce or judgment of nullity, or six years after the day the spouses begin to live separate and apart. An application may not be brought after the date of death. See section 17.4 of Chapter 17, "Family Property", for a description of the types of assets that are considered family property in Prince Edward Island.

- *Powers of Attorney.* Separation has no effect on a spouse's power of attorney for finances or health care directive.

- *Estates.* Separation will generally have no impact on a spouse's will or estate plan (see section 19.6 of Chapter 19, "Distribution of an Estate", for a discussion as to the rights of a spouse at the time of death). However, where the deceased spouse died without a will, a surviving spouse will not inherit any part of the estate where they had left the deceased and were living in adultery at the time of death (although they may have an outstanding family property claim against the estate).

## 6.7.11 Quebec

### *6.7.11.1 De Facto and Civil Union Couples*

- *Support.* In Quebec, unmarried couples (which are referred to as "*de facto* couples") are not entitled to apply for support at the time of relationship breakdown, but individuals who have entered into a "civil union" may. For civil union spouses, there is no time limit for making an application for support.

- *Family Property. De facto* couples are not entitled to make an application for a division of the "family patrimony". However, if the couple has registered their relationship as a civil union, then they will have the same family property rights as a married couple. For civil unions, see section 17.4 of Chapter 17, "Family Property", for a discussion as to which types of assets are considered family property in Quebec.

- *Mandate in Case of Incapacity.* Separation will have no impact on a *de facto* or civil union partner's mandate in case of incapacity.

- *Estates.* The separation of a "*de facto*" couple will have no impact on a partner's will or estate plan (see section 3.9 of Chapter 3, "Common-Law Couples", for a discussion as to the rights of a *de facto* partner at the time of death). However, if the couple has registered as a civil union, and they then terminate that union, a surviving partner will no longer be entitled to inherit any part of the estate where the deceased died without a will. If a former civil union spouse dies with a will, then all gifts to the surviving former civil union spouse are revoked unless the will indicates to the contrary. A civil union can be terminated upon death of one of the parties, a court judgment or a notarized joint declaration.

### 6.7.11.2 Married Couples

- *Support.* There is no time limit for making an application for support.

- *Family Property.* There is no time limit for making an application for a division of family property. See section 17.4 of Chapter 17, "Family Property", for a discussion of the types of assets that are considered family property in Quebec.

- *Mandate in Case of Incapacity.* Separation will have no impact on a mandate in case of incapacity.

- *Estates.* Separation will generally have no impact on a spouse's will (see section 19.6, of Chapter 19, "Distribution of an Estate", for a discussion as to the rights of a spouse at the time of death). However, if you have made any beneficiary designations on an insurance policy in favour of your spouse, be sure to obtain their consent to change the beneficiary designation as part of your separation agreement. This is because in Quebec, a beneficiary designation is considered to be irrevocable unless it is expressly made revocable. Where an irrevocable designation has been made, the policy owner must obtain the consent of the beneficiary to alter or revoke the designation, assign the policy, withdraw funds, transfer ownership or change the policy coverage.

## 6.7.12 Saskatchewan

### 6.7.12.1 Common-Law Couples

- *Support.* A common-law partner who had been living with their partner for at least two years may be entitled to make a claim for support, and there is no time limitation for making this application.

- *Family Property.* A common-law partner who had been living with their partner for at least two years may make a claim for family property, if they make the claim within 24 months of separation. See section 17.4 of Chapter

17, "Family Property", for a description of the types of property that are considered family property in Saskatchewan. Generally, only assets that were acquired after the couple have been living together for two years are shareable (except a family home and household goods, which may be shareable no matter when acquired).

- *Powers of Attorney*. If a common-law partner has appointed the other partner as their attorney, the appointment is terminated as soon as they cease to cohabit as spouses as a result of an intention to end their spousal relationship.

- *Estates*. A separation will impact a common-law partner's estate plan as follows:

  - A separation of at least 24 months from a common-law partner will cause the will to be interpreted as if the separated common-law partner predeceased their partner.

  - If a partner dies without a will, and the surviving partner is living in a conjugal relationship with someone else, the surviving partner will not inherit any part of the estate.

However, the surviving common-law partner could still have an outstanding family property claim against the estate. See section 3.9 of Chapter 3, "Common-Law Couples", for a discussion as to the rights of a common-law partner at the time of death.

### 6.7.12.2 Married Couples

- *Support*. There is no time limit by which a separated spouse must make an application for support.

- *Family Property*. A separated spouse may bring an application for a division of family property against their separated spouse, if they make the claim prior to the time of divorce. See section 17.4 of Chapter 17, "Family Property", for a discussion of the types of assets that are considered family property in Saskatchewan.

- *Powers of Attorney*. If a spouse has appointed the other spouse as their attorney, the authority is terminated as soon as they cease to cohabit as spouses as a result of an intention to end their spousal relationship.

- *Estates.* Separation will generally have no impact on a spouse's will or estate plan (see section 19.6 of Chapter 19, "Distribution of an Estate", for a discussion as to the rights of a spouse at the time of death). However, if a spouse dies without a will, and the surviving spouse is living in a spousal relationship with someone else, they will not inherit any part of the estate, unless they have an outstanding family property claim.

## 6.7.13 Yukon

### *6.7.13.1 Common-Law Couples*

- *Support.* Opposite-sex, common-law partners who have cohabited in a relationship of some permanence, may, during cohabitation or not later than three months after the cohabitation has ceased, apply to a court for an order for support. Currently, same-sex, common-law couples do not have the ability to apply for support.

- *Family Property.* Common-law partners are not entitled to make an application for a division of family property, unless they had entered into a cohabitation agreement providing for such division, or they pursue one of the other legal remedies discussed in section 3.4.2.1 of Chapter 3, "Common-Law Couples".

- *Powers of Attorney.* Separation will have no impact on a common-law partner's power of attorney for finances or health care directive.

- *Estates.* Separation does not impact a common-law partner's will or estate plan. See section 3.9 of Chapter 3, "Common-Law Couples", for a discussion as to the rights of a common-law partner at the time of death.

### *6.7.13.2 Married Couples*

- *Support.* There is no time limit for bringing an application for spousal support.

- *Family Property.* An application for a division of family property may be made any time after the time of separation and prior to the time of divorce. See section 17.4 of Chapter 17, "Family Property", for a description of the types of assets which are considered family property in the Yukon.

- *Powers of Attorney*. Separation does not impact a common-law partner's power of attorney for finances. However, unless a directive regarding health care decisions states otherwise, an appointment of the maker's spouse as a proxy is revoked if the marriage is terminated by divorce.

- *Estates*. Separation will generally have no impact on a spouse's will or estate plan (see section 19.6, of Chapter 19, "Distribution of an Estate", for a discussion as to the rights of a spouse at the time of death). However, if a separated spouse dies without a will, and if the spouses had:

  - immediately before the death of one spouse, separated for not less than one year with the intention of living separate and apart; and

  - during that period not lived together with the intention of resuming cohabitation,

  then the surviving spouse will not inherit any part of the estate unless they have an outstanding family property claim.

# 6.8 CASE STUDIES

## 6.8.1 Separated, Living Common-Law, No Children

Iris separated from her common-law partner, Andrew, six weeks ago. Iris and Andrew currently live in New Brunswick (reference will be made to the differences in other jurisdictions at the end of the case study). Iris and Andrew do not have any children, and they lived together for five years. Iris and Andrew have structured their affairs as outlined below.

- Iris and Andrew lived in a home purchased by Iris prior to their relationship. Although Andrew lived in the home for five years, title to the home remains in Iris's name alone. Andrew contributed to the mortgage payments while he lived in the home.

- Since Iris made more money than Andrew, she decided to make a $5000 spousal RRSP contribution in his name so that their income would be more equitable at the time of their retirement.

- Iris has RRSPs worth approximately $50,000, and Andrew has spousal RRSPs worth approximately $10,000. Neither of them has any non-registered investments.

- Iris earns $60,000 per year, and Andrew earns $40,000 per year.

- Iris has named Andrew as the direct beneficiary of her RRSPs and insurance policies.

- Iris signed a power of attorney giving Andrew control of her finances only in the event she became mentally incapable of handling her own affairs.

- Iris signed a power of attorney for personal care giving Andrew the right to make medical decisions on her behalf in the event she became mentally incompetent.

- Iris and Andrew do not have a cohabitation agreement or wills.

Now that Iris and Andrew have been separated for a few weeks, Iris has decided that it would be a good idea to speak to an advisor to see what, if any, issues need to be discussed in relation to the separation.

- Since Iris and Andrew currently live in New Brunswick, neither of them will have the right to apply for a division of family property under the provincial family law legislation. From Iris's perspective, this is both a good thing and a bad thing. She is relieved that Andrew will not be able to apply for half of the value of her home, but she is worried that she may not be able to recover the $5000 spousal RRSP contribution she made to Andrew's RRSP.

- However, Iris's advisor also points out that Andrew may be able to make an argument that Iris has been "unjustly enriched" by the relationship, and the mortgage payments he made towards her home are being held in a "constructive trust". Therefore, she may have to pay part or all of the money back. Since Iris and Andrew do not have a cohabitation agreement, Iris's advisor cannot give her any certainty as to how much she will have to pay Andrew until they reach a settlement, or until a court makes an order if they are unable to reach a settlement. If Andrew sues her for the mortgage payments, Iris may ask to have any amount owing to Andrew offset by the $5000 spousal RRSP contributions, again, using the constructive trust doctrine.

- Iris tells her advisor that she feels that it is unlikely that she and Andrew will re-unite. Iris's advisor tells her that she should write a will to clarify how she would like her estate to be distributed at the time of her death. Iris chooses to name her father as her personal representative in her will, and leaves her estate equally to each of her parents. Iris knows that although she has changed her will, Andrew may still have a claim against the estate if he wins the unjust enrichment argument, and this claim will have to be paid from the estate before her parents will be able to receive the remainder.

- Iris's advisor also tells her to review all of her beneficiary designations on her RRSPs and insurance policies. Iris's advisor tells her that she should remove Andrew as a beneficiary, and the simplest solution would be to designate the estate as her beneficiary, since there could be complications if she appoints someone else as a beneficiary (see Chapter 2, "Single", for a further discussion on the potential negative consequences of appointing a direct beneficiary).

- Iris chooses to rewrite her powers of attorney for finances and personal care. She names her father as her primary power of attorney for finances, and her mother as the alternate. Since she has spoken with her mother about her health care philosophies, she chooses to appoint her mother as her primary attorney for personal care, with her father as her alternate.

- Iris asks her financial planner to create a new financial plan for her to ensure that she is saving adequate amounts for her retirement, now that she is single. She also cancels the credit card which indicates Andrew as the supplemental cardholder, and obtains a new card in her name only.

### *6.8.1.1 Jurisdiction Differences for this Case Study*

Note that there are many differences between the Canadian jurisdictions regarding whether or not common-law partners have a right to a division of family property when a common-law relationship ends. Although Iris and Andrew would not have the ability to apply for a division of family property in many jurisdictions (as was the case in the case study), they would have had the right to apply for a division of family property in the following circumstances:

- Manitoba — either if they lived together for a minimum of three years, or registered their relationship under *The Vital Statistics Act*;
- Northwest Territories – if they lived in a conjugal relationship for a period of two years, or in a relationship of some permanence with a child;
- Nova Scotia — if they registered their relationship as domestic partners;
- Nunavut – if they lived in a conjugal relationship for a period of two years, or in a relationship of some permanence with a child.
- Quebec — if they entered into a civil union; or
- Saskatchewan — if they lived together for a minimum of two years.

However, the assets that comprise family property are different in each jurisdiction, so it is important to speak with a family lawyer prior to entering into a common-law relationship to determine which assets are divisible, and which are not. If appropriate, a cohabitation agreement should be signed to clarify the understanding between the parties as to how they want their assets to be divided in the event of a relationship breakdown. See Chapter 3, "Common-Law Couples", for a further discussion on this issue and the rules applicable in each of the jurisdictions. Also see Chapter 17, "Family Property", for a discussion regarding what is considered family property in your jurisdiction if common-law partners have the right to a division of family property in your jurisdiction.

The other major difference in some of the jurisdictions is the fact that a separated common-law partner may be entitled to receive part of their partner's estate, even if the partner dies without a will. Therefore, in some jurisdictions, it would have been very important for Iris to sign a new will. See section 6.7, "Jurisdiction Differences", and section 19.6 of Chapter 19, "Distribution of an Estate", for further information on the rights of a separated common-law partner in your province to receive part of an estate where there is no will.

## 6.8.2 Separated, Married, No Children

If Iris and Andrew had been married at the time of their separation, not much of the advice given to Iris by her lawyer in Case Study 6.8.1 would have changed. However, there are some exceptions.

- Regardless of where they lived, each of Iris and Andrew would have been entitled to make an application for a division of family property under the provincial or territorial family law legislation, assuming they made the application within the prescribed time as required in their province or territory. See Chapter 17, "Family Property", for a discussion of the types of property which are considered family assets of married couples in your province or territory.

- It would have been extremely important for Iris to sign a new will to ensure that Andrew did not receive part of her estate at the time of death (other than any amount owing as a result of a division of family property). In most jurisdictions, married spouses are entitled to receive some or all of their spouse's estate, even if they are separated. See sections 6.7 and section 19.6 of Chapter 19, "Distribution of an Estate", for a description as to the rights of a separated spouse at the time of death.

## 6.8.3 Separated, Living Common-Law, With Children

Jacques and his former common-law partner, Shelley, have two children, Sam who is seven years old, and Sally who is five. Jacques and Shelley have separated after a ten year relationship. They currently live in Alberta (see below for the jurisdiction differences in this case study). Jacques would like all of his estate to go to Sam and Sally, since he does not want to leave his estate to Shelley. Jacques goes to see his advisor, who advises as outlined below.

- Jacques needs to rewrite his power of attorney for finances and personal directive. Jacques appoints his brother as his primary attorney in both documents, and his sister as his alternate.

- Jacques also needs to rewrite his will. Jacques signs a new will that leaves his entire estate to his two children equally, although he understands that Shelley may still be able to make a claim against the estate if she is successful in making a claim for unjust enrichment against Jacques (see section 3.4.2.1 of Chapter 3, "Common-Law Couples", for a further discussion regarding the types of claims which common-law partners can make even in jurisdictions where they do not have the ability to make a family property claim). If Jacques does not specify to the contrary, his children will be entitled to receive their portion of the estate when they reach the age of majority, which is 18 in Alberta. Jacques decides instead to leave his estate to his two children in trust, and gives the trustees of these trusts the right to encroach upon the capital as they see necessary for the best interests of his children. Jacques further provides that at age 18, each of his children will be entitled to receive the annual income from their respective trust. The children will be entitled to receive one-quarter of the capital when they reach 21 years of age, half of the remainder when they reach 25, and all of the remaining capital when they reach 30 years of age.

- Jacques appoints his brother as his personal representative in his will and his sister as the alternate executor and guardian of his children, after discussing the responsibilities of each job with them. (In the event of Jacques' death, Shelley will have the first right to act as guardian, so the proposed guardian would only take care of the children in the event Shelley predeceased Jacques).

- Jacques then changes the beneficiary designations on his RRSPs to his estate, so that the funds will be managed by his personal representative. If he appoints his children as the beneficiaries of his RRSPs, the funds will have to be managed by the provincial trustee or guardian, resulting in unnecessary expense. Jacques has been advised against designating his brother or sister as the beneficiary of his RRSPs, since the funds will then go to them, and they will not be obligated to use the funds for the benefit of Sam or Sally. In addition, if he appoints his brother or sister as the beneficiary of his RRSPs, his estate will be liable for paying the tax on the amount held in his plan, even though the beneficiary will be entitled to the funds, and will not have to pay any tax unless the estate has insufficient funds to pay the tax.

- Jacques decides to establish an insurance trust with his insurance proceeds so that he can minimize probate fees, yet still allow the insurance proceeds to be managed by his personal representative. See section 22.3.7 of Chapter 22, "Probate", for a further discussion on insurance trusts.

- Jacques also reviews his life insurance requirements with his financial planner. Since he is not choosing to rollover his RRSP or other assets to his children, there may be a significant tax liability at the time of his death (see Chapter 21, "Taxation at Death", for a discussion as to how to calculate the tax liability at the time of death). For example, if Jacques has $100,000 in his RRSPs, and he had left them to Shelley, Shelley could have contributed that sum to her own RRSP, deferring the taxation of that amount until she made withdrawals or died. Now that he is instead choosing to leave the RRSPs to his estate to be divided equally between his children, tax will be owing at the time of his death, leaving only a fraction of that amount for his children. Jacques must consider what the *after-tax value* of his estate will be, and consider whether or not he will need additional insurance to ensure he leaves a sufficient amount for his children. (Note that although the children can purchase a registered annuity with RRSP funds if they were financially dependent upon the deceased, and were either under the age of 18 or were financially dependent due to a mental or physical infirmity, in many cases it is still not recommended that RRSP proceeds be left directly to a child. Even if an annuity is purchased, the payments must all be received prior to the child's 18th birthday, which in many cases is too young, since they will not have adequate maturity to manage such sums.)

### *6.8.3.1 Jurisdiction Differences for this Case Study*

The main difference which may have been relevant in other jurisdictions is the ability of common-law partners to make a claim for a division of family property in some jurisdictions. See section 6.8.1.1 for a listing of the jurisdictions in which such a claim can be made by a former common-law partner.

## 6.8.4 Separated, Married, With Children

The issues for Jacques would not be much different from Case Study 6.8.3 if he and Shelley were married. However, married couples may make a claim for a division of family property in every jurisdiction, and are generally entitled to inherit part of the estate in the event a separated spouse died without a will. Note that the family property rules vary in each jurisdiction, so reference should be made to section 17.4 in Chapter 17, "Family Property", for further information on the family property rules in your jurisdiction of residence. Also see section 19.6 of Chapter 19, "Distribution of an Estate", for the rules in your jurisdiction regarding who will receive an estate when there is no will.

# CHAPTER 7



# DIVORCED



Divorced individuals should review their estate plan in generally the same manner as a separated person (see Chapter 6, "Separated"). However, here is a brief review of some of the additional issues you should consider, as there are some considerations which are unique to divorced persons.

## 7.1 FINANCIAL PLANNING

The financial planning issues for divorced individuals are essentially the same as those for separated individuals. See Chapter 6, "Separated", for more information on this subject.

## 7.2 TAX PLANNING

The tax planning issues for divorced individuals are essentially the same as those for separated individuals. See Chapter 6, "Separated", for more information on this subject.

## 7.3 FAMILY LAW ISSUES

Prior to obtaining your divorce, it is important that you receive professional advice regarding the family laws in your jurisdiction. For a further discussion of these issues, see Chapter 6, "Separation", and Chapter 17, "Family Property".

It is also important to have all the documentation respecting your divorce drafted by a professional to ensure that you are protected from future claims. For example, a divorced spouse may be able to make a claim for a division of family property or spousal support even after the time of divorce, so it is important that the divorce order include a final release of all claims in this regard, although it should be noted that with respect to support, a court can overlook any agreement between the parties, and award support as necessary. Under the federal *Divorce Act*, there is no limitation period for bringing an application for spousal support.

## 7.4 DISABILITY PLANNING

Review your powers of attorney for both finances and health care, and write new ones if necessary. Divorce generally does not impact a power of attorney for finances or health care, although there are some exceptions (see section 7.7 for the rules in your jurisdiction). Therefore, if you become incompetent, and you have not changed your power of attorney, your ex-spouse may still be the person with authority to deal with your affairs. If your ex-spouse chooses not to exercise that authority, another family member may have to go to court to be appointed as committee of your affairs. If you do choose to change your power of attorney, you should give notice to anyone who received notice of your previous power of attorney that you have terminated the prior appointment and made a new one.

If you did not have a power of attorney for finances or health care previously, consider the issue carefully, as you can no longer assume that your spouse will look after you in a time of need. Consider your choice carefully, and be sure to speak with your intended attorneys prior to appointing them (see Chapter 18, "Powers of Attorney", for more information on these issues).

Also review your disability insurance to ensure that it is adequate for your new circumstances. This may be particularly important if you are no longer insured under the group plan of your former spouse's employer. Also, if you are supporting a family, it may be even more crucial that your income be protected in the event of disability. Speak to a financial advisor to ensure that your insurance coverage is appropriate for your needs.



## 7.5 ESTATE PLANNING

Many of the issues regarding your estate plan are similar to those you should consider at the time of separation (see Chapter 6, "Separated", for more information). However, here are some additional issues to consider in the case of divorce.

### 7.5.1 Review Your Will

When you are divorced, you should review your will and other estate planning documents to ensure that they are consistent with your intentions. In some jurisdictions, if your spouse is still indicated as your personal representative or beneficiary in your will, a court will consider him or her to have predeceased you, and they will instead appoint the alternate or co-representatives in his or her place. It is for this reason that it is important to always appoint an alternate beneficiary and personal representative. However, even if you have an alternate, this is a good time to review your estate plan, and do a new will. If you live in a jurisdiction where your spouse is not deemed to have predeceased you, then it is imperative that you re-write your will so that your ex-spouse does not receive your estate. (See section 7.7 for the rules in your province.)

One other reason to review your will is to ensure that your estate is distributed properly, especially if you have young children. If you live in a jurisdiction where a divorced spouse is deemed to have predeceased you, then your estate will go to your alternate beneficiaries, which could include children who are minors. Therefore, it is particularly important to ensure that your will includes the proper trust conditions, so that your children do not receive the property when they are too young to manage it. If money is left to minors, even inadvertently, it is quite likely that the provincial or territorial authorities will be required to manage the funds until the children reach the age of majority.

If you do not have a will, it is important to sign a will, especially if young children could be potential beneficiaries. See section 19.6 of Chapter 19, "Distribution of an Estate", for a discussion as to how your estate will be distributed in your jurisdiction if you die without a will.

## 7.5.2 Review Your Beneficiary Designations

Ensure that all of the beneficiary designations on any pensions, RRSPs, RRIFs, segregated funds and insurance plans are changed if necessary. Divorce does not automatically affect a beneficiary designation in favour of a spouse even if you have reached a settlement indicating that all property matters are settled between you. In many cases, the recommended course of action will be to designate your estate as the beneficiary. Please see section 6.5.4 of Chapter 6, "Separated", for a discussion of some of the issues to consider when designating a direct beneficiary after a separation or divorce.

If you do not change your beneficiary, and your divorced spouse receives your RRSP or RRIF, your estate will be responsible for paying the tax on the RRSP or RRIF proceeds, even though your ex-spouse received the funds. If you were still married to your spouse at the time of your death, these funds could have been contributed to an RRSP or RRIF in your spouse's name, thereby deferring the tax until the spouse withdrew the funds or died (although the recipient spouse does not have to defer the tax, even if married). However, since you are now divorced, the rollover will no longer be available, so your estate will be taxed on the full amount of the proceeds, even though the asset went to your ex-spouse. Changing beneficiary designations on an RRSP is very important when you divorce. If you still want your ex-spouse to receive the registered funds, then ensure that your estate will have sufficient funds to pay the tax.

# 7.6 INSURANCE PLANNING

See Chapter 6, "Separated", for some of the insurance issues you should consider in the case of relationship breakdown.

# 7.7 JURISDICTION DIFFERENCES

## 7.7.1 Alberta

- *Powers of Attorney.* Divorce has no impact on a power of attorney or personal directive, so you may want to change these documents if your spouse was appointed as your attorney for finances or health care decisions.

- *Estates.* Divorce or annulment has no effect on a will, so you will need to re-write your will if you want to exclude your ex-spouse as a beneficiary or personal representative (assuming you had named them in a previous will, which was executed sometime after the date of marriage).

## 7.7.2 British Columbia

- *Power of Attorney.* Divorce has no impact on a power of attorney. However, if you have named a former spouse as your representative in a representation agreement, that appointment will cease upon divorce unless you have indicated to the contrary in the document and you have completed a consultation certificate indicating that you want the appointment to survive a divorce.

- *Estates.* Divorce or annulment will revoke any gifts or appointments made to a former spouse (e.g. if you named them as your personal representative), and the will takes effect as if the former spouse had predeceased the deceased, unless the will expresses an intention to the contrary.

## 7.7.3 Manitoba

- *Powers of Attorney.* A divorce has no impact on a power of attorney. However, if you have appointed your spouse as your proxy in a health care directive, the directive will be automatically revoked at the time of divorce, unless the document provides to the contrary.

- *Estates.* Divorce or annulment will revoke any gifts made to a former spouse as well as any appointments in their favour (e.g. if you named your former spouse as your personal representative), and the will takes effect as if the former spouse had predeceased the deceased, unless the will expresses an intention to the contrary.

## 7.7.4 New Brunswick

- *Powers of Attorney.* Divorce has no impact on a power of attorney for finances or personal care, so you may want to change these documents if your spouse was appointed as your attorney for finances or health care decisions.

- *Estates.* Divorce or annulment has no effect on a will or its clauses. The gifts and powers of appointment made to an ex-spouse under a pre-divorce will are still valid. However, it is possible for a divorce to *revive* a previous will. For example, if you wrote a will before you got married, and did not write a new will while you were married, although the will is not effective while you are married (except in limited circumstances), it can become effective again once you divorce, if there were no children of the marriage. If you wrote a will prior to your marriage, you should review it, and, if necessary, sign a new one.

## 7.7.5 Newfoundland

- *Powers of Attorney.* Divorce has no impact on a power of attorney for finances. However, if a spouse has been appointed as their substitute decision maker in an advance health care directive, a divorce will revoke the appointment of the spouse.

- *Estates.* Divorce or annulment has no effect on a will or its clauses. The gifts and powers of appointment made to an ex-spouse under a will made before the time of divorce are still valid.

## 7.7.6 Northwest Territories

- *Powers of Attorney.* Divorce has no impact on a power of attorney for finances or an advanced health care directive, so you may want to change these documents if your spouse was appointed as your attorney for finances or health care decisions.

- *Estates.* Divorce or annulment has no effect on a will or its clauses. The gifts and powers of appointment made to an ex-spouse under a will made before the time of divorce are still valid.



## 7.7.7 Nova Scotia

- *Powers of Attorney.* Divorce has no impact on a power of attorney, so you may want to change this document if your spouse was appointed as your attorney for finances. For personal directives for health care decisions, unless the personal directive expressly provides otherwise, once the spouse is no longer a spouse, any appointment of the spouse as delegate is revoked.

- *Estates.* For divorces that occurred prior to August 18, 2008, divorce or annulment has no effect on a will or its clauses. The gifts and powers of appointment made to an ex-spouse under a will before the time of divorce will remain valid. However, for divorces that occurred on or after August 18, 2008, divorce or annulment will revoke any gifts made to a former spouse as well as any appointments in their favour (e.g., if you named your former spouse as your personal representative), and the will takes effect as if the former spouse had predeceased the deceased, unless the will expresses an intention to the contrary.

## 7.7.8 Nunavut

The rules in Nunavut are generally the same as in the Northwest Territories. See section 7.7.6.

## 7.7.9 Ontario

- *Powers of Attorney.* Divorce has no impact on a power of attorney for finances or personal care, so you may want to change these documents if your spouse was appointed as your attorney for finances or health care decisions.

- *Estates.* Divorce or annulment will revoke any gifts or appointments made to a former spouse (e.g. if you named them as your personal representative), and the will takes effect as if the former spouse had predeceased the deceased, unless the will expresses an intention to the contrary.

## 7.7.10 Prince Edward Island

- *Powers of Attorney.* Divorce has no impact on a power of attorney for finances. However, when a spouse is appointed proxy for health care decisions, the appointment is revoked upon divorce, unless the document includes an indication to the contrary.

- *Estates.* Divorce or annulment will revoke any gifts or appointments made to a former spouse (e.g. if you named them as your personal representative), and the will takes effect as if the former spouse had predeceased the deceased, unless the will expresses an intention to the contrary.

## 7.7.11 Quebec

- *Mandate in Case of Incapacity.* Divorce has no impact on a mandate in case of incapacity, so you may want to change these documents you have appointed your spouse as your attorney.

- *Estates.* Divorce or annulment will revoke any gifts or appointments made to a former spouse (e.g. if you named them as your personal representative), and the will takes effect as if the former spouse had predeceased the deceased.

## 7.7.12 Saskatchewan

- *Powers of Attorney.* If a spouse has appointed the other spouse as their power of attorney, the authority is terminated as soon as they cease to cohabit as spouses as a result of an intention to end their spousal relationship. If a spouse had appointed the other spouse as their proxy in their health care directive, the appointment is terminated at the time of divorce, unless the directive indicates to the contrary.

- *Estates.* Divorce or annulment will revoke any gifts or appointments made to a former spouse (e.g. if you named them as your personal representative), and the will takes effect as if the former spouse had predeceased the deceased, unless the will expresses an intention to the contrary.



### 7.7.13 Yukon

- *Powers of Attorney.* Divorce has no impact on a power of attorney for finances, so you may want to change this document if your spouse was appointed as your attorney for finances. However, unless a directive regarding health care decisions states otherwise, an appointment of the maker's spouse as a proxy is revoked if the marriage is terminated by divorce.

- *Estates.* Divorce or annulment has no effect on a will or its clauses. The gifts and powers of appointment made to an ex-spouse under a pre-divorce will are still valid.

## 7.8 CASE STUDIES

Since many of the issues relevant at the time of divorce are also relevant at the time of separation, reference should be made to the case studies in section 6.8 of Chapter 6, "Separated". Depending upon the jurisdiction, it is usually the issues below that are relevant at the time of divorce, in addition to the issues discussed in Chapter 6 regarding separation.

- In the event of divorce, any gifts or appointments in favour of an ex-spouse in a will or power of attorney for finances or health care decisions may be automatically revoked (see section 7.7 for the rules in your jurisdiction).

- Divorced spouses are generally not entitled to any part of their ex-spouse's estate if they die without a will (unless they can make a dependant's relief application — see section 19.6 of Chapter 19, "Distribution of an Estate", for a description of the types of claims which may be made against an estate).

If you have updated your wealth plan after the time of your separation, it is possible that it will not necessarily need to be changed again as a result of your divorce. Speak to a qualified professional to determine if any further changes are required.

# CHAPTER 8

# BLENDED FAMILIES

It is becoming increasingly common for Canadians to be a member of a blended family. Blended families are families where one or both spouses (or common-law partners) have been in a previous relationship, and have children from that relationship.

Although individuals involved in a second marriage or common-law relationship may not consider themselves to be unique from a social perspective, there are still many issues they should discuss to ensure that their wealth will be distributed in a manner which includes both their new spouse (or partner), as well as their children from their previous relationship (and perhaps from the current relationship as well). Couples who are in common-law relationships should also read Chapter 3, "Common-Law Couples", and couples who are married should read Chapter 5, "Married". For the purposes of this chapter, we will refer to a spouse or common-law partner as a "spouse".

## 8.1 FINANCIAL PLANNING

Blended families often come together at a time when both spouses are more mature, and perhaps have already developed very specific philosophies towards money. Since money disputes are one of the leading causes of relationship breakdown, it is imperative that couples communicate early on in their relationship about their views towards money and debt. If one spouse has accumulated significant wealth, and the other has not, this can cause animosity if there is no clear understanding from the beginning as to how expenses will be shared, and the amount which should be saved on a regular basis.

Different financial histories can cause even more difficulties when both parties are bringing children into the relationship. The couple should review the amounts which they have saved for each branch of the family, and determine if adjustments need to be made in order to give each child a similar level of post-secondary education. For example, do the RESPs of one branch of the family exceed the RESPs of the other? If this discussion does not take place until the children are older, it may become difficult to rectify the problem if a large amount of money is required in a short amount of time. If the amount saved for each child is compared early in the relationship, then it may be possible to direct more resources to the RESPs of the children who have not had as much saved for them.

## 8.2 TAX PLANNING

Whether you are living as a common-law or a married couple, you will be required to file your tax returns as a couple. This brings with it both advantages and disadvantages. Be sure to review the tax planning strategies discussed in section 5.2 of Chapter 5, "Married", which apply to both married and common-law couples. If you are living common-law, you may also want to review sections 3.1 and 3.3, of Chapter 3, "Common-law Couples", which outline when common-law couples must file their income tax returns as a couple, and the consequences of filing as a couple.

## 8.3 FAMILY LAW ISSUES

In many cases, individuals in blended families have acquired significant assets, since they are entering into this relationship later in life. In many first marriages or common-law relationships, spouses or partners are not as concerned about how their assets will be distributed if the relationship ends, since neither one of them has brought many (if any) assets into the relationship. If you have significant assets, or you are concerned about protecting your assets for your children, it will become more important for you to be familiar with the family property rules in your jurisdiction. For example, in Newfoundland, Ontario and Saskatchewan, a marital home may be shareable, even if it was purchased by one of the spouses prior to the marriage. In British Columbia and Nova Scotia, many different types of family assets may be shareable, even those acquired prior to the date of marriage. These are just some of the anomalies which exist across the country. Refer to section 17.4 of Chapter 17, "Family Property", for a discussion on the family property rules in your jurisdiction. If you are in a common-law relationship, you may not have the right to a division of family property, although you may have other legal remedies. See section 3.9 of Chapter 3, "Common-Law Couples", for the rules in your jurisdiction.

If you need to enter into a pre-nuptial agreement, marriage contract or cohabitation agreement to protect certain assets (such as a business, or assets acquired before the relationship), be sure to speak with an advisor who is experienced in this area, and who will be able to address your concerns. Under no circumstances should both spouses speak with the same advisor — it is crucial that both parties obtain independent legal advice when entering into a domestic contract.

# 8.4 DISABILITY PLANNING

Although the issues regarding disability are essentially the same in any relationship, there can be some complicating factors in blended families. If, for example, you do not change your power of attorney, and you had previously named your adult children as your power of attorney for financial matters, your children could have more power over your financial affairs than your new spouse in the event of your incapacity. It is crucial that you discuss your wishes with your new spouse and your children regarding what should happen in the event of a disability, and ensure that your documentation is in proper order. Depending upon the relationship of the parties involved, you may wish to appoint your new spouse and adult children as joint attorneys, or perhaps give your adult children the ability to review the accounts on a periodic basis. Spouses usually have more authority than children when making medical decisions, but you may not feel that is appropriate in your situation. Review section 3.5 in Chapter 3, "Common-Law Couples", or section 5.4 in Chapter 5, "Married", for more information on disability planning, and also see Chapter 18, "Powers of Attorney".

# 8.5 ESTATE PLANNING

## 8.5.1 Potential Estate Planning Problems

Estate planning for blended families is particularly difficult, as there are competing interests — generally you will want some of your estate to go to your new spouse, but you will not want to disinherit your children from a previous relationship. Many blended families do not structure their estate plan properly, with the result being that one branch of the family receives the entire estate, and the other branch of the family receives nothing.

### *8.5.1.1 Potential Problems if Assets Left to Spouse*

Most couples choose to draft "mutual" wills, which state that, upon one's death, everything is to go to the surviving spouse or common-law partner, and upon the death of the second spouse or partner, everything is to be divided equally between all of their children. In other cases, the couple does not draft a will, but places all assets in joint ownership with a right of survivorship. However, this type of planning is generally not recommended for blended families, and is generally not sufficient to ensure that your children will receive any part of your estate after you are gone. Consider the scenarios below.

- Let's assume that you die first and leave your entire estate to your spouse and then he or she remarries. Marriage renders all previous wills void (except in Quebec), meaning that the will which your spouse signed with you is no longer in effect due to their remarriage. If your spouse does not sign a new will after they remarry, they will effectively die intestate, meaning that all of their assets will go to their new spouse and their children only, since the intestate succession legislation does not include step-children (i.e. your children). Even if they do sign a new will, their new spouse will be entitled to a portion of their estate, and it is very likely that your children will not receive any of the estate. A court may give some consideration to the fact that you have previously drafted wills leaving assets to both branches of the family, but there are no guarantees that your children will win any argument on that basis.

- Let's assume that you die first and leave your entire estate to your spouse, who then decides to re-write his or her will, leaving everything to his or her new spouse and children, and nothing to your children. If you want your spouse to be bound by the original wills, then you must both sign a contract agreeing not to change your wills after the death of the first spouse. Without an agreement to this effect, there is no guarantee that the original document will not be changed.

- Let's assume that you leave everything to your spouse, and your spouse has a will that includes your children. However, prior to the time of their death, they decide to do "probate planning", meaning that they add joint owners with a right of survivorship to their property (not applicable in Quebec), or designate their child as a direct beneficiary of their estate. If the surviving spouse has lost contact with your children (their step-children), it is more likely that they will name their own children as joint owners or direct beneficiaries of their property. Many people do not realize that by doing this, they are circumventing the provisions of their will (although in the case of joint ownership, your children may be able to argue that the asset is being held "in trust" for the estate). Even if the surviving spouse provides in their will that your children are to receive a part of their estate, if they have managed to remove all of their assets from their estate, the fact that they have a will is not sufficient to ensure your children will ever receive anything. If your children are not children of your spouse, they may not even be entitled to make a dependants' relief claim.

From the above, it is obvious that after the time of your death, you will not have any control over whether or not your children receive any part of your estate if you give everything directly to your spouse. In many cases, the surviving spouse has not chosen to disinherit their step-children, but it has still happened inadvertently. If you want to ensure that your children will receive something after the time of your death, you must take specific steps to ensure that that happens.

## *8.5.1.2 Potential Problems if Assets Left to Children*

Because of the concern that a child from a previous relationship will never see any part of their estate, many parents in blended family situations try to leave money directly to their children. However, this brings with it its own set of challenges.

### 8.5.1.2.1 Family Property Claims

It is important to keep in mind that regardless of the terms of your will, your spouse may be entitled to some or all of your estate. Do not assume that you can simply choose to leave as much as you want to your children — your spouse may have a claim against your estate for more than you anticipated, which could mean that your estate will not be distributed as you intended.

Some people assume that they can leave all of their estate to their children, since they feel that their surviving spouse will receive "enough" by virtue of being the joint owner of their home, or the direct beneficiary of their registered assets or insurance policies. In many jurisdictions, however, when calculating the amount of assets that the surviving spouse is entitled to, jointly held assets, or assets which are paid directly to a beneficiary, are disregarded. In many cases, the only assets that are considered for the purposes of family property rights are the assets that pass through the estate. This may mean that the surviving spouse will receive considerable assets by virtue of joint ownership rights or direct beneficiary designations, but still be entitled to make a claim against the estate assets. In this case, the children may not receive the amount you intended them to receive.

See section 19.6 of Chapter 19, "Distribution of an Estate", for further information on what your spouse or common-law partner may be entitled to, regardless of the terms of your will.

### 8.5.1.2.2 Failure to Write a New Will After Remarriage

Another common misconception of many individuals is that their children from a previous relationship will receive part or all of their estate, since they wrote a will before entering into this new relationship that left everything to their children. However, getting married will void any previous wills (except in the

Province of Quebec). You must rewrite your will after you get married, unless your will was drafted in contemplation of marriage (and in Prince Edward Island, within 30 days of that marriage). It is important to remember that a will must be drafted in contemplation of *that particular marriage*. A will which simply says that children from a previous relationship are to inherit your estate even "if I ever marry again" is not sufficient. In some jurisdictions, entering into a common-law relationship will also render a will void after a certain period of time, or upon registration of the relationship with the provincial government. See section 3.9 of Chapter 3, "Common-Law Couples", if you are in a common-law relationship.

#### 8.5.1.2.3 Rights of Spouse on Intestacy

Many individuals in first marriages choose not to do a will right away since they do not have many assets, and they are not concerned with how their assets will be distributed. However, in the case of blended families, one or both of the spouses may have acquired significant assets. It is for this reason that it may be even more important to do a will right away, since if you die without a will, a spouse may be entitled to a preferential share, even if you were only married for a few days. For example, in Ontario, the preferential share is $200,000, plus a portion of the remainder of the estate. If you have only been married a short time, you may choose to leave far less than that to your spouse, with the remainder to your children, which is why it is important to write a will (see 19.6 of Chapter 19, "Distribution of an Estate", for a description of how much your spouse would be entitled to if you died without a will).



#### 8.5.1.2.4 Triggering Capital Gains Tax

If you intend to leave assets directly to children, keep in mind the tax consequences of doing so. When assets are transferred to a spouse or common-law partner, any unrealized capital gain can be deferred until the spouse or common-law partner sells the asset or dies. However, when assets are transferred to a child, any unrealized capital gain will usually be triggered at the time of the parent's death, possibly resulting in a tax liability for the estate sooner than anticipated.

## 8.5.2 Estate Planning Strategies

Given the above challenges, what is the solution? Here are a few strategies commonly used by individuals in blended families.

### 8.5.2.1 Spousal or Common-Law Partner Trusts

Many individuals in second relationships choose not to leave their estate outright to their surviving spouse or common-law partner. Instead they choose to leave their estate to their spouse or common-law partner in a spousal trust or common-law partner trust (we will refer to both types of trusts collectively as "spousal trusts"). These types of trusts work in the manner outlined below.

- The surviving spouse is entitled to receive all the income generated by the trust during their lifetime.

- No one other than the surviving spouse is entitled to use any of the capital of the trust, so long as the spouse is alive.

- Upon the death of the second spouse, the capital in the trust will be distributed according to the will of the first spouse, not according to the will of the second spouse to die. This is because the assets never became the property of the surviving spouse — they are the property of the trust. The terms of the spousal trust can provide that upon the death of the surviving spouse, all the assets are to be distributed among the children of the first spouse (or to trusts in favour of those children).

- Assuming all the conditions set out in the *Income Tax Act* are met, the assets can roll over to the spousal trust, without triggering any capital gains at the time of death of the first spouse, in the same manner as if they had been transferred directly to the surviving spouse.[1]

---

1 The conditions set out in the *Income Tax Act* are as follows:

1. The deceased must have been a resident of Canada immediately before the time of death.

2. The trust must be a resident of Canada, which essentially means that the trustees of the trust must be residents of Canada. The Canada Revenue Agency will look to where the mind and management of the trust is, which is usually where a majority of the trustees are resident, so at a minimum, a majority of the trustees should be resident in Canada. However, if the non-resident trustees are the trustees who control the trust, it is still possible that the trust could be considered non-resident, even if the non-residents form the minority of the trustees.

3. The assets must vest indefeasibly within the trust within 36 months of the date of death. This essentially means that the assets must be the assets of the trust — if the assets are subject to someone else having the right to buy them, they will not vest within the trust. This is sometimes the case where shares in a privately owned business are subject to a buy-sell provision in a shareholders' agreement.

One important item to keep in mind if you want to have your assets distributed in this manner, is that your assets must pass through your estate. If you have arranged your affairs so that none, or very few, of your assets pass through your estate, this type of planning will be ineffective. For example, many couples often hold title to their assets in joint names so that they will pass to the survivor automatically. If the assets pass directly to the surviving spouse, then they will not be subject to the conditions set out in the will. *In many blended family scenarios, it is not recommended that assets be held jointly, or that spouses be named as direct beneficiaries on registered assets or insurance policies.* Some individuals disregard the potential problems this may cause their family simply in order to save a small amount in probate fees (for a further discussion of the problems with probate planning, see Chapter 22, "Probate"). However, what they fail to recognize is that if the assets go through probate upon the death of the first spouse and are then held in trust, they will not have to go through probate upon the death of the second spouse, so spousal trusts do not really result in any additional probate being paid. *Individuals in blended families should be very careful when arranging their affairs — probate planning is generally the least important concern in these types of relationships.*

If you would like to hold assets jointly with your spouse, consider holding title as *tenants in common* as opposed to *joint tenants.* This means that upon the death of one of the spouses, their interest in the property will pass through their estate (and effectively through the trust), and will not automatically pass to the surviving spouse.



### 8.5.2.2 Leaving Assets Directly to Children

It is possible that a spousal trust may not be practical in your situation, for a number of reasons.

- If your new spouse is close in age to your children, it is quite possible that your children will not receive any part of the capital during their lifetime,

4. The spouse must be entitled to receive all of the income from the trust every year.

5. No one other than the spouse may have access to any of the capital of the trust prior to the death of the spouse. This condition will not be met where, for example, the deceased transfers a vacation property into the trust, but gives the children the right to use the vacation property for a period of time each summer.

since your children are only entitled to receive the trust capital upon the death of your spouse.

- If you feel that your surviving spouse and your children will not be able to co-operate after the time of your death, a spousal trust may not be practical. If your spouse and children are not likely to agree on the degree to which the spouse may encroach upon the capital of the trust, this could lead to protracted arguments and, potentially, litigation. When you use spousal trusts in your will, your spouse will have to waive their right to apply for a family property accounting — if they do not waive their right to receive a portion of the estate directly, then they could "break" the trust after the time of your death. Generally speaking, most spouses will only agree to waive their family property rights if the trust provides that they have the right to encroach upon the capital, since they will not be inheriting the assets in their own name. However, if the surviving spouse chooses to encroach on the capital, this means there obviously will be less for the children when the second spouse dies, which could lead to arguments.

- If your spouse is a spendthrift and you are not comfortable that there will be anything left in the trust by the time of their death, then a spousal trust might not work.

If you think that the spousal trust mechanism is not feasible for any of the above reasons, then there may be other options.

One option that may be available to those who have significant assets is to leave a portion of your estate directly to your spouse, and leave different assets directly to your children. It is imperative that you speak with an experienced estate planning lawyer to determine how much your spouse will be entitled to, to make sure that they will not have a claim against the assets meant for your children. It may also be important that none of your assets be held in joint ownership with your spouse, to ensure that sufficient assets pass through your estate in order to leave enough for everyone. If everything is held jointly with your spouse, the terms of your will are irrelevant, since everything will pass directly to your spouse (except in the province of Quebec). Also, if assets are left directly to your children, this could trigger a tax bill, for which planning is required (see Chapter 21, "Taxation at Death", for information on how a person is taxed at the time of death).

### 8.5.2.3 Using Insurance to Fund Obligations

If you do not have sufficient assets to both leave enough to your spouse to satisfy their family property claim, yet still leave enough for your children, it may be simpler to leave your entire estate to your spouse, and instead make your children the beneficiaries of a life insurance policy. This will ensure that each party will receive the desired amount, and each party will be free to use their inheritance as they see fit. Be sure that you speak with an experienced estate planning advisor prior to implementing this type of planning. For example, you would not want to leave your estate to your children, with the insurance proceeds to go to your spouse, since the spouse could choose to make a claim against the estate, effectively receiving both the insurance proceeds and a portion of the estate.

Beware when designating children as the direct beneficiaries of an insurance policy, as a spouse could potentially make a claim against the insurance policy if they live in a jurisdiction where the dependant's relief legislation provides that insurance policies are to be included in the estate. For example, if the spouse is left an estate worth $100, and the children are left an insurance policy worth $100,000, your spouse may still have a claim against assets that were meant for your children. Also, in some jurisdictions, the amount left to persons other than your spouse may be subject to a family property claim by your spouse, even if they do not pass through your estate (see section 19.6 of Chapter 19, "Distribution of Your Estate"). It is crucial that members of blended families speak to an experienced estate planning lawyer when structuring their estate plan.

Also be careful when using this strategy if your children are young. If your children are minors, or even if they are young adults, it may not be a good idea to name them as the direct beneficiary of an insurance policy. This is because the Public Trustee will have the authority to manage the funds until they attain the age of majority, resulting in unnecessary expense, and then your children will be entitled to the funds when they are potentially still too young to manage them. If your children are young, speak to your lawyer about placing the insurance proceeds in an insurance trust for your children, so that a trusted family member can manage the funds and distribute them over a period of time, until the children are old enough to manage them. See section 10.5 of Chapter 10, "Children", for a further discussion of the issues to be considered regarding your children when structuring your estate.

When purchasing insurance to fund an estate for your children, be sure to purchase a policy which will pay out at the time of your death, not a joint last-to-die policy which will only pay out at the time of death of the second spouse.

Although many couples choose to purchase joint last-to-die policies, this is not appropriate where the intent is for the insurance to be payable upon your death alone. If the child also has to wait for the step-parent to die, they may not receive the funds in their lifetime, particularly if your new spouse is much younger than you.

## 8.5.2.4 *Registered Investments*

Registered investments can cause unique concerns when developing an estate planning strategy for blended families. Here are some issues to consider.

### 8.5.2.4.1 Placing Registered Investments in a Spousal Trust

If you are using the spousal trust strategy, then consider whether your registered investments should go into the trust. Generally speaking, most individuals prefer to put non-registered assets in a spousal trust, since registered assets, such as RRSPs and RRIFs cannot be rolled over into a spousal trust without triggering tax. The registered plan must be collapsed at the time of the death of the plan holder if you want the assets to go into a trust. Many people choose not to do this, however, due to the tax ramifications. Therefore, there are effectively two options, as follows:

- have these assets go into your spousal trust, in which case they must be included in your taxable income in the year of death, and then the after tax amount will go into the trust; or

- leave the registered investments directly to the surviving spouse, which is generally done through a direct beneficiary designation (although direct beneficiary designations on some forms of registered investments are not effective in Quebec) or a designation in your will, thereby possibly deferring the tax on these assets until the death of the second spouse. If your spouse chooses, they can elect to have the value of your registered assets included in their tax return, and then make a contribution to their RRSP or RRIF in order to continue to defer the tax. However, if your spouse does not choose to make such an election, your estate will remain liable to pay the tax on the registered investments, and your spouse will receive the gross amount. If your spouse is the only beneficiary of your estate, this may not be a problem. However, if your children are also beneficiaries of the estate, and will now have to pay a disproportionate amount of the tax, this could be an issue. In addition, it is quite possible that your children will not receive any of these funds when the second spouse dies.

Therefore, you must decide which is more important — potentially deferring tax until the death of the second spouse, or placing the after-tax funds in the trust so that you can continue to control the funds after your death, and any capital remaining upon the death of the second spouse will be distributed to your children. If you are concerned that if you choose to leave the assets to your estate, the tax consequences will leave an insufficient amount for your heirs, then consider purchasing insurance to restore the value of your estate.

#### 8.5.2.4.2 Designating Direct Beneficiaries on a Registered Investment

If you are using the strategy which involves giving some of your estate directly to your spouse, and some directly to your children, it is generally not a good idea to leave your RRSPs or RRIFs directly to your children if you have the option to leave them to a spouse and give something else to the children. RRSPs and RRIFs are taxable at the time of your death, unless the plan is rolled over to an RRSP or RRIF in the name of your spouse or common-law partner. (There are other exceptions if registered assets are left to minor or disabled children, although the drawbacks of doing this are discussed in section 21.2.5 of Chapter 21, "Taxation at Death"). If you can, leave the RRSPs or RRIF to your spouse, so that the tax on these amounts can be deferred until the time of their death.

However, if your spouse receives the RRSP directly and the children receive the estate, then depending upon your jurisdiction of residence, your spouse may be able to claim that they did not receive any of the estate, and could make a claim against the assets intended for your children. Alternatively, if they have not agreed in advance to defer the tax, they may choose to receive the gross value of the registered assets, leaving the tax liability to be paid by the estate. Always speak to an experienced advisor when structuring your estate plan to accommodate both spouses and children.

A particular problem can arise in the context of pensions and locked-in accounts. Generally speaking, spouses and common-law partners (as defined under the applicable pension legislation) are entitled to receive pension and locked-in payments, regardless of whether or not a beneficiary designation has been made in favour of someone else. Therefore, if you designate a child as a direct beneficiary of a pension and you have a surviving spouse, the direct designation in favour of the child will be treated as void, and the payments will be made to the spouse, which was obviously not your intention. In some cases, a spouse may be entitled to waive their rights to the payments, but in the case of locked-in accounts, the estate is still liable for the tax payable on the plan if the payments are made to a non-spouse, assuming there is no tax deferral available when the proceeds of the locked-in plan are paid to the child. If the spouse is the beneficiary of the estate, they may not want to waive their entitlement to the locked-in funds if the payment of the tax liability for the locked-in plan may result in he or she receiving less than anticipated. Be very careful when dealing with pensions and locked-in plans as the prevailing pension legislation may operate at cross-purposes with your intentions.

### *8.5.2.5 Alter Ego or Joint Partner Trusts*

If you are concerned that your children or beneficiaries may challenge your will or the distribution of your estate after the time of your death, you may also wish to consider whether or not it would be advisable to use an alter ego trust, or joint partner trust, which is a trust created during your lifetime and can set out the distribution of the trust assets at the time of your death. However, there are numerous tax disadvantages to creating this type of trust during your lifetime, so be sure to speak with an experienced estate planning lawyer prior to embarking on this type of planning. There is more information on alter ego and joint partner trusts at sections 22.3.5.2 and 22.3.5.3 in Chapter 22, "Probate".

## 8.5.3 Funerals

If you are in a blended family, you should discuss with your children where you would like to be buried. In many cases where a previous relationship ended with a death as opposed to a divorce, children want to have one parent buried next to the other, but a new spouse may have different intentions. A discussion in this regard may prevent disputes after you are gone, when the atmosphere could be emotionally charged.

## 8.5.4 Guardianship

Choosing a guardian may be especially complicated if there are children from previous relationships, as well as children from the current one. In blended families, the choice of guardian must be considered very carefully. See section 10.5.1 of Chapter 10, "Children", for a further discussion on this issue. Also remember that even if you have previously appointed a guardian for your children, all of your previous wills are voided at the time you remarry (except in Quebec), and in some jurisdictions, even when you enter into a common-law relationship. Do not assume that your previous planning will be sufficient now that you have entered into a new relationship.

### 8.5.5 Personal Representatives

Choosing a personal representative (commonly referred to as an "executor") may also be more complicated in a blended family situation — will you appoint your new spouse? Your adult children from a previous relationship? Do they get along with the new spouse? These decisions should not be made lightly, and should be discussed with all family members. In some cases, it may be best to have a spouse act as personal representative over part of your estate, with your children acting in respect of other assets (perhaps a business or an art collection which they may be more intimately familiar with). In other cases, it may be best to appoint an independent third party such as a trust company. See Chapter 20, "Personal Representatives", for further information on the issues to consider when appointing a personal representative.



### 8.5.6 Common Disasters

In the case of blended families, it is important to have a will to ensure that all beneficiaries are treated as intended in the case of a common disaster. Section 19.6 of Chapter 19, "Distribution of an Estate", describes the implications of a common disaster — in some jurisdictions the older spouse is deemed to die first, and in others, both spouses are deemed to have predeceased each other. This may cause inequities — for example, if the older spouse is deemed to die first, and their will provides that everything is to go to the younger spouse, then it is possible that the beneficiaries of the younger spouse will receive a larger portion of the combined estate. If the beneficiaries of both spouses are identical, this may not be a problem, but if the beneficiaries are different, this may cause disputes. This is another reason why it is imperative for individuals in blended families to have a proper will.

### 8.5.7 Personal Effects

In many cases, the items which are of most importance to children from previous relationships are family mementos and heirlooms. You should not assume that your children will be happy to simply receive the portion of the estate that they are allowed by virtue of provincial legislation if you choose not to do a will. Sentimental items are often the items which cause the most strife among family members, and you should try to ensure that these disputes are minimized after you are gone. When items such as photographs, china, jewellery and art are inadvertently left to a new spouse as opposed to children from a previous relationship, this can lead to disappointment, anger, family tensions, and in some cases, litigation.

Obviously, one solution is to leave certain personal effects to your children in your will. However, if there are some items which you want your children to have sooner rather than later (for example, personal items from a deceased parent), you may wish to consider giving them to your children before you die, to minimize potential problems later if the will is challenged for some reason. The discussions around personal items can often be very emotional, so be sure to discuss this issue with all immediate family members prior to making a decision.

### 8.5.8 Pension Survivor Benefits

You may be entitled to receive survivor benefits under the Canada Pension Plan or Quebec Pension Plan, if your deceased spouse contributed to either of those plans (although in the case of a common-law relationship, see section 3.6.1 of Chapter 3, "Common-law Couples", for information on when common-law partners will qualify for these benefits). You should apply for survivor benefits as soon as possible after the time of death.

In addition, you may be entitled to survivor benefits under an employee pension plan if your deceased spouse was a member of such a plan. However, you should not assume that you will qualify for a pension. If you were married after your spouse had already started receiving the pension (and he or she elected to receive higher individual payments instead of choosing lower payments with a survivor pension), then your spouse may no longer be able to change the payments in order to provide for a survivor pension. In fact, if your spouse was married to a previous spouse at the time he or she began to receive the pension, it may be the previous spouse who is entitled to receive the survivor benefits. Speak to your financial planner about whether or not you will be entitled to receive survivor benefits under your spouse's pension — if not, you will have to factor this into your financial plan when determining how much you need to save for your retirement.

## 8.6 INSURANCE PLANNING

Do you have spousal support obligations to a previous spouse? If so, the current amount of life insurance that you have may not be sufficient. Ensure that your assets at the time of death will be sufficient to fund any obligations from a previous relationship, as well as take care of your current dependants, which may include a spouse and/or children. See section 5.6 of Chapter 5, "Married", for a discussion of the types of insurance which couples should consider. Also see section 8.5.2.3 for a discussion as to how insurance can help to provide an estate both for a new spouse as well as children from a previous relationship.

## 8.7 JURISDICTION DIFFERENCES

Please refer to Chapter 3, "Common-Law Couples", Chapter 5, "Married", Chapter 17, "Family Property", and Chapter 19, "Distribution of an Estate", to determine if there are any unique rules in your province or territory which may apply to your situation.

## 8.8 CASE STUDY

### 8.8.1 Blended Family, Living Common-Law, No Will

Allison and Bob have been in a common-law relationship for the past five years. Allison has a child, Aurele, age 20, from a previous relationship. Bob has two children from a previous marriage, Sandra, age 33, and Cathy, age 35. Allison is 50 and Bob is 60 years of age. Both of them have acquired substantial assets during their lifetime, as a result of having received insurance proceeds upon the death of their respective first spouses. Each of them would like to ensure that the survivor is sufficiently taken care of so long as they are alive, but upon the death of the survivor, they would each like their respective estates to go to their children from their previous relationships.

Allison's estate is comprised of the following:

1. Her 50% interest in their home in West Vancouver worth $900,000, or $450,000. Given that they intend to use the principal residence exemption in respect of this asset, the after-tax value is $450,000.

2. Her 50% interest in their condo in Whistler worth $500,000, or $250,000. Since their condo has grown appreciably in value since it was first purchased (meaning that there will be a tax liability on the gain), her after-tax interest is $200,000.

3. An RRSP worth $500,000. Assuming a 45% tax-rate, her after-tax value is $275,000.

4. Non-registered investments worth $700,000. Since there are some unrealized capital gains in respect of these investments, their after-tax value is $600,000.

Total value: $1,900,000

Total after-tax value: $1,525,000

Bob's estate:

1. His 50% interest in their home in West Vancouver worth $900,000, or $450,000. Given that they intend to use the principal residence exemption in respect of this asset, the after-tax value is $450,000.

2. His 50% interest in their condo in Whistler worth $500,000, or $250,000. Since their condo has grown appreciably in value since it was first purchased (meaning that there will be a tax liability on the gain), his after-tax interest is $200,000.

3. An RRSP worth $300,000. Assuming a 45% tax-rate, his after-tax value is $165,000.

4. Non-registered investments worth $300,000. Since there are some unrealized capital gains in respect of these investments, their after-tax value is $250,000.

Total value: $1,300,000

Total after-tax value: $1,065,000

(See Chapter 21, "Taxation at Death", for an explanation as to how tax is calculated at the time of death).

Allison and Bob would therefore like their estates to be distributed as follows upon the death of the survivor of them:

- Aurele — $1,525,000 (i.e. all of Allison's estate)
- Sandra — $532,500 (i.e. half of Bob's estate)
- Cathy — $532,500 (i.e. half of Bob's estate)

Allison and Bob hold their non-registered and registered investments in their own names personally. However, they have designated each other as the direct beneficiaries of their registered investments. Also, they own their home and condo as joint tenants. What are the relevant issues that they should consider?

First of all, they need to review their estate plan to ensure that it meets their objectives. Since they are living common-law, reference should be made to Case Studies 3.10.1 and 3.10.2 for a discussion of the issues regarding powers of attorney, division of property in the event of relationship breakdown, and the distribution of assets at the time of their death.

However, an overriding consideration in this case will be to ensure that the children are treated fairly at the time of their deaths. As currently structured, it is very possible that either Aurele, or alternatively Sandra and Cathy, could receive far less than their parents would like. For example, if Bob dies first, consider what will happen:

- Allison will be entitled to the home in Vancouver and the condominium in Whistler, since those properties are held as joint owners with a right of survivorship (note that if they lived in Quebec, there would be no right of survivorship). Since the properties are worth $1,400,000, they comprise a significant portion of their combined estates.

- Bob also has $600,000 in investments. However, $300,000 is held in an RRSP, and he has designated Allison as the direct beneficiary of those funds.[2] Therefore, only the $300,000 in non-registered assets held in his sole name will pass through his estate. Since they have been living in a common-law relationship for more than two years, and he does not have a will, Allison will be entitled to a portion of the estate (note that common-law partners are not entitled to inherit their partner's estate in every jurisdiction — see section 3.9 of Chapter 3, "Common-Law Couples", to determine if common-law partners have rights at the time of death in your province or territory). If a common-law partner dies without a will in British Columbia, their partner is entitled to the first $65,000 of the estate, plus one-third of the remainder if they have more than one child. Therefore, Allison will be entitled to $65,000, plus one-third of ($300,000 – $65,000), which is 33% of $235,000, or $78,333, for a total of $143,333. (The assets which pass to Allison will roll over at their cost base, so no capital gains will be triggered on these assets until Allison sells them or

2 For the purposes of this example, we will assume that Allison chooses to include the RRSP in her tax return and make a corresponding contribution to her own RRSP. If she chooses to receive the gross amount held in the plan, there will be even less left in the estate, as the estate will be responsible for paying the tax on the registered assets.

dies.) This will leave Sandra and Cathy with ($300,000 – $143,333), or $156,667, out of their father's total estate of $1,065,000. The after-tax value of these assets is about $120,000 (since there is generally no rollover on assets passed to children).

What will happen when Allison dies?

- Assuming that she also fails to make a will prior to the time of her death, her son will be entitled to all of the value of her estate (assuming she does not remarry or enter into a new common-law relationship). We will assume for the purposes of this example that the real property does not change in value and the investments also do not change, as Allison uses the annual income or gains for her living expenses. Therefore, since her estate was originally worth $1,900,000, plus she inherited Bob's half of the properties ($700,000), his RRSPs ($300,000), and $143,333 from the remainder of his estate, her estate is now worth over $3,000,000, less any amounts owing for taxes. (Although Allison was able to contribute $300,000 to her own RRSP to defer the taxes owing at the time of Bob's death, no such deferral will be available when the RRSPs are transferred to her adult child.)

- Let's assume that there is $2,500,000 remaining in the estate after all the taxes and expenses have been paid. Since Allison has not written a will specifically leaving anything to Sandra or Cathy, her estate will be transferred to Aurele, since the legislation which determines how an estate is distributed where there is no will does not include step-children. Therefore, Aurele will receive $2,500,000.

Therefore, the after-tax estates of both Bob and Allison have been distributed as follows:

- Aurele — $2,500,000

- Sandra — $60,000 (50% of $120,000)

- Cathy — $60,000 (50% of $120,000)

After comparing these numbers with the initial distribution Bob and Allison calculated, it is obvious that Bob and Allison's estates were not distributed as intended. Where did they go wrong? First of all, they should not have held their property as joint tenants, or designated each other as direct beneficiaries of their RRSPs. By doing so, they allowed the survivor to inherit the bulk of the estate of the first to die. Also, by not writing wills, they did not ensure that step-children were included. However, even if the survivor had written a will

(Allison in this case), there is no guarantee that she would have included Sandra and Cathy in the distribution of her estate. So what are the alternatives?

1. Allison and Bob could have held their property as tenants in common, in which case their half of the property would not have gone automatically to the survivor. In their will, they could have then provided that the survivor would be entitled to live in the property during their lifetime, but upon their death, their half of the property would be transferred to their children, not the children of the survivor. This mechanism is referred to as a spousal trust. See section 8.5.2.1 or section 5.5.2 of Chapter 5, "Married", for a further discussion of how trusts can be established in your last will and testament.

2. Allison and Bob should have considered the implications of designating each other as the direct beneficiaries of their RRSPs. Since RRSPs are taxable at the time of death unless transferred to the RRSP of a surviving spouse, many couples choose to designate their spouse as the beneficiary of the RRSP, even if that means that their children will never see the money. However, in that case, many people also purchase a separate insurance policy which names the children as the beneficiaries, so that the surviving spouse receives the RRSP, and the children from the previous relationship will receive the insurance proceeds. In many cases this is a simpler mechanism than using a spousal trust, since there is no guarantee that the surviving spouse will not encroach upon the capital in the trust, or that the child will live long enough to receive their part of the estate.

3. Bob could have left a part of his estate directly to Sandra and Cathy. However, Bob would have had to ensure that he left a significant amount of his estate to Allison, or she could make a claim against the estate (married couples, and, in some jurisdictions, common-law partners, are entitled to a portion of their spouse's estate, regardless of what the will states). Therefore, Bob could not leave his entire estate to Sandra and Cathy, and assume that Allison would be satisfied receiving the house, the condo and the RRSPs. Bob may have had to restructure his affairs so that part of those assets would go through his estate (perhaps by holding one of the properties in his name only, or designating the estate as the beneficiary of the RRSPs). He could have then left the home or the RRSPs to Allison in the will, and left Sandra and Cathy something else, like the unregistered assets. The same comment would apply to Allison's estate.

Regardless of which strategy they decide to use, the important element to their plan will be to work with an advisor who is experienced in the area of estate planning, and who will be able to customize their estate plan according to their needs.

# CHAPTER 9

# WIDOWED





Suffering the loss of a spouse is generally considered to be one of the most traumatic events a person can experience. In many cases, the surviving spouse is too distraught to deal with any issues other than those which are urgent. However, if possible, speak to an advisor as soon as possible, since in many cases they will be able to help you in this difficult time. Below are a few things to consider when you experience the loss of a spouse.

## 9.1 FINANCIAL PLANNING

### 9.1.1 CPP Benefits

Surviving spouses or common-law partners may be entitled to receive a survivor benefit from the Canada Pension Plan ("CPP"). (The definition of common-law partner for these purposes includes a partner who has lived with the deceased in a conjugal relationship for at least 12 months). If your deceased spouse or common-law partner made sufficient contributions to the CPP, then you will receive benefits based on the amount contributed to the plan, your age at the time of your spouse's death, and whether you also receive a CPP disability or retirement pension. To avoid losing the entitlement to any of these benefits, you should apply for the benefits as soon as possible after the time of death, as retroactive payments are only allowed up to 11 months.

In order to be eligible to receive survivor benefits, the deceased must have contributed to the CPP for at least three years. If the period of time in which the deceased would have been eligible to make CPP contributions was longer than nine years, they must have contributed in one-third of those calendar years, or ten calendar years, whichever is less.

A survivor's pension is paid to the person who was the deceased's spouse *at the time of death*. Therefore, if there is a surviving spouse, but they were separated from the deceased at the time of death, and the deceased had been living with a common-law partner for a sufficient period of time prior to their death, the common-law partner will receive the survivor's pension. A separated spouse may qualify for a survivor's pension if the deceased did not have a common-law partner at the time of death. Separated common-law partners are not entitled to receive survivor benefits.

Surviving spouses or common-law partners may also be entitled to receive a death benefit from the CPP equal to six months of retirement pension, up to a maximum of $2500. The lump-sum death benefit can be included on the income tax return of either the beneficiary or the estate. The personal representative for the deceased can determine which tax return to use so that the amount of tax owing is minimized.

If the deceased had children, they may be entitled to receive Orphans' Benefits under the CPP. See section 10.5.8 of Chapter 10, "Children", for more information.

## 9.1.2 Investing Your Inheritance

As it is very likely that you will have inherited assets from your deceased spouse, you should speak to a financial advisor to determine the best way to invest those assets. Investing a lump sum of money should not be done hastily, and your advisor will be able to tell you which asset allocation is appropriate for your needs and risk tolerance, and whether you should invest the funds over a period of time, using the "dollar cost averaging" approach. Do not make any investment decisions while you are in a state of shock — if possible, place the funds in a liquid investment like a money market mutual fund, and then invest for the long term once you have had a chance to recover from the shock of what has occurred. Once you are less distraught, consider your options carefully. The key is to not lock into something before you are ready to make decisions regarding your future.

## 9.2 TAX PLANNING

Generally speaking, the death of an individual can result in a large income tax bill. However, if your deceased spouse's estate was left primarily to you, the tax ramifications can be deferred until the time of your death. It may still be in your best interests though to speak with an experienced tax accountant, as there may be opportunities to structure your affairs so that the tax bill at the time of your death is minimized. Here are a couple of things to which you may want to pay particular attention.

- If your deceased spouse or common-law partner had unused RRSP room, and there will be taxable income in the year of death, consider whether or not the estate should make a spousal RRSP contribution. After death, the personal representative will no longer be able to make a contribution to the RRSP owned by the deceased, but they can make a spousal RRSP contribution (if the deceased was survived by a spouse or common-law partner) and there was unused contribution room. If the personal representative is going to make a spousal RRSP contribution, it must be made within 60 days of the end of the calendar year following death or the contribution room will be lost. Therefore, if the deceased died in November or December, there may not be much time to make this decision.

- If the deceased had any unused capital losses, be sure to use them to the extent possible. If possible, elect out of the rollover on some assets in order to trigger unrealized capital gains or include some RRSP income in the tax return of the deceased.



The details for these strategies and many others are found in Chapter 21, "Taxation at Death". Refer to that chapter for a further discussion of the methods used to minimize taxes in the year of death, and plan for the tax bill at the time of death of the second spouse. You (or the estate's personal representative, if that is not yourself) should seek the advice of an experienced tax accountant as soon as possible after the time of death in order to take maximum advantage of any tax planning opportunities.

## 9.3 FAMILY LAW ISSUES

As a surviving spouse, under provincial law you may be entitled to receive a certain portion of the estate of your deceased spouse, and you may also have the right to remain in the family home, even if you were not on title to the property. If you have not been left a significant portion of your spouse's estate, speak to your lawyer about whether or not you can make a claim against the estate under either the family law legislation or dependant's relief legislation in your jurisdiction. See section 19.6 of Chapter 19, "Distribution of an Estate", for a further discussion of the rules in your jurisdiction.

## 9.4 DISABILITY PLANNING

When you are widowed, you should review your disability plan to ensure that it is updated to reflect your new life situation. For example, many individuals appoint their spouse as their attorney for finances and health care decisions. These documents should be updated to appoint new attorneys for those positions, and new alternate attorneys, to ensure you always have a back-up. You may wish to appoint different people for different purposes if you feel that one person does not have the necessary skills to perform both jobs. See Chapter 18, "Powers of Attorney", for more information on this issue.

You should also speak with your advisor to ensure that you have adequate insurance in the event of disability or illness. If you were relying on the insurance available from your spouse's employer, you may have to purchase an individual policy now that you will no longer be covered by your spouse's group insurance. If you are not employed, critical illness insurance and long-term care insurance may be the answer for you. See Chapter 25, "Insurance", for more information on these products.

## 9.5 ESTATE PLANNING

### 9.5.1 Will Planning

Your will should be reviewed to see if any changes need to be made in respect of the distribution of your estate, and the appointment of a new personal representative. If your deceased spouse was named as the primary beneficiary and personal representative, the will should be changed. See Chapter 20, "Personal

Representatives", for a discussion of the attributes to look for in a personal representative.

### 9.5.2 Minor Children

If you have children who are still minors, review your will to ensure that their inheritance will be managed by trustees until the children attain an age at which they are more likely to be capable of handling large sums of money, such as 25 or 30. (See section 10.5.3 of Chapter 10, "Children", for more information on leaving inheritances to children.) Many individuals structure their estate so that upon the death of both parents, their children will receive the combined estates. However, if there are no trust provisions, the provincial authorities will step in to manage the funds if the children are minors, resulting in additional costs for the estate. As well, the provincial authorities will transfer the estate assets to the children as soon as they reach the age of majority, which in most cases is still too young to manage a large sum of money. Review your will with your lawyer to ensure that any amounts left to your children will be distributed in an appropriate manner.

If your deceased spouse was the other parent to your children, you will also need to consider the issue of guardianship even more carefully. Most parents indicate in their will that the surviving parent is to act as guardian, and then appoint an alternate. You will now need to choose a new alternate guardian, in case the primary guardian is unable to act. (See section 10.5.1 of Chapter 10, "Children", for more information on choosing a guardian.)

Please see section 9.8.1 for a case study of this situation.

### 9.5.3 Adult Children

If you are survived by financially responsible adult children, you may still wish to consider the possibility of leaving your inheritance to them in trust. This is because testamentary trusts (being trusts created in your last will and testament) are often used for tax savings purposes as well as control purposes (as described in section 9.5.2 when leaving money to children who are minors). If you anticipate that your children will be relatively high income earners, and will choose to invest all or a significant portion of their inheritance, speak to them about whether or not they would prefer to receive their inheritance in trust. If they invest the inheritance in the name of the trustees of the trust, then any income or capital gains earned by that trust can be taxed as a separate taxpayer, gaining access to another set of graduated tax rates. If your children are high income earners, then every additional dollar they earn on the investments will be taxed at a high rate. Please see section 9.8.2 for a case study of this situation, and section 10.5.4 of Chapter 10, "Children", for more information.

## 9.5.4 Beneficiary Designations

Be sure to review all beneficiary designations on RRSPs, RRIFs or insurance policies. Sometimes, when people lose a spouse, they appoint their children as direct beneficiaries of their registered investments and insurance policies. However, in many cases, this is not recommended, particularly if the children are minors. This is because the proceeds may have to be managed by the Public Trustee or Children's Lawyer (depending upon your province or territory), and the children will be entitled to the entire lump sum upon attaining the age of majority.

In many cases, it is a better idea to appoint the estate as the beneficiary of the assets. Assuming the will is properly structured, the personal representative will then be able to manage the funds without the interference of any government agencies, and assuming a trust has been created for the children, they will not receive the money until age 25, 30 or any other age which has been chosen. Although there may be a relatively small probate cost to doing this, the advantages usually far outweigh this cost.

Some advisors recommend that a minor be appointed as beneficiary of an RRSP or RRIF, since there may be tax advantages to doing so. When an RRSP or RRIF is paid to a financially dependent child who is under the age of 18, or to an adult child who was financially dependent upon the deceased as a result of a mental or physical infirmity, then the estate may not be responsible for paying the tax on the funds. The child can purchase a registered annuity, which must either be paid out by the time the child reaches age 18 if they are not disabled, or by age 90 if they are disabled. Generally speaking, in the case of minor children who are not disabled, this is not recommended, as they are too young to manage the funds. The annuity payments will have to be managed by the Public Trustee or other government authority until the child reaches the age of majority, and then the child will be entitled to receive the funds, when they are still potentially too young to properly manage them. In many cases, it would be best if the funds were paid into the estate, all taxes paid, and then have the remaining funds managed by a trustee. If there is a concern that there will be insufficient funds remaining for a child after the taxes are paid, then consideration should be given as to whether or not life insurance will be necessary to fund the tax liability.

Even if the children are adults, again, it is usually not recommended that children be named as direct beneficiaries. The reasons for this are numerous, and discussed more fully in section 10.6.2 of Chapter 10, "Children". One example of the problems which can occur is a situation where two children have been appointed as direct beneficiaries, and one of the children then predeceases their parent. If that deceased child had children of their own, those grandchildren may receive no part of the asset, and the surviving child may receive the entire asset, as they are the only living beneficiary named on the document. Wills usually contemplate these scenarios, and provide for contingencies in the event a child predeceases a parent. However, direct beneficiary designations usually do not include the same contingency plans. Also, if a child receives an asset directly through a beneficiary designation, then some of the tax planning techniques that are available at the time of death will no longer be available, such as the use of testamentary trusts. (See section 10.5.4 of Chapter 10, "Children", for more information on this strategy.) Always speak to an advisor prior to naming a child as a direct beneficiary of any asset.

In no case should someone other than the intended beneficiary be named as a direct beneficiary on an insurance policy, RRSP or RRIF. There have been cases where uncles, aunts and other individuals have been appointed as the direct beneficiary on a registered plan or insurance policy, on the assumption that they would manage the assets for the deceased's children after the time of their death. Unfortunately, in some cases, the recipient of the funds has not chosen to use the funds in the best interests of the children, as they have taken the position that they are the proper beneficiary. Even though a will may indicate that all funds are to be used in the interests of their minor children, if an asset flows to someone outside of the estate (i.e. by way of joint ownership or direct beneficiary designation), then those assets will not be subject to the terms of the will, and it is possible that the intended heirs will never receive the funds. See Chapter 22, "Probate", for a discussion on the dangers of distributing assets outside of an estate. Note that in Quebec, beneficiary designations on RRSPs and RRIFs are not effective (unless the plan is in the form of an annuity), and the surviving owners of a jointly held property are not automatically entitled to receive the interest of the deceased owner in that property.



## 9.6 INSURANCE PLANNING

After the death of a spouse, it is important to review all insurance policies, since many survivors lose their entitlement to medical insurance coverage on their spouse's death. If the deceased had an employee pension plan, the survivor should review it very carefully. Although the plan may allow you to receive a lump sum benefit, consider whether it may be more beneficial to continue to receive monthly payments if that means the extended health care benefits can continue.

Also, the disability and life insurance plans for the surviving spouse should be reviewed to ensure that they are sufficient to care for any children who might be dependent upon the survivor, since there will now only be one source of income, instead of two, if both parents were employed.

## 9.7 JURISDICTION DIFFERENCES

There are no jurisdiction differences for this chapter.

## 9.8 CASE STUDIES

### 9.8.1 Widowed, With Minor Children

Let's assume all of the same facts as in the previous example, but in this case, Jane and Myron are minors. Giselle is concerned about several things.

- She had originally appointed Gerry as guardian for the children. Now that Gerry is deceased, she asks her brother, Bruce, if he would be willing to act in this capacity. Bruce agrees, and her sister Shannon agrees to act as the alternate guardian.

- At the time of Gerry's death, Jane is 14 and Myron is 12. Giselle appoints her sister Shannon as her personal representative in her will, and indicates that Shannon is to hold any money which is intended for Jane or Myron until they turn 18. At that time, Jane and Myron may receive the annual income from the assets held in the trust. Jane and Myron may receive the capital in the trust in the following increments — one-quarter at age 21, half of the remainder at age 25, and all of the remainder at age 30.

- Giselle appoints her sister Shannon as her power of attorney for finances, and her proxy for making health care decisions, but indicates that her power of attorney for finances is not effective until she is no longer capable of handling her own affairs. (Her power of attorney for personal care is not effective until such time as she is incapacitated, regardless of the terms of the document.)

- Giselle changes the beneficiary on all of her insurance policies and registered assets to indicate "estate". Although she knows that it might be more tax effective for the registered assets to roll over to Jane and Myron, she does not want the Public Trustee to manage the funds while they are minors, and she does not want Jane and Myron to have access to the funds at age 18 since the value of her registered assets is quite high. She knows that the proceeds of her registered assets will be taxable at the time of her death, but her estate will receive a significant amount of insurance. She would rather see the after tax proceeds from the registered assets paid into the trusts for the children, and managed by people she knows and trusts. Giselle considers appointing Shannon as the direct beneficiary of her registered assets in order to avoid probate, and then thinks better of it — although she trusts Shannon, she knows that Shannon runs a business, and creditors could seize those funds if she was insolvent at the time she received them. Giselle decides to appoint her estate as the beneficiary of her registered assets. By doing this, she feels more comfortable knowing that the after-tax amount of her registered assets will go directly to the trusts established for her children in her will, and neither Shannon, nor any of Shannon's potential creditors, will be able to use the money for their own purposes.

### 9.8.2 Widowed, With Adult Children

Giselle was recently widowed. Giselle has been appointed personal representative of her husband's estate and is the sole beneficiary. Her husband, Gerry, had unused RRSP contribution room of $20,000, and very little taxable income in the year of death, as he died in February. Gerry also owned stocks with unrealized capital gains of $50,000 (Gerry purchased the shares for $40,000 and they are now worth $90,000). Although Giselle could "roll over" the stock to herself at their cost base ($40,000), and defer the capital gain until she sells the stock, her accountant tells her instead to elect to transfer the shares to herself at their fair market value ($90,000), which will trigger the capital gain. Giselle will then include 50% of the capital gain (or $25,000) on the terminal year return for Gerry. Giselle then makes a $20,000 spousal RRSP contribution to an RRSP for which she is the annuitant (Giselle can no longer make a contribution to Gerry's RRSP, as he is now deceased). Giselle then deducts the $20,000 RRSP contribution against the $25,000 of taxable income she reported in Gerry's terminal year return. The estate pays very little tax, and when Giselle sells the shares a few years later for $100,000, she only has a capital gain of $10,000 ($100,000 – $90,000), as opposed to $60,000 ($100,000 – $40,000).

Giselle then reviews her estate plan. She notices that she has named Gerry as her personal representative in her will, her power of attorney for finances, and her proxy for making all health care decisions. She changes all of these documents to indicate that her two children, Jane and Myron, will carry out these roles. In the event either Jane or Myron predeceases Giselle, their survivor will continue to act.

Giselle then reviews all of her beneficiary designations on her insurance policies and RRSPs. She had originally named Gerry as her direct beneficiary, but she changes all of her beneficiary designations to indicate "estate". Giselle chooses not to indicate either of her children as the beneficiaries, since both of her children have children of their own, and she is concerned that if one of her children predeceases her, the surviving child will receive the entire asset, and the children of the deceased child will receive nothing. Also, both of her children are in relatively high tax brackets, so she wants the money to be left to them in a trust created in her will in order to minimize any tax they might have to pay. (See section 10.5.4 of Chapter 10, "Children", for more information.)

Finally, Giselle applies to receive payments in respect of Gerry's contribution to the Canada Pension Plan within a few months of Gerry's death to ensure that she receives any survivor benefits to which she may be entitled.

# CHAPTER 10

# CHILDREN

Having children changes your life dramatically. Unfortunately, many people do not adequately change their financial and estate plan to accommodate this major life change. This chapter will discuss some of the things you should consider if you are a parent.

## 10.1 FINANCIAL PLANNING

### 10.1.1 CPP Benefits

If you were out of the workforce for a period of time due to the fact that you were raising a child under the age of seven, be sure to mention this when applying for your Canada Pension Plan ("CPP") benefits. The CPP will make contributions on your behalf for these years to ensure that your benefits are not unduly decreased due to the fact that you were out of the workforce. This provision is referred to as the Child Rearing Dropout Provision and you must specifically request it when applying for CPP, or they may not be aware of it.

### 10.1.2 Registered Education Savings Plans

Given the ever-increasing cost of post-secondary education, many parents are concerned about saving sufficient funds for their children's education. One of the most tax-effective ways to save for a child's education is through the use of a Registered Education Savings Plan ("RESP"). Generally speaking, here is a description of how these plans work.

- Subscribers are entitled to make contributions to an RESP, which will be held in trust for the child. The lifetime maximum amount of contributions that can be made for any one child is $50,000. However, the federal government will also match 20% of your contributions to the plan, up to a maximum of $500 annually (which would require a $2500 contribution from the subscriber), or $7200 over the child's lifetime. This government money is referred to as the Canada Education Savings Grant (the "CESG"). If you do not make a $2500 contribution in every year, then you can carry forward the "room" (up to certain limits, as discussed later in this section), although only contributions made for children under the age of 18 will qualify for CESG. The amount of the CESG increases if your family income is less than approximately $78,000 per year. A CESG will only be made to beneficiaries resident in Canada at the time the CESG is made.

- RESP contributions are not tax deductible. However, taxation on any income or growth earned on the contributions as well as the CESG is deferred until such time as it is withdrawn from the plan.

- When the child begins to attend a post-secondary institution, the funds can be withdrawn and taxed in the hands of the child, who will likely be in a lower tax bracket than the parent, and who will usually pay less tax on the withdrawals. The child may also be able to reduce the amount of tax owing through the use of education, textook or tuition tax credits.

- Children of families receiving the National Child Benefit as part of the Canada Child Benefit may also be entitled to receive the Canada Learning Bond ("CLB"). The government will contribute $500 to the child's RESP in the first year of eligibility (plus $25 in the year in which the plan is opened in order to cover any administration fees) and $100 per year thereafter to a maximum of $2,000. There are no "matching" requirements — i.e. no contributions need to be made to the RESP for the RESP to receive CLB. Only children born in 2004 or later are eligible to receive CLB. If no RESP is opened for the child, the government will keep track of the CLB payments to which the child is entitled, and will pay them out as soon as an RESP is opened and a CLB application received, but no interest will be paid on these amounts. So, even if a low-income parent is unable to make contributions to an RESP while their children are young, they should still open an RESP for them in order to maximize the growth on the CLB. Applications for the CLB can be made until just before a child's 21st birthday. Accumulated CLB will be forfeited at age 21 if it has not been transferred to an RESP prior to that time. There are also other provincial programs for residents of Alberta and Quebec, so be sure to speak to a financial advisor to ensure you are receiving the maximum amount of benefit for your child.

- The "subscriber" of the RESP (usually the child's parent) may withdraw earnings in the plan if none of the intended beneficiaries is pursuing post-secondary education by age 21 and the plan has been in place for at least ten years. Earnings will be taxable income when withdrawn, but if the subscriber has sufficient RRSP room, they may be rolled over to the RRSP of the contributor or their spouse or common-law partner, up to a maximum of $50,000. Plan earnings received by the contributor which are not contributed to an RRSP are subject to a special tax of 20% in addition to regular tax payable. The Canada Education Savings Grant ("CESG") must be repaid to the government if the child does not attend post-secondary education. If one of your children chooses not to attend post-secondary education, it may be possible to change the beneficiary of the plan to a sibling, or if the subscriber is a grandparent, then it may even be possible to change the beneficiary to a cousin. However, if you do change the beneficiary, then any CLB paid in respect of that beneficiary (as described previously) must be returned, as those amounts can only go to the original beneficiary.

- Although you can withdraw the original contributions tax free at any time, it is usually best to wait until the beneficiary is in school, or you could lose the government grants paid on those contributions. Once the beneficiary is attending an eligible post-secondary educational institution, the earnings on the contributions can be withdrawn and can be reported by the student as taxable income. These withdrawals are referred to as "educational assistance payments" ("EAPs"), and it may be best to withdraw EAPs before your contributions, in case the beneficiary does not complete their schooling. However, one potential advantage to spreading the EAPs out over a number of years is that the beneficiary may pay more in tax if larger taxable amounts are taken out in fewer years. Normally you would only withdraw contributions once the taxable amounts are all withdrawn. However, if you do need your contributions back earlier, try to at least wait until the student is eligible to receive EAPs so that you do not need to repay any government funds.

- Contributions cannot be made to an RESP for more than 31 years, and the plan must be wound up within 35 years. Also, no contributions under a family RESP may be made in respect of a beneficiary who is 31 years of age or older.

When contributing to an RESP, consider these strategies.

- While CESG matching grants can be carried forward, contributions made in a year in excess of the maximum amount considered for CESG purposes cannot be carried forward to the following calendar year for the purpose of attracting the CESG in that year. For example, if you contribute $5000 in Year 1 and $0 in Year 2, the RESP will receive $500 in CESG in Year 1 and nothing in Year 2. It may be better to spread out the contribution over two years, or contribute the entire amount in Year 2. The RESP would have received $500 in CESG in each of Year 1 and Year 2 if you contributed $2500 in each of Year 1 and Year 2, or $1000 in CESG if the entire contribution was made in Year 2. However, if the entire amount had been contributed in year 2, then the RESP would not have earned any income during Year 1, so it is always better to contribute as early as possible in order to maximize the compounding. However, contributing too much early in the life of the plan may cause you to lose some of the CESG.

- Parents who have family income of less than approximately $78,000 will receive a CESG of 30% of the first $500 of contributions (the remaining $2000 is subject to the normal matching rate of 20%). Parents with family income of less than approximately $39,000 have a matching rate of 40% on the first $500 of contributions. However, this enhanced CESG cannot be carried forward. Therefore, if you are in a low- to mid-income level and you are trying to maximize the amount of education savings for your children, you should try to contribute at least $500 every year, in order to maximize the grant.

- Although you can establish several RESPs for the same beneficiary, the contribution limits remain the same, so you should communicate with other potential subscribers (e.g. grandparents), or there could be a 1% penalty charged on over-contributions.

- If you are unable to make any contributions for your child when they are first born due to financial constraints, beware that the maximum amount of contribution that can be made each year and still qualify for the grant is $5000 (resulting in a $1000 grant, assuming no enhanced grant). Therefore, at a minimum, you must start contributing to the child's RESP by the time they reach age ten, and you must contribute the maximum each year until they reach 18, in order to maximize the grant received. You cannot wait until the last minute and then contribute a large sum of money, and expect to receive the entire CESG. In fact, if you have not made at least four annual contributions of $100 each, or $2000 in total contributions before the child turns 16, contributions for a 16- or 17-year-old child will not attract any CESG.

- Before any contributions can be made for a beneficiary, their Social Insurance Number ("SIN") must be provided. Therefore, do not delay in obtaining a SIN number for your child, so that contributions can be made as soon as possible.

- You may also wish to open a TFSA for the purpose of saving for your children's future. With an RESP, if a child does not attend a post-secondary institution, the Canada Education Savings Grants paid into the RESP have to be repaid (unless the amounts can be transferred to another child). In addition, if the RESP had generated earnings, the parents are liable for taxes on that income. Some families may prefer to save more through their TFSA if they are unsure if their child will attend a post-secondary institution (although if you are in a low-income tax bracket, it may still be advisable to open a plan simply to receive the CLB, as no contributions are required). Other families may wish to save within a TFSA in order to supplement the amount in their RESP. Although you will not be able to open a TFSA for your child until they turn 18, you may wish to save in your own TFSA for this purpose.

- If you are in a position to contribute the maximum amount each year, consider contributing $15,000 in the first year and $2500 in each of the next 14 years (to reach the lifetime maximum of $50,000 and also maximize the amount of CESG received). If you are going to make additional contributions that do not qualify for the CESG, it is best to make them as early as possible, in order to maximize the tax deferral. However, there is no uniform answer to the question of how much you should contribute to an RESP, since it really depends upon what other uses you may have for the funds, and the likelihood of your child attending a post-secondary educational institution.

If you feel that the amount which you will be able to save in an RESP will not be sufficient for the type of education you want your children to have, then you should consider whether or not it would be advisable to invest additional funds for them. Generally, informal "in-trust" accounts are not recommended, so speak to your advisors about the best way to structure this arrangement (see section 10.1.3 for more information). Also, a discussion of some of the issues to be considered if a grandparent will be making contributions to an RESP is found in section 11.1.1 of Chapter 11, "Grandchildren".

## 10.1.3 Placing Money in Trust for a Child

If you have significant sums of money that you do not require for your own purposes, there may be strategies that you can implement to have more of your income taxed in the hands of your children (which is desirable if they are in a lower tax bracket than you). One such strategy may be to create a trust (formally referred to as an *inter vivos* trust). However, *inter vivos* trusts are generally only recommended for very high net worth individuals, and only after discussing the strategy with a well qualified tax lawyer. Testamentary trusts, which are trusts created at the time of your death, are recommended much more frequently (see sections 10.5.3 and 10.5.4 for more information on how to create a trust at the time of your death). *Inter vivos* trusts, sometimes also known as "family trusts", may also be recommended for families who own businesses – further discussion is found in section 16.5.2 of Chapter 16, "Business Owners" if this applies to you.

### *10.1.3.1 Informal Trusts*

Many individuals set up investments or bank accounts for their children with the words "in trust" on the account. This is often referred to as creating an "informal" trust. However, in many cases, the "in trust" designation causes nothing more than confusion and disagreement, and there are generally no advantages to creating this type of structure. At law, there is no such thing as an informal trust — either there is a trust, or there is not. If the intent is to create a trust, then all the formalities must be respected — separate tax returns must be filed for the trust every year in which it has taxable income, and separate records must be kept for the trust. If these formalities are not adhered to, it is very likely that the Canada Revenue Agency will find that there is no trust, and the funds still belong to the parents, meaning that they are responsible for all income and capital gains earned on the money. If there is in fact a trust, but no documentation indicating when the child will be entitled to the money, the child will be entitled to the funds upon attaining the age of majority, at which point the parent will cease to have any control over the funds. This fact alone is usually enough to dissuade most parents from establishing an informal trust.

From a tax perspective, informal trusts are usually of little or no benefit. Any income earned by the trust that is taxed in the hands of the trust will be taxed at the highest marginal rate. Even if the income or capital gains are instead paid out to a beneficiary, the income will be attributed back to the parent and taxed in their hands as if they had never established the trust. This is because with most informal trusts, the parent continues to maintain complete control over the funds, so they will not avoid the attribution rules with respect to any income or capital gains earned by the trust (unless the funds contributed to the trust are from the Canada Child Tax Benefit or the Universal Child Care Benefit). Although it is possible for the capital gains to be taxed in the hands of a child, this is only if the parent does not retain control over how the assets are distributed and does not access the funds in the account for their own personal use. Generally speaking, this would only be the case with a formal trust, where the consent of the parent is not required in order to make distributions. Since a parent who creates an informal trust usually acts as sole trustee of the trust, all income and capital gains will be attributed back to the parent, even once the child becomes an adult (by which point most informal trusts are wound-up in any event). If the parent who did not contribute the money to the trust acts as sole trustee of the trust, it is possible that the contribution rules may not apply, but it will be important to keep documentation proving which spouse made the contribution and which spouse is in control of the trust. Some individuals who choose to contribute funds to an account where their spouse is the sole trustee (in order to avoid the attribution rules) come to regret this decision if their marriage later comes to an end.

Another problem which often arises with informal trusts is the fact that the lack of documentation can lead to unintended consequences. Since informal trusts generally have little, if any, written documentation, and, therefore, since there are no formal terms for the trust, the provisions of the provincial Trustee Act will apply. This will usually mean that the trustee (generally the parent) is limited to making investments authorized by law. Although this may include most forms of mutual funds, stocks and bonds, if you invest in an asset that is speculative, you may have to answer to the beneficiary (the child) at a later date. The parent is in effect liable to their child for any losses if it is found that they did not comply with the governing Trustee Act.

Informal trusts do not really accomplish much, but they may require a parent to fulfill certain obligations, which they would not have had, had they simply kept the money in their own name personally and designated where they wanted the money to go in their will. They may also regret the decision to establish the account if their young adult child spends the money in a way that was not intended, or experiences a "starter marriage" that results in the loss of part of the funds to a former spouse. Before placing any money in an informal trust, be sure to speak with your advisor about the potential disadvantages of using this strategy.

### *10.1.3.2 Formal Trusts*

If the amount of money a parent wants to leave to their child is significant, and they want to specifically ear-mark it for them, then they could consider whether or not it would be a good idea to establish a formal trust. A trust is a legal relationship where one person (the trustee) holds property in trust for another person (the beneficiary). A trust agreement needs to be drafted by a lawyer to ensure that it meets all of the desired objectives (see Chapter 23, "Trusts", for more details on trusts in general). Here is how a formal trust for children typically works.

- A relative or third party establishes the trust with a gold coin (a gold coin is used to settle trusts in order to avoid the attribution rules discussed previously). The gold coin is usually kept in a safety deposit box by the trustee.

- The parent can be designated as one of the trustees of the trust in order to maintain some control. However, if the parent is the sole trustee and has complete control over who receives the money and when, then both the income and capital gains earned in the trust can be attributed back to him or her. It may be best if the parent is only one of three trustees, and decisions are made by majority vote, instead of requiring unanimous consent.

- The parent would appoint their children (and perhaps their grandchildren as well) as the beneficiaries of the trust, so that they will be the persons who eventually receive the assets in the trust.

- The parent would lend a sum of money to the trust, and invest that money in income and capital-gains producing assets. If the children are minors, they may prefer to invest in capital-gains producing assets, since the attribution rules apply to income paid out to related minors, but not to capital gains (assuming the trust is properly structured). This means that any income paid out to a minor will be taxable in the hands of the parent, but any capital gains paid out to a minor will be taxable in the hands of the minor. If you want the trust to invest in income producing assets, then you will need to charge a rate of interest as prescribed by the Canada Revenue Agency. For some trusts, the requirements to pay this annual interest may be cumbersome, particularly in years when the assets experience a decline in value. For this reason, assets that primarily result in capital gains, such as corporate class mutual funds, may be a better investment, particularly in you want the loan to be non-interest bearing.

- However, it is important that the trust not invest too speculatively, since losses incurred inside the trust will be trapped in the trust and cannot be flowed out to beneficiaries. Although the parent may prefer to invest in equities in order to earn capital gains as opposed to income, they must be sure that the equities they choose are not likely to lose too much of their value.

- If the intent is to use the money for a specific item, such as post-secondary education costs, consider triggering capital gains from time to time, to avoid having all of the gains taxed at one time when the funds are withdrawn. Also, if the funds are to remain in the trust for more than 21 years, again consider triggering some of the capital gains a few years prior to the 21st anniversary of the trust, since there is a "deemed disposition" of all of the gains at that time. However, keep in mind that if you want the capital gains to be taxed in the hands of the beneficiary, the taxable portion of the gain will have to be paid out to them. This can be done by issuing a promissory note to the child (as opposed to making a cash payment), but once the child reaches the age of majority, they will be able to demand payment of the promissory note, which may or may not be a problem, depending upon the amount in question. Alternatively, distributions from the trust could be used to pay for annual expenses incurred in favour of the child, such as private school tuition and/or costs related to musical or sports activities.

Unlike with contributions to an RESP or a universal life policy for a child (which are discussed in sections 10.1.2 and 10.6.5, respectively), there are no limits on the amount of funds which can be lent to a trust. At the time of the parent's death, the loan would be paid back, and the funds could be distributed according to the terms of their will. However, one drawback with a trust is that any unrealized capital gains that are earned inside the trust will be "deemed" to have been disposed of every 21 years, so the parent will want to distribute the capital within 21 years of creating the trust. Therefore, it may not be recommended that a trust be established while the children are quite young, or you may have to distribute the assets while the children are still too young to properly manage them. However, if the intent is to pay out the capital gains on a regular basis to the children, this may not be a concern.

If you lend money to a trust for a child, the loan receivable is still an asset of your estate. Therefore, the amount of the loan is subject to probate at the time of your death, and could be exposed to the creditors of your estate. Instead of lending the money to a trust, you could transfer the assets to the trust, but that would mean less control, as you will not be able to demand the repayment of the loan in the future. As well, the funds will no longer form part of your estate, so they will not be available to form a testamentary trust at the time of your death. In many cases, the best strategy is to wait to give the money to the children when they actually need the funds (e.g. to purchase a home or buy a business) and establish testamentary trusts in your will for the part of your estate that you do not give to them prior to your death. Testamentary trusts are an excellent income-splitting technique which may provide your estate with several advantages. (See section 10.5.3 regarding the use of trusts when leaving money to minors and section 10.5.7 for children who are adults, as well as Chapter 23, "Trusts". Also see Case Study 10.8.3 for an example of a trust established for a minor.)

## 10.1.4 Lending Money to a Child

If your children are adults, then you may want to lend money to them for major purchases, such as purchasing a home or starting a business. However, be sure to put sufficient safeguards in place to protect these funds, especially when lending significant amounts of money. Consider the following when lending money to your children:

- *Legal Documentation.* Always ensure that the proper documentation is in place, including a loan agreement and promissory note. You should seek the advice of a lawyer to ensure that the terms are properly understood, and to ensure that you will be able to get your money back in the event you need to. Here are a few examples of why you may need such documentation:

  - There have been situations where parents have lent money to children for the purpose of purchasing a home or vacation property, but no documentation was put in place. Then at a later date when difficulties arose, for example, the death of the child or the breakdown of their marriage, there was no proof that the amounts given were meant as a loan, and the loan proceeds were either inherited by the son- or daughter-in-law, or divided in a family property accounting. If the amounts being lent are meant to be repaid in the case of certain events, this must be properly documented.

  - If you lend money to one child only, and there is no documentation in place, it is possible that the child who has borrowed the money will receive more of your estate than their siblings. If the intention is that the loan is to be taken into account when dividing your estate between all of your children, then your will should state so, and you should keep a copy of the loan documentation with your will so that the personal representative is able to deduct the appropriate amount from the borrowing child's portion of the estate.

- ○ Formal loan documentation may be required if anyone ever challenges the validity of the loan. For example, if you lend money to a child to purchase a home and the child then separates, their former spouse may allege that there never was a loan. In fact, even if loan documentation is put in place, there is still a risk that it will be considered a sham if no interest or principal payments are ever made, or if the documents are allowed to become statute-barred. For example, if the loan is a non-interest bearing demand note on which no payments are ever made, then at a minimum, a new promissory note should be signed every few years (the length of time in which a contract may become unenforceable will vary between the jurisdictions). If you want the security to be enforceable, then you should ensure that it is drawn up and registered by a lawyer.

- *Security*. Be sure to take security on the property being purchased with the loan proceeds. For example, if the child is purchasing a home, register a mortgage against the property. In the event the child goes bankrupt, you will want to ensure that your loan will rank ahead of unsecured creditors. If the child is starting a business, register a general security agreement in the personal property security registry. Although this will not ensure that you will receive all of your money back in the event the business fails, it will ensure that at a minimum, you will rank ahead of unsecured creditors. If you do not have security, you will only receive your money back after all of the secured creditors have been paid, which, in the case of insolvency, may mean that you will receive nothing at all.

- *Lending to Minors*. Lending money to minors can be problematic. Minors do not have the capacity to contract, so they will not be required to repay the loan. Some parents lend money to their children so that the income will be taxable in the child's name, thereby resulting in less tax. However, there are rules in the *Income Tax Act* that prevent this. All income earned on property transferred or lent to a related minor (which includes a niece or nephew) will be attributed back to the transferor for tax purposes. If you file an improper tax return and the Canada Revenue Agency reassesses you, not only will the tax be payable, but interest and penalties may also be assessed. Note that only the income will be attributed back. Capital gains and income earned on the income (i.e. second generation income) may not be attributed back if the borrower is a minor, but in many jurisdictions, any money earned in the hands of a minor must be managed by the provincial authorities. When faced with the prospect of losing control over the funds, many parents do not feel that the tax savings are worth the risk. If you are very intent on income splitting with a child, consider creating a formal trust with the help of a qualified professional. Generally speaking, in-trust accounts are not recommended (see section 10.1.3 for a discussion on the problems with informal "in trust" accounts).

- *Attribution.* As mentioned above, any income earned on amounts lent to minors will be attributed back to the parent for tax purposes. Although the attribution rules are generally not applicable for adult children, if the sole purpose for making the loan was to reduce the taxable income of the parents, the income earned on the loaned money may be attributed back to the parents for taxation purposes, even if the children are adults.

## 10.1.5 Giving Money to a Child

If you wish to give money to a child, as opposed to lending it to them, then there are other issues to consider since you will be giving up control over the asset.

### *10.1.5.1 Tax Issues*

The first issue to consider is the impact the gift may have from an income tax perspective. If you give your child a stock, mutual fund or other asset that has an unrealized capital gain, the transfer of that asset to your child will trigger that gain immediately. You will be required to report 50% of the gain in the tax return for the year in which you gave the gift, and you will then be required to pay tax on the taxable portion of the gain at your marginal tax rate. Remember that even a gift of real property, such as a vacation property, could trigger such a gain, so you must be prepared for the potential tax bill (see section 15.1.4 of Chapter 15, "Vacation Properties", for a further discussion of this issue). If your intention is to give cash or other tax-paid funds to your child, then this will obviously not be an issue.

The next issue revolves around who will be responsible for paying the tax on any income earned by the asset in the future. Some individuals are under the impression that if they invest money in the name of their child, that any income or capital gains will be taxable in the hands of that child, who would presumably be in a lower tax bracket, and therefore pay less tax. Unfortunately, the "attribution" rules will apply to attribute back to the parents any income earned on the assets if the children are minors. Although there is no attribution on capital gains, the capital gain must be paid out to the child in order to have it taxed in the hands of the child, and the parent cannot have any control over the funds, or it is possible that even capital gains could be attributed back to the parents. The loss of control in many cases is not worth the potential tax savings.

### *10.1.5.2 Control Issues*

As already alluded to, the issue of control must also be considered. If a parent gives money to a child who is still a minor, and simply puts the money in an investment or bank account in the name of the minor, then they will no longer have any control over the money, nor any ability to dictate when and how it can be used in the future. Who has the authority to manage the money until the child attains the age of majority? In most provinces, the provincial government has that authority, in the form of the Public Trustee or Children's Lawyer. The provincial authorities will charge a fee for providing this service, and there is no guarantee that they will invest the money in the manner in which you would have. Once the child reaches the age of majority, the child will be entitled to use the funds however they wish, which may mean that the funds are used to purchase a new sports car, not university tuition.

### *10.1.5.3 Protecting a Gift from a Family Property Claim*

Another concern when making a gift to a child is whether or not it may become subject to a family property division in the future. In most jurisdictions, gifts and inheritances are exempt from a division of family property (see Chapter 17, "Family Property", for a description of the family property rules in your child's jurisdiction of residence). It should be noted, however, that if your child chooses to spend the funds on a sharable asset, such as a home or vacation property, the asset may become sharable, regardless of whether or not it was funded by a gift or inheritance.

If you want to give money to a child while you are still alive, and you want to ensure that the money is protected from a family property claim, then the gift should either be structured as a loan, in which case all of the proper loan documentation and security should be put in place (see section 10.1.4), or, if possible, consider buying the asset in your name, and lending it to your child. If the asset is not in the child's name, it will not be divisible in a family property accounting. The asset can then be left to your child in your will.

In some jurisdictions, it may also be helpful to sign a "Declaration of Gift" that indicates that the asset itself and growth in value of such asset are not meant to be sharable. If you are concerned that the asset will grow significantly in value during the course of the marriage, but you do not want such growth to be sharable, a declaration of gift may be very important. This may be particularly important where the gift is a special asset, such as shares of a family business, or a vacation property. However, in some jurisdictions marital homes (which can include vacation properties) are shareable even if they are received as a gift or inheritance. See section 17.4 of Chapter 17, "Family Property", for a description of the rules in this regard in your jurisdiction.

Given the complications that may arise in giving a gift to a child, many parents choose to simply keep the funds in their own name, or establish a formal trust, which is discussed below.

## 10.2 TAX PLANNING

The following discussion includes many of the tax credits and benefits available from the Canada Revenue Agency, although you should also refer to section 10.1 for information about certain financial planning strategies that may also provide tax savings, such as registered education savings plans and formal trusts.

### 10.2.1 Canada Child Tax Benefit

Parents of children under the age of 18 are entitled to a tax credit of $2101 multiplied by the lowest personal tax rate, which is currently 15% (resulting in approximately $315 of tax savings). Where a child resides with the child's parents throughout the year, either of those parents may claim the credit. In other cases, the credit will be claimable in respect of a child by the parent who is eligible to claim the wholly dependent person credit for the year in respect of the child (or who would be eligible to claim that credit if the child were the parent's only child).

### 10.2.2 Universal Child Care Benefit

Families supporting a child under the age of six are entitled to receive a monthly payment of $100 per child per month, regardless of the income of the parents. If you are already receiving the Canada Child Tax Benefit ("CCTB"), you will not need to apply for the Universal Child Care Benefit ("UCCB"), but if you are not already receiving the CCTB, you will need to apply for the UCCB in order to receive it. You will need to apply by completing Form RC66, *Canada*

*Child Benefits Application*, as soon as possible after your child is born, or a child under the age of six starts to live with you. The form can be found at *www.cra.gc.ca/forms*. This payment is taxable, and no amount will be withheld for taxes, so you need to plan for the tax liability when you receive it.

## 10.2.3 Child Care Expenses

If you are raising a child, be sure to claim any child care expenses to which you may be entitled. The annual limit is $7000 for a child under the age of seven, $4000 for children between the ages of seven and 16, and $10,000 for children who qualify for the disability tax credit. This is further restricted to weekly maximums of $175 for children under the age of seven, $100 for children between the ages of seven and 16 and $250 for children who qualify for the disability tax credit.

Regardless of which parent pays for the expenses, the amount generally can only be claimed by the lower income-earning spouse, and the amount cannot exceed two-thirds of their income. Although child care expenses must generally be claimed by the lower income-earning spouse, there are some exceptions to this rule, such as where one spouse is attending post-secondary education, or is confined to a wheelchair. However, there are a number of restrictions, so be sure to refer to IT-495R3 on the Canada Revenue Agency ("CRA") Web site, which is *www.cra-arc.gc.ca*. Note that for these purposes, the definition of "spouse" includes a common-law partner who has been living with you in a conjugal relationship for a period of 12 months, or a shorter period of time if you are raising a child together.

Below are some strategies for maximizing the amount of eligible child care expenses.

- If you have child care expenses during the summer months, consider whether these costs are deductible. You cannot claim tuition expenses, transportation costs or athletic activities, but you can claim expenses relating to a nursery school, child-care centre, day camp, overnight camp, or an adult individual who takes care of your children, so long as you have a receipt with their SIN number on it.

- You can only deduct the cost of child care if you are not "otherwise available" to take care of your children. For example, teachers who are off during the summer would not be able to claim camp costs as a child care expense unless they were taking a course.

- The courts have allowed parents to claim expenses related to extra-curricular activities as child care expenses where the primary reason for the activity was to provide before- or after-school care. If your child is enrolled in activities in order to provide child care during certain portions of the day, consider whether the fees for these activities may qualify as a child care expense.

- If your child is attending a private school, can a portion of the tuition be attributed to "child care expenses"? For example, does the school offer an "after hours" program to take care of children until their parents are off from work? Can the school itemize the amount paid for these additional programs? Tuition paid for private schools is generally not considered a child care expense.

- Child care expenses cannot be carried forward, so be sure to claim them in the year incurred.

- If you have one child who is an adult, you can deduct payments made to them for the purposes of taking care of your younger children.

- Child care costs can include the costs to advertise or use a placement agency to find a child care provider.

You are required to keep any receipts regarding these expenses in order to properly claim them. The Quebec provincial government does not allow the $7 a day provincial day care fee to be included in child care costs, although the federal government does.

## 10.2.4 File a Tax Return

If you are the parent of a child, and you are not already filing a tax return, consider filing one in order to qualify for certain tax benefits. For example, the Canada Child Tax Benefit ("CCTB") is paid to parents whose income does not exceed a certain level (which varies depending upon the number of children in the family). These payments are tax free, and are paid until the child turns 18. However, in order to qualify, both parents must file a tax return along with an application giving proof of the child's birth.

Entitlement to the Canada Learning Bond is also determined by the income of the parents. Children of families earning less than approximately $39,000 will be entitled to receive a $500 contribution to their RESP (plus $25 for the cost of opening the RESP) plus $100 annually until age 18 (assuming their family income does not exceed the annual thresholds). Therefore, even if you do not earn an income, or do not earn much income, it may be in your best interests to file a tax return if you have young children.

## 10.2.5 Children's Fitness Tax Credit

Parents may claim a non-refundable tax credit of up to $500 in fees for the enrolment of a child in an eligible program of physical activity. The credit may be claimed by either parent in respect of each child under the age of 16. You should keep all of your receipts respecting any amounts paid for fitness programs, since they must be provided in order to receive the credit.

## 10.2.6 Public Transit Pass Credit

If you purchase public transit passes for your children, you may be able to claim the public transit pass credit. There is no limit on the amount of the credit, but in order to claim it, you must purchase a pass on a bus, streetcar, commuter train or ferry which is either monthly or weekly (as long as the passes are purchased for four consecutive weeks). Electronic payment cards used for at least 32 one-way trips in any given month also qualify.

## 10.2.7 Encourage Your Child to File a Tax Return

If you have a child who is earning an income, encourage them to file an income tax return, regardless of how low their income is. Many low-income Canadians choose not to file a tax return, since they know that if they earn less than the personal exemption amount (which is currently $10,382), they will not need to pay any tax. However, there are some advantages to filing a tax return.

- When your child files a tax return, they will begin to accumulate RRSP "room". Contributions to an RRSP are limited to the amount of "room" that has been accumulated, and is calculated based on 18% of your previous year's earned income. Although your children may have no interest in making an RRSP contribution at this time, any accumulated RRSP room may be carried forward indefinitely, allowing them to use it later when they have sufficient funds to make a contribution. "Earned income" generally includes items such as salary and wages, but does not include passive income such as interest and dividends.

- If your child's income is below a certain threshold (which is approximately $30,000), they may be entitled to receive a GST credit. The GST credit is available to residents of Canada who are 19 years of age or older. However, a person who is under the age of 19, and either has (or had) a spouse or common-law partner, or is a parent and lives (or lived) with their child, may also be entitled to receive the benefit.

## 10.2.8 Tax-Free Savings Accounts

Individuals may contribute up to $5000 annually (which amount will be indexed, but only in $500 increments) to a tax-free savings account ("TFSA") in which none of the income, capital gains or withdrawals are taxable. Although the name implies that this is a form of savings account, in fact, the contributor may invest in any of the same types of investments which would be offered in an RRSP or RESP, including mutual funds, stocks and bonds. Any Canadian 18 years of age or older is allowed to open a TFSA, and there is no attribution on any of the amounts. Therefore, if you have children 18 years of age or older, you will be able to make contributions to a TFSA in their name (or encourage them to do so, perhaps by making matching contributions), and all the income earned on those contributions will accrue to the child tax free. TFSAs may be of particular benefit to parents who want to supplement the amount they would like to save for their child's education beyond the maximum amount allowed to be contributed to an RESP. Also, for parents who are unsure as to whether or not their child is likely to attend post-secondary education (perhaps because the child has shown more of an inclination to pursue alternative activities such as starting a business or becoming a performer or athlete), then maximizing contributions to a TFSA may provide more flexibility than an RESP (although the grants and bonds available with RESPs are not available for TFSAs – please see section 10.1.2 for more information on RESPs).

Speak to your financial advisor about the benefits of opening a TFSA both for yourself and your child. One particular problem that may be of concern if you make a contribution to a child's account is the possibility that the amount may be shareable in the event of relationship breakdown, or it may become subject to other creditors of the child.

## 10.2.9 Starting an RRSP for Your Child

Once your child has sufficient disposable income, discuss with them the importance of saving for the future, and perhaps contributing to an RRSP. Many young people are not aware of the advantages of contributing to an RRSP, and retirement savings is often not a priority for young people, especially if they are not earning significant amounts of income. However, if they are able to make a contribution to an RRSP, those funds will grow on a tax-deferred basis inside the RRSP, and the contribution receipts can be carried forward indefinitely and used in a year when the child is in a higher tax bracket. Your child can then begin to benefit from the advantages of tax-deferred compounding, and can invest more aggressively than individuals who start investing for retirement later in life, since they will have a longer investment horizon.

If your child is under the age of 18, it may be difficult to find a financial institution willing to open an RRSP account for him or her, if they want to trade securities, but they should be able to purchase things like a savings bond, or alternatively your child can carry forward any RRSP room they have created, and make the RRSP contributions once they are old enough to open an account. Most children do not have sufficient disposable income to make an RRSP contribution or use the tax deduction until they reach age 18, but the earlier they start, the better.

Keep in mind that although a minor can contribute to an RRSP, they are not allowed the $2000 of over-contribution "room" that adults are allowed before they must pay a penalty tax. If your child is going to make contributions to an RRSP, they should ensure that they know the exact amount of their contribution room, so they do not make an over-contribution.

If your child is over the age of 18, and therefore eligible to begin making contributions to a TFSA, it may be better to maximize TFSA contributions first, especially if your child does not have sufficient taxable income to use the RSP deduction.

## 10.2.10 Income Splitting

If you have a child who is in a low tax bracket (perhaps because he or she is in school or taking time off from a career), think about whether there might be ways to split part of your taxable income with them, so that you will be paying less tax as a family.

- If you are self-employed, consider employing your child in your business and paying them a salary. You will be able to deduct the salary from your income, and they will pay tax on their income at a lower rate. However, the child must actually be providing services to your business, and the salary must be reasonable in comparison to the services they are providing.

- If you have assets that will create taxable capital gains or other forms of income in the future, consider transferring or lending the asset to your child or a trust of which they are a beneficiary so that these taxable amounts will be taxed in their name. Once your child is over the age of 18, the attribution rules will no longer apply, so the income and capital gains earned on the asset will be taxed in their hands (unless the assets are loaned to the child, and the sole purpose for the loan is the avoidance of tax, in which case the attribution rules will still apply). However, prior to doing this, you must understand that the transfer itself will trigger any unrealized capital gains and you will lose control of the asset once it is given to your child. Also, if the transfer is a loan, be sure to have proper documentation in place. See sections 10.1.3, 10.1.4 and 10.1.5 for more information on these strategies.

- If you own shares in a business or investment company, consider doing an "estate freeze" that would freeze your interest in the corporation and transfer the future growth to the new shareholders, which could be your adult children, or more usually, a family trust that includes your adult children as beneficiaries of that trust. See section 16.5.2.4 for a further discussion on the use of estate freezes. Note that if your child is a beneficiary of a family trust, which is a shareholder of a passive investment corporation instead of an active business corporation, they should be prohibited from receiving any dividends from the trust until they attain the age of 18, or there could be negative tax consequences.

## 10.2.11 Tuition, Textbook and Education Tax Credits

Students are entitled to claim a non-refundable credit for tuition fees paid to a university, college or other institution where post-secondary level courses are offered. The eligible fees include tuition, library and lab charges, computer service fees and ancillary fees (sports, insurance, etc.), but do not include student association fees or costs for goods of enduring value.

Students may also claim an education amount of $400 per month based on the number of months of full-time study in a post-secondary education program. Part-time students may claim a tax credit of $120 per month. However, part-time students who qualify for the disability tax credit (or suffer from a significant impairment) may be entitled to claim the full $400 per month. Students may also claim a textbook tax credit of $65 per month for every month in which a student qualifies for a full-time education credit, or $20 per month for part-time students.

If you have a child who has unused tuition, textbook or education tax credits, a portion of their tuition and mandatory ancillary fees can be transferred to a supporting parent, grandparent or spouse to a maximum of $5000 less the excess of the student's income over the basic personal credit amount (unused credits cannot be transferred on the Quebec income tax form). The transferable portion of the credits is the amount by which the combined credits exceeds the credit necessary to reduce student's tax payable to zero. This is the case regardless of who paid the tuition. Any amounts not used or transferred are automatically carried forward indefinitely (since 1997). However, if the child chooses to carry the credit forward, they may not transfer that amount to a supporting person at a later date.

If you have a child with a disabililty, tuition costs may be claimed as a medical expense in some cases, even if the tuition is not in respect of a post-secondary educational institution. Please see section 12.2.5.6 of Chapter 12, "Disabled Persons", for more information.

## 10.2.12 Moving Expenses

If your child attends university full-time, and had to move more than 40 kilometres away, they will be able to deduct their moving expenses from scholarship income, employment or self-employment income earned in the location where they attend school. If the student is not able to deduct all of the expenses because they did not earn enough income in the year in which they moved, they can carry forward the expenses to the next year.

## 10.2.13 Scholarships

The total of all scholarships and bursaries received in connection with a student's enrolment in an elementary or secondary school are exempt from tax.

These amounts are also exempt when received in connection with post-secondary education if the student qualifies for the education tax credit (meaning they are enrolled in a designated financial institution) or the amount is to be used by the student in the production of a literary, dramatic, musical or artistic work. However, if the student does not meet these conditions, then the exemption is limited to $500.

## 10.2.14 Interest Payments on Student Loans

If your child takes out a student loan, they can claim a tax credit for any interest paid on that loan (so long as the loan is kept separate from any other borrowings, and it is clear that the amount was used for education purposes). Although this credit cannot be transferred to a parent, it can be carried forward by the student for up to five years.

Be careful if you are considering refinancing your student loan. The loan must be one made under the *Canada Student Loans Act* in order for the interest payments to qualify for the tax credits, so make sure that any potential interest rate savings upon refinancing more than outweigh the loss of the tax credit.

## 10.2.15 Eligible Dependant Credit

If you are not living with a spouse or common-law partner and you are not claiming the spousal tax credit, you may be able to claim the eligible dependant credit if you are raising a child. If your child is a minor, and earning less than the personal tax credit (which is $10,382), then you will be able to claim a credit in respect of your child until he or she reaches age 18 (unless he or she is mentally or physically infirm).

Generally, you must be living with the child in order to claim the credit, although it may be possible to claim the credit where you have joint custody with a separated or divorced spouse. However, only one parent will be entitled to claim the credit in respect of any one child, so the parents should negotiate who will be able to claim the credit. (See section 6.2.4 of Chapter 6, "Separated", for more information.) If you are paying child support payments to your spouse in respect of the child, you will not be entitled to claim the eligible dependant credit.

## 10.2.16 Tax Deduction for Adoption Expenses

Parents can deduct expenses relating to a completed adoption for a child under the age of 18 years. Eligible adoption expenses include:

- fees paid to a provincially licensed adoption agency;
- legal, administrative and translation fees;

- reasonable travel and living costs for the child and adoptive parents; and
- mandatory fees paid to a foreign institution.

The maximum eligible expense is $10,975, which may be divided between two adoptive parents. The adoptive parent must submit proof of an adoption in the form of a Canadian or foreign adoption order, and can only claim the expense in the year in which the adoption is finalized (although at that time, they will be able to claim expenses from prior years relating to that adoption effective from 2005).

## 10.3 FAMILY LAW ISSUES

Once you have children, you will be legally liable to support them, usually until the age of majority, but in many cases, even beyond that. This may be the case even if the child is not a natural or adopted child. If you take on a parental role, and become what is known as "in loco parentis", you will generally have the same legal liability as a natural or adoptive parent. In addition, a court can ignore any domestic contract where a child's parent purports to release you from any legal liability in respect of a child after the time of your separation. Once you accept a parental role, you will have to incorporate that responsibility into your wealth plan for a potentially long period of time. Child support obligations are generally based on the amount of money you make and the number of children you are supporting — do not assume that simply because the child has two natural parents that you will not be obligated to pay support. Some children may have several supporting parents, and the courts do not take these obligations lightly.

It is also important to understand that in some jurisdictions, you may be liable for damages caused by your child. For example, in Manitoba, parents may be liable for up to $7500 of any property loss experienced by an owner of property as a result of an act of a child.

## 10.4 DISABILITY PLANNING

As referred to in the previous chapters, it is imperative that you plan for disability so that an already traumatic situation does not become worse due to your lack of planning.

When children are added to the equation, the need to plan for disability becomes even more critical. Have you reviewed your disability insurance to ensure that it meets all of your needs? Now that you have children, you will not be the only person to suffer if your income decreases dramatically as a result of a disability. Critical illness insurance may also be recommended if you want to ensure that you can pay for various services (like housekeeping services or cooking) if you are dealing with a major illness.

Later in life when your children reach adulthood, you may want to appoint them to act as your power of attorney for financial or health care issues. If you have several children and you are concerned that all of your children would not be able to agree with respect to decisions regarding your health and personal care matters, you can use your Power of Attorney for Personal Care to appoint one or more of your children whom you feel will best represent your interests in the event that you become incapable of making health and personal care decisions for yourself (this document has different names in different jurisdictions — see Chapter 18, "Powers of Attorney"). The child or children you appoint will have priority over children whom you do not appoint with respect to the matters set out in the document. No matter whom you appoint, it is very important to discuss these issues with your family. The person you appoint may not feel comfortable taking on the responsibility, and the people you do not appoint may feel offended. Also, do not assume that your children's marriages will be permanent — think twice before appointing a son-in-law or daughter-in-law as your attorney for finances or health care purposes.

## 10.5 ESTATE PLANNING

It is very important to ensure that you have planned adequately for an untimely death, especially when you have children. Here are a few things you need to consider.

### 10.5.1 Guardianship

If your children are still minors, who will take care of them in the event neither you, nor the children's other parent, is able to? Nominating a guardian for your children in your will is potentially one of the most important parts of your estate plan. Some people feel that it is not necessary to nominate a guardian because they have many family members who would be more than capable of doing the job — which may be precisely the problem. If various family members feel that they are the better parents, your orphaned children could find themselves embroiled in a custody battle. Reduce the stress for all involved by nominating the person you feel is the most appropriate person for the job. Give serious consideration to the issue, and be sure to speak with the person you wish to nominate. It is possible that the person you wish to nominate as guardian is not willing to accept the position — it is better to find this out sooner rather than later.

You should also talk to that person about your views and perspectives on parenthood so that they have an understanding of how you would like your children to be raised. Here are some of the issues you may wish to discuss with your proposed guardian.

1. Can they afford to take care of your children? Will they require regular payments of funds from any money left to the children from your estate? Do the guardians have the type of lifestyle that would allow them sufficient time to raise a child?

2. Do you and your proposed guardian have the same philosophies regarding discipline? Does your guardian have similar religious beliefs? Are there any cultural or language issues which may pose difficulties?

3. Do you have the same philosophies regarding money? For example, do you expect your children to do chores before earning an allowance? Or are you comfortable simply giving them money upon request? Do you expect they will get a summer job when they are older? Or do you want their post-secondary education, and perhaps summer travel costs paid for?

4. Does you guardian know the extent to which education and/or certain extra-curricular activities are to be encouraged? For example, do you want your children to go to private school? University? Take music lessons? Sports?

5. Does your guardian live close by? Although geography may be a consideration of lesser importance, choosing someone in your local community may result in less upheaval for your children, especially if they can continue in their previous school and maintain friendships.

Once you are gone, it will be too late to convey your wishes in this respect. Here are some additional considerations to take into account when choosing a guardian.

- Consider the age of the guardian, and their ability to raise children for a potentially long period of time. Some people automatically assume that their parents are the best choice for acting as guardians. However, your parents may not always be the best choice because they may not outlive you, and even if they do, they may be elderly or unable to act. When choosing a guardian, consider that it is a potentially lengthy responsibility.

- Once you have decided upon a guardian, consider whether or not you want to nominate a married couple as guardians, or if you are only really concerned that one individual have that authority (for example, you want to nominate your sister or brother, but not necessarily their spouse or partner). If you nominate both the intended guardian and their spouse, what will happen if that couple separates or divorces? Who will be entitled to act as guardian in that instance? It is generally better to nominate one person only, in order to avoid these types of disputes.

- Ensure that you nominate an alternate in the event that the person you have chosen to act as guardian is not able to fulfill the role as originally planned.

- A guardianship nomination in a will is not binding on a court, and a court may appoint someone else if they feel that your choice is inappropriate for some reason (e.g. the person you have chosen has developed an addiction, and is not fit to parent your children). However, although your choice is not binding, it will carry quite a bit of weight with a court, so you should make your wishes known in your will. Be sure to speak with your family about your choice, so that they have an opportunity to ask any questions, and understand why you have chosen the person over other individuals. This discussion in advance may help to avoid a custody battle after the time of your death.

- When choosing a guardian, do not simply assume that the guardian should be the same person as you have chosen to be the personal representative for your estate. It is often advisable to make the guardian and your personal representative different people in order to prevent a conflict of interest between preserving the estate, and caring for the children.

- If your guardian will need financial assistance from the estate in order to raise the children, ensure that your will allows your personal representatives to make payments to the guardians as and when needed. Also consider the personalities of your guardian(s) and personal representative(s) and their ability to get along.

- In Quebec, parents may appoint a guardian, which is referred to as a "tutor" in Quebec, for any children who are minors, either in their will, in a mandate given in anticipation of incapacity or by filing a declaration to that effect with the Public Curator.

Choosing a substitute parent for your child is obviously one of the most important decisions you will have to make when structuring your estate plan. Consider the decision carefully prior to making your choice.

## 10.5.2 Distribution of Your Estate

Another reason why it is so important to have a proper estate plan in place once you have children is because the birth of a child can severely impact how your estate will be distributed. Many people assume that when they die, their spouse will inherit their entire estate. However, in most jurisdictions, that is not the case once you have a child. Although a surviving spouse may be entitled to a "preferential share" of your estate, as well as a portion of the remainder, your child may also be entitled to a portion of your estate if you die without a will, and in some jurisdictions, even if you die with a will that has specifically excluded your children (see section 19.6 of Chapter 19, "Distribution of an Estate"). There have been many cases where one parent has died without a will while the children were still young, and although the surviving spouse was entitled to a portion of the estate, the children were entitled to a portion of the house, the investments and the RRSPs. This is a problem for several reasons.

1. If the child is under 18 or 19 (the age of majority varies between the jurisdictions — see section 10.7, "Jurisdiction Differences") the money may have to be held by the provincial authorities if there is no will, or if no trustee for the child's inheritance was appointed in the will. Do not assume that surviving parents automatically have the right to manage their child's estate.

2. Generally speaking, estate assets (such as investments, property and heirlooms) can roll over to a surviving spouse without triggering capital gains or losses. In the same manner, RRSPs or RRIFs can be transferred to the RRSP or RRIF of the surviving spouse without any tax consequences at the time of death (see Chapter 21, "Taxation at Death", for further information). However, the same is generally not true when assets are transferred to a child. If the children become entitled to a portion of the estate, then tax may become owing on some of the assets at the time of death of the first parent, potentially necessitating the sale or liquidation of some of the assets or registered investments sooner than if everything had been left to the surviving spouse.

3. Once the children reach the age of majority, they will be entitled to spend the money however they see fit. Whereas the surviving spouse may prefer to keep the money invested in order to fund his or her child's education or the parent's retirement, the child may prefer to spend the money on items such as a new car. If the parent died without a will, or did not put sufficient controls in the will, there will be nothing to stop the child from spending the money however they please once they become an adult.

As you can see, the consequences of not drafting a will can cause difficulties for the estate, and particularly for the surviving spouse. If the parents had assumed that the surviving spouse would inherit all of the assets, it will be a nasty surprise to discover that your children are entitled to a portion of the estate, especially if the surviving spouse requires all of the estate assets in order to preserve the family's standard of living. This may be particularly difficult if the funds inherited by the child must be held in trust by the provincial authorities until he or she reaches the age of majority. Be sure to review your estate plan with a professional once you have children to ensure that your estate will be distributed in the manner you intended.

## 10.5.3 Leaving Money to Minors

If you have children who are minors (or even young adults), you should give consideration as to what types of controls you may need on the distribution of your estate. Even if you are married or in a common-law relationship, and you have provided that your estate is to go to your spouse or partner in the event of your death, what would happen in the event of a common disaster? If you are single, separated, divorced or widowed, your will may provide that your children are your primary beneficiaries — would your children be capable of managing your estate if you were to die tomorrow?

If you leave money directly to a child who has not yet reached the age of majority, the provincial authorities may have the right to manage that money until the child becomes an adult, depending upon the jurisdiction. However, in many cases, this is not the optimal result. The public trustee will charge a fee in order to manage your estate, and they may not manage the funds in the manner you would like (for example, they may feel that certain expenses, which you would have approved, are not good uses of the money). Also, once your child attains the age of majority, he or she will be entitled to their inheritance in one lump sum. Do you believe that an 18- or 19-year-old is capable of managing hundreds of thousands of dollars? Millions?

Generally speaking, when questioned about the topic, most parents do not want their children to receive their entire inheritance at age 18 or 19. However, if you do not take steps to specifically ensure that your estate is held in trust until a later date, it is very possible that your children could receive a large lump sum of money when they are too young to manage it. It is generally recommended that parents with young children provide that any amounts inherited by their children are to be held in trust until reaching the age of majority, if not longer (see section 10.5.4 as well as Chapter 23, "Trusts", for further information on the structure of a trust). Trusts established for children are generally managed by the deceased's personal representative (see Chapter 20, "Personal Representatives", for further information on choosing a personal representative). The personal representative may be given the power to encroach upon the capital of the trust for the benefit of the children. It is generally a good idea to speak to your personal representative about the types of expenditures which you would like them to authorize — private school? Travel? Private music or sporting lessons?

The next decision is whether or not you want the trust provisions to continue past the age of majority. In many cases, parents feel that even 18 or 19 is too young to be able to manage a large lump sum of money. Young adults may be prone to impulse buying, or perhaps have creditor exposure, or may even experience a bad marriage that results in part of the funds passing to a former spouse. In order to prevent these problems, many parents provide in their wills that their child's inheritance is to be held in trust past the age of 18 or 19. For example, in many cases parents provide that their children are entitled to an annual income from the trust once they attain the age of majority, but they cannot encroach upon the capital at that time without the consent of the trustee. The capital of the trust is generally paid out in stages — for example, one-quarter of the capital at age 21, half of the remaining capital at age 25 and all of the remaining capital at age 30. Keep in mind that every situation is different — be sure to speak with your professional advisors about how long you would like to keep the trust in place. There are tax advantages and disadvantages to keeping a trust in place, so you may need to balance these tax issues with the issues of control.

Be sure to keep in mind when you are structuring your estate that the only moneys which will be held in trust are those which pass through your estate. If you provide that your children are to receive assets outside of your estate, then it is very possible that even though you provided in your will that your children were not to receive a large sum until they were old enough to manage it, they may still receive a large lump sum much earlier than intended. For example, if you add your children as joint owners on an account or asset, or if you designate them as the direct beneficiaries of an RRSP or insurance policy, they will receive the funds immediately, and the assets will not form part of your estate (except in some cases where assets are held in joint ownership with an adult child, and in some cases in Quebec). If you want your assets to be held in trust, then it is generally not a good idea to make a child a joint owner or direct beneficiary of an asset. As mentioned before, if a child receives money prior to reaching the age of majority, the provincial authorities may step in to manage the money, which is often not the preferred state of affairs.

Sometimes you may hear that there are tax advantages to naming a minor child as a beneficiary of an RRSP, since the RRSP proceeds will not be taxable immediately at the time of death, as they otherwise would (see Chapter 21, "Taxation at Death", for more information). Although this is true, the tax deferral is not forever, and at the time of death, a registered annuity must be purchased for the child which pays out prior to the child's 18th birthday (unless the child suffers from a disability). Although this may result in some tax advantages, this also means that the child will be entitled to a potentially large sum of money while they are very young. In many cases, it is a better idea to plan for the tax liability (perhaps by purchasing insurance), and have the RRSP payable to the estate, so that the funds are de-registered at the time of death, but then the after-tax proceeds will be held in trust until the desired time. Saving a little bit of money on tax will be small consolation if your child spends the money recklessly as soon as they receive it!

If you are concerned about leaving extremely large amounts to children, and the impact it may have on their motivation to become contributing members of society, then you may need to be more original in your approach to distributing the money. For example, you may provide in your will that money is only to be distributed as follows:

- on a dollar-for-dollar matching basis with the child's salary (although this may in fact be a disincentive if the child wishes to pursue a career which does not pay a high salary, but does provide community advantages, such as charitable or relief work);

- on a matching basis if a child invests in a business; or

- on a bonus basis upon achieving certain goals, such as a university degree, or upon having a child.

Some parents are concerned about their children suffering from "affluenza", and prefer to put conditions in their will to ensure that their children are motivated to achieve as much as they can in their life, although many advisors warn against this type of planning. If you do use an "incentive" trust, be sure to carefully consider what type of behaviour you wish to motivate.

## 10.5.4 Tax Planning for Adult Children

Even if your children are adults, you should still give consideration as to whether or not it would be appropriate to leave their inheritance to them in a trust. In some cases, this is because the child suffers from a disability, and the parents want to preserve the child's right to receive social assistance payments (see section 12.3.1 in Chapter 12, "Disabled Persons"). In other cases, it is simply because the children are earning significant amounts of income, and want to minimize the amount of income tax they are paying. Assuming your child is competent to manage money, and the trust is being established primarily for tax savings, here is how this type of trust would work:

- Instead of leaving your estate to your children directly, you would provide in your will that it is to be held in trust.

- The trustees of the trust could be your personal representatives. Given that many parents choose their adult children to act as trustees upon the death of the second parent, it is likely that the children will be acting as the trustees of their trusts. It is generally not recommended that a child act as the sole trustee of their own trust, since there may be a question as to whether or not you have truly established a trust. If at all possible, try to include another person (perhaps a sibling) as a trustee, if the children get along. If a child does not want siblings involved in his or her trust, then perhaps include a provision that states that the capital in the trust is also to be held for the benefit of grandchildren after the child dies. In this way the child will be acting as trustee of a trust not only in his or her favour, but also in favour of the grandchildren, which will give more evidence of a true trust.

- Generally, if there are no concerns about control, the trustees will be given the power to encroach upon the capital at any time.

- If the child does not require all of the assets in the trust immediately, then those assets can remain in the trust, and the income can be taxed in the name of the trust. Trusts are treated as separate taxpayers under the *Income Tax Act*, so there may be some tax savings if the children are in mid- to high-tax brackets (see Case Study 10.8.2 for an example).

- Generally, trusts established for individuals other than a spouse are wound up within 21 years. This is because the *Income Tax Act* provides that all of the assets in the trust will be deemed to be disposed of every 21 years. This means that if there are assets in the trust that have an unrealized capital gain, then that capital gain will be triggered on the 21st anniversary of the creation of the trust. Therefore, most trusts established for children allow the trustees to wind up the trust within 21 years, so that the assets can be transferred to the children on a tax-deferred basis (in most cases), avoiding the deemed disposition on the 21st anniversary.

- If the beneficiary of the trust is a Canadian resident, then the assets can be "rolled out" of the trust at their cost base, and no capital gains will be triggered until the child disposes of the asset, or dies (which is the same result as if the asset had been given to the child immediately at the time of the death of the second parent).

The tax advantages referred to above are generally only available for testamentary trusts. Trusts that are established during a person's lifetime are referred to as "*inter vivos*" trusts. Every dollar of income earned within an *inter vivos* trust is taxed at the highest marginal rate, so the income-splitting advantages referred to above are not available (although *inter vivos* trusts may provide income splitting advantages in limited circumstances, as discussed in section 10.1.3.2).

In order to obtain maximum tax advantage, one trust should be created for each beneficiary, although the *Income Tax Act* prohibits more than one trust being created for the same beneficiary by the same person. Speak to an experienced tax professional to ensure that the structure does not offend the rules in the *Income Tax Act*. Also see Chapter 23, "Trusts", for more information on trusts generally.

### 10.5.5 Protecting Assets Given to Children from Family Property Claims

In many jurisdictions, property received by way of gift or inheritance is exempt from a division of family property at the time of marriage breakdown (and in some jurisdictions, also at the time of the breakdown of a common-law relationship). If you intend to leave a significant inheritance for your child, it may be worthwhile to include a clause in your will that states that the inheritance is meant solely for the benefit of your child, and is not to be included in the calculation of net family property. You may also wish to indicate that any growth on the property is also to remain separate (although this type of clause may not be effective in every jurisdiction). Although there is no guarantee that your child will not simply use the money to purchase a family asset, thereby squandering the opportunity to keep the money from becoming sharable, a clause of this type may be useful in cases where children are conscientious about keeping their money separate. See section 17.4 of Chapter 17, "Family Property", for a discussion of the family property rules in the jurisdiction where your child resides. Remember that even though your child may not reside in a jurisdiction where a clause of this type would be effective now, they may move to another jurisdiction in the future, or the laws of their jurisdiction could change. For example, common-law partners now have rights to a division of family property in many jurisdictions, so even if your child is not married, you should not discount the importance of this type of clause.

### 10.5.6 Leaving Money to Spendthrift Children

As mentioned in section 10.5.3, when a parent is concerned about the ability of their children to manage money, the usual solution is to place the funds in a trust. Although these trusts are usually only in effect until a pre-determined age, such as 25 or 30, some parents are sufficiently concerned about the ability of their children to manage money that they choose to create trusts that will exist for much longer than that, or which are managed by professional trustees who have complete discretion over when to pay the funds out to the children. If you are concerned about leaving large sums of money directly to your children, consider including such a trust in your will.

Another strategy that is sometimes utilized when there is concern about a beneficiary's ability to handle money is an annuity. The personal representative of the estate could be directed to purchase an annuity with the beneficiary's inheritance, thereby providing the beneficiary with a fixed stream of income, but not allowing the beneficiary to receive a lump-sum all at one time. If the annuity is to be paid over the course of the beneficiary's life, then it will have no cash value, and it will be difficult to pledge. However, the entire estate will be depleted by the purchase of the annuity, leaving nothing for future generations, unless the beneficiary uses part of the annuity payments to pay for insurance in order to replenish their estate, or invests the payments as they are received.

## 10.5.7 Personal Representatives

Once your children become adults, you may consider appointing them as personal representatives of your estate. (Personal representatives are also sometimes referred to as "executors" — see Chapter 20, "Personal Representatives", for more information.) Parents often choose children as alternate personal representatives in the event their spouse predeceases them, or is unable to act on their behalf, or perhaps if they do not have a spouse. Although appointing a child as your personal representative is a natural choice, and often the best choice, consider the following factors.

- If you appoint several children to act as your personal representatives, consider whether or not your will should provide for decisions to be made by majority vote. If your will does not specify that your personal representatives can make decisions in this manner, in most cases, unanimous consent of all the personal representatives will be required for each and every decision they make.

- The residence of the personal representatives is important for determining the residence of your estate. If one or more of your children is no longer a resident of Canada, consider whether or not they are the best person to act in that position.

- If you are appointing one of several children to be your personal representative, it may be wise to provide for a clause in your will giving reasonable compensation to your personal representative, perhaps utilizing a formula such as a percentage or a set fee. If you do not express this wish, the children who are not personal representatives may put pressure on the child who is a personal representative not to take compensation even though the responsibilities can be quite onerous. Fees for acting as personal representative are taxable, so it is possible that the child acting as the personal representative may choose not to take such fees.

- Do not assume that your child's marriage will be permanent — think twice before appointing a son-in-law or daughter-in-law as a personal representative.

## 10.5.8 CPP Orphan Benefits

Upon the death of a parent, a child may be entitled to receive what is sometimes referred to as an "orphan benefit" or "children's benefit" from the Canada Pension Plan ("CPP") if their deceased parent has made sufficient contributions to the CPP. This benefit is paid to a dependent, natural or adopted child of the deceased contributor, or a child in the care and control of the deceased contributor at the time of death. The child must be either under age 18, or between the ages of 18 and 25 and in full-time attendance at a school or university.

A child may receive two benefits if:

- both parents paid into the CPP for the minimum number of years, and
- each parent is either disabled (according to CPP rules) or deceased.

If the child is under the age of 18, the benefit is normally paid to the person with whom the child is living. However, if the child is 18 or older and qualifies because of full-time attendance at a school or university, the benefit is paid directly to him or her. In order to receive this benefit, you child (or their guardian) must apply. If your child's other parent is deceased, you should ensure that your children are receiving all benefits they are entitled to.

## 10.5.9 Protecting Your Child's Estate

Many people who are in traditional first marriages draft their wills so that their spouse will receive everything upon their death, and upon the death of the second spouse, the estate is to be divided equally between their children. Although this appears to be the easiest solution in many cases, there are some disadvantages to writing a will this way. For example, what happens if the surviving spouse remarries? Generally, upon the death of the surviving spouse, the new spouse will receive some (or potentially all) of the estate, and it is possible that the children from the first marriage could be left out. If you want to ensure that at least your portion of your estate will eventually go to your children regardless of what your spouse chooses to do later in life, then it may be advisable to set up spousal trusts in your will.

A spousal trust is a trust which essentially allows the surviving spouse to use the income from the trust assets every year, and it may or may not allow the spouse to encroach on capital. Since the capital is held by the trust as opposed to the surviving spouse, it will not be impacted by a future marriage by the surviving spouse. In this way, when the surviving spouse dies, the assets in the trust are distributed to the children from the first marriage. In a perfect world, the surviving spouse would ensure that his or her children from their first marriage are taken care of — the sad reality is that one branch or another of a blended family is often disowned (see Chapter 8, "Blended Families", for more information on how children in blended families can be disinherited). If you want to ensure that your estate will go to your children even if your spouse fails to properly plan for them in the future, a spousal trust is a good idea.

When structuring your estate, keep in mind that only assets which pass through your estate will be included in the spousal trust. For example, assets that are held in joint names with your spouse, or that will pass directly to your spouse by virtue of a direct beneficiary designation will not pass through your estate (except in most cases in Quebec). Therefore, if you want the majority of your assets to go into the trust, you must ensure that they will pass through your estate. Although this may mean paying more in probate fees at the time of death of the first spouse, in many cases there are other more valuable tax advantages that will arise by using a trust (and it usually results in lower probate fees at the time of the death of the second spouse). See section 5.5.2 in Chapter 5, "Married", for more information on these issues, and be sure to speak with a qualified professional about the advantages of using a trust in your will.

## 10.5.10 Disowning a Child

Although these circumstances are rare, there are situations where for one reason or another, a parent does not want to leave assets to a child, or wants to leave one child a smaller portion of their estate, rather than distributing it equally. If you are contemplating doing this, consider the following factors.

- If the child is a minor, or an adult still attending a post-secondary educational institution, and therefore financially dependent upon you, the child, or his or her guardians, may have the ability to apply to the court for an award under the provincial dependant's relief legislation. Generally speaking, the law does not allow parents to leave financially dependent children out of their will. In fact, in some jurisdictions, even financially independent adult children may be able to make a claim against the estate for failing to fulfill a "moral" obligation. See section 19.6 of Chapter 19, "Distribution of an Estate", for more information on this subject.
- If you want to disown a child, consider including them in your will, but only give them a nominal amount, such as $100. By doing this, it is clear that you did not forget to include them, but chose to give them nothing. Although there is no guarantee that the child will not choose to challenge the will, this gesture will at least signal to the court that you did not simply forget about this child. However, as mentioned above, in some jurisdictions even financially independent children are entitled to apply to the court to have the will varied if they feel that they were not left a sufficient

amount. Some advisors do not feel that a clause of this nature is necessary, but it may be helpful if the deceased happens to die while domiciled in a U.S. state where state laws permit "pretermitted heirs" to receive a portion of the estate. Pretermitted heirs are children (or grandchildren) whom you fail to expressly mention in your will, so expressly naming the child and then giving them a nominal amount may preclude these types of claims.

- If you want to exclude a child from a will, consider writing a letter separate and apart from the will which sets out your reasons for doing so. Although such letter will be non-binding, it may help prevent disputes among your children by clearly setting out your reasoning. The rationale for listing the reasons in a separate document is so that the reasons will remain confidential, and not be filed in the public probate court along with the rest of the will.

- If you believe the disowned child may challenge the validity of the will, consider obtaining a medical opinion stating that you were of sound mind on the date that you made the will, so even if you lose your mental capacity later, it is clear that you were of sound mind at the time you intended to leave the child out of your will. Also consider adding a provision which indicates that if a child challenges your will, they will receive no part of the estate (which is obviously only a deterrent if they have received at least a small portion of the estate).

- If you think that disowning a child may lead to litigation, consider leaving your estate equally to your children, but then doing things outside the will to give others more of the estate. For example, you could:

    - add some children as joint owners of your property (although if they are adults, you will also need to sign a document indicating that the asset is not to be included in your estate, and is to go to the surviving joint owner);

    - make some children direct beneficiaries of some of your property;

    - give gifts of property during your lifetime to some children; or

    - establish alter ego trusts so that your estate is distributed according to the trust rather than according to the will.

See Chapter 22, "Probate", for a discussion about some of the advantages and disadvantages of these strategies. Although *these strategies are generally not recommended*, since they can lead to unequal divisions of an estate as well as tax problems, they may be an option worth considering in severe cases. Be sure to speak with an advisor about the advantages and disadvantages of this type of planning before implementing any of these strategies.

- Make sure that you really want to leave the child out of your will. Many children and parents reconcile later in life, but if the reconciliation happens too late for you to change your will, your child will still receive nothing.

## 10.5.11 Estate Planning for Pets

Although not everyone would consider their pet equivalent to a "child", there are certainly some people who do. If you are concerned about the welfare of your pet(s) in the event something happens to you, here are a few things you and/or your family should consider.

- Ask a trusted individual if they would be willing to care for your pet(s) in the event of an emergency. Make sure they either have a set of keys to your home or know where to find them, as well as any required information regarding your pet's food and care, and the contact information for the pet's veterinarian.

- Make sure that your friends, family and neighbors know the name and phone number of the pet caregiver, so that they can call them in the event of emergency. If possible, carry a card in your wallet that has the contact information for your pet's caregivers on it.

- Place notices on the front and back windows of your home to indicate what type of pet(s) you own, and how many there are, so that emergency workers will look for them. Also consider placing emergency phone numbers on the inside of your front and back doors with the contact information listed for the pet's caregivers.

You should also ensure that there will be sufficient financial resources to care for your pet. Consider designating someone as the beneficiary of a sum of money in your will, on the condition that they agree to care for your pet. Although this is obviously not a guarantee that they will care for your pet in the manner that you would have, if you speak to the caregiver in advance, and explain to them the type of care you would like for your pet, the chances are higher that your pet will be well cared for.

You should not indicate in your will that you will give a certain sum of money to anyone who agrees to take the pet — this will only prompt unethical individuals to agree to take the pet, but will not ensure their well-being. Always talk to the proposed pet caregiver in advance and ensure that the amount of money left for the pet is reasonable, but not so much as to encourage people to act in anything other than your pet's best interests.

Another possibility is to speak to your local Humane Society or animal shelter to see if they have any programs for placing animals in new homes after their owner has died.

## 10.6 INSURANCE PLANNING

Having adequate insurance is extremely important — especially if you are concerned about the standard of living you want your children to have. Ensure that you have reviewed your life insurance needs to incorporate the needs of your children.

### 10.6.1 Reviewing Your Insurance Needs

If you have dependants, it will be important for you to review your insurance needs with your financial planner. Although the amount of insurance you had previously may have been sufficient to support a spouse in the event of an untimely death, it may not be sufficient to support your children, especially if your spouse decides to quit their job or work part-time in order to care for them. Given that the needs of your children could continue for many years, including past age 18 if they decide to attend a post-secondary educational institution, carrying the appropriate amount of insurance may be more important now than at any other point in your life.

### 10.6.2 Designating a Child as a Direct Beneficiary

In recent years, it has become increasingly common to designate a direct beneficiary on insurance policies. Although there are advantages to doing this between spouses, especially where the intent is to save probate and to avoid creditors, there are also many drawbacks, which are discussed in the previous sections of this chapter and section 22.3.6 in Chapter 22, "Probate". If you do not have a spouse to designate as the direct beneficiary of your insurance policy, do not automatically assume that you should then appoint your children.

In many cases this is not a good idea, since the insurance company may have to pay the insurance proceeds into court or to the Public Trustee to be held until the children are 18 or 19. In many cases it is better to have the insurance proceeds paid to your estate, and distributed in accordance with your will. As discussed in section 10.5.3, your will can ensure that your children do not receive the money until they are mature enough to manage it.

Also, what happens if one of your children predeceases you? If you have named more than one child on the insurance policy, the surviving children will receive all of the proceeds, but any children of the deceased child may receive nothing. If the proceeds had instead been paid to your estate, they would have been distributed according to your will, which would probably provide that upon the death of one of your children, their children would receive the deceased's child's portion.

One instance where designating a child as a beneficiary may be advisable is if you have creditor exposure. In certain cases, designating certain individuals (such as children) may protect the insurance from seizure by a creditor, since certain family members are considered to be in a "protected class" of beneficiaries. However, if at all possible, attempt to avoid naming a minor child as the beneficiary, and consider putting a trust agreement in place so that it is clear as to how the insurance proceeds are to be distributed. Speak to an advisor if you are in this situation, and see section 25.4 of Chapter 25, "Insurance", for a list of the "protected class" of beneficiaries in your jurisdiction.

### 10.6.3 Insurance Trusts

In previous sections we discussed the use of testamentary trusts, and the need to have the assets pass through your estate if you want them to be held in trust. The consequences of having an asset pass through an estate are generally that the asset will have to be included in the value of your estate for probate purposes, potentially increasing the amount of probate tax payable by your estate, and also potentially exposing the asset to creditors of the estate.

However, there is one type of asset that can be placed in a testamentary trust without having to pass through probate — a life insurance policy. Ask your lawyer if it would be advisable to include a life insurance trust as part of your will, so that the proceeds of the life insurance policy will be held in trust for a spouse or child (in order to protect the assets from claims, and to reduce taxes, as discussed in sections 10.5.3 and 10.5.4). Once your lawyer has incorporated an insurance trust into your will (or a separate declaration), they will contact your insurance provider to ensure that the funds are paid to the proper person. See section 22.3.7 in Chapter 22, "Probate" for more information on insurance trusts.

### 10.6.4 Insurance for Children

Although children generally do not have dependants, it may be worthwhile to consider whether or not a life insurance policy should be placed in their names. The death benefit could be used to pay for funeral expenses, etc., in the event of a premature death, although the more usual reason for considering insurance for a child is to guarantee insurability. Many young people have been diagnosed with serious diseases in their youth or young adulthood, which has resulted in an inability to obtain insurance later in life when they need it.

Generally, a separate insurance policy is not taken out for the child. Rather, a rider is attached to a policy in the name of the parent, which provides for a relatively small death benefit to be paid at the time of their death. However, once they become adults, they can convert the rider into a permanent policy, without taking a medical exam. The death benefit for the permanent policy can be worth several times the amount of the original rider, so the rider will guarantee insurability to a certain extent. The rider generally needs to be converted to a permanent policy by the time the child reaches the age of 25.

### 10.6.5 Using Insurance to Shelter Income

If you have extra funds that you do not require in order to fund your lifestyle, it may be worthwhile to consider purchasing a whole life insurance policy that insures your child. Any income earned on the premiums placed in the policy will grow on a tax-free basis (so long as it is not withdrawn from the policy). You will retain control over the policy during your lifetime, and the policy can be transferred to a child without incurring probate fees. You will also be able to access the funds during your lifetime either by making withdrawals (which are taxable) or using the funds as collateral for a loan.

If you add a child as the contingent owner, then the policy will pass to them tax free at the time of your death. Your child can then either use the funds as collateral for a loan, or make taxable withdrawals. Alternatively, if your children will not need the funds, the death benefit could be paid on a tax-free basis to the next generation (or a trust in their favour), allowing the contributions to grow tax free within the policy for many years.

As mentioned above, a policy can be transferred tax free to a child. For these purposes, a "child" includes any natural or adopted child, a grandchild, step-child or a daughter-or son-in-law.

## 10.7 JURISDICTION DIFFERENCES

The age of majority is 18 in:

Alberta
Manitoba
Ontario
Prince Edward Island
Quebec
Saskatchewan

The age of majority is 19 in:

British Columbia
New Brunswick
Newfoundland
Northwest Territories
Nova Scotia
Nunavut
Yukon

## 10.8 CASE STUDIES

### 10.8.1 Married, With Minor Children

Miranda and her husband Richard have two children, Mikayla and Hailey. Both Mikayla and Hailey are natural children of both Miranda and Richard (for situations where there are children from a previous relationship(s), see Chapter 8, "Blended Families"). Mikayla is eight and Hailey is six. Since Miranda and Richard live in Nova Scotia, they know that if they do not have a will, that Mikayla and Hailey will be entitled to a portion of their estate, even if the other parent is still alive (see section 19.6 of Chapter 19, "Distribution of an Estate", for a description of how an estate is distributed in your jurisdiction where there is no will). They speak with their advisors to ensure that they have proper wills, powers of attorney and insurance. They also review how title is held on all of their assets (e.g. Sole names? Joint ownership?) and review all of their direct beneficiary designations.

Miranda and Richard have appointed each other as their personal representatives, and sole beneficiaries in each of their wills. Although they have left their entire estate to each other upon the first to die, they have left it to each other in trust. The trust provides that the survivor is entitled to the income every year, and may encroach upon the capital as necessary. However, any capital remaining in the trust at the time of death of the survivor will not form part of the survivor's estate — it will instead be distributed to Mikayla and Hailey. If they leave their entire estate to each other without using a trust, and then the survivor gets remarried, it is possible that Mikayla and Hailey will not receive their intended inheritance. For example, assume Miranda dies first and leaves everything to Richard. If Richard decides to remarry, and adds his new wife as a joint owner of all of his assets, then Richard's new wife will inherit those assets upon his death, and Mikayla and Hailey would not receive Miranda's (and potentially not even Richard's) estate. (Note that in Quebec, there is no right of survivorship on jointly held assets). If Miranda instead leaves her assets to Richard in trust, and then he remarries and subsequently dies, all that his new wife may inherit are the assets in his name — the assets in Miranda's trust will go to Mikayla and Hailey.

Miranda and Richard then provide that upon the death of the survivor of them, their estate is to be divided equally between Mikayla and Hailey, after payment of all debts and taxes. Any amounts to be given to Mikayla and Hailey are to be held in trust for their benefit. Miranda and Richard have appointed Miranda's sister, Jennifer, as their alternate personal representative (they have appointed each other as their primary personal representative), and they have indicated that Jennifer is to act as trustee of the trusts created for Mikayla and Hailey. Jennifer has the power to encroach upon the capital of the trust as she feels necessary for the benefit of Mikayla and Hailey. Miranda and Richard have discussed their views with Jennifer, and they have told her that they would like Mikayla and Hailey to be able to continue to attend private school, and someday attend a post-secondary educational institution.

The trusts further provide that when Mikayla and Hailey attain the age of majority (which is 19 in their province), they will be entitled to the annual income. However, the capital will remain in the trust, although Jennifer will continue to have the right to encroach upon the capital as she feels necessary. The capital of the trusts will be distributed as and when Mikayla and Hailey reach certain ages. Miranda and Richard feel that it would be best if they were each allowed to receive one-quarter of the capital upon attaining the age of 21, half of the remainder upon attaining the age of 25, and all of the remaining capital upon attaining the age of 30.

Miranda and Richard's lawyer points out to them that if they were to die tomorrow, the trusts would continue in existence for more than 21 years, given the children's current ages. Trusts are deemed to dispose of all of their assets every 21 years, and tax must be paid on any unrealized capital gains at that point. Although Miranda and Richard understand that there is the potential for an unwanted tax bill at that time, they feel that the possibility that they will both die in the near future to be small, and they are more concerned about leaving the assets in the trust for a longer period of time to ensure that the money is properly managed.

Finally, Miranda and Richard carefully consider whom they would like to nominate as guardian for Mikayla and Hailey in the event they both die while the children are still minors. After discussing the issue with Richard's brother to ensure that he is willing to accept the position, they decide to name Richard's brother, John, as the primary guardian, with Miranda's sister, Jennifer, named as the alternate guardian. Although both John and Jennifer are married, Miranda and Richard do not name their brother- or sister-in-law, in the event either one of the marriages should breakdown.

## 10.8.2 Married, With Adult Children

Colin and Marie-Claude have been married for 35 years and they have two children, Paul and Bridget. Paul is 33 and earns about $80,000 per year. Bridget is 31 and earns a similar amount, but her income is expected to increase dramatically as time goes on, as her business is doing very well. Both Paul and Bridget have indicated to their parents that they do not intend to spend their inheritance immediately, and would prefer to have their inheritances left for them in a testamentary trust, as that could result in tax advantages.

Colin and Marie-Claude decide to leave their estate to each other in trust (for further information on spousal trusts, see Case Study 5.8.2). However, at the time of death of the survivor of them, their estate is to be divided equally and transferred into two trusts, one for Paul and one for Bridget. Colin and Marie-Claude have indicated that Paul and Bridget are to act jointly as their alternate personal representatives once they are both deceased (the survivor of Colin and Marie-Claude will act as primary personal representative). Colin and Marie-Claude have also indicated that the personal representatives will act as trustees for each of the trusts, meaning that Paul and Bridget will act as trustees for each of Paul's trust and Bridget's trust.

When Colin and Marie-Claude pass away, their combined estate is worth $1,000,000 on an after-tax basis. Paul and Bridget place $500,000 in a trust for Paul, and $500,000 in a trust for Bridget. Since many of the assets are invested in capital gains producing assets, the trust does not produce excessive amounts of annual income, but it does produce about $20,000 per year, and significantly more in some years when they decide to rebalance portfolios and trigger capital gains. By the time Colin and Marie-Claude pass away, both Paul and Bridget are in the highest marginal tax bracket. If the $20,000 in annual income were taxed in their hands, they would have to pay approximately $9000 in tax annually. However, because the income is taxed in the lowest marginal tax bracket in the trust, they only pay about $5000 in taxes (note that trusts are not entitled to claim the personal tax exemption of $10,382). Over a period of 20 years, this results in a significant savings for them (over $80,000 in total). Just prior to the 21st anniversary of the creation of the trust, Paul and Bridget transfer all the remaining assets held in the trusts into their personal names on a "rollover" basis in order to avoid the deemed disposition of the assets within the trusts.

The trusts also have one other side benefit — five years after the death of his parents, Paul went through a messy divorce. Since his inheritance was locked away safely in the trust, his ex-wife was not able to claim any portion of the funds. Although inheritances are generally safe in most jurisdictions from a family property division (but not necessarily the growth), many beneficiaries fail to adequately separate the inherited money, and spend it on a family asset such as a car or home. By keeping the money clearly separate, there were no arguments as to whether or not the funds were sharable. Also, Bridget's business deteriorated suddenly about 15 years after her parents died. Although her creditors seized many of her personal investments, they were not able to seize her inheritance, as it was kept out of her personal name.

## 10.8.3 Establishing a Formal Trust for a Child

Ned has decided that he would like to set aside $500,000 for his three children, Marc, Milan and Marcial, who are all under the age of 18. After speaking with his lawyer, Ned decides to establish a formal trust. Ned asks his mother Nicole to establish the trust with a gold coin. A gold coin is used to settle trusts in order to avoid the attribution rules. If the attribution rules apply, Ned will have to pay tax on any income distributed to Marc, Milan or Marcial.

Ned's lawyer drafts the trust agreement, and Ned decides to designate himself as one of the trustees of the trust so that he may maintain some control. However, Ned also appoints his spouse and a non-related friend as trustees of the trust, and the trust agreement provides that decisions are to be made by majority vote, not unanimously. Ned then appoints Marc, Milan and Marcial as the beneficiaries of the trust, and gives the trustees complete discretion as to when income or capital may be paid out.

Ned decides that instead of transferring the funds to the trust, he will lend the $500,000 to the trust, and invest that money in capital-gains producing assets, so that any capital gains paid out to the children are taxable in their names, not Ned's. Ned then changes his will so that when the loan is repaid at the time of his death, those funds will go into a testamentary trust for Marc, Milan and Marcial, which will be managed by his executors. When Marc, Milan and Marcial turn 35, Ned's will provides that they will be entitled to receive all of the capital of the trust.

# CHAPTER 11

# GRANDCHILDREN



The arrival of grandchildren is an exciting event which can provide both wealth planning complications and opportunities. Here are some of the issues which may arise when grandchildren arrive on the scene.

## 11.1 FINANCIAL PLANNING

### 11.1.1 Giving or Lending Money to a Grandchild

Although the birth of a grandchild in and of itself generally does not necessitate the need to change your wealth plan, many individuals do review their financial and estate plan when they have grandchildren to see if there are ways in which they can benefit their grandchildren. This may be a result of several factors.

- The cost of post-secondary education is rising dramatically, and is expected to continue to do so in the future. Many grandparents want to designate money specifically for the education of their grandchildren.

- One phenomenon that has evolved as a result of our ever increasingly wealthy society is the individual who has accumulated not only sufficient wealth for themselves, but also for their children. In cases where both the grandparents and parents are sufficiently provided for, the focus of attention may shift to the next generation.

- Some individuals feel that leaving all of their assets to their children is a bad idea, since their children have proven to be spendthrifts. Alternatively, their children may have experienced failed marriages or businesses, and the grandparents do not want their assets drained by their children. Therefore, some grandparents want to leave money directly to their grandchildren since they feel that is the only way they can ensure the money will reach them.

Unfortunately, many individuals do not plan adequately when leaving money to grandchildren. If you are considering giving money to a grandchild, review sections 10.1.3, 10.1.4 and 10.1.5 of Chapter 10, "Children", for an in-depth discussion of the problems that can result when gifts are given without the proper controls, and how the use of trusts may be important when giving money to children or grandchildren. In many cases, it is better to keep the funds under your control, and only pay them out as appropriate. Another potential problem with leaving money to a grandchild is that you could potentially have more grandchildren after the date of your death. If you give money to some grandchildren, but others are born too late to receive similar gifts, this could cause animosity and resentment between family members. For these reasons, it is often not recommended that gifts be made directly to grandchildren, unless you have received appropriate advice from your lawyers as to how to structure the gift.

Despite the drawbacks mentioned above, if you do decide to set aside some money for your grandchildren immediately, see Case Study 10.8.3 for a discussion of the issues to consider.

The issues involved with lending money to a grandchild are similar to those that arise when lending money to a child. See section 10.1.4 in Chapter 10, "Children", for a discussion of the issues that should be considered when entering into this type of arrangement.

## 11.1.2 Registered Education Savings Plans

As discussed in section 10.1.1 of Chapter 10, "Children", parents and grandparents can establish Registered Education Savings Plans ("RESPs") for minors in order to save for their post-secondary education. Contributions made to the RESP are not tax-deductible, but the income accrues on a tax-deferred basis, until such time as it is withdrawn for educational purposes, at which point it is taxable in the hands of the child, who presumably will be in a lower tax bracket than the contributor. In addition, the federal government will match 20% of any contributions (and in some cases, 30 or 40%) made for a minor who is a resident of Canada, subject to certain rules that are discussed in section 10.1.1 of Chapter 10, "Children". The government contributions are known as the Canada Education Savings Grant (the "CESG"). It is important to ensure that contributions are made in a manner that maximizes both the amount of CESG as well as the tax-deferred compounding.

However, be careful when establishing an RESP for a grandchild. Here are a couple of issues that can arise when the grandparent chooses to create an RESP, and therefore acts as the "subscriber" of the plan.

- As discussed in section 10.1.2 of Chapter 10, "Children", if a child does not pursue post-secondary education, then the contributor to the RESP may be able to transfer a portion of the accrued income into their RRSP without penalty (to a maximum of $50,000). Any income and growth not transferred to their RRSP is subject to tax as well as a penalty. If the subscriber is over 71, however, they cannot reduce the amount subject to tax by transferring the income and growth to an RRSP, since you cannot make contributions to an RRSP after the year in which you turn 71. There is no corresponding provision in the *Income Tax Act* that allows for the transfer of funds in an RESP to a RRIF, so the penalty tax could be much higher if the contributor is over 71 at the time the grandchild decides not to pursue post-secondary education.

- Only the original subscriber is entitled to transfer the income and growth to their RRSP as referred to above. If a grandparent was the original subscriber, but they have passed on before the grandchildren made the decision not to attend a post secondary educational institution, then, again, the penalty tax may be higher than if a parent had been an original subscriber to the RESP (if a parent becomes a subscriber to the RESP upon the death of a grandparent, they will not be entitled to rollover such amounts to their RRSP).

Contributors must also realize that there is a limit as to how much can be contributed to an RESP. Although the lifetime limit is $50,000, CESG will only be paid on a maximum of $2500 of contributions each year (CESG "room" can be carried forward, but CESGs will not be paid on more than $5000 of contributions in any one year.) This means that contributions must be started by the time the grandchild reaches the age of ten in order to receive the maximum CESG, and the contributor must make $5000 in contributions for seven years, and then $1000 in the eighth year. Grandparents must be careful when establishing RESPs to ensure that the parents have not already established a plan for the grandchild. Although several RESPs may be established for the same beneficiary, the contribution limits remain the same, so the subscribers should communicate with each other as to how much they have contributed, or there could be a 1% penalty charged on over-contributions. Also, multiple plans are generally not a good idea from an investment perspective, as it may be more difficult to develop a sufficiently broad asset allocation with smaller amounts.

If grandparents want to assist their children in saving for the educational needs of their grandchildren, it may be best if they simply give the money to their children, and have them make the contributions to a plan where the parent is the subscriber. In that way, there is less chance of an overcontribution, and in the event the child does not pursue a post-secondary education, the parents may be able to roll the contributions over into their RRSPs (although only if they have sufficient room available to allow for such a rollover). Note that if a beneficiary of an RESP does not use the money on post-secondary education, the CESG will have to be refunded to the government.

However, giving money to a child to contribute to a grandchild's RESP may not be appropriate in all cases.

- The grandparents must be comfortable giving up control of their contributions to the RESP, and understand that once they give the money to their child, the child will be entitled to manage the funds in the RESP, or withdraw them, without the grandparents' consent.

- There is no creditor protection for RESPs, so if their child has creditor exposure, it may not be appropriate to give the money to them. In some cases, the contributions could even be included in a division of family property in the event of relationship breakdown. If this is a concern, then again, it may not be appropriate to give the money to the child first.

If the grandparent wishes to make contributions above those allowed for in an RESP (either because the parent is already maximizing their contributions, or because the grandchild would like to take an educational program that is particularly expensive), they may prefer to establish a trust, since there is more flexibility as to how the funds can be used, and there is no maximum on the amount that can be contributed. A grandparent could also make himself or herself a beneficiary of the trust, or make their children the capital beneficiaries, with grandchildren being the income beneficiaries, which may allow for more flexibility in using the funds. See section 10.1.3 of Chapter 10, "Children", for a discussion of the issues to be considered when establishing a trust. However, strategies involving a trust are generally only appropriate where large sums of money are involved. If a grandparent simply wants to supplement a grandchild's educational expenses, the simplest method, other than providing sums to a child to invest in a grandchild's RESP, is to simply provide such sums directly to the grandchild as and when required.

## 11.2 TAX PLANNING

If you are raising a grandchild as a child, review section 10.2 of Chapter 10, "Children", for a discussion of the tax planning strategies you can use to minimize taxes. Generally speaking, you will be able to claim the same expenses and credits when raising a grandchild as you would when raising a child.

## 11.3 FAMILY LAW ISSUES

If you are raising a grandchild as a child, review section 10.3 of Chapter 10, "Children", for a discussion of the family law issues to be considered.

## 11.4 DISABILITY PLANNING

If you are raising a grandchild as a child, review section 10.4 of Chapter 10, "Children", for a discussion of the disability planning strategies you should consider to protect you and your grandchild in the event of disability.

# 11.5 ESTATE PLANNING

## 11.5.1 Review Your Estate Plan

The birth of a grandchild may be a good time to review your estate plan to ensure that all family members will be treated equitably. Without realizing it, many individuals have structured their estate plan in a way which could potentially leave one branch of their family with less than the other(s). Here are a few examples of how grandchildren can be disinherited inadvertently.

- If your will was written some time ago, it may have stated that if any of your children predeceased you, their share of the estate was to go to their siblings. Now that your children have children of their own, it is important to ensure that the will states that if a child predeceases you, that their share is to be divided equally between their own children, if that is the intent.

- If you have an insurance policy, segregated funds, or a RRSP or RRIF with a direct beneficiary designation, it may be useful to review those designations. For example, the beneficiary of this type of plan (or alternate beneficiary, if the spouse is the primary beneficiary) may be all of your children. Again, if one of the children predeceases you, the children of that deceased child may not be entitled to any of those funds, and the assets may pass directly to the surviving children. (Note that direct beneficiary designations on RRSPs and RRIFs are not effective in all cases in Quebec.)

- If you are holding an asset in joint names with your children with a right of survivorship, then upon the time of your death, the joint owners may receive the property. Again, if one of your children predeceases you, the children of that deceased child may not receive any of that jointly held property. (Note that jointly held property does not have a right of survivorship in Quebec.)

Many of the strategies listed above are often undertaken for the purposes of saving probate fees. However, in many jurisdictions, the probate fees are not significant, and the disadvantages inherent in attempting to save probate are not properly understood. See Chapter 22, "Probate", for further information.

If part of an estate will be left directly to a grandchild through your will or by way of a direct beneficiary designation, it is important to ensure that proper controls are placed on the gift, especially if the grandchild is a minor. See sections 10.5.3 and 10.6.2 in Chapter 10, "Children". If the grandchild is disabled, then it is particularly important that the will be structured in a way which will provide maximum advantage to the grandchild. If your grandchild is disabled, see Chapter 12, "Disabled Persons", for a discussion regarding the methods by which social assistance payments can be preserved, and inheritances can be received in an appropriate manner.

## 11.5.2 Leaving Money to Grandchildren in a Will

If you are going to leave a grandchild a gift in your will, here are some of the issues you should keep in mind.

- Is it possible that you could have more grandchildren after you are gone? If a grandparent leaves a certain portion of their estate to be divided equally between the grandchildren who are alive at the time of their death, it is quite possible that grandchildren born after that date will feel resentment for receiving less of the estate. If a grandparent simply leaves their estate to their children, then their children can divide their estate equally between their children, including any grandchildren born sometime after the grandparents are gone.

- Do your children truly have sufficient assets of their own? Although your children may appear to be financially self-sufficient, it is possible that they are concerned about saving for their own retirement and long-term care costs. If money is left to a grandchild, it is possible that a grandchild could have more disposable income than their parent, causing resentment and angst between family members. There have been frequent instances where parents have found it impossible to discipline children who have received money from their grandparents, since the grandchildren feel that they have the money, and, therefore, the power to do as they please. In other cases, the money has been given on the condition that it be held in trust until the child reaches a certain age — if the parents are not financially comfortable, then instead of the money being used to improve the standard of living for the grandchild, it may have to be kept invested for a long time.

- When do the grandparents anticipate that the grandchildren should receive their inheritance? If no age is specified in the will, they will receive the sum at the time they reach the age of majority. See section 10.5.3 in Chapter 10, "Children", for a discussion about the need to apply conditions when minors will receive their inheritance, and the use of testamentary trusts.

- The grandparents should also think carefully about who they will appoint as their personal representative for their estate. If they appoint only one of their three children (for example, because the other two are non-residents of Canada — see Chapter 20, "Personal Representatives"), and the personal representative is also to act as trustee of any testamentary trusts, then it is possible that the appointed child will be acting as trustee for a trust established for one of his or her nieces or nephews. Depending upon the family dynamics, this may or may not result in disagreements.

- Many grandparents want to leave a small amount of money to their grandchildren as a token only. However, if the money is to be held in trust until they attain a more mature age (such as 21 or 25), consider how practical it will be to hold a small sum in trust for a long period of time. If you have grandchildren who are two or three years old when you die, and you leave them $5000 each in trust, the personal representative of your estate will be very limited in what they can invest in, and it may become very cumbersome to file tax returns for each of the trusts. Although you may have the best intentions when making the gift, if you have quite a few young grandchildren, and you are leaving small sums to each of them, consider carefully whether or not it would be better to simply leave your estate to your children.

Although leaving a legacy to a grandchild through a will is a generous and usually appreciated gesture, care must be taken to ensure that the gift achieves the desired objectives. In many cases, upon examining the issues, the grandparents choose to simply leave their estate to their children, and choose not to further complicate matters by making a direct gift to a grandchild.

## 11.6 INSURANCE PLANNING

See section 10.6 of Chapter 10, "Children", for some of the issues to consider if you would like to purchase insurance for a grandchild, or name them as a beneficiary on one of your existing policies.

## 11.7 JURISDICTION DIFFERENCES

There are no jurisdiction differences for this chapter.

# 11.8 CASE STUDIES

## 11.8.1 Leaving Money to a Grandchild in a Will

Quinn and Quinten decide that they have left more than enough money to their children, Ria and Ray in their will. They would like to leave some money in their will directly to their grandchildren, Stephanie and Steven, to help fund their post-secondary education. Stephanie and Steven are currently ten and twelve, and Quinn and Quinten are fairly certain that Ray and Ria will not be having any more children. Quinn and Quinten discuss the issue with their lawyer, and decide to leave $20,000 to each of Stephanie and Steven in their will.

Due to the young ages of Stephanie and Steven, however, Quinn and Quinten do not want them to receive the money immediately. In fact, if Quinn and Quinten were to die soon, it is quite possible that the money would have to be managed by the provincial authorities, which is not what Quinn and Quinten intended. Therefore, they provide in their wills that Ray and Ria are to act as trustees of trusts established for Stephanie and Steven. Ray and Ria can pay out the income and encroach upon the capital of the trust whenever they deem it to be appropriate although Stephanie and Steven will be entitled to receive all the annual income upon reaching the age of majority. The trust capital is to be paid out to Stephanie and Steven in stages — one quarter when they turn 21, half of the remainder when they turn 25, and all of the remaining funds when they reach the age of 30. Quinn and Quinten further provide that the gift is not meant to be a divisible asset under the prevailing family law legislation.

# CHAPTER 12



# Disabled Persons

Coping with a disability, or caring for a loved one with a disability, can bring many unique challenges. Whether the disability is physical or mental, you will want to ensure that you have taken advantage of any tax or social assistance benefits that may be available to you. If you are taking care of a disabled person, you also will want to ensure not only that you are aware of any services that may be available to them now, but that they are properly taken care of after you are gone. This chapter discusses some of the planning opportunities and issues to consider if you or a family member has a disability.

## 12.1 FINANCIAL PLANNING

### 12.1.1 Social Assistance Payments

Many jurisdictions offer social assistance to individuals who have few assets and/or low income. If you or your child is not able to earn an income, inquire with the municipal or provincial authorities as to the requirements for obtaining social assistance. (See section 12.5, "Jurisdiction Differences", for more information on the rules regarding social assistance in your jurisdiction.)

### 12.1.2 CPP Disability Benefits

If you have a "severe and prolonged" disability, you may be eligible to receive Canada Pension Plan ("CPP") disability benefits. In order for a disability to be considered "severe", you must not be able to work regularly at any job, and in order for it to be "prolonged", your condition must be long term.

In order to receive disability payments, you must have contributed to the CPP during four out of the six years previous to the disability. If you qualify, benefits will start four months after you have been classified as disabled, and will continue until you begin to receive CPP retirement benefits, or the time of your death, whichever is earlier. You must be between the ages of 18 and 65 to qualify.

If you qualify to receive a disability benefit and if you have a dependant child under 18 years of age, or a child who is between 18 and 25 and who is attending school full time, they may also be entitled to receive a monthly benefit.

CPP disability benefits are generally considered taxable income, but no deductions will be made from the payments unless you request them. You should try to calculate the amount of tax you may have to pay as a result of receiving the payments, and either save the appropriate amount each month or fill out the form entitled *Request for Voluntary Federal Income Tax Deductions* to have the appropriate amount deducted from your cheque.

If you live in Quebec, you may be entitled to receive payments under the Quebec Pension Plan ("QPP"). Please see section 12.5.11 for a description of the rules in Quebec.

### 12.1.3 Registered Disability Savings Plans

Registered disability savings plans ("RDSPs") are a long-term savings vehicle for persons with disabilities. They operate in a manner somewhat similar to RESPs, in that contributions are not tax deductible, but they grow on a tax-deferred basis within the plan, and may attract the payment of government grants and bonds. However, unlike RESPs, unless the contributor is also the beneficiary of the plan (i.e. the disabled person), they are not entitled to withdraw their contributions – only the disabled person may withdraw any funds in the plan. In order to open a plan, the beneficiary of the plan must be eligible for the disability tax credit (as discussed in section 12.2.1), and be a resident of Canada at the time any contributions are made. Only one account may be opened in respect of any one beneficiary, and there is a lifetime contribution limit of $200,000, although there are no annual contribution limits. Contributions are not allowed after the year in which the disabled beneficiary turns 59.

Contributions to an RDSP may result in the payment of a Canada Disability Savings Grant ("CDSG") based on the "family net income" of the beneficiary and the amount contributed. The government will match the first $500 in contributions with a CDSG in the amount of 300% of the contribution, if the family earns less than approximately $75,000 annually, and 200% of the next $1,000 contributed in a taxation year, to a maximum annual grant of $3,500. This means that a contribution of $1,500 can result in $3,500 in grants, for a total of $5,000 in the RDSP in any given year. The maximum amount of grant that may be received by any one beneficiary over the course of their lifetime is $70,000.

In addition, families with very low income levels may qualify for a Canada Disability Savings Bond ("CDSB") of up to $1000 per year, with a $20,000 lifetime limit. Disabled persons who are from very low income families should open an RDSP simply to obtain the CDSB, since the bond is payable even if no contribution is made. Once a beneficiary turns 18, it is only their income (and their spouse's) which is relevant when calculating "family net income", so adult disabled persons who earn less than $20,000 should open an RDSP simply to receive the $1000 bond, although they will not be able to immediately withdraw this money without penalty, as discussed below. The maximum CDSB grant is $1,000 for eligible individuals with incomes below approximately $20,000. This bond is indexed, with no CDSB available for incomes over approximately $37,000. CDSGs and CDSBs will not be payable after the year in which the beneficiary turns 49.

If the family earns more than approximately $75,000, no CDSG or CDSB will be paid. However, once the beneficiary turns 18, it is only their income that will be included in the calculation of family income, not their parents', so it may be worthwhile for higher income families to wait until their children are adults before making contributions.

When contributions are withdrawn, they must go to the disabled beneficiary, not the contributor (unless the contributor is also the beneficiary). Therefore, if the beneficiary suffers from a mental illness, such as schizophrenia, making contributions to an RDSP may not be recommended. No withdrawal of the contributions can be made without some portion of the withdrawal representing taxable amounts (which could include the government grants and bonds, as well as income or growth on the investments in the plan). These amounts will be taxed in the hands of the beneficiary. However, once the money goes into the plan, it has to stay there for ten years before the disabled person can take it out without penalty. Any time a withdrawal is made from an RDSP, it will trigger a full clawback of the "assistance holdback amount", which consists of the total amount of grants and bonds paid into the plan in the preceding ten-year period. Therefore, RDSPs are generally recommended in situations where it is anticipated that the beneficiary will not require the funds for many years.



Contributions can be made to the RDSP up until the end of the year the beneficiary turns 59. At that time, the total RDSP must be used to purchase an annuity for the beneficiary. The monthly amount received would be dependent on the life expectancy of the beneficiary (which can vary tremendously depending upon the disability) and the amount accumulated in the plan. Here are a few additional points of interest regarding RDSPs.

- Withdrawals from an RDSP will not impact how much Old Age Security a beneficiary may be entitled to.

- The plan must be wound up if the beneficiary ceases to qualify for the disability tax credit, resulting in the repayment of the government benefits and the taxation of amounts earned in the plan. Therefore, if the disability is of a nature that may be "cured" in the future (an example may be a situation where a person suffering from a hearing problem is able to have implants in the future), then you should consider carefully whether or not an RDSP is appropriate for you, particularly if you are from a high-income family.

- RDSPs are not a replacement for Henson trusts, which are discussed in section 12.3.1. Inheritances to a disabled child should still be left to a Henson trust, but consideration should be given to allow the trustee to make contributions to an RDSP in favour of the beneficiary (and also relieve them from liability if they choose not to do so).

### 12.1.4 RESPs for Disabled Students

The concept of an RESP is discussed in section 10.1.2 of Chapter 10, "Children". However, there are some modifications to the rules for RESPs to address the special needs of students with disabilities.

- The requirement that a beneficiary be enrolled on a full-time basis will not apply where the beneficiary cannot reasonably be expected to be enrolled as a full-time student because of a mental or physical impairment. A medical doctor or a medical practitioner, such as an optometrist, audiologist, psychologist or occupational therapist, as applicable, must certify in writing that the beneficiary has such an impairment.
- Normally contributions may only be made over a 31-year time period. For disabled students, the contribution period is extended to 35 years.
- Normally all funds in an RESP must be withdrawn within 35 years from the date on which the RESP was established. For disabled students, this time period is extended to 40 years.

## 12.1.5 Study Grants for Disabled Students

In addition to the other forms of financial assistance that governments make available to students (e.g. Canada Student Loans and Millennium Scholarships), there are two types of federal grants developed particularly for post-secondary education students with disabilities.

1. *The Canada Study Grant for the Accommodation of Students with Permanent Disabilities.* This grant is worth up to $8000, and is intended to fund education expenses to accommodate the special needs of persons with disabilities such as tutoring, note takers and sign language interpreters.
2. *The Canada Access Grant for Students with Permanent Disabilities.* This grant is worth up to $2000, and is intended to fund educational costs such as tuition, books, supplies and other education-related expenses for students who demonstrate financial need.

You can find more information regarding these programs at *www.hrsdc.gc.ca/eng/learning/canada_student_loan/grant2.shtml.* You can find out more about additional local provincial programs by contacting your Minister responsible for education.

## 12.1.6 Lifelong Learning Plan

The Lifelong Learning Plan ("LLP") is a federal program that allows individuals to withdraw $20,000 from an RRSP for the purpose of funding their post-secondary education. Normally, the LLP may only be used for the purpose of funding post-secondary education if the student is attending classes full-time. However, students suffering from a disability may make withdrawals under the LLP even if they are only attending classes part-time. This concession is available if the student cannot reasonably be expected to be enrolled as a full-time student because of a certified mental or physical impairment, and the educational program requires the student to spend ten hours or more per week on courses or work in the program.



### 12.1.7 Home Buyer's Plan

The Home Buyer's Plan ("HBP") allows "first-time" home buyers to withdraw $25,000 from their RRSP for the purpose of buying a home. Normally, withdrawals may only be made under the HBP where the taxpayer has not owned a home within the last five years. However, for individuals with a disability, you do not need to be a first-time home buyer if you are using the funds to purchase a home that is more accessible for, or better suited for the care of, an individual with a disability.

## 12.2 TAX PLANNING

There are a myriad of income tax benefits available for persons with disabilities. In addition to the information provided below, there is information available on the Canada Revenue Agency Web site at *www.cra-arc.gc.ca* or their guide RC4064, *Information Concerning People with a Disability*. Due to the complexity of our tax system, and the intricacies involved in claiming all of these credits, you should speak to a tax professional prior to filing your income tax return to ensure you are maximizing the use of these credits, and claiming the credits properly.

### 12.2.1 Disability Tax Credit

If you or your child suffers from a disability, you or your child may qualify for the disability tax credit of $7239. However, if you qualify for the disability tax credit, you may also qualify for many other tax benefits, since the ability to claim the disability tax credit is usually one of the criteria for claiming other amounts or accessing other programs (such as the ability to open an RDSP). Here are some of the things you will need, and some things to consider, when applying for the credit.

### *12.2.1.1 Disability Tax Credit Certificate*

In order to receive the disability tax credit, you will need to complete Form T2201, "Disability Tax Credit Certificate", and file it with your tax return. The certificate must describe:

- the nature of the impairment;
- the manner in which the impairment has affected your (or your child's) ability to perform a basic activity of daily living; and
- the expected duration of the impairment, which must be for a continuous period of at least 12 months.

Part of the certificate must be completed by a qualified practitioner (as described in section 12.2.1.3), and the Canada Revenue Agency must validate the certificate before you will be entitled to receive the credit.

### *12.2.1.2 Basic Activities of Daily Living*

There are effectively three criteria for eligibility for the disability tax credit. You will be entitled to claim the credit if:

1. you are blind (even with the assistance of corrective lenses or medication);
2. you are markedly restricted in your ability to perform a basic activity of daily living; or
3. you would be markedly restricted were it not for extensive therapy to sustain a vital function.

Basic activities of daily living are described as:

- perceiving, thinking and remembering;
- feeding yourself;
- dressing yourself;
- speaking;
- hearing;

- eliminating (bladder or bowel functions); and
- walking.

An individual may also qualify for the disability tax credit if the individual has multiple symptoms that, on a cumulative basis, have an impact similar to a marked restriction on any one activity of daily living.



Individuals who have a severe and prolonged impairment do not need to prove a marked restriction in a basic activity of daily living if they can prove that they would have such a restriction if they were not receiving therapy that:

- is essential to sustain a vital function;
- is required to be administered at least three times each week for a total duration averaging not less than 14 hours a week; and
- cannot reasonably be expected to be of significant benefit to persons who are not so impaired.

### *12.2.1.3 Qualified Practitioners*

The individuals who are qualified to complete the Form T2201 are:

- medical doctors;
- optometrists (for vision impairment);
- audiologists (for hearing impairments);
- occupational therapists (for walking, feeding and dressing impairments);
- psychologists (for mental function impairments);
- speech language pathologists (for speaking impairments); and
- physiotherapists (for walking or mobility impairments).

### 12.2.1.4 Ask for a Review if Your Claim is Denied

If you are originally denied your claim for the disability tax credit, consider asking the Canada Revenue Agency for a second review. This second review will be carried out by a different staff person, and may lead to a different result, but you must generally ask for the review in order to receive it (the Canada Revenue Agency generally will not volunteer them). If the claim is still denied, a Notice of Objection can be filed with the Canada Revenue Agency for a formal review of the decision.

### 12.2.1.5 Transfer Unused Credits to a Supporting Person

If you are (or your child is) unable to use the disability tax credit due to low income, it can be transferred to a "supporting person", which includes a spouse or common-law partner, a parent, grandparent, child, grandchild, brother, sister, aunt, uncle, nephew or niece of the individual. (For these purposes, a common-law partner is an individual who has lived with the taxpayer in a conjugal relationship either for a period of one year, or for a lesser period of time, but they are raising a child together.)

### 12.2.1.6 Attendant Care Costs

You may not claim the disability tax credit if you claim attendant care or nursing home expenses as a medical expense, other than certain attendant care costs that do not exceed $10,000 (as described in section 12.2.5.2). Speak to your accountant about which option is more beneficial for you.

### 12.2.1.7 Additional Amount for Children

If your child qualifies for the disability tax credit, they may also be able to claim the disability tax credit supplement that is available for children with severe and prolonged disabilities. The maximum amount of the supplement is a tax credit of an additional $4223. However, the amount of the supplemental tax credit is reduced dollar-for-dollar by the amount of child care expenses or attendant care expenses that are claimed as a medical expense over $2473.

## 12.2.2 Wholly Dependent Person Credit

You will be entitled to claim the wholly dependent person credit if you are providing support in your home to:

- a related adult who suffers from an infirmity;
- a relative under the age of 18; or
- a parent or grandparent.

The dependant must be wholly dependent upon you for support at some time during the year, and unless he or she is your child, the dependant must be resident in Canada. The support can be provided jointly with another person or persons, but only one person may claim the credit, or the parties must agree as to how the credit will be shared.

The maximum amount of the credit is $10,382, but this is reduced on a dollar-for-dollar basis based on the dependant's net income.

You may not claim this credit if you are married or in a common-law relationship, although you may claim the credit if you are separated and not receiving support from your spouse or common-law partner or paying support to your spouse or common-law partner. This credit is sometimes referred to as the "equivalent to spouse" credit, since you may not claim both this credit and the spousal credit at the same time. You may not claim this credit for more than one person.

If you claim this credit in respect of an individual, you may not claim the caregiver credit or the infirm dependant credit discussed in sections 12.2.3 and 12.2.4 below. However, you may apply for an additional amount in cases where the value of the caregiver credit or the infirm dependant credit (had you been able to claim either of those) would have exceeded the value of the wholly dependent person credit.

## 12.2.3 Caregiver Credit

You may be entitled to claim the caregiver tax credit if you provide in-home care to:

- an adult relative (including an adult child or grandchild, parent, grandparent, brother, sister, aunt, uncle, niece or nephew of either yourself or your spouse or common-law partner) who is dependent upon you due to a mental or physical infirmity; or

- a parent or grandparent over the age of 65.

You cannot claim this credit in respect of care given to a spouse or common-law partner and you will not be entitled to claim this credit if you deduct support payments made to a spouse or a common-law partner. The maximum credit is approximately $4200, and is reduced dollar-for-dollar once the dependant's net income reaches approximately $14,400, so that it is fully phased out once the dependant's net income is approximately $18,600.

If you choose to claim the caregiver credit in respect of a dependant, then you will not be entitled to claim the wholly dependent person credit or the infirm dependant credit described in sections 12.2.2 and 12.2.4 in respect of that same dependant, and vice versa. Also, if you claim one of these two credits in respect of a dependant, no other person may also claim either of these two credits in respect of that same dependant. However, two taxpayers may split the maximum allowable credit in respect of that dependant.

## 12.2.4 Infirm Dependant Credit

You may be able to claim the infirm dependant credit if you support a child, grandchild, niece, nephew, parent, grandparent, brother, sister, aunt or uncle who is:

- 18 years of age or older; and
- dependent upon you due to a mental or physical infirmity.

You cannot claim this credit in respect of a spouse or common-law partner or if you are deducting support paid to a spouse or common-law partner. The amount of the credit is approximately $4200, which is reduced dollar-for-dollar by the dependant's income over approximately $6000, being completely eliminated when the dependant's income reaches approximately $10,200.

If you claim the infirm dependant credit in respect of a dependant, you will not be entitled to claim the wholly dependent person credit or the caregiver credit described in sections 12.2.2 and 12.2.3 in respect of that same dependant, nor will anyone else.

## 12.2.5 Medical Expense Credit

### *12.2.5.1 Claiming the Medical Expense Credit*

Under the *Income Tax Act,* you may claim a medical expense tax credit for medical expenses incurred by you, your spouse or common-law partner, or children under the age of 18, which exceed the lesser of 3% of your net income, or a set threshold, which is approximately $2000. You must provide receipts for any medical expenses you wish to claim. You may not claim a medical expense that has been otherwise reimbursed.

There is no limit on the amount of medical expenses that you may claim if they were incurred for the benefit of yourself, your spouse or common-law partner, or minor children. However, you may also claim medical expenses incurred for a dependent relative, such as a parent, grandparent, brother, sister, aunt, uncle, niece or nephew, so long as those expenses do not exceed $10,000. If you are claiming medical expenses in respect of a dependent relative, then you may claim expenses in excess of the lesser of the current threshold (which is approximately $2000) or 3% of the *dependant's* net income, not yours.

Medical expenses cannot be carried forward. However, you can choose any 12 month period ending in the tax year, and the 12 month period does not need to be the same every year, so try to time expenses so that they are maximized in one year, so that more expenses exceed the threshold.

Medical expenses can be pooled between spouses (which could include married couples, or common-law couples who have cohabited for at least a year, or for a lesser period of time, but who are raising a child together). It may be easier to exceed the threshold if you pool your expenses together and then claim them on one return.

Expenses that are claimed as an attendant care deduction or disability support deduction may not also be claimed as a medical expense. See section 12.2.7 and 12.2.8 for further discussion on these types of deductions.

### *12.2.5.2 What Qualifies as a Medical Expense*

The following items will qualify as a medical expense for the purposes of the medical expense tax credit:

- an amount paid to a medical practitioner, dentist or nurse or a public or licensed private hospital in respect of medical or dental services (this includes amounts paid to provincially licenced chiropractors, masseuses, naturopaths and optometrists, in those jurisdictions that recognize these disciplines). Hospital costs over and above what is covered by the province are eligible medical expenses (e.g. the cost of a private room), as are costs incurred outside of Canada (which are not reimbursed);

- remuneration for one full-time attendant (other than the patient's spouse or common-law partner, or a person under the age of 18), or for full-time care in a nursing home;

- remuneration for attendant care provided in Canada if:

  - the patient qualifies for the disability tax credit (see section 12.2.1);

  - the attendant is not the patient's spouse or common-law partner, or a person under the age of 18;

  - the amounts are not deducted as attendant care costs (see section 12.2.7); and

  - the expenses do not exceed $10,000;

- remuneration for care or supervision in a group home operated exclusively for the benefit of individuals who have a severe and prolonged impairment, if:

  - the patient qualifies for the disability tax credit (see section 12.2.1);

  - the amounts are not deducted as attendant care costs (see section 12.2.7); and

  - each receipt contains the payee's social insurance number;

- remuneration for one full-time attendant in the patient's home if:

  - the patient has been certified in writing by a medical practitioner to be a person who, by reason of mental or physical infirmity, is likely to be dependent on others for their personal needs indefinitely;

  - the attendant is not the patient's spouse or common-law partner, or a person under the age of 18; and

  - each receipt contains the payee's social insurance number;

- an amount paid for full-time care in a nursing home for a patient who has been certified by a medical practitioner in writing to be a person who, by reason of lack of normal mental capacity, is dependent upon others for their personal care;

- for the care and training at a school or institution of a patient who has been certified in writing to be a person who by reason of a physical or mental handicap, requires special care or training;

- amounts paid for items such as ambulance fees, artificial limbs, braces, eyeglasses, guide dogs, wheel chairs, organ transplants and other related items; and

- the cost of prescription drugs and medications used in the diagnosis, treatment or prevention of a disease or disorder.



Many expenses that persons with disabilities incur in order to go to work or school are eligible for the medical expense tax credit, including tutoring for persons with learning disabilities, sign language interpreter fees and talking textbooks.

The above list is not exhaustive. If you are unsure as to whether or not an expense will qualify as a medical expense, go to the Canada Revenue Agency Web site at *www.cra-arc.gc.ca*, and review the list of allowable expenses in Interpretation Bulletin IT-519R2.

### *12.2.5.3 Home Construction and Renovations*

If prescribed, you can include reasonable expenses relating to the construction, renovation or alteration of a dwelling as a medical expense for a patient who lacks normal physical development or has a severe and prolonged mobility impairment, to enable the patient to gain access to, or to be mobile or functional within the dwelling. However, the expense must not typically be expected to increase the value of the home, and the expense must be of a type that would not typically be incurred by persons without such an impairment. Therefore, it is unlikely that items such as hardwood floors or hot tubs would qualify as a medical expense.

### *12.2.5.4 Travel and Meal Expenses*

Transportation costs are allowed if you must travel a distance in excess of 40 km to obtain services that are not otherwise available closer to home. If the patient is unable to travel without the assistance of an attendant, travel costs will also be allowed for one additional person.

Meal costs are allowed if you must travel at least 80 km in order to receive the medical treatment. If the patient is unable to travel without the assistance of an attendant, meal costs will also be allowed for one additional person.

### *12.2.5.5 Disability Tax Credit*

If any amounts in respect of remuneration for an attendant or care in a nursing home are claimed as a medical expense, other than the maximum deduction of $10,000 referred to in section 12.2.5.2 above, the disability tax credit will be denied.

### *12.2.5.6 Tuition Fees*

If you have a child with a disability, tuition fees paid to a private school may be claimed as a medical expense in some cases, although it is relatively difficult to meet the conditions for claiming tuition fees as a medical expense. Here are the four requirements that must be met.

- The taxpayer must pay an amount for the care, or care and training, of the patient at a school, institution or other place.

- The patient must suffer from a mental or physical handicap.

- The school, institution or other place must specifically provide to the patient suffering from the handicap, equipment, facilities or personnel for the care or the care and training of the person suffering from the same handicap. This condition may be hard to meet if all the students, regardless of special needs, have access and benefit to the same services, although a "mixed-function" school or institution may satisfy the requirements.

- An appropriately qualified practitioner must certify that the mental or physical handicap is the reason the patient requires that the school specially provide the equipment, facilities or personnel for the care or the care and training of individuals suffering from the same handicap. The certification must specify:

- the mental or physical disability suffered by the patient; and

- the equipment, facilities or personnel required to obtain the care or training needed to deal with that disability.



### 12.2.6 Refundable Medical Expense Supplement

The refundable medical expense supplement helps to pay for medical expenses, since many disabled people experience a decrease in social assistance payments when they start to earn an income from employment. You and your spouse must earn at least $3000 in employment or business income in order to qualify for this supplement. The amount of the supplement is decreased by 5% of family income in excess of $23,000.

The maximum refundable medical expense supplement is 25% of the allowable portion of expenses that can be claimed under the medical expense tax credit plus 25% of the amount claimed under the disability supports deduction (discussed in section 12.2.8), up to a maximum of approximately $1000. This credit is also relatively unique in that it is refundable, which means that a taxpayer will be entitled to a refund if the amount of the supplement exceeds their net federal tax.

When calculating the credit, you need to use the same 12 months of expenses as you used for the medical expense credit.

### 12.2.7 Attendant Care Costs Deduction

If you incur costs for the purposes of hiring an attendant so that you can work, run a business or go to school, you may be able to deduct these costs from your income, to the extent that you have not been otherwise reimbursed. Attendant care costs may be deducted where:

- you have a mental or physical infirmity;

- the attendant care services are provided in Canada;

- the services are provided by a person who is an adult who is neither your spouse nor common-law partner; and

- you either qualify for the disability tax credit (as discussed in section 12.2.1), or a medical practitioner has certified in writing that because of your infirmity, you are likely to be indefinitely dependent on others for your personal needs and care, and therefore require a full-time attendant.

The maximum amount that can be claimed is two-thirds of your earned income from work or business. If you are in school, then the maximum amount that can be claimed is two-thirds of your earned income from work or business plus the least of:

- $15,000;
- $375 times the number of weeks during which you are in attendance; and
- your taxable income other than earned income.

If you are not employed, running a business or going to school, you may be able to claim your attendant care costs as a medical expense (see section 12.2.5). Generally speaking, using the attendant care tax deduction is more valuable than the medical expense credit under the circumstances described below.

- A tax deduction will lower your taxable income on a dollar-for-dollar basis, unlike a tax credit, which is applied to your tax payable, and is calculated by multiplying the amount by the lowest tax rate (i.e., 15% federally). Therefore, for those with income above the lowest tax bracket, it would be more beneficial to receive the attendant care tax deduction, which avoids having income taxed in the highest tax bracket, than to receive the medical expense tax credit based on the lowest tax bracket.
- Expenses claimed as attendant care costs are 100% deductible — with the medical expense credit, only expenses which exceed a certain threshold may be included in the credit.
- A tax deduction immediately lowers your net income, making it easier to qualify for social assistance payments. With a tax credit, your tax payable is decreased, but your net income is not affected, making it more likely that you will not receive as much in social assistance payments.

In most cases, it will be more beneficial to claim the amount as a tax deduction, but if you do not qualify for the attendant care tax deduction, then you may still obtain some benefit by claiming the amount as a medical expense.

## 12.2.8 Disability Supports Deduction

The cost of disability supports that are purchased for the purpose of employment or education is fully deductible, to the extent that the expense has not been otherwise reimbursed. Individuals do not have to be eligible for the disability tax credit in order to claim these expenses as a tax deduction (unlike the attendant care deduction, which is discussed in section 12.2.7), but they must file receipts to evidence payment for the supports and file the prescribed form. Although the list of disability supports eligible for the tax deduction is too extensive to enumerate here, the list does include sign-language interpretation services, real-time captioning services, deaf-blind intervening services, teletypewriters or similar devices, optical scanners and similar devices and electronic speech synthesizers. The type of support allowed will depend upon the impairment in question. A complete list can be found on the Canada Revenue Agency's Web site at *www.cra-arc.gc.ca.*



The maximum amount that can be claimed is the lesser of:

- the total expenses paid in the year, to the extent they are not reimbursed; and
- two-thirds of your earned income from work or business.

However, if you are attending a designated educational institution, then it is the lesser of the amount of un-reimbursed expenses or two-thirds of your earned income plus the least of:

- $15,000;
- $375 times the number of weeks during which you are in attendance; and
- your taxable income other than earned income.

If the disability support was purchased for a purpose other than employment or education, then the taxpayer may be able to claim the expense as a medical expense (see section 12.2.5). If you deduct the expense as a disability support for employment or education, then you will not also be entitled to claim the expense as a medical expense. Any unused deduction cannot be carried forward or transferred to a spouse or a non-supporting person. However, it may be possible for the disabled person or a supporting person to claim the unused amount as a medical expense. See section 12.2.7 for a discussion as to why tax deductions such as the disability supports deduction are usually more valuable than tax credits such as the medical expense tax credit.

## 12.2.9 Education Tax Credit

Students who qualify for the disability tax credit are entitled to claim the $400 monthly education tax credit even if they are only part-time students (normally a student must be in full-time attendance to claim this credit). The student must be enrolled in a program which is at least three weeks long and requires at least 12 hours of course work per month in order to be eligible. If the disabled student does not qualify for the disability tax credit, they may still qualify for the education tax credit if they cannot reasonably be expected to enroll full time because of a certified mental or physical impairment.

## 12.2.10 Child Care Expense Deduction

There are two enhancements to the child care expense deduction that may be available where either you or your child is disabled.

1. Section 10.2.3 of Chapter 10, "Children", discusses the ability to deduct certain child care expenses from your taxable income. If your child qualifies for the disability tax credit, you will be entitled to deduct $10,000 in annual expenses, as opposed to the $4000 or $7000 amounts otherwise allowed. In addition, the child does not have to be under age 16 in order for you to claim these expenses.

2. Normally the deduction must be claimed by the lower income-earning spouse (or common-law partner), which may limit the amount of the expenses that can be claimed. However, if one of the spouses (or common-law partners) is incapable of caring for their children due to a mental or physical infirmity, then the expenses may be claimed by the higher income-earning spouse (subject to the limitations discussed in section 10.2.3 and above). The infirmity needs to be certified in writing by a medical doctor.

## 12.2.11 Canada Child Tax Benefit Supplement

If your child is eligible for the disability tax credit (see section 12.2.1), then depending upon your family income you may be entitled to receive the Child Disability Benefit, which is a supplement to the Canada Child Tax Benefit. The full amount of the Child Disability Benefit (which is approximately $2500) is paid for each eligible child to families with net income below the amount at which the National Child Benefit Supplement is no longer available. The Child Disability Benefit is reduced as your family income increases. For more information regarding eligibility for this supplement, see the Canada Revenue Agency Web site at *www.cra-arc.gc.ca*, or their pamphlet T4114, *Your Canada Child Tax Benefit*.

### 12.2.12 File a Tax Return

If you are disabled, you should file a tax return, even if you do not have any taxable income, in order to receive non-taxable items such as workers' compensation benefits or social assistance. Certain types of benefits are based on taxable income, including the GST credit, the Canada Child Tax Benefit and some provincial benefits (e.g. medical or dental benefits, subsidized housing and public transportation), so it may be in your best interest to indicate that your taxable income is, in fact, very low.



### 12.2.13 File a T1 Adjustment

If you believe that you would have qualified for a credit in a previous year, but you did not file a tax return or did not complete it properly, consider filing a T1 Adjustment to receive credits up to ten years in the past.

## 12.3 ESTATE PLANNING

Generally speaking, parents of disabled children have the same concerns as other parents when structuring their estate plan, although there are some additional wrinkles.

- If the child is mentally disabled, there may be a concern as to how an inheritance will be managed.
- If the child is receiving social assistance from the provincial government, there may be a concern that the social assistance will be discontinued once the child receives the inheritance, since most jurisdictions will not give social assistance to a disabled person who has income or assets beyond a certain level (see section 12.5, "Jurisdiction Differences").

We will discuss some of the estate planning strategies used when there are beneficiaries who have a disability, as well as some of the issues to be considered when implementing these strategies.

## 12.3.1 Henson Trusts

If you are leaving an inheritance to a beneficiary with a disability, it is generally not recommended that you simply leave their inheritance to them directly. In most cases, it is recommended that any inheritance be left in a "Henson trust", which may help to preserve the beneficiary's right to receive any social assistance payments that they may currently be receiving. In the case of a mentally disabled beneficiary, using a trust will also help to avoid the intervention of the Public Trustee in the management of the trust property. Below are some examples of how such a trust could work.

- The parents provide in their will that any amount left to their disabled child is to be held in trust. The terms of the trust are to be completely discretionary, meaning that the trustee is to have complete discretion over when the beneficiary will receive the capital, and in what amounts. This type of planning was challenged in the courts in Ontario in the *Henson* case, which is why these trusts are commonly referred to as "Henson trusts". Even if the child is physically disabled (as opposed to mentally), and fully capable of managing the funds on his or her own, if the intent is to preserve the right to receive social assistance payments, it is imperative that the trust funds not be accessible by the disabled child at their discretion. In order for this strategy to be effective, it must be the trustee or trustees who have control over the funds in the trust.

- If parents of a disabled child want to do this type of planning, it is very important that they have the appropriate type of will. If a parent of a disabled child dies without a will, then their child may inherit a part or all of their estate directly, which could potentially impact their ability to receive social assistance payments. If a mentally disabled child is not capable of managing an inheritance, the Public Trustee will usually step in to manage the estate. If you would like to dictate who the trustee of the trust will be, and the powers the trustee is to have, it is imperative that you set this out in a properly drafted will.

- If the proper trust provisions are not placed in the parents' will, it may not be possible to rectify the problem after the time of death. In many jurisdictions, a disabled person will not be able to transfer assets into a trust after they have received them, as this is considered a disposition of assets (i.e. they gave away something they were entitled to, so the social assistance is discontinued regardless of whether or not they still have the asset). Also, even if they are able to create a trust, the trust will be considered an *inter vivos* trust and not a testamentary trust, since it was not created in the parent's will, so it will not have access to the same tax advantages as a testamentary trust. See section 23.2 in Chapter 23, "Trusts", for a further discussion of the taxation of trusts.

- Given that the funds will be managed by a trustee once you have passed on, and the disabled child may be vulnerable to abuse, it is obviously very important to pick the right trustee. If you do not have a family member who would be an appropriate choice, then you should consider whether or not it would be more appropriate to choose a corporate trustee. Although choosing a corporate trustee may be more costly in some cases, it may also provide for less abuse and better management of the trust assets.

- If you choose a sibling of the beneficiary to act as trustee of the trust, then you should not appoint that sibling as capital beneficiary of the trust assets upon the death of the disabled beneficiary. This is because it will put the trustee in a conflict of interest — the more they distribute to the disabled beneficiary during the beneficiary's lifetime, the less there will be for them after the disabled beneficiary has passed on. Siblings are often a good choice for trustee, but they should not be named as contingent beneficiaries of the trust assets. However, it is generally recommended that a contingent beneficiary of some sort be indicated, for trust law purposes. One suggestion may be to name any children of the disabled child as the contingent beneficiaries. If the disabled child does not have any heirs, and is not capable of writing a will, then it is very likely that their siblings will inherit the disabled child's estate in any event under the prevailing intestacy legislation.

- If you want to ensure that the majority of your assets remain in the trust, then you will need to ensure that your estate passes to the disabled beneficiary through your estate, and not by some other means. For example, you should not hold any assets in joint names with the disabled child, since they may receive that asset outright upon your death, and the asset may not form part of the trust (except in Quebec, where there is no right of survivorship). Also, you should not appoint your disabled child as direct beneficiary on any of your RRSP or insurance proceeds, since they will receive those assets outright (except in Quebec, where beneficiary designations on many registered investments are not effective). In order for the Henson trust strategy to work, the child cannot indirectly receive any assets outside of the estate. (If you would like to save some probate fees, consider using an insurance trust if some of the assets intended for the trust are proceeds from an insurance policy – see section 22.3.7, "Insurance Trusts" in Chapter 22, "Probate", for more information.)

- If the disabled beneficiary meets certain conditions, he or she may be able to take advantage of the "preferred beneficiary election", which is provided for in the *Income Tax Act*. This election provides that certain persons may report the income earned in the trust in their own tax return, yet have the income itself remain in the trust and continue to be managed by the trustee of the trust. If the beneficiary is in a very low tax bracket, it may be beneficial to have the trust income taxed in their name personally, even if the trust is a testamentary trust. This is because only individuals are entitled to claim the personal tax exemption (which is currently $10,320), meaning that a portion of the income will be essentially received tax free. In order to use the preferred beneficiary election, the beneficiary must be either the spouse or common-law partner of the person who created the trust, or a lineal descendant or spouse or common-law partner of a lineal descendant. This can include a child, step-child, grandchild, step-grandchild, great-grandchild or step-great-grandchild or a spouse or common-law partner of any of those persons. However, the amount of taxable income reported by the beneficiary could impact their ability to receive social assistance payments.

- Leaving a gift in trust avoids the necessity of having to go to court to appoint a committee for the disabled person and require that person to provide an annual accounting to the court.

- Henson trusts usually continue for the lifetime of the disabled beneficiary. Therefore, they often exist beyond 21 years. Under the *Income Tax Act*, there is a "deemed disposition" of all of the assets in the trust on the 21st anniversary of the creation of the trust. With many other trusts, the trustees choose to wind up the trust before the 21st anniversary in order to avoid the deemed disposition, but in the case of a Henson trust, that may not be appropriate. Therefore, the trustees of the trust should give consideration to triggering some of the capital gains in the trust a few years before the 21st anniversary, to avoid having all the gains taxed at one time.

- All trusts are required to maintain records and to abide by any terms in the trust documents (typically spelled out in the will). These may include instructions on how to invest and acceptable investment vehicles. In addition, a T-3 trust return must be filed annually by the trustee.

- Trustees are entitled to an annual fee, which is a percentage of assets, typically in the range of 2 to 2.5%.

As is evident from the above discussion, a parent with a disabled child needs to ensure that their will is properly drafted so that their disabled child is adequately taken care of after they are gone. It is imperative that individuals in this situation speak with an estate planning lawyer who specializes in this area.

### 12.3.2 Purchasing an Annuity

If the disabled beneficiary will not be eligible to receive social assistance, there may be no need for a Henson trust. In fact, if the person is physically disabled, then the estate planning may not be much different than that done for any other child (see section 10.5 of Chapter 10, "Children"). However, if the beneficiary is mentally disabled, and there is no appropriate person capable of managing their inheritance (and the amount in question does not justify the use of a corporate trustee), it may be easier to simply purchase a life annuity for the disabled person. In this way, they will regularly receive an amount that they can use to live on, but they will not have access to the entire lump sum.



If you want your personal representatives to carry out this strategy, it may be recommended that you indicate in your will that you would like them to use the funds designated for the disabled child for the purpose of purchasing a life annuity. However, in some cases annuities may be overly restrictive, since the annuitant is only entitled to the monthly payments, which may be problematic if they require a lump sum. In addition, there will be nothing remaining to pass on to other beneficiaries after the time of the disabled person's death. This strategy may only be appropriate in the limited circumstances outlined above.

### 12.3.3 Designating a Disabled Child as Direct Beneficiary on an RRSP

Normally, when a taxpayer dies, any amounts held in an RRSP or RRIF are taxed in the estate, unless the amounts are transferred to the deceased's spouse or common-law partner, or a financially dependent child under the age of 18. These individuals are then usually able to contribute a corresponding amount to their own RRSP or purchase an annuity in order to continue deferring the tax for some period of time (see section 21.2.5 of Chapter 21, "Taxation at Death", for a further explanation). However, it is also possible to transfer amounts to an RRSP or RRIF of a disabled child who is over age 18 if certain conditions are met. In order for amounts to be transferred on a tax-deferred basis, the child must have been financially dependent upon the deceased due to a mental or physical infirmity. The financial dependency threshold is significantly higher than the threshold applicable to a non-infirm child — the disabled child may earn up to approximately $17,000 and still be considered financially dependent upon someone else. Because many disabled children would qualify for this tax deferral, some parents choose to name their disabled child as the direct beneficiary of their registered investments, or name them as the direct beneficiary in their will (in Quebec, direct beneficiary designations are not effective on all registered investments, so in most cases the designation would have to be made in the will).

However, there are significant drawbacks to naming a child as a direct beneficiary of an RRSP or RRIF, or designating them as the beneficiary of such an asset in a will.

- If they receive the asset directly, it may affect their eligibility for social assistance payments. As mentioned in section 12.3.1, it is usually not recommended that disabled beneficiaries receive any assets directly, but rather, the assets should be placed in a trust so that they are not considered when applying for social assistance (although see section 12.5 for details as to whether this strategy is effective in your province or territory).

- If the beneficiary has a mental disability, they may not be capable of managing the funds. If they receive the funds directly, then the Public Trustee will intervene to manage the funds, usually charging a fee. It may be preferable to choose a trusted relative, friend, or corporate trustee to manage the funds, again by placing them in a trust.

- The tax deferral mechanism referred to above is not available unless the funds are transferred to an individual's RRSP or RRIF, not to a trust. Although there are proposed amendments that will make it possible to transfer such amounts to a trust, under the current legislation, the Henson trust mechanism is not available if a disabled beneficiary is named as the direct beneficiary of a registered plan.

- When the funds are withdrawn from the RRSP or RRIF, they are subject to tax. If equal amounts of the estate are left to various beneficiaries, but the amount received by the disabled beneficiary is an amount from an RRSP or RRIF, they will in fact receive less than the other beneficiaries on an after-tax basis.

Although the *Income Tax Act* does allow a transfer of registered assets on a tax-deferred basis, it is not always recommended as an estate planning strategy. Although it usually makes sense to take advantage of the deferral upon the death of the first spouse, it becomes much more complicated after the second parent dies, so at that point the plan is usually de-registered and the taxes paid. Once the taxes are paid, the after-tax amount can be divided equally between all of the beneficiaries, and any amounts intended for disabled beneficiaries can be left in a Henson trust, or used to purchase an annuity, as discussed in section 12.3.2. If there is a concern that there will not be a sufficient amount left for the disabled beneficiary on an after-tax basis, then consideration should be given to purchasing additional insurance to address the tax liability, and ensure that all of your dependants will receive enough to sustain themselves after you are gone.



## 12.4 INSURANCE PLANNING

If you have a disabled child, review your insurance needs. Depending upon the severity of your child's disability, they may need financial assistance long after they become an adult, and in fact many years after you are gone. In addition, they may have additional financial needs, if they require medical treatment, home care, or special equipment. The amount of life insurance that you applied for prior to having the disabled child, or prior to realizing the extent of their disability, may no longer be adequate if you intend to leave a sufficient amount for them to live on for the remainder of their life.

As discussed in section 12.3.1, if you have included a Henson trust in your will, you will probably not want to name your child as the direct beneficiary on any of your insurance policies. In order for the Henson trust strategy to be effective, you will need to ensure that your assets pass through your will, and do not pass directly to your disabled child. If you are concerned about probate costs, consider establishing an insurance trust, which is discussed in section 22.3.7 of Chapter 22, "Probate".

## 12.5 JURISDICTION DIFFERENCES

### 12.5.1 Alberta

The regulations allow a disabled person to have the following assets and still qualify for social assistance:

- a principal residence;
- one vehicle that is adapted to accommodate the handicap; and
- insurance received to replace exempt property.

An individual cannot have more than $100,000 in non-exempt assets, or they will not qualify for assistance. Unfortunately, the *Assured Income for the Severely Handicapped Act* currently does not allow for the use of Henson trusts. The legislation deems all amounts held in trust for a disabled person to be the property of the disabled person, thereby discontinuing their social assistance if they have more in the trust than allowed under the legislation. For more information, see *www.seniors.gov.ab.ca/aish/*.

## 12.5.2 British Columbia

The *Employment and Assistance for Persons with Disabilities Act* provides social assistance to disabled individuals whose assets do not exceed certain thresholds. Individuals cannot have assets of more than $3000, and not more than $5000 if they have a dependant. When determining eligibility, certain types of assets are exempt from the calculation, such as a place of residence and a motor vehicle.

A disabled person may also have up to $100,000 in a non-discretionary trust, and up to any amount in a discretionary trust. However, even if the amount of the anticipated estate is less than $100,000, it may still be recommended that all amounts be left in a discretionary trust, especially if the disabled person has a disability which may prevent him or her from being able to manage money in any amount. Also, if a smaller amount is left in a non-discretionary trust, but it then grows in value to over $100,000, social assistance benefits may stop until such excess amounts are spent.

For more information, please see *www.hsd.gov.bc.ca/PUBLICAT/VOL1/Part3/3-5.htm* and *www.hsd.gov.bc.ca/PUBLICAT/bcea/trusts.htm*.

## 12.5.3 Manitoba

*The Employment and Income Assistance Act* provides that social assistance will be paid to disabled individuals to the extent that their assets do not exceed the following:

- the cash surrender value of life insurance policies, up to a maximum total value of $2,000;
- equity in the home in which the applicant or recipient resides and the property on which it is located that is essential to the home;

- inventory and equipment essential to carrying on a viable farming or business operation;
- liquid assets up to $4000 for a single person and up to $6000 for a person with one dependant and $1000 for each additional dependant, to a maximum of $8000 per household;
- personal property essential to the health and well-being of members of the applicant's or recipient's household, including household furnishings and personal clothing; and
- gifts of a non-recurring nature received while in receipt of income assistance or general assistance, of a value up to $100 each.



Individuals can also receive lump-sum payments and accumulate them within a non-discretionary trust fund of no more than $100,000. Disbursements for the purchase of disability-related items or services are not included in calculating an applicant's financial resources.

Although a disabled person may have up to $100,000 in a non-discretionary trust, they can receive an inheritance of any amount in a discretionary trust. Even if the amount of the anticipated estate is less than $100,000, it may still be recommended that all amounts be left in a discretionary trust, especially if the disabled person has a disability which may prevent him or her from being able to manage money in any amount. Also, if a smaller amount is left in a non-discretionary trust, but it then grows in value to over $100,000, social assistance benefits may stop until such excess amounts are spent.

For more information, see *www.gov.mb.ca/fs/eiamanual/index.html.*

## 12.5.4 New Brunswick

The *Family Income Security Act* provides that when determining eligibility for social assistance, the following assets are exempt:

- liquid assets to a maximum of $3000 for each person in the household who is disabled, plus $1000 for each household member who is not disabled, to a maximum of $4000;
- your residence;

- a vehicle used for routine transportation, work, medical reasons or shopping;
- an RDSP with up to $200,000 in contributions, $70,000 in grants and $20,000 in bonds;
- the principal and accumulated interest of a documented trust fund, to a maximum of $200,000, of which the principal and accumulated interest are intended and are used solely to assist in maintaining a disabled, blind or deaf recipient to live in the home or the community; and

There are a number of other exempt items listed in section 8(2) of the *Family Income Security Act*. For more information, see *www.gnb.ca/0048/index-e.asp*, and in particular, the Financial Aid tab.

Although a disabled person may have up to $200,000 in a non-discretionary trust, they can receive an inheritance of any amount in a discretionary trust. Even if the amount of the anticipated estate is less than $200,000, it may still be recommended that all amounts be left in a discretionary trust, especially if the disabled person has a disability which may prevent him or her from being able to manage money in any amount. Also, if a smaller amount is left in a non-discretionary trust, but it then grows in value to over $200,000, social assistance benefits may stop until such excess amounts are spent.

## 12.5.5 Newfoundland

People who are unable to support themselves due to a mental or physical infirmity may qualify for social assistance if they have liquid assets that do not exceed the following limits:

- $3000 for one adult; or
- $5500, for a family, where either the adult is disabled, or the family has a child who is disabled.

For more information, see *www.hrle.gov.nl.ca/hrle/disabilities/poverty.html*.

A disabled person is also allowed to be the beneficiary of a trust that does not exceed $100,000 where the disabled adult or family annually receives the total interest and income from the trust plus 2% of the liquid assets of the trust and the trust is established and maintained in a manner and under terms and conditions that the minister may establish or approve.

Although a disabled person may have up to $100,000 in a non-discretionary trust, they can receive an inheritance of any amount in a discretionary trust. Even if the amount of the anticipated estate is less than $100,000, it may still be recommended that all amounts be left in a discretionary trust, especially if the disabled person has a disability which may prevent him or her from being able to manage money in any amount. Also, if a smaller amount is left in a non-discretionary trust, but it then grows in value to over $100,000, social assistance benefits may stop until such excess amounts are spent.



## 12.5.6 Northwest Territories

The *Social Assistance Act* provides that social assistance payments may be made to disabled persons. The following items are exempt when determining eligibility:

- the value of real property used as the residence of the applicant unless the property is in excess of the reasonable needs of the applicant;
- the value of real property and equipment necessary for the operation of a viable business of the applicant;
- in respect of a person who is disabled, the value of assets to a total of $50,000;
- the value of household furnishings and appliances of the applicant which are reasonably required by the applicant; and
- the value of a motor vehicle that is specially adapted to accommodate a physical disability of the applicant or his or her dependant, or not worth more than $20,000.

In determining the amount of social assistance a person is entitled to, the social services officer will include "moneys held in trust for a child and available for distribution", but will not include "moneys held in trust for a child and not available for distribution". Therefore, if you intend to leave an inheritance to a disabled child, it may be recommended that you leave the assets in a completely discretionary Henson trust.

For more information, see *www.ece.gov.nt.ca/PDF_File/IncSuptPolicyMan.pdf.*

## 12.5.7 Nova Scotia

The *Employment Support and Income Assistance Act* provides that disabled individuals may receive social assistance if their assets do not exceed a certain level. If the family size is one person, no assistance can be granted where the assets exceed $500, and if the family is comprised of more than one person, the family's assets cannot exceed $1000. The definition of "assets" includes all real property and liquid assets, but does not include:

- a primary residence that is assessed at less than twice the average assessed value of single family dwellings in the municipality in which the residence is located;
- a cash surrender value of under $500 of a life insurance policy;
- a motor vehicle used for basic transportation;
- tools or equipment directly related to a trade or profession;
- an RESP established for the education of a child;
- any portion of an RRSP that is part of an employment pension program; and
- prepaid funeral arrangements to a maximum of $5000.

Given the relatively low thresholds, if you intend to leave an inheritance to a child, you should consider leaving the assets in a discretionary Henson trust. It is important that the trust be completely discretionary, as money that is left in a trust will affect social assistance payments where it is feasible that the beneficiary would be able to support themselves from the trust.

For more information, see *www.gov.ns.ca/coms/employment/income_assistance/ESIAManual.html*.

## 12.5.8 Nunavut

The *Social Assistance Act* provides that social assistance payments may be made to disabled persons. The following items are exempt when determining eligibility:

- the value of real property used as the residence of the applicant unless the property is in excess of the reasonable needs of the applicant;
- the value of real property and equipment necessary for the operation of a viable business of the applicant;
- in respect of a person who is disabled, the value of assets to a total of $5,000;
- the value of household furnishings and appliances of the applicant which are reasonably required by the applicant; and
- the value of a motor vehicle that is specially adapted to accommodate a physical disability of the applicant or his or her dependant, or not worth more than $20,000.



In determining the amount of social assistance a person is entitled to, the social services officer will include "moneys held in trust for a child and available for distribution", but will not include "moneys held in trust for a child and not available for distribution". Therefore, if you intend to leave an inheritance to a disabled child, it may be recommended that you leave the assets in a completely discretionary Henson trust.

For more information, see *www.canlii.org/en/nu/laws/regu/rrnwt-nu-1990-c-s-16/latest/rrnwt-nu-1990-c-s-16.html* and *www.canlii.org/en/nu/laws/regu/nu-reg-003-2002/latest/nu-reg-003-2002.html.*

## 12.5.9 Ontario

The *Ontario Disability Support Program Act* provides social assistance payments to disabled individuals where their assets do not exceed certain limits. The prescribed limit for assets is equal to the sum of:

- $5000; plus
- $2500 if there is a spouse or common-law partner; plus
- $500 for each dependant other than a spouse or common-law partner.

The following are not included as assets when determining the right to social assistance:

- a person's interest in a principal residence (which they are occupying);
- a motor vehicle;
- assets held in trust for the person that are derived from an inheritance or life insurance policy, so long as the amount does not exceed $100,000 (an "exempt trust");
- the combined capital of an exempt trust and the total cash surrender value of a life insurance policy, if held, which does not exceed $100,000; and
- interest or dividends earned on the capital amount of an exempt trust that are reinvested in the trust, provided the capital does not exceed the $100,000 limit.

Amounts received in excess of $100,000 should be placed in a completely discretionary Henson trust in the will. Payments and interest earned from an exempt trust (derived from an inheritance or life insurance policy) or a Henson trust that are used for the following purposes are exempt as income:

- the purchase of approved disability-related items and services (such as aids and assistive devices) that will not otherwise be reimbursed;
- educational or training expenses incurred as a result of the applicant/recipient's disability that will not otherwise be reimbursed; and
- expenses for any purpose up to $6000 in a 12-month period.

The cash surrender value of a life insurance policy is viewed as an exempt asset (up to $100,000), so it may be possible to purchase a permanent life insurance policy and transfer it to the disabled child on a tax-deferred basis. Another strategy may be to purchase segregated funds up to a maximum of $100,000 (since they are considered a "life insurance policy"), although the Minister may "claw-back" any benefits to be received within one year of doing this, and in some cases, up to three years, so be sure to confer with a qualified professional prior to implementing this strategy.

For more information, see *www.mcss.gov.on.ca/mcss/english/pillars/social/directives/ODSP_incomesupport.htm*.

## 12.5.10 Prince Edward Island

The *Social Assistance Act* provides that financial assistance may be granted to an applicant who:

- has a disability, no dependants and has liquid assets not exceeding $900 in value; or
- lives with a spouse and either or both of the applicant and spouse have a disability and combined liquid assets that are valued at not more than $1800 plus $300 for each dependent child up to a maximum total liquid assets of $2400.

In determining the financial resources of an applicant, all of the resources of the applicant that may be used for the support of the applicant will be included, but the following assets are exempt:

- the applicant's principal residence to the value approved by the Director;
- real and personal property essential for the operation of a business;
- approved personal belongings;
- a vehicle, to an approved maximum value;
- earned monthly income of $75 plus 10% of the excess if single, or $125 plus 10% of the excess if there is a spouse or dependants; and
- various other government payments and insurance amounts.

Since the rules and regulations regarding which assets and/or income may or may not be exempt for the purposes of determining eligibility for social assistance are quite detailed, see *www.canlii.org/pe/laws/regu/2003r.396/20080818/whole.html* for more information.

Given the relatively small amounts that a person is allowed to have yet still be entitled to social assistance payments, if you are leaving an inheritance to a disabled person, it may be recommended that you leave the assets in a Henson trust.

## 12.5.11 Quebec

### *12.5.11.1 Quebec Pension Plan*

If you are disabled, and you have made sufficient contributions to the Quebec Pension Plan ("QPP"), you may be entitled to a disability pension. To be declared disabled, you must:

- have made sufficient contributions to the QPP;
- be under age 65; and
- have a severe and permanent disability which is recognized by the QPP's medical advisors and that renders you unable to do any type of substantially gainful work because of your state of health (substantially gainful work is work which would pay at least $13,000 a year).

You will have made sufficient contributions to the QPP:

- if you have contributed for at least two of the last three years in your contributory period;
- if you have contributed for at least five of the last ten years in your contributory period; or
- if you have contributed for half of the years in your contributory period, and for at least two years.

For more information on the QPP program, please see *www.rrq.gouv.qc.ca/en/invalidite/*.

### *12.5.11.2 Social Assistance*

To be eligible for employment assistance benefits, you may not have more than certain specified amounts in cash, or in assets that can readily be converted into cash. The rules in Quebec are quite detailed — please see *www.mess.gouv.qc.ca/index_en.asp* for more information.

#### *12.5.11.3 Medical Expenses*

On the provincial tax return, there is no minimum threshold as in the federal system, so all expenses in excess of 3% of net income may be claimed. However, net income is based on the combined income of both spouses, as opposed to the income of the lower income-earning spouse, so many residents do not qualify for this credit provincially.



### 12.5.12 Saskatchewan

*The Saskatchewan Assistance Act* provides that disabled persons may receive social assistance payments so long as their assets do not exceed certain limits. Recipients are entitled to have certain assets, as follows:

- cash and liquid assets not exceeding $1500 for a single recipient or $3000 for a recipient and one dependant, plus $500 for each additional dependant;
- the cash surrender value of any policy of life insurance, but not the amount of any benefits paid;
- amounts received as a result of inheritances not exceeding $1500 if single or $3000 if there is a dependant plus $500 for each additional dependant; and
- the home they are residing in.

Monies held in trust for children are not considered an asset if they are not available for distribution, so a Henson trust may be a good solution if you would like to leave a significant inheritance to a disabled person.

As the list of exempt items is quite detailed, please see *www.qp.gov.sk.ca/documents/English/Regulations/Regulations/SR78-66.pdf* for more information.

### 12.5.13 Yukon

Individuals with disabilities may receive a Territorial Supplementary Allowance. Individuals who apply for this allowance may earn up to $3900 annually without affecting their ability to receive benefits. Due to the relatively low income limits, it may be recommended that any inheritances left to a disabled person be left in a Henson trust.

For more information, see *www.hss.gov.yk.ca/disabilites.php*.

# 12.6 CASE STUDY

## 12.6.1 Disabled Child, Henson Trust

Greg and Pam have a child, Jonathon, who suffers from a permanent disability. Jonathon has a severe mental disability, and he requires personal care 24 hours a day, as he cannot feed himself, bathe himself, or walk. Pam has quit her job to stay at home and take care of Jonathon. Greg and Pam have confirmed with their accountant that they are maximizing the use of any and all tax credits that may be available to them. However, their main concern is what will happen to Jonathon at the time of their deaths. Greg and Pam live in Manitoba, and they have heard that in their will they may be able to place their assets in a trust so that they can appoint someone to manage the assets on Jonathon's behalf, and so that Jonathon can continue to qualify for social assistance, as he will have no means of supporting himself. This type of strategy for maximizing social assistance benefits is available in every province except Alberta.

Greg and Pam's lawyer advises them to create a Henson trust in their will, which will be established upon the death of the second spouse. In their wills, they appoint each other as their primary personal representative, and appoint their other children, Debbie and Heather, as their alternate personal representatives. They indicate that upon the death of the first spouse, all of the assets are to pass to the survivor, but upon the death of the second spouse, all of the assets are to be divided equally among their three children. However, the portion of the estate which is meant for Jonathon is to be held in trust for his entire lifetime. Greg and Pam indicate that their personal representatives (who will be Debbie and Heather after the death of both Greg and Pam) will have complete discretion in deciding whether to pay out any income or capital to Jonathon, and may use the funds for any purpose that is in Jonathan's best interests.

Greg and Pam also indicate that after Jonathan passes away, the assets in the trust are to pass to his issue (the term "issue" means lineal descendents, such as children, grandchildren or great-grandchildren). Although Greg and Pam are fairly certain that Jonathan will never have any children, they want to ensure that there is a contingent beneficiary so that there is no question that there is a valid trust, and the funds do not unconditionally belong to Jonathan. They also do not want to appoint Debbie or Heather as the contingent beneficiaries, as that would put them in a conflict of interest, and prevent them from having the ability to make decisions about the trust funds. Greg and Pam know that if Jonathan dies without heirs, that the funds will revert to Debbie and Heather in any event under the provisions of the intestacy legislation.

Greg and Pam also indicate in their wills that they have nominated Debbie to act as guardian for Jonathan. Although a court does not have to accept this nomination, it is likely that unless someone else can prove Debbie to be a bad choice, a court will accept the wishes of Greg and Pam.

Greg and Pam then speak to their financial advisor about their estate plan, and the fact that they have created a Henson trust for Jonathan. Their financial planner tells them the following regarding the structure of their assets.

- Although there is no problem with them holding assets in joint ownership right now, when the first spouse dies, they should not add any of their children as joint owners on any of their property or investments. If they do so, it is possible that those assets will pass directly to those beneficiaries, and will not be available to be divided equally, and will not be included in Jonathan's trust. It may be possible to add the children as joint owners and still have the assets form part of a Henson trust, but they should ensure that they have a separate agreement drawn up with respect to the joint account to ensure that is what happens.

- Until the first spouse dies, it will not be a problem for them to designate each other as the direct beneficiaries of their registered investments and insurance. Since they have not created spousal trusts in their wills, the direct beneficiary designations will allow them to save probate. (Although if they had lived in Quebec, a beneficiary designation on a registered asset would not have been effective in some cases.) However, once the first spouse dies, the survivor should designate the estate as the direct beneficiary of any registered assets or insurance policies. Although that will generally mean that the assets will have to pass through probate, it will also mean that the assets will be available to go into the Henson trust for Jonathan (and if Debbie and Heather should one day be in a high tax bracket themselves, Greg and Pam may even create testamentary trusts for Debbie and Heather for tax reasons — see Case Study 10.8.2). In any event, the probate fee in Manitoba is less than 1% of the value of the estate, so Greg and Pam agree that it should not be the driving force in their estate plan, and they agree that the primary focus should be ensuring that there are effective controls on Jonathan's inheritance.

- Greg and Pam's financial advisor also tells them that if Jonathan survives them for a period of 21 years, there will be a "deemed disposition" in the trust for tax purposes. This means that any unrealized capital gains in the trust on the 21st anniversary of the creation of the trust will be deemed to have been realized on that date, and tax will be owing accordingly. However, Greg and Pam have discussed the issue with Debbie and Heather, who have agreed that they will attempt to pay out capital gains to Jonathan as appropriate to save tax, but if no payments from the trust are necessary, they will simply pay the tax and leave the remainder in the trust, as again, control issues are more important than taxes for their purposes.

# CHAPTER 13

# ELDERLY PARENTS

Given the advances in medical technology, people are living longer and longer. As a result, many people may find that their parents will require medical care and attention much longer than previously anticipated. Although you may feel uncomfortable raising the issues of death and disability with your parents, it is important to ensure that adequate planning has been done. Here are a few of the issues you should consider discussing with your parents.

## 13.1 FINANCIAL PLANNING

The financial issues for seniors and retirees are discussed in section 14.1 of Chapter 14, "Seniors and Retirees".

## 13.2 TAX PLANNING

The tax planning issues that an older Canadian should consider are discussed in section 14.2 of Chapter 14, "Seniors and Retirees". However, there are some additional tax planning opportunities for those who are caring for an elderly person.

### 13.2.1 Eligible Dependant Credit

If you provide care in your home for a parent or grandparent who is suffering from a mental or physical infirmity, you may be eligible to claim an "eligible dependant credit". An individual who does not claim a spousal tax credit for the year and who, at any time in the year, was not married, or was married but did not support nor live with his or her spouse and was not supported by his or her spouse, may claim an equivalent-to-spouse tax credit for a qualified relative (subject to the amount of the qualified relative's income for the year) if, at that time:

- the individual maintained a residence either alone or with other persons;
- the individual lived in the residence; and
- the individual supported a qualified relative in the residence.

The eligible dependant tax credit is reduced as the dependant's income rises. Therefore, this credit is generally only available if the dependant earns relatively little income.

### 13.2.2 Caregiver Credit

You will be able to claim a "caregiver tax credit" if you lived with and provided in-home care for a parent or grandparent aged 65 or older (although the parent or grandparent can be younger if they are suffering from a mental or physical infirmity). See section 12.2.3 of Chapter 12, "Disabled Persons", for more information on this credit.

### 13.2.3 Infirm Dependant Credit

If you are providing support to a mentally or physically infirm parent or grandparent, you can claim the "infirm dependant credit" in respect of them, as long as they reside in Canada. See section 12.2.4 of Chapter 12, "Disabled Persons", for more information on this credit.

### 13.2.4 Disability Tax Credit

If you have a parent who is in failing health, consider whether he or she would now meet the eligibility criteria for claiming the disability tax credit (which is discussed more fully in section 12.2.1 of Chapter 12, "Disabled Persons"). This tax credit may be available if the cumulative effects of your parent's disability are such that they are now markedly restricted in their abilities. If such is the case, ask their doctor to certify that their impairment is severe enough to make them eligible for the disability tax credit. You may send in the certificate at any point, so send it in as early as possible rather than just at the time of filing their tax return, as this can help to avoid delays in assessing the return. If your parent will not be able to use the entire credit, the remainder can be transferred to a supporting child.

### 13.2.5 Nursing Care Costs

If you are paying nursing care costs on behalf of a parent you may be able to claim these as a medical expense. An individual can claim medical expenses paid for a dependent relative to the extent that the amount paid exceeds the lesser of 3% of the dependant's income or approximately $2000, to a maximum of $10,000 annually. To maximize the tax benefit in relation to these costs, it may make sense for the children to each pay a portion of the cost, so that they can each use the $10,000 credit. However, if a full-time attendant care or nursing home care medical expense claim is made, the disability tax credit cannot be claimed by anyone in respect of that individual. Even so, it is still important to obtain the certification for the disability tax credit, since full-time care costs will only qualify as a medical expense if the individual meets the criteria for the disability tax credit.

There is the ability to claim both the disability tax credit and up to $10,000 of total attendant care costs under the "part-time attendant care rules". However, this would only be used if it produced a higher claim than claiming the full-time care costs.

## 13.3 FAMILY LAW ISSUES

In most jurisdictions in Canada, adult children are legally liable for caring for their parents. Generally, adult children are liable to pay parental support if their parent supported them financially when they were minors. The support provided by the parent during childhood does not have to have been luxurious — so long as your parents supported you, you will be expected to support them once you reach adulthood, to the extent that you are able. Parental support may also be payable to a step-parent if that step-parent supported you when you were a child.

The factors that a court will examine in determining the amount of support to award will vary from case to case, and are dependent upon the facts of the case. The issue to keep in mind is that you should speak to your parents about their financial stability, and if you foresee financial problems in the future, speak to your parents as early as possible about how to plan for their retirement. You should also ask them if they would consider long-term care insurance to cover long-term medical costs or home-care costs. If necessary, it may be advisable for you to pay the premiums in order to avoid large lump-sum payments in the future.

See section 13.7, "Jurisdiction Differences", regarding the potential parental support liability in your jurisdiction.

# 13.4 DISABILITY PLANNING

## 13.4.1 Powers of Attorney

If the intent is that you and/or your siblings will be the people who will manage your parents' affairs once they are no longer capable of doing so, you should ensure that they have proper powers of attorney in place, and you know where they are kept. Children do not automatically have the right to manage their parents' affairs in the event of their incapacity, so it is imperative that this issue be addressed while they are still of sound mind, and able to sign the required documents. A relatively inexpensive power of attorney kit purchased at a retail outlet could turn into a very expensive court application if your parents have not signed the proper documents. Encourage your parents to speak with an experienced professional to ensure that they have the appropriate documentation.

If no power of attorney is in place, then you can apply to act as "committee" for your parents, but your actions will be monitored by the court, and limited according to provincial legislation. If your parents want you to have the unlimited power to manage their affairs to the best of your ability, they need to give you that right. For a more complete discussion regarding powers of attorney, see Chapter 18, "Powers of Attorney".



## 13.4.2 Health Care Directives and Living Wills

Another issue you should discuss with your parents is their medical care. Do they want you to have the ability to make medical decisions on their behalf in the event they cannot do so? If so, then they should sign a document giving you those powers. This document is variously referred to in different jurisdictions as a living will, representation agreement, health care directive, advanced health care directive, power of attorney for personal care or mandate in case of incapacity. See Chapter 18, "Powers of Attorney", for a more complete discussion about these documents and the rules applicable in each jurisdiction. Again, it is important that your parents prepare such a document while they are still of sound mind, so that when the time comes, there is no dispute as to who has authority to make medical decisions on their behalf. This is a document that they should discuss both with their doctor and lawyer to ensure that it properly sets out their wishes.

Your parents should also consider whether or not they would like to have life-prolonging medical care discontinued in the event there is no chance for recovery. Although not legally enforceable in every jurisdiction, a living will can carry significant weight with health care professionals when determining the appropriate course of action. Again, this is a document which should be discussed both with medical and legal professionals.

## 13.4.3 Long-Term Care Insurance

Long-term care insurance is a form of insurance that pays out monthly amounts to insured individuals, generally once they have lost the ability to perform two of the following five basic life skills:

- feeding;
- bathing;
- dressing;
- using the washroom; and
- transferring positions (e.g. getting in and out of a bathtub or bed).

The amounts paid to the insured vary depending upon the coverage, and can be used for any expenses the insured chooses. Given that most individuals would prefer to remain in their home for as long as possible, this insurance can pay for home care or other services that your parents may need in order to carry out their daily lives. Although many children would like to be able to provide as much of the required care as possible themselves, in many cases it is not feasible for people to quit their jobs or cease to take care of their own family so that they can care for a parent or parents on a full-time basis. If your parents' assets will not be sufficient to pay for personal care over an extended period of time, you should consider whether or not long-term care insurance is the answer. For many children, they themselves are willing to pay the premiums to ensure that their parents are cared for as they desire.

Please see section 25.1.3 of Chapter 25, "Insurance", for more information on Long-Term Care Insurance.

### 13.4.4 Critical Illness Insurance

Critical illness insurance is another form of insurance that your parents may need in order to protect themselves and their estate in the event of a critical illness. This type of insurance pays out a lump-sum of money in the event of a critical illness (e.g. stroke, heart attack, cancer, etc.). This money may be used for any purpose, including private medical care, home care or home renovations. Speak to your insurance advisor about whether or not this type of insurance would be appropriate. See section 25.1.2 of Chapter 25, "Insurance", for more information.

## 13.5 ESTATE PLANNING

### 13.5.1 For the Parent

An individual who has an elderly parent may want to ensure that their parent has an estate plan in place. Below are some of the issues the child may want to confirm with the parent.

- Does the parent have a will that has been prepared with the assistance of a qualified professional? See Chapter 19, "Distribution of an Estate", for a further discussion on the importance of wills.

- If the parent has charitable intentions, does their estate plan contemplate giving a charitable gift at the time of their death? If so, has the gift been structured in the most tax-effective manner possible? See Chapter 24, "Charitable Giving", for a further discussion about the different options available when giving a charitable gift.

- If the parent has foreign property, do they have a will that will be accepted in the jurisdiction in which the foreign property is located? Are they aware of any possible foreign tax liability?

- If they have a particular asset that they would like to keep in the family, such as a vacation property or a business, have they made arrangements to ensure that their children will be able to pay for any tax liability that may arise at the time of their death? If not, consider whether or not insurance may be necessary in order to keep the asset within the family, and also consider whether or not the children should pay the insurance premiums. Are they sure that their children will be able to share the asset? If not, have they structured their estate so that the other child or children will receive something of equal value? See Chapter 15, "Vacation Properties", or Chapter 16, "Business Owners", for a further discussion about these issues.

- If the parents have substantial assets, have they arranged their estate so that their children will receive their inheritance in the most tax-effective manner possible? See section 13.5.2, "Tax Effective Inheritances", for a further discussion on this issue. Also see Chapter 21, "Taxation at Death", and Chapter 22, "Probate", for a review of how taxes at the time of death can be minimized. Remember that minimizing income taxes and minimizing probate fees are two different objectives, and attempting to minimize probate fees should not be the driving force in your estate. In most cases, maximum savings will be achieved by minimizing income taxes, not probate fees.

## 13.5.2 Tax Effective Inheritances

The amount of money that your parents choose to leave to family, friends and favourite charities, and the manner in which they leave it, is strictly their prerogative, and children should not try to exercise undue influence when discussing the issue with their parents. However, many parents do not realize that rather than just leaving an estate directly to their children in their will, there may be a more tax effective way to leave their estate to their children.

If you are in a relatively high tax bracket, it may be more tax effective if you receive your inheritance from your parents by way of a testamentary trust, as opposed to receiving it directly in your name. Many people structure their will so that money is held in trust until their children reach a minimum age (for example, 25 or 30), but then provide that the entire amount is to be paid to the child. This is done in order to protect the inheritance from bad management on the part of a young child, or exposure to creditors or family property claims.

However, testamentary trusts are not just useful for young children. Older children may prefer to receive their inheritance via a trust, since a trust forms a separate taxpayer. This means that any income or capital gains earned on investments held within the trust will be taxable in the trust, as opposed to in the hands of the beneficiary. If you do not anticipate that you will require the funds at the time of your parents' deaths, consider asking your parents to structure their will so that any money left to you is left in trust. The trust can be discretionary so that you can still access the capital as and when you need to, but until such time, the income and capital gains can be earned within the trust. Although a trust cannot claim any personal tax credits, a testamentary trust is taxed using the graduated rates of tax applicable to individuals, so the first dollars of income will be taxed at a lower rate in the trust than in the hands of the beneficiary (assuming the beneficiary is not already in the lowest tax bracket).

In fact, this type of planning may also be of benefit to your parents themselves. They may prefer to receive each other's inheritance in trust, as they may wish to minimize their taxable income in order to preserve their right to receive Old Age Security payments. If the income on the inheritance is taxed in the hands of the trust instead of taxed in the survivor's name, they may be able to pay less tax overall.

Keep in mind, however, that assets that are held in joint names, or that will pass directly to a beneficiary by way of a direct beneficiary designation *may not be available to form part of a testamentary trust.* Your parents may wish to review with their advisor whether or not it would be better to hold all of their assets in individual names, and designate their estate as the beneficiary on their RRSPs, RRIFs or insurance policies. See Chapter 23, "Trusts", for a further discussion about testamentary trusts, as well as Case Studies 5.8.2 in Chapter 5, "Married", and 10.8.2 in Chapter 10, "Children".



### 13.5.3 Protecting Inheritances from Family Property Claims

In many jurisdictions, property received by way of gift or inheritance is exempt from a division of family property at the time of marriage breakdown (and in some jurisdictions, at the time of the breakdown of a common-law relationship). If you anticipate that your parents will be leaving you a significant estate, it may be worthwhile for them to include a clause in their will that states that the inheritance is meant solely for your benefit, and is not to be included in the calculation of net family property (although this type of clause may not necessarily be effective in every jurisdiction). They may also wish to indicate that any income or growth on the property is also to remain separate. Although there is no guarantee that the money may not become shareable at a later date (particularly if you choose to use the money for the purposes of buying a family asset), if you are conscious about keeping your money separate, a clause of this type may be useful. Even if you do not currently live in a jurisdiction where this clause may be useful, consider asking your parents to include such a clause in their wills in case you later move to a jurisdiction where it would be effective. See section 17.2.2 of Chapter 17, "Family Property", for a discussion as to the best ways in which to give a gift or inheritance to a child, and 17.4 for the rules in your jurisdiction in particular.

## 13.5.4 Where Parents are Non-Residents of Canada

If your parents are non-residents of Canada, it may be possible for you to receive your inheritance in a manner that allows for a tax deferral. If your parents' will provides that the amount to be left to the Canadian resident beneficiary is to be left in a trust that will not itself be a resident of Canada (meaning that the trustees of the trust are not residents of Canada and the "mind and management" of the trust is not resident in Canada), the income in the trust may accumulate on a tax-free basis for a period of five years, assuming the investments within the trust do not attract taxation in the trust's jurisdiction. The capital can later be distributed on a tax-free basis to the Canadian resident. This strategy is often referred to as a "non-resident inheritance trust", and is something you should speak to your advisors about to determine if it would be useful for you. Your parents should also consult with an advisor in their jurisdiction to ensure that their will is structured in the most tax effective manner possible.

## 13.5.5 Funeral Arrangements

Another awkward and sometimes unpleasant conversation that you may consider having with your parents once they reach a more advanced age, revolves around whether or not they have made any funeral arrangements. Some people feel very strongly about the type of service they want to have or do not want to have, but they fail to convey these feelings to their heirs. Also, in the case of blended families, a discussion regarding funeral arrangements can dredge up many unpleasant feelings — for example, children in blended family situations may want to have their parents buried next to one another, but a new spouse may feel quite differently. You also may wish to discuss the type of service your parents want, whether or not they wish to be cremated, and where they would prefer to be buried. Discussing this in advance and documenting any decisions can help to minimize disputes between family members once your parents have passed on.

You may also wish to discuss the issue of prepaid funeral arrangements with your parents. This strategy has many benefits.

- It allows your parents to have more control over their funeral, and plan those aspects of their funeral about which they feel strongly. This can also help to avoid arguments that often arise when children are left to decide all of the details, since one child may want a more elaborate service than another.

- The cost is fixed by paying for it in advance, and therefore inflation-protected.
- Amounts paid into a prepaid funeral account (up to a maximum of $35,000) will grow on a tax-deferred basis (assuming the amounts are not withdrawn prior to the time of death).
- By pre-paying the cost of the funeral, it ensures that there are sufficient funds available at the required time. Often, family members are forced to pay for a funeral themselves, and then wait for reimbursement once the estate has been settled. Depending upon your own financial circumstances, and those of your siblings, it may be less stressful to have the funeral prepaid.

Any amounts remaining after the funeral and cemetery expenses have been paid for will be refunded to the contributor or the contributor's estate. Only the amount that represents investment income will be taxable.

When purchasing a pre-paid funeral plan, confirm whether or not the funds paid to the funeral home are guaranteed in the event the funeral home experiences financial difficulty. You should also confirm that the services are portable to another community.



## 13.5.6 Dependants' Relief Claims by a Parent

If an individual is supporting an elderly parent, and the parent becomes financially dependent upon them, that financial obligation could impact the child's own estate. In some jurisdictions, parents have the right to make a court application for a portion of their child's estate if they were not left much, if any, of the estate, and they were financially dependent upon the deceased. If an adult child is supporting an elderly parent, and wants to ensure that a sufficient amount will be left to their spouse, common-law partner, children or other heirs, then they must ensure that there will be sufficient funds in their estate to cover all of these potential liabilities. Individuals in this "sandwich generation" situation may need to review their life insurance policies to ensure that all of their dependants, including their parents, will be properly taken care of in the event they were to die prematurely. See section 19.6 of Chapter 19, "Distribution of an Estate", for a description of the types of individuals who may be able to make a claim against your estate in your jurisdiction.

## 13.5.7 Compensation for Providing Personal Care to a Parent

Sometimes a child cares for a parent or other relative in the expectation that compensation will be received, generally after the time of death of the parent. If you have provided significant levels of personal care to your parent and you are expecting compensation, it is recommended that your parent's will be changed to reflect this agreement. If the will does not provide for this payment, it is possible that the other beneficiaries will not agree to make such payment out of their portion of the estate after the time of death.

Another alternative is to enter into a "care agreement" between the parent and child, where the child would receive a fee, or perhaps live with their parents rent free. The child may even be given the right to remain in the home after the parent is deceased. However, the implications of doing this should be discussed with a professional, and all the other beneficiaries, so that they understand why one child is receiving more from their parents than they are, and to minimize disputes after the time of death. Since any payments received by a child for care services rendered to a parent are a fee for services, the child must also understand that the amount received (or deemed to have been received in the form of free accommodation, for example) will be taxable.

Instead of changing their will or paying a fee, some individuals add children as joint owners of property, believing that the child will inherit that property. However, the Supreme Court of Canada has held that this type of arrangement between a parent and an adult child will be considered a trust arrangement, unless the child can prove that the parent did in fact intend to give them the property. If there is no evidence that the parent intended to give that property to the child at the time of their death, the asset will be considered to be an asset of the parent, and will be divided according to their will, even if only one child was listed as a joint owner. If the parties decide to sign a document confirming that the child is a true joint owner of the property, the parties need to further understand that this may cause disputes among other children who were not aware of the agreement. As well, the gift of the property can cause tax problems both at the time the joint owner is added and at the time of death, since the joint owner will receive the property (except in Quebec, where there is no right of survivorship), but the estate will still be liable for the capital gain on the portion of the property the deceased owned at the time of death (unless the property was the parents' principal residence). Before your parents agree to add any joint owners to any property, encourage them to speak with a professional to ensure that they understand how that strategy will affect their estate, and if possible, document their intentions to prevent disputes once they are gone. See Chapter 22, "Probate", for further information on the implications of adding joint owners or gifting property during your lifetime.

## 13.6 INSURANCE PLANNING

If your parents have assets that have a significant tax liability (perhaps in the form of an unrealized capital gain, or because of registered investments that will be taxable at the time of death), discuss with them whether or not the payment of this tax liability could result in the sale of estate assets that their beneficiaries might like to keep (for example, a vacation property, a family business, or art or other heirlooms). See Chapter 21, "Taxation at Death", for a discussion of how the tax liability is calculated at the time of death, and speak to your parents about obtaining sufficient insurance to cover this liability. If necessary, consider paying the premiums yourself in order to ensure that you will be able to keep the desired asset after your parents are gone.

If your parents have charitable intentions, and they have permanent life insurance policies that they no longer need for their own purposes, they may wish to consider using the insurance for the purposes of making a charitable donation at the time of their death. See Chapter 24, "Charitable Giving", for a further discussion of the planning strategies that may be available with insurance.

Earlier in this chapter we also discussed the potential need for a child to obtain additional insurance if their parents are financially dependent upon them. If you are supporting a parent, consider whether you should purchase additional term insurance until such time as your parents are deceased, in order to ensure there will be sufficient funds in your own estate to take care of both your parents, and any other dependants you may have. See Chapter 25, "Insurance", for a description of the different types of life insurance available.

## 13.7 JURISDICTION DIFFERENCES

### 13.7.1 Alberta

There is no legislation requiring a child to financially support a parent.

### 13.7.2 British Columbia

An adult child is liable to maintain and support a financially dependent parent having regard to the other responsibilities and liabilities and the reasonable needs of the child. A "parent" means a father or mother dependent upon a child because of age, illness, infirmity or other economic circumstance.

### 13.7.3 Manitoba

A son or daughter is liable for the support of his or her dependent parents if it appears that the son or daughter has sufficient means to provide for the parent. A parent will be considered to be dependent if, by reason of age, disease or infirmity, he or she is unable to maintain himself or herself without assistance.

### 13.7.4 New Brunswick

Every person who has attained the age of majority has an obligation to provide support, in accordance with need, for his or her parent who has cared for and provided support for that person, to the extent that the person is capable of doing so.

### 13.7.5 Newfoundland

Every child who is not a minor has an obligation to provide support, in accordance with need, for his or her parent who has cared for or provided support for the child, to the extent that the child is capable of doing so.

### 13.7.6 Northwest Territories

A child who has attained the age of majority has an obligation to provide support, in accordance with need, for his or her parent to the extent that the child is capable of doing so, where the parent:

- cared for or provided support for the child over a significant period of time, including any period during which care or support was provided by the parent after the child attained the age of majority; and

- is unable to support himself or herself.

### 13.7.7 Nova Scotia

A court may order a child who is of the age of majority to pay maintenance for a dependent parent. When determining the amount of maintenance, the court will consider:

- the reasonable needs of the dependent parent;
- the ability of the dependent parent to contribute to his or her own maintenance; and
- the reasonable needs and ability to pay of the child obliged to pay.

### 13.7.8 Nunavut

See section 13.7.6. The rules in Nunavut are essentially the same as in the Northwest Territories.

### 13.7.9 Ontario

Every child who is not a minor has an obligation to provide support, in accordance with need, for his or her parent who cared for or provided support for the child, to the extent that the child is capable of doing so.

### 13.7.10 Prince Edward Island

Every child who is not a minor has an obligation to provide support, in accordance with need, for his or her parent who has cared for or provided support for the child, to the extent that the child is capable of doing so.

### 13.7.11 Quebec

A child is liable for the support of a dependent parent.

### 13.7.12 Saskatchewan

A child is liable for the support of a dependent parent. A parent is deemed to be dependent if he or she is unable to maintain himself or herself.

### 13.7.13 Yukon

Every child who is not a minor, has an obligation to provide support in accordance with need, for their parent who has cared for or provided support for the child, to the extent that the child is capable of doing so.

## 13.8 CASE STUDY

### 13.8.1 Elderly Parents with Adult Children

Chris wants to ensure that his parents, Armand and Anita, are prepared for their "golden years", and their estate plan is in order. After discussing a few issues, Armand and Anita decide to update their documents to indicate the following circumstances.

- In the event either Armand or Anita should become incapacitated, they have named each other as their power of attorney for finances, naming Chris as the alternate. They do the same with their health care directives.

- Armand and Anita review their finances with their financial advisor, and determine that they should take out a long-term care policy to fund their health care costs in the future.

- Armand and Anita decide to change their will so that Chris will receive his estate in a trust, as Chris is already in the highest tax bracket. When Chris receives his inheritance, he will invest it in the name of the trustees of the trust, and the first dollars of income earned in the trust will be taxed at a lower rate than if they were taxed in Chris's hands.

- Armand and Anita also decide that it would be more tax effective if they each received their inheritances from each other in trust, so they hold all of their assets in individual names, as opposed to joint names. When the first of the spouses dies, their inheritance will go to a spousal trust, and the income will not impact the survivor's ability to collect Old Age Security payments.

- Armand and Anita discuss their funeral plans between themselves and with Chris, and decide to pre-arrange their funeral to minimize stress in the future

# CHAPTER 14

# SENIORS AND RETIREES

This chapter contains information related to people who are 60 years old or over and/or contemplating retirement. In our modern economy, many individuals are choosing not to retire until well into their 70s or 80s, and in our ever-aging society, people who are 60 hardly seem "senior". However, for lack of a better label, this chapter should provide some planning ideas for those in the "golden years".

# 14.1 FINANCIAL PLANNING

## 14.1.1 CPP Benefits

### *14.1.1.1 When to Start Receiving CPP*

If you have been contributing to the Canada Pension Plan ("CPP"), you will be entitled to start receiving a monthly pension as early as age 60. However, the normal retirement age is considered to be age 65, so if you choose to start receiving payments earlier than that, your payments will be reduced by .5% for each month prior to age 65 that you elect to begin receiving payments. If you choose to defer receipt of your CPP benefits past age 65, your payments will be increased by .5% for each month after age 65, with no increases after age 70. Therefore, if you start receiving payments at age 60, your payments will be

30% lower than the payments you would be entitled to at age 65, and if you start receiving payments at age 70, your payments will be 30% higher. If you apply for CPP after age 65, you can receive retroactive payments for up to one year.

When making a decision as to when to begin receiving payments, it is important to discuss the issue with your financial planner to ensure you are making the right decision. In many cases, it is best to start receiving payments as early as possible. For example, even though your payments may be lower at age 60, in many cases you would have to live well past 75 in order to receive more from the plan by waiting until age 65. Also, once you begin to receive payments, you will no longer need to make contributions to the plan (even if you decide to go back to work), which, depending upon your income, could save you up to approximately $2000 on an annual basis, and double that amount if you are self-employed.

If you want to start receiving payments before age 65, you must actually retire from your current occupation, although there is nothing to prevent you from starting to work again once you have met the initial conditions for receiving payment. Therefore, if you are under age 65 and you retire from your current position, you could start to receive CPP so long as you have no earnings, or earnings less than the maximum monthly CPP retirement benefit, *both* in the month prior to and *the actual month* that your benefit begins. Once you start receiving your CPP pension, you can work as much as you want without your earnings affecting your pension amount, but you will not be able to contribute to the CPP on those earnings. Once you reach age 65, you will be entitled to begin receiving CPP payments even if you are still working.

Another reason to consider starting your CPP payments early is if you are not working between the ages of 60 and 65. You should consider the impact that these non-contributory years may have on the amount of pension you will be entitled to at age 65 compared with the amount of a reduced pension taken earlier. However, if you are earning a significant income between age 60 and 65 and you did not have much opportunity to contribute to the CPP prior to that (or not at a high level), you may prefer to wait until age 65 or older to start collecting a pension.

Regardless of when you decide to start to receive CPP benefits, and how you decide to receive them, always remember that you must apply for these benefits in order to receive them, and no tax will be deducted from the payments, so you must plan for the tax liability that must be paid on these amounts.

For more information on the benefits of splitting CPP payments with a spouse or common-law partner, see section 14.2.1.3.1.

### *14.1.1.2 Child-Rearing Dropout Provision*

If you are eligible to receive CPP payments, and you were out of the workforce for a period of time due to the fact that you were raising a child under the age of 7, ensure that the government is aware of this fact. Your CPP payments will be calculated based on the number of years in which you contributed to the plan, versus the number of years you could have contributed, so you do not want your payments to be decreased unnecessarily simply because there were a number of years in which you could have contributed to the plan, but chose to stay at home in order to raise a family. In order to ensure that your payments are as high as possible, be sure to fill out the form regarding The Child Rearing Dropout Provision, which is a separate form (except in Quebec). Service Canada will not be aware of your personal circumstances unless you tell them, so it is important to inform them of the number of years in which you were at home raising your family.

## 14.1.2 Old Age Security and Guaranteed Income Supplement

The Old Age Security ("OAS") and Guaranteed Income Supplement ("GIS") are two income-tested benefits provided by the federal government for seniors. OAS is available to anyone over the age of 65 who has met certain Canadian residency requirements. The amount of the benefit is income-tested, and is clawed back by 15% of any net income earned over approximately $67,000, such that it is completely eliminated for individuals with a net income of approximately $108,000. OAS payments are taxable. You should apply for OAS at least six months prior to your 65th birthday in order to ensure you will start receiving benefits as soon as possible. If you apply after your 65th birthday, the maximum amount of benefits that can be paid in arrears is 11 months, plus the month in which your application was received. Please see section 14.2.1 for a discussion on a number of strategies you may be able to employ to reduce your net income, as it is your income that the government will look to when determining eligibility for benefits, not your assets. In fact, there are some very wealthy Canadians who have manipulated their income so that they can receive OAS (and in some cases, even GIS, as discussed below). Since OAS payments are based on individual incomes, not net combined family income, income splitting with your spouse or common-law partner may be particularly beneficial. Maximizing your TFSAs and investing in T-Class or Corporate Class mutual funds may also assist in maximizing your OAS payments..

The GIS provides additional monies to low-income individuals, and is paid in addition to OAS. To be eligible to receive GIS benefits, you must be receiving OAS and not exceed certain income amounts. When determining whether or not you are eligible for GIS, any OAS payments will be deducted from the amount of your income. For couples who are legally married or who have been living in a common-law relationship for a period of at least one year, their income is combined when determining eligibility for the benefits. If you have been living apart voluntarily, then your GIS will be recalculated as if you were single. If you are living apart involuntarily (i.e., one of you is confined to a hospital or nursing home), then each spouse will be considered a single person if it is to their advantage.

If your spouse or common-law partner is entitled to receive both OAS and GIS, and you are 60-64 years of age and meet certain Canadian residency requirements, you may also be entitled to receive what is known as the Allowance. The amount of this benefit is calculated based on the combined annual income from the previous year of both you and your spouse or common-law partner. At age 65, most people who receive the Allowance will become entitled to receive OAS and GIS, depending upon their income.

You need to apply for both of these benefits annually, and no withholdings for taxes will be made against any of these payments unless you request it, so you must plan for any tax liability you may owe in respect of these payments.

## 14.1.3 Nursing Care Costs

Nursing care costs are becoming a larger and larger concern for many families in Canada. Although there is some planning that can be done in advance to try to minimize the amount that you will have to pay for nursing care, in many cases it involves taking drastic steps like giving all of your assets away so that you are essentially destitute. This type of planning is generally not recommended, and you should speak with a financial advisor prior to taking any drastic step so that you understand the tax consequences and financial implications of doing so. Also, in many jurisdictions, the government will look back over transactions made over the past several years, so you would have to give your assets away well in advance of actually needing to go into the nursing home. How can you predict when that might be, and how will you support yourself in the interim?

However, some jurisdictions, nursing care costs are based on net income as reported on your income tax return, as opposed to your asset level (see section 14.6, "Jurisdiction Differences"). If that is the case in your jurisdiction, see section 14.2.1, "Reducing Your Net Income", for a list of strategies that may help you to minimize your net income. Be sure to speak with a financial advisor prior to implementing any of these strategies.

## 14.1.4 Pharmaceutical Expenses

In many jurisdictions, you must complete a special provincial form to calculate your deductible for medication. Given the high cost of drugs, it is worth talking to your financial advisor about whether or not there are methods by which you can minimize these costs.

## 14.1.5 Locked-In Retirement Plans

If you contributed to a pension that was later transferred to a locked-in plan such as a life income fund (a "LIF"), then there will be minimum and maximum amounts that you can withdraw from the plan each year. Even if you do not need the maximum amount allowed, consider withdrawing the maximum amount each year, and transferring the unnecessary amounts to a RRSP (if you are under 71) or a RRIF using Form T2030. The transfer is tax deferred (if transferred to a registered plan), and the withdrawal of these funds in the future will no longer be restricted, meaning that in case of emergency, you will be able to withdraw a lump sum from your RRSP or RRIF, which is something you cannot do with a locked-in plan. Another reason to transfer the funds to an RRSP even if they are not required right away is because the investment earnings will also be "unlocked", giving you even more flexibility in the future. However, if you are a business owner or you have other reasons to be concerned about creditor protection, speak to your advisors prior to transferring excess amounts to your RRSP, since locked-in plans are generally less subject to seizure by creditors than unlocked plans.

However, if you do want to transfer any amounts to your RRSP or RRIF, you must arrange to have this sum transferred directly. If you withdraw the amount from the locked-in plan, you will need to pay tax on that amount, and you will only be able to contribute the after-tax amount to an RRSP if you have sufficient RRSP room. If the intention is to roll over an amount to an RRSP, this must be done directly, without the funds being transferred to you first.

### 14.1.6 Charitable Gifts

If you have planned well for your retirement, you may now be in a position where you have sufficient income to sustain you for the rest of your life, and you may start to think about making charitable contributions. If so, ensure that you are making these contributions in the most tax-effective manner. See Chapter 24, "Charitable Giving", for a further discussion on this topic.

One strategy you could consider once you start receiving payments from your RRIF is to use the after tax RRIF payments to pay the insurance premiums on a policy given to charity, if you do not need the RRIF payments for your current needs. If the insurance policy is owned by a charity, you will receive a charitable tax credit for each of the premiums paid, which can help offset the RRIF income inclusion. However, there are advantages and disadvantages to making the charity the owner of the insurance policy, which are discussed more fully in Chapter 24.

## 14.2 TAX PLANNING

### 14.2.1 Reducing Your Net Income

Although minimizing taxes is a key objective for most Canadians, the issues are a little more complex for seniors. This is because a number of benefits that seniors are entitled to are not determined by the amount of tax they pay, but are determined by their *net income* for tax purposes. Here are a few examples.

- *Old Age Security.* Individuals aged 65 or over may be entitled to start receiving OAS, as well as the GIS and the Allowance, all of which are discussed in more detail in 14.1.2. These social assistance programs are income-tested, with all amounts clawed back for individuals making in excess of $108,000. Therefore, once you reach age 65, it may be in your best interests to minimize your net income for tax purposes in order to maximize the amount of social assistance to which you may be entitled.

- *Age Credit.* Individuals aged 65 or over may claim an amount for the "age credit" on their income tax return. The amount of the age credit is clawed back by 15% of any net income earned above a prescribed threshold, which is indexed annually. The income threshold is currently approximately $33,000, so once your income reaches approximately $75,000, you will no longer be entitled to receive any of this credit

- *Nursing Care Costs.* As mentioned in section 14.1.2, in many jurisdictions, the amount you pay for nursing care is determined by the amount of your net income for tax purposes. (See section 14.6 for the rules in your jurisdiction).

Therefore, as you can see, it is the reduction of net income for tax purposes, not necessarily the reduction of the amount of tax you pay, that is of most concern to most seniors and retirees.

### 14.2.1.1 Tax-Free Savings Accounts

All Canadian residents over the age of 18 are entitled to make annual contributions to a Tax-Free Savings Account ("TFSA"). Although contributions to a TFSA are not tax-deductible in the same manner as an RRSP, all withdrawals from a TFSA are completely tax free, including any income or growth on the original contributions. Unlike RRSPs, you do not have to start making withdrawals from this type of plan at a specific age, so these vehicles may be particularly useful for retirees who are forced to start making withdrawals from their RRIF at age 71. Currently, the annual contribution limit is $5000, which is the same amount granted to every adult, regardless of income. This amount will be indexed in increments of $500 based on the rate of inflation.

Although the name implies that this is simply a "savings account", you may in fact invest in any type of qualified investments, which are essentially the same types of investments as allowed for RRSPs, including mutual funds, stocks and bonds. This may be a particularly good place for seniors to put their dividend paying stock, since as referred to in section 14.2.1.6, although dividends are not necessarily highly taxed due to the dividend tax credit, they do have a very punitive effect when calculating your net income for the purposes of determining your entitlement to certain social assistance benefits such as OAS. However, since losses incurred within a TFSA cannot be used against taxable capital gains, it may not be wise to invest too aggressively within these types of plans.

### 14.2.1.2 T-Class Mutual Funds

T-Class mutual funds are tax-advantaged funds that include a return of capital component in the distributions. When you receive a return of your capital, this portion of the payment is tax free, although it will "grind-down" your cost base in the fund, meaning that you will have a higher capital gain when you sell the fund in the future. Therefore, although the fund allows you to receive cash flow, your investments can continue to grow, since the number of shares you own in the fund will remain the same. Over time, your adjusted cost base will continue to go down until it reaches zero. At that point, any additional payments will be considered capital gains, which are only 50% taxable, so it will continue to be a more preferred investment if your intent is to minimize taxable income.

These funds allow you to receive a consistent tax-efficient monthly income, and are therefore sometimes also referred to as "monthly income funds" or T-series or T-SWPs. The amount you can receive from these funds is greater than what you might receive if you were simply earning interest on a traditional GIC, since part of the payment is in fact a return of your original investment. Also, interest payments are 100% taxable, and therefore not as tax-efficient. These funds are appropriate for non-registered investments, and may be particularly appropriate if you have maximized all of your RRSP contributions. However, the strategy is obviously only as good as the investment you choose, so it is still important to confer with a financial advisor to invest in the appropriate fund.

As mentioned previously, the return of your capital over a period of time will reduce your adjusted cost base, possibly resulting in a larger capital gain at the time of sale or the time of death. If you intend to leave a charitable gift in your will, consider giving your personal representative the ability to give the T-class mutual fund to the charity, since the capital gains inclusion rate is 0% for publicly traded mutual funds given to qualified donees.

### *14.2.1.3 Income Splitting*

One way in which to reduce your net income to the greatest extent possible is to have some of your income included on the tax return of a lower income-earning spouse or common-law partner. Although the *Income Tax Act* generally prohibits you from reporting income on the tax return of anyone other than yourself, there are a few limited instances in which it is allowed, and which we will review in this section.

However, do not always assume that it is better to income-split. In some cases, transferring income from the high income-earning spouse to the low income-earning spouse may mean that the low income-earning spouse will receive fewer social assistance benefits (for example, if their Old Age Security benefits are now clawed back). Always speak to a professional to determine the most optimal way in which to report the income of both spouses.

### 14.2.1.3.1 Splitting CPP Benefits

If both you and your spouse are 60 or over and retired, you can split your CPP benefits so as to each receive an equal benefit. For example, if you are entitled to $6000 in CPP benefits per year, and your spouse is entitled to $10,000 per year, you could split the benefits so that you each receive $8,000 per year. Depending upon the income you receive from other sources, this income-splitting technique may help you pay less tax overall. For example, if the person entitled to $10,000 in CPP is also entitled to a $50,000 pension, and the person entitled to $6,000 in CPP has no other source of income, it is obviously in your best interests to have as much of your combined CPP payments taxed in the hands of the lower income-earning spouse as possible. The amount of your CPP benefit that is shareable will depend upon the number of years during which you were married or living common-law. Contact your local Income Security Program of Human Resources Development Canada for more details.

Sharing of CPP pension benefits will stop, and benefits will return to their original value when:

- either spouse or common-law partner dies;
- a non-contributing spouse or partner starts contributing to the CPP;
- both parties provide a written request to cease the division of benefits;
- the parties have been voluntary separated for at least one year; or
- the parties are divorced.

### 14.2.1.3.2 Pension Income Splitting

Up to 50% of income that qualifies for the federal pension income tax credit can be transferred to a spouse or common-law partner for tax reporting purposes. Whether or not income qualifies as pension income for the pension income tax credit depends upon the age of the spouse who receives the income, and then transfers it (i.e., the age of the spouse with whom the taxpayer is splitting the income for tax purposes is not relevant). Payments that qualify for pension income splitting will continue to be paid to the person originally entitled to the payment, but there will be an ability to allocate some of that income to a spouse or common-law partner on your tax return on an annual basis (unlike when CPP or QPP benefits are split, in which case the payment itself is actually paid to the spouse or common-law partner directly).

For those individuals aged 65 and over, eligible pension income includes the following:

- lifetime annuity payments under a registered pension plan or a foreign pension plan;

- lifetime annuity payments under a registered retirement savings plan or a deferred profit sharing plan;

- payments from a registered retirement income fund, a life income fund, a locked-in retirement income fund or a prescribed retirement income fund; and

- any interest paid as part of a non-registered annuity.

Other types of income, including OAS and GIS payments, lump-sum RRSP withdrawals and income from a retirement compensation arrangement, do not qualify as pension income for these purposes.

For those under age 65, eligible pension income includes lifetime annuity payments under a registered pension plan (or a foreign pension plan) and some payments received upon the death of a spouse or common-law partner. Payments from a locked-in retirement fund or life income fund are not qualified pension income, since the fund is not a life annuity.

In order to split income that qualifies for the pension income tax credit, you must report all the pension income you receive, and then deduct up to 50% of it on your tax return, and your spouse or common-law partner must include the corresponding amount on their tax return. You may choose to allocate any amount up to 50% of your pension income on your spouse's return, but no more than 50%. In some cases, depending upon the incomes of each spouse, it may not be advisable to allocate any income to either spouse.

However, in some cases, the ability to allocate pension income to a spouse may provide the following benefits:

- less tax may be paid by the couple as a result of some income now being taxed in a lower tax bracket;

- if the recipient spouse was not using the $2000 pension income tax credit, they may now be able to use it. However, although the recipient spouse of pension income does not have to be 65 in order to allocate pension income on their tax return, he or she must be 65 in order to claim the pension income credit;

- benefits and tax credits that are calculated based on the pooled amount of income of both spouses or common-law partners — such as the Guaranteed Income Supplement, the GST/HST credit, Canada Child Tax Benefit, and related provincial or territorial benefits, such as nursing care subsidies — will not change as a result of pension splitting. However, pension splitting will affect any tax credits and benefits that are calculated using an individual's net income, such as the age amount, the spousal credit and Old Age Security benefits. In some cases, pension income splitting will be helpful, as it may allow a high income-earner to receive more of these benefits. In other cases, it may not be advisable if the amount transferred to a lower income-earning spouse means they are now eligible for fewer of these benefits;

- where the lower-income spouse is not subject to tax, pension income splitting may increase the amount of medical expenses you can claim as part of the medical expense tax credit as a result of the lower-income spouse now earning more taxable income.

- both Ontario and Quebec's health care premiums are based on the taxable income of each taxpayer, so pension income splitting may help to reduce the health care premium.

Before deciding how much pension income to transfer, you should speak to your financial advisor to determine how to pay less tax as a couple.

### 14.2.1.3.3 Other Forms of Income Splitting

Here are some other strategies for splitting income with a spouse or common-law-partner.

- If you have significant investment assets, the higher income-earning spouse could lend money to the lower income-earning spouse at an interest rate acceptable to the Canada Revenue Agency, and then the lower income-earning spouse could invest that money. The lower income earning-spouse could then report all of the income earned on those investments, although the higher income-earning spouse would obviously have to report the annual income payments they receive. Speak to your financial advisor as to whether or not this type of prescribed rate loan would assist you, as they should be aware of the current rate of interest that has been set by the Canada Revenue Agency for these types of loans. Please refer to section 5.2.1.5 of Chapter 5, "Married", for more details regarding prescribed rate loans.

- Another method by which to shift more taxable income into the hands of a lower-income earning spouse is to arrange your financial affairs so that the lower-income earning spouse uses their income for family savings, and the higher income-earning spouse uses their income for family expenses. This will allow more of the investment income to accrue in the hands of the lower-income earning spouse. However, this strategy may not be appropriate for common-law couples who reside in jurisdictions where there is no ability to divide family property in the event of a relationship breakdown as they may want to keep all of their assets in their own name (see section 17.7 of Chapter 17, "Family Property", for more information on the rules in your jurisdiction).

- If your spouse or common-law partner will be in a lower tax bracket than you in retirement, you could make your RRSP contributions to a "spousal" RRSP that lists your spouse or common-law partner as the annuitant. Payments from the spousal RRSP can then be paid to the lower-income earning spouse, thereby paying less tax as a couple. However, there are a couple of issues to keep in mind when using spousal RRSPs:

  - If your spouse or common-law partner withdraws the money in the year in which you make any contribution, or in either of the next two calendar years, then the amount of the withdrawal will be taxed in the contributor's name. Therefore, if you make a spousal RRSP contribution in 2006, your spouse should not withdraw any funds from the spousal RRSP in 2006, 2007 or 2008 if you want the funds taxed in your spouse's name. Also note that if you make a subsequent contribution in 2008, the time period for the attribution rules will start again since you will not be able to designate the withdrawal as being in respect of the 2006 contribution. In fact, if your spouse withdraws the funds in 2009, but you make a contribution later in 2009, the attribution rules will still apply, since the withdrawal occurred in the same year in which you made a contribution to the spousal RRSP.

  - If you are in a common-law relationship, it may not be recommended that you make a spousal RSP contribution if you have not entered into a cohabitation agreement. This is because you may want to keep your assets separate if you live in a jurisdiction where common-law couples are not required to divide their family assets at the time of relationship breakdown. See section 17.4 of Chapter 17, "Family Property", for more information on the rules in your jurisdiction.

Section 5.2.1 in Chapter 5, "Married", has more information on strategies that married or common-law couples could consider to split their income for tax purposes.

### 14.2.1.4 Invest in Capital Gains Producing Assets

One tax-effective form of income is capital gains income, which is only 50% taxable, and can be deferred for as long as you hold the asset. Capital gains are usually earned on investments such as equities or real estate. However, some of these types of investments may be more risky, so they may not be appropriate if you have a very short time horizon for your investment, or if you are very risk adverse. However, despite the increased risk inherent in some individual investments, a financial advisor should be able to construct a well-balanced portfolio for you that includes some equities, but also minimizes your risk.

### 14.2.1.5 Corporate Class Mutual Funds

Mutual funds that use a corporate structure will allow you to move from fund to fund within the corporation without triggering any capital gains. Therefore, you can continue to defer the payment of any capital gains on your investments, yet at the same time make changes to your portfolio (so long as you do not leave the corporate structure). Also, fixed income payments made from a corporate structure generally are taxed as capital gains, not regular income, further reducing your net income. Using a corporate structure may allow you to have some fixed income in your portfolio, while at the same time, minimizing your annual net income for tax purposes.

### 14.2.1.6 Minimize Dividend Income

While many people understand that capital gains are the best type of income to receive if you want to minimize your net income, many people do not realize that dividend income from a Canadian public corporation is the worst type of income to receive in this respect. That is because these types of dividends are "grossed up" by 41% when calculating your net income. For example, if you earned $10,000 in dividends from a Canadian public corporation, you would actually have to report $14,100 in taxable income. Although you will receive a dividend tax credit that will in fact result in the dividends being taxed at a relatively low rate of tax, the dividend tax credit is not relevant for the purposes of determining your net income. *It is net income that is relevant for most of the benefits you are entitled to, not your tax payable.* Therefore, if you are looking for methods by which to decrease your net income, interest income and foreign source dividends are actually preferable to Canadian source dividends in this instance, and, of course, capital gains are even better.

Some dividends are subject to a lower "gross-up" rate than 41%. As mentioned above, the 41% rate is applied to dividends paid from public corporations resident in Canada (and, in fact, is also applied to dividends paid by Canadian-controlled private corporations ("CCPCs") subject to tax at the general corporate tax rate and dividends paid by Canadian corporations that are not CCPCs). However, when a CCPC earns income that is eligible for the small business deduction, any dividends paid in respect of that income will only be subject to a gross-up of 25% (and accordingly, a lower dividend tax credit). Generally speaking, these dividends (which are referred to as "ineligible dividends") are also not desirable when trying to minimize your taxable income, but they are not as detrimental as "eligible dividends" (being those which qualify for the 41% gross-up rate). The higher the gross-up rate, the more the dividend will erode at your ability to receive social assistance, etc.

Foreign source dividends are not subject to any gross-up. This means that they also don't qualify for any sort of dividend tax credit, so they are not taxed as favourably as Canadian source dividends. However, if your intent is to lower your net income for the purpose of maximizing social assistance, they actually produce the least detrimental result. However, always confer with a financial advisor before investing in any foreign investment and pay particular attention to whether or not holding a US stock could result in a US estate tax liability.

### *14.2.1.7 Minimize Withdrawals from Registered Assets*

As you grow older, the withdrawals you make from your registered investments (e.g. RRSPs or RRIFs) could comprise one of the most significant income receipts on your tax return. Generally speaking, you will want to defer the receipt of this income as long as possible. Here are a few strategies to consider.

- In the year in which you turn 71, your RRSP will mature, and you will either be required to purchase an annuity, or transfer the proceeds into a RRIF. If you transfer the assets to a RRIF, you will be required to withdraw annual amounts, based on your age. If you have a spouse or common-law partner who is younger than you, you can choose instead to have the withdrawals based on your spouse or common-law partner's age, meaning that the amount you will be required to withdraw each year will be lower than if the withdrawals were based on your age.

- Prior to age 71, it is usually recommended that you pay all administration fees from your non-registered funds in order to keep as much as possible in the plan, as all funds in the plan grow on a tax-deferred basis. However, once you turn 71, it may be advisable to pay these fees with funds inside the plan, as this will be considered a withdrawal, lowering the amount you will need to include in your taxable income.

- If you are not earning much income, it may be advisable to start making withdrawals prior to age 71, in order to smooth out your taxable income in later years. Income tax rates are assessed on a graduated basis, meaning that the more income you earn, the higher the tax rate. If you are in a low tax bracket now, it may be advisable to pay some tax earlier at a lower rate, rather than withdrawing large sums later, some of which may be taxed at a high rate. However, if you are going to withdraw funds from your RRSP sooner than you are required to because you are in a low-income tax bracket, monitor your withdrawals carefully. It is probably best not to withdraw an amount which would put you in an income tax bracket higher than the lowest threshold, which is approximately $41,000, since the income tax rates increase significantly after that point. Speak to your financial advisor to determine if this strategy is appropriate for you.

### *14.2.1.8 Maximize Tax Deductions*

When attempting to minimize your taxable income, also consider whether or not you are maximizing any tax deductions that may be available to you. The most popular tax deduction is the deduction given for making a contribution to an RRSP. Here are some strategies that may maximize the use of this deduction.

- In the year in which you turn 71, if you are still working or earning "earned income", try to anticipate the amount of RRSP room you will generate that year, and make an RRSP contribution before December 31st based on that estimated amount. Since your RRSP will mature by the end of the year, you will not be able to make an RRSP contribution in the next year, even if you had earned income that year. Although there will be a penalty for over-contributing in the year in which you turned 71 (the penalty is 1% of the amount of the over-contribution), the penalty will be minimal given that you will only be charged the penalty for one month, assuming you make the over-contribution in December.

- After the year in which you turn 71, you will no longer be able to make contributions to an RRSP. However, if your spouse or common-law partner is under the age of 71, you will still be able to make RRSP contributions to an RRSP that has your spouse or common-law partner as the annuitant (this is referred to as a "spousal RRSP"). If you continue to have earned income, you will be able to continue making these contributions, regardless of whether or not you are over 71. (However, if you are in a common-law relationship, you may not want to make spousal RRSP contributions if you want to keep your property separate in case of relationship breakdown – see section 17.4 of Chapter 17, "Family Property", to see if common-law partners have the right to a division of family property in your jurisdiction.) After you turn 71, any unused RRSP contribution room will not be reported on your Notice of Assessment, so you will need to contact the Canada Revenue Agency in order to obtain this information.

- Another planning technique that you may want to consider is to make RRSP contributions prior to age 65, but save the receipts until turning age 65, and use them at that time to reduce your taxable income so you qualify for certain government programs such as Old Age Security.

It is important to remember that an RRSP contribution is a *tax deduction,* which will decrease your net income on a dollar-for-dollar basis. Unfortunately, maximizing the amount of tax *credits* that you are entitled to will not help to minimize your net income. For example, the charitable tax credit will not reduce your net income. Although it will reduce the amount of tax you have to pay, it will not help to reduce your net income, which is the only item relevant in most jurisdictions when determining whether or not you are entitled to certain benefits. The tax credit available for employees who exercise employee stock options and the dividend tax credit work in the same way as the charitable tax credit — they help to reduce your total tax payable, but will not assist you in minimizing your net income.



### *14.2.1.9 Annuities and GMWBs*

As discussed in section 14.2.1.2, it may be possible to decrease your net income by purchasing investments that include a "return of capital" as part of their payments. If your investment portfolio consists mainly of conservative investments such as GICs which produce income that is taxable on an annual basis (e.g. interest), then it may be better to take the capital currently invested in the GIC and purchase an annuity. (Although if the assets used to purchase the annuity are equities, you may trigger immediate capital gains when you sell those assets.) Since part of the annuity payment will represent a return of capital (which is non-taxable), your net income for tax purposes should be lower than if you were to receive a regular interest payment.

Annuities are generally only recommended if you do not require the capital for other purposes, since you are only entitled to a fixed monthly amount. Another drawback with the use of an annuity is that your estate will not receive any of the remaining capital unless there is some sort of guaranteed payment period. However, the annuity payment is often higher than the interest payment you would have otherwise received, and you will be paying less in taxes. This additional income can be used to purchase a life insurance policy so that the capital will be returned to your estate at the time of your death. You should review this strategy with your tax professional to ensure that the additional cost of the insurance premiums does not exceed the tax savings.

Another potential risk inherent in using an annuity is the fact that the annuity payment is fixed, so your purchasing power will decrease if interest rates increase. Therefore, it may be a good idea to have some investments in equities as a hedge against inflation.

Instead of purchasing an annuity, you may prefer to consider a segregated fund with a guaranteed minimum withdrawal benefit ("GMWB"). This type of fund is similar to an annuity in that it provides a guaranteed income stream so long as you don't withdraw more than the allowed amounts. However, unlike an annuity, it may still have a market value at the time of death. This type of fund does not include a return of capital, so it is less tax efficient.

## *14.2.1.10 Receiving Inheritances Through a Trust*

If you anticipate receiving an inheritance from an elderly parent or a spouse, review their estate plan with them to see if there is a more tax-effective manner in which you could receive the inheritance. For example, if you receive the inheritance in your own name, and then invest the money, all of the annual income will be taxable in your name. However, if the inheritance is instead left to you in a trust, that trust will be considered a separate taxpayer, reducing the amount of income taxable in your own name, and maximizing the amount of Old Age Security to which you may be entitled. If you feel comfortable discussing finances with the person who will be giving you the inheritance, ask them about the possibility of changing their will to include a testamentary trust (see Case Studies 5.8.2 in Chapter 5, "Married", and 10.8.2 in Chapter 10,

"Children", for examples of when a testamentary trust may help a beneficiary pay less tax).

### *14.2.1.11 Permanent Life Insurance*

Another way in which you may be able to reduce your taxable income is through the use of a whole life or universal life insurance policy. With these types of permanent insurance, any income earned within the policy accrues on a tax-deferred basis, and the beneficiaries receive the death benefit and cash surrender value tax free. If you should need the funds at a future date, a portion of the cash surrender value can be withdrawn tax free as a loan, and then repaid at the time of death using the insurance proceeds (sometimes referred to as an "insured retirement plan"). Although many older people do not perceive themselves to be in need of insurance, that is generally because they are not aware of the tax liability that may arise at the time of their death. If you want to preserve a specific asset for your children (for example, a vacation property or a business), it may be particularly important to ensure that you have adequate insurance so that your heirs will not have to sell the asset to pay the tax liability. See Chapter 21, "Taxation at Death", for a further discussion of how your registered investments (including RRSPs and RRIFs) and any unrealized capital gains are taxed at the time of your death. Also see Chapter 15, "Vacation Properties", or Chapter 16, "Business Owners", if you have one of these types of assets and section 25.2.3 of Chapter 25, "Insurance", for more information on permanent life insurance.

### *14.2.1.12 Holding Corporations*

If you have significant non-registered investments, it may be worth considering whether or not these investments should be transferred to a holding corporation. Any income earned on the investments would be taxable to the holding corporation, which would not affect your net income for Old Age Security purposes. If the transfer is structured as a loan, you will also be able to remove funds from the corporation on a tax-free basis by having the corporation make loan repayments. However, if you need the annual income generated by the investments to support your standard of living, then the income will need to be paid out as a dividend, which will of course be taxable, and may put you in a worse position than if you had simply earned the income in your own name. (This is because dividends from Canadian corporations must be "grossed up" by 41%. Although the tax on Canadian source dividends is reduced by the dividend tax credit, this does not reduce your net income. See section 14.2.1.6

above for more information.) However, if you do not need the income, then this strategy may be helpful.

Speak with your tax advisors prior to implementing this sort of structure, as there are ongoing administrative costs with a corporation, and you will need to transfer a significant sum of money into the corporation in order to make the strategy cost effective.

The use of a holding company may also provide a potential probate fee savings if you can use the multiple will strategy in your jurisdiction. See section 22.3.9 of Chapter 22, "Probate", for more information on this strategy.

### *14.2.1.13 Timing Receipt of Income*

If you are attempting to minimize your income, particularly for the purpose of maximizing your Old Age Security payments, try to time the receipt of various income items so that the amounts are received in a tax-advantaged manner. For example, try to avoid buying mutual funds near the end of a calendar year. Most mutual funds will make their annual distributions of capital gains dividends just prior to the end of December. If you buy a mutual fund in late December, you will receive a tax slip respecting capital gains, even though you will not have received any cash. Although the taxable amount of any capital gain realized when you sell the mutual funds will be decreased in the future, this does not help you in the year in which you received the dividend. Receipt of this dividend income will be included in your tax return in the year it was received, potentially affecting the amount of Old Age Security you will be entitled to receive (depending upon your total net income). Therefore, if possible, defer any purchases of mutual funds until the next calendar year, unless your financial advisor knows that the mutual fund in question will not be making any such distribution that year.

Another way in which your net income could be adversely affected is if you sell or transfer an asset with a large unrealized capital gain, such as a vacation property, since 50% of the entire capital gain will have to be reported in your tax return for the year in which the asset is sold or transferred. If you are considering transferring the property to a family member prior to the time of death, consider having the purchase price paid to you over a five-year period, so that the capital gain can be spread out over five years of tax returns. See section 15.1.4 in Chapter 15, "Vacation Properties", for more information on this strategy, and be sure to discuss the issue with a financial advisor prior to transferring the asset.

### *14.2.1.14 Transferring Assets to a Trust*

Some people attempt to reduce their net income by transferring their assets into a "trust". However, there are a set of rules in the *Income Tax Act* referred to as the attribution rules which attribute income back to you in certain circumstances. When you transfer assets to a trust, you must essentially give up control over the assets in the trust, or the attribution rules will apply. If you are found to control the trust, or if it is at all possible that the assets could come back to you in the future, the *Income Tax Act* will attribute all capital gains and income earned in the trust to you, and you will not have achieved your objective of minimizing your net income.

Also, when determining the amount you must pay for nursing care costs, some jurisdictions will look back at any transactions completed in the last few years, so transferring your assets into a trust a short time before going into a nursing care facility may not be effective in reducing those costs. Speak to a lawyer prior to implementing any strategy of this type.

## 14.2.2 Pension Credit

Taxpayers 65 years of age or older are entitled to claim a tax credit in respect of the first $2000 in annual pension income. Pension income includes:

- periodic (but not lump sum) payments received from a private pension plan created by your employer; and
- periodic payments received from a RRIF, but not lump sum payments received from an RRSP.

However, amounts received from a public pension or social assistance plans such as the CPP or Old Age Security are not considered pension income.

If you are not receiving $2000 of eligible pension income, you can create additional eligible pension income by:

- converting all or part of an RRSP into a life annuity or RRIF (for example, consider transferring enough of your RRSP to your RRIF to withdraw $2000 per year); or
- purchasing an ordinary life annuity with unregistered funds.

If you are under 65, you may also be entitled to claim the pension credit if you are receiving pension income in the form of an annuity, but lump sum amounts received from an RRSP or RRIF will not qualify for the pension credit in this case.

### 14.2.3 Medical Expense Credit

As you grow older, your medical expenses may begin to increase dramatically. The medical expense credit allows you to claim a tax credit for medical expenses in excess of 3% of your total income, or all amounts over a certain threshold, which is approximately $2000 (although the amount is indexed annually, and the rules are different in Quebec — please see section 12.5.9.3 of Chapter 12, "Disabled Persons", for more information on claiming medical expenses in Quebec). Although you may not have had sufficient medical expenses to take advantage of this credit in the past, do not forget about it once your medical expenses start to increase. See section 12.2.5 of Chapter 12, "Disabled Persons", for more details regarding the medical expense tax credit.

### 14.2.4 Disability Tax Credits

Many seniors qualify for the disability tax credit, and the other tax credits associated with having a disability. In many cases, family members can also benefit from the tax credits given to caregivers. See section 12.2 of Chapter 12, "Disabled Persons", for a description of the types of tax credits that may be available to you if you suffer from a disability.

Although you may not suffer from any individual disability that would normally prompt you to apply for the disability tax credit, the *Income Tax Act* now acknowledges that the cumulative effect of a number of conditions may qualify as a disability. Speak to your physician to see if he or she will certify that you qualify for this credit.

## 14.3 DISABILITY PLANNING

As discussed in previous chapters, you should ensure that your disability plan is up-to-date, and you have a proper power of attorney for finances as well as health care decisions. You should also review your disability and illness insurance needs, particularly long-term care insurance, which is discussed in section 14.5 below.

If you suffer from a disability, also review Chapter 12, "Disabled Persons", which discusses the tax credits and other issues relevant to disabled individuals.

## 14.4 ESTATE PLANNING

As discussed in previous chapters, it is imperative that you have your estate plan in order, particularly your will, beneficiary designations and joint ownership arrangements. See the chapter that addresses your current marital status, and/or family situation for further information. Also see the discussion on prepaid funerals in section 13.5.5 of Chapter 13, "Elderly Parents".

One point that seniors need to remember regarding their estate plan is that when you transfer an RRSP into a RRIF you will need to specifically designate a beneficiary on your RRIF if you want it to be the same person or entity that was designated on your RRSP. A direct beneficiary designation will not automatically roll over from an RRSP to a RRIF, so you should confirm with your financial advisor that you want the designation to be made on your RRIF.

## 14.5 INSURANCE PLANNING

Although many older individuals do not perceive there to be a need for insurance once their children are financially independent, and once they themselves have saved enough for their own retirement, you may still have need for certain types of insurance, which are discussed below.

### 14.5.1 Medical Insurance

If you plan to retire, review how much medical insurance coverage you have through your pension plans, and whether they provide dependant coverage. If you or your spouse relies on dependant coverage, be aware of the fact that many survivors lose their entitlement to medical insurance coverage upon the death of their spouse or common-law partner. You may need to make alternate arrangements in advance so that either you or your spouse or common-law partner will have coverage for as long as required.

## 14.5.2 Life Insurance for Tax Liabilities

If your assets have grown considerably in value, there could be a significant tax bill to pay at the time of your death (or at the time of death of your spouse or common-law partner, if everything is transferred to them — see Chapter 21, "Taxation at Death"). If the assets involved are simply investments, and your children are not financially dependent upon you, then you may not be concerned about the fact that your estate will have to liquidate part of your portfolio to pay the taxes. However, if the assets in question include a vacation property, a family business or other sentimental item (such as art, an heirloom, a stamp collection or other valuables), then you may want to ensure that there is adequate insurance in place so that your heirs do not have to sell the asset in order to pay the tax bill. See Chapter 15, "Vacation Properties", and Chapter 16, "Business Owners", for further information regarding the issues involved with these types of assets.

## 14.5.3 Long-Term Care Insurance

You should also consider the benefits of long-term care insurance. Current demographics indicate that governments may not be able to sustain the current level of healthcare. Also, in many cases, people would prefer to stay in their own homes as long as possible, so they want to be able to afford home care, or other services such as assistance with housecleaning and cooking. Even though your savings may be sufficient to pay all of your normal expenses, will they be enough to pay for additional daily services? If not, you should give consideration to long-term care insurance. Long-term care insurance provides for monthly lump-sum payments, which can usually be spent however the insured wishes. The payments usually begin once the insured has lost the ability to perform two of the five functions associated with normal daily life, which are feeding, bathing, dressing, using the washroom and transferring positions (such as getting in and out of bed or a bathtub).

Another reason to consider long-term care insurance is because the daily rates in many nursing homes are based on your income earned as a couple. Costs are usually based either on your level of income, or your level of assets, and in many cases, do not take into account that the spouse who is not in a nursing home still has to maintain a household. Therefore, one spouse could experience a serious deterioration in their standard of living in order to support the other spouse who is living in a nursing home. Long-term care insurance may help the spouse who is not in a nursing home to maintain their lifestyle.

Please see section 25.1.3 of Chapter 25, "Insurance", for more information on long-term care insurance.

### 14.5.4 Critical Illness Insurance

Consider whether or not you should have critical illness insurance. This type of insurance pays a lump sum benefit once you are diagnosed with one of the illnesses listed in the policy. This lump sum payment may give you the freedom to obtain the type of medical care you need, complete home renovations or obtain home care. See section 25.1.2 of Chapter 25, "Insurance", for more information on this product.

## 14.6 JURISDICTION DIFFERENCES

### 14.6.1 Alberta

Nursing care costs are based on the type of room (e.g. private, semi-private), not income or asset level. However, low-income earners can receive assistance through the Alberta Seniors Benefit, the Assured Income for the Severely Handicapped and Supports for Independence, so it may still be beneficial to speak to your financial advisor to determine if there are ways in which you can lower your income in order to qualify for these benefits, including those listed in section 14.2.1.

### 14.6.2 British Columbia

Nursing care costs are based on an income test. You will be required to pay a rate based on your net income (and your spouse's if applicable) minus income tax paid, a basic income amount deduction (which varies based on family size) and earned income up to a maximum of $15,000. The remaining annual income is then matched to one of the daily client rates (see *www.healthservices.gov.bc.ca/hcc/fees.html*). Residential care rates are calculated in two ways (i.e., both combined income for the couple, and individual income) and the lowest rate is applied. Speak to your financial advisor to determine if there may be appropriate strategies to reduce your net income, including those discussed in section 14.2.1.

## 14.6.3 Manitoba

Nursing care costs are based on your assessed income, which is based on your net income less total taxes payable as reported on your income tax notice of assessment. Speak to your financial advisor to determine if there may be appropriate strategies to reduce your net income, including those discussed in section 14.2.1.

Although your assets are generally not considered when calculating your income, the province has a one year look-back rule, so for example, if you withdraw all amounts in your RRIF and then go into a nursing home, the withdrawal will be included on your tax return, and you will be expected to keep those funds for future use.

## 14.6.4 New Brunswick

Nursing care costs are based on your net family income. In New Brunswick, the policy states that an individual's family will include the individual, his or her spouse or common-law partner, and any financially dependent children who are either under 19, under 25 and enrolled full-time in an educational institution, or over 18 and disabled.

The Standard Family Contribution Policy currently defines "net family income" as total income from all sources, of all family members, whether taxable or non-taxable, net of all statutory and other employer deductions including CPP, EI, and income tax, net of any health insurance premiums, and excluding income exempted under the policy. The ministry has also informally made the following statements.

- 100% of any capital gain will be added to "net family income". There will be no 50% inclusion rate, and no recognition of exemptions such as the principal residence exemption.

- The actual amount of any dividend income, and not the grossed-up amount of the dividend, will be added to "net family income".

Speak to your financial advisor to determine if there may be appropriate strategies to reduce your net income, including those discussed in section 14.2.1.

### 14.6.5 Newfoundland

Nursing care costs are based not only on your annual income, but also all "liquid assets", which include cash, securities, GICs, bonds and T-bills. Since it is generally not recommended that assets be transferred to family members prior to the time of death, in many cases there will not be much you can do to reduce your nursing care costs.

### 14.6.6 Northwest Territories

There is no income or asset test when determining the amount payable for nursing care costs.

### 14.6.7 Nova Scotia

Nursing care costs are based on assessed income, not assets. An individual's assessed income is based on "net income" less "total taxes payable" as reported on your income tax return. The regulations also indicate that once admitted to a long-term care facility, you cannot transfer or reduce your income in order to qualify for a lower accommodation charge. Therefore, although you should still be able to make legitimate changes to your portfolio that may in effect reduce your taxable income, other strategies, such as transferring all of your assets to a child or a trust, may not be effective if there is no legitimate reason for the transfer other than to reduce the accommodation charge. See section 14.2.1 for a description of some of the strategies you may be able to use to reduce your net income for tax purposes, although you should speak to a financial advisor prior to implementing them.

### 14.6.8 Nunavut

There is no income or assets test when determining the amount payable for nursing care costs.

### 14.6.9 Ontario

Nursing care costs are based on an income test. Speak to your financial advisor to determine if there may be appropriate strategies to reduce your net income, including those discussed in section 14.2.1.

### 14.6.10 Prince Edward Island

Nursing care costs are based on income, not assets, when assessing whether an individual is eligible for a subsidy with respect to accommodation costs. Although you may be able to employ some of the strategies listed in section 14.2.1 to reduce your income, the rules do include a two-year "look-back" rule, so if you reduce your income within two years of applying for assistance, they may reassess your application based on previous income levels. Please see *www.gov.pe.ca/law/regulations/pdf/L&16-1.pdf* for a description of the rules and regulations for receiving subsidies for long-term care.

### 14.6.11 Quebec

All income and assets are considered when determining the amount payable for nursing care costs. There is a two year look-back rule if you try to transfer assets to a family member to reduce your estate. Since it is generally not recommended that you give away all of your assets to family members prior to the time of your death, it may not be possible to reduce the amount you must pay for nursing care.

### 14.6.12 Saskatchewan

Nursing care costs are based on an income test. Speak to your financial advisor to determine if there may be appropriate strategies to reduce your net income, including those discussed in section 14.2.1.

For married residents (including common-law couples), the couple's income is combined, divided equally, and then a formula is applied. Married residents who live in separate dwellings for reasons beyond their control may choose to complete an Optional Designation Form for the purpose of determining the resident charge. With this designation only the resident's income is considered when calculating the charge. This option is only of benefit in situations where the resident's income is lower than that of their spouse.

### 14.6.13 Yukon

There is no income or asset test when determining the amount payable for nursing care costs

# CHAPTER 15

# VACATION PROPERTIES



Vacation properties are often one of the most difficult assets to address when developing a wealth plan.

- Unlike monetary assets, a vacation property is not divisible. Unless an individual is lucky enough to come from a family that owns more than one vacation property, a decision generally has to be made as to which child will receive the property, or how it will be shared between the children.

- Values for vacation properties have risen dramatically across Canada in recent years. Although this may generally be considered a good thing for many property owners, it does bring with it one major problem — capital gains tax. Many people assume that since the capital gain on their principal home is exempt, that the capital gain on all of their other properties will also be exempt. Unfortunately, this is not true. Families are generally only allowed to designate one property as their principal residence, which means that the gain on any of their other properties will be taxable. Unless the vacation property itself is designated as the family's principal residence, the sale or disposition of a vacation property will generally lead to a tax liability.

- Vacation properties are very special assets in many families. They are a place of nostalgia and emotional attachment. In many cases, children already have a principal residence of their own, but they may not have a vacation property. Therefore, even though the logical thing in many cases may be to sell the property and divide the proceeds, many families want to preserve their specific property at all costs — even if some or all of their children have moved far away. A vacation property may be a favourite location for family reunions or other family gatherings, so emotions may prevail over logic.

These are just a few of the reasons as to why vacation property planning can become very complex. This is why it is particularly important for people to discuss their plans regarding their vacation property with their professional advisors.

## 15.1 TAX PLANNING

One of the major issues you will need to consider if you own a vacation property is the potential tax liability that may arise when you sell the property, or are deemed to have sold it at the time of your death. Assuming you do not designate your vacation property as your principal residence for tax purposes, the sale of the property may trigger a gain (or loss) that will be the difference between your "proceeds of disposition", less the "cost" of the property, and any expenses incurred in disposing of the property. Fifty percent of the capital gain must be reported in your tax return as a taxable capital gain in the year of disposition. Unfortunately, if you experience a loss on the property, you will not be entitled to claim that loss against other capital gains, as the losses on "personal use property" are deemed to be nil.

If you do not sell your property during your lifetime, then it will be deemed to have been disposed of at the time of your death, unless you leave it to a spouse or common-law partner (or a trust in favour of a spouse or common-law partner), in which case the property will be deemed to be disposed of in the year in which your surviving spouse or common-law partner sells the property or dies. When a vacation property is transferred to a family member (other than a spouse or common-law partner), either by way of gift or sale, the transfer will result in a disposition for tax purposes (which is explained more fully in this chapter). Therefore, it is in your best interests to ensure that the amount of the gain is minimized to the extent possible.

### 15.1.1 Proceeds of Disposition

Obviously, the less you receive for your property (or the lower your "proceeds of disposition"), the less tax you will have to pay. As a result, many families try to structure transactions so that it appears that they have not received much, if anything, when they transfer the vacation property to a family member. However, your "proceeds of disposition" for disposition cannot be manipulated in order to minimize the tax liability, as the Canada Revenue Agency has developed a set of rules outlined below.

- If the property is sold or transferred to someone acting at "arm's length" from you, then the proceeds of disposition will be the amount received from the arm's length party.

- If the property is sold or transferred to a non-arm's length party other than a spouse or common-law partner (for example, a child), then the owner will be deemed to have received fair market value for the property, even if the new owner paid less than fair market value or was gifted the property. (See section 22.3.3 of Chapter 22, "Probate", for a discussion on how double taxation can occur if a property is sold to a non-arm's length person for less than fair market value — this course of action is generally not recommended.)

- If you do not sell your property prior to the time of your death, then at the time of death, the property will be deemed to have been disposed of at fair market value (unless you leave the property to a spouse or common-law partner, or a spousal or common-law partner trust, in which case the deemed disposition occurs at the time the survivor sells the property or dies).

Therefore, no matter how the disposition is structured, the proceeds of disposition will either be the amount received from an arm's length party, or the amount the Canada Revenue Agency deems you to receive, which will be the fair market value either at the time of transfer or sale to a family member (other than a spouse or common-law partner or trust in favour of a spouse or common-law partner), or at the time of death. See section 15.1.4, "Transferring the Property to a Family Member", for a further discussion on some of the strategies that you may wish to consider if you want to pass the property to a non-arm's length person. Also see Case Study 15.4.1, "Transfer of Property to a

Child", for an example of the tax consequences that can arise when a child is added as a joint owner to a vacation property.

## 15.1.2 Cost

Obviously, if the amount of your proceeds of disposition cannot be minimized, then the only way to minimize the amount of the capital gain will be to maximize the "cost base", since the higher the cost base, the lower the capital gain.

Many people fail to properly calculate the full cost of their vacation property. The "cost" amount includes more than simply the amount paid for the vacation property — it also includes any amounts that have been spent on the vacation property over the years in order to increase its value. For example, amounts spent on renovations or improvements to a vacation property can be included in the cost base, but the cost of annual repairs such as a new coat of paint, cannot be included. The cost of the property only includes the amount of any cash outlays — therefore, the value of your labour will not be included, although the amount spent to hire others to provide the labour can be included. This is why *it is very important to retain any receipts for amounts spent on materials, supplies or contracted labour for your vacation property*. Be sure to keep these receipts in one place, with any other documentation relating to the vacation property. Also, your personal representatives (i.e. your executors) should be made aware of where such documentation is kept, so that they are able to provide the documentation to the Canada Revenue Agency at the time of death, and minimize the amount of the capital gain.

If you own two properties, then it is also recommended that you save your receipts not only in respect of capital improvements made to your vacation property, but also in respect of any capital improvements that you make to your home. This is because you may decide at some point in the future that you would prefer to designate your vacation property as your principal residence, meaning that the gain on your home will now be taxable (the principal residence exemption is discussed in section 15.1.3). At that point, you will want to minimize the capital gain on your home, which can be done by maximizing the cost base, and keeping good records regarding any capital improvements.

Also keep in mind that prior to 1992, individuals were allowed a $100,000 lifetime capital gains exemption on capital gains realized upon the sale or deemed disposition of any real property, not just principal residences. If an election was made to trigger part or all of the capital gain earned on one of your properties up until that time, it will be important for your personal representatives to know where the documentation regarding this election is kept. By triggering the capital gain prior to the deadline, your cost base will effectively have increased, and it will be important for your personal representatives to know that the cost base is higher as a result of the election. If the election was not made at the required time, neither you nor your personal representatives will be able to make this election in the future, as all deadlines for making the election or requesting an extension have now passed.

### 15.1.3 Principal Residence Exemption

If you designate a property as your "principal residence", then any capital gain triggered by the actual disposition or deemed disposition of that property is exempt for tax purposes. However, the *Income Tax Act* does not require that your "principal residence" for tax purposes be the home where you spend the most time. All that is required is that you must "ordinarily inhabit" the property. You do not need to spend a lot of time at a particular property in order to consider it your principal residence, so a vacation property that you visit on an annual basis could be considered your principal residence for tax purposes, even if you only spend a short period of time there (although the case law indicates that only one day per year would not be sufficient). In certain situations it is even possible to make an election to continue to designate a property that you have not inhabited in that year as your principal residence (e.g. if you move to another location for a few years for employment reasons), although you generally cannot make the election for more than four years. However, you cannot designate a residence as your principal residence unless you were a resident of Canada in that year.

The principal residence exemption is calculated as follows:

$$\frac{\text{Number of years property is designated as your principal residence} + 1}{\text{Number of years in which property is owned by you since 1971}}$$

The result of this fraction is then multiplied by the total capital gain to determine what portion of the capital gain is exempt. Therefore, if you choose to designate your vacation property as your principal residence during every year in which you owned it, the gain will be completely exempt. However, if you only designate it as your principal residence for a few of the years in which you owned the property, then only a portion of the gain will be exempt. For example, let's assume you owned both a primary residence and a vacation property for many years. You then decide to sell your primary residence and move to your vacation property. If you designate your primary residence as your principal residence in every year in which you lived there, you will not be able to use the principal residence exemption on your vacation property for those years. However, you may decide to designate your vacation property as your principal residence once you sell your primary residence. This does not mean that the capital gain on your vacation property will be completely exempt at the time of sale. The Canada Revenue Agency will only allow you to designate one property as your principal residence in any one year, so it is possible that part of the capital gain on your vacation property will be exempt, and part may be taxable. See Case Study 15.4.2, "Calculation of the Principal Residence Exemption", for an example.

There are some other rules regarding the principal residence exemption of which property owners should be aware.

- Prior to 1982, couples were allowed to have two principal residences. Since 1982, families have only been entitled to claim one principal residence exemption (a family would include a taxpayer, their spouse or common-law partner, and any children under the age of 18). If a property-owner owned both of their residences prior to 1982, they should see whether their affairs were structured so that at least part of the gain on the second property owned before 1982 is exempt. It is important to speak with an accountant regarding this issue to ensure that the exemption has been maximized to the extent possible.

- If a property was used as a rental property for a period of time, then the calculation may be impacted by the value of the property on the date on which the property changed uses from being a rental property to a "personal use" property (or vice versa). Since you can only claim the principal residence exemption for a property that you "ordinarily inhabit", a rental property will not qualify for the exemption. Your tax accountant will be able to assist you in determining how much of the capital gain can be sheltered.

- Although you must be a resident of Canada in order to designate your property as your principal residence, your principal residence for the purposes of the principal residence exemption does not need to be located in Canada — you can choose a property located anywhere in the world. However, do not confuse your principal residence for the principal residence exemption with your "residence" for the purposes of determining where you are taxed. You could be a resident of Canada for tax purposes, but designate a vacation property in another country as your principal residence for the principal residence exemption. Although the capital gain on the foreign property would not be taxable in Canada, you would continue to be taxed in Canada, as that is where you are "resident". The principal residence designation will not impact your residence for tax purposes. (Keep in mind, however, that you may continue to be liable for tax on the capital gains on the foreign property in the jurisdiction where the property is located. Unless you can claim a foreign tax credit for the capital gains tax paid in the foreign jurisdiction, designating a foreign property as your principal residence for the principal residence exemption may not be recommended.)

- If you were in a opposite-sex common-law relationship prior to 1993, or a same-sex common-law relationship prior to 2001 (and you did not elect to be treated the same as a married couple prior to that time), you and your partner may be able to each designate a property as a principal residence for the years prior to that, since opposite-sex common-law partners were only taxed in the same manner as married couples beginning in 1993, and same-sex common-law partners only began receiving that treatment in 2001 (although they could elect to be taxed in the same manner as a married couple beginning in 1998).

In order to maximize the benefit of the principal residence exemption, it may be important to discuss these issues with your professional advisors long before the sale or transfer of the vacation property is even contemplated. For example, if the primary residence is being sold, and another one is being purchased, it may be important to pay the capital gain on the primary residence in order to preserve the ability to use the principal residence exemption for the vacation property. In many cases, these decisions will not be easy to make without the assistance of a tax professional.

### 15.1.4 Transferring the Property to a Family Member

Many people assume that if they transfer their vacation property to a family member prior to the time of their death, they can avoid paying tax on the capital gain. Nothing could be further from the truth. When a property is transferred to a family member (other than a spouse or common-law partner), this will trigger any unrealized capital gain immediately, and in fact accelerate the payment of the capital gains tax. See section 22.3 of Chapter 22, "Probate", for a more complete discussion of how capital gains are taxed when a property owner adds a joint owner, gifts the property or sells the property, and see Case Study 15.4.1 for an example. Note in particular the potential for double taxation when a vacation property is sold for less (or more) than fair market value. If you intend to sell the cottage to a family member during your lifetime, then ensure that the transaction is properly structured. For example, as discussed in Chapter 22, gifting the cottage to a child is usually more advantageous from a tax law and family law perspective than selling it for $1. This is just one example of some of the unanticipated consequences of a poorly structured transfer.

In many cases it may be most appropriate to defer the transfer of the property until both the parents are deceased, and give the property to the children at that time. However, if you want to transfer or sell the property to a child during your lifetime, then it will be important to structure the transaction properly to avoid the double taxation issue that can arise if a property is sold for less than fair market value. One option is to sell the cottage to the family member for fair market value, and then take back some (if not all) of the purchase price by way of a promissory note with no interest. This ensures that the child will have a high cost base when or if they sell the property. This also ensures that the outstanding amount of the loan will be offset against any amount the child is to receive from the estate at the time the parents die. If the intention is that the debt of the child is to be forgiven at the time at which the parents die, then the will should indicate that.

However, because the property has been sold for fair market value, the parents will have to report any capital gain on their tax return for the year in which the property was sold. If the parents have unused capital losses, this may help to minimize the tax consequences resulting from the sale of the property, since the capital losses can be used against the capital gain resulting from the sale of the property. If they do not receive all of (or any of) the purchase price on the date of sale, then they may be able to spread the recognition of the capital gain over a five-year period. The portion of the gain that may be deferred for tax purposes is required to be a reasonable portion of the gain, subject to certain minimums. The "reasonable" portion is determined by calculating the ratio of the capital gain to the total proceeds of disposition, and applying this ratio to the amount not payable until after the end of the year:

$$\frac{\text{capital gain}}{\text{selling price}} \times \text{amount payable after the end of the taxation year} = \text{reserve}$$

However, the other restriction is that a minimum of 20% of the capital gain must be reported in the year of disposition, and 20% in each of the next four years. If you receive a large lump sum when the transaction closes, you may have to report more than 20% at that time – 20% is the minimum, but this amount will not apply if you have received more than that amount. In order to claim a capital gains reserve, you must file Form T2017 with your return.

The benefit of using the capital gains reserve is that you may be able to have some of the gain taxed at lower tax rates, and if you are expecting your child to make regular payments to you, it may alleviate some cash flow difficulties. However, if the parents' income is in the $67,000 to $110,000 range, then spreading out the capital gain over five years could mean losing all or part of their entitlement to receive Old Age Security ("OAS") payments. If the gain is really significant, then not only might it impact the parent's OAS clawback in the year the property is sold, but there will be extra amounts included in their tax returns for the next four years. So, although they may be able to spread the capital gain out over a number of years to have part of it taxed in lower tax brackets, they could lose five times as much of their OAS than if they had simply reported the entire gain in the year of sale. Depending upon the situation, it may in fact be better to simply report all the gain in the year of sale in order to preserve OAS payments in later years.

One of the drawbacks of selling a vacation property, as opposed to gifting it, is that the property will not be exempt from a division of family property if the child is married (or living common-law). Some people attempt to resolve this issue by selling the property to their children for fair market value, but then place a mortgage against it for essentially the entire value. However, in that case the growth is still shareable because it was not a gift. If the intent is that the asset is not to be shareable, the child will either have to enter into a domestic contract with their spouse or common-law partner, or it may be more advisable to consider a gifting strategy (although in some jurisdictions gifts are not exempt if they are a family home, including a cottage). See Chapter 17, "Family Property", for a description of the family property rules in your jurisdiction.

Another risk with this strategy is the possibility that your child will experience creditor problems, making it difficult for them to repay the loan, and in a worse case scenario, resulting in the vacation property being seized by a creditor. If you take back a promissory note, be sure to take security against the property so that you rank ahead of any other creditors who may attempt to seize the property at some point in the future.

If the intention is that the property will be transferred to a child at the time of death, see the issues discussed in section 15.2, "Estate Planning".

## 15.2 ESTATE PLANNING

In most cases, after the family discusses the best way to transfer the vacation property, it is determined that the most practical time to transfer the property is after the time of death. Here are some of the issues to consider if you intend to pass your vacation property on to your beneficiaries as part of your estate.

## 15.2.1 Capital Gains Tax

As discussed in section 15.1, the sale of a vacation property usually results in a capital gain. If you do not sell the property during your lifetime, then you will be deemed to have sold it at the time of your death, unless you transfer the property to a spouse or common-law partner, in which case the deemed disposition will not occur until they sell it or the time of their death. Unless the property is designated as your principal residence, 50% of the gain must be reported in your tax return for the year of sale or death. If you will have sufficient liquid assets in your estate to pay this tax liability, then the capital gain may not be a concern to you. However, in many cases, the capital gain on a vacation property may be very high, and the estate may not have sufficient funds to pay the tax, especially if it has been depleted due to long-term care costs.

Speak to your financial advisor to determine the amount of capital gain that may be triggered at the time of your death (or the death of your spouse or common-law partner). If there is a concern that your estate will not have sufficient assets to pay the anticipated tax liability, then you may consider purchasing insurance in order to fund this liability. Since the liability will generally only arise at the time of death of the second spouse, determine which spouse will have the lower insurance premiums, as you will only need to insure one spouse. (If the insured spouse dies first, then the funds will be available even sooner than the tax liability itself.) If you do not have sufficient cash flow to fund the premiums, speak to the individuals who will be inheriting the cottage to determine if they would be willing to pay the premiums. In many cases, children are willing to pay the insurance premiums, as it is usually a small price to pay to ensure that they will not have to sell the cottage when their parents die.

## 15.2.2 Choosing a Beneficiary

Many people simply assume that after their death (and/or the death of their spouse), the vacation property should automatically be divided equally between all of their children. Although this may be a feasible alternative in some families, in many families the decision as to how to deal with the vacation property has resulted in disputes that have permanently torn their family apart. Here are a few of the considerations that should be kept in mind when deciding who should receive the vacation property.

- Speak to your children about whether or not they would like to receive the vacation property, or perhaps something else instead. Upon discussion with family members, it sometimes becomes apparent that not all of the children are interested in keeping the vacation property. Although all of the children may be interested in visiting the vacation property so long as their parents are alive, their vacation patterns may change once their parents are deceased. Also, if one or more of the children lives a far distance away, they may become less inclined over time to travel long distances when they may prefer to own a vacation property closer to their primary residence. On the other hand, one or more children may be very adamant about keeping the vacation property and never selling it. It is these types of differences that can lead to explosive disputes once both of the parents are gone. If a resolution can be reached in advance, it is more likely that the family will be able to continue to co-operate throughout their lives. In most cases it will be best to leave the property to one child only, but the parents may not have a large enough estate to give one child the vacation property, yet give assets of equal value to the other children. In that case, insurance has often been used as a way to equalize an estate — and, if necessary, by having the children pay the insurance premiums.

- If more than one child would like to keep the vacation property, then a decision must be made as to how title to the property will be held, and the terms of the co-ownership arrangement. If there will be more than one owner, they should sign a co-ownership agreement, and, if possible, the agreement should be negotiated before the parents' death. If an agreement cannot be reached, that is a sign that perhaps a co-ownership arrangement is not appropriate. See section 15.2.3 for more information on the various types of co-ownership arrangements.

These are just a few of the issues that should be discussed with family members and advisors when determining whether or not it will be feasible for the vacation property to be passed down to other family members. In many cases, it is far more practical to sell the vacation property and divide the proceeds, or simply give the vacation property to one of the children, while ensuring that the other siblings have received other assets of similar value (which may involve the use of insurance if there are not sufficient assets currently in the estate). However, without discussing the issue in advance, it will be impossible to know how your children view the vacation property, and their level of interest in keeping it.

## 15.2.3 Co-ownership Arrangements

If a decision is made to transfer the vacation property to more than one beneficiary after the parents are gone, a decision must be made as to how this would be best accomplished. Here are some of the alternatives.

### *15.2.3.1 Joint Ownership*

In many cases, if the will does leave the property to more than one child, the simplest and most effective structure is to simply register the property in the joint names of the children. However, in many cases, the preferred form of registration is as "tenants in common" as opposed to "joint tenants". If an asset is held by "joint tenants", then each tenant will have a right of survivorship, meaning that if one owner dies, the other owner (or owners) will receive the deceased owner's interest in the property (note: there is no right of survivorship in Quebec). If the intent is to pass down a person's interest to the next generation, then the preferred form of registration may be to hold the property as "tenants in common", which does not have a right of survivorship, so the property will pass to the beneficiaries of the deceased. In many jurisdictions, if the registration does not indicate whether the property is being held as joint tenants or tenants in common, the law will presume the property to be held one way or another. Be sure to discuss the issue in advance with your lawyer, and ensure that the proper specification is made on the title.

Regardless of how title is held, it is also necessary to ensure that each of the owners signs a co-ownership agreement in order to avoid disputes in the future. In many cases, the co-ownership agreement is attached to the will, and the beneficiary must sign the agreement as a condition of the inheritance. Here are some of the clauses that can be included in a co-ownership agreement.

- Who will have the right to use the vacation property, and when? If several siblings will own the vacation property jointly, then they must have the type of relationship that will allow them to negotiate the use of the vacation property without resulting in a major argument. There may be certain weeks in the summer when all of the siblings want to use the vacation property, or perhaps there is one sibling who intends to use the vacation property the entire summer. Is the intent that the families can visit the vacation property simultaneously? Or does each family want a period of exclusive use? Depending upon the number of children each sibling has, sharing one property may or may not be feasible. The agreement could also include a provision where the parties "bid" for prime summer weeks, meaning that if you want to stay at the cottage during the most desirable weeks, you will pay a larger proportion of the expenses incurred that year. Regardless of the mechanism chosen, it should be agreed to in advance.

- Who will be responsible for performing the maintenance, or arranging for it to be done? Although administrative items such as who will clean out the septic tank are usually not dealt with in a written contract, there should at least be a general discussion as to who will be responsible for what and how expenses will be covered. There have been many cases where one sibling lives closer to the vacation property, and therefore becomes responsible for visiting the vacation property more frequently and taking care of it. Although this may enable them to receive more enjoyment from the vacation property, this may also lead to resentment if they feel that the other sibling is not making an equal contribution.

- What are the future plans for development of the property? For example, is the intent to keep the vacation property looking "rustic"? Or are all the siblings in agreement that the structure needs serious renovations? Can some of the owners build other buildings on the property? Can an owner rent out the property during their allotted time? Frequently there are family situations where one sibling has a significant income, whereas another sibling may not. If the vision of one child is significantly different than that of the other(s), and there is a similar disparity in their resources, the vacation property may become a lightening rod for disputes, and may in fact have to be sold. If a decision is made to renovate or upgrade the property, it is possible that one child may be able to make a monetary contribution, while the other is capable of contributing "sweat equity" — both contributions may be of equal value, but that should be agreed upon in advance.

- Who can the property be sold to in the future? If the agreement indicates that the property cannot be sold to anyone outside of the family, then that will obviously have a serious effect on the marketability of the property. Although it may seem romantic to require that the property be kept in the family, understand that this could effectively make your interest worthless if your family is not willing or capable of buying you out in the case of dispute.

- What will happen in the case of dispute? Can one party make an offer to buy out the other? If the person who receives the offer does not want to sell their interest, should they then be forced to buy out the other party? Provisions such as these are often referred to as "shot-gun" clauses, as they require one person or the other to "pull the trigger". Without a clause such as this, disputing parties could be forced to keep the property for some time, if both parties refuse to sell their interest. In a worst case scenario, a court application would have to be made to sell the property, resulting in high litigation fees, and, in many cases, a less than optimal selling price for the property. A buyout provision could help alleviate going to court to resolve the issue, but again, may cause resentment if one sibling has significantly more resources than the other, and uses the shot-gun clause to purchase the property from under them.

- What will happen in the event of marriage or relationship breakdown? If a claim is made against one of the owners by a former spouse or common-law partner, would the relevant party be prepared to pay over a portion of the value of the property to that spouse? Does each sibling have sufficient assets to be able to satisfy a family property claim without having to transfer their interest in the vacation property to a former spouse? Will each owner be required to ask their spouse or common-law partner to sign a domestic agreement, in which they acknowledge that they have no interest in the property? What will happen if the spouse or common-law partner refuses to enter into such a contract?

- What will happen in the event of bankruptcy or insolvency? If one party becomes exposed to creditor liability, will the other owner be entitled to buy them out? Again, will the siblings have the financial ability to buy out the bankrupt sibling, or will the property have to be sold?

- What will happen in the case of death? Will the surviving owner have the right to buy out the interest of the estate? Or will the surviving brother-in-law or sister-in-law be entitled to receive the interest of the deceased owner? If the deceased had children, will they all be entitled to take over the interest of the deceased? If the children are minors, will the other owners be prepared to deal with the Public Trustee or other governmental authority? Or has a trustee been appointed in the parent's will to manage the property of the minor?

- Is there sufficient insurance to fund a buyout at the time of death? For example, if the surviving owner is to have the right to buy out the deceased owner at the time of death, will they have the financial assets to do so? Or will they require insurance in order to fund such a buyout? If the heirs of the deceased are to inherit the interest of the deceased, will they have sufficient assets to pay the tax liability that may arise at the time of death? Or will the Canada Revenue Agency seize the property in order to pay the taxes?

As can be seen, there are many issues that must be considered before agreeing to own a property jointly with a sibling or another party. Often these issues are best discussed before the death of the parents, with the form of agreement attached to their will. If an agreement cannot be reached prior to the time of the parents' death, this may be a signal that the parties will not be capable of sharing the property.

### *15.2.3.2 Trusts*

Another possible alternative when leaving a vacation property to more than one family member is to leave it to a trust. The trustees of the trust could be one or more individuals who would have the power to make certain decisions, and the beneficiaries could include not only children, but potentially grandchildren or other relatives. The advantage to using a discretionary trust is that none of the beneficiaries have any vested right to the property — they will only be entitled to use the property as the trustees allow, and/or when the trustees decide to distribute the property to them. In the meantime, if a beneficiary dies, there will be no tax liability resulting from their interest in the trust, and if they suffer a marriage breakdown or experience creditor issues, they will have a stronger argument that they have no interest in the vacation property, and it therefore should not be subject to seizure.

However, the use of a trust does have several disadvantages, and arrangements must be put in place to ensure that the trustees deal with the vacation property in the intended manner. For example, who will be entitled to use the vacation property? What will happen if the trustees cannot agree as to who will receive the vacation property in the future? It is still necessary to have a trust agreement drafted by a well qualified lawyer that addresses the issues discussed in section 15.2.3.1. In many cases, the use of a trust only adds another level of administration, and simply postpones the date by when a difficult decision must be made. There is also potential for abuse on the part of the trustees — if one of the siblings dies, then the other sibling may be under no requirement to ever transfer any interest in the vacation property to the children of that deceased sibling. If the intent is to give each child an equal interest in the vacation property, then using a discretionary trust may not be recommended.

Trusts also have unique tax issues that must be kept in mind:

- When an asset is transferred into a trust, the transfer will trigger a deemed disposition of any unrealized capital gains (except in the case of a spousal, alter ego or joint partner trust which are described in section 23.5.10 of Chapter 23, "Trusts"). If a cottage is transferred into a trust for family members after the time the parents die, then generally speaking, the capital gain will already have been triggered at the time of death, and the estate will have paid any capital gains liability. However, in addition, there will be a "deemed disposition" of the property held by the trust every 21 years thereafter. This means that any unrealized capital gain in the value of the vacation property will be triggered on the 21st anniversary of the trust and the tax will have to be paid regardless of whether or not any of the beneficiaries have died or sold their interest in the vacation property. If the vacation property is distributed to the beneficiaries prior to the 21st anniversary, then this disposition can be avoided and the capital gain will only be realized at the time of sale or death of the owner. Therefore, at some point, a decision will still have to be made — to whom will the vacation property be transferred? How will the vacation property be dealt with if the new owners come to a major disagreement, or if one of them dies? The problem with a trust is that instead of dealing with only two or three children, by the time the 21st anniversary comes around, the decisions may now involve the interests of many, many grandchildren, and children who were originally not very interested in the vacation property may suddenly start to make their opinions known if their children have grown to love the property.

- If money is left in the trust for the purpose of maintaining the property, and those funds earn income which is then used to pay for expenses incurred in respect of the property, then the beneficiaries will receive a taxable benefit for the amount of income used to pay expenses. If the expenses are instead paid out of the capital of the trust, then there is no problem, because that is effectively tax paid money. The point is that the trust cannot avoid paying tax on the income by using those funds to upkeep a property. The beneficiary's right to use the trust property (i.e. the cottage), however, does not create a taxable benefit.

- Another drawback for using a discretionary trust for a cottage is if there are several beneficiaries, and one of the beneficiaries chooses to designate the cottage as their principal residence for the principal residence exemption. If this happens, then none of the other beneficiaries of that trust will be able to use the principal residence exemption for any of those years.

If you are interested in using a trust structure, you should speak with an estate planning lawyer to determine if it is a good option for you.

### 15.2.3.3 Corporations

Although it is technically possible to have a vacation property registered in the name of a corporation, this is generally not recommended for a number of reasons.

- Every time a shareholder uses the vacation property, they will have to report a "shareholder benefit" on their tax return equal to the value they received when they were entitled to use the vacation property without paying rent to the corporation.
- Unlike a trust, a vacation property cannot be "rolled out" to a shareholder without triggering a disposition of any unrealized capital gain.
- You will lose the ability to designate the property as your principal residence, which may be unfortunate if the capital gain on the property is greater than the capital gain on your primary residence.
- There is the potential for double taxation at the time of death. At the time of death of the shareholder, there will be a deemed disposition of his or her shares of the corporation (unless the shares are transferred to a spouse or common-law partner) and the shareholder will recognize a capital gain on any increase in the value of the shares. However, this deemed disposition of the shares does not impact the corporation's adjusted cost base of the vacation property. Therefore, if the corporation sells the cottage (rather than the estate selling the shares of the corporation), this will result in the gain on the cottage being taxed twice.
- There are administrative expenses involved in running a corporation, particularly in the form of filing annual information returns and annual tax returns, as well as updating minutes, resolutions and shareholders agreements. These administrative requirements usually result in the need to hire professional advisors.

Therefore, there is no tax advantage to using a corporation and there is no administrative advantage, since corporations are expensive to incorporate and administer, and a shareholders' agreement dealing with the issues discussed in section 15.2.3.1 will still have to be executed. Whether the joint owners are simply co-owners of the property, or shareholders in a corporation, there will still be a need for a contract setting out their rights and obligations.

#### *15.2.3.4 Unincorporated Associations*

Another possible structure is the use of an unincorporated association, but again, this is generally not recommended. Like a corporation, the asset cannot be rolled out to the members of the association without triggering taxation, but unlike a corporation, where an asset can be rolled into the structure without triggering a capital gain, a vacation property cannot be transferred to the structure without triggering any gain. As well, a set of by-laws or rules dealing with the issues raised in section 15.2.3.1 will still have to be drafted so that all of the members of the association understand what their rights and obligations are with respect to the use of the vacation property. These structures are generally not recommended.

## 15.3 JURISDICTION DIFFERENCES

There are no jurisdiction differences for this chapter.

## 15.4 CASE STUDIES

### 15.4.1 Transfer of Property to a Child

Archie owns a vacation property in British Columbia that is currently worth over $800,000. He purchased the property over 20 years ago for $150,000, and has made $50,000 of capital improvements, so the unrealized capital gain is $600,000 ($800,000 – ($150,000 + $50,000)). Archie also owns a home in Vancouver that he intends to designate as his principal residence, so he will not be able to shelter any of the gain from the sale of his vacation property, and he had already used his $100,000 lifetime capital gains exemption prior to 1992, so he did not file an election to increase the cost base of the vacation property.

Archie has one adult child, Gloria. Archie has heard that probate fees are high in British Columbia, so he decides to transfer the cottage to Gloria on the understanding that he is still entitled to use the property as he wishes, and Gloria will only be entitled to exclusive use of it after the time of his death.

Unfortunately, the transfer of the cottage has ramifications of which Archie is not aware. Consider the circumstances outlined below.

- As soon as Archie transfers the property to Gloria, he is deemed to have disposed of it for fair market value. The total unrealized gain is $600,000, so Archie must report $300,000 of taxable income (since 50% of the $600,000 capital gain is taxable) and pay about $120,000 in tax, even though Gloria has not actually paid him anything for the cottage. Archie was not aware of this in the year in which he transferred the property to Gloria, so he did not pay the proper amount of tax. By the time the Canada Revenue Agency becomes aware of the situation, not only must he pay the $120,000 in tax, but significant interest and penalties as well.

- A few years later, Gloria separates from her husband Joseph, and Joseph claims the cottage as part of their family property. Gloria cannot afford to pay him $400,000. (The cottage is worth $800,000 and Joseph is entitled to 50% of this amount.) Archie does not want to lose the ability to use the cottage, so he pays Joseph the $400,000 out of other funds so that Gloria can keep it.

Unfortunately, giving Gloria the cottage has cost Archie quite a bit of money (both in taxes and in her divorce settlement). Since Archie intended to use the cottage until the time of his death, it would have been better for him to have held the cottage in his name alone, and had it distributed as part of his estate. If Gloria was concerned about the ability to pay the capital gains taxes, she could have obtained an insurance policy on Archie's life. This would have resulted in the deferral of the capital gains tax for as long as possible, and allowed Archie to use the cottage throughout his lifetime without having to worry about Gloria's potential creditors.

### 15.4.2 Calculation of the Principal Residence Exemption

Ted and Susan own two properties as joint owners — a home in Winnipeg and a cottage property in Kenora. Ted and Susan purchased their home in Winnipeg in 1983, and lived there until 2006 when they retired and moved out to the cottage full time. They purchased their cottage in 1986 and did not sell it. Unfortunately, Susan dies in 2009, leaving her entire estate to Ted who dies in 2010, leaving his entire estate to their three children, Stuart, Jacqueline and Amanda.

Jacqueline is their personal representative and is trying to determine how the capital gain on their cottage will be calculated. Jacqueline cannot find any documentation regarding the 1992 lifetime capital gains exemption election, and after making some enquiries with the Canada Revenue Agency, she determines that they did not make an election to increase the cost base on either of their properties. However, they have saved all of the receipts from any improvements they have made to the properties (other than basic repair and maintenance, such as paint), and after examining her parents' tax returns for 2006, she determines that they did not report the capital gain relating to their home at that time, so they will be deemed to have designated it as their principal residence for all the years in which they owned it. Therefore, the issue to be determined is the amount to be paid in respect of the cottage. Here is the information Jacqueline has been able to gather.

*Kenora cottage*

| | |
|---|---|
| Purchased in 1986 for | $60,000 |
| Capital improvements/renovations | $50,000 |
| Total Cost Base | $110,000 |
| | |
| Fair market value in 2010 | $500,000 |

Using the above information, Jacqueline calculates the capital gain owing by Ted's estate as a result of the deemed disposition of the cottage to be as follows:

Total gain = $500,000 – $110,000 = $390,000

Total number of years in which Ted owned the property = 25 (Calculated as 2010-1986 + 1, since both 2010 and 1986 must be included)

Number of years Ted can designate the property as his principal residence = 5 (including the years 2006, 2007, 2008, 2009 and 2010, even though he died part way through 2010). The year 2006 is still available because Ted and Susan did not need to use it to shelter 100% of the gain when they sold their house in 2006 — this is because of the "+1" in the numerator of the equation.

Portion of gain which is exempt = $\$390{,}000 \times \frac{5 + 1}{25} = \$93{,}600$

Portion of gain which is taxable = $390,000 – $93,600 = $296,400 x 50% = $148,200

As a result of the deemed disposition of the cottage, Ted's estate owes over $60,000 in tax (based on $148,200 times the relevant tax rate) to the Canada

Revenue Agency. Unfortunately, there is almost nothing in the estate other than the cottage, since Ted and Susan spent all of the money from the sale of their home on travel and increased medical costs. Since Stuart, Jacqueline and Amanda are unable to pay the tax bill from their own funds, the cottage must be sold, with the after-tax proceeds being divided three ways. Just because Ted and Susan were living in the vacation property as their principal residence at the time of their death does not mean that the entire capital gain was exempt.

# CHAPTER 16

# BUSINESS OWNERS

Business owners have some very unique wealth planning issues. This chapter examines both the issue of how a business affects an owner's personal planning as well as the difficult question of business succession.

# 16.1 FINANCIAL PLANNING

Unfortunately, many business owners are too busy running their business to worry about personal financial planning. Here are some issues that business owners should consider.

## 16.1.1 Payment of Salary vs. Dividends

When making distributions from a corporation, ensure that some of the funds come in the form of salary, not just dividends. Some business owners decide that they only want to receive dividends, as dividends are generally taxed at a lower rate due to the dividend tax credit. However, here are some of the problems that can arise if you do not receive a salary.

- You will not have any "earned income" for RRSP purposes, so you will not be able to make an RRSP contribution.

- Your CPP contributions will be based on your salary, so if you do not receive a salary, you will not be making CPP contributions. This means that you will not be eligible to receive CPP at the time of your retirement (although in some cases, the amount you will lose in CPP may be less than the premiums you would have had to pay).

- Your salary may be important when determining the amount of a monthly disability insurance payment, as the payment is usually based on the salary you have received in years prior to the disability.

It is very important that business owners speak with a tax advisor to optimize their dividend/salary mix.

## 16.1.2 Proper Diversification

Although your business may be very successful, having all of your eggs in one basket is generally not a good idea. If you are receiving all of your income from your business (and if your family members are as well), and you are relying on your business to provide you with a retirement income at the time you decide to sell it, you are not properly diversified. Do not underestimate the importance of investing outside of your business to ensure you have a safety net in the event the business fails.

### 16.1.3 Creditor Protection

When structuring your personal investments, consider whether or not you may be exposed to liability resulting from your business activities. Here are some strategies you may wish to consider in order to protect your personal assets in the event of business failure, or a lawsuit stemming from the operation of your business.

- *Incorporation.* In many cases, it may be best to incorporate your business so that you are not personally liable for debts of the corporation. If the business is not incorporated, then the owner or owners may be personally liable for all of the debts or liabilities of the business. However, once the business is incorporated, then the owners are shareholders, and any contracts or loans are taken out in the name of the corporation, which is a separate legal entity. As a shareholder, you would usually only be liable for the corporation's business debts if you had co-signed or personally guaranteed those debts. In addition, if you are a director of the company, there are certain types of liabilities from which you cannot protect yourself (e.g. remittances to the Canada Revenue Agency, and many types of environmental or human rights claims). Please see section 16.2.1 for more information regarding incorporation.

- *Segregated Funds.* Another strategy you may want to consider to protect your assets is to invest in segregated funds, as they can provide more creditor protection than other investments. Whether you are a sole proprietor, partner, unincorporated professional, or owner of a corporation, consider whether your personal investments are adequately protected. Segregated funds generally cannot be seized by creditors if you name specific family members as beneficiaries, if they fall into the "protected class" of beneficiaries. See section 25.4 of Chapter 25, "Insurance", for further information regarding who is considered to be in the protected class of beneficiaries in your jurisdiction.

- *Permanent Life Insurance.* Another option may be to invest in a permanent life insurance policy, as the cash surrender value in the policy is protected if the beneficiary of the policy is a member of the "protected class" of beneficiaries. See section 25.4 of Chapter 25, "Insurance", for further information regarding who is considered to be in the protected class of beneficiaries in your jurisdiction.

- *Individual Pension Plans.* Individual pension plans ("IPPs") may also help to protect some of your assets, as the assets held within the plan are protected from creditors in the way any form of registered pension assets are. Please see section 16.1.4 for more information on IPPs.

- *Place Assets in the Name of Your Spouse.* If your assets are placed in your spouse's name before you begin to incur any debts or liabilities, the assets now owned by the spouse should be protected, to a certain degree, from your creditors. However:

  - Having the assets in the name of your spouse could be a concern from a family property perspective, particularly if those assets could otherwise have been exempt from a division of family property, had they been kept in your name alone (such as an inheritance). This may be of particular concern if you are in a common-law relationship and live in a jurisdiction where common-law partners do not have family property rights at the time of relationship breakdown or death.

  - If there is a mortgage on the family home, then the lending institution may prefer that the mortgage be against a home where you are both liable to make any outstanding payments. However, it may be sufficient for your spouse to pledge the house as security and perhaps for you to guarantee your spouse's mortgage payments.

  - From an income tax point of view, if you are putting income-producing assets, such as mutual funds, in your spouse's name, the spousal attribution rules will usually apply to attribute the first generation income and capital gains back to you.

- *Place Your Assets in an Inter Vivos Trust.* This may have tax consequences, but doing so may provide some creditor protection. However, the more difficult you make it for your creditors to access the trust property, the less control you will have over access to the property. In other words, this option may not be practical depending upon the circumstances.

- *Receive Inheritance through a Testamentary Trust.* If you anticipate that your parents might leave you a substantial inheritance, you should talk with them about receiving that inheritance through a testamentary trust under which you and your family are discretionary beneficiaries. That way, the inheritance will be less likely to be available to creditors than it would be if it were left to you directly. See section 13.5.2 of Chapter 13, "Elderly Parents", for more information about receiving an inheritance through a trust.

However, creditor protection is not guaranteed in all circumstances and many of these strategies will not prevent a claim by a former spouse or the CRA. This type of planning must be completed well before you become aware of any potential liability – if you try to transfer your assets after the liability has arisen, the transaction may be set aside as a fraudulent conveyance.

## 16.1.4 Retirement Savings and IPPs

Business owners should not assume that they will be able to fund their retirement by selling their business or continuing to receive cash payments from the business indefinitely into the future. If you own a business, you should accumulate retirement savings outside of the business, both to help you diversify, and to help protect you and your dependants from business creditors. Although RRSPs are a useful savings tool, they are not protected in all cases if you are sued or experience a business failure. A better alternative may be to establish an individual pension plan ("IPP"), where the funds are invested outside of the business, although these plans generally require regular contributions, which may be problematic if the cash flow generated by your business is erratic. IPPs generally allow owners, managers and executives of incorporated businesses who earn a stable income of at least $75,000 annually and who are at least 45 years of age to make larger tax deductible contributions than allowed for an RRSP. Since IPPs are a form of registered pension plan, they are more creditor proof than RRSPs, although they may still be subject to a division of family property in the event of relationship breakdown.

IPPs are defined benefit pension plans, so there are no contribution limits (unlike RRSPs), although a "maximum funding valuation" must be prepared. An actuary must determine how much money needs to be contributed to the plan to fund the desired retirement benefits based on the individual's annual employment income. All contributions and expenses associated with maintaining an IPP are tax-deductible by the employer. As with any pension plan, the contributions are not taxable to the employee until such time as they start receiving payments from the plan.

When the IPP is created, the employer may make an initial contribution based on past service for any years in which the individual was an employee after 1991. This prohibits professionals who have just incorporated their business from making past service contributions, but may be another reason for professionals to incorporate, so that they can accumulate contribution room. When calculating the past service contributions, individuals must transfer a sum of money that is equal to their "past service pension adjustment" from their RRSP – this amount is transferred between the plans on a tax-deferred basis. All future contributions to the IPP will affect the individual's RRSP contribution room.

In the event the employer experiences financial trouble, the IPP will be protected from creditors, as long as the plan was not set up to defraud creditors in anticipation of pending insolvency. If the plan experiences poor returns resulting in the value of the investments being insufficient to fund future payments, additional contributions may have to be made to make up for deficiencies (depending upon the pension legislation in your jurisdiction – in some provinces there is no requirement to fund deficiencies). If funds are borrowed to make additional contributions, the resulting interest expenses are tax-deductible. RRSPs do not provide the ability to make up for investment losses, and the interest payable on RRSP loans is not tax-deductible.

The employee may start receiving a pension as early as age 50, at which time they may income split these amounts with their spouse, unlike payments from an RRSP or RRIF, which are not subject to income splitting until the annuitant is 65. A surviving spouse may receive 2/3 of the pension after the employee's death (although this amount may be increased). However, there are some disadvantages. Unlike with an RRSP, the money is locked in the plan, and cannot be accessed. There are also higher costs associated with an IPP, since the parties will need to sign a trust agreement and actuarial valuations are required every three years.

## 16.1.5 Retirement Compensation Arrangements

If you are a very high income earner, and you feel that the contribution limits for an IPP are too low, consider whether or not a retirement compensation arrangement ("RCA") would be appropriate for you as well. An RCA is not subject to the same contribution limits as an IPP, but 50% of any of your contributions to the RCA must be paid to the Canada Revenue Agency, so only 50% of your contributions will grow within the plan. (Although depending upon your tax bracket when you withdraw sums from the RCA, you may be able to obtain a refund of a large part of the amount sent to the Canada Revenue Agency). RCAs are also a popular strategy for companies that need cash, since you can leverage the RCA and lend the money back to the company. If you are planning to emigrate from Canada in the future, and do not expect to withdraw the funds from the RCA until you are a non-resident, then depending upon the withholding rate in place for the country you emigrate to, an RCA may in fact provide a permanent tax savings.

### 16.1.6 Cash Damming

Cash damming is a strategy which allows individuals to convert some of their personal debt into business debt so that the interest payments are tax deductible. Effectively, this involves segregating borrowings related to business expenses and keeping them separate from borrowings related to personal expenses. As the personal debt is paid off, the debt related to deductible purposes (such as running a business or investing for the purpose of producing income) can be increased, converting non-deductible debt into deductible debt. This strategy is appropriate for individuals who have an unincorporated business, with significant business expenses, good cash flow and non-deductible debt. It is also important to be able to trace the use of the borrowed funds for the Canada Revenue Agency, so the appropriate product must be used to adequately track the use of funds for tax purposes.

Also, if you are married or in a common-law relationship, you should consider whether or not this strategy may result in more debt against your business (which may or may not be shareable) and less debt against your personal assets (which may be shareable). If you live in a jurisdiction where businesses aren't shareable or you have entered into a domestic contract that exempts your business from a division of assets, then you may want to consult with your advisors before shifting too much of your debt to an exempt asset. See section 5.3.1.5 of Chapter 5, "Married", for more information.

## 16.2 TAX PLANNING

Here are some tax planning opportunities that may be appropriate for business owners, although it is important to speak to a tax professional before implementing any of them.

### 16.2.1 Incorporation

One of the first issues that a business owner must consider is whether or not to incorporate their business. Here are some of the factors to review when making this determination.

- If you are expecting to experience losses in the first few years of the business, it may be best to wait to incorporate until such time as you are in a profit position. This is because losses inside a corporation are trapped within that corporation, whereas losses incurred by an unincorporated business can be used against other income earned personally by the business owner.

- Once the business is in a profit position, then incorporation may be more beneficial, especially if you do not intend to withdraw all of the profits, either because you want to reinvest them in the corporation, or because you do not need all of the profits to fund your standard of living. By keeping profits inside the corporation, you can defer paying personal income tax on those profits until you pay yourself a salary or a dividend. Although tax will be paid on the corporate profits, the corporate tax rate is quite low on the first $500,000 of active business income earned in Canada by a Canadian-controlled private corporation.

- So long as your business is making a profit, it may be beneficial to incorporate even if you do need the funds generated by the business. This is because you can choose to defer the payment of the profits in the form of a bonus or dividend until after the end of the calendar year. Therefore, business income that is earned in 2009 will be taxed at the corporate level in 2009, but if these profits are not paid out to you until January of 2010, the bonus will only be taxable to you in 2010. A bonus must be paid out within 180 days of company's year end in order to deduct it in that year.

- Regardless of the tax advantages or disadvantages of incorporation, if you are involved in a business where there is a risk of liability, it may be a good idea to incorporate in order to shield your personal assets from exposure to lawsuits or creditors. In many cases, the creditor protection issues are an important consideration, so do not discard the option of incorporation even if you are not sure if you will be in a profit position in the first few years. (However, incorporation may not protect your assets from all types of creditors in all situations, so speak to your legal advisors if creditor protection is of paramount importance to you, and see section 16.1.3 for more creditor protection strategies.)

- If your business is in the practice of providing professional services (e.g. you are a lawyer, doctor, accountant, veterinarian, etc.), then you may not be allowed to incorporate, so do not do so until you speak with an advisor. Also keep in mind that while incorporation may allow you to limit liability regarding business debts, it does not generally limit liabilities regarding professional acts. For example, if an accountant negligently prepared a tax return for a client, the client could sue the accountant (and his or her professional corporation) for compensation for the resulting damage. Most professions that allow their members to incorporate only allow the professional corporation to minimize business liabilities, such as lease payments, etc. Also, although you may be able to "roll" assets into a corporation without triggering any unrealized capital gains or losses, you cannot roll assets out on a tax-deferred basis, so do not incorporate your practice until you have confirmed with your tax advisors that this is the appropriate thing to do.

### 16.2.2 Income Splitting With Family Members

It is very common for business owners to involve family members in their business. In many cases, the reason for doing this is to "income split". Due to the graduated system of tax in Canada, it is usually beneficial to have profits divided between as many taxpayers as possible so that more income is taxed at a lower rate of tax. However, the *Income Tax Act* includes a number of rules referred to as the "attribution" rules, which in many cases, attribute income back to the person who actually earned the income. In addition, involving family members in your business can create other problems. Here are some points to consider.

- Income splitting with family members may be possible if you pay them a "reasonable" salary for services that they provide to the business. For example, if you have a spouse or child who is employed in the business, you can pay them a salary, which will result in some of the income from the business being taxed in their hands instead of yours (meaning that the income may be taxed in a lower income tax bracket). When you are employed (as opposed to running a business), it is much more difficult to transfer part of your income to a family member. However, in order for a family member to receive a salary from the business, they must actually be employed by the business, and provide a level of services that is commensurate with the salary they are receiving. Also, any salary paid to a family member must be deposited in their own bank account, which they control. Loss of control of these funds, especially when paid to young children, may negate any tax benefits of paying a salary. Also, when the salary has been paid to a related minor, care should be taken to ensure that money earned by way of salary is saved and invested separately from gifted monies on which income attribution applies. Interest earned on invested salaries is taxed in the children's hands.

- If you want to income split with an adult child who is not working for the corporation, consider having the corporation lend money to the adult child. Since the amount is a loan, as opposed to salary, the corporation will not be allowed to deduct the payment, and if the loan is not repaid within one year of your company's year-end, the loan will be taxed in the hands of the child. However, if the child is in a low tax bracket when they receive the loan, they will pay tax on the payment at a very low rate of tax, and if the child ever repays the loan, they will be entitled to a tax deduction when they are potentially in a much higher income tax bracket.

- If you incorporate, and you want to add family members such as a spouse or child as a shareholder so that you can pay them dividends, be sure to consult with an experienced lawyer prior to issuing shares to them. In many cases it is not advisable to issue shares directly to these family members, especially children (and, in fact, there are generally no circumstances where it would be recommended that a minor become a shareholder). It is usually more advisable to make them beneficiaries of a family trust that then subscribes for shares in the corporation. You can be a trustee of the trust in order to have some control as to how and when dividends are paid out to the beneficiaries. Also consider issuing a different class of shares to the trust so that you can pay dividends out either to yourself only or the trust only, which would therefore give you more flexibility. If you do wish to add family members as shareholders, either directly or through a trust, the strategy generally used to achieve this on a tax-deferred basis is through an estate freeze, as discussed in section 16.5.2.4.

- If you do choose to make an adult family member a direct shareholder in the business, it is extremely important that all of the shareholders enter into a shareholders' agreement at the same time as the shares are issued. It is almost impossible to negotiate an agreement once tensions arise between the parties, so it is best to set out your agreement in writing while everyone is co-operating. Issues such as what will happen in the case of death, disability, dispute and relationship breakdown should be addressed, along with many others that your lawyer can review with you. See section 16.5.2.3 for more information.

- In many cases, it only makes sense to introduce family members (or a family trust) as shareholders if the corporation is a small business corporation. The attribution rules are an issue for investment companies, although there may be some tax advantages to using an investment corporation if there are adult children who are in a very low tax bracket. If a family trust is issued shares in an investment corporation, the trust agreement should prohibit any payments to a spouse, common-law partner or related minor of the original owner of the corporation.

## 16.2.3 $750,000 Capital Gains Exemption

If you own shares in a corporation that may qualify for the $750,000 capital gains exemption, there are a number of factors which you should consider in order to maximize the availability of the credit.

- *Monitor Level of Passive Assets.* Although the tests for using this exemption are too extensive to include here, one of the main problems business owners experience when attempting to use this exemption is the fact that they have too many passive assets in their corporation. In order to use the exemption, 90% of the assets of the corporation must be used to produce active business income in the year in which the shares are sold, and 50% of the assets must be used to produce active business income in the 24 months prior to the date of sale. Even if you do not anticipate selling the company in the next 24 months, it may still be worthwhile "purifying" the company on a periodic basis, since the capital gains exemption can only be used if 90% of the assets are active business assets at the time of disposition, which could include the time of death. If the corporate structure is such that purification can be achieved simply by paying out dividends to a trust and then a holding company, consider paying out these passive dividends regularly, so that the estate does not lose the ability to use the $750,000 exemption.

- *Multiply the Use of the Exemption.* The $750,000 exemption is available for each individual shareholder (i.e. more than one person may claim the exemption in respect of shares of the same company). Therefore, to the extent your family members have not already used their exemptions, consider introducing them as shareholders of your corporation in order to multiply the use of the exemption. In many cases, it is not appropriate to make spouses or children direct shareholders of a corporation, but it may be acceptable to make them beneficiaries of a trust which is a shareholder of the company, and which is controlled by you and/or your spouse. In this way, although your children are not direct owners of the shares of the corporation (and therefore cannot create havoc by refusing to vote for resolutions beneficial to the company, or expose the shares to a division of family property in the event of relationship breakdown), they may be able to have capital gains flowed to them through the trust, sheltering more of the capital gain at the time of sale. Structuring this type of arrangement properly can become very complicated, particularly if trying to avoid the attribution rules in the case of a spouse or common-law partner. Also, if you have a family member who is also a shareholder of another corporation, you may not want the two corporations "associated" as defined in the *Income Tax Act*, as that may limit the ability for one of the corporations to use the small business deduction on the first $500,000 of active business income. Always speak to a tax professional before embarking on this type of planning.

- *Consider Whether the Exemption Is Likely to be Used.* The capital gains exemption is only available to residents of Canada who sell shares in a small business corporation. Therefore, there is no capital gains exemption in respect of the sale of assets of a business. In many cases, purchasers prefer to buy assets of a business, as opposed to shares of a company, as they do not want to inherit any of the liabilities of the company. Therefore, it is quite possible that when you sell your business that you will not be able to use the exemption. Having said that, if do you not structure your corporation so that the exemption is available, you will not be able to use that as a bargaining chip when negotiating the price of the business (i.e. if the exemption is available, you may be able to demand more for the assets than if the purchaser agrees to buy shares). However, there are a number of businesses for which there may never be a buyer, such as the case with many professional practices, where there is no "goodwill" in the value of the business. Another example is a corporation which primarily owns rental properties. It will likely be considered to be a specified investment business unless it employs more than five employees, so the capital gains exemption may not be available. If you know that there is no chance that you will ever be able to sell the assets of your corporation, then there is no point in undergoing expensive planning processes to preserve an exemption that you will never be able to use.

Again, as the use of this exemption can be quite complicated, speak to your tax advisors before implementing any strategy that could affect your ability to use it.

## 16.2.4 Charitable Contributions

If you have a corporation, it is often best to make all charitable contributions in your personal name, especially if you are in a low tax bracket, and your contribution is large enough to result in a tax credit at the high rate. This is because contributions made by corporations are treated as a tax deduction and do not result in a tax credit in the same manner as when made personally. However, if you are contributing to an organization that is not a registered charity, it may be best to make the contribution corporately if you can deduct the contribution as a promotional cost. See Chapter 24, "Charitable Giving", for more information on how best to structure a charitable donation.

# 16.3 FAMILY LAW ISSUES

Although no one likes to consider the possibility of relationship breakdown, the implications of a division of property can be particularly onerous for business owners. If you are in a relationship, or contemplating entering into one, consider the factors discussed below when structuring your business affairs.

- In some jurisdictions, business assets are shareable in the same manner as any other type of asset. Refer to section 17.4 of Chapter 17, "Family Property", for further information on the family law rules in your jurisdiction of residence.

- Be careful when intermingling personal and business assets for maximum tax advantage. For example, some business owners or self-employed individuals structure their affairs so that their personal assets, including homes, cottages, cars and boats are debt-free, or as debt-free as possible. They instead choose to shift as much of their debt as possible towards their business. This is generally done so that the interest paid on the debt becomes tax deductible. (Interest is generally only tax deductible where the loan is entered into for the purpose of earning income.) However, a problem may arise where a couple then separates, and the non-business owner spouse receives more of the family assets than was anticipated, since the house is either free and clear of any mortgage, or the amount of the mortgage is artificially low due to the refinancing of the business. If the debt that the business-owning spouse is responsible for is shareable, then the division of assets may be more equitable, but in many cases, debt is not shareable, or there could be an agreement indicating that the business is not part of the family assets, leaving the business owner with all of the debt. If a business person wants to embark on this type of planning, they should consult with their legal advisors prior to doing so.

- If children purchase shares as part of an estate freeze (as discussed in section 16.5.2.4), the shares are likely to be included in a division of family property, since they were not a gift or inheritance. If the intent is that these shares are not to be a divisible asset, a pre-nuptial contract should be entered into to that effect. In some cases, it may be better to have the parents give the shares to the children so that they fall under the exception given to gifts and inheritances (which is not available in every jurisdiction), but speak with your professional advisors prior to doing this to ensure that there will be no detrimental tax effects (e.g. the application of the attribution rules).

- A relationship breakdown can also seriously affect the future of the business, especially if a spouse with no business experience is entitled to a portion of the shares. If you are in business with another individual (including a family member), be sure to sign a partnership or shareholders' agreement so that it is made clear what will happen in the event of relationship breakdown. See section 16.5.2.3 for more information on shareholders' agreements.

## 16.4 DISABILITY PLANNING

Although every adult Canadian should plan for the possibility that they may suffer from a disability at some point in the future, this type of planning is particularly important for business owners.

### 16.4.1 Powers of Attorney

Having a power of attorney for property is crucial for business owners. It is necessary that someone be given authority to step in and manage the business if for some reason you are not able to, even for a relatively short period of time. Significant damage can be done to a business if it has to cease operations for even a short time period. If no one other than the business owner has authority to make decisions, write cheques or enter into contracts, even a short-term disability can have long-term ramifications. When discussing your power of attorney with your lawyer, consider the provisions below, in addition to the standard provisions which are usually included in such documents (see Chapter 18, "Powers of Attorney", for a discussion of some of the more common clauses found in a power of attorney document).

- If you want your attorney to preserve your business, even if it experiences a downturn, you should specifically authorize your attorney to retain the shares of the family business, if they conclude that is the best decision in the circumstances. You should also indemnify the attorney from damages that may result from failing to sell the shares of the company, since some beneficiaries may feel that retaining a business that is in a loss position is not a good idea.

- Consider whether you want to give the attorney the ability to sign contracts on behalf of the business, or have other powers specific to the business.

- Think carefully about appointing someone as your attorney if they own a corporation themselves. Although it would seem to make sense to appoint someone with similar experience, from a tax perspective, this may not be a good decision. The *Income Tax Act* contains a series of "associated company" rules which provide that two companies are associated if they are controlled by the same person or group of persons. Unfortunately, the Canada Revenue Agency takes the position that an attorney controls the shares of the donor of a power of attorney, so if the attorney owns a company, it could be seen to be associated with the donor's company. This is a problem because associated companies must share the "small business deduction". The small business deduction allows companies to pay a very low rate of tax on the first $500,000 of active business income. Obviously if you and your attorney want to preserve the ability to use the small business deduction, you will not want your companies to be associated. One small concession is that if the power of attorney is a "springing" form of attorney, meaning that it only comes into force in the event a certain thing happens (e.g. mental incapacity), then the attorney will only be seen to control the donor's shares at the time of the event.

### 16.4.2 Disability Insurance

If you own a business, review your disability insurance needs with your advisors. You may require disability insurance not only to replace an income stream, but potentially also to fund a buyout of your interest in the business if you have business partners. If the business is completely reliant upon you in order to generate a profit, then it will be particularly important to ensure that you and your family are protected in the event you are not able to work, even for a relatively short time period.

### 16.4.3 Partnership or Shareholders' Agreements

If you are not the sole owner of your business, you should ensure that you enter into a partnership or shareholders' agreement setting out what will happen in the event of disability. For example, will the other shareholders be obligated to buy out your interest in the corporation if you are disabled for a certain period of time (e.g. 12 months)? If you do not have a provision addressing this issue in a written document, it is possible that you will not be able to sell your interest on the open market, and there may be no way in which to force your partners to buy you out. Again, it is important to ensure that the other partners or shareholders will have sufficient liquid assets to fund such a buyout — these liquid assets are usually obtained through the use of insurance.

# 16.5 ESTATE PLANNING

This part of the chapter is divided into two parts, since a business owner must consider not only how his or her personal estate plan will be affected as a result of owning a business, but they must also ensure that they have a proper business succession plan in place in order to ensure a smooth transition after the time of their death, in order to preserve the value of the business.

## 16.5.1 Personal Planning

If you own a business, ask your advisors how this will impact your personal estate plan, and how you can minimize both the stress on your beneficiaries, as well as income taxes payable both at the time of death, and on future earnings.

### *16.5.1.1 Will Planning*

Business owners should consider the scenarios described below when structuring their will.

- If you originally left your business assets to a specific beneficiary in your will when your business was not incorporated, and then later choose to incorporate your business, be sure to change your will after you incorporate to ensure that it is clear that the beneficiary will now receive the shares of the corporation as opposed to the business itself. Since the assets of the business will now be owned by the corporation, not the individual, the will must be changed, or the gift will fail.

- If you have not incorporated your business, and you want to leave it to a specific beneficiary or beneficiaries, you should ensure that all the appropriate assets used in the business are left to that beneficiary. For example, if you want to leave a business to a specific beneficiary, simply leaving them all "land, buildings and equipment" may not be sufficient. Consider all the relevant parts of the business, including unsold inventory, prepaid accounts, or other assets used in the business. If the intent is to leave the entire business, then the will must be sufficiently clear in that regard.

- In order to avoid potential double taxation, the will should instruct the executors to wind up a holding company within the estate's first taxation year, triggering tax in the holding company on the distribution, but allowing a carryback of a capital loss on the shares' redemption.

- If you have executed a shareholders' agreement that will allow the other shareholders or the corporation to purchase your shares at the time of your death, you will not be able to give the shares to a beneficiary. Ensure that the terms of your will are consistent with the terms of any shareholders' agreement.

### *16.5.1.2 Choosing a Personal Representative*

In the case of business owners in particular, the choice of personal representative is very important (many jurisdictions refer to this person as an "executor" — see Chapter 20, "Personal Representatives", for more information). Here are a few issues that business owners must consider when choosing their personal representative.

- Although every individual should ensure that they have a properly drafted will with a carefully chosen personal representative (and alternate), for business owners it is especially important that you have a personal representative in place who can step into your shoes immediately — a business can decline dramatically in value if an owner dies and no succession plan is in place. This is particularly true if the business is a sole proprietorship, where there are no other directors or officers with authority to act.

- Many business owners choose to appoint one of their business partners as their personal representative. Although this may be a good choice in the sense that your partner may be very familiar with your business, they could also be in a conflict of interest. For example, if you appoint your partner as personal representative, and you and your partner are also parties to a partnership agreement or a shareholders' agreement that includes a buy-out provision in the case of death, then it is possible that your partner will be negotiating both on behalf of themselves in the purchase of your interest, and on behalf of your estate in the sale of your interest. This is obviously a conflict of interest that may result in a less than fair price being received by your estate. Although a business partner may be a good choice in some instances, beware of potential conflicts of interest when making your decision.

- For business owners, there are certain tax planning techniques that must be completed within one year after the time of death. For this reason, it is important to have a personal representative appointed in your will, so that they will be able to start administering the estate immediately, without having to make a court application. It is also important for this reason to choose someone who is diligent, and who will not procrastinate after the time of death — the implications for the estate can be quite significant if there is a business and the personal representative is not competent to address the issues.

### 16.5.1.3 Probate Planning

If you own a business, there may be methods of reducing probate that you should consider.

- In other chapters, there have been numerous references to the perils of probate planning, and the need to consider whether or not it is more effective to do income tax planning as opposed to probate planning (in particular, see Chapter 22, "Probate"). However, there is one probate planning technique that achieves both objectives — minimizing probate fees while at the same time allowing the assets to be distributed according to your last will and testament, which allows for income tax planning. The concept is the use of "multiple wills", which involves distributing any assets that must be probated in one will, and distributing assets that do not need to go through probate in another will. For example, land, mutual funds and bank accounts are assets that often cannot be distributed to your heirs without letters probate, so these assets should be dealt with in one will. However, shares of privately held corporations often do not need to go through probate, since the directors of the corporation are usually close family members or colleagues, who are willing to transfer the shares to the heirs without requiring formal letters probate. Where this is the case, consider multiple wills for the purpose of probate planning. See section 22.3.9 of Chapter 22, "Probate", for more information on this strategy, and be sure to speak to your lawyer about this strategy, as it is not effective in every jurisdiction.

- Probate fees are generally assessed against the gross value of an estate, less the value of any debts secured by real property (see section 22.4 of Chapter 22, "Probate", for the rules in your jurisdiction). Unfortunately, personal debt related to the purchase of a business usually will not reduce the value of that business for probate purposes. However, if investments or business assets are transferred into a holding company, and the corresponding debt is also transferred to the holding company, then the value of the asset for probate purposes will effectively be reduced, since the net value of the shares of the holding company will be the value of the assets, less the amount of debt.

#### *16.5.1.4 $10,000 Tax-Free Death Benefit*

A maximum of $10,000 can be received tax free if it is a death benefit from the deceased's employer in recognition of the deceased's years of service. The payments must be made from a pension plan (or similar type of plan), or represent unpaid sick leave. Therefore, if you own a private corporation, consider passing a resolution indicating that $10,000 is to be paid to your estate (or your beneficiaries) at the time of your death, either from a pension plan, or in recognition of unpaid sick leave.

### 16.5.2 Business Succession Planning

If you own a business, not only will you have to consider how this will affect your personal documents, such as your will and power of attorney, but you will probably also need to do some additional planning in order to ensure that the business passes either to your family members, or is sold after the time of your death in a smooth fashion. If you have not done sufficient business succession planning, then it is very likely that your family will either not be able to continue to run the business, or they will only be able to sell it for a fraction of its true value. Here are some of the primary issues you should consider in your business succession plan.

#### *16.5.2.1 Transfer or Sale of the Business*

One of the first issues that you must consider is how you think the business should be dealt with after the time of your death. Do you want your personal representatives to transfer the business to a family member, or sell it on the open market to the highest bidder? Many people who own a business want to pass it on to their family, but in some cases this is not realistic because there are no family members capable of running the business. It is important to speak to your family and your business partners when structuring your estate plan to ensure that you know what they would like to see after the time of your death. It is of no use to structure your estate plan so that a child can take the business over if neither the child nor your business partners wants to see this happen.

If you do have a child who is interested in purchasing the business and you want to sell it to them prior to the time of your death, it may be possible to sell the business to that child for fair market value and take back a promissory note payable over a 10 year period (not on demand). You will need to recognize at least 10% of the capital gain every year, but this strategy may at least help to spread the gain out over a longer period of time, and perhaps result in less tax being paid if some of the gain is paid in years when you are in a lower tax bracket. However, if you do this, you will need to register a security interest against the business assets to protect your interest in the event your child experiences financial difficulties or a marital breakdown. If you do not intend to actually receive any payments from your child, then you can indicate that the promissory note is not to bear interest, and any outstanding amounts at the time of your death can be forgiven in your will. (*Note*: there may be tax disadvantages to forgiving a loan prior to the time of your death.) You should speak with a qualified professional prior to embarking on this type of transaction.

### *16.5.2.2 Planning for Tax at Death*

If you want to leave the business to your children after you die, the next step in the process should be to calculate how much tax will be owing at the time of your death as a result of the deemed disposition of the business assets (or the shares of the corporation that owns the shares), and determine whether or not your estate has sufficient liquid assets to pay this tax, or if the business will have to be sold in order to satisfy this liability (see Chapter 21, "Taxation at Death", if you are not aware of the manner in which assets are taxed at the time of death). If you want your beneficiaries to be able to keep the business after the time of your death, life insurance is often necessary. Many people are aware of the fact that the first $750,000 in capital gains on shares in a qualified small business corporation ("QSBC") are exempt from taxation. However, the QSBC exemption is very complicated, and a number of conditions must be met before you or your estate will be able to claim it (see section 16.2.3 for more information regarding this exemption). Be sure to speak with your advisors to try to determine the amount of your tax liability at the time of your death, and, if necessary, insure this liability as appropriate.

### *16.5.2.3 Shareholders' Agreements*

If you are not the sole owner of your business, then you need to have either a partnership or shareholders' agreement in place. A partnership or shareholders' agreement is necessary even if you are in business with a family member, and perhaps even more crucial between family members than with other individuals. It is not uncommon for business partners to come to a disagreement regarding the direction in which they want to take the business, and the manner in which profits are to be divided. Under no circumstances is it recommended that you enter into a business relationship on a "gentlemen's agreement", or hand shake. Some of the more important provisions in a partnership or shareholders' agreement include those listed below.

- *Death*. Will the survivors be obligated to buy out your interest? Will there be life insurance available to fund this buyout? Will your family members be entitled to remain as shareholders?

- *Disability*. Will the other shareholders or partners be obligated to buy out your interest in the business if your disability is long term? Is there sufficient insurance in place to fund such a buyout?

- *Relationship Breakdown*. If you separate or divorce, will your spouse or partner be entitled to some of the shares of the business? Are your partners amenable to this? Or will they have the option to buy out a former spouse?

- *Disagreement*. What will happen if you can no longer agree as to the future of the business? Will one partner or the other have the option to buy you out? Will you have the option to buy them out? Is this a plausible solution, or is it a situation where the business would have to be sold on the open market?

If some of the above listed events are to be funded with insurance, be sure to speak with your insurance professional to ensure that the ownership and beneficiary designation on the insurance policy is consistent with the terms of the agreement. These are only some of the issues that should be addressed in a partnership or shareholders' agreement. Your lawyer will be able to explain how these clauses as well as a number of others will work to protect both you and your family.

### *16.5.2.4 Estate Freezes*

If you intend to transfer your business to your family in a few years, or you anticipate selling your business, consider whether or not an estate freeze would be a good strategy for you. Here is how an estate freeze essentially works, assuming your business is incorporated.

- The value of any common shares that you own in the corporation will be "frozen" so that your interest in the corporation does not increase in value in the future. This is done by exchanging your common shares for fixed value preference shares. The shares that you exchange must be worth exactly the same as the shares you receive, or the Canada Revenue Agency may assess you as having triggered a capital gain. If the company pays you non-cash consideration for your shares (such as a promissory note or cash), this could create a tax liability, so you need to speak with a professional to ensure that the transaction occurs on a tax deferred basis.

- A new shareholder can then purchase new common shares in the corporation for nominal value. For example, you could create a family trust with your family members as beneficiaries of the trust, and the trust could then subscribe for new common shares at $1 per share. As a result of the trust purchasing the common shares, all the future growth in the company will now accrue to the family trust, not to you (although you can make yourself a beneficiary of the trust in order to receive dividends in the future, or transfer the shares back into your name). You can maintain voting control by being a trustee of the trust (perhaps with a spouse and a trusted third party).

- If your children are mature enough to be direct shareholders in the company, then you could purchase the new common shares and then gift them to a child, since in many jurisdictions gifts are exempt from a division of family property. In most cases, however, it is usually more appropriate to introduce new family members through the use of a family trust, rather than by direct share ownership, since many parents do not want to lose any control over the corporation until they are ready to retire. The appropriate mechanism should be reviewed with your advisor. Since there is a deemed disposition of the assets held in a trust every 21 years, the trust would usually be wound-up by its 21st anniversary.

- Even after the estate freeze is complete, you will still own a potentially large portion of the value of the business, since your interest was simply "frozen", not sold. Over time, the corporation can either purchase your preference shares for cancellation, which will result in you receiving taxable dividends (unless the payments are made from a non-taxable account called the capital dividend account), or the new shareholders could purchase your shares from you, resulting in a capital gain, which may be exempt from tax if the conditions are met for the $750,000 capital gains exemption.

- Over time, as the value of the new common shares increases, and your preference shares are either purchased for cancellation by the corporation or sold to the new shareholders, your interest in the business will decrease. If some of the amounts received by you are taxable, the tax will be paid gradually over a long period of time, and potentially not all at the highest tax rate.

- If you choose to retain your shares, then life insurance should be put in place to ensure that the other shareholders are able to buy out your shares at the time of your death, pay the tax liability, and retain the business. Your estate can then be distributed easily between those family members who are involved in the business, and those who are not. It may be advisable to purchase corporately-owned insurance which designates the corporation as the beneficiary so that the corporation has the necessary funds at the required time.

- If the business is later sold to a third party and the $750,000 capital gains exemption is available, not only will you be able to claim the exemption, but other family members may be able to as well if part of the capital gain has accrued while they owned shares (or were beneficiaries of a trust which owned shares). In order to claim the capital gains exemption, a shareholder generally must hold the shares for at least two years, which is why it is important to do this type of planning well in advance of the time at which you intend to sell the business.

- If payment for shares of a small business corporation is not received all at once, a reserve can be claimed over a five-year period, although at least 20% of the purchase price must be reported every year (the time period is extended to ten years in certain circumstances where the purchaser is the taxpayer's child and the child resides in Canada). Although this spreads the capital gains liability out over a longer period of time, be sure to obtain security if you are not receiving the purchase price immediately at the time of sale.

An estate freeze is a popular mechanism for transferring a business to family members, as it overcomes the usual problems of the children not having sufficient funds to purchase the business and the parents not wanting to trigger a large tax liability all at one time. As estate freezes can be quite complicated, be sure to speak with an advisor who specializes in dealing with business owners before implementing this type of strategy. Also, the process itself can be quite expensive, so it is usually not advisable to implement an estate freeze unless the business is expected to grow significantly in the next few years, and the original owner is only a few years away from retirement (although the freeze should be done at least two years prior to the time of sale).

## 16.6 INSURANCE PLANNING

Insurance is generally a very important part of a properly structured business succession plan. Be sure to speak with your financial advisor about the best type of insurance for your needs.

### 16.6.1 Amount of Insurance Required

When you own a business, there are a number of reasons why you may need life and/or disability insurance. In particular, when purchasing insurance, consider the factors below when determining how much you will need.

- If you were to die, how much life insurance would the business need in order to buy out your interest? If you are the sole shareholder and your family intends to sell the business after the time of your death, this may not be an issue, but if you have business partners who are not interested in selling the business, it will be important for the corporation or your partners to have insurance on your life so that your estate will be able to sell your interest in the business to your partners.

- At the time of your death, tax will be payable on any increase in value of the shares since the date you purchased them (or the increase in value of the assets of the business if it isn't incorporated), unless the shares are transferred to a spouse or common-law partner (see Chapter 21, "Taxation at Death", for more information). Even though you have not sold the business, you will be "deemed" to have sold it for fair market value. For example, if you originally purchased the shares for $100, and they are now worth $500,000, your estate would have a $499,900 capital gain, 50% of which would be taxable. Although it is possible that your estate may be able to make use of the $750,000 capital gains exemption, you should confirm with your tax advisors that this exemption is available. If it is not, then 50% of the entire capital gain will be taxable. Be sure to properly calculate the amount of the capital gain when determining how much insurance you need. If you do not plan for the tax liability, it is likely that your family will have to sell the business to pay the tax bill, which may not have been your intention.

- Consider whether you need personal life insurance in order to leave a legacy to children or other beneficiaries who may not be receiving a part of the business. Corporate owned life insurance may assist those family members who need insurance to pay the tax liability resulting from the business, but it may not be of any assistance to those family members who are not involved in the business. If you have some family members who will be taking over the business, and others who will not, personal life insurance is a good solution for equalizing your estate.

- Ensure that the amount of life insurance is sufficient to support your family after the time of your death, regardless of the value of your business. There are some businesses that have a relatively low value for insurance purposes, yet provide a significant annual income for their owners. Be sure that you have enough life insurance for the needs of your family, with the proceeds received from the buyout of your shares possibly forming only a portion of what you need.

- Do you need life insurance to pay for interim management of the business in the event of an unexpected death? Your beneficiaries may have sufficient funds to keep the business from being seized by the Canada Revenue Agency, but if they do not have the skills necessary to run it, they may require additional funds to hire an external manager. In business, liquidity is crucial. This type of insurance is often referred to as "key person" insurance. Consideration should also be given to purchasing key person critical illness insurance, since the business could also be in jeopardy if you are unable to manage it in the event of a critical illness.

- If a policy is payable to a corporation, the death benefit (less the adjusted cost base of the policy) will be deposited into the corporation's capital dividend account, and can be paid out on a tax-free basis to the shareholders, since the death benefit would have been received tax free had it been paid to the shareholders directly. Any amount paid in premiums over and above the net cost of pure insurance will be taxable when received by the corporation, so it may be necessary to purchase more insurance to ensure that the after-tax amount received by the corporation is sufficient.

- As discussed in section 16.4, "Disability Planning", adequate disability insurance is necessary not only to ensure that your interest in the business can be bought out in the event of disability, but also to ensure an adequate income stream in the event you are no longer able to work.

## 16.6.2 Structuring the Insurance Policy

Once you have determined how much insurance you will need, you then need to consider how to structure the policy, and what type of insurance is best suited to your needs.

- Life insurance purchased to fund obligations under a buy-sell agreement typically takes the form of a whole life policy, or some related form of insurance that builds up a cash surrender value over time. By building up a cash surrender value, the owners of the policy can also cash in the policy to purchase the interest of a retiring owner, as long as this is permitted by the buy-sell agreement.

- Be sure that the beneficiary of any life insurance purchased for the purpose of funding a buyout at the time of death is the company or a surviving shareholder — not the estate of the deceased shareholder or the surviving spouse! The company or the surviving shareholder will need the funds in order to buy out the estate. Many people automatically appoint a family member as the beneficiary of all of their insurance policies, but in the case of an insurance policy established for the purpose of funding a corporate buyout, this may not be appropriate. If the policy is corporately held, then it may be advisable to have the corporation designated as the beneficiary of the policy. If a shareholder is designated as the beneficiary of a policy paid for by the corporation, that designation could result in a taxable shareholder benefit.

- If life insurance is intended to be paid to a family member, then there are advantages if certain individuals are named as beneficiary (these individuals are members of the "protected class" of beneficiaries, and are listed in section 25.4 of Chapter 25, "Insurance"). In that case, the policy's cash value, as well as the death benefit payable to the beneficiary, is generally exempt from seizure by creditors of the policyholder. This creditor protection is a distinct advantage for professionals or business owners who want to consider using insurance as an investment vehicle.

- Even if you don't have any relatives who fall into the "protected class" of individuals referred to above, you may still be able to protect your life insurance proceeds from creditor claims by designating an irrevocable beneficiary. However, remember that if you designate a beneficiary irrevocably, you cannot change that designation without the consent of that beneficiary.

- If your corporation requires life insurance in order to obtain financing, then consider whether or not the corporation should be the owner of the policy, as it may be possible to deduct the premiums (or a portion of the premiums) from the corporation's income. The "net cost of pure insurance" will be deductible if the corporation is the owner and beneficiary of the policy. Review the terms of the financing carefully with your tax advisors, however. If the policy is personal in nature, then the premiums may not be deductible, and in fact may result in a taxable shareholder benefit to the person who will be receiving the benefit from the policy.

- Consider whether it may be beneficial to own a universal life insurance policy with a "split-dollar arrangement". The usual type of split-dollar arrangement is where the corporation owns the cash-value portion of the policy and the employee owns the life-insurance component. The employee would pay the minimum amount to fund the life insurance component, and the corporation would overfund the policy above the minimum. The employee's estate or beneficiaries would then receive the death benefit, and the corporation would receive the cash surrender value, which it may need to cover the costs of replacing the employee. The reverse is also possible, and may be beneficial to executives who would like to take advantage of the tax-deferral opportunities available with universal life policies, yet have their corporation fund the insurance cost. At the time of retirement, the policy can be transferred to the employee, who can choose to continue paying the premiums if he or she would like to keep the insurance in place. Since the employer will pay the premiums up until then, the employee will have received a substantial benefit.

- When considering whether to purchase insurance in the names of the shareholders or the name of the corporation, keep in mind some of the potential problems associated with corporate-owned insurance:

    - the cash surrender value and death benefit may be exposed to creditors of the corporation;

    - if for any reason the parties want to transfer the policies into their personal names (for example, if the shareholders sell the company to a third party but want to retain the insurance for personal purposes), the transfer of the policy may result in tax exposure for the company and shareholders; and

    - cash values of a permanent insurance policy are not considered active business assets for the purposes of the $750,000 capital gains exemption.

These issues can usually be dealt with by placing the insurance policy within a holding company. The operating company can pay dividends to the holding company on a tax-free basis to fund the premiums. This insulates the policy from the operating company's creditors and allows the shares of the operating company to be sold while retaining control of the insurance policies. If properly structured, the use of a holding company to own the insurance policies may also allow the shares of the operating company to continue to qualify for the capital gains exemption.

It is important to review your insurance plan with your advisors when you are still young and insurable at a reasonable cost. Insurance is often the best solution for funding a buyout of your business in the event of disability or death, so do not put your financial future, or the financial future of your beneficiaries, in jeopardy by waiting too long to obtain adequate coverage.

## 16.7 JURISDICTION DIFFERENCES

There are no jurisdiction differences for this chapter.

## 16.8 CASE STUDY

### 16.8.1 Estate Freeze

Karin and Terry, ages 49 and 51 respectively, own a successful chain of flower shops that they started on their own in 1980. Although the business is now worth about $2 million, when they first incorporated their business, each purchased 50 common shares for $1 per share. Karin and Terry have two children, Joel, age 25, and Carole, age 21, both of whom have indicated an interest in taking over the business. However, Joel and Carole are still too young to take over the business, and Karin and Terry are not ready to retire. Karin and Terry either want to transfer the business to Joel and Carole, or sell the business in about ten years time, so they ask their advisor what type of planning they should consider.

Karin and Terry's advisor reviews their financial situation, and it is agreed that Karin and Terry will have enough to retire on, since they started an individual pension plan some years ago, and, additionally, they have been making regular investments in non-registered segregated funds. They are concerned about the almost $2 million unrealized capital gain that has already accrued in their hands, and, if possible, they would like to pass on some of the future gains to their children. They are also concerned that if the capital gain at the time of their death is too significant, their beneficiaries will have to sell the business in order to satisfy the tax liability. The capital gains liability is calculated as follows:

| | |
|---|---|
| Fair market value | $2,000,000 |
| Adjusted cost base | ($100) |
| Capital gain | $1,999,900 |
| Taxable capital gain (50%) | $ 999,950 |
| Tax liability (assuming 45% tax bracket) | $ 449,977.50 |

Karin and Terry's accountant tells them that if they each qualify for the $750,000 capital gains exemption for qualified small business shares, they may be able to reduce that liability by 75%, since the capital gain would be reduced by $1,500,000. However, they will have to ensure that the corporation continues to meet the tests set out in the *Income Tax Act.* In particular, at least 50% of the assets of the corporation must be used to produce active business income in the two years prior to the time of sale, and at least 90% of the assets of the corporation must be used to produce active business income at the time of sale.

Karin and Terry decide that it is time to do an estate freeze. Therefore, they each exchange their 50 common shares for 1,000,000 preference shares, for a total of 2,000,000 preference shares with a fair market value of $2,000,000. Since they still have shares worth $2,000,000, the share exchange does not have any tax consequences.

They then create a family trust with themselves and a close friend as the trustees, and Terry's parents as the "settlors". Terry's parents "settle" the trust with a gold coin, and have no involvement in the trust after that point. Terry, Karin, Joel and Carole, as well as any future children of either Joel or Carole, are all designated as beneficiaries of the trust. Since the trust is completely discretionary in nature, the trustees can choose which beneficiary will receive distributions from the trust, and in what amount. The trustees of the trust then borrow $100 from a bank and use these funds to then subscribe for 100 new common shares in the corporation, for $1 per share. This borrowed money should be repaid as soon as the corporation pays $100 in dividends to the trust.

Over time the business continues to increase in value. However, the value of the shares owned by Terry and Karin stays constant at $2,000,000. Terry and Karin purchase a joint last-to-die life insurance policy with a face value of $500,000 so that at the time of the last to die, their estate will have sufficient funds to pay the tax owing on the shares. Although Terry and Karin know that the tax liability could be much lower than $500,000 if they each qualify for the $750,000 capital gains exemption, they decide that they would like to have the additional insurance just in case the tax bill is larger than they anticipated.

Over the years, Terry and Karin continue to receive a salary from the company, and dividends are paid to the common shareholder (the trustees of the trust) on a periodic basis. Terry and Karin make distributions to the beneficiaries of the trust from time to time, although the distributions are often made to different people in different amounts. For example, Terry and Karin gave Carole $30,000 every year while she was still in university in order to pay for her tuition and living expenses, even though they did not pay out the same amount to either Joel, or themselves.

About six years after completing the estate freeze, Terry and Karin receive an offer to purchase their business for over $5,000,000. Terry and Karin are now very close to retirement, and neither Joel nor Carole has really indicated a strong interest in continuing to run the business, although they would like to continue to be employed there. Terry and Karin decide to sell the business at this point. They receive $2,000.000 for their shares, and, because the shares meet all the required tests at that time for the capital gains exemption ($750,000 each), their tax liability is only $112,477.50 (calculated using the total gain of $1,999,900 less $1,500,000 = $499,900 x 50% inclusion rate x 45% tax rate). The trustees of the trust receive the remaining $3,000,000 of the purchase price. Since Joel and Carole are beneficiaries of the trust, they can also each use the $750,000 capital gains exemption, so a further $1,500,000 of the purchase price is sheltered from taxation. The remaining $1,500,000 in capital gains is distributed back to Terry and Karin. Although Joel and Carole are in a lower tax bracket than Terry and Karin, both of them are in shaky relationships, so Terry and Karin want to distribute as little as possible to them, while still using the $750,000 capital gains exemption. The taxable portion of the gain (or $375,000) must be distributed to each of Joel and Carole if they want to use the capital gains exemption, and Terry and Karin encourage Joel and Carole to invest the funds separately, and enter into a pre-nuptial or cohabitation agreement regarding these funds prior to getting married or beginning to live with someone. Since Terry and Karin made themselves beneficiaries of the trust, they decide to distribute the remaining purchase proceeds back to themselves, and they indicate in their will that their estate is to be left equally to Joel and Carole, in testamentary trusts (see Case Study 10.8.2, "Married, With Adult Children", for a discussion on how testamentary trusts can be used to reduce taxes for the beneficiaries of an estate).

If Terry and Karin had chosen not to sell the business, they could have retained their shares for many years without tax ramifications. However, they probably would have decided to wind the trust up by its 21st anniversary, in order to prevent what is known as a "deemed disposition". If, for example, it was decided at that time that Carole would continue on with the business, and Joel would not, then all the common shares held by the trust could be "rolled out" to Carole without tax consequences, assuming she was a resident of Canada at that time. Terry and Karin would then enter into a shareholders' agreement with Carole at that time, setting out what would happen in the event of death, disability, dispute, relationship breakdown, retirement, etc. Carole would need to ensure that the company purchased life insurance in the amount of $2,000,000 in order to fund the buyout of her parents' shares at the time of the last to die, and Terry and Karin could indicate in their will that Joel would receive an extra $500,000 (or whatever amount they feel is fair) from the estate to account for the fact that he would not be receiving the business.

# Part III

# Reference Chapters

# CHAPTER 17



# FAMILY PROPERTY

Discussions regarding the division of family property are often very complex and emotionally charged. Although this chapter will help to give you an idea as to how family assets may be divided in your jurisdiction, *it is extremely important that you speak with an experienced family lawyer prior to entering into any agreement with your spouse, common-law partner or future spouse or common-law partner regarding family property.* The area of family law is continually changing, so it is possible that the rules set out in this chapter may have changed since the date of publication, or your situation requires unique considerations. The division of property is made even more complicated by the tax consequences that must be considered prior to transferring an asset to a spouse. With those caveats in mind, here is a brief overview of the family property rules which may be applicable to you.

## 17.1 DIVIDING FAMILY PROPERTY

The process involved in dividing family assets varies quite dramatically across the country. In some provinces, separated spouses are not actually entitled to a portion of any particular asset that their spouse may own, but rather, they are entitled to an "equalization payment". The process essentially involves totalling the net assets owned by each spouse on the date of separation, subtracting the assets owned on the date of marriage, and then the spouse with more assets pays an amount to the other spouse so that their assets are equalized. In other provinces, all assets are shareable, including assets brought into the marriage or those acquired after the date of separation but prior to the time of divorce. This is obviously an extremely simplified explanation of what can become a very complicated and arduous process. Here are just a few of the issues that must be resolved as part of this process.



1. Which assets must be included in the calculation? All assets owned by either spouse? Or will some assets be "exempt" (i.e. the value of assets brought into the relationship? Inheritances and gifts? Businesses? The value of assets acquired after the date of separation?)

2. How much are the various assets worth? Is there an inherent tax liability that must be taken into account to determine each asset's after-tax value? Should the value of the asset be discounted to take account of the fact that it may not be accessible for some time (e.g. a pension)?

3. How will "payment" be made from one spouse to the other? Most individuals don't have thousands of dollars in liquid funds available to make a large payment. Will one spouse transfer their interest in the family home to the other? Rollover some of their Registered Retirement Savings Plans ("RRSPs")?

Generally speaking, only married couples will be able to make a court application to have their assets divided according to provincial legislation. However, a few jurisdictions have amended their legislation to provide that common-law partners are entitled to make an application for a division or equalization of family property after meeting certain pre-conditions, such as living together for a certain period of time or registering their relationship with the provincial government. In addition, a common-law partner may be able to claim in the courts that their partner has experienced an "unjust enrichment", which may entitle him or her to receive certain assets using a "constructive trust" argument. For further information on family property rights or other legal remedies for common-law couples in your jurisdiction, see sections 3.4.2 and 3.9 of Chapter 3, "Common-Law Couples". There is also some information in section 17.4 of this chapter.

These are just some of the myriad of issues that can arise when trying to reach a settlement of family property issues. It goes without saying that all individuals experiencing a separation or divorce should speak to an experienced family lawyer prior to agreeing to any settlement.

## 17.1.1 Which Assets Are Shareable upon Separation or Divorce?

The assets subject to provincial or territorial family law legislation vary from jurisdiction to jurisdiction. Generally speaking, all family assets that were acquired during the marriage are shareable, including homes, cottages, vehicles, furniture and personal effects. In addition, pensions, RRSPs, RRIFs or other retirement assets are generally shareable to the extent that they were acquired over the course of the marriage.

However, the legislation regarding businesses, gifts and inheritances may vary between the different jurisdictions. Note that it is generally the law of the jurisdiction in which you resided at the time of separation that is relevant when determining how your property will be divided, not the jurisdiction in which you were married. Therefore, if you move to a new jurisdiction during the course of your marriage, be sure to review the rules in the new jurisdiction to understand what their rules are regarding the division of family property. It is possible that the rules of your new jurisdiction will not apply if you have not lived there for very long, so again, be sure to speak to a family lawyer to determine which rules will apply to you.

Please see section 17.4, "Jurisdiction Differences", for a discussion on the types of assets that are shareable in your jurisdiction.

## 17.1.2 Family Home

Regardless of the manner in which the value of the family assets is calculated, the family home is a special asset, with special rights. Spouses are generally entitled to stay in the family home as long as they are legally married spouses (see section 3.9 of Chapter 3, "Common-Law Couples", to see if common-law partners have a right of possession to the family home in your jurisdiction). In many jurisdictions, spouses cannot agree in advance that they will not have a right of possession in the family home, and, in many cases, the right of possession extends for a period of time after the time of death of the spouse who owns the home.

If you are married, or contemplating marriage, or if you are in a common-law relationship in a jurisdiction that gives common-law partners rights of possession in family homes, speak with your lawyer about the need to include a provision regarding the family home in a domestic contract, and if this type of provision is enforceable. If your spouse owns your family home, be aware that the right to possession is not indeterminate, and will end either at the time of divorce, possibly after a certain period of time after the time of death (depending upon your jurisdiction of residence), or in the event the court grants possession to the other spouse.

Keep in mind that the right to stay in the home for a period of time is not the same as a right to a division of the value of the property. Just because you may be entitled to occupy the home for a period of time does not mean that the entire value of the property will be shareable. However, in some jurisdictions, spouses are entitled to a division of the entire value of the family home, regardless of whether or not it was purchased by one spouse prior to the time of marriage (or the common-law relationship). If you or your partner owns a home, this issue should be discussed with your advisor, and see section 17.4 to see if there are any special rules regarding family homes in your jurisdiction.

If you and your spouse or partner live in a home that neither of you own, then you may have little or no protection in the case of relationship breakdown or death. Some individuals are surprised to learn that their home is owned not by their spouse, but by their spouse's parents, in which case you will not have the right to occupy the home in the same way as if your spouse owned it.



## 17.1.3 Division of Federal Pensions

Although the division of most property is governed by provincial law (including the division of pensions governed by provincial legislation), some assets are divided according to federal legislation – particularly, federal pensions, including the Canada Pension Plan ("CPP").

### *17.1.3.1 Pensions for Federally Regulated Industries*

The *Pension Benefits Standards Act* (Canada) applies to all federally regulated industries such as airlines and banks. A member of a federal pension may assign all or part of his or her pension benefit to his or her spouse, effective on marriage breakdown or separation. If a joint and survivor benefit is to be divided, the pension may be paid as two separate pensions as long as the sum of the present values of the two pensions does not exceed the present value of the joint and survivor pensions. The *Pension Benefits Standards Act* also states that the definition of spouse has the same definition as it has under the applicable provincial legislation, so in some jurisdictions this will include a common-law partner, depending upon how long the couple has lived together. Spouses cannot apply for a division of benefits until they have been separated for at least one year, and they must provide a written and signed separation agreement or court order. Once the pension is divided, the spouse will no longer qualify for survivor benefits.

The *Pension Benefits Division Act* applies to all federal public service plans. This statute provides for a division of a member's benefits between the member and spouse or former spouse upon separation or divorce. The division is generally done by transferring 50% of the value to the plan of the spouse (if the spouse's plan permits), or to an RSP for the purpose of purchasing an annuity. The definition of "spouse" for the purposes of the *Pension Benefits Division Act* includes both married spouses and common-law couples who have lived together in a conjugal relationship for at least one year. Note that unlike some other federal legislation (notably, the *Income Tax Act*), simply living together in a conjugal relationship with a child will not meet the test for being considered a spouse – the parties must live together for at least one year in order to meet the test in this legislation.

#### *17.1.3.2 Canada Pension Plan*

Couples who have been married for at least one year are entitled to receive a share of their spouse's CPP benefits after they have been separated for 12 months, or after the time of divorce. There is no time limit for making an application for receiving these benefits. In Quebec, Quebec Pension Plan ("QPP") payments cannot be divided once the couple is either legally separated or divorced.

Common-law spouses are also entitled to CPP credit splitting if they lived together for at least one year and were separated for 12 months before making the application to split the credits (note that simply living together with a child for a period of less than 12 months is not sufficient). The application for credit splitting must be made within four years of the date of separation.

### 17.1.4 Limitation Periods

Property division is typically a time sensitive matter. In some provinces, a spouse may be able to apply for a division or equalization of family property during the marriage and possibly even after the time of divorce. In other provinces, a spouse may only be able to make an application once the couple has been separated for a certain period of time. See section 6.7 of Chapter 6, "Separated", for more information regarding the time periods in which you may make an application. Also speak to your family lawyer to ensure you meet all necessary requirements.

### 17.1.5 Claims Against an Estate

In some jurisdictions, a surviving spouse may make an application for a division of family property against the estate of a deceased spouse. The surviving spouse may be able to make an application for an equalization of family property against the estate instead of receiving the amount provided under the will, or the amount they are entitled to under the intestacy legislation if there was no will. Depending upon the jurisdiction, a spouse may choose to do this where they were not included in the deceased's will, or were not left as much as they would receive upon a division of family assets. Again, the rules in each jurisdiction differ in this regard. See section 19.6 of Chapter 19, "Distribution of an Estate", for more information on this subject.



### 17.1.6 Unequal Division of Assets

It is possible in some circumstances that a court may order an unequal division of assets if the facts warrant it. However, unequal divisions are not common, and the factors considered by a court will vary from case to case, so speak to a family lawyer if you feel that an unequal division is warranted in your case.

### 17.1.7 First Nations Canadians

Provincial or territorial family law legislation may not apply to Indian reserve lands. There can be no partition and sale of Indian reserve land, as it belongs to the Crown in trust. No order for exclusive occupancy can be made either. The Supreme Court of Canada has found that where the court is unable to award an interest in Indian reserve lands, it may order compensation in respect of those provisions of the provincial or territorial property legislation that allow for the division of family assets between spouses.

## 17.2 STRATEGIES FOR PRESERVING FAMILY ASSETS

Although it is not always possible to protect assets from claims by a former spouse or partner, it may be possible to protect some of your assets by taking a few precautionary measures. Please note that the majority of these strategies must be implemented well in advance of the time of separation or divorce, so, if possible, you should speak with a family lawyer prior to entering into a common-law relationship or getting married. If you know how the family property laws work in advance, you will be more likely to preserve a greater portion of your assets in the event of separation and/or divorce.

## 17.2.1 Assets Acquired Prior to the Time of the Relationship or Marriage

Many people assume that it is only the assets that are acquired during the course of marriage that are shareable. However, in some jurisdictions (particularly Newfoundland, Ontario and Saskatchewan), family homes (which can include a cottage) may be shareable even if acquired before the date of marriage. In British Columbia and Nova Scotia, many different types of assets may be shareable, regardless of when they were acquired, and in Manitoba and New Brunswick, assets acquired in contemplation of marriage may be shareable.

In addition, many jurisdictions have amended their legislation to include assets acquired during the course of a common-law relationship as well. Be aware of the rules in your jurisdiction, as they may operate in a manner that you would not expect (see section 17.4 for a description of the rules in your jurisdiction).

For some individuals, this may be a significant concern, especially if they are entering into the relationship later in life, after having acquired significant wealth. Although they may be prepared to share their wealth with their new partner or spouse if the relationship is successful, or in the event of death, they may be particularly concerned about protecting their assets in the event of relationship breakdown if they have children from a previous relationship and want to preserve their assets for their children.

Here are a few things to consider if you would like to protect assets acquired prior to the time of the relationship.

- It will be important to establish your net worth before you get married (or start a common-law relationship). Prepare a balance sheet for your personal assets (including all assets and liabilities), and maintain copies of the following documents to provide a basis for the value of your assets as of the start of your relationship or marriage:
  - bank, mutual funds and other investment account statements;
  - RRSP, RPP, TFSA, RESP, RDSP, and DPSP statements;
  - stock option plan statements;

- financial statements from closely-held corporations; and
- real estate appraisals.

Although you may be able to obtain some of this information after the fact, it may be very difficult to obtain confirmation of your investment account balance on the date of marriage, after you have been married for ten years. You should keep copies of these documents as of the date of marriage (or the commencement of the common-law relationship) in a separate file where they can be easily accessed in the event of separation and/or divorce.

- If you want an asset to remain separate, avoid adding a spouse as a joint owner of the property. It is possible that a court will interpret the addition of a spouse as a joint owner of a property as an indication that you intended to share the asset with them equally. Although in many cases spouses purport to do this only for the purpose of saving probate fees, keep in mind that probate fees are extremely low across Canada, and in most cases an estate can save more in income taxes if the probate planning is not done (see Chapter 22, "Probate", for a further discussion on the dangers of probate planning).

- Consider specifically protecting these assets in a domestic contract, which is discussed further in section 17.2.5 (particularly if you live in a jurisdiction where assets acquired prior to the marriage or relationship are not exempt).

### 17.2.2 Gifts, Inheritances and Loans from Family Members

In many jurisdictions, gifts or inheritances received from third parties are exempt from a division of family property. However, there are certain issues that you must keep in mind when you receive a gift or inheritance.

- In order to remain exempt, the gift or inheritance should not be used to purchase a family asset. Therefore, if you want the gift or inheritance to remain exempt, you should not use the funds to purchase a family home or other form of family asset. In some jurisdictions, it is not even advisable to use the income generated by the inheritance for family purposes, or the asset could be considered a "family asset" and therefore become shareable.

- In some jurisdictions, any growth on the gift or inheritance will be shareable, unless the person who gave the gift indicated that not only the gift itself, but also any income or growth is meant to benefit the recipient only.

Therefore, if you are aware that a family member intends to leave you a significant gift or inheritance, ask them to ensure that the declaration of gift or their will includes a clause to that effect.

- If you live in a jurisdiction where there are no specific exceptions respecting gifts or inheritances, or it is possible that you could move to a jurisdiction which does not have such an exception, it may be best to include a provision regarding this issue in a domestic contract.

- In some jurisdictions, there is a distinction between gifts and inheritances received prior to the time of marriage, and those received after. Therefore, you should not assume that all gifts and inheritances will be exempt from a division of family property. If this issue is of concern to you, speak to your family lawyer about entering into a domestic contract to protect these assets.

- Avoid adding a partner or a spouse as a joint owner on a gift or inheritance. You will not want to infer in any way that the spouse is an equal owner of this asset.

As the rules vary between the jurisdictions, see section 17.4, "Jurisdiction Differences", for a description of the rules in your jurisdiction.

If you are going to be transferring money to a child during your lifetime, then in many jurisdictions it would be best to structure the advance as a gift, since in most jurisdictions, gifts are exempt. The parents should sign a declaration of gift, indicating that the amounts are not meant to be shareable, including any income or growth. However, if the money will be used to purchase a family home, then the funds may become shareable, since in some jurisdictions, family homes are shareable, even if received by way of gift. One way in which to protect the amount given may be to transfer the funds in the form of a loan as opposed to a gift. However, there are steps you should take to ensure the loan is enforceable and not considered a sham.

- You should register a mortgage against the property in order to provide evidence that the amounts are meant to be repaid. Promissory notes and loan agreements are also helpful, but generally speaking, you should have all legal documents drafted by a lawyer so that they are properly executed and witnessed.

- It is important that these documents be done at the time the advance of funds is made, since you will need to establish your intent at the time of advance (these documents are not as persuasive if done in contemplation of separation or litigation). In addition, all future documentation should be consistent. For example, if a child completes a balance sheet with a financial institution when applying for a loan, they should indicate that there is an outstanding amount owing to their parents.

- It is not absolutely necessary that interest be charged on the loan, but where the loan has specific terms of interest, and the interest is not paid, this may be a factor in favour of a finding that the loan was later forgiven. If it is anticipated that the loan will be outstanding for some time, however, then either regular payments of principal and/or interest should be made, or the loan may become statute-barred, meaning that the parents will not be able to recover the loan. It may also be necessary to sign a new promissory note from time to time to re-start the limitation period. It will be important to establish that there was an intent to repay the loan if you want to protect those funds in the event of relationship breakdown.

- If there is a previous history of loans being made to a child (or a sibling) which were then repaid, you should retain evidence of this, as it will illustrate that your behavior (and/or your child's behavior) was consistent with the intent to make a loan as opposed to a gift.



However, if the funds are advanced by way of loan, then obviously the parent will only be entitled to receive the principal plus any accrued interest. If the intent is that the parent wants to receive a portion of the equity, then they will need to become a co-owner of the property.

If parents are loaning money to a child to acquire a business asset, and the intent is to forgive the loan at the time of death, the forgiveness should be in the will of the parent, not in the promissory note or loan agreement. If the loan is forgiven prior to the death of the parent, or upon death but not by means of the will, this may result in negative tax consequences.

## 17.2.3 Business Assets

Do not assume that business assets will be exempt from a division of family property. Although business assets are exempt in some jurisdictions, they are not exempt in every jurisdiction. Also, in some cases, the growth in the business is not exempt (see section 17.4 for a discussion of the rules in your jurisdiction). If you have a business you want to keep separate from a division of family property, or you are concerned about moving to a jurisdiction where business assets are not exempt, speak to a family lawyer about entering into a domestic contract that will address this concern.

As mentioned in section 17.2.2, gifts and inheritances are exempt property in some jurisdictions, so in cases where parents are passing a business down to children, it may be better to structure the transaction as a gift rather than a sale. For example, when one generation wishes to start passing a business down to the next generation, they will usually do an "estate freeze", and then the children will subscribe for new shares by paying a nominal price. If the parents (and children) are concerned about protecting these shares from a division of family property, it may be better to have the parents subscribe for the new shares, and then gift them to the children. See section 16.5.2.4 of Chapter 16, "Business Owners", for more information on estate freezes.

## 17.2.4 Jointly Held Assets

As mentioned above, one issue that many individuals do not consider carefully enough when entering into a new relationship is the effect of adding their new spouse or common-law partner as a joint owner of their assets. The law generally presumes that when a spouse adds their spouse as a joint owner to an asset, that the spouse intended to make a gift of part of the asset now, and the surviving spouse will be entitled to the entire asset at the time of death (unless you added your spouse as a "tenant in common", in which case there is no right of survivorship, and except in Quebec, where there is no right of survivorship). If you are attempting to preserve your assets, joint ownership generally will not be recommended, whether with or without a right of survivorship. The laws regarding which property is or is not exempt in a particular jurisdiction are generally only relevant to those assets that are in the name of one or the other spouse alone. If the asset is held in joint names, a court may infer that the asset is shareable. As well, if you sign a domestic contract indicating that each party is to retain any assets held in their own name, it is quite likely that the contract will not apply to any asset you hold in joint ownership, since the act of adding your spouse as a joint owner may be an indication to the court that you no longer wished to keep the asset separate. Please keep this in mind before adding a joint owner to any asset.

## 17.2.5 Domestic Contracts

If you do not like the manner in which family assets are divided in your jurisdiction, it is possible that you and your spouse or common-law partner may be able to enter into a domestic contract that provides for a different division. Domestic contracts are referred to by different names:

- cohabitation agreements, for common-law couples;

- pre-nuptial agreements, for couples who intend to get married;
- marriage contracts, for married couples; and
- separation agreements, for couples who have separated.

Why might you want a domestic contract?

- If you are in a common-law relationship and live in a jurisdiction where common-law partners do not have the right to apply for a division of family property in the event of relationship breakdown, then you may need a cohabitation agreement if you would like your assets (and the assets of your partner) to be shareable in the same manner as a married couple.
- If you live in a jurisdiction where assets acquired *prior* to the time of marriage or cohabitation are shareable, you may wish to include a provision in the contract indicating that only assets acquired after the date of cohabitation or marriage are shareable.
- If you live in a jurisdiction where there are no exceptions for business assets, you may want an agreement that indicates that business assets are not shareable in the event of relationship breakdown, nor is any of the growth in the business asset.
- If you live in a jurisdiction where gifts and inheritances are not exempt from a division of family property, or the growth in those assets is not exempt, you may want a contract that indicates that all gifts and inheritances, and any growth on those assets, are exempt.

You may also wish to enter into a domestic agreement to provide more certainty in the future.

- What if the laws in your jurisdiction are changed in the future? Would you be comfortable if all of a sudden you had to share more of your property than you originally anticipated?
- What if you and your spouse or partner move? Are you familiar with the rules in every jurisdiction? Are you comfortable with the thought that your property could be subject to an entirely different property regime?

Because of this uncertainty, you may want to "lock-in" the current rules, and try to avoid the retroactive application of laws, which may be passed in the future.

However, you must keep in mind that there will be some items you will not be able to address in a domestic contract. For example, in most jurisdictions, a spouse has a right to possession of a family home. Although you may be able to provide in the contract that your spouse is not entitled to share in the value of the home that was brought into the relationship, you will not necessarily be able to evict them from the house immediately at the time of separation. Also, clauses dealing with children are generally not enforceable, particularly those addressing custody or support (unless the agreement is a separation agreement). You can address spousal support in the agreement, but if the situation has changed since the date of the agreement, it is possible that a court will ignore the spousal support provisions if necessary.

The requirements for these agreements vary between the different jurisdictions, and certain conditions may have to be met before they will become enforceable. Speak to your family lawyer about the technical requirements for these agreements (for example, marriage contracts in Quebec must be written by notaries). In addition, given the acrimonious nature of many divorces, you do not want to run the risk of your spouse successfully challenging the validity of the agreement later in court. Here are a few suggestions for decreasing the chances of a court finding that the agreement is unenforceable.

- Start the process well before the wedding (or before moving in together). In many cases, the most important aspect of a domestic contract is the financial disclosure provided by each party. Valuing your assets could take several weeks and, in the case of a business, months. Also, since each party should obtain independent legal advice, it could take some time for both lawyers to review the terms of the agreement and explain it to you and your spouse. The process may also involve the signing of new wills and powers of attorney. If the process is rushed, resulting in the agreement being signed the day of the wedding, this may lead to an inference of duress, which you want to avoid.

- Ensure that there is complete financial disclosure – hiding assets may result in the contract being set aside. If there is inadequate disclosure, the other party may argue that they did not realize what they were giving up or signing away – your spouse will want to know what assets you own, and what they are worth – just saying you own "a company" may not be sufficient.

- Each party should obtain independent legal advice – if you both go to the same lawyer, there may be an inference that the lawyer had a bias towards one party or the other.

If you are entering into a separation agreement, there may also be certain tax and other considerations that should be taken into account in the preparation of the agreement. See section 6.3 of Chapter 6, "Separated", for a discussion of the issues relevant to separation agreements.

## 17.3 SPOUSAL AND CHILD SUPPORT



The right to spousal support or child support is completely separate from the right to a division or equalization of family property. For example, a spouse may be entitled to a division of equalization of family property, as well as spousal and/or child support. As each fact scenario is different, it is important to speak to an advisor to determine whether or not you will be entitled to receive (or be required to make) a support payment.

The amount of spousal support to be paid will vary depending upon the circumstances of the spouses. However, when determining the amount of child support to be paid, the court will usually look at the Federal Child Support Guidelines for your province or territory. The amount of support is generally determined by the amount of your income, and who has custody of the child. The amount to be paid is based upon where you live, unless you live outside of Canada, in which case the courts will use the guidelines for the province where the child lives. The court can deviate from the Guidelines if the amount provided would cause "undue hardship" to either the parent or the child. A parent can also be responsible for sharing "special" or "extraordinary" expenses of the child, which is added to the base amount set out in the Guidelines. Examples of special expenses could include child care expenses, medical or dental premiums attributable to the child, health-related expenses such as orthodontic treatment or glasses, private school tuition or certain ex-curricular activities.

If you are involved in a common-law relationship, you will only be entitled to apply for spousal support if you meet the tests set out in the family laws of your jurisdiction. To find out the rules for your jurisdiction, see section 3.9 of Chapter 3, "Common-Law Couples", for more information. However, you may be responsible for paying child support to a child of your former common-law partner, even if you were not the natural or adoptive parent of that child. See section 3.4.3 of Chapter 3, "Common-Law Couples", for further discussion on paying child support to a child of a common-law partner.

# 17.4 JURISDICTION DIFFERENCES

## 17.4.1 Alberta

### *17.4.1.1 Assets that Are Shareable and/or Exempt*

Generally, all assets are shareable if they were acquired during the course of the marriage, including business assets. However, certain property is exempt from distribution. The value of the following property at the time of marriage or on the date on which the property was acquired by the spouse, whichever is later, is exempt:

- property acquired by gift from a third party, or by inheritance;
- property acquired before the marriage;
- an award or settlement of damages in tort (unless the award is for a loss to both spouses); and
- proceeds of an insurance policy that is not insurance in respect of property, unless the proceeds are compensation for a loss to both spouses.

Such property still must exist or be traceable into existing property. Property may lose its exempt status, in whole or in part, if it is seen as being gifted to the other spouse, usually by a transfer to joint ownership.

The increase in value in exempt property from the date of marriage or date of acquisition is shareable unless there is an agreement to the contrary. Therefore, if you bring property into a marriage, or you have received an inheritance, and you would like the growth on any of those assets to remain exempt, it may be advisable to enter into a domestic contract providing for this.

In Alberta, the value of assets is generally determined as of the date of trial, not the date of separation, so even assets acquired after the date of separation may be shareable.

#### *17.4.1.2 Common-Law Couples*

Only married spouses can make an application for an equalization of property under the *Matrimonial Property Act.* Common-law couples (referred to as "adult interdependent partnerships") do not have the right to make an application for an equalization of marital property, unless they enter into an agreement providing for such, or file a lawsuit for unjust enrichment. See section 3.4.2 of Chapter 3, "Common-Law Couples", for more information.



### 17.4.2 British Columbia

#### *17.4.2.1 Assets that Are Shareable and/or Exempt*

Generally speaking, in British Columbia, any family asset owned or used by either spouse and used for a family purpose is shareable, and each spouse is generally entitled to one-half of all property. There are almost no exemptions for any types of property, including assets that were acquired prior to the time of marriage, so if you are bringing assets into a marriage, you should consider signing a domestic contract indicating that they are not to be shareable.

It is possible that an asset not used for a "family purpose" will be exempt from a division of family property. Therefore, if you receive an inheritance, and you do not want it to be shareable, it is important that you keep the inheritance separate, and not use it to purchase a family property, such as a house or cottage. It may even be advisable to refrain from using the income generated on such property for a family purpose. This onus is on the person attempting to keep the asset outside of a division of family property to prove that the asset does not have a family purpose, so the best alternative may be to sign a domestic contract if you want the asset to be exempt.

If business assets are owned by one spouse only, and the non-owning spouse does not make any direct or indirect contribution to the acquisition of the property by the other spouse or to the operation of the business, the property is not a family asset. An indirect contribution includes savings through effective management of household or child rearing responsibilities by the spouse who holds no interest in the property. Therefore, if the intent is that business assets are to be kept separate, this should still be set out in an agreement.

The legislation in British Columbia provides for a deferred community of property regime, meaning that at the time of the separation agreement or court order, each spouse is deemed to own a 50% interest in each asset that is a family asset, as opposed to providing for an equalization payment system as described in 17.1. Also, the legislation specifically provides that even where there is a domestic contract in place, a court may award an unequal division of assets where the circumstances warrant it.

#### *17.4.2.2 Common-Law Couples*

Only married spouses can make an application for a division of property under the *Family Relations Act.* Common-law couples do not have the right to make an application for a division of marital property, unless they enter into a domestic contract, or make a claim for unjust enrichment. See section 3.4.2 of Chapter 3, "Common-Law Couples", for more information.

However, if a common-law couple enters into a domestic contract for one purpose, then many other laws regarding the division of family property may also apply to them, so you should speak with an experienced family law lawyer before entering into such an agreement in British Columbia.

### 17.4.3 Manitoba

#### *17.4.3.1 Assets that Are Shareable and/or Exempt*

Generally all family assets are shareable, including assets used for shelter or transportation, or for household, educational, recreational, social or aesthetic purposes, including a family home, less any liabilities. However, *The Family Property Act* also specifically exempts certain assets from an equalization of family property, including:

- any asset acquired by a spouse by way of gift or trust benefit from a third person, unless it can be shown that the gift or benefit was conferred with the intention of benefiting both spouses;
- the proceeds of the surrender or the cash surrender value of any insurance policy where the premiums of the policy were paid by a third person by way of gift in favour of a spouse, unless it can be shown that the premiums were paid with the intention of benefiting both spouses;
- an asset acquired by a spouse by way of inheritance, unless it can be shown that the inheritance was devised or bequeathed with the intention of benefiting both spouses; and

- any income from, or appreciation or depreciation in the value of the above assets, unless it can be shown that the gift was conferred or the inheritance devised or bequeathed, as the case may be, with the intention that the income or appreciation should benefit both spouses.

However, any income from or appreciation in the value of an asset referred to above will be included in any accounting if the income or appreciation is used for the purchase of a family asset.



Although assets acquired by a spouse before marriage generally will not be shareable, they are shareable if:

- the asset was acquired when the spouse was cohabiting in a conjugal relationship with the other spouse immediately before their marriage; or

- the asset was acquired before, but in specific contemplation of, the cohabitation with, or the marriage to, the other spouse.

Any income from or appreciation in the value of an asset acquired prior to the time of the marriage or common-law relationship (and therefore exempt as discussed above) will be included in any accounting, unless it was a gift or inheritance. However, a negative value will not be deducted if the combined depreciation exceeds the combined appreciation.

The value of the proceeds of any damage award or settlement or insurance claim made in favour of a spouse for personal injury, or disability will not be included in the equalization calculation, except to the extent that the proceeds are compensation for loss to both spouses.

There is no exclusion for business assets, although a business could be exempt if received as a gift or inheritance. A life insurance policy or an accident and sickness insurance policy is not a family asset where the purpose of the policy is to provide funds that the beneficiary of the policy will likely require, or compensation for loss that the beneficiary of the policy will likely suffer, in respect of a business undertaking, in the event and as a result of the death, injury, illness, disability or incapacity of the person insured.

### 17.4.3.2 Common-Law Couples

Common-law couples who have registered a common-law relationship under *The Vital Statistics Act*, or who have cohabited with their partner in a conjugal relationship for a period of at least three years may apply for an equalization of property under *The Family Property Act*. Common-law couples who do not meet these criteria are not entitled to apply for such an equalization of assets, unless they enter into a domestic contract providing for such. Common-law couples may have other remedies available to them, such as making a claim against their partner for unjust enrichment. See section 3.4.2 of Chapter 3, "Common-Law Couples", for more information.

Although *The Family Property Act* may apply to common-law couples in certain circumstances as set out above, the legislation does not apply to the value of any asset acquired by a common-law partner:

- while living separate and apart from his or her common-law partner;
- while in a common-law relationship with a former common-law partner unless the asset was acquired while living separate and apart from the former common-law partner and it can be shown that the asset was acquired in contemplation of the common-law relationship with the present common-law partner; or
- before the commencement of cohabitation.

However, the statute does apply to any asset acquired by common-law partners before, but in specific contemplation of, their common-law relationship.

## 17.4.4 New Brunswick

### *17.4.4.1 Assets that Are Shareable and/or Exempt*

Family property includes family assets acquired while the spouses cohabited, or acquired in contemplation of marriage, except:

- a business asset;
- gifts from one spouse to the other, including income from that property; and
- gifts made by third parties to one spouse only, including any income from that property.

However, family property does not include property that the spouses have agreed by a domestic contract is not to be included in family property.

Where family property to be divided includes a family asset that was acquired:

- before the spouses married, or
- by one spouse as a gift from the other spouse or as a gift, devise or bequest from any other person,

the court may exclude that family asset from the division of family property if, in the discretion of the court, it would be unfair and unreasonable to the owner to include the family asset in the division of family property.



#### *17.4.4.2 Common-Law Couples*

Only married spouses can make an application for a division of property under the *Marital Property Act*. Common-law couples do not have the right to make an application for a division of family property, unless they enter into an agreement providing for such division, or make a claim for unjust enrichment. See section 3.4.2 of Chapter 3, "Common-Law Couples", for more information.

### 17.4.5 Newfoundland

#### *17.4.5.1 Assets that Are Shareable and/or Exempt*

Family assets include all real and personal property acquired by either or both spouses during the marriage, with the exception of,

- gifts or inheritances (other than a family home) received by one spouse from a third party and any appreciation in value of them during the marriage;
- personal injury awards, except the portion of the award that represents compensation for economic loss;
- personal effects;
- business assets;
- property exempted under a marriage contract or separation agreement;
- family heirlooms; and

- real and personal property acquired after separation.

The division of family assets can include a family home acquired *before* the marriage, and includes a family home acquired by gift, settlement or inheritance.

Although business assets are generally exempt from a division of family property, where one spouse has contributed work, money or money's worth in respect of the acquisition, management, maintenance, operation or improvement of a business asset of the other spouse, the contributing spouse may be awarded compensation in respect of their contribution.

### 17.4.5.2 Common-Law Couples

Only married spouses can make an application for a division of property under the *Family Law Act*. Common-law couples do not have the right to make an application for a division of family property unless they enter into an agreement providing for such division or make a claim for a finding of unjust enrichment. See section 3.4.2 of Chapter 3, "Common-Law Couples", for more information.

## 17.4.6 Northwest Territories

### 17.4.6.1 Assets that are Shareable and/or Exempt

Essentially everything owned by the spouses at the time of separation can be considered family property. The following assets may be exempt from a division:

- the spouse's debts and other liabilities as of the date of separation;
- the value of property that the spouse owned on the date of marriage (or as of the date the couple had cohabited for a sufficient period of time) after deducting the spouse's debts and other liabilities on that date;
- where the following types of assets were acquired after the time of marriage (or after the date on which the couple had cohabited for a sufficient period of time to be considered a spousal relationship), the lesser of the values of the following property on the date of acquisition and the date of separation:
    - property that was acquired by gift or inheritance from a third person,

  - proceeds or a right to proceeds of a policy of life insurance that are payable on the death of the life insured, and

  - property into which property referred to in the subparagraphs above can be traced.

Where a spouse owns property in the following categories, the value of the property, if it was owned by the spouse prior to the marriage (or the date on which a common-law couple had been cohabiting for a sufficient period of time), is not included in the calculation of the spouse's net family property:

- property that is excluded by domestic contract;

- damages or a right to damages for personal injuries or other harm to the person or the part of a settlement that represents those damages, and

- property into which this property can be traced.

The value of a spouse's debts and other liabilities that are related to the above described property is not included.

#### *17.4.6.2 Common-Law Couples*

Common-law couples who have been living together in a conjugal relationship for a period of at least two years, or who are in a relationship of some permanence where together they are the natural or adoptive parents of a child are subject to the provisions of *The Family Law Act* in generally the same manner as married spouses. Common-law couples who do not meet these criteria are not entitled to apply for such a division of assets, unless they enter into a domestic contract providing for such. Common-law couples may have other remedies available to them, such as making a claim against their partner for unjust enrichment. See section 3.4.2 of Chapter 3, "Common-Law Couples", for more information.

### 17.4.7 Nova Scotia

#### *17.4.7.1 Assets that Are Shareable and/or Exempt*

The legislation provides that all assets are presumed to be family assets, unless proven to fall into an excluded category. It is important to note that family assets include all property acquired during the marriage, *and brought into the marriage*. Where parties cohabit and ultimately marry, the duration of the entire relationship is considered in the division of property. However, the definition of family assets does not include:

- gifts or inheritances received from a third party, unless used for the benefit of both spouses or their children;
- an award or settlement of damages in favour of one spouse;
- insurance proceeds paid to one spouse;
- reasonable personal effects;
- business assets (unless the spouse contributed to the business);
- property exempted under a marriage contract or separation agreement; and
- real and personal property acquired after separation unless the spouses resume cohabitation.

If funds have been deposited into a business account, but they are used for family purposes, then those funds will be considered a family asset.

### *17.4.7.2 Common-Law Couples*

Common-law couples who have registered their relationship as domestic partnerships are subject to the provisions of the *Matrimonial Property Act* in the same manner as married spouses.

Common-law couples who have not registered their relationship as domestic partnerships do not have the right to make an application for a division of family property unless they enter into an agreement providing for such division or make a claim for a finding of unjust enrichment. See section 3.4.2 of Chapter 3, "Common-Law Couples", for more information.

## 17.4.8 Nunavut

See section 17.4.6. The rules in Nunavut are generally the same as in the Northwest Territories.

## 17.4.9 Ontario

### *17.4.9.1 Assets that Are Shareable and/or Exempt*

Shareable property includes all family property that a spouse owns on the date of separation or death, after deducting:

- the spouse's debts and other liabilities; and
- the value of property, other than a family home, that the spouse owned on the date of marriage, after deducting the spouse's debts and other liabilities, calculated as of the date of the marriage.

Therefore, in Ontario a family home may be shareable even if it was acquired prior to the date of marriage. If you are bringing a family home into the relationship (which could include a cottage), you will have to enter into a domestic contract with your spouse if you do not want it to be included in an equalization of family property.

The following property is excluded when calculating the amount owing by one spouse to the other:

- property, other than a matrimonial home, that was acquired by gift or inheritance from a third person after the date of marriage;
- income derived from such property if the donor or testator expressly stated that the income is to be excluded;
- damages or a right to damages for personal injuries, nervous shock, mental distress or loss of guidance, care and companionship, or the part of a settlement that represents those damages;
- proceeds or a right to proceeds of a policy of life insurance that are payable upon the death of the life insured;
- property, other than a family home, into which any of the previously listed types of property can be traced; and
- property that the spouses have agreed by domestic contract to exclude.

Note that if a gift or inheritance from a third party is received prior to the date of marriage, the value of the gift or inheritance is exempt from a division of family property, unless it is used to purchase a family home (generally all assets brought into a marriage are exempt except for family homes). However, although the value of the gift or inheritance may be exempt, the growth in value is not exempt. If you want any growth on the gift or inheritance received prior to the date of marriage to be exempt from a division of family assets, you should enter into a domestic contract to that effect.

In contrast, if the gift or inheritance from a third party is received after the date of marriage, not only is the value of the gift or inheritance exempt, but any increase in value may also be exempt if the person giving you the gift or inheritance includes a clause in the declaration of gift or will that both the gift and any increase in value of the gift are not to be shareable. (However, if the gift or inheritance is a family home, it will be shareable.) Therefore, if you would like a gift or inheritance to remain exempt, you should ask the person giving you the gift or inheritance to put it in writing that the growth in value is to be exempt, and you should keep the asset separate and ensure it is not used to purchase a family home.

Business assets are not exempt from a division of property under the *Family Law Act* unless the business was received as a "gift or inheritance" (although even in that case, it is possible that the growth in value will not be exempt). Therefore, if you want to protect a business, you should enter into a domestic contract specifically providing that it will be exempt.

### *17.4.9.2 Common-Law Couples*

Only married spouses can make an application for a division of property under the *Family Law Act*. Common-law couples do not have the right to make an application for a division of family property, unless they enter into a domestic contract, or make a claim for a finding of unjust enrichment. See section 3.4.2 of Chapter 3, "Common-Law Couples", for more information.

## 17.4.10 Prince Edward Island

### *17.4.10.1 Assets that Are Shareable and/or Exempt*

The value of all assets acquired during the marriage is shareable at the time of marriage breakdown subject to certain exceptions. Family property includes all property owned on the date of separation, including the income from the property, less:

- the spouse's debts and other liabilities on the separation date;
- the value of property that the spouse owned on the date of the marriage, valued at the date of the marriage, less the spouse's debts and other liabilities on the date of the marriage;
- the value of a gift or inheritance received from a third person after the date of the marriage and owned by the spouse on the valuation date, or the value of property into which a gift or inheritance acquired after the date of marriage can be traced; and
- the value of property owned by the spouse on the valuation date which is subject to a domestic contract.

The valuation date is generally the date of separation. There is no exception for business assets (unless they were received as a gift or inheritance), so if you would like certain business assets, or the growth in those assets, to be exempt from a division of family property, you should enter into a domestic contract to that effect.



### *17.7.10.2 Common-Law Couples*

Only married spouses can make an application for a division of property under the *Family Law Act.* Common-law couples do not have the right to make an application for a division of family property, unless they enter into a domestic contract, or make a claim for a finding of unjust enrichment. See section 3.4.2 of Chapter 3, "Common-Law Couples", for more information.

## 17.4.11 Quebec

### *17.4.11.1 Assets that Are Shareable and/or Exempt*

The assets that are shareable in the event of marriage breakdown are referred to as the "family patrimony". The family patrimony is comprised of:

- family residences;
- furnishings and household goods;
- family vehicles;

- retirement plan benefits, except in the case of death where the retirement plan awards the right to the death benefit to the surviving spouse (all sums accrued in an RRSP prior to marriage or civil union, together with any increase in value, are excluded);

- QPP earnings, except in the case of death; and

- gifts from one spouse to the other.

The family patrimony does not include a number of items, including:

- inheritances, or any increase in value;

- non-registered investments;

- bank accounts;

- businesses;

- company shares, dividends and stock-savings plan;

- life insurance policies; or

- salaries, wages, child tax benefits and family allowances.

Assets acquired and *entirely* paid for prior to the marriage or civil union are not included. You may be able to deduct the value of a contribution to a family patrimony asset made from an inheritance, if you can prove that the contribution did in fact derive from the inheritance. Couples cannot "contract out" of the family patrimony rules at the beginning of a civil union or marriage, although they can waive their rights at the time of separation.

In addition to the family patrimony rules, couples will also be subject to a matrimonial regime or a civil union regime, which determines the division of property that is not included in the family patrimony at the end of the relationship. There are three regimes.

1. *Separation as to Property.* This regime is only applicable if the couple has signed an agreement stating that it will apply. Each spouse will retain their own debts and assets unless it is unclear as to which spouse owns the asset or is responsible for the debt.

2. *Partnership of Acquests.* This regime will automatically apply to all married and civil union couples unless they agree otherwise. Generally, all assets are shareable, unless they are personal property. Personal property includes:

    - property brought into the marriage or civil union; and

    - inheritances received during the marriage or civil union, and if the testator so provides, the income on the inheritance.

3. *Community of Property.* This regime applies to couples married prior to July 1, 1970, unless they contracted out (or married after that time, but contracted in). Family property is divided into three types of assets – private property, common property and property reserved to the woman.



Inheritances are generally exempt from a division of family property unless the couple agrees otherwise. If you would like the growth on an inheritance to also be exempt, you should ask the person leaving the inheritance to you to put a clause to that effect in their will.

The family property rules in Quebec are quite complex. Be sure to speak with an experienced advisor to determine how the rules will apply in your situation.

### *17.4.11.2 De Facto and Civil Union Spouses*

Couples who have entered into a civil union will have the family property provisions of the *Civil Code of Quebec* apply to them in the same manner as a married couple.

*De facto* couples who have not entered into a civil union will not be subject to those provisions, and therefore must sign a cohabitation agreement or pursue other legal remedies in order for there to be a division of family property.

## 17.4.12 Saskatchewan

### *17.4.12.1 Assets that Are Shareable and/or Exempt*

The definition of family property includes almost every form of real and personal property owned by either spouse at the time the application for a division of property is made. However, subject to the court ordering an unequal division, the fair market value, at the commencement of the spousal relationship (which in the case of common-law couples does not occur until the parties have been living together for at least 24 months), of family property, other than a family home or household goods, is exempt from distribution where that property is:

- acquired before the commencement of the spousal relationship by a spouse by gift from a third party, unless it can be shown that the gift was conferred with the intention of benefiting both spouses;
- acquired before the commencement of the spousal relationship by a spouse by inheritance, unless it can be shown that the inheritance was conferred with the intention of benefiting both spouses (note that the growth is shareable, as are gifts acquired after the commencement of the spousal relationship); or
- owned by a spouse before the commencement of the spousal relationship.

A family home or household good is shareable in Saskatchewan even if it was acquired prior to the date of the marriage or common-law relationship. If you want a family home and household goods to be exempt, you must sign "an interspousal contract". Household goods means personal property that is ordinarily used, acquired or enjoyed by one or both spouses for transportation, household, educational, recreational, social or aesthetic purposes, but does not include heirlooms, antiques, works of art, clothing, jewelry or other articles of personal use, necessity or ornament or any personal property acquired or used in connection with a trade, business, calling, profession, occupation, hobby or investment.

There is no specific exception for gifts or inheritances received after the beginning of the spousal relationship. Gifts and inheritances received after the time of marriage, or at the two-year mark in a common-law relationship, and the growth on all gifts and inheritances whenever received, are shareable unless you sign a domestic contract stating the contrary. In Saskatchewan, a declaration by the donor of the gift or inheritance stating that the assets are not to be shareable may not be effective.

Business assets are not exempt from a division of property under *The Family Property Act*. It is possible that a business could be exempt if it was received as a "gift or inheritance" prior to the beginning of the spousal relationship, although even in that case, the growth in value may not be exempt.

Family property, other than a family home or household goods, is also exempt where that property is:

- an award or settlement of damages in favour of a spouse, unless the award or settlement is compensation for a loss to both spouses;
- money paid or payable pursuant to an insurance policy that is not paid or payable with respect to property, unless the proceeds are compensation for a loss to both spouses;
- property acquired after a declaration of divorce, a declaration of nullity of marriage or a judgment of judicial separation is made with respect to the spouses or, where the spouses are common-law partners, property acquired more than 24 months after cohabitation ceased;
- property acquired as a result of an exchange of the above property; or
- appreciation on or income received from and property acquired by a spouse with the appreciation on or income received from the above property.



In order for a property to be exempt, it must be in existence at the time the proceedings are commenced or, if not, then it must be directly traceable to another property acquired in exchange.

Family property will be valued as of the date of the application, not the date of separation.

### *17.4.12.2 Common-Law Couples*

Common-law couples who have cohabited with their partner as spouses continuously for a period of not less than two years may apply for a division of property under *The Family Property Act*. Only those assets acquired from the date on which the couple has been living together for two years will be included in the calculation of the division of property, unless it is a family home or household good.

Common-law couples who have not lived together for a period of at least two years are not entitled to apply for such a division of assets, unless they enter into a domestic contract providing for such division. Common-law couples who are not subject to *The Family Property Act* may have other remedies available to them, such as making a claim against their partner for unjust enrichment. See section 3.4.2 of Chapter 3, "Common-Law Couples", for more information.

## 17.4.13 Yukon

### 17.4.13.1 Family Assets

The definition of family assets is quite broad, and generally means a family home, and property owned by one spouse or both spouses, and ordinarily used or enjoyed by both spouses or one or more of their children while the spouses are residing together for shelter or transportation or for household, educational, recreational, social or aesthetic purposes.

Although business assets are not specifically exempt from a division of property under the *Family Property and Support Act,* the definition of "family assets" includes only those assets which were ordinarily used by either spouse or the children for family purposes, so it is possible that a business may not be shareable.

### 17.4.13.2 Common-Law Couples

Only married spouses can make an application for a division of property under the *Family Property and Support Act.* Common-law couples do not have the right to make an application for a division of family property, unless they enter into a domestic contract, or make a claim for unjust enrichment. See section 3.4.2 of Chapter 3, "Common-Law Couples", for more information.

## 17.5 CASE STUDIES

See the following case studies, which include a description of family law issues:

- 3.10.1 — Living Common-Law, Jurisdiction Generally Does Not Recognize Status
- 3.10.2 — Living Common-Law, Jurisdiction Generally Recognizes Status
- 4.8.1 — Engaged, One Spouse Owns a Home
- 4.8.2 — Engaged, One Spouse Owns a Business
- 6.8.1 — Separated, Living Common-Law, No Children
- 6.8.2 — Separated, Married, No Children
- 6.8.3 — Separated, Living Common-Law, With Children
- 6.8.4 — Separated, Married, With Children

# CHAPTER 18

# POWERS OF ATTORNEY

A power of attorney is potentially the most important document in your wealth plan. Without one, there will be no one authorized to act on your behalf in the event you become incapacitated, even for a short period of time. If you choose not to have a power of attorney, you may personally bear the consequences of that decision, since your assets may be managed by someone you may not have chosen, and in a manner of which you do not approve. If you recover from your incapacity, you may find that your assets have been depleted as a result of court costs, mismanagement, and costly delays in decision making, especially if a business is involved. For all of these reasons, it is important that every adult Canadian have a power of attorney.

There are essentially two types of powers of attorney:

1. a power of attorney for finances authorizes your attorney to make financial decisions on your behalf; and

2. a power of attorney for health care (sometimes referred to as a health care directive, advance health care directive, personal directive, representation agreement, power of attorney for personal care or living will) authorizes an individual to make health care decisions on your behalf.

In this chapter, references to the person who is giving the power of attorney will be to the "donor", and references to the person who is given the power to act will be to the "attorney".

# 18.1 POWER OF ATTORNEY FOR FINANCES

Every adult should have a power of attorney for finances, no matter how old they are, and no matter how many assets they have. It is possible for any person to be incapacitated even for a short period of time due to an accident, and it is very important to have someone available to take care of your affairs in the event you are not able to.

## 18.1.1 Why Do I Need a Power of Attorney for Finances?

A power of attorney is a document that appoints someone to act on your behalf when you are incapable of doing so. This may be because you have suffered an illness or you are out of the country and unable to sign an important document when required. If you have not appointed a power of attorney, it is possible that your family members will have to apply to a court in order to obtain the necessary powers to deal with your assets, since no one will have the authority to act as your attorney unless you give them that power. A court application can be expensive, and it is possible that a court may inadvertently appoint someone that you do not trust, given that you may not be able to provide your opinion on the subject. Consider the situations outlined below.

- Many married couples are under the mistaken impression that their spouse automatically has the ability to manage their affairs, but that is not the case. Couples should not assume that they automatically have the right to act for each other — even if you are married, you need to give your spouse a power of attorney if you want them to be able to handle your financial affairs when you are not able to. In fact, in some jurisdictions, a spouse may be the one person who is not allowed to act as your attorney in respect of certain assets, particularly when dealing with the family home (see section 18.4, "Jurisdiction Differences", below). All married individuals should have a power of attorney which appoints both a primary and an alternate attorney.

- If you do not have a power of attorney for finances, a court will usually grant authority to your spouse or next-of-kin (generally the person appointed will be called your "committee"). In many cases, your next-of-kin may be the best choice, but in some cases, this may not be what you would want. For example, common-law partners in many jurisdictions rank behind a separated spouse and next-of-kin when making such an application. Would you really prefer to have a separated spouse act on your behalf rather than your common-law partner? If you want a specific person to act on your behalf, you should ensure that you make your wishes known in a power of attorney.

- Even once a relative or friend does receive permission from a court to act on your behalf, they may be limited in what they can do. For example, some courts have been very restrictive when allowing relatives to sell assets or carry out tax planning strategies in respect of businesses or corporations. If your assets are extensive or complicated, or if you are a business owner, you will likely want and need a power of attorney that gives your attorney broader powers.

- If no one has the authority to manage your assets, some of your investments may automatically be reinvested (e.g. GICs) for the same term as they are currently invested. For example, if you purchased a five-year GIC when interest rates were high, that investment may automatically be rolled over into another five-year term at the time of maturity, even though interest rates may be very low at that time. You will want to ensure that someone has authority to manage your investments in the most optimal manner.

A court application in many cases can cost several thousand dollars. A power of attorney will generally not cost more than a few hundred dollars, and will relieve your family of additional stress and administrative headaches.

Unfortunately, many people feel they do not need a power of attorney if they have a will — however, a will does not take effect until you die. Therefore, your personal representatives named in your will do not have any authority to manage your affairs while you are still alive. A power of attorney document will be effective during your lifetime (although in some cases it is not effective until the time of a mental incapacity), but it will cease to be effective at the time of your death. When you die, it is your will that becomes effective.

## 18.1.2 Factors to Consider When Appointing an Attorney

Generally speaking, your attorney should be:

- trustworthy;
- responsible;
- knowledgeable about your assets (for example, if your attorney will have to run a business, then business experience would be an advantage); and
- a resident of Canada, and, preferably, a resident of your home jurisdiction. Although you can choose an attorney who is not a resident of Canada, that is almost tantamount to choosing no one at all, since in many cases your financial advisors will generally be prohibited from taking instructions from a non-resident. The securities laws in some countries (particularly the United States) are very stringent, and most Canadian financial advisors do not have the required licensing to take investment instructions from residents of other countries.

Here are some general matters that you should consider when preparing a power of attorney for finances.

- *Choose Your Attorney Carefully.* Do not assume that your spouse will have the requisite degree of knowledge to manage your affairs, particularly if you own a business. Also, you must have complete trust in the person or persons you are appointing, since a Power of Attorney is a very powerful document. A power of attorney gives another person the right to manage your assets and money, including selling property and cashing out your investments without your consent. If the attorney has the ability to manage your assets when you are incompetent, you must trust that they will act in your best interests, not their own.
- *Speak to Your Attorney in Advance.* Be sure to speak with the person you have designated to ensure that they are willing to take on the position, and to ensure that they know where your power of attorney is kept in the event they need it.
- *Designate an Alternate.* Always ensure that you have a "back-up" person designated in case your first choice is not able to act when you need them. Again, speak to the alternate in advance and ensure that they know where you keep your important documents. In cases where a person designates

a spouse as their attorney, it is important to designate an alternate, since in some jurisdictions a spouse is not entitled to sign documents on behalf of an incapacitated spouse when selling or mortgaging the family home. See section 18.4, "Jurisdiction Differences", for further details.

- *Consider Granting Wide Powers of Investment.* Although most provincial legislation allows attorneys relatively broad powers of investment, this legislation is subject to change at the whim of the government. If you want your attorney to have the ability to do anything you could do if you were able to, you should specify this in the power of attorney, or your attorney will be restricted to making investments that are allowed under provincial legislation.

- *Compensating the Attorney.* People acting under a power of attorney often have to spend a considerable amount of time taking care of the donor's affairs. In most jurisdictions, if the document does not specifically allow the attorney to take compensation, they will not be entitled to any unless a court approves such payment (except in certain provinces like Ontario, where the legislation allows compensation at a prescribed rate). In most cases, it would be appropriate for the attorney to receive some compensation for the services they are providing, so consider whether or not you want to include a clause allowing compensation to your power of attorney.

- *Designate a Monitor.* When you appoint an attorney, consider appointing a "monitor" in the document as well. You could provide that the attorney has to give an accounting to the monitor on an annual basis, and/or obtain consent from the monitor for major transactions.

- *Avoid Conflicts of Interest.* Try to choose a person who will not be in a difficult position when making decisions. For example, although it may seem like a good idea to appoint a business partner as attorney over your business assets, if there is a possibility that they will exercise the power for their own benefit, think carefully before choosing that individual. Another example of a potential conflict of interest is where someone who receives remuneration for your care is also appointed attorney to look after your property. This type of scenario should be avoided if possible.

If you cannot find an individual who is suitable for the job, consider appointing a corporate attorney. Corporations who provide these services are generally more knowledgeable and capable than a lay person, and less likely to encounter conflicts of interest. However, they will obviously charge for their services, so this may not be an option for everyone. Keep in mind, however, that many individuals will also charge for their services, so do not discount the use of a corporate attorney if that would be the most appropriate choice. However, a corporation cannot serve as a power of attorney for health care decisions — that power can only be given to an individual.

If you like, you can appoint two attorneys — for example, your two children. In some cases, appointing all your children may not be practical. For example, if you have several children, it may only be practical to appoint two or three of them. However, if you want to ensure that the children who are not appointed do not feel left out, you can give those individuals the right to demand an accounting once a year from the attorneys in order to review the accounts, and confirm that no assets have been used improperly. It is also common to see one child appointed as the primary attorney, with another child appointed as the alternate attorney, in the event the first child is unable or unwilling to act.

It is important to discuss with your advisors how decisions will be made, and how disputes will be resolved. For example, if you have several attorneys, can decisions be made by majority rule? If this is not set out clearly in the document, the governing legislation will dictate how decisions are made. Some jurisdictions also provide that in the event of disagreement, the attorney who is named first in the document will have the authority to make a final decision. It is possible that the legislation will not be consistent with your wishes.

If you own a business, there are some issues you should specifically consider. See section 16.4.1 of Chapter 16, "Business Owners", for a further discussion.



## 18.1.3 What Type of Document Do I Need?

### *18.1.3.1 Standardized Forms*

Generally speaking, pre-prepared power of attorney "kits" are not recommended. It is recommended that you ask an experienced lawyer to prepare a power of attorney for you that meets your needs and is broad enough to encompass all of your assets. Also, the rules regarding who may act as witness, how the document must be prepared, and the minimum age for the donor and attorney are different in every jurisdiction. Without proper advice, it is possible that the document you prepare on your own will not be effective at the time you need it (by which point, it will be too late to fix the problem).

Many people feel that if they have a power of attorney at their bank, that this should be sufficient for their purposes. This is generally not true. Generally, bank powers of attorney give your attorney power to deal with your bank only — any assets outside of your bank, including your home, your business or your car, will usually not be included in a standard form banking document. It is generally recommended that you have a broader power of attorney that allows your attorney to deal with all of your assets. Also, be careful if you decide to sign a bank power of attorney in addition to a general power of attorney, since you do not want the bank document to revoke your other power of attorney.

### *18.1.3.2 Enduring Powers of Attorney*

Every Canadian jurisdiction allows individuals to create what is referred to as an "enduring power of attorney". This is a power of attorney that will endure during a mental incapacity. It is very important that you speak with an estate planning professional when drafting your power of attorney. If the power of attorney does not include the proper wording, the power will cease upon a mental incapacity, which is generally the time when you will most need someone to act on your behalf.

### *18.1.3.3 Springing Powers of Attorney*

Unless your power of attorney states to the contrary, your attorney will have the power to begin dealing with your assets from the date on which the document is signed (except in the case of medical decisions, which can only be made upon mental incapacity of the donor). However, if you choose, you can sign what is known as a "springing" form of attorney, which will not take effect until some point in the future, after certain designated events have taken place. For example, you could specify that your attorney will not have power to act on your behalf until such time as two medical doctors have certified that you are no longer capable of handling your affairs.

Alternatively, you could leave the document with a trusted, objective third party (such as your lawyer) with instructions to only release the document once you become incapable of managing your own affairs, since some people feel that the need to obtain a medical certificate is too cumbersome, and delays your ability to use the power of attorney. Some documents also specify that the problem must be a mental incapacity, which may not be what you need if you suffer a severe physical injury, and are unable to take care of your affairs. Again, if you would like a springing form power of attorney, it is crucial that you speak to an estate planning lawyer.

#### *18.1.3.4 Health Care Decisions*

Generally, a power of attorney for finances is limited to financial issues. If you want your attorney to have the power to make medical decisions on your behalf, then you should consider a power of attorney for health care. It is usually not recommended that the power of attorney for finances and the power of attorney for health care be incorporated into the same document, as you may not want your financial institutions to have access to a document that also discusses health concerns. See section 18.2 for further information on powers of attorney for health care decisions.

### 18.1.4 Are There Any Limits on What an Attorney Can Do?

Generally speaking, an attorney can do anything you could have done, except make a will on your behalf or give away your assets. An attorney is a "fiduciary", meaning that they must always act in your best interests, not theirs. For example, an attorney should not designate themselves as the direct beneficiary of your insurance policies or registered investments or add themselves as joint owners of your assets in order to receive all of your assets directly at the time of your death, circumventing your will. Also, if they sell any of your assets, they are obligated to invest the proceeds in accordance with trust law, and cannot use the funds for their own purposes.

In some cases, you may wish to give your attorney powers that are broader than that contemplated under provincial law. For example, you may wish to give your attorney broad powers of investment, and the ability to undertake certain business transactions. Your lawyer will review the types of clauses that should be included in your power of attorney to ensure that it gives your attorney sufficient power to manage your assets properly.

There are some jurisdictions which allow attorneys to make gifts up to specific limits, or in specific circumstances. See section 18.4, "Jurisdiction Differences", for information regarding the limitations in your jurisdiction.

### 18.1.5 Impact of Marriage, Separation and Divorce

There are certain instances in which a power of attorney may be automatically revoked. For example, in some jurisdictions, a power of attorney is automatically revoked at the time of separation or divorce if the attorney is a former spouse. See section 6.7 of Chapter 6, "Separated", or section 7.7 of Chapter 7, "Divorced", for information on your jurisdiction.

However, marriage will not impact a power of attorney. If you get married, or enter into a common-law relationship, review your power of attorney document to ensure that it is consistent with your current wishes.

## 18.1.6 What If I Have Property in More than One Jurisdiction?

If you have property in different jurisdictions, you should ensure that your document is reviewed by a qualified lawyer in every applicable jurisdiction, and, if necessary, prepare different powers of attorney where required. The execution requirements for a power of attorney are different in different jurisdictions. For example, in British Columbia, if you sign what is known as a "representation agreement" (which is a power of attorney that can allow your attorney to deal with health care decisions as well as financial decisions), it must be signed and witnessed by specific individuals, including a lawyer. If you live in a jurisdiction where this is not required, but you have property in British Columbia or later move there, your power of attorney may not be accepted if it does not meet these requirements.

This may be especially important if you have assets outside of Canada, where the requirements may be quite different. In some cases, your advisors may recommend that you have a different form of attorney simply for convenience purposes. For example, even if it turns out that the execution requirements in one jurisdiction are the same as in another, if the authorities in another jurisdiction are used to seeing a specific format, or the document needs to be translated into a different language before it is accepted, there may be unnecessary delays in the handling of your assets. However, if you do sign a second power of attorney in a foreign jurisdiction, make sure that it does not revoke the power of attorney you want to have in effect in your home jurisdiction.

## 18.1.7 First Nations Canadians

The Minister of Indian Affairs and Northern Development has exclusive authority over the estate of a Status Indian who has become incompetent. Although provincial legislation will govern the process by which the aboriginal person is declared incompetent, the administration of the person's estate is governed by the Minister or their delegate.

# 18.2 POWERS OF ATTORNEY FOR HEALTH CARE

If you would like to appoint someone else to make health care decisions on your behalf, it is generally recommended that you sign a document dealing with this issue. Although the name and form of the document will vary from jurisdiction to jurisdiction (see section 18.4, "Jurisdiction Differences", for more information on your jurisdiction), for the purposes of this chapter, we will refer to this document as a power of attorney for health care. The following are some considerations you should take into account.

- You do not have to appoint the same person as your attorney for finances, and for health care decisions. The skills and background for each position may necessitate choosing different people for each position.

- Generally speaking, your health care attorney will be limited to making decisions regarding whether or not to prolong your life, and whether or not to proceed with life extending medical treatment. An attorney cannot choose to have you undergo elective or cosmetic surgery while you are incompetent.

- Although a power of attorney for finances can be drafted in a manner that allows it to become effective immediately, a power of attorney for health care will only become effective upon incapacity.

- Since you may not be capable of communicating to anyone that you have a health care directive once you become incapacitated, it will be important for you to inform your attorneys and your doctors that you have such a document, and where to locate it in times of emergency. In some cases it may be recommended that you keep a card in your wallet indicating that you have such a document, and instructing your doctors to contact a specific individual in case of emergency.

- Unlike a will, you can have several original copies of your power of attorney for health care. Consider giving one copy to your attorney and one to your doctor. Having only one copy, and leaving that copy in your safety deposit box, may make the document inaccessible at the very time that you need it.

- Although an attorney for health care decisions is generally not paid a fee, consider including a clause in the document that at least allows the attorney to be reimbursed for expenses, and if appropriate, paid a fee.

- There are certain instances in which a power of attorney may be automatically revoked. For example, in some jurisdictions, a power of attorney is automatically revoked at the time of separation or divorce. See section 6.7 of Chapter 6, "Separated", or section 7.7 of Chapter 7, "Divorced", for information on your jurisdiction.

- Marriage will not impact a power of attorney for health care. If you get married, or enter into a common-law relationship, review your power of attorney documents to ensure that they are consistent with your current wishes.

- If your power of attorney for health care decisions contains provisions regarding the withholding or withdrawal of life-sustaining procedures (such as a "do not resuscitate" clause), it should be clear that these procedures are to be withheld or withdrawn only if the attending physician has determined that its use will only artificially prolong the dying process, and that they should be applied when it may restore or improve your state of health.

The difference between a power of attorney for health care and a living will is that a power of attorney appoints someone else to make decisions on your behalf, while a living will simply sets out your wishes regarding the type of medical care you would or would not like, in order to act as a guide for your medical advisors. Not all jurisdictions recognize living wills, and there is no guarantee that a foreign country will recognize such a document. If you reside in a different province or country for part of the year, ensure that your living will complies with the laws of that jurisdiction. It is best to consult with a lawyer in both jurisdictions, and have two separate living wills, if necessary.

## 18.3 ALTERNATIVES TO A POWER OF ATTORNEY

There are some alternatives to signing a power of attorney if you would like someone else to manage your affairs. You may choose to transfer your assets into an alter ego trust, allowing the trustees to manage the trust funds on your behalf. However, you may not be able to transfer all of your assets into a trust (e.g. registered investments), and there may be some negative tax consequences to establishing the trust. See section 23.5.10 of Chapter 23, "Trusts", for more information. Speak with an estate planning lawyer if you feel that a trust would be a better option for you.

# 18.4 JURISDICTION DIFFERENCES

## 18.4.1 Alberta

### *18.4.1.1 Finances*

Both enduring and springing forms of attorney are authorized. In addition to their normal powers, an attorney may provide for the maintenance, education, benefit and advancement of the donor's spouse and dependent children (including the attorney if the attorney is the donor's spouse or dependent child). An attorney can make gifts if the donor specifically granted the attorney the right to make the gift or was in the habit of making such gifts. Attorneys in Alberta must invest the donor's funds in accordance with the *Trustee Act* (see section 23.6 of Chapter 23, "Trusts"). There is no prohibition on a spouse acting as attorney for a spouse when selling the family home.

### *18.4.1.2 Health Care Decisions*

Individuals may sign a "personal directive" giving someone else authority over their health care decisions once they become incapable of making these types of decisions on their own. A personal directive can give the attorney the power to make decisions in a number of areas, including health care and accommodation.

## 18.4.2 British Columbia

### *18.4.2.1 Finances*

Both enduring and springing forms of powers of attorney are authorized. There is no prohibition on a spouse acting as attorney for a spouse when selling the family home. In British Columbia, you can also sign what is known as a "representation agreement" that can address both financial and health care decisions. Representation agreements are usually used for health care decisions, with powers of attorney being used for financial decisions.

#### *18.4.2.2 Health Care Decisions*

As noted above, you can sign a document called a representation agreement that can address both financial and health care decisions. However, it is generally recommended that you sign a power of attorney for financial decisions and a representation agreement for health care decisions. There are fairly stringent requirements regarding the form of a representation agreement and who must witness it.

### 18.4.3 Manitoba

#### *18.4.3.1 Finances*

Both enduring and springing forms of power of attorney are authorized. Where two or more attorneys are appointed to act jointly,

- a decision of the majority is deemed to be a decision of all; and
- if one or more of the attorneys die, renounce the appointment, become bankrupt or mentally incompetent, or are unwilling or, after reasonable inquiries by another attorney, not available to make a decision, the remainder of the attorneys may make the decision and the decision of the majority of the remainder is deemed to be the decision of all.

In an enduring power of attorney, unless otherwise provided, where two or more attorneys are appointed to act jointly, but are unable to make a majority decision, the attorney first named in the document may make the decision.

Under *The Homesteads Act* of Manitoba, an individual cannot consent to the disposition (meaning a sale or mortgage) of a homestead on behalf of his or her spouse or common-law partner, even in situations where they are acting under a power of attorney. An individual may give such power to someone other than their spouse or common-law partner, but only if the power of attorney expressly authorizes the attorney to give consent under *The Homesteads Act*, and only if a specific form (Form 9) is executed with the document. Thus, when a person drafts a power of attorney in Manitoba in favour of his or her spouse or common-law partner, the person will usually specifically appoint a different individual as his or her attorney for the limited purposes of giving consent to a disposition of the homestead. Under *The Homesteads Act*, a common-law partner includes only those persons who have registered their relationship or who have lived together for at least three years – living together for one year with a child is not sufficient.

### *18.4.3.2 Health Care Decisions*

Individuals are allowed to designate someone as their proxy for making health care decisions by signing a health care directive. If two or more proxies who are appointed to act jointly disagree about the making of a health care decision and there is no majority decision, the proxy first named in the directive may make the health care decision on behalf of the donor.

## 18.4.4 New Brunswick

### *18.4.4.1 Finances*

Both enduring and springing forms of powers of attorney are authorized. There is no prohibition on a spouse acting as attorney for a spouse when selling the family home.

### *18.4.4.2 Health Care Decisions*

An individual may sign a power of attorney for personal care that appoints someone to make personal care decisions on their behalf.

## 18.4.5 Newfoundland

### *18.4.5.1 Finances*

Both enduring and springing forms of powers of attorney are authorized. There is no prohibition on a spouse acting as attorney for a spouse when selling the family home.

#### *18.4.5.2 Health Care Decisions*

Individuals may sign an advance health care directive in which the donor sets out instructions or general principles regarding his or her health care treatment, or in which the donor appoints a substitute decision maker, or both. If there is no substitute decision maker, health care professionals will look to your spouse, and then your children, parents, siblings, grandchildren, etc., to make a decision on your behalf, but not your common-law partner. If you are in a common-law relationship and you would like your common-law partner to have the ability to make health care decisions on your behalf in the case of incapacity, you should appoint them as your proxy in an advance health care directive.

### 18.4.6 Northwest Territories

#### *18.4.6.1 Finances*

Both springing and enduring forms of power of attorney are authorized. Not only does the attorney have the authority to do anything on behalf of the donor that the donor may lawfully do, but they may also exercise their authority for the maintenance, education, benefit and advancement of the donor's spouse and dependent children (including the attorney if he or she is the donor's spouse or dependent child). There is no prohibition on spouses acting as an attorney when dealing with the family home.

If a donor appoints two or more attorneys in a springing or enduring power of attorney without indicating whether they are to act jointly or successively, the attorneys shall act successively in the order in which they are named in the document. A majority vote will be sufficient; if there is a tie, the decision of the first-named attorney prevails. If one attorney is no longer capable of acting, the remaining attorneys may continue to act.

#### *18.4.6.2 Health Care Decisions*

There is no legislation in the Northwest Territories allowing individuals to appoint others to make health care decisions for them.

## 18.4.7 Nova Scotia

### *18.4.7.1 Finances*

Both enduring and springing forms of powers of attorney are authorized. There is no prohibition on a spouse acting as attorney for a spouse when selling the family home.

### *18.4.7.2 Health Care Decisions*

The *Personal Directives Act* permits someone to write a personal directive, authorizing someone who is of the age of majority (unless the minor is a spouse) to make, on the maker's behalf, decisions regarding the maker's personal care. A delegate may make, on the donor's behalf, decisions regarding personal care. A health care decision is defined to include instructions, consent and refusal, and withdrawal of consent with respect to health care.

## 18.6.8 Nunavut

See section 18.6.6. The rules in Nunavut are substantially the same as in the Northwest Territories.

## 18.4.9 Ontario

### *18.4.9.1 Finances*

Both enduring and springing forms of power of attorney are authorized. An attorney acting under an enduring power of attorney is allowed to make gifts or loans to the donor's friends and relatives, and to make charitable gifts, in certain situations. In making the gifts, the attorney cannot impoverish the donor. The gifts or loans should only be made if there is reason to believe, based on intentions the person expressed before becoming incapable, that he or she would make them if capable, and the amount of charitable gifts should generally not exceed 20% of the donor's income.

Spouses may not act as attorney for their spouse when selling or mortgaging the family home, so it is important to appoint an alternate if you have appointed your spouse as your primary attorney.

A continuing power of attorney will automatically be terminated upon the execution of a new one, unless the donor provides that there will be multiple continuing powers of attorney.

### *18.4.9.2 Health Care Decisions*

An individual is allowed to give someone else the ability to make health care decisions on their behalf by using a power of attorney for personal care. The grantor can give specific instructions within the document about the types of medical treatment they do or do not want, and those instructions are legally binding.

## 18.4.10 Prince Edward Island

### *18.4.10.1 Finances*

Both enduring and springing forms of power of attorney are authorized. There is no prohibition on a spouse acting as attorney for a spouse when selling the family home.

### *18.4.10.2 Health Care Decisions*

An individual may sign a health care directive giving someone else authority to make health care decisions on their behalf. A directive may:

- stipulate treatment, procedures or medication that the donor authorizes or refuses to consent to, or directs to be discontinued in the circumstances set out in the directive;

- stipulate circumstances in which the donor will be permitted to die a natural death, receiving only palliative care intended to reduce pain and suffering;

- appoint a proxy;

- specify an event or condition upon which the directive becomes effective; or

- make any other direction concerning health care or treatment of the donor.

## 18.4.11 Quebec

### *18.4.11.1 Finances*

A "mandate given in anticipation of incapacity" allows the mandator to name another person or trust company to make decisions on their behalf in the event of mental incapacity. One document can be used to name your mandate for finances, personal care and organ donation. Your mandatary must apply to the courts to certify your incapacity before the mandate becomes effective. The application to the courts may require a psychological and medical assessment of your incompetency. There is no prohibition on a spouse acting as attorney for a spouse when selling the family home.

### *18.4.11.2 Health Care Decisions*

You may sign a mandate regarding health care decisions. However, if your attorney is considering consenting to any treatment that could have serious medical risks or permanent side effects, court approval may be necessary before the treatment is allowed.

## 18.4.12 Saskatchewan

### *18.4.12.1 Finances*

Both enduring and springing forms of power of attorney are authorized. If the power of attorney was written prior to January 1, 2005, it will be deemed to be a power of attorney for property only. If it was written after that time, it will be deemed to be a power of attorney over both the donor's personal care as well as their property, unless the attorney states otherwise. Personal care decisions include items such as food, clothing, personal hygiene, accommodation and social activities. A power of attorney will not govern health care decisions — those need to be put in a health care directive (see section 18.4.12.2).

An attorney may provide for the maintenance, education, or benefit of the donor's spouse and dependent children (including the attorney if the attorney is the donor's spouse), but they cannot make gifts. There is no prohibition on a spouse acting as attorney for a spouse when selling the family home.

### *18.4.12.2 Health Care Decisions*

You may sign a health care directive giving someone else authority to make medical decisions on your behalf. There are three types of directives:

1. a general directive that is to be used for guidance as to the wishes of the person;

2. a specific health care directive that anticipates and gives directions relating to the treatment for the specific circumstances that exist; and

3. appointment of a proxy that gives the power to make health care decisions for the person making the directive.

## 18.6.13 Yukon

### *18.6.13.1 Finances*

Both enduring and springing forms of power of attorney are authorized. The attorney may exercise their authority for the maintenance, education, benefit and advancement of the donor's spouse and dependent children (including the attorney if the attorney is the donor's spouse or dependent child). There is no prohibition on a spouse acting for a spouse when selling the family home.

### *18.6.13.2 Health Care Decisions*

Individuals may sign a directive giving another person power to make health care decisions on their behalf.

# CHAPTER 19

# DISTRIBUTION OF AN ESTATE

At the time of your death, how will your estate be distributed? This is not as easy a question as it may initially appear. There are many factors that may play into the division of your estate, including the following:

- the provisions of your last will and testament;
- the rules in your jurisdiction regarding "intestacy" (which means dying without a will), if you die without a will, or a will that neglects to distribute all or part of your estate;
- the ability for a surviving spouse or common-law partner to make an application for a division of family property, regardless of the terms of your will;
- the ability for someone who was financially dependent upon you prior to the time of death to make a dependant's relief claim against your estate;
- the possibility that certain family members may make a claim against an estate if you live in a jurisdiction that allows certain family members to make a claim for "moral obligations";
- the extent to which your estate has been distributed outside of your will, by virtue of:
    - gifts given during your lifetime;
    - assets sold during your lifetime;
    - assets that pass to a surviving joint owner by virtue of a right of survivorship;
    - the provisions of any trust agreements; and
    - direct beneficiary designations on registered assets and life insurance products; or
- the provisions of any contractual arrangements, such as:

- a pre-nuptial agreement, cohabitation agreement, marriage contract, separation agreement or divorce order; and

- a unanimous shareholders' agreement or other business contract.

As you can see, there are many factors that can affect the distribution of your estate. This chapter will review how these factors work together, and how you can arrange your estate in order to ensure that the final distribution is consistent with your intentions. For more information on the issues of joint ownership and strategies that involve transferring assets outside of your estate, also see Chapter 22, "Probate".

## 19.1 WHAT IS THE PURPOSE OF A WILL?

A will is a legally binding document that sets out how you would like your assets to be distributed after the time of your death. If you do not write a will, your estate will be distributed according to the laws of intestacy in the jurisdiction where you resided at the time of your death (see section 19.4, "What Happens if I Die Without a Will?"). Having a properly written will is one of the cornerstones of an effective wealth plan. Every adult Canadian who either has dependants or assets should have one. Unfortunately, many adult Canadians do not have a will, and of those who do, many of them are poorly drafted. Here are some of the reasons why you need a properly drafted will.

### 19.1.1 Control the Distribution of Your Estate

It is important to understand how the laws of intestacy work in your jurisdiction of residence. Here are some of the most common scenarios in which a will is crucial.

- Many people believe that if they die without a will, their spouse will receive their entire estate. In most jurisdictions, this is not the case if you have children. See section 19.6 for a description of the intestacy rules in your jurisdiction.

- If you have young children or grandchildren, and they become entitled to a part of your estate, the Public Trustee may have the authority to manage any monies left to them until they reach the age of majority, and then they will be entitled to receive all of the monies directly. In many cases, this results in young adults receiving large sums of money when they are not mature enough to manage it. See section 10.5.3 of Chapter 10, "Children", for more information on this issue.

- Individuals in blended families often assume that step-children will inherit in the same way as a natural or adopted child, which is not true, leading to many instances where step-children are inadvertently disinherited. See section 8.5 of Chapter 8, "Blended Families", for more information on this issue.

- Common-law partners often assume that they will be treated the same as a married spouse at the time of death. Depending upon which jurisdiction you live in, this may or may not be true. See section 3.9 of Chapter 3, "Common-Law Couples", for more information on this issue.

- If the funds are given directly to a disabled child, the provincial government may discontinue payment of any social assistance. If the inheritance is instead left to the child in a testamentary trust through your will, it is possible that the disabled child will be entitled to keep receiving social assistance. See section 12.3 of Chapter 12, "Disabled Persons", for more information on this issue.

- Some people feel that they do not need a will, since they do not have many (or any) assets. However, even if you don't currently have any assets, it is quite possible that your estate will in fact have assets to distribute, either in the form of insurance proceeds or a settlement award from a lawsuit after an accident. Also, even if you have designated direct beneficiaries on all of your assets, if your beneficiaries predecease you, there could still be assets in your estate. It will be impossible to predict the exact value of your estate in advance, so it is important to always have a will that plans for these contingencies.

These are just some of the reasons why it may be important to have a will. It is crucial that you review the laws of your jurisdiction with a well qualified estate planning lawyer. Keep in mind that even if you are comfortable with how the current rules would divide your estate in the event you died without a will, these laws are subject to change at any time, and you will be subject to a different regime every time you move to a different jurisdiction. Writing a will allows you to take control over how your estate will be distributed (although there are certain limits on your ability to leave your assets to whomever you want, which are discussed in section 19.2.2).

## 19.1.2 Choose a Guardian to Care for Your Children

If you have young children, one of the most important reasons to have a will is to ensure that you have designated someone to act as guardian in the event you die before they reach adulthood. The act of naming a guardian in your will is a nomination only, meaning that your choice of guardian must be approved by a court. However, a court will give significant weight to the fact that you had a specific preference as to who would care for your child(ren). This is obviously a very important decision, and care must be taken when nominating a guardian. See section 10.5.1 of Chapter 10, "Children", for more information on the factors to consider when making this decision.

## 19.1.3 Choose Your Personal Representative

Writing a will also allows you to choose a personal representative (or executor) who will distribute your estate. If you do not have a will, no one will have the legal authority to manage your assets until the court appoints an administrator. If an asset decreases in value immediately after your death, your beneficiaries may lose some of the value of your estate, simply because they were not able to act quickly enough. This can be especially important for business owners, or those with significant holdings in volatile investments. Although a court will have the ability to appoint an administrator if you do not appoint a personal representative, that person may not receive authority to act for several weeks or months. In addition, the person the court appoints may not be the person you would have chosen. For example, in some jurisdictions, a common-law partner does not have priority over next-of-kin when applying to the court to act as administrator of your estate. It is very important that you appoint a personal representative to administer your estate, as well as an alternate.

See Chapter 20, "Personal Representatives", for more information on choosing a personal representative, and the importance of choosing the right person or corporate trustee.

## 19.1.4 Give Personal Representatives Necessary Powers

A will can also give your personal representatives more flexibility than they might otherwise have had if you did not have a will. For example, most jurisdictions provide that a personal representative must invest the assets of the estate in the same manner as a "prudent person" would. If the estate is comprised mostly of the shares of a small business, a prudent person might sell those shares and diversify the investments. However, if the small business is the family business, the beneficiaries may not want the personal representative to take that course of action. It is a good idea in many cases to give your personal representatives broad powers of investment, so they are not limited by the prevailing legislation, or the whims of provincial governments, which could choose to change the legislation at any time.

You may also want to give your personal representatives the authority to use their discretion when paying off your loans. If you do not give them these powers, the prevailing legislation could require them to pay any debt in full as soon as possible, which could mean that the estate may have to incur significant early penalty payments. The same issue arises with liquidating estate assets and distributing them to your heirs. You may want your personal representatives to be able to sell assets at the most opportune time, instead of being pressured to sell them as soon as possible. In addition, you may want your personal representatives to give assets to your beneficiaries in their current form, as opposed to liquidating everything and then distributing cash.

### 19.1.5 Protect Inheritances from Family Property Claims

As mentioned in section 19.1.1, if you do not put conditions on when your children will receive their part of your estate, they will automatically become entitled to receive it upon reaching the age of majority. Therefore, if you want to ensure that your children do not receive their inheritance until they are more mature, you will need to indicate in the will that their inheritance is to be held in trust until they reach a more mature age, such as 25 or 30.

Some parents are also concerned about the prospect of their child's inheritance becoming subject to a family property claim in the event of marriage or relationship break-down. Inheritances are exempt from a division of family property in some jurisdictions, but in many cases, only if the property is kept separate from the family assets. Also, in many jurisdictions, even if the inheritance itself is not shareable, the growth on the inheritance may be shareable. See section 17.7 of Chapter 17, "Family Property", for a description of the family property rules in your jurisdiction. If a parent or other relative wants not only the gift, but also any increase in value of a gift or inheritance to be excluded from a division of family property, they should write a will that includes a clause indicating that. Although this type of clause may not be effective in every jurisdiction in Canada, it is still recommended that you include it in your will, since it is impossible to predict where your heirs will be living at the time of your death.

### 19.1.6 Tax Planning Strategies

There are numerous estate planning strategies that can help to save taxes, particularly the use of testamentary trusts. For the most part, if you want to take advantage of these tax strategies, you must do so through the use of a will. Please note that when referring to "tax savings", the "tax" in question is income tax. Probate planning techniques are those techniques that are often done outside of your will, and often do not result in a significant savings. For examples of some of the tax planning strategies you may wish to consider, see section 5.5.2 of Chapter 5, "Married", section 8.5.2 of Chapter 8, "Blended Families", section 10.5.4 of Chapter 10, "Children", and section 12.3 of Chapter 12, "Disabled Persons".

The reasons for having a will vary from individual to individual. Please refer to the chapter that discusses your personal situation, either in terms of your marital status, your children, or the types of assets you own for a more complete explanation as to why you may need a will in your personal circumstance.

## 19.2 THINGS TO KEEP IN MIND WHEN WRITING A WILL

### 19.2.1 Use a Professional

Always use a professional when writing a will — a pre-prepared will kit is not recommended under any circumstance. Here are some of the reasons to use a qualified lawyer when writing your will.

- Every individual has unique issues that should be discussed with their lawyer. In many cases, individuals have assumed that their situation was "simple", only to find out from their lawyer that there were a number of unique considerations they needed to take into account.

- If you use a will kit and make a mistake, there is no insurance to rectify the problem. If you use a lawyer, and he or she makes a mistake, his or her liability insurance will reimburse your beneficiaries.

- You need to ensure that your will is enforceable in every jurisdiction where you have property. For example, although holograph wills are accepted in most Canadian jurisdictions, they generally are not accepted in British Columbia or Prince Edward Island (or Nova Scotia if written prior to August 18, 2008). Holograph wills are wills prepared entirely in your own handwriting, and do not require any witnesses. If you live in a province such as Alberta, which accepts holograph wills, but you have real property in British Columbia, which generally does not accept holograph wills, your real property in British Columbia will be distributed as though you did not have a will, since British Columbia will take the position that you died without a valid will. A lawyer can ensure that your will is enforceable in every jurisdiction where you have property.

- Dealing with foreign property outside of Canada is another scenario that generally is not addressed in pre-prepared will kits. For example, will kits generally start out with a clause that revokes any previous wills. If you need dual wills as a result of owning property in different jurisdictions, you will not want one will to revoke the other.

Be sure to use a lawyer who is well experienced in the area of estate planning when writing your will. Most lawyers will tell you that they are capable of writing a will, but very few lawyers actually specialize in the area of estate planning. If you want your estate to be distributed equitably and in the most tax-effective manner, you need to confer with advisors who regularly practice in this area.

Do not procrastinate in writing a will. If you wait too long, or you are in a serious accident that affects your mental capacity, you may lose the opportunity to write a will. It is also important to keep in mind that you cannot delegate the job of writing a will. Once you become incapable, your power of attorney or heirs will not be allowed to write a will for you.



## 19.2.2 Limitations on Testamentary Freedom

You can generally leave your estate to whomever you want, once you have satisfied your obligations to your spouse and dependants. Every jurisdiction has family property legislation that requires individuals who are legally married, and in some cases, in a common-law relationship, to leave all or a portion of their estate to their spouse or common-law partner. See section 19.6 for a description of the family property rights in your jurisdiction. If you are in a common-law relationship, see section 3.9 of Chapter 3, “Common-Law Couples”, to determine if your province gives common-law partners any family property rights at the time of death.

Also, if you were financially supporting a family member prior to your death, that person may be able to make a dependant’s relief application against your estate in the event you do not leave a sufficient amount to them. Depending upon the jurisdiction, dependants can include spouses and minor children, and, in some cases, adult children, parents, siblings and common-law partners. See section 19.6, "Jurisdiction Differences", for a description of the types of individuals who may be considered dependants in your jurisdiction. If you know that an individual will be able to make a claim against your estate, ensure that your estate plan accounts for this claim so that your other beneficiaries will not receive less than you intended for them.

Another area where there may be some limits on your ability to distribute your estate is in respect of your pension. Generally speaking, your spouse (and in some cases your common-law partner) will be entitled to receive the survivor benefits from your pension, regardless of whom you designate as beneficiary. Speak to a professional before appointing anyone other than a spouse or common-law partner as the beneficiary of your pension, as the gift may be ineffective.

There is one other limitation on your ability to distribute your estate — the gift cannot be contrary to public policy. For example, a condition that indicates that a beneficiary will not inherit any part of your estate if they get married would probably be void for public policy reasons.

## 19.2.3 Personal Effects

Making a decision regarding your personal effects and family heirlooms is often one of the most difficult parts of the estate planning process. In some cases, individuals spend so much time agonizing over who will receive various personal effects that they die before they are able to finalize their will. In many cases, it is best if the distribution of personal effects is kept out of your will. Certain large items can be included if you want, but you should not let the issue delay the signing of your will. Once you have a properly drafted will that deals with the division of your estate, you can always change it at a later date to include specific gifts of personal items.

Many people list the people who are to receive specific items in a separate letter or memorandum. Although this memorandum is not binding in many cases, it will provide your personal representative with instructions, which in many cases are followed quite closely. As discussed in Chapter 20, "Personal Representatives", it is essential that you choose a trustworthy personal representative who will carry out your wishes, even if they are not legally required to do so.

If you want the memorandum to be legally binding, it must be in existence prior to when you signed your will, and it must be referenced in your will. The memorandum will also have to be probated with the will, which means that it will have to be filed publicly with the probate court. Also, since you will not be able to change the memorandum without changing your will, consider carefully whether or not a binding document is necessary. In most cases, individuals feel sufficiently comfortable with their personal representative to let them distribute their effects in accordance with a non-binding letter. Also be aware of the fact that if you create a binding memorandum that indicates that certain personal effects are to be given to beneficiaries who are minors, the estate may incur significant costs in storing and preserving the effects until the beneficiaries reach the age of majority.

If you do not want to list which of your heirs is to receive which of your personal effects in advance, you can establish a mechanism in your will that allows your heirs to each choose one item in turn, until all the items have been chosen. In order to make things more equitable, you could also provide that the person who chooses first in the first round, will choose last in the next round, and so on. If some of your personal effects are worth significantly more than the others (for example, a piece of art), then you could provide that the person who chooses that item will receive a lesser amount of the remainder of the estate (for example, $10,000 less of the monetary assets). Some people also put masking tape or recipe cards on the back of more valuable items to indicate who should receive the item, along with any other historical or nostalgic information.

There is no "right" or "wrong" way to distribute personal effects. In many cases, people choose to give some of their effects away prior to their death in order to ensure that specific people receive specific items. This is especially true in the case of second marriages, where one spouse would like some of his or her personal effects (or the effects of a deceased spouse) to go to their children, rather than their new spouse. This can be a delicate issue, but it should be discussed in advance in order to ensure that there are no disputes at the time of death.



### 19.2.4 Specific Gifts

If possible, try to allow for as much flexibility as possible in your will, as it is quite possible that your personal circumstances will change between when you write the will, and the time of your death. For example, some individuals leave very specific assets to certain beneficiaries, as opposed to leaving them a portion of the entire estate. Although this may seem like a good idea at the time, specific gifts can often cause problems if the deceased does not own the specific item at the time of their death (for example, they sold the cottage referred to in the will, and purchased a different one). In other cases, the gift fails due to the fact that the description of the gift was not specific enough, so it is unclear as to the intent of the deceased. If you intend to leave a specific item to a specific beneficiary, discuss the issue carefully with your family members and your lawyer before including it in your will.

You should also confirm how title to each of your assets is held. Some individuals have attempted to give a certain asset to a beneficiary in their will, but after the time of their death, it was discovered that they did not have the right to bequeath the asset, as it was held jointly with another person. Speak to your lawyer about how title to each of your assets is held so you can ensure you have a clear picture as to the extent of your estate that will pass by your will.

## 19.2.5 Foreign Property

If you own property in a jurisdiction outside your jurisdiction of residence, it may be advisable to have a separate will that meets the requirements of the jurisdiction in which the property is located. This will ensure that the transfer is completed as smoothly as possible. In some cases, however, it may also be better to use an international will instead of dual wills, although your lawyer will be able to tell you whether or not that is appropriate. When dealing with foreign property, it is imperative that you obtain professional advice.

## 19.2.6 Common Disasters

It is also important to have a properly drafted will to ensure that there are no inequities in the case of a common disaster. As you will see in section 19.6, "Jurisdiction Differences", some jurisdictions provide that in the case of a common disaster, where it is not possible to determine which person predeceased the other, the older person will be deemed to have predeceased the younger person. In other jurisdictions, they will both be deemed to have predeceased each other.

This is potentially unfair. For example, in situations where the older person is deemed to have predeceased the younger person, the estate of the older person will first go to the younger person (to the extent the will or the intestacy legislation provides for that), and then the estate of the younger person will be distributed to his or her beneficiaries. Therefore, the beneficiaries of the younger person will inherit more than the beneficiaries of the older person. If the beneficiaries are the same, this is obviously not an issue. However, in the case where the beneficiaries are different (such as in the case of blended families), this can cause inequities.

Many people include a clause in their wills indicating that their spouse or common-law partner will inherit their estate only in the event they survive them for a specified period of time (e.g. 14 days or 30 days). In the event they do not survive for such time period, the estate assets are to flow to the alternate beneficiaries. This serves two purposes — first, it alleviates the potential inequities referred to above in jurisdictions where the older spouse is deemed to have predeceased the younger spouse, and, secondly, it alleviates the need to probate the same assets twice (first when they flow through the estate of the older spouse, and then again when they flow through the estate of the younger spouse). Discuss the need for this type of clause with your estate planning lawyer.

## 19.2.7 Legal Terms

Here are some legal terms you may find in a will.

*Intestate*: to die without a will.

*Issue*: lineal descendants. If a person has "issue", this means that they have surviving children, grandchildren, or great-grandchildren, etc. Step-children are not included in the definition of this term.

*Per Stirpes*: to be divided by branch. When an estate is divided by branch, all of the surviving issue of one generation will receive the same share. If someone of one generation has predeceased the deceased, then their children will share their portion of the estate. For example, let's assume that Anna indicates in her will that her estate is to be divided among her issue *per stirpes*. Anna had three children, Joe, Brent and Dave. Unfortunately, Dave predeceased her, but left two children, Ashley and John. Anna's estate generally will be divided as follows:

Joe – 1/3
Brent – 1/3
Ashley – 1/6 (1/2 of Dave's 1/3)
John – 1/6 (1/2 of Dave's 1/3)

The definition of *per stirpes* has been interpreted differently in different jurisdictions, so speak to your lawyer if you become involved in a *per-stirpes* distribution.

# 19.3 PROPERTY THAT PASSES OUTSIDE OF A WILL

It is important to keep in mind that your will only governs the distribution of assets that pass through your estate. Therefore, if an asset passes outside of your estate, the instructions set out in your will are not relevant. Here are some of the common ways in which assets may pass outside of your estate:

- by appointing direct beneficiaries of your pension plans, registered investments or insurance policies (these assets will pass directly to the designated beneficiary, regardless of what your will says, although in Quebec, direct beneficiary designations are not effective on all types of registered investments);

- by giving assets away prior to the time of death;

- by adding a joint owner on a property so that it will pass directly to the survivor at the time of their death (although the right of survivorship is not effective in all cases when assets are held in joint ownership with an adult child, and there is no right of survivorship on jointly held assets in Quebec. See Chapter 22, "Probate" for more information);

- by selling the asset during your lifetime; or

- by agreeing in a contract to transfer an asset in a certain manner at the time of your death (e.g. examples of such contracts could include a pre-nuptial agreement or unanimous shareholders' agreement).

Although there may be good reasons for arranging your affairs so that some or all of your assets pass outside of your estate, many individuals do not realize the problems that can be experienced by your heirs in doing so. For example, there have been numerous lawsuits where a parent added one of several children onto a joint account in order to save probate at the time of their death, but still believed that their other children would inherit their portion of the account, since the will provided that the estate was to be divided equally. If the account passes to the child who is a joint owner of the account, it is quite possible that the co-owning child will be able to convince a court that the funds were meant for him or her alone, thereby disinheriting their siblings of that part of the estate. Before arranging your affairs in this manner, be sure to read Chapter 22, "Probate", for a discussion regarding the dangers of having assets pass outside of your estate, and consult with an estate planning professional prior to making any adjustments to your estate plan.

# 19.4 WHAT HAPPENS IF I DIE WITHOUT A WILL?

If you do not write a will, then your assets will be distributed to your next-of-kin in accordance with the intestacy rules of the jurisdiction in which you resided at the time of your death. (The word "intestacy" refers to an estate where there is no will). Here are some of the problems that can be experienced with intestacy legislation.

## 19.4.1 Different Rules in Different Jurisdictions

The rules regarding a distribution on intestacy vary quite dramatically from jurisdiction to jurisdiction. In fact, in some jurisdictions, some people, such as a common-law partner, may inherit a significant portion or all of your estate, whereas in another jurisdiction, that person may receive nothing. If you do not have a spouse, common-law partner, children or grandchildren, your estate will generally go first to your parents, then siblings, nieces and nephews, and then more distant relatives. If you die without any next-of-kin, your estate may go to the government, even though you may have preferred to give your estate to a charity or other organization. See section 19.6, "Jurisdiction Differences", for an explanation of the rules in your jurisdiction regarding immediate family.

## 19.4.2 Rules May Change in the Future

The rules regarding a distribution on intestacy can vary whenever the provincial government chooses to change them. If you die without a will, you will be leaving the distribution of your estate in the hands of others.

## 19.4.3 Property May Be Subject to More than One Set of Rules

If you have real property in a jurisdiction other than the jurisdiction in which you resided at the time of your death, then different rules may apply for different types of property. Generally, all personal property will be distributed according to the rules of the jurisdiction in which you were residing at the time of death. However, real property will be distributed according to the rules of the jurisdiction where it is located.

### 19.4.4 Property May Pass Directly to Children

You will note from the description of the intestacy distributions set out in section 19.6 that spouses (and in some jurisdictions common-law partners) are generally entitled to a "preferential share" of their deceased spouse's estate, plus a portion of the remainder. However, in most jurisdictions, a surviving spouse or common-law partner is not entitled to the entire estate when the deceased has children. This can be a problem in several respects.

- The surviving spouse may have needed the entire estate in order to maintain his or her standard of living. The couple may not have anticipated that their children would be entitled to anything, and, therefore, the surviving spouse may not be able to support themselves and their family on only a portion of the estate.

- If the children are minors, the surviving spouse may require the consent of the Public Trustee or the Children's Lawyer (depending upon the jurisdiction of residence) before dealing with the assets (for example, selling or mortgaging the family home, if some or all of that asset now belongs to their child).

- If the children are adults, and no longer living in the family home, they may require that the home be sold in order to receive their portion of the estate.

- Although assets can generally roll over on a tax-deferred basis to a surviving spouse or common-law partner, there is no such rollover to children (except in rare circumstances, such as with qualified farm property). Therefore, the estate may have to pay income tax much earlier than would have been required if the entire estate had passed to the surviving spouse or common-law partner.

If you have children, be sure to have a properly drafted will. See section 10.5 of Chapter 10, "Children", for more information. If you are in a blended family, see section 8.5.2 of Chapter 8, "Blended Families", since you may want your children to receive a portion of your estate immediately at the time of your death as opposed to leaving everything to your new spouse. Each situation is unique, so again, discuss the issue with a qualified lawyer to ensure your estate plan is consistent with your objectives.

### 19.4.5 Intestacy Does Not Consider Personal Circumstances

Dying without a will can be problematic. For example, if you have minor children, a court will choose who will act as their guardian, regardless of who you may have wanted. Your children will also have access to all of their inheritance at the age of majority (which is age 18 or 19, depending upon their jurisdiction of residence), which is still very young. Prior to that, the provincial government will be responsible for managing their estate, which can be costly. For those with disabled children, the ramifications can be even more severe, since the receipt of the inheritance directly, as opposed to through a trust, can result in the discontinuance of social assistance payments. Blended families and common-law couples also usually require a will in order to ensure that their estate will be distributed as intended. Generally speaking, every adult Canadian should have a will to ensure that their estate is distributed in accordance with their intentions, in order to minimize disputes between their beneficiaries.

## 19.5 FIRST NATIONS PROPERTY

There are certain rules that apply only to Status Indians who reside on a reserve and there are also certain rules that only apply to reserve property. Here are a few of the issues unique to these circumstances.

- If you are a Status Indian, you may only transfer real property that is located on a reserve to a person who is entitled to reside on the reserve.
- The will of a Status Indian does not have to comply with the formalities of the legislation of the province in which he or she resides. It can simply be a written instrument signed by the Status Indian.
- Where a Status Indian dies without a will:
    - if the net value of the estate does not exceed $75,000, the estate will go to the surviving spouse or common-law partner (for these purposes, common-law partner means someone who lived with the deceased in a conjugal relationship for a period of one year);
    - where the net value of the estate exceeds $75,000, $75,000 will go to the surviving spouse or common-law partner, and:

- if the deceased left no descendants, the remainder will go to the survivor;
- if the deceased left one child, one-half of the remainder will go to the survivor and one-half will go to the child; and
- if the deceased left more than one child, one-third of the remainder will go to the survivor and two-thirds will be divided equally between the children.

- if the deceased did not leave a surviving spouse or common-law partner, the entire estate will be divided equally between the children.

- If any child of the deceased died during the lifetime of the deceased, but left children or grandchildren of their own, they will share the deceased child's portion of the estate; and

- notwithstanding the above:

  - where in any particular case the Minister of Indian Affairs is satisfied that any children of the deceased will not be adequately provided for, he or she may direct that all or any part of the estate that would otherwise go to the surviving spouse will go to the children;
  - the Minister may direct that the surviving spouse will have the right to occupy any lands in a reserve that were occupied by the deceased at the time of death.

- The Minister may administer or provide for the administration of any property to which infant children of Indians are entitled, and may appoint guardians for that purpose.

# 19.6 JURISDICTION DIFFERENCES

## 19.6.1 Alberta

### *19.6.1.1 Dying Without a Will*

In Alberta, if you die without a will, your surviving spouse or adult interdependent partner will receive the first $40,000 of the value of the estate (see section 3.9 of Chapter 3, "Common-Law Couples", to determine who will be considered an adult interdependent partner). The remainder of the estate will be distributed as follows:

- the spouse or adult interdependent partner will receive all of the remainder if there are no descendants;
- if the deceased left a surviving spouse or adult interdependent partner and one child, one-half of the remainder will go to the surviving spouse or adult interdependent partner, and the other half will go to the child;
- if the deceased left a surviving spouse or adult interdependent partner and more than one child, one-third of the remainder will go to the surviving spouse or adult dependent partner and the other two-thirds will be divided between the children.

If any child of the deceased died during the lifetime of the deceased, but left children or grandchildren of their own, they will share the deceased child's portion of the estate.

If the deceased had both a spouse and an adult interdependent partner at the time of death, the person who was living with the deceased at the time of death (or who was last living with the deceased) will inherit the amounts referred to above, and the other will receive nothing.

In certain cases, separated spouses or adult interdependent partners will not receive anything upon intestacy. See section 6.7.1 of Chapter 6, "Separated", for more information.

### *19.6.1.2 Common Disasters*

In a common disaster, the older person is deemed to have died first. With an insurance policy, unless the contract provides otherwise, if a person insured, or group person insured, and a beneficiary die at the same time or in circumstances rendering it uncertain which of them survived the other, the insurance money is payable as if the beneficiary had predeceased the person insured or group person insured.

### *19.6.1.3 Family Property*

A surviving spouse can make an application for a division of family property after the death of the other spouse, but only if they would have been entitled to make such an application prior to the time of death, which, generally speaking, can only be done if the parties were separated or divorced (see section 6.7.1.2 of Chapter 6, "Separated", for the conditions to be met before making an application, or section 17.4.1 of Chapter 17, "Family Property", for a description of the types of assets that are considered family property in Alberta). When a family property order is made in favour of a surviving spouse, the court will take into consideration any benefit received by the surviving spouse as a result of the death of the deceased spouse. An application by a surviving spouse for a family property order must be made within six months of the date of issue of a grant of probate or administration of the estate of the deceased spouse.

Only legally married spouses are entitled to make an application for a division of family property, although adult interdependent partners may agree to such a division in a written agreement. Since a common-law partner (who is not an adult interdependent partner) is not entitled to make an application for a division family property in the event of relationship breakdown, they will not be able to make such an application in the event of death (unless they have an agreement to the contrary). However, a surviving common-law partner may be able to make an unjust enrichment claim – see section 3.4.2 of Chapter 3, "Common-law Couples", for more information on the types of claims common-law couples may be able to make.

The proceeds of life insurance on a spouse, in favour of the surviving spouse, are exempt and specifically not considered to be family property.

A surviving spouse (who was legally married to the deceased) has the right, for the remainder of their life, to live in the family home and keep the personal property of the deceased spouse. This right may not be available if the spouses are separated at the time of death, or if the home was owned in joint names with a third party.

### 19.6.1.4 Dependant's Relief Applications

A dependant may make an application under the *Dependant's Relief Act* where a deceased has not made adequate provision for them. A dependant is defined as including the spouse or adult interdependent partner of the deceased, a child who is a minor at the time of death, and a child of the deceased who is over 18 at the time of death and is unable by reason of mental or physical disability to earn a livelihood. (For information on who may be considered an adult interdependent partner, see section 3.9 of Chapter 3, "Common-Law Couples".)

An adult child who does not have a disability may not make a claim against their deceased parent's estate. However, the deceased's step-child of any age may make such a claim against their step-parent's estate if they can prove that over time, an adult interdependent relationship was established. (In Alberta, no conjugal relationship is necessary in order to prove that you are an adult interdependent partner, but a parent and their natural child would not be considered an adult interdependent relationship unless they entered into an agreement to that effect.)

A dependant's relief application must be made within six months from the grant of probate or administration.

## 19.6.2 British Columbia

### *19.6.2.1 Dying Without a Will*

In British Columbia, if you die without a will, your spouse or common-law partner (who is defined as a person who lived with the deceased in a marriage-like relationship for at least two years immediately prior to the time of death) will receive the first $65,000 of the value of the estate plus any household furnishings. In addition, the surviving spouse or common-law partner will be entitled to the following portion of the remainder of the estate:

- if the deceased left no descendants, then all of the estate;
- if the deceased left a surviving spouse or common-law partner and one child, one-half of the remainder will go to the surviving spouse or common-law partner, and the other half will go to the child (or their descendants);
- if the deceased left a surviving spouse or common-law partner and more than one child, one-third will go to the surviving spouse or common-law partner, and two-thirds will be divided between the children (or their descendants)

If any child of the deceased died during the lifetime of the deceased, but left children or grandchildren of their own, they will share the deceased child's portion of the estate.

If there are two or more individuals who meet the definition of spouse or common-law partner, then they will share the spousal share in the portions determined by the court, although it is unclear as to who would get the spousal home and furnishings.

The personal representative of the deceased owner of a family home holds the home in trust for the life of the surviving spouse, despite any provision to the contrary in the will.

In certain cases, separated spouses or partners will not receive anything upon an intestacy. See section 6.7.2 of Chapter 6, "Separated", for more information.

### 19.6.2.2 Common Disasters

In a common disaster, the older person is deemed to have died first. If, however, a life insured and the beneficiary under the life insurance policy die under these circumstances, the beneficiary is presumed to have predeceased the life insured, unless a contrary intention appears in the beneficiary designation.

### 19.6.2.3 Family Property

At the time of death, surviving spouses and common-law partners do not have the right to make an application for a division of family property, but they do have the right to apply to the court for a variation of the will, according to the *Wills Variation Act*. The court has complete discretion when determining how much to award the surviving spouse or common-law partner. A surviving spouse or common-law partner has six months from the date on which probate has been granted to make a wills variation application.

### 19.6.2.4 Dependant's Relief Applications

In British Columbia, the legislation that allows an individual to make a claim against an estate where they believe they have not been left a sufficient amount under a will is called the *Wills Variation Act*. If the deceased died without a will, there is no legislation that will permit an individual, even one who was financially dependent upon the estate, to challenge the distribution of the estate.

Only a spouse, common-law partner (meaning a partner who lived with the deceased for at least two years immediately prior to the time of death) or a child (of any age) will be considered a dependant for the purposes of the *Wills Variation Act*. However, it is not necessary for the dependant to be financially dependent upon the deceased in order to make a claim against the estate, and the child does not have to be a minor in order to make an application. A dependant can make a "moral" claim, and receive a portion of the estate (or a larger portion than they were given in the will), if they can convince the court that the will should be varied.

It is not possible for a married couple or common-law couple to "contract out" of the *Wills Variation Act*, even at the time of separation. A court may consider the provisions of an agreement when determining whether or not to make an award, but they will always have the right to make an order where they feel it is appropriate.

If you are concerned about the provisions of the *Wills Variation Act*, consider the circumstances described below.

- The legislation applies to separated spouses, but not divorced ones, so you should not assume that a separation agreement will be sufficient to remove the possibility of your separated spouse making a claim after you are gone. A divorce order will be required in order to preclude a former spouse from making a wills variation application.

- If you have children that you specifically wish to leave out of your estate, then it may be best to distribute part or all of your estate outside of your will. This can be done by way of joint ownership, direct beneficiary designations, or other techniques such as alter ego trusts. However, these strategies may bring other complications, so review Chapter 22, "Probate", before making any changes to your estate in this regard, and speak with a professional about the most effective manner in which to distribute your estate.

- A wills variation application must be made within six months of the date on which probate is granted, not within six months of the date of death. If you are concerned about the potential for a wills variation application to be made in the future, you should instruct your personal representative to apply for probate as soon as possible, even if probate is not technically required in order to administer the assets. If the estate is not probated, the limitation period will never expire.

## 19.6.3 Manitoba

### *19.6.3.1 Dying Without a Will*

In Manitoba, if a person dies without a will, their surviving spouse or common-law partner will be entitled to the greater of $50,000 or one-half of the estate. The remainder will be divided as follows:

- if the deceased left a surviving spouse or common-law partner, and no descendants other than descendants who are also descendants of the surviving spouse or common-law partner, then the remainder of the estate will go to the surviving spouse or common-law partner; or

- if the deceased left a surviving spouse or common-law partner, as well as descendants who are not also descendants of the surviving spouse or common-law partner, the surviving spouse or common-law partner is entitled to one-half of the remainder, and the other half will be divided among the descendants of the deceased.

For the purposes of the intestate succession legislation, "common-law partner" means an individual who:

- lived with the deceased in a conjugal relationship for at least three years;

- lived with the deceased in a conjugal relationship for a period of one year while raising a child together; or

- registered their relationship with the deceased at the Vital Statistics office.

If the deceased is survived by both a spouse and a common-law partner (or partners), the claim of the spouse or partner who most recently lived with the deceased will have priority.

If some of the estate is distributed by a will, and some is distributed on an intestacy, the amount received by the spouse or common-law partner will be reduced by the value of any benefits received under the will.

In certain cases, separated spouses or common-law partners will not receive anything upon an intestacy. See section 6.7.3 of Chapter 6, "Separated", for more information.

A beneficiary must survive the deceased by at least 15 days in order to receive any part of the deceased's estate.

### 19.6.3.2 Common Disasters

In the case of a common disaster, both parties are deemed to have predeceased each other. If property is jointly held, and the owners die in a common disaster, they will be deemed to hold the property as tenants in common, and each will be deemed to retain their proportionate interest.

In the case of insurance, unless a contract or declaration otherwise provides, where the person whose life is insured and the beneficiary die at the same time or in circumstances rendering it uncertain which of them survived the other, the insurance money is payable as if the beneficiary had predeceased the person whose life is insured.

### 19.6.3.3 Family Property

A surviving spouse or common-law partner has the ability to make a family property application, and take those assets in lieu of the amount left to them in the will (see section 17.4.3 of Chapter 17, "Family Property", for a discussion as to the types of property considered family property in Manitoba). If the spouse or partner received any assets from the estate on intestacy, those assets will be factored into the amount received when dividing the family property. For the purposes of this legislation, a common-law partner includes only common-law partners who lived with the deceased for at least three years, or who registered their relationship with the deceased at the Vital Statistics branch.

It should be noted that for the purposes of a family property accounting made after the time of death, the following assets will be included in the value of the deceased's estate, regardless of whether or not they formed part of the estate for probate purposes:

- any gifts made on the deceased's death bed to a person other than the surviving spouse or common-law partner;
- property held with a right of a survivorship (if the deceased held assets jointly with a third party, they will be included in the division of family property unless the deceased received adequate consideration in respect of that asset);

- an RRSP, RRIF or annuity, or a pension, or other profit-sharing fund or scheme payable to a person other than the surviving spouse or common-law partner;
- the cash surrender value of life insurance payable to someone other than the surviving spouse or common-law partner; and
- life insurance proceeds payable to the estate, unless:
  - the insurance is for business purposes;
  - the insurance was taken out in compliance with a court order made under the *Divorce Act* or *The Family Maintenance Act*; or
  - the insurance is in compliance with a maintenance agreement between the deceased spouse or common-law partner and a person other than the surviving spouse or common-law partner.

Therefore, if you wish to leave a significant amount of your estate to your children, adding your children as joint owners to your property may not be an effective strategy, since property jointly owned with a third party will still be considered a divisible family asset. If you want to leave certain property to a child, it may be advisable to transfer the asset during your lifetime. However, note that there may be tax implications if property is transferred to a child (see Chapter 22, "Probate"), and if you die within two years of the transfer, the surviving spouse may be able to set the transaction aside.

Also, if you want to leave a significant portion of your estate to someone other than your spouse or common-law partner, adding your spouse as joint owner on some of your property, and then leaving other assets to third parties through your will may not be an effective strategy. Assets held in joint ownership with a surviving spouse or common-law partner are excluded from any division of family property, so even though the surviving spouse or common-law partner may have received a significant portion of your assets by virtue of their right of survivorship on jointly held assets, they may still be entitled to make an application against the estate for additional assets if they were not left very much in the will.

Here are some strategies you may consider to avoid this problem.

- Put assets in your name only and give the asset to your spouse or common-law partner as part of the estate (although the assets will then be exposed to estate creditors and probate fees).

- Change assets held as "joint tenants" to "tenants in common" so that there is no right of survivorship. This will ensure that your spouse or common-law partner must account for one-half of the asset when dividing the family property (note, however, that your half of the assets will still be exposed to estate creditors and probate fees).

- Give the asset to your spouse or common-law partner during your lifetime, so it is included in their assets when dividing the family property.

Life insurance and pensions (including retirement savings plans) payable to the surviving spouse are excluded from a division of family property. If you want to have those amounts included in the calculation, they must pass through the estate, meaning the spouse should not be designated as the direct beneficiary on these plans. In order to save probate fees on insurance proceeds, consider using an insurance trust, as discussed in section 22.3.7 of Chapter 22, "Probate".

Spouses have a life interest in the marital home, regardless of who it is left to in the will. Only the claims of creditors may erode the homestead rights since those claims have priority over legacies in a will. Only one spouse or common-law partner can have homestead rights in a particular home. Subsequent spouses or partners will not acquire homestead rights until the previous spouse or common-law partner's homestead rights have been resolved, for example by a release. Under *The Homesteads Act*, a common-law partner includes only those persons who have registered their relationship or who have lived with the deceased for at least three years – living together for one year with a child is not sufficient. A homestead is defined as a residence occupied by the owner and their spouse, consisting of not more than six lots or one acre if in the city, or not more than 320 acres if outside the city. A person may only have one homestead at any one time.

A surviving spouse or common-law partner may not make application for a division of family property more than six months after the grant of letters probate or letters of administration.



### 19.6.3.4 Dependant's Relief Applications

A dependant may make an application to the court that reasonable provision be made out of the estate of the deceased for the maintenance and support of the dependant. A dependant means:

- a spouse;

- a divorced spouse, in whose favour an order or agreement for maintenance and support was subsisting at the time of the deceased's death;
- a common-law partner who:
  - was living with the deceased at the time of the deceased's death;
  - had lived with the deceased within three years of the deceased's death; or
  - was being paid or was entitled to be paid maintenance and support by the deceased under an agreement or a court order at the time of death;
- a child of the deceased:
  - who was under the age of 18 years at the time of the deceased's death;
  - who, by reason of illness, disability or other cause was, at the time of the deceased's death, unable to withdraw from the charge of the deceased or to provide himself or herself with the necessaries of life; or
  - who was substantially dependent on the deceased at the time of the deceased's death;
- a grandchild of the deceased who was substantially dependent on the deceased at the time of the deceased's death;
- a parent or grandparent of the deceased who was substantially dependent on the deceased at the time of the deceased's death; or
- a brother or sister of the deceased, whether related to the deceased by the whole blood or the half blood, who was substantially dependent on the deceased at the time of the deceased's death.

A common-law partner includes a person who, with the deceased, registered their relationship as a common-law relationship or who cohabited with the deceased in a conjugal relationship either for a period of at least three years or for a period of at least one year and they were together the parents of a child. A child can include a step-child.

A dependant may make an application under the legislation regardless of whether they received any part of the estate under the will or on an intestacy.

No application for an order may be made after six months from the grant of letters probate or administration, although an application can be made later than that in respect of the undistributed portion of the estate.

## 19.6.4 New Brunswick

### 19.6.4.1 Dying Without a Will

In New Brunswick, when a person dies without a will, their estate will be distributed as follows:

- the entire estate will go to the spouse if the deceased left no descendants;
- if the deceased left a surviving spouse and one child (or children of a deceased child), then one-half of the estate will go to the spouse and one-half of the estate will go to the child (or their descendants); or
- if the deceased left a surviving spouse and more than one child (or children of a deceased child), then one-third of the estate will go to the spouse and two-thirds of the estate will be divided between the children (or their descendants).

The definition of spouse does not include common-law partners, so it is very important for common-law couples to make wills if they want to leave their estates to each other.

If a child dies leaving descendants and such descendants are alive at the date of the intestate's death, the surviving spouse will take the same share of the estate as if the child had been living at that date. If an intestate dies leaving descendants, his or her estate will be distributed, subject to the rights of the surviving spouse, if any, *per stirpes* among such descendants.

### 19.6.4.2 Common Disasters

In the case of common disaster, the property owner is deemed to survive the other. Parties are deemed to have died at the same time if they die within ten days of each other. If property is jointly held, the parties are deemed to hold the property as tenants in common, and each is deemed to retain their proportionate interest. Family property is deemed to be held in equal shares, unless there is a written agreement to the contrary.

With an insurance policy, unless a contract of insurance provides otherwise, where a person whose life is insured and a beneficiary die at the same time or in circumstances rendering it uncertain which of them survived the other, the insurance money is payable as if the beneficiary had predeceased the person whose life is insured.

### *19.6.4.3 Family Property*

When a legally married spouse dies, the surviving spouse is entitled to have the family property divided in equal shares, and a court may grant the survivor the use of the deceased spouse's interest in the family home and household goods (see section 17.4.4 of Chapter 17, "Family Property", for a description of the types of assets considered family property in New Brunswick). A family property application must be made within four months of the date of death.

Common-law partners are not entitled to make an application for a division of family property. However, a surviving common-law partner may be able to make an unjust enrichment claim – see section 3.4.2 of Chapter 3, "Common-law Couples", for more information on the types of claims common-law couples may be able to make.

### *19.6.4.4 Dependant's Relief Applications*

A dependant can make an application for support if there is a will or upon an intestacy. A dependant means:

- children, including adult children who are unable to withdraw from the charge of their parents or to obtain the necessaries of life by reason of illness, disability, pursuit of reasonable education or other cause;
- parents;
- spouses; and
- common-law partners if they have lived together:
    - continuously for a period of not less than three years in a family relationship in which one person has been substantially dependent upon the other for support; or

- in a family relationship of some permanence where there is a child born of whom they are the natural parents,

and have lived together in that relationship within the preceding year.

A dependant's relief application must be made within four months of the date of death.

## 19.6.5 Newfoundland

### *19.6.5.1 Dying Without a Will*

In Newfoundland, when a person dies without a will, their estate will be distributed as follows:

- the entire estate will go to the spouse if the deceased left no descendants;
- if the deceased left a surviving spouse and one child (or children of a deceased child), then one-half of the estate will go to the spouse and one-half of the estate will go to the child (or their descendants); or
- if the deceased left a surviving spouse and more than one child (or children of a deceased child), then one-third of the estate will go to the spouse and two-thirds of the estate will be divided between the children (or their descendants).

Note that the family home does not form part of the division of the estate where there is a surviving spouse. A surviving spouse is entitled to receive the family home. For the purposes of this legislation, the definition of spouse does not include a common-law partner.

Where a child has died leaving issue and the issue is alive at the date of the intestate's death, the spouse will take the same share of the estate as if the child had been living at that date.

### *19.6.5.2 Common Disasters*

In a common disaster, the older person is deemed to have died first. If, however, a life insured and the beneficiary under the life insurance policy die under these circumstances, the beneficiary is presumed to have predeceased the life insured, unless a contrary intention appears in the beneficiary designation.

### 19.6.5.3 Family Property

A surviving spouse may make an application for a division of family property (see section 17.4.5 of Chapter 17, "Family Property", for a discussion as to the types of property considered family property in Newfoundland). This right is in addition to rights that the surviving spouse has as a result of the death of his or her spouse, whether that right arises on intestacy or by will. Common-law partners do not have the right to apply for a division of family property under provincial family law legislation. However, a surviving common-law partner may be able to make an unjust enrichment claim – see section 3.4.2 of Chapter 3, "Common-law Couples", for more information on the types of claims common-law couples may be able to make.

Title to the family home vests in the surviving spouse without the need for probate or the administration of an estate of the deceased spouse. The family home is not included in the division of family assets.

Unlike in most jurisdictions, the personal representative of the deceased spouse may sue the surviving spouse for an equal or unequal division of family assets. The personal representative will not normally make such a claim where the entire estate is going to the spouse. However, where the estate is going to other beneficiaries, or where there are unpaid creditors, the personal representative is liable if he or she fails to maximize the estate by suing the surviving spouse, unless the spouses had signed a domestic contract prior to the time of death.

An application for a division of family property must be made within one year of the first spouse's death.

### 19.6.5.4 Dependant's Relief Applications

A dependant can make an application for support from the estate even if they inherited all or part of the estate under a will or upon an intestacy. The term "dependant" includes the widow, widower or child of the deceased. There is no age limit on the definition of "child", and there is no requirement that the deceased must have been supporting the dependant at the time of death. Common-law partners do not have the right to make a dependant's relief application.

The application must be made within six months after the grant of probate of the will or grant of administration.

## 19.6.6 Northwest Territories

### *19.6.6.1 Dying Without a Will*

When someone dies without a will in the Northwest Territories, the surviving spouse is entitled to the greater of the first $50,000 of the value of the estate, or the house instead of the $50,000 where the value of the home is in excess of $50,000, or as part of the $50,000 where the value of the home does not exceed $50,000. In addition, the surviving spouse is also entitled to the following portion of the remainder:

- if the deceased had no descendants, the entire estate;
- if the deceased left a surviving spouse and one child, one-half will go to the surviving spouse, and one-half will go to the child (or their descendants); or
- if the deceased left a surviving spouse and more than one child, one-third will go to the surviving spouse and two-thirds will be divided between the children (or their descendants).

Common-law partners are given the same rights as legally married spouses. A common-law partner is defined as a person who lived with the deceased in a conjugal relationship for a period of two years, or in a relationship of some permanence with a natural or adopted child.

Where a child of the intestate dies during the lifetime of the intestate leaving issue, one or more of whom are alive at the date of the death of the intestate, the surviving spouse shall take the same share of the estate of the intestate as if the child had been living at that date.

In certain cases, separated spouses will not receive anything upon an intestacy. See section 6.7.6 of Chapter 6, "Separated", for more information.

### 19.6.6.2 Common Disasters

In a common disaster, the older person is deemed to have died first. In an insurance contract, where the person whose life is insured and a beneficiary die at the same time or in circumstances rendering it uncertain which of them survived the other, the insurance money is payable as if the beneficiary had predeceased the person whose life is insured.

### 19.6.6.3 Family Property

After the time of death, a surviving spouse may choose to make an application for a division of family property, instead of receiving the allocated amount under the will or upon an intestacy (see section 17.4.6 of Chapter 17, "Family Property", for a discussion as to the types of assets that are considered family property in the Northwest Territories). Spouses have six months from the date on which probate is granted to make an application for a division of family property. The definition of spouse includes common-law couples who have been living together for at least two years or who are in a relationship of some permanence where together they are the natural or adoptive parents of a child. Where there is more than one spouse and/or common-law partner at the time of death, the court can make any order it considers fair and equitable.

A spouse who has no interest in a family home but is occupying it at the time of the other spouse's death, is entitled, for 60 days after the spouse's death, to retain possession, rent free, as against:

- the deceased spouse's estate; and
- a person who, at the time of the deceased spouse's death, owns an interest in the family home as a joint tenant with the deceased spouse.

### 19.6.6.4 Dependant's Relief Applications

A dependant may make an application under the *Dependant's Relief Act* where a deceased has not made adequate provision for them. The definition of dependant includes:

- the surviving spouse or common-law partner of the deceased (for these purposes, common-law partner means a person who had cohabited with the deceased for at least two years, or in a relationship of some permanence with a natural or adopted child);

- a child of the deceased who is under the age of 19 years at the time of the death of the deceased;
- a child of the deceased who has attained the age of 19 years at the time of the death of the deceased and is unable by reason of mental or physical disability to earn a livelihood;
- a person who cohabited with the deceased for one year immediately before the time of the death of the deceased and was dependent on the deceased for maintenance and support;
- a person who at the time of the death of the deceased was cohabiting with the deceased and between whom one or more children were born; or
- a person who at the time of the death of the deceased was acting as a foster parent of the children of the deceased in the same household and who was dependent on the deceased for maintenance and support.

The legislation in this territory is somewhat unique, in that the definition of "child" for these purposes includes a step-child.

For the purposes of a dependant's relief application, the value of the following items will be included in the net estate of the deceased:

- gifts made on the deceased's deathbed;
- money held in trust by someone else, but which belonged to the deceased;
- money held in joint tenancy, to the extent that the money was the property of the deceased; and
- any amount payable under an insurance policy on the life of the deceased owned by the deceased, where there was no irrevocable designated beneficiary.

A dependants' relief application may not be brought more than six months after the grant of probate or administration.

## 19.6.7 Nova Scotia

### *19.6.7.1 Dying Without a Will*

When an individual dies in Nova Scotia without a will, the spouse is entitled to the first $50,000 of the value of the estate. However, they may also elect to receive the house *instead* of the $50,000 where the value of the home is in excess of $50,000 or as part of the $50,000 where the value of the home does not exceed $50,000. The remainder of the estate will be distributed as follows:

- if the deceased left only a surviving spouse, they will receive the remainder of the estate;
- if the deceased left a spouse and one child (or descendants of a deceased child), one-half of the remainder will go to the surviving spouse, and one-half will go to the child or his or her descendants; or
- if the deceased left a surviving spouse and more than one child (or descendants of a deceased child), one-third will go to the surviving spouse, and two-thirds will go to the deceased's children (or their descendants if a child has predeceased the deceased).

If a common-law couple registered their relationship as a domestic partnership, then a surviving domestic partner will inherit in the same manner as a spouse. Otherwise, a surviving common-law partner will not inherit any part of the estate where the deceased died without a will. In Nova Scotia, it is not possible to be survived by both a spouse and a registered domestic partner. This is because a couple cannot register their partnership unless both parties are unmarried, and neither is already party to a different registered partnership.

In certain cases, a separated spouse or domestic partner will not receive anything upon an intestacy. See section 6.7.7 of Chapter 6, "Separated", for more information.

### *19.6.7.2 Common Disasters*

In a common disaster, the older person is deemed to have died first, unless one of the individuals was a beneficiary of the will of the other person, and there is a gift over in the will. In that case, the gift will go to the contingent beneficiary of the older person's will.

If a life insured and the beneficiary under a life insurance policy die under similar circumstances, it is presumed that the beneficiary predeceased the life insured, unless a contrary intention appeared in the beneficiary designation.

### *19.6.7.3 Family Property*

Surviving spouses and domestic partners are entitled to make a claim against the estate of the deceased for a division of family property (see section 17.4.7 of Chapter 17, "Family Property", for a discussion as to the types of assets considered family property in Nova Scotia). However, a surviving common-law partner may be able to make an unjust enrichment claim – see section 3.4.2.1 of Chapter 3, "Common-law Couples", for more information on the types of claims common-law couples may be able to make. An application for a division of family property must be made within six months after probate or administration of the estate is granted.

Family property rights are *in addition* to rights a surviving spouse or domestic partner has as a result of the death of the other spouse or domestic partner, whether by intestacy or will. If the entire estate is not going to the spouse or domestic partner, it may be important to indicate that the spouse's or partner's inheritance is to take into account any amount they may be entitled to under the family property legislation, the spouse or domestic partner can make an application for a division of family property in addition to what they received in the will, and any jointly held assets.

The surviving partner of a common-law couple who did not register their relationship as a domestic partnership will not be entitled to make an application for a division of family property.

### *19.6.7.4 Dependant's Relief Applications*

Only a child or surviving spouse or domestic partner of the deceased may make an application for a portion of an estate if it can be established that adequate provision has not been made for their proper maintenance and support. The court will not only consider whether or not the applicant was financially dependent upon the deceased, but it will also consider whether or not the deceased has breached a "moral duty". This moral duty can extend to a financially independent adult child. Common-law partners who are not parties to a registered domestic relationship are not entitled to make this type of application.

An application may not be made where the deceased died without a will. In that case, the estate will be distributed as provided in section 19.6.7.1, and a dependant will not be entitled to claim any more.

The application must be made within six months of the grant of probate or administration.

## 19.6.8 Nunavut

See section 19.6.6. The rules in Nunavut are essentially the same as in the Northwest Territories. However, the definition of common-law partner for some purposes includes only opposite-sex partners, so a same-sex, common-law partner may not have the same rights, unless they were able to successfully challenge the legislation.

## 19.6.9 Ontario

### *19.6.9.1 Dying Without a Will*

When an individual dies without a will in Ontario, the surviving spouse is entitled to the first $200,000 of the value of the estate. The remainder of the estate will be distributed as follows:

- if the deceased had no descendants, the surviving spouse will receive the remainder of the estate;
- if the deceased had one child (or descendants of a deceased child), one-half will go to the surviving spouse and one-half will go to the child (or their descendants); or
- if there is a surviving spouse and more than one child (or descendants of a deceased child), one-third will go to the surviving spouse and the remaining two-thirds will be divided between the deceased's children (or their descendants *per stirpes* if a child is deceased).

If a spouse has already received some property under a will, that amount will be deducted from the amount they would be entitled to under the division set out above. For these purposes, "spouse" strictly means a married spouse, and does not include a common-law partner.

If a child has died leaving issue, and the issue is alive at the date of the intestate's death, the surviving spouse of the deceased child shall take the same share of the estate as if the deceased child had been living at that date.

### *19.6.9.2 Common Disasters*

In Ontario, where two people die simultaneously, they are deemed to have survived each other. Jointly held property is deemed to be held as tenants in common.

For an insurance policy, unless the contract provides otherwise, where a person insured, or a group person insured, and a beneficiary die at the same time or in circumstances rendering it uncertain which of them survived the other, the insurance money is payable as if the beneficiary had predeceased the person insured or group person insured.

### *19.6.9.3 Family Property*

A surviving spouse may apply for a division of family property, or "equalization payment", within six months of the date of death (see section 17.4.9 of Chapter 17, "Family Property", for a discussion as to which types of assets are considered family property in Ontario). If the spouse makes such an application, they will not receive anything under the will, or any distribution in the case of an intestacy.

One-half of the value of a jointly owned property will be included in the assets of the deceased person when determining the amount of the equalization payment. However, this can be problematic as the asset itself has now been transferred to the survivor, and therefore will not be available to satisfy a family property equalization payment.

The proceeds of any insurance policy or lump sum payments under a pension plan owned by the deceased and paid to the surviving spouse will offset any equalization payment owing to that person. In fact, if there is an excess, the personal representative is allowed to recover it for the estate.

Common-law partners do not have the right to apply for an equalization payment upon relationship breakdown. However, a surviving common-law partner may be able to make an unjust enrichment claim – see section 3.4.2.1 of Chapter 3, "Common-law Couples", for more information on the types of claims common-law couples may be able to make.

In the event of death, the non-owning spouse only has a right to retain possession of the family home for 60 days after the spouse's death. If a spouse dies owning an interest in a family home as a joint tenant with a third person and not with the other spouse, the joint tenancy will be deemed to have been severed immediately before the time of death. This means that the deceased's interest will form part of his or her estate and may or may not go to the surviving joint tenant, depending upon the terms of the will.

### *19.6.9.4 Dependant's Relief Applications*

In Ontario, the following individuals will be entitled to make a claim against the estate if they were financially dependent upon the deceased at the time of death:

- a spouse (which could include a former spouse);
- a common-law partner, where the couple had cohabited together in a conjugal relationship continuously for at least three years;
- a child, including a step-child or grandchild;
- a parent, including a step-parent or grandparent; and
- a sibling.

For the purposes of making a dependant's relief order, the court will consider certain assets to be part of the estate, even though those assets did not form part of the estate for probate purposes. These assets will include:

- gifts made on the deceased's death bed;
- money (and interest), in an account in the name of the deceased in trust for another;
- joint bank accounts held by the deceased and a third party;
- any other disposition of property made by a deceased whereby property is held at the date of his or her death by the deceased and another as joint tenants;
- any disposition of property made by the deceased in trust or otherwise, to the extent that the deceased at the date of his or her death retained a

power to revoke such disposition, or a power to consume or dispose of the principal (but this clause does not affect the right of any income beneficiary to the income accrued and undistributed at the date of the death of the deceased);

- proceeds of any insurance policies effected on the life of the deceased and owned by him or her, notwithstanding that these proceeds are payable to a designated beneficiary;
- any amount payable on the death of the deceased under a policy of group insurance; and
- any amount payable under a designation of a beneficiary.

Therefore, if the deceased leaves a spouse who was financially dependent upon him or her, and the deceased had an insurance policy or an RRSP plan that was payable to children from a previous marriage, it is possible that the spouse could make a claim against those assets. With jointly held property, the value to the estate will be the amount of the deceased's interest in the property.

A dependant's relief application must be made within six months from the date on which letters probate or letters of administration are granted.

## 19.6.10 Prince Edward Island

### *19.6.10.1 Dying Without a Will*

In Prince Edward Island, when a person dies without a will, their estate is distributed as follows:

- if they are survived by a spouse and no descendants, then the entire estate will go to the surviving spouse;
- if they are survived by a spouse and one child (or descendants of a deceased child), then one-half of the estate will go to the spouse, and one-half to the child (or their descendants);
- if they are survived by a spouse and more than one child (or descendants of a deceased child), then one-third of the estate will go to the spouse, and the remaining two-thirds will be divided between the children (and/or their descendants); and

- if the deceased is not survived by a spouse, then the estate will be divided between his or her children (and/or their descendants).

Common-law partners will not inherit any part of the deceased's estate where there is no will.

In certain cases, separated spouses will not receive anything upon an intestacy. See section 6.7.10 of Chapter 6, "Separated", for more information.

### 19.6.10.2 Common Disasters

In a common disaster, the older person is deemed to have died first. If a life insured and the beneficiary under the life insurance policy died in a common disaster, the beneficiary is presumed to have predeceased the life insured, unless a contrary intention appears in the beneficiary designation.

### 19.6.10.3 Family Property

A surviving spouse does not have the ability to commence a family property claim after the time of death. If they feel that they have not been left a sufficient amount under the will, or on an intestacy, their only recourse will be to launch a claim under the *Dependant's Relief Act.*

### 19.6.10.4 Dependant's Relief Applications

Where a deceased has not made adequate provision for the proper maintenance and support of one of his or her dependants, the dependant may make an application against the estate for support. For the purposes of making a dependant's relief application, a dependant will include:

- a surviving spouse;

- a child under the age of 18, or over the age of 18 who is unable to earn a livelihood due to mental or physical disability;

- a grandparent, parent or descendant of the deceased, who for a period of at least three years immediately prior to the date of the death of the deceased, was dependent upon him or her for maintenance and support;

- a divorced spouse who, for a period of at least three years immediately prior to the date of death of the deceased, was dependent upon the deceased for maintenance and support; and

- a person of the opposite sex to the deceased not legally married to the deceased who, for a period of at least three years immediately prior to the date of the death of the deceased, lived and cohabited with the deceased as the spouse of the deceased and was dependent upon the deceased for maintenance and support (note that this does not include same-sex partners).

For the purposes of making a dependant's relief application, the following assets will be considered part of the deceased's estate, regardless of whether or not they formed part of the deceased's assets for probate purposes:

- gifts made in contemplation of, and conditioned upon, the death of the donor;

- assets held in trust by the deceased or for the deceased;

- assets held in joint tenancy with another party; and

- any amount payable under a policy of insurance on the life of the deceased and owned by him or her.

In certain cases, a person who has received a gift from a deceased person within a year of their death may be required to pay support to the dependants of the deceased.

An individual who wishes to make an application for an order for support must do so within six months of the date of the grant of probate of the will or letters of administration.



## 19.6.11 Quebec

### *19.6.11.1 Dying Without a Will*

In Quebec, when a person dies without a will, their estate is divided as outlined below.

- If the deceased was survived by a spouse, the spouse is entitled to their portion of the family patrimony in priority to all other claims (see section

17.4.11 of Chapter 17, "Family Property", for a discussion as to the types of assets considered to be part of the family patrimony in Quebec). A surviving spouse may also be entitled to a share of the estate if their property was governed by one of the other matrimonial regimes. The remainder of the estate will be divided as follows:

- if the deceased had a spouse and descendants, the surviving spouse would receive one-third of the remainder of the estate and the descendants will receive the other two-thirds; or

- if the deceased had a spouse and no children, the surviving spouse would receive two-thirds of the remainder of the estate and the deceased's family would receive one-third.

- If the deceased had no spouse, but had children, the children would receive the entire estate.

- If the deceased had no spouse or children, his or her parents would receive 50% of the estate and the deceased's siblings would receive 50%.

In Quebec, only married spouses are entitled to inherit under the rules governing intestate estates. However, couples who enter into a civil union have the same rights as a legally married couple. Couples in a *de facto* relationship do not have the right to inherit any part of a deceased partner's estate in the event of intestacy.

### 19.6.11.2 Common Disasters

In the case of common disaster, the property owner is deemed to survive the other.

### 19.6.11.3 Family Property

A surviving spouse is entitled to make a claim against the estate of the deceased spouse for their share of the "family patrimony". See section 17.4.11 of Chapter 17, "Family Property", for a discussion regarding the types of assets included in the family patrimony. Although surviving common-law partners (referred to as "de facto" spouses in Quebec) are not entitled to any share of the family patrimony, individuals who were in a registered civil union with the deceased are entitled to make a family patrimony claim in the same manner as a legally married spouse.

#### *19.6.11.4 Dependant's Relief Applications*

Certain individuals may make a claim against the estate if they were financially dependent upon the deceased. These individuals include the surviving spouse or civil union spouse, as well as parents and children. The maximum award will be 50% of the amount the applicant would have been entitled to on an intestacy, less any amounts actually received under the will.

The application must be made within six months of the date of death.

### 19.6.12 Saskatchewan

#### *19.6.12.1 Dying Without a Will*

If an individual dies in Saskatchewan without a will, their surviving spouse is entitled to the first $100,000 of the value of the estate. The remainder of the estate will be distributed as follows:

- if the deceased did not leave any direct descendants, then all of the estate will go to the spouse;
- if the deceased left a surviving spouse and one child (or descendants of that child), one-half of the remainder will go to the surviving spouse and the other half will go to the child (or their descendants);
- if the deceased left a surviving spouse and more than one child (or descendants of those children), one-third of the remainder will go to the surviving spouse and the other two-thirds will be divided between the children (or their descendants); or
- if the deceased dies without a spouse, the estate will be divided equally between the children (or their descendants).

A common-law partner is included in the definition of spouse, as being a person who:

- cohabited with the deceased as a spouse continuously for a period of not less than two years; and

- at the time of death, was continuing to cohabit with the deceased, or had ceased to cohabit with the deceased within the 24 months before their death.

If the deceased left both a surviving spouse and a surviving common-law partner, then the spouse will inherit the "spouse's share", unless it can be shown that the spouse had left the intestate and was cohabiting with another person in a spousal relationship at the time of the intestate's death.

In certain cases, separated spouses or common-law partners will not receive anything upon an intestacy. See section 6.7.12 of Chapter 6, "Separated", for more information.

### *19.6.12.2 Common Disasters*

In the case of a common disaster, the parties are deemed to survive each other. Two parties are considered to have died together if they die within five days of each other. If property is jointly held, it will be held as tenants in common, and each owner will be deemed to retain their proportionate interest, unless there is a written agreement to the contrary.

### *19.6.12.3 Family Property*

A spouse can make an application for a division of family property at the time of death if they were the spouse of the deceased at the time of death (see section 17.4.12 of Chapter 17, "Family Property", for a discussion regarding the types of assets considered family property in Saskatchewan). A spouse includes a common-law partner who lived with the deceased for a period of not less than two years.

The surviving spouse must make an application within six months of the date of death. The rights of the spouse to any amount upon an intestacy are not to be taken into account when determining the division of family property, but the amount received under the will is to be taken into account.

### *19.6.12.4 Dependant's Relief Applications*

Certain individuals may be able to make a claim for support against the estate if they were financially dependent upon the deceased. In Saskatchewan, a dependant includes:

- a spouse;
- a common-law partner, if:
  - he or she cohabited with the deceased continuously for a period of not less than two years, or
  - he or she was in a relationship of some permanence with the deceased and together they were the parents of a child;
- a child who is under the age of 18;
- a child who is older than 18, but is unable to earn a livelihood by reason of mental or physical disability; and
- a child who is older than 18, and who alleges that by reason of need or other circumstances, ought to receive a greater share of the deceased's estate.

The application must be made within six months from the date of grant of letters probate or letters of administration.

## 19.6.13 Yukon

### *19.6.13.1 Dying Without a Will*

In the Yukon, if a person dies without a will, their surviving spouse is entitled to the first $75,000 of the value of the estate. In addition to the preferential share, the spouse is also entitled to the following portion of the remainder:

- if the intestate dies without leaving any descendants, the entire estate;
- if the intestate dies leaving one child (or descendants of that child), one-half will go to the surviving spouse, and one-half will go to the child (or his or her descendants);
- if the intestate dies leaving more than one child (or descendants of those children), one-third will go to the surviving spouse, and two-thirds will go to the children (or their descendants).

If an intestate dies leaving issue, subject to the rights of the spouse, if any, the person's estate must be distributed *per stirpes* among the issue.

The person who becomes beneficially entitled to the family home must hold it in trust for the life of the surviving spouse, or so long as the surviving spouse wishes to retain the estate for life (subject to any rights of foreclosure from outstanding debts) and the household furnishings go to the surviving spouse.

In certain cases, separated spouses will not receive anything upon an intestacy. See section 6.7.13.2 of Chapter 6, "Separated", for more information. If the spouses had been living separate and apart, an application to the Court must be made within six months of the date of the issue of letters of administration.

If an intestate leaves a common-law spouse, the Court may order that there be retained, allotted and applied for the support, maintenance, and benefit of the common-law spouse so much of the net real or personal estate, or both, of the intestate as the court sees fit to be payable in the manner the court directs. An application to the court may not be made unless it is made within six months of the date of the issue of letters of administration, and notice must be given to any widow, widower or child (or their guardian) of the intestate. A common-law partner is defined as a person who has cohabited with the deceased as a couple for at least 12 months immediately before the time of death. A common-law spouse who brings an action for a portion of the estate in the event of an intestacy is barred from bringing an application under the *Dependant's Relief Act*.

### *19.6.13.2 Common Disasters*

In the case of common disaster in the Yukon, the property owner is deemed to survive the other. If property is held jointly, it is deemed to be held as tenants in common, and each joint owner is deemed to retain their proportionate interest.

### *19.6.13.3 Family Property*

A surviving spouse does not have the ability to commence a family property claim after the time of death. If they feel that they have not been left a sufficient amount of the estate, their only recourse will be to begin an application for dependant's relief.

### *19.6.13.4 Dependant's Relief Applications*

A dependant may make an application under the *Dependant's Relief Act* where a deceased has not made adequate provision for them. The definition of dependant includes:

- the widow or widower of the deceased;
- a child of the deceased who is under the age of 16 years at the time of the deceased's death;
- a child of the deceased who is 16 years of age or over at the time of the deceased's death and unable because of mental or physical disability to earn a livelihood;
- a grandparent, parent or descendant of the deceased who, for a period of at least three years immediately before the date of the death of the deceased, was dependent on the deceased for maintenance and support;
- a person divorced from the deceased who, for a period of at least three years immediately before the date of death of the deceased, was dependent on the deceased for maintenance and support; or
- the common-law spouse of the deceased.

A common-law partner is defined as a person who cohabited with the deceased as a couple for at least 12 months immediately before the time of death. A common-law spouse who brings an action for a portion of the estate in the event of an intestacy is barred from bringing an application under the *Dependant's Relief Act*.

An application for dependant's relief must be made within six months from the grant of letters probate of the will or of letters of administration.

If a deceased attempts to transfer certain assets outside of his or her estate prior to the time of their death, or transfers assets upon his or her death outside of the estate, certain types of transactions will be ignored for the purposes of determining the right of a dependant to a portion of the estate, including:

- gifts made on the deceased's death bed;
- money in an account in the name of the deceased in trust for another or others;

- any disposition of jointly held property by right of survivorship; and
- any amount payable under a policy of insurance effected on the life of the deceased and owned by him.

Where a deceased gave away property within a year prior to their death, the court may order the person who received the property to use such amount for the proper maintenance and support of the dependant.

# CHAPTER 20

## PERSONAL REPRESENTATIVES



A "personal representative" is the legal term for the person who will represent you after you are deceased. This person is most commonly known as your "executor" or "executrix", but we will refer to them as your personal representative, since some jurisdictions do not use the term executor. For example, in Quebec, the term is "liquidator", and in Ontario it is "estate trustee". For those who die without a will, your personal representative may in fact be called an "administrator". An administrator is the person appointed by the court to act on your behalf should you fail to appoint someone in a will. Also, your personal representative could be acting in a capacity of "trustee" if you have created any trusts in your will. For the purposes of this book, the term "personal representative" will encompass executors, liquidators, estate trustees, administrators and trustees.

# 20.1 CHOOSING A PERSONAL REPRESENTATIVE

The choice of personal representative is extremely important. This person will make many very important decisions on your behalf after you are deceased, including the manner in which your estate will be distributed. Although your personal representative will have to act in accordance with your will or the prevailing intestacy legislation (which is the legislation that dictates how your estate will be distributed in the event you do not have a will, or all or part of your will is deemed to be invalid), you should still choose someone who is trustworthy and responsible, or the court will choose someone for you. The list of tasks to be performed by a personal representative can be quite long, and can be particularly onerous if you have business interests or extensive assets.

Here are some of the characteristics that you may want to look for when choosing a personal representative:

- trustworthy and honest;
- organized and responsible;
- intelligent and discreet; and
- has sufficient time to complete the job.

Do not choose someone simply because you believe they will be offended if you do not choose them — choose someone willing and capable of doing the job. When making your choice, consider the following:

- *Confirm Acceptance.* Always ask your potential personal representative in advance if he or she is willing to do the job — do not assume that he or she will automatically accept the position. If you do not ask the person in advance, it is possible that he or she will not accept the position, putting you in the same position as if you had not chosen anyone at all. This can have detrimental effects on your family and the distribution of your estate.

- *Evaluate Their Skill Set.* Consider whether or not there should be different personal representatives for different purposes. For example, if one person is particularly knowledgeable about a business or art collection, perhaps they should be appointed to deal with that asset, while a different person handles the remainder of the estate.

- *Choose a Canadian Resident.* In many cases it will be important to ensure that your personal representative or representatives are residents of Canada, for tax reasons. See section 20.2, "The Importance of Canadian Residency", for a further discussion regarding this issue.

- *Avoid Conflicts of Interest.* You will want to avoid choosing individuals who may be in a conflict of interest. See section 20.3, "Conflicts of Interest", for a further discussion regarding this issue.

- *Consider Vulnerable Persons.* Be particularly careful when choosing a personal representative if you also intend for that person to act as trustee of a trust in favour of a disabled person. If the beneficiary is mentally disabled, they will be in a very vulnerable position, so you must pick someone very responsible and trustworthy.

- *Decision Making.* If you choose more than one personal representative, think about how decisions will be made. If possible, choose an uneven number of individuals, and provide that decisions may be made by majority rule. If you do not specify in your will that decisions are to be made by majority rule, all decisions will have to be made unanimously (except in Quebec). In many cases, this may not be realistic.

- *Avoid Appointing Too Many.* If possible, try not to appoint more than three personal representatives. Each personal representative will have to participate in each decision, and sign the documentation, etc. It may become very difficult to administer the estate if there are too many personal representatives, particularly if some of them live far away.

- *Corporate Trustees.* In some circumstances, a corporate trustee is the best choice to act as your personal representative. Some situations where a corporate trustee may be appropriate include situations where:

    - the administration of the estate will require specialized skills;

    - the duties are too onerous for an individual to complete;

    - the assets must be held for a long period of time;

    - there are conflicting interests (see section 20.3, "Conflicts of Interest");

    - you are not comfortable with the abilities of the family members who might be willing to carry out the job; or

    - you do not have any family or friends available to act for you.

A family member could act in conjunction with the corporate trustee to ensure decisions are made in the context of the family history.

- *Appoint an Alternate.* Always be sure to choose an alternate. If your chosen personal representative is for some reason unable to act, you will want to ensure that there is an alternate in place. In some jurisdictions, if you do not choose an alternate, the personal representative of the estate of your personal representative will take over at the time of their death. In other jurisdictions, the court will decide on an alternate. In either case, you will not be the person choosing this individual. In order to maintain control of the distribution of your estate, ensure that your will designates an alternate or alternates.

- *Consider Family Dynamics.* It is often recommended that if you are going to appoint children as your personal representatives, that all of your adult children be appointed in order to avoid family conflict. However, this may not always be appropriate. See section 20.4, "Family Dynamics", for a further discussion on this issue.

## 20.2 THE IMPORTANCE OF CANADIAN RESIDENCY

When choosing a personal representative, choose a person who is resident in Canada, if at all possible. There are several reasons for doing this.

- If the personal representative is not a resident of Canada, they may have to post a bond in order to administer the estate. This may be a significant cost to the estate that may have been unnecessary if there were Canadian residents equally qualified to do the job.

- Generally speaking, your estate will be probated in the jurisdiction in which you were resident at the time of your death. Your final tax return will also be filed in that jurisdiction. However, if it takes some time to administer your estate (which is not unusual), or your will creates testamentary trusts that are to continue for some time, your estate or the testamentary trusts will have to file tax returns themselves. Your estate and testamentary trusts will be resident wherever the "mind and management" of the estate or trust is resident. This generally means that the estate or trust is resident wherever a majority of your personal representatives are resident, unless you can prove that one person in particular had control over all of the decisions of the estate or trust. *If you want your estate and/or any testamentary trust created under your estate to be taxed in Canada, then it is crucial that your personal representative, or a majority of your personal representatives, be resident in Canada.* There are some instances in particular where residence of the estate is crucial for tax purposes. For example, if the will establishes a spousal or common-law partner trust, it will qualify for rollover treatment only if the trust is resident in Canada. If the spousal or common-law partner trust is not resident in Canada, there will be a deemed disposition of all of the assets of the deceased at the time of death (see Chapter 21, "Taxation at Death", for more information on deemed dispositions at the time of death).

If you have property in a foreign jurisdiction, it may be appropriate to appoint a foreign personal representative to deal with that property, and appoint Canadian representatives to administer the remainder of your estate.

## 20.3 CONFLICTS OF INTEREST

It is important to ensure that your personal representative is not in a conflict of interest. Here are some examples of when that might occur.

- If you are in a second marriage, and you establish a spousal trust in your will, the personal representative may have to make decisions regarding when and if to encroach on the capital for the benefit of the surviving spouse (see section 8.5.2.1, in Chapter 8, "Blended Families", for more information on spousal trusts). If you appoint your spouse as your personal representative, it will obviously be in his or her best interests to encroach on the capital in his or her favour whenever he or she chooses. If your children from a previous relationship are the contingent beneficiaries (meaning they will receive the capital that is left in the trust after the death of the surviving spouse), and you appoint them as your personal representative(s), it will obviously be in their best interests to refuse any requests made by your surviving spouse for a payment of capital. It is evident that in this case, neither the surviving spouse, nor the children from the previous relationship may be appropriate choices as trustees of the spousal trust. This is one example where an independent party (possibly a corporate trustee) may be the best choice.

- If you appoint a business partner as your personal representative, that business partner may have to participate in negotiations regarding your interests in the business. In many cases, you and your business partners will be parties to a partnership agreement or shareholders' agreement that allows the surviving partner (or partners) to buy out any interest in the business from the estate of a deceased partner. If you appoint your business partner as your personal representative, then it is possible that your partner will be negotiating both on behalf of him- or herself in the purchase of your interest, and on behalf of your estate in the sale of your interest. This is obviously a conflict of interest that may result in a less than fair price being received by your estate.

The above examples illustrate the need to choose a personal representative who can act objectively and without bias. Choosing someone who lacks a personal interest in your affairs can help to avoid many potential problems.

## 20.4 FAMILY DYNAMICS

The ability of family members to get along with each other is another issue that should not be overlooked. Do the beneficiaries respect the personal representative? Or will they be challenging every decision the personal representative makes? Many individuals choose their spouse as their personal representative, and in the event their spouse predeceases them, appoint all of their adult children as the alternates, regardless of their level of business acumen, since they do not want to cause resentment among their children. Although this is a valid concern, appointing children who are not capable of managing the assets can lead to other problems. If possible, speak to all of your children in advance, and discuss the issue with them. You may find that they are not all interested in acting as personal representative, or may prefer an objective third party to act instead. If you do decide to leave out some of your children, or choose someone other than a child as a personal representative, be sure to explain your choice to your children so that friction after the time of your death is minimized. If your children are expecting to act as your personal representatives, they could consider their omission as a slight, which could lead to acrimony in the distribution of your estate.

If you are in a non-traditional family, the issue can be even more sensitive. For example, if you have remarried later in life, and you have adult children from a previous relationship, you should carefully consider who to appoint as your personal representative. Although your children may have expected that they would manage your estate, you may prefer to appoint your new spouse (or vice versa). Communicate your decision to your family members, and allow them to raise any concerns they may have well in advance of the time of your death. This will help to avoid family dissention after you are gone.

## 20.5 WHAT HAPPENS IN THE CASE OF SEPARATION OR DIVORCE?

If you appoint your spouse as your personal representative, then you cannot assume that the appointment will automatically change in the event you separate or divorce. In some jurisdictions, separation or divorce will automatically impact the appointment in favour of your spouse, so if you have not appointed an alternate, you will effectively have no personal representative. However, in other jurisdictions, separation or divorce will have no impact, meaning that your former spouse will still have the authority to act on your behalf after you die. If you are separated or divorced, and you have appointed your spouse as your personal representative in your will, it is imperative that you change your will as soon as possible to ensure your wealth plan is up-to-date.

For more information on whether or not a separation or divorce impacts the ability of a spouse to act as personal representative of your estate in your jurisdiction, see section 6.7 of Chapter 6, "Separated", or section 7.7 of Chapter 7, "Divorced".

## 20.6 IF YOU FAIL TO APPOINT A PERSONAL REPRESENTATIVE

It is very important when preparing your will and estate plan that you seek the advice of a qualified professional, so that they can prepare a proper will that includes the appointment of a personal representative. If you do not appoint a personal representative, then your heirs will be entitled to apply to a court to act as administrator. However, this may lead to the court appointing a person you would not have chosen to act in that capacity. For example, in many jurisdictions, a spouse has priority when applying to act as administrator, but a common-law partner does not. Would you rather have your separated spouse act as administrator of your estate as opposed to your current common-law partner?

If you fail to appoint a personal representative, and no one applies to be appointed as administrator, the court may appoint the Public Trustee. However, the Public Trustee is entitled to charge trustee fees for estates on which it is required to act as trustee (although for small accounts or for people on social assistance, they may waive the fee). Also, the Public Trustee may manage the funds in a more conservative manner than you would have liked. They may choose to sell assets you would have liked to pass on to family members, or deny applications made by family members to encroach on the capital of your estate. This can be an especially important issue if you have young children who are not capable of managing the estate, and you have no other close relatives. Generally speaking, the appointment of the Public Trustee is a measure of last resort, so be sure to appoint a personal representative of your choosing — if necessary choose a corporate trustee, and discuss your philosophies regarding the distribution of your estate with them in advance.

## 20.7 FEES

Personal representatives are entitled to charge a fee. However, in many cases, family members will not charge such a fee, especially if they are also a beneficiary of the estate, since personal representative fees are taxable. Therefore, it may be more tax effective to charge nothing for the personal representative services, thereby leaving more in the estate to be received by way of inheritance.

If there is more than one personal representative, they will be required to share the allowed fee. Although the fee is prescribed by regulation in some jurisdictions, in many jurisdictions, personal representatives may charge an amount that is "reasonable". A personal representative can apply to the court for a higher fee if the duties involved in administering the estate or any trusts are particularly onerous.

If only one of several children of the deceased will be acting as personal representative, and they therefore would need to charge a fee in order to receive a larger portion of the estate, then in many cases it is best if the will contemplates the payment of a fee, as some personal representatives feel uncomfortable about charging a fee to the estate. Acting as personal representative is a time-consuming and thankless task that should be compensated accordingly. A personal representative is assuming potential liability and a high degree of responsibility by agreeing to act in such capacity.

## 20.8 HOW YOU CAN MAKE THEIR JOB EASIER

There are a few things you can do to ensure that your estate will be administered smoothly, and to ensure that your personal representative experiences the minimum amount of stress.

- Talk to them about what type of funeral service or arrangements you would like. This may prevent arguments, for example, where one child believes you would have wanted an elaborate funeral, whereas another child believes a smaller funeral is more appropriate.

- Ensure that there are some liquid funds available to pay for the service, or arrange to have the funeral pre-paid. (See section 13.5.5 of Chapter 13, "Elderly Parents", for more information on prepaid funerals.)

- Ensure that your personal representative knows where to find your important documents and assets — for example, if you deal with several different financial institutions, be sure that they are aware of that.

- Keep your financial and administrative papers in order so that they can find the assets easily when they need to.

- Let them know the name of your lawyer, accountant, financial planner and/or business partners so they know who to contact when the time comes.

- Document important wishes that you want the personal representative to respect, possibly by letter or memorandum, if there are issues that you do not want made public in your will (although keep in mind that only the provisions in your will are legally binding, unless the memorandum meets certain requirements, which your lawyer can explain to you).

## 20.9 JURISDICTION DIFFERENCES

There are no jurisdiction differences for this chapter.

# CHAPTER 21

# TAXATION AT DEATH



Most Canadians know that they will probably have to pay "tax" at the time of their death. However, many Canadians do not know how to estimate the amount of tax they will have to pay at death. As well, there is a significant amount of misunderstanding regarding the difference between income taxes and probate fees (or estate administration taxes as they are known in Ontario). This chapter will focus on how *income taxes* are calculated at the time of death. Chapter 22, "Probate", discusses how probate fees are calculated, and the problems that can arise as a result of organizing your estate only with the avoidance of probate fees in mind. At the end of this chapter, we will look at examples of how, in most cases, it is more advisable to do income tax planning than probate planning.

## 21.1 CALCULATING TAX AT THE TIME OF DEATH

After a person has passed away, their personal representative must file a tax return on their behalf in respect of the "terminal year". The terminal year is the period from January 1st to the date of death. The terminal year return will include numerous items.

1. *Regular Income.* All the regular income that the deceased earned from January 1st to the date of death must be reported on the terminal year return. This can include employment income, business income, interest, pensions, RRIF payments, annuity payments, royalties, dividends and any other types of income received by the deceased during the year of their death. In some cases, even if the income has not yet been received, the Canada Revenue Agency will require the personal representative to include an "accrued" amount representing the portion of the payment that accrued up to the date of death (e.g. the portion of an interest payment earned to the date of death, even though the full interest payment is not made until after the date of death).

2. *Unrealized Capital Gains.* All capital property owned by the deceased will be deemed to be disposed of immediately before the time of death and 50% of any resulting capital gains or losses are also included in the terminal year return. For example, if the deceased owned stocks for which he or she originally paid $1000, and those stocks were worth $10,000 immediately before the time of death, there will be a deemed disposition of these stocks at $10,000, triggering a $9000 capital gain ($10,000 minus $1000). Fifty percent of the capital gain, or $4500, must be included in the deceased's terminal year return, even though he or she did not actually sell the stock before he or she died, and has not received any cash proceeds from the stock.

3. *Registered Investments.* The full value of any registered investments owned by the deceased, including the full value of their RRSPs and RRIFs, will be included in the terminal year return. For example, if the deceased had an

RRSP worth $300,000 at the time of his or her death, his or her personal representatives would have to include $300,000 in his or her terminal year return. (However, if a death benefit is paid under a pension plan, that amount is taxed in the hands of the beneficiary who receives the death benefit, not the deceased.)

Although the first category includes items that you might normally see on your tax return, the second and third categories are somewhat unique to the year of death. Although you may sell assets from time to time and trigger some capital gains in some years, or you may take money out of your RRSP or RRIF during your lifetime, it is unlikely that you would ever sell all of your capital property and de-register all of your registered assets in any one year. This is why it is very likely that the largest tax bill you (or in fact, your personal representative) will ever have to pay will arise in the year of your death.

The large potential tax liability that arises at the time of death could lead to problems such as those described below.

- Not only could your taxable income be very high in the year of death, but a large portion of the income may be taxed at the highest marginal rate, since large amounts of taxable income are all being included on the same tax return.

- Your estate may not have sufficient liquid assets to pay the tax liability, so your personal representatives may have to sell assets that you may have wanted to leave to your beneficiaries, such as a vacation property or family business.

- Overall, less of the estate will be left for your beneficiaries, and if you have not done proper planning, some of your heirs may have to pay a larger portion of the tax bill than others (for example, if you leave your RRSPs to one child and the remainder of your estate to the other child, the child who receives the estate will be responsible for paying the tax bill on the RRSPs, even though they have not received any of them).

So what can be done to plan for this tax? The rest of this chapter will discuss ways in which to defer the tax, avoid the tax or ensure there are sufficient funds to pay the tax.

# 21.2 HOW TO MINIMIZE TAX PAYABLE AT THE TIME OF DEATH

There may be strategies which your personal representative can take advantage of to minimize the tax liability for your estate. This is one of the many reasons why it is important to choose the right personal representative when preparing your will. You should encourage your personal representative to confer with a tax professional when preparing the tax returns for your estate, as these tax returns can become quite complicated. Here are some of the strategies that may be appropriate to minimize taxes for your estate.

## 21.2.1 Spousal Rollover

If you are married or in a common-law relationship, you can "rollover" most assets left to your spouse or common-law partner. (See section 3.3 of Chapter 3, "Common-Law Couples", for a description of when an individual is considered to be a common-law partner for income tax purposes. For the purposes of this chapter, the term "spouse" will also include common-law partners as defined in the *Income Tax Act*). This means that if you left stock to your spouse that you paid $1000 for, the stock will be inherited by your spouse at a "cost base" of $1000, even if it is worth $10,000 on the date of your death. The unrealized capital gain will not be triggered until your spouse later sells the asset, or at the time of his or her death, whichever comes first (unless your spouse transfers the asset to a new spouse or common-law partner). Therefore, although the capital gain can be deferred, it will not be eliminated (unless, of course, the stock decreases in value back down to $1000 or lower). This "rollover" treatment also applies in most cases to "spousal trusts", which are trusts created for a spouse or common-law partner that meet certain conditions set out in the *Income Tax Act*. The concept of "spousal trusts" or "common-law partner trusts" is discussed in section 5.5.2 of Chapter 5, "Marriage", and section 8.5.2.1 of Chapter 8, "Blended Families".

Although most individuals use the spousal rollover in order to defer the taxation of the gain until the death of the second spouse, there may be instances where your personal representative might want to trigger the capital gain. Examples of some of these instances are outlined below.

- If a deceased individual has unused capital losses at the time of death, it may be a good idea to trigger capital gains so that these losses are not "lost". Capital losses cannot be transferred to a spouse, so the personal representative should ensure that the deceased had no unused capital losses.

- If the deceased did not have much other income in the year of death (for example, if he or she died in January), it may be a better idea to trigger capital gains in the year of death, rather than transfer them to a spouse, since the gains may be taxed at a lower rate in the hands of the deceased than if transferred to the spouse.

- If the asset is one that qualifies for a capital gains exemption (e.g. shares of a qualifying small business corporation or qualified farm property), and the deceased has not yet used his or her $750,000 lifetime limit, it may be advisable to trigger the capital gain on these assets so that the exemption may be claimed. If the exemption is not used by the personal representatives at the time of death, the beneficiaries of these assets will not be entitled to use the unused portion of the deceased's exemption at a later time.

- If the deceased owned an asset that is in a loss position, it may be advisable to trigger the loss in order to offset other amounts that are taxable in the year of death (this is the case even if the other income is not in the form of a capital gain, as capital losses can be applied against any form of income in the year of death and the year prior to death).

Therefore, the personal representative will have to decide which is the better strategy — roll over the assets or trigger some of the capital gains so that the spouse does not have to pay tax on the gains later? If a decision is made to trigger capital gains in the year of death, the personal representative will have to trigger all of the capital gain on any one asset as the personal representative cannot elect to trigger only part of the gain. Although the personal representative and the spouse cannot choose to trigger only a portion of the capital gain on any one asset, a decision can be made to trigger the capital gains on some assets and not on others in order to manage the amount of the gain that is taxable in the year of death.

One type of asset that generally may not "rollover" to a spouse or common-law partner at the time of death is a segregated fund. A segregated fund is a contract that has an owner, a beneficiary and an annuitant. If the annuitant passes away, the contract ends, and the death benefit is paid to the beneficiary. Therefore, if one spouse owns the segregated fund and is the sole annuitant, but has designated their spouse as the beneficiary, then any unrealized capital gains will be taxed when the sole owner dies, even though the proceeds are payable to a surviving spouse. However, in a case where the contract has provided for a joint or successor annuitant, the death benefit is paid on the death of the last annuitant. Therefore, when the second annuitant dies, the owner (or his or her estate) will be liable for the tax on any deemed gain that is realized at that point. If the owner is not the annuitant, the policy will remain in effect even after the owner dies, and ownership will pass to the new owner as designated by the deceased's estate. In this case, the transfer of ownership is treated like any other deemed disposition of capital property, so the property can be rolled over if the new owner is a spouse or common-law partner.

## 21.2.2 Principal Residence Exemption

The principal residence exemption is one of the few tax exemptions that has not been eliminated by the federal government over the years. The principal residence exemption provides that any capital gain realized upon the disposition of a residence that you "ordinarily inhabit" will be exempt from tax. The term "ordinarily inhabit" does not necessarily mean that you have to live in the property each day. Therefore, a vacation property could be designated as a principal residence, so long as you used it on a regular basis each year. However, an individual can only designate one residence as their principal residence in any one year, and if you are married or in a common-law relationship, then your family unit can only designate one principal residence in any one year (a family unit also includes children under the age of 18).

If you own only one principal residence, the use of this exemption is obviously not much of an issue. However, if you own more than one property that you use for personal purposes, then your personal representative should try to minimize taxes for your estate by using the exemption in the most tax-effective manner. Generally, your personal representative will want to designate the residence with the highest capital gain as your principal residence. For example, if you purchased a home in 1984 for $100,000, and it is worth $200,000 at the time of your death, it would have a $100,000 capital gain. If you also purchased a vacation property in 1984 for $100,000, and it is worth $300,000 at the time of your death, it would have a $200,000 capital gain. Obviously, it would be more tax effective for your personal representative to designate your vacation property as your principal residence for tax purposes, and pay the tax on the gain on your home, since the capital gain on your vacation property is larger.

The principal residence exemption is calculated by taking the number of years during which the property was designated as the principal residence after 1971, adding one to that number, and dividing that total by the total number of years the property was owned after 1971. For example, let's look at a situation where an individual purchased a family home in 1987 for $100,000, and they then purchased a vacation property in 1995 for $100,000. Let's further assume that at the time of their death in 2006, the family home is worth $300,000, and the vacation property is worth $400,000, and they are not survived by a spouse or common-law partner. Here is how the capital gain would be calculated on each property:

*Family Home*

The home is deemed to have been disposed of in 2006 for $300,000. Since it was originally purchased in 1987 for $100,000, the total capital gain is $200,000. Since we know that the capital gain on the vacation property is larger ($400,000 – $100,000 = $300,000), the personal representative will generally only use the principal residence exemption on this property for years where this was the only property they owned (i.e. 1987 to 1995, or nine years). Although the deceased owned two properties in 1995, designating the family home as the principal residence in that year will not affect the calculation for the vacation property, due to the addition of one year in the numerator of the calculation. The equation is:

$$\frac{9 + 1}{20} \times \$200{,}000 = \$100{,}000 \text{ of the capital gain is exempt}$$

Therefore, $100,000 of the capital gain is not exempt (50% of this amount, or $50,000, will be included in the terminal year return for the deceased).

*Vacation Property*

At the time of death, the vacation property is deemed to be disposed of for fair market value, which is $400,000. Since the deceased paid $100,000 for the property, the capital gain is $300,000. The personal representative would like to completely eliminate the gain on this property, since it has the larger gain of the two properties. The personal representative designates the vacation property as the principal residence for each year from 1996 to 2006 (the year 1995 was used for the family home). Therefore, the portion of the capital gain that is exempt is calculated as follows:

$$\frac{11+1}{12} \times \$300{,}000 = \$300{,}000 \text{, or 100\% of the capital gain is exempt}$$

This is a fairly straightforward example. There are many ways in which the calculation can become much more complicated, which is why it is highly recommended that personal representatives seek the assistance of a tax professional when attempting to maximize the use of the principal residence exemption in the terminal year return. Below are some of the other issues that may arise.

- Capital gains were not taxable prior to 1972, but the calculation for determining the cost base as at December 31, 1971, can become complex. Your personal representative should speak with an advisor if you owned the property prior to 1971.

- It was possible for a family to designate two properties as principal residences prior to 1982, and it may still be possible to designate two properties for those years, if each property was owned in the sole name of each spouse. If the properties were owned jointly, this may not be possible, unless each spouse gifts their interest in one property to the other.

- Prior to 1992, it was possible to shelter capital gains on any type of property using the $100,000 lifetime capital gains exemption. Many property owners had their properties appraised at that time in order to shelter all or a part of the capital gain that had accrued to that time. If you took advantage of this exemption, your cost base may be significantly more than what you paid for the property.

- If a property was used as a rental property for a period of time, then the calculation may be impacted by the value of the property on the date on which the property changed uses from being a rental property to a "personal use" property (or vice versa). Your tax accountant will be able to assist you in determining how much of the capital gain can be sheltered in that case.

These are just some of the ways in which the calculation of the principal residence exemption can become very complex. In order to ensure you are using the principal residence exemption in a manner which maximizes its value, you (or your personal representative) should be sure to speak with an experienced tax accountant prior to using the exemption. There is more information on this subject in Chapter 15, "Vacation Properties", particularly in section 15.1 and Case Study 15.4.2.

## 21.2.3 Using Capital Losses

It is possible that during your lifetime you had capital losses that you were not able to use. For example, if you had purchased stock for $10,000, and it then decreased in value to $1000 on the date you sold it, you would have a $9000 capital loss ($1000 – $10,000), $4500 of which could be claimed on your tax return ($9000 x 50%). However, since capital losses can only be used against capital gains, it is possible that you were not able to take advantage of the $4500 capital loss if you did not have any capital gains resulting from the sale of other assets. If you cannot use a capital loss in any one year, you can carry it back to be used on a tax return in any one of the three previous years, or carry it forward indefinitely.

It is possible that at the time of your death, you have unused capital losses, either as a result of losses incurred on property you still own, or losses that were previously incurred, and carried forward from previous years. Not only could these capital losses reduce the amount of any capital gains included on your terminal year return as a result of the deemed disposition of your assets, but in the year of death, they can also be used to reduce *any* type of taxable income. In addition, your personal representative can carryback unused capital losses to the year prior to death, and use them against any type of income in that year as well. If there is not sufficient income in the year of death or the year prior to death to use all of the losses, consider other strategies that may maximize the use of the losses, such as triggering capital gains instead of transferring the asset on a rollover basis to a spouse (see section 21.2.1). The use of unutilized capital losses can become extremely complicated, so it is best for the personal representative to confer with a tax professional in order to maximize their value.

If the personal representative is unsure as to whether or not the deceased had unused capital losses, it may be advisable for them to contact the Canada Revenue Agency to obtain a history of any unused amounts.

## 21.2.4 Spousal RRSP Contributions

If the deceased had unused RRSP contribution room, and they have a surviving spouse or common-law partner who is under the age of 71, their personal representative should consider making an RRSP contribution to the deceased spouse's or common-law partner's RRSP (assuming the will allows for that). Although an RRSP contribution cannot be made to the deceased's RRSP after the time of death, a contribution may be made to the RRSP of a spouse or common-law partner within 60 days of the end of the calendar year in which the deceased died. In cases where the deceased died in November or December, the personal representative will not have much time to act on this issue, which is one of the reasons why personal representatives should confer with an advisor as soon as possible after the time of death.

## 21.2.5 Refund of RRSP or RRIF Premiums

If some of your assets are held within an RRSP or RRIF, it may be possible to defer the taxation on these funds until a date later than the date of death. This is possible in the circumstances described below.

1. *Transfer to Spouse.* (In this paragraph, all references to "spouse" also include common-law partners, as defined in the *Income Tax Act.*) If you designate your spouse as the beneficiary of your RRSP or RRIF, or if you leave all or a portion of your estate to your spouse, and your personal representative and your spouse elect that part of the spouse's inheritance is to be comprised of the registered funds, it may be possible to defer the taxation on these assets past the date of your death. If your spouse receives registered assets, he or she can report the taxable income on his or her tax return as a "refund of premiums". That means that the personal representative will not have to include that amount on the terminal year return for the deceased. If the spouse is under the age of 71, they may then be able to make a contribution to their own RRSP up to the amount that they have received as a refund of premiums, thereby reducing the amount of taxable income received in respect of that asset down to zero. The spouse does not need to have any available RRSP "room" in order to make this contribution. This is a special contribution allowed as a result of reporting the refund of premiums. Obviously, when the spouse withdraws the funds from their own RRSP or RRIF, the amounts will become taxable. Any amounts remaining in their RRSP or RRIF at the time of their death will be taxable in their terminal year return (unless, of course, they pass the amounts onto a new spouse or common-law partner). If the spouse is over age 71, then they may continue to defer tax on the refund of premiums by purchasing a registered life annuity, or a registered term annuity to age 90, which provides for regular payments beginning in the year of purchase.

2. *Transfer to a Minor.* If the RRSP proceeds are left to a child or grandchild who is under the age of 18 and financially dependent upon the deceased, there may be an opportunity to defer the taxation of the RRSP. "Financially dependent" generally means that their income is not more than the amount of the personal tax exemption, which is currently $10,382. If the RRSP proceeds are left to such a child, then the child will report the amount on their tax return as a refund of premiums so that the personal representative does not have to report those amounts on the terminal year return of the deceased. Then, if a registered annuity is purchased that pays out all of the proceeds by the child's 18th birthday, the child will be able to deduct a corresponding amount from their tax return for purchasing the annuity, and no tax will be owing at that time. However, as the annuity payments

are received by the child, the payment amounts must be included in the income of the child, meaning that all the tax will become payable prior to the child turning 18 (although presumably the child will be in a lower tax bracket than the deceased was in the year of death, and the payments may be spread out over several years, depending upon how old the child was at the time of death of the parent).

Be very careful when doing this type of planning — if you transfer the RRSP to the child while they are still a minor, the Public Trustee may have the authority to manage the funds until the child attains the age of majority. Once the child attains the age of majority, the funds will be given to them without any conditions. In many cases, even young adults do not have sufficient maturity to manage large sums of money, and it would be more advisable to pay the tax in the year of death and have the after tax amounts transferred to a trust for the benefit of the child. See section 10.5.3 of Chapter 10, "Children", for more information on the issues involved when leaving money to minors.

3. *Transfer to a Disabled Child.* The taxation of an RRSP or RRIF may also be deferred if the proceeds are left to children or grandchildren who are financially dependent upon the deceased, and their financial dependency is as a result of a mental or physical infirmity. In this context, "financially dependent" means that the disabled child or grandchild has taxable income of less than approximately $17,000. Again, the RRSP proceeds will be reported on the tax return of the disabled child or grandchild, and they will not need to be reported on the terminal year tax return for the deceased, so tax will not be payable until the child or grandchild receives the money. Generally, an annuity is purchased for the child or grandchild and payments are made over the course of their lifetime, to age 90.

   However, be careful when doing this type of planning, since it is often more advantageous for the tax to be paid on such amounts, with the after-tax amount held in a trust, for a couple of reasons:

   - if the child is mentally infirm, then they may not be capable of managing the payments as and when they are received, usually necessitating the involvement of the Public Trustee in the management of those funds; and

   - if the child is receiving social assistance, then the receipt of the annuity payments may make them ineligible for part or all of their social assistance payments.

Disabled children require special considerations when doing estate planning. See Chapter 12, "Disabled Persons", for a discussion of some of these issues. Be sure to discuss your estate plan with your financial advisor before naming a disabled child or grandchild as a direct beneficiary of an RRSP or RRIF.

## 21.2.6 $750,000 Capital Gains Exemption

The personal representative should ensure, to the extent it is available, that the $750,000 capital gains exemption is utilized for qualified small business corporation shares or qualified farm property. The conditions for qualifying for either of these exemptions are extensive, and beyond the scope of this book. Please see section 16.2.3 in Chapter 16, "Business Owners" for more information on this topic. Speak to a tax professional to see if these exemptions are available for the deceased.

## 21.2.7 Rollover of Farm Property to a Child or Grandchild

In some cases, farm property can roll over to a child or grandchild of the deceased at its cost base. Normally, at the time of death, property can only roll over to a spouse or common-law partner (or a trust established for a spouse or common-law partner that meets the conditions in the *Income Tax Act*), and property given to anyone else will be transferred at fair market value. However, in the case of farm property, a rollover may be available to a child or grandchild, so speak with a tax professional to see if this rollover is available. Briefly, here are some of the conditions that must be met in order to roll over qualified farm property to a child or grandchild without triggering capital gains at the time of death:

- the child must have the right to the property within 36 months of the date of death;
- the property must have been used in the business of farming by the deceased, or their spouse or common-law partner, or any of the deceased's children (or their spouse or common-law partner), immediately prior to death; and
- the child must be a resident of Canada immediately before the time of death.

For the first condition, be aware of the fact that using a trust to hold the property for a child may result in this condition not being met. However, in some cases individuals feel that it is more important to leave the property in trust until the child is mature enough to manage the property rather than giving the property to the child on a rollover basis.

For the second condition, renting the land under a crop-share or cash lease will not qualify as using the property "in the business of farming" unless the deceased rented the land to a spouse, child or grandchild who carried on the business of farming.

Once the child receives the property, they do not have to use the farm property in the business of farming. It is the deceased's use of the property that is relevant for determining whether or not rollover treatment is available.

## 21.2.8 Filing Separate Tax Returns

It is possible that your personal representative may be able to include some of your income from the year of death on a separate tax return. This is obviously beneficial, since our tax system is based on graduated rates of tax, so it is better to have income spread out over more than one tax return, as opposed to having it included all on one tax return. Although the ability to file separate returns is limited, it is available in the circumstances described below.

- *Rights and Things.* Where the deceased had "rights and things", which can include dividends that were declared but unpaid, unused vacation leave credits and inventory for farmers who report income on a cash basis, these amounts can be included on a separate return.

- *Business Income.* If the deceased earned business income, and the fiscal year for the business ended before the death of the deceased, the personal representative can include a pro-rated amount of business income earned in the next fiscal year, but prior to the date of death, in a separate tax return.

- *Testamentary Trust Income.* If the deceased was a beneficiary of a testamentary trust that had a taxation year that ended before the death of the deceased, the personal representative can include a pro-rated amount of trust income earned after the end of the trust's taxation year, but prior to the date of death, in a separate tax return.

The calculation of how much income can be reported on each separate return can become quite complex, so the personal representative should confer with a qualified tax accountant prior to filing any of these types of returns.

## 21.2.9 $10,000 Tax-Free Death Benefit

If the deceased, or the spouse, common-law partner or child of the deceased, receives a death benefit from the deceased's employer in recognition of the deceased's years of service, it is possible that up to $10,000 of the death benefit can be received tax free if the payments are made from a pension plan (or similar type of plan), or represent unpaid sick leave. If the estate or a beneficiary receives such an amount, the personal representative should ensure that the first $10,000 is indicated as being tax free when the income tax returns are filed.

## 21.2.10 Charitable Contributions

If the terms of the will allow for it, or a charitable giving strategy was put in place prior to the time of death, the personal representative may be able to reduce the amount of tax paid by the deceased or the estate by making a charitable contribution. See Chapter 24, "Charitable Giving", for more information on this subject.

## 21.2.11 Carryback of Losses Incurred by the Estate

As mentioned previously, unless the assets rollover to a spouse or common-law partner (as defined in the *Income Tax Act*), generally speaking, there will be a deemed disposition of all capital assets owned by the deceased on the date of death, triggering any unrealized capital gains accrued to that date. These capital gains are reported on the terminal year return of the deceased, with all future capital gains being reported by the estate or the beneficiaries. However, it is possible that some of the assets held by the estate could decrease in value after the date of death, resulting in a capital loss for the estate. If these losses occur within one year of the date of death, the personal representative will be able to carry these losses back, and use them against capital gains realized in the hands of the deceased in the final tax return. It is imperative that personal representatives are diligent in selling assets within one year of the date of death, if they want to use this carryback provision. This provision may also be helpful when a family business or farm is being sold. In many cases, it may be important to complete the transaction within one year of the date of death, in order to take advantage of the loss carryback provision.

### 21.2.12 Holding Companies

Owners of shares in private holding companies should be aware that there is the potential for double taxation in respect of these shares at the time of death. At the time of death, the shareholder will be deemed to have disposed of the shares at fair market value. This will result in an increase in the cost base of the shares when the estate or beneficiary later sells them. However, it will not result in a corresponding increase in the cost base of the underlying assets which are owned by the holding corporation. In order to avoid this double taxation, the personal representatives of an estate should be given sufficient authority to wind-up the company within one year of the death of the shareholder, or alternatively, transfer the shares of the holding company to a new company in exchange for a promissory note. Although the mechanics of this type of planning are too involved to discuss here, the topic should be raised with an experienced estate planning lawyer to ensure that your will contains the necessary provisions to minimize tax at the time of your death. Again, if this transaction does not happen within a year of the date of death, the estate may no longer be able to take advantage of this strategy, which is why you should choose a diligent personal representative who will speak to a qualified professional as soon as possible.

## 21.3 TAX PLANNING STRATEGIES PRIOR TO THE TIME OF DEATH

There may be some strategies that can be implemented prior to the time of death to minimize the tax owing by an estate.

### 21.3.1 Charitable Giving

One option that is becoming very popular for reducing taxes at the time of death and leaving a legacy is charitable giving. If you are interested in leaving a gift to charity at the time of your death, see Chapter 24, "Charitable Giving", for a review of the different strategies available.

### 21.3.2 $10,000 Tax-Free Death Benefit

A maximum of $10,000 can be received tax-free if it is a death benefit from the deceased's employer in recognition of their years of service. The payments must be made from a pension plan (or similar type of plan), or represent unpaid sick leave. Therefore, if you own a private corporation, consider passing a resolution indicating that $10,000 is to be paid to your estate (or your beneficiaries) at the time of your death, either from a pension plan, or in recognition of unpaid sick leave.

### 21.3.3 Estate Freezes

If you own a corporation, consider if it would be appropriate to effect an "estate freeze" in order to freeze the amount of capital gains tax you will have to pay at the time of your death in respect of that asset. See section 16.5.2.4 of Chapter 16, "Business Owners", for a further discussion as to how this strategy can help to reduce tax for your estate.

### 21.3.4 Testamentary Trusts

In many cases it may not be possible to significantly reduce the amount of income tax owing at the time of death, but it may be possible to reduce the amount of income tax your beneficiaries will have to pay on the income earned on their inheritances through the use of a testamentary trust. A testamentary trust is a trust created in your last will and testament, and the income earned in the trust will be taxed in the hands of the trust, not in the name of the beneficiary, which could result in significant tax savings. See sections 5.5.2 of Chapter 5, "Married", 8.5.2.1 of Chapter 8, "Blended Families", 10.5.3 and 10.5.4 of Chapter 10, "Children" and 12.3.1 of Chapter 12, "Disabled Persons" for more information on when testamentary trusts may be useful in your particular circumstances. It is important to keep in mind that if you wish to use a testamentary trust, only the assets which flow through your estate will be included in that trust, which is why probate planning will not be recommended in many cases as most probate planning techniques involve the distribution of assets outside of your estate.

### 21.3.5 Joint Ownership

Many individuals are under the mistaken belief that if they add a joint owner to an asset that has an unrealized capital gain they will not have to pay tax on that gain at the time of their death. Not only is this not true, the addition of a joint owner could in fact accelerate the time at which payment for part of the tax is owing. See section 22.3.1 in Chapter 22, "Probate", for a discussion regarding joint ownership.

# 21.4 PLANNING FOR THE TAX

Even after taking advantage of as many planning strategies as possible, there may still be tax owing as a result of the terminal year return, and it may be a significant amount. Although the tax can usually be kept to a minimum so long as one spouse or common-law partner is still alive (since assets can be rolled over to them), generally, when the assets are transferred to the next generation, tax will be owing. The question then arises, how will it be paid? Here are some of the most common solutions.

- If the estate has sufficient liquid assets, the personal representative can liquidate as many assets as are necessary to pay the tax bill, and simply divide the remainder.

- If the estate does not have sufficient assets, or you know that your heirs will require a certain amount to maintain their standard of living (for example, when you have a financially dependent spouse or child), then you should consider insurance. Speak to your financial advisor to ensure that you have sufficient insurance, and the appropriate type of insurance to protect your estate. See section 25.2 of Chapter 25, "Insurance", for an explanation of the different types of products available to provide the necessary liquidity for an estate.

- Even if you know that your heirs could maintain their standard of living in the event that certain estate assets had to be sold to pay the taxes, you may wish to leave certain specific assets to them. For example, do they want to be able to keep the family vacation property after you are gone? How about the family business? It may be difficult, if not impossible, to sell just a portion of these assets to pay the tax bill, and insurance may be necessary to equalize the estate if the property or business is not to be divided between all the beneficiaries. The personal representative may be in a position where he or she is forced to sell an asset that the family wanted to keep. Again, in many cases, planning for the tax in advance and obtaining sufficient amounts of insurance in order to pay the tax is the best planning technique in many cases.

It is important to speak with an advisor about these issues sooner rather than later. There have been many instances where owners of businesses or vacation properties have not addressed the issue until later in life, by which time they are either uninsurable, or the insurance is prohibitively expensive. Not addressing the problem will not make it go away — in fact, over time, it will only get worse as your assets grow in value, increasing the tax liability. Speak to an advisor about the potential tax liability of your estate, and how you can minimize it, or plan for it.

Even if you do not personally feel that you can afford the insurance, your children or business partners may be willing to pay the premiums in order to keep the asset after you die.

## 21.5 JURISDICTION DIFFERENCES

There are no jurisdiction differences for this chapter.

## 21.6 CASE STUDIES

### 21.6.1 Taxation at Death — Individual

Caroline has significant investments, a home, a vacation property and RRSPs. She is concerned about how much income tax she may have to pay at the time of her death. The value of her assets is as follows:

| Asset | Cost Base | Fair Market Value | Unrealized Capital Gain |
|---|---|---|---|
| Mutual Funds | $10,000 | $100,000 | $90,000 |
| Vacation Property | $100,000 | $200,000 | $100,000 |
| RRSPs | Nil | $150,000 | Nil |
| Home | $150,000 | $200,000 | $50,000 |

Caroline earns an annual income of $60,000 per year. Caroline dies on September 30th. Her personal representative must file her terminal year tax return for the period from January 1st to September 30th. Caroline's terminal year tax return will include the following items:

| | |
|---|---|
| Employment Income | $45,000 (9 months of income) |
| Deemed dispositions: | |
| Mutual funds | $45,000 (50% of $90,000) |
| Vacation Property | Nil (designated as her principal residence) |
| Home | $25,000 (50% of $50,000) |
| Registered assets | $150,000 (100% taxable) |
| TOTAL TAXABLE INCOME | $265,000 |

Depending upon the jurisdiction in which Caroline resided at the time of her death, her personal representative may have to pay tax on a significant part of her income at rates of approximately 40 to 45%. Since Caroline is single, her personal representative will simply sell the assets, and distribute the remaining proceeds among her beneficiaries. However, in some cases, this is not so easy — what if Caroline had children, and they needed her $200,000 in investments as well as the family home to maintain their standard of living? Caroline should ensure that she has sufficient assets to pay any tax owing at the time of death, and still provide adequately for her children.

## 21.6.2 Taxation at Death — Married Person

Sonia and Kyle are married and own the following assets:

| Asset | Title | Cost Base | Fair Market Value | Unrealized Capital Gain |
|---|---|---|---|---|
| Home | Joint | $200,000 | $300,000 | $100,000 |
| Business | Sonia | $100 | $1,000,000 | $999,900 |
| Mutual funds | Kyle | $200,000 | $20,000 | ($180,000) |
| Mutual funds | Sonia | $70,000 | $220,000 | $150,000 |
| Spousal RRSP | Kyle | Nil | $200,000 | Nil |
| RRSP | Sonia | Nil | $200,000 | Nil |

Sonia and Kyle have each written wills that leave their entire estate to the survivor, so when the first person dies, no income tax will be payable (although there may be some probate fees since not all of the assets are held in joint names). Sonia and Kyle have specifically chosen not to hold all assets in joint names, as they have created spousal trusts in their wills in order to allow the survivor to income split with the trust (see Case Study 5.8.2 in Chapter 5, "Married", for more information on spousal trusts).

However, Sonia and Kyle also have three children, Horatio, Gertrude and Esmeralda, and they want to know how their estate will be taxed at the time of death of the survivor. Let's assume that Kyle dies first. Although Kyle's RRSP could be transferred to Sonia on a tax-deferred basis, because he has $180,000 of unused capital losses, Sonia decides to trigger the capital loss (which results in a taxable loss of $90,000), and includes $90,000 of Kyle's RRSPs in his terminal year return. Therefore, only $110,000 of his RRSP's are transferred to her RRSPs. Assuming no changes in value, Sonia's estate would have the following tax liability at the time of her death:

| | | |
|---|---|---|
| Home | - | Nil (principal residence exemption) |
| Business | - | $999,900 capital gain, $750,000 of which is exempt |
| | | $249,900 x 50% = $124,950 |
| Mutual funds | - | $150,000 x 50% = $75,000 |
| RRSPs | - | $200,000 + $110,000 (from Kyle) = $310,000 |

Total taxable estate = $509,950
Total tax payable = approximately $200,000 – $250,000
(depending upon the province of residence at the time of death)

Total probate payable = maximum of $28,600
(depending upon Sonia's province of residence at the time of death)

Prior to Sonia's death, she decides that she wants to save as much "tax" as possible for her beneficiaries. Since she does not understand the difference between probate fees and income taxes, she thinks that by transferring assets outside of her estate she will be doing the right thing for her beneficiaries. This is what Sonia does:

- she makes Horatio the joint owner of her mutual funds and principal residence and signs a document indicating that Horatio is not holding these assets in trust for her estate;
- she adds Gertrude as the direct beneficiary of her RRSPs; and
- she leaves the remainder of her estate to Esmeralda.

In fact, although she has saved probate fees on the business and the RRSPs, her estate plan is very flawed. Horatio receives the mutual funds and principal residence free and clear, Gertrude receives the RRSPs, and Esmeralda receives the business (being the only asset left in the estate). Although Esmeralda's portion of the estate is reduced by the tax liability of the estate, she still receives more than 1/3 of the estate (and Esmerelda had to sell the business in order to pay the tax liability on the RSPs). Although Sonia has saved some probate fees, she has not saved any income taxes. (In fact, the transfer of the mutual funds has accelerated the payment of tax, as she would have triggered a partial deemed disposition when she added Horatio as a joint owner. She has also lost the ability to use the principal residence exemption on Horatio's half of the principal residence, as he does not live there. See 22.3.1 in Chapter 22, "Probate", for a discussion as to the disadvantages of adding joint owners to property). Also, Sonia has established testamentary trusts in her will for her children, but since almost nothing passes through her estate, there is essentially nothing to put in the trusts, wasting a valuable tax planning opportunity.

### 21.6.3 Principal Residence Exemption

See section 21.2.2 for an example of how the principal residence exemption can be maximized.

# CHAPTER 22



# PROBATE

In recent years, many individuals have become interested in doing probate planning. However, in many cases, they are not completely sure as to the advantages and disadvantages of doing this type of planning, and the alternatives that are available. When reading this chapter, keep in mind that *probate planning should not be the driving force in your wealth plan. In many cases it can detrimentally affect the distribution of an estate and the ability to do income tax planning.* In fact, in most cases it is more advantageous to do income tax planning rather than probate planning (examples of how this may be the case are described throughout this chapter). Since income tax planning and probate planning are often mutually exclusive, be careful not to compromise any income tax savings by doing probate planning instead.

## 22.1 THE PROBATE PROCESS

Probate is the process in which the personal representative takes the last will of the deceased, and brings it to the provincial probate court for approval. The court will approve the will and issue what is referred to in most jurisdictions as "letters probate", unless someone challenges the validity of the will. In order for the court to provide this approval, the will must be prepared in an acceptable method (for example, some jurisdictions do not allow holograph wills), and the personal representative must provide an "inventory" of all of the assets that pass through the estate.

Not every estate will have to go through the probate process. For example, if all of the assets held by the deceased were held in joint ownership with a spouse, then it is possible that there will not be any assets in the estate (note that this example does not apply in Quebec, where there is no right of survivorship on jointly held assets). However, in many cases, there will be assets that are registered solely in the deceased's name. If the personal representative does not obtain probate, it is likely that third parties (such as mutual fund companies, banks and land titles offices) will refuse to transfer any of the deceased's property, as they will have no way of knowing if the will was in fact the last will of the deceased, or if it is valid. By obtaining letters probate (or letters of administration, if there is no will), these third parties will be given assurances that they are transferring the assets to the proper beneficiaries. If these third parties simply acted on the instructions of anyone coming forward with what they claimed to be a last will and testament of the deceased, they would risk a lawsuit if that will was later found to be invalid, or a more recent will was located.



Probate gives protection to both the third parties who are asked to transfer assets, and to personal representatives who are administering the estate. This is because if a personal representative administers an estate without obtaining probate, he or she could be liable if a beneficiary produces a later will with a different distribution scheme. As well, certain limitation periods run from the date on which the will was probated – if the will is never submitted for probate, these limitation periods will never expire, leaving the personal representative continually at risk.

For example, in several jurisdictions, it may be possible for certain individuals to make claims against the estate if they are a spouse or child of the deceased, or in some cases where they are a more distant relative who is financially dependent upon the deceased. The parties allowed to make such dependant's relief claims and the conditions required to make such a claim are described briefly in section 19.6 of Chapter 19, "Distribution of an Estate". The issue to keep in mind is the time limit these individuals have for making a claim. In many instances, the claim must be made within six months of obtaining the grant of probate or letters of administration, *not* six months from the date of death. If probate is never obtained, then these time limits may never expire. If there is any concern about the ability of a relative to make a claim against the estate, then it may be worth the cost to go through the process of obtaining probate, simply to ensure that there are no nasty surprises later.

Some people may also want to go through the probate process in order to protect the personal representative. There is a risk to a personal representative who chooses to administer an estate without the protection of a formal court grant. If another will is subsequently located that names another individual as personal representative and provides for an alternative scheme of distribution, the personal representative may face liability.

## 22.2 PROBATE FEES

Generally speaking, probate fees are charged on the "gross value" of your estate as indicated in the estate inventory provided by your personal representative to the probate court. The gross value of your estate in most jurisdictions is calculated by taking the fair market value of all of your assets and subtracting only liabilities that have been secured against real property (for example, the amount of an unsecured line of credit would not reduce the value of your estate). A percentage rate (which varies from jurisdiction to jurisdiction — see section 22.4, "Jurisdiction Differences") is then applied to this amount. Your personal representative will be required to pay probate in the jurisdiction in which you resided at the time of your death. In most jurisdictions you will be required to pay probate on all real property located in that jurisdiction, as well as all of your personal property, regardless of where it is located. Any real property that is located in another jurisdiction may also be subject to probate in the other jurisdiction. For example, if you died in Alberta, owning $500,000 in personal property and $200,000 in real property located in Alberta along with $300,000 in real property located in British Columbia, you would have to pay probate on a gross estate of $700,000 in Alberta and $300,000 in British Columbia (although there are exceptions to this rule — see section 22.4, "Jurisdiction Differences"). Depending upon which jurisdiction you live in and in which jurisdictions you have property, it is possible to pay probate twice on the same asset (e.g. if your province of residence requires you to pay probate on all of your real property, and then you are required to pay probate again on real property located in another jurisdiction).

In Ontario, probate fees are referred to as "estate administration taxes". For the purposes of this chapter, we will refer to estate administration taxes as probate fees.

## 22.3 PROBATE PLANNING

Until relatively recently, having an estate go through probate was not seen to be a major problem. Although the probate process can cause delays and results in the filing of an inventory of the deceased's assets in a public registry, many people were not too concerned about trying to avoid the process altogether. However, in the early 1990s, the government of Ontario increased its probate fees from .5% to 1.5% of the gross value of the deceased's estate, and some other provinces followed suit. (See section 22.4, "Jurisdiction Differences", for an explanation of the probate fees in your jurisdiction). This led to a marked increase in the interest in doing probate planning. However, in many jurisdictions the fees are much less, and in a couple of cases (e.g. Alberta and Quebec), almost nothing at all. Even in jurisdictions with the "highest" probate fees, the costs of doing probate planning may far outweigh the benefits.

Before examining each technique individually, here are some of the more common reasons for doing probate planning:

- avoiding probate fees;
- avoiding the delays involved in the probate process;
- minimizing legal and trustee fees. Legal fees and trustee fees are sometimes calculated on the basis of the value of the "estate". For these purposes, the value of the "estate" is calculated based on those assets that pass through probate. Obviously, the less of your estate that passes through probate, the lower your legal and trustee fees may be, although many professionals will negotiate their fee on an hourly basis, and do not charge a percentage rate. (Note: if you do probate planning without the assistance of a qualified professional, and this planning results in a lawsuit, the legal fees involved in the litigation of the lawsuit may far exceed any legal fees that might have been payable had your estate been probated.);
- avoiding wills variation claims (generally only an issue in British Columbia) or in some cases, a claim by a dependant or other creditor; or
- avoiding public disclosure of estate assets. The probate process involves filing a copy of the will along with an inventory of assets with the provincial probate court. If you are extremely wealthy, or a media personality, confidentiality may be an issue for you. If you want to keep all of your personal details confidential, it may be best to try to avoid the probate process.

What are some of the disadvantages of avoiding the probate process? Although we will examine these issues more closely later in this chapter, here is a brief description of the major issues.

- Probate planning often involves the transfer of an asset to another person prior to the time of your death. This can result in a loss of control that usually is not desirable.
- A transfer of assets can also expose the asset to the creditors and family property claims of the person to whom it is transferred.

- A transfer of assets can result in a capital gain for tax purposes much earlier than necessary. The amount of the tax payable on the capital gain will far exceed the probate savings in many cases.

- When assets are distributed according to a will, they are usually distributed in an orderly and fair manner. When assets are distributed to beneficiaries in advance of death, they are often distributed in a hap-hazard way, without any regard for the tax implications. In many cases, one or two beneficiaries will receive an asset transferred prior to death, leaving the other beneficiaries with less of the estate, as the estate will be decreased due to the tax liability on those assets.

- If assets are given to children outside of a will, children of a deceased child are often left out. If the asset had been distributed according to a will, it is more likely that the children of a deceased child would have received their proportionate share.

- If some of your assets are distributed to a child while he or she is still a minor, this may necessitate the involvement of the Public Trustee in the management of these assets, which can be costly and frustrating for all involved. This also usually results in the child obtaining the assets once they reach the age of majority, which is far too young in many cases. If assets are instead left to a child or grandchild in a will, they can be managed by a trustee, and held in trust until the child is older, perhaps 25 or 30.

- In some cases, when property is transferred to another person, the transfer will result in land transfer tax, if the property in question is real property. If the property is personal property, then commissions or transfer fees may be charged to change an account registration or re-register share certificates. Also, if the property is real property that is subject to a mortgage, the approval of the lender will have to be obtained prior to completing the transfer. In fact, if the property is completely transferred to a new owner, this may result in a breach of contract for the purposes of a mortgage, or a mortgage insurance policy, which could lead to a loss of benefits. The process may also involve legal and accounting fees when transferring the property, appraisal costs and GST.

- The probate process in many cases provides protection to the personal representative and the estate. For example, in many jurisdictions, spouses, common-law partners and other dependants have a certain period of time in which to make claims against the estate, and these time periods often start from the date on which the estate was probated. If the estate never goes through the probate process, it is possible that one of these claims could arise in the future, long after the estate has been distributed. This could lead to potential liability for the personal representative.

In fact, in most cases, it makes more sense to do income tax planning than probate planning — see the chapter that discusses your current life scenario to see if there are any tax or estate planning strategies from which you or your beneficiaries could benefit, which would be hampered by probate planning. Also speak to a tax planning professional prior to implementing any probate planning techniques.

With these warnings in mind, here are some of the types of probate planning techniques that are used from time to time.



## 22.3.1 Adding a Joint Owner

In almost every province (except Quebec), individuals may hold their assets in joint ownership with another person with a "right of survivorship". This means that when one of the owners dies, the other owner or owners will become the owner(s) of the property, and the estate of the deceased person will not be entitled to any portion of the property. Since the asset does not pass through the estate of the deceased owner, no probate fees are payable on jointly held assets. (Note that there are two types of joint ownership — "joint tenants", and "tenants in common". If a property is held as tenants in common, there is no right of survivorship, so many of the issues discussed here will not be relevant. For the purposes of this discussion, we will assume that any jointly held property is held as joint tenants, with a right of survivorship.)

The Supreme Court of Canada has ruled that when an asset is held in joint ownership with an adult child (or children), the presumption will be that the child (or children) is holding the asset as a trustee only, and the asset will still form part of the parent's estate. Therefore, if the parent's estate does not need to go through probate for any reason at all, no probate will be payable on the asset held in joint ownership, and the asset will be distributed as per the will. However, if even one asset requires a probated will (for example a piece of real estate in the deceased's name), then all the estate assets will have to be included as part of the estate when calculating the probate fees, including any assets held in joint ownership with an adult child. Therefore, it is very likely that in many cases, adding a child as a joint owner will not avoid probate. In addition, there could still be arguments over what the parent really wanted – if the child who is a joint owner argues that the asset was meant as a gift to them alone, and the asset is not to form part of the estate, then it is possible that they will be able to rebut the presumption that the asset is being held for the estate, and keep the property for themselves. If you decide to add a child as a joint owner of an asset, then it will be very important that you sign an agreement indicating what your intentions were when they were added. Under no circumstances is it recommended that a minor child be added as a joint owner, as in many cases the provincial Public Trustee will be required to consent to any transaction involving an asset owned (or partly owned) by a minor.

Joint ownership can bring with it many, many problems. In fact, unless the joint owners are spouses in a first marriage, generally speaking, it may be better if the assets were either held by one person only, or as tenants in common, meaning that the portion of the asset held by each person would go through their estate at the time of their death (although this could obviously involve the payment of additional probate fees). Even in traditional first marriages, in many cases, it would be preferable to hold the assets separately, which may allow for more favourable tax planning, through the use of testamentary trusts in your wills (see section 5.5.2 of Chapter 5, "Married", for more information). Here are some of the potential pitfalls of adding a joint owner.

### 22.3.1.1 Triggering Capital Gains Tax

The addition of a new owner may trigger a "deemed disposition" of part of the asset, and, potentially, the payment of capital gains tax. A capital gain will not arise when a spouse or common-law partner is added as a joint owner, so long as the other spouse or common-law partner was the sole owner of the property before the other spouse or common-law partner was added as a joint owner. However, when the new owner is not a spouse or common-law partner (e.g. a child), a capital gain may be triggered. As mentioned above, normally when an adult child is added as a joint owner of an asset, they are presumed to be holding the asset as a trustee only. However, if the parties make it clear that the child is in fact a true owner with a right of survivorship, then part of any unrealized capital gain on the asset will be triggered when that child is added as an owner. Here is a case study that illustrates how the gain is calculated.

> Let's assume that Murray has a vacation property worth $500,000. We will further assume that Murray has already used his principal residence exemption on his home in the city. Murray decides to add his adult daughter, Josee, as a joint owner on the vacation property. Murray only paid $100,000 for the vacation property, with the remaining $400,000 representing unrealized capital gains that have accrued on the vacation property since he purchased it. When Murray adds Josee as a true joint owner to

the vacation property, he will trigger 50% of the capital gain, or $200,000 (calculated as follows: 50% of the fair market value of the asset is $250,000, and 50% of the cost of the asset was $50,000. The difference between $250,000 and $50,000 is $200,000).

Even though Josee has not paid Murray anything for her half of the vacation property, Murray will have to include $100,000 in taxable income in his tax return for that year (capital gains are only 50% taxable, so $200,000 x 50% = $100,000). Depending upon Murray's jurisdiction of residence, he may have to pay almost $45,000 in income taxes, even though he has not sold his vacation property, and has no cash with which to pay this tax. If Murray had simply appointed Josee as his beneficiary in his will, his vacation property could have continued to increase in value on a tax-deferred basis, with the capital gain becoming payable only upon his death.



If Murray had added two joint owners, then he would have been deemed to have disposed of two-thirds of the property, instead of one-half. The deemed disposition is calculated on a pro rata basis, based on how many owners there were prior to adding the joint owner, and how many joint owners there are after adding the joint owner.

### *22.3.1.2 Loss of Control*

Once you add a joint owner to the asset, you give up control over the asset. Since there will now be more than one owner, you will no longer be able to simply mortgage the property or sell the asset without the consent of the other owner. Some people soon come to regret their decision to add a joint owner when they realize the headaches inherit in obtaining consent to deal with the property. There have been situations where parents have added several children as joint owners of a property, and then been shocked to learn that some or all of their children are not willing to give consent to the sale of the property when the parents decide that is what they would like to do. If you are truly ready to hand over an asset, then in many cases it is usually better to gift it completely. Owning an asset with another individual can lead to complications and disputes between family members.

If the asset is one where any joint owner may deal with the property (for example, a bank account), then you may be able to access funds without the other owner's consent — the problem is that the other owner will be able to do that as well, so they could choose to deplete the account without your knowledge.

### 22.3.1.3 *Unintentional Unequal Treatment of Beneficiaries*

Many parents who add a child as a joint owner of an asset do so solely for the purpose of saving probate. However, if the asset is held with a right of survivorship, the child will receive the asset at the time of the parent's death, and it is possible that the other children or beneficiaries will never know that the asset existed. Even though the parents may have intended to share their assets equally between all of their children (and in fact stated so in their will), they are taking a significant risk of this not happening if they only add one child as a beneficiary. Although the law presumes that amounts held in joint ownership with an adult child are held in trust for the estate, this presumption may be rebutted. If the child argues that the asset was a form of payment for care services provided to the parent, for example, they may be able to convince a court that they should keep the asset, and share in the remainder of the estate as well.

Some parents feel the way to avoid this problem is to add all of their children as beneficiaries. However, this does not alleviate the possibility that a beneficiary will be disinherited. Let's look at our example again.

> Let's assume that Murray added both of his children, Ron and Josee, as joint owners of his vacation property and signed a document indicating that they were true joint owners of the property. He also made them each 50% beneficiaries of his estate, which did not include very much. He did this so that each of Ron and Josee would receive an equal interest in the vacation property, and as equal beneficiaries of his estate, would each be responsible for bearing an equal portion of the tax burden prior to receiving anything from the estate.
>
> Unfortunately, Ron dies shortly before Murray dies, and Murray does not have an opportunity to change his estate plan prior to his death. As a result of the death of both of Ron and Murray, Josee remains the sole owner of the vacation property. Also, as a result of the tax liability on the vacation property, there is almost nothing left in the estate after the tax bill is paid.
>
> However, a problem arises because Ron had two children, who have now been completely disinherited. Not only did they not receive the vacation property, but there is nothing left in the estate due to the tax liability. To make matters worse, since Ron was a joint owner, Ron's estate is responsible for paying tax on part of the capital gain on the vacation property, even though Ron's beneficiaries will never receive that asset. Murray's intention had been to treat Ron and Josee equally, with the intent that if either of them predeceased him, their share would go to their children. Although this

is what his will said, this was not what resulted, since the vacation property was not distributed according to his will. In the end, Josee received almost the entire estate, and Ron's children were left with nothing. Although Murray thought that adding a joint owner was a simple and smart thing to do, it turned out to be just the opposite. Murray should have conferred with his professional advisors prior to carrying out this plan.



### 22.3.1.4 Exposure to Family Law Claims

Once the property is jointly owned with someone else, the asset could become exposed to a family property claim. If the asset is "acquired" during the course of a marriage (and in some jurisdictions, during the course of a common-law relationship), or increases in value, all or part of the asset could become shareable in a division of family property. Also, in some jurisdictions, if the asset is a "family home" (which could include a vacation property that a child and his or her spouse and children use), then a separated or divorced spouse could potentially have a claim against the asset even if it was acquired prior to the marriage or common-law relationship (see section 17.4 of Chapter 17, "Family Property", for an explanation of the family property rules in each jurisdiction).

In some provinces, it is possible to state in a will that amounts given to a beneficiary are not to be considered family property, and the growth on the asset is not to be divisible. If the beneficiary keeps the inheritance separate from the family assets, it is possible that the inheritance will be exempt from a division of family property. However, if an asset is given to a beneficiary by virtue of joint ownership, you will have lost the opportunity to add this condition to the gift. If you want to ensure that any amounts left to your beneficiaries are not divisible, then it may be recommended that you leave the asset through your will (or a declaration of gift), and include the proper clause. However, this provision is not effective in every jurisdiction. See section 17.4 of Chapter 17, "Family Property", for a discussion of the rules in your jurisdiction.

### 22.3.1.5 Tax Liability for Estate

At the time of death, the automatic transfer of the asset to someone other than the estate could result in inequities in the payment of taxes resulting from the asset since the estate will owe taxes on an asset it no longer owns. This is not an issue if prior to the time of death, the only owners of the property were two individuals who were either legally married, or living common-law, as defined in the *Income Tax Act*, since most assets can rollover to spouses and common-law partners on a tax-deferred basis (see section 3.3 of Chapter 3, "Common-Law Couples", for a description of when a couple is considered to be living common-law under the *Income Tax Act*). Also, if the joint owner is an adult child who is holding the asset in trust for the estate, then the asset will form part of the estate and will be available to cover any tax liability. However, if the surviving joint owner is someone other than a spouse or common-law partner and the joint owner is a true owner who receives the asset upon the death of the original owner, this could be problematic. Let's look at our example again.

> Murray had a vacation property worth $500,000 and he added only his daughter Josee as a joint owner (and indicated in writing that she was to receive the asset at the time of his death). Murray originally paid $100,000 for the vacation property, but was deemed to have disposed of 50% of it when he added his daughter Josee as a joint owner. Therefore, Murray's cost base on his remaining 50% ownership is $50,000.
>
> At the time of Murray's death, the vacation property is worth $600,000, and it is transferred into Josee's name only, since she is the joint owner, with a right of survivorship. Murray also had a son, Ron. Murray decided to leave Ron his home and other assets, which were worth approximately $600,000. Murray assumed that he was treating Ron and Josee equally, since he left them each $600,000 in assets. He also thought he was doing a good thing for the estate as a whole, since the $600,000 vacation property that went to Josee did not have to go through probate, which would have resulted in over $6000 in probate fees in Murray's jurisdiction.
>
> Unfortunately, Murray forgot about the fact that he still owned half of the vacation property for tax purposes. At the time he added Josee as a joint owner, he paid tax on the first half of the capital gain (as calculated in section 22.3.1.1). However, at the time of his death, his estate will be responsible for paying tax on the other 50% of the capital gain, even though his estate did not receive the asset itself. At the time of his death, Murray's half of the vacation property was worth $300,000, and his cost base was $50,000. Therefore, the amount of the capital gain will be $250,000 (calculated as $300,000 – $50,000), half of which ($125,000) must be included in his final tax return. His estate will be responsible for paying over $50,000 in taxes.
>
> Unfortunately, it will be Ron who will be responsible for paying the entire amount of the taxes, since he is the sole beneficiary of the estate. Josee will be entitled to keep the vacation property, but the estate must pay the $50,000 tax bill before transferring anything to Ron. This means that Ron

will only receive $550,000 instead of $600,000, and since the assets he was to inherit were the principal residence and personal effects, he may have to sell some of them to pay the taxes. Obviously, Murray did not achieve his objective of leaving his children equal amounts of his estate.

### 22.3.1.6 Lost Opportunities to Use a Trust



Another problem with adding a joint owner is the inability to transfer the asset into a testamentary trust. In many of the chapters in this book, we have discussed the advantages of using testamentary trusts for control purposes, and for income splitting purposes. Below is a summary of some of the situations where we discussed the importance of using testamentary trusts.

- Where the beneficiaries are in a high tax bracket and do not require the immediate use of the funds, it may be better to put the funds in trust, so that the beneficiary can income-split with the trust, and pay less tax overall. (See section 5.5.2 of Chapter 5, "Married", and section 10.5.4 of Chapter 10, "Children".)

- In a blended family situation, one of the potential strategies for distributing an estate, which considers both the new spouse or common-law partner and the children from a previous marriage, is to give the assets to the new spouse in trust. Although the spouse may use the assets during his or her lifetime, he or she will not be entitled to give the estate assets away to whomever he or she pleases at the time of his or her death. At the time of death of the second spouse, the assets will revert back to the children of the first spouse, ensuring that no one will be disinherited. (See section 8.5.2.1 of Chapter 8, "Blended Families".)

- Where some of the potential beneficiaries are minors, trusts can be used to ensure that the minors do not receive the trust funds until they are mature enough to manage them, and the will can designate who will act as trustee of the trust, so that the provincial authorities will not step in (see section 10.5.3 of Chapter 10, "Children").

- Where there is a disabled beneficiary, and the intent is to preserve that beneficiary's right to social assistance payments, an individual may wish to use what is commonly known as a Henson trust so that the disabled person does not have direct access to the funds (see section 12.3.1 of Chapter 12, "Disabled Persons").

If for these (or any other) reasons a testamentary trust has been established in a will, then it will be very important that the assets that are intended to go into the trust, do actually pass through the will. If the assets pass by way of joint ownership, then the provisions of the will are irrelevant. For example, in a blended family situation, if the parents establish testamentary trusts in their wills, but then proceed to put all of their assets in joint ownership, none of the assets will be held on the conditions set out in the will. That will mean that upon the death of the first spouse, all of the assets will pass to the second spouse. At the time of death of the second spouse, it is very likely that their assets will go to their children only, or perhaps a new spouse, completely disinheriting the children of the first spouse. (Note that this is not relevant in the province of Quebec, as jointly held property in that province does not include a right of survivorship.)

### *22.3.1.7 Nullify Domestic Contracts*

Adding a joint owner can nullify the provisions of a domestic contract. If two spouses or common-law partners enter into a domestic contract in which they agree that if they separate, any property that was in their names at the time of the marriage will continue to be theirs, this agreement could be nullified, with respect to a particular asset, if a joint owner is added. When a spouse is added as a joint owner to an asset, the presumption is that the intent is to share the asset. If the parties have entered into a domestic contract, extreme caution should be used prior to adding a spouse or common-law partner as a joint owner to an asset.

Even if there is no domestic contract, adding a joint owner to a property can still affect the division of property at the time of marriage breakdown. For example, some jurisdictions specifically exempt certain types of property (such as property acquired prior to the time of marriage, or property received as an inheritance). In order to maintain this exempt status, it is usually necessary that this property be kept separate from the family assets. By adding the other spouse as a joint owner to the property, it is likely that the asset will lose its exempt status, and become shareable at the time of marriage breakdown. In some jurisdictions, these rules also apply to common-law relationships. See section 17.4 of Chapter 17, "Family Property", for a description of the family property rules in your jurisdiction.

### *22.3.1.8 Joint Ownership with a Resident of Quebec*

As mentioned above, there is no right of survivorship when a property is held jointly in Quebec. The anomaly between the law in the common-law jurisdictions and the law in Quebec can cause some uncertainty when one or more of the joint owners is a non-resident of Quebec, and one or more of the joint owners is a resident of Quebec — is there a right of survivorship, or isn't there? The answer may depend upon whether the non-resident of Quebec dies first. Due to the uncertainty, it is recommended that all parties document the relationship to indicate that there is no right of survivorship, and then amend their will to ensure that their interest in the property is properly distributed at the time of their death.



As can be seen from the above discussion, adding a joint owner can bring with it more problems than it is worth. Although it may appear to be an innocuous thing to do, and the probate savings are attractive, it may in fact be the worst thing you could do for your estate. Be sure to confer with a professional prior to changing the registration on any of your assets. There are some situations where adding a joint owner may be appropriate, and some lawyers are able to draft documents indicating that the joint ownership arrangement is for probate purposes only, avoiding many of the problems listed above. However, if you do not receive the appropriate advice, adding a joint owner can be very problematic for your estate.

## 22.3.2 Gifting Property

Giving an asset will have many of the same results as adding a joint owner, except obviously, title to the entire asset is transferred to the new owner, not just a portion of it. Gifting an asset could result in a capital gains liability, the original owner will lose control over the property, and the property may become exposed to the creditors of the new owners, or become the subject of a family property claim.

It is also possible that family members could be treated differently at the time of death. For example, if one child was to receive the gifted asset, and another child was to be left the assets in the estate, the child who received the estate may receive less than expected, if the estate is smaller than anticipated due to long-term care costs incurred by the parent, or a tax liability. Since part of the estate will have passed to a beneficiary directly due to the gift, the personal representatives will not have the ability to equalize the estate.

From a tax perspective, the one major difference between giving a gift and adding a joint ownership is that when a gift is made, the entire capital gain will be triggered, whereas with joint ownership, only a portion of the gain is triggered at the time of adding a joint owner, and a portion at the time of death. Note that when a property is gifted (either completely, or partially by adding a joint owner), that the cost base to the new owner is equal to the fair market value of the property on the date of the gift. Let's go back to our example.

> If Murray gives the entire vacation property to Josee at a time when it is worth $500,000, her cost base will be $500,000 and Murray will have an immediate capital gain of $400,000 ($500,000 - $100,000 cost base), half of which ($200,000) is taxable. Any capital gain that accrues from that date forward will be taxable in Josee's name only, not Murray's. If he adds her as a joint owner only, her cost base will be $250,000, and she will be responsible for paying tax on 50% of the gain from that date forward (if, in fact, there was an intention to transfer part of the property, and not simply make Josee a trustee of the property).

If you do decide to make a gift, try to either time the gift when the gain is lower (if the asset fluctuates in value), consider a series of gifts over a few taxation years to spread the tax payable over a number of years, or make the gift when you have unused capital losses, as a capital gain can be offset by a capital loss.

## 22.3.3 Selling the Property for Less than Fair Market Value

Some people think that they can avoid paying taxes on the capital gain by selling the asset for a small amount. Unfortunately, this is generally not true. If you sell an asset to a non-arm's length party (for example, a child), then you will be deemed to have received fair market value for the property, even if you have received much less. In addition, a sale for less than fair market value to a non-arm's length party can effectively lead to double taxation. Let's go back to our case study.

> What would have happened if Murray had sold the vacation property to Josee instead of adding her as a joint owner or gifting it to her? Murray decides that he no longer needs the vacation property, and he does not want it to form a part of his estate when he dies. He believes that not only will he save probate fees by doing this, but this will also reduce the income tax bill for his estate. Murray decides to sell the vacation property to Josee for $100,000, which is the amount he originally paid for it, even though it

is currently worth $500,000. He believes that by doing this, he will avoid all of the capital gain.

Unfortunately, because Josee is Murray's daughter, and they therefore do not act at arm's length, the Canada Revenue Agency will deem Murray to have received $500,000 for the vacation property, which is its fair market value at the time it is transferred to Josee. This will result in a $400,000 capital gain for Murray, $200,000 of which must be included in his tax return for that year. Murray may be responsible for paying almost $90,000 in tax (depending you where you live), even though Josee only paid him slightly more than that.



An even bigger problem arises when Josee decides that she needs the money to buy a house, so she wants to sell the vacation property. As we mentioned above, if Murray had given the vacation property to Josee, her cost base would have been $500,000. Therefore, if she sold it for $600,000 at a later date, her capital gain would be $100,000, resulting in approximately $22,000 in tax (a $100,000 capital gain results in $50,000 of taxable income). Unfortunately, if Murray sells it to Josee for $100,000, her cost base is only $100,000, since that is all she paid for it. Therefore, if she later sells the vacation property for $600,000, her capital gain will be $500,000 ($600,000 minus $100,000), resulting in a taxable gain of $250,000, and about $110,000 in tax.

The conclusion is that from a tax perspective, selling an asset for less than fair market value can result in double taxation. Not only did Murray have to pay tax on the capital gain over his $100,000 cost base, but Josee had to as well. If you are making a decision as to whether or not to gift an asset, or sell it for less than fair market value (e.g. for $1), it is much more tax effective to gift the asset, since the recipient's cost base will be the fair market value of the asset at the time of the gift. If you sell the asset for $1, the purchaser's cost base will only be $1, even if the asset was worth far more than that on the date of sale.

### 22.3.4 Selling an Asset for More than Fair Market Value

Problems can also arise if a person sells an asset for more than fair market value. Let's look at our example again.

Let's assume that Murray is experiencing financial difficulties, whereas Josee is financially well-off. They decide that Murray is going to sell his vacation property to Josee for $600,000, even though they know that it is only worth $500,000. When Murray files his tax return for that year, he will have to report the fact that he sold the vacation property for $600,000. Since his cost base was only $100,000, he will have a capital gain of $500,000, $250,000 of which will be taxable.

Later on, Josee decides that she would like to sell the vacation property. The vacation property has risen in value from $500,000 to $600,000, but Josee believes that she will not have to pay tax on the gain, since she paid $600,000 for the vacation property, so that should be her cost base. Unfortunately, Josee is mistaken. Since Josee was not dealing at arm's length with Murray, her cost base will be the fair market value for the property at the time at which she purchased it, which was $500,000. Therefore, Josee will have to pay tax on 50% of the difference between $500,000 and $600,000, even though Murray has already paid tax on the same gain. This plan has resulted in double taxation — obviously Murray and Josee should have conferred with their tax advisors prior to embarking on such a plan.

## 22.3.5 Transferring the Asset into a Trust

Another method that can be used to avoid probate is the use of an *inter vivos* trust, which is a trust established during your lifetime (as opposed to a testamentary trust, which is a trust established in your last will and testament). *Inter vivos* trusts are only useful in very limited circumstances (unlike testamentary trusts, which are used quite frequently in estate planning). When an asset is transferred to a trust, legal title to the asset is held in the name of the trustee or trustees for the benefit of the beneficiaries. Therefore, when an individual transfers an asset into a trust, they will no longer hold legal title to the asset, and the asset will not need to go through probate at the time of their death. After the original owner dies, the trustees will transfer the asset to the beneficiaries pursuant to the terms of the trust, and no probate fees will be payable. Also, if the original owner wants to avoid the probate process for some reason (e.g. confidentiality), this strategy will help them to achieve that objective.

From a tax perspective, assets that are transferred into a trust will generally be deemed to have been disposed of at the time of transfer into the trust.

In our example, if Murray transfers the vacation property to a trust when it is worth $500,000, he will trigger a $400,000 capital gain, since his cost base is only $100,000.

However, in certain circumstances, the Canada Revenue Agency will allow you to transfer assets into a trust on a "rollover" basis, meaning that the capital gain on the asset will not be triggered at the time of the transfer. There are three types of trusts where this is allowed: spousal trusts, alter ego trusts and joint partner trusts. Here are the conditions that must be present in order to have a trust that allows a rollover of property under the *Income Tax Act*:



### 22.3.5.1 Spousal Trusts

In order to have a valid spousal trust under the *Income Tax Act*, here are some of the conditions that must be met:

- the spouse must be entitled to receive all of the income generated by the trust every year;
- no one other than the spouse may be entitled to use any of the capital of the trust until the time of the spouse's death;
- the trust must be created by a Canadian resident; and
- the trust itself must be a resident of Canada, meaning that the trustee, or a majority of the trustees, should be resident in Canada (please see section 23.4.1 for a further discussion regarding the residency of a trust).

With a spousal trust, a disposition of the assets will occur upon the death of the spouse, even if the original owner is still alive. Note that all references to a spouse include a common-law partner, as defined in the *Income Tax Act* (see section 3.3 of Chapter 3, "Common-Law Couples", for a description of when an individual is considered a common-law partner under the *Income Tax Act*).

Although spousal trusts are used quite regularly when established as testamentary trusts, they are very rarely used as *inter vivos* trusts for probate planning.

### 22.3.5.2 Alter Ego Trusts

In order to have a valid alter ego trust under the *Income Tax Act*, here are some of the conditions that must be met:

- the person who transferred the assets into the trust (the "transferor") must be entitled to receive all of the income generated by the trust, every year;

- no one other than the transferor may be entitled to use any of the capital of the trust until the time of the transferor's death;
- the transferor must be at least 65 years of age at the time of transfer;
- the trust must be created by a Canadian resident; and
- the trust itself must be a resident of Canada, meaning that the trustee, or a majority of the trustees, should be resident in Canada (please see section 23.4.1 for a further discussion regarding the residency of a trust).

With an alter ego trust, a disposition of the assets will occur upon the death of the original owner.

### 22.3.5.3 Joint Partner Trusts

In order to have a valid joint partner trust under the *Income Tax Act*, here are some of the conditions that must be met:

- the transferor must be entitled to receive all of the income generated by the trust, every year;
- no one other than the transferor, or their spouse or common-law partner, may be entitled to use any of the capital of the trust until the time of death of the transferor and their spouse or common-law partner;
- the transferor must be at least 65 years of age at the time of transfer;
- the trust must be created by a Canadian resident; and
- the trust itself must be a resident of Canada, meaning that the trustee, or a majority of the trustees, should be resident in Canada (please see section 23.4.1 for a further discussion regarding the residency of a trust).

With a joint partner trust, a disposition of the assets will occur upon the death of the last of the transferor and their spouse or common-law partner.

### 22.3.5.4 Disadvantages to Using an Inter Vivos Trust

Unfortunately, there are many disadvantages to using these types of *inter vivos* trusts — in fact, too many to discuss here. However, below is a brief discussion of some of the major disadvantages.

- Every dollar of income earned in an *inter vivos* trust is taxed at the highest marginal tax rate (as opposed to testamentary trusts, which have access to the graduated rates of tax). If the assets are transferred to an *alter ego trust,* then at the time of the death of the transferor, all of the assets in the trust will be deemed to have been disposed of in the trust, meaning that the entire amount will be taxed at the highest marginal rate (this will happen at the time of death of the spouse or common-law partner in the case of a spousal trust, or at the time of death of the last survivor in the case of a joint partner trust). Had the disposition occurred in the name of the deceased, it is possible that some of the gain would have been taxed at a lower tax rate.

- At the time of death, the trustees will distribute all of the trust assets to the beneficiaries. If the terms of the trust provide that the trust assets are to be given to certain beneficiaries in trust (for example, because the beneficiaries are minors, or one of the beneficiaries is disabled), then that new trust will also be considered to be an *inter vivos* trust because it was created by an *inter vivos* trust. Therefore, all of the income earned in that trust will also be taxed at the highest marginal rate. If the trust had instead been established in a will, it would have been considered a testamentary trust, and the tax paid on the income earned in the trust may have been much less. By using an *inter vivos* trust to save probate, the estate may potentially pay much more income tax overall, by losing the ability to create testamentary trusts after the time of death.

- If the assets that are transferred into the trust experience a loss, then that loss may go unused. That is because losses inside of a trust cannot be transferred out to the beneficiaries. Therefore, if the deceased had income in the year of death that is taxable (for example, due to the de-registration of his or her RRSPs), and the trust had losses, the estate will not be able to use the losses to offset the income in the year of death. If the deceased had simply kept the assets in his or her own name, it is possible that the losses could have been used to reduce the taxable income owing by the deceased in the year of death. Once again, the desire to save a relatively small amount of probate, could result in a larger income tax bill.

- Since these trusts must be drafted in a very specific manner in order to meet the conditions previously discussed, you will need to see a lawyer to ensure that the trusts are created properly, which can result in significant expense, depending upon the complexity of the terms of the trust. In addition, there may be administrative requirements in terms of additional bank accounts, tax returns, etc.

As can be seen, the use of a trust must be considered carefully before it is used as part of an estate plan. If you believe that an *inter vivos* trust may be useful in your situation, confer with an estate planning expert prior to implementing this type of plan.

## 22.3.6 Designating a Direct Beneficiary

Another mechanism that is often used to save probate is the use of direct beneficiary designations. These designations, which are permitted with certain types of plans, such as insurance policies, segregated funds, Registered Retirement Savings Plans and Registered Retirement Income Funds, allow funds to be paid directly to a beneficiary, by-passing the probate process. However, as with transferring assets prior to the time of death, direct beneficiary designations have many traps for the unwary, and careful consideration should be given prior to designating anyone as a direct beneficiary. Below are some of the issues that should be considered when designating a beneficiary.

- If the asset in question is an RRSP or a RRIF, then consideration must be given to the tax implications to the estate. If the beneficiary is a spouse, common-law partner, minor child or disabled child, then the tax consequences can be deferred by transferring the funds to the RRSP of the spouse or a registered annuity for the child (see section 21.2.5 of Chapter 21, "Taxation at Death", for more information). However, if the beneficiary is someone other than the spouse, common-law partner, minor child or disabled child, then generally speaking, the estate will be responsible for paying tax on the entire amount in the plan at the time of death. Therefore, if one adult child is designated as the beneficiary of an RRSP worth $300,000, and the other adult child is given the estate which is also worth $300,000, the child who receives the estate will in effect receive much less than the child who receives the RRSP. This is because the estate will be responsible for paying all the taxes on the RRSP (as well as paying any other taxes owing on the estate assets), and only the remainder will be given to the beneficiary of the estate. In contrast, the person who receives the RRSP proceeds will receive the gross amount held in the plan. Only once the estate has been completely depleted will the Canada Revenue

Agency approach the beneficiary of the RRSP to cover the remaining tax liability. (Direct beneficiaries on registered assets are not effective in all cases in Quebec.)

- In many cases, individuals designate beneficiaries who are not capable of managing the funds themselves. For example, if a minor child is designated as a direct beneficiary, then it is likely that the Public Trustee, or other governmental authority will have authority to manage the funds, causing unnecessary expense for the estate. In addition, the child will be entitled to receive the funds upon attaining the age of majority, which may still be too young to use the funds responsibly. As discussed in section 10.5.3 of Chapter 10, "Children", in many cases it is necessary to put controls on the funds, and distribute them gradually over a period of time. If you want the terms of the trust to prevail, then all of your assets must pass through the estate. If the assets pass directly to a beneficiary, the terms of the will become irrelevant.

- Many estate plans incorporate the use of testamentary trusts in order to achieve their objectives. For example, a spousal trust may be used in a blended family scenario, a Henson trust may be used for a disabled beneficiary, or testamentary trusts may be used for income splitting where the beneficiaries are in high tax brackets and wish to reduce the amount of income tax payable. If assets are distributed to a beneficiary directly, then these objectives will not be met, as the trust will be circumvented. Many individuals do not realize that they could be sabotaging their estate plan when they add a direct beneficiary — if you have a properly drafted will that includes a testamentary trust, be sure to confer with your professional advisors prior to designating any direct beneficiaries on any of your assets.

- Insurance is often required as part of an estate plan, either to pay creditors or other liabilities (such as taxes), or in order to equalize an estate (for example, where one child is to receive a large asset such as a vacation property or family business, and the insurance proceeds are to be given to another child). If the insurance proceeds are paid directly to a beneficiary, then the personal representative of the estate may not be able to use the insurance proceeds in the anticipated manner. It is very important that any funds intended to be used by the estate be paid to the estate.

- In some jurisdictions, courts will "claw-back" assets that have been distributed outside of an estate in the event a claim is made by a dependant of the estate. For further information on whether this is an issue in your jurisdiction, see section 19.6 of Chapter 19, "Distribution of an Estate".

Therefore, the person you intended to receive the money may not in fact receive it.

- A particular problem can arise in the context of pensions and locked-in accounts. Generally speaking, spouses and common-law partners (as defined under provincial pension legislation) are entitled to receive pension and locked-in payments, regardless of whether or not a beneficiary designation has been made in favour of someone else. Therefore, if you designate a child as a direct beneficiary of a pension and you have a surviving spouse, the direct designation in favour of the child may be treated as void, and the payments may be made to the spouse, which was obviously not your intention. In some cases, a spouse may be entitled to waive their rights to the payments, but in the case of locked-in accounts, the estate is still liable for the tax payable on the plan if the payments are made to a non-spouse, assuming there is no tax deferral available when the proceeds of the locked-in plan are paid to the child. If the spouse is the beneficiary of the estate, the payment of the tax liability for the locked-in plan may result in him or her receiving less than anticipated. Be very careful when dealing with pensions and locked-in plans, as the prevailing pension legislation may operate at cross-purposes with your intentions.

Despite all of the disadvantages to adding a direct beneficiary, there are some cases where there may be an advantage.

- If you confirm with your advisors that no harm will be done to your estate by designating a beneficiary, then the payment of funds directly to a beneficiary may help to reduce probate fees.

- The payment of assets outside of an estate can help to avoid creditors of the estate. In fact, in some cases, the designation of a direct beneficiary can even help to protect an asset from creditors while the owner is still alive. For example, in some jurisdictions, the cash value of a life insurance policy that designates a spouse, child, grandchild or parent of the life insured as a beneficiary is protected from creditors, so long as the policy was not purchased with the intent to defraud creditors. This protection may be available even if the beneficiary is not one of the above listed individuals, if the designation is irrevocable. See section 25.4 of Chapter 25, "Insurance", for a list of "protected beneficiaries" in your jurisdiction.

When you transfer an RRSP into a RRIF, be sure to designate the beneficiary on the RRIF in the same manner as it was designated on the RRSP. A beneficiary designation will not automatically continue in the new plan.

## 22.3.7 Insurance Trusts

As discussed in section 22.3.6, designating a direct beneficiary on a life insurance product will result in that asset going directly to the designated beneficiary, and, therefore, probate will not be assessed against that asset. However, this strategy can lead to many problems and inequities, and in many cases is not recommended. However, one strategy that does provide for a probate savings while avoiding the problems discussed in section 22.3.6 is the use of an insurance trust.

The insurance legislation in most jurisdictions allows funds to be distributed according to the deceased's will, but still avoid probate, if there is an insurance trust that refers to the proper provision in the relevant insurance statute. It is possible to distribute the assets according to an insurance trust either in the will or in a document separate from the will. However, if the insurance trust is created in a separate declaration, it is important that the trust not be effective until the time of death, as the tax treatment of a testamentary trust is more favourable than for trusts created prior to the time of death. Insurance trusts sometimes need to be created outside of a will, particularly if the insurance is owned by more than one person. A person can create an insurance trust in their will only if they are the sole owner of the insurance policy.

One potential drawback with an insurance trust is the potential to lose the ability to protect the cash surrender value of the insurance policy from the insured's creditors during the lifetime of the insured person. In some cases, the cash surrender value of an insurance policy may be protected from creditors if an individual in the "protected class" is designated as the beneficiary of the policy (the protected class usually includes spouses and children, but see section 25.4 of Chapter 25, "Insurance", for a description of the individuals who are considered to be in the protected class in your jurisdiction). If you designate a trustee of an insurance trust as the beneficiary of the policy, and the trustee is not a member of the protected class, the cash surrender value will not be protected from creditors. In these cases, it may be recommended that you file a beneficiary designation with the insurance company before the will or separate insurance declaration is signed. The insurance trust declaration in the will or separate declaration is then signed to indicate that it is an insurance trust, but the designation on file with the insurance company will still indicate that the insurance policy is protected. However, in some provinces, adding a direct beneficiary will not prevent the insurance proceeds from a potential claim by a dependant (see the Dependants' Relief section of section 19.6 of Chapter 19, "Distribution of an Estate", for information on your jurisdiction). Speak to your lawyer about this issue if creditor protection is a concern for you.

There is also some question as to whether or not these types of trusts are effective in Quebec. If you are resident in Quebec, speak with your lawyer prior to implementing this strategy.

By creating an insurance trust as part of your estate plan, you can ensure that your insurance proceeds are properly distributed, and subject to the types of controls that are usually placed on assets held in trust. In addition, the disadvantages of direct beneficiary designations may be avoided, and no probate is payable. Speak to your estate planning lawyer about how to word the beneficiary designation on your insurance policy to ensure this strategy is effective.

## 22.3.8 Reducing the Net Value of an Estate

If an asset must go through probate, probate fees are calculated against the gross value of the estate, without taking into account any taxes or liabilities that may be owing in respect of those assets. The one major exception to this rule is the deduction of real property mortgages — if debt has been secured by a mortgage registered against real property, this amount usually may be deducted from the amount of the estate that is subject to probate fees. If you own real estate with no mortgage, and you also owe money (perhaps on a line of credit or a car loan), consider having the debt converted to a line of credit or mortgage secured against the real estate. It may then reduce the value of the real estate for probate purposes.

Another strategy to consider if you have large amounts of unsecured debt is to transfer all of your assets along with the debt to a corporation. At the time of your death, the value of your estate will include the value of your shares, but their value will be reduced by the amount of debt inside the corporation, regardless of whether or not the debt is registered as a real property mortgage. However, you should exercise caution if you are transferring assets to an active corporation. Shares of a qualifying small business corporation may qualify for the $750,000 capital gains exemption, but only if the assets of the corporation meet the various tests in the *Income Tax Act*, including the need to limit the amount of passive assets in the corporation. Therefore, if you have an active business corporation, it may be better to transfer passive assets into a separate corporation in order to preserve the ability to use the $750,000 capital gains exemption on the shares of the active corporation. Due to the costs involved, this strategy should not be implemented without speaking to an advisor.

## 22.3.9 Multiple Wills

In some jurisdictions, it may be possible to have two wills, each distributing a part of the estate — one will to distribute assets that must go through probate (e.g. real property), and one will to distribute assets that do not need to go through probate (e.g. shares in a private corporation where the directors are willing to transfer title without a probated will). Since there have been very few cases addressing this issue, the effectiveness of this strategy in many jurisdictions is still open to debate. So far, only the courts in Ontario have specifically allowed this strategy.

If you live in a jurisdiction where multiple wills are effective (or may be effective), it is extremely important that you speak to an estate planning lawyer with expertise in this area, as multiple wills are somewhat difficult to draft. For example, the first clause in most wills revokes all previous wills — if you want more than one will to be in effect simultaneously, this revocation clause will obviously have to be worded differently. Also, you will need to consider how to allocate taxes and debts between the different assets to ensure that the net effect of the distribution is as you intended.

This strategy could prove to be particularly effective if you first transfer some or all of your assets into a holding company. If the directors of the holding company are family members, it is likely that they will agree to transfer the shares to the beneficiaries named in your will without demanding a grant of probate. Since your estate will be comprised only (or mostly) of shares in the holding company that can be transferred through the will that does not have to go through probate, the amount paid in probate fees will be minimized.

## 22.3.10 Buying Property in Alberta

Generally, an estate is probated in the jurisdiction in which the deceased was domiciled at the time of death. However, if you would prefer to have your estate probated in Alberta (where probate fees are almost non-existent), consider buying real property there. Alberta allows anyone who owns real property in that province to have their estate probated there. Keep in mind, however, that you may need to have your will "resealed" in another province if you own real property in another province. You should not implement this strategy without speaking to an estate planning specialist.

If you want to ensure that your estate will not need to go through probate in any other province, consider transferring all of your real property to a corporation. At that point, only the shares of the corporation will need to be probated (which will not be a significant problem if you are able to probate your estate in Alberta), or you may be able to use the multiple will strategy discussed in section 22.3.9.

## 22.3.11 Proper Will Drafting

Some of the simplest methods to avoid unnecessary probate fees involve the inclusion of proper clauses in your will.

- If you are leaving your entire estate to a spouse or common-law partner, ensure there is a common disaster clause that indicates that if you both die within a short period of time (e.g. usually 10-30 days), your estate will automatically go to your contingent beneficiaries. If this clause is not inserted in the will, and you and your spouse die in a common accident, all of your assets may first have to go through probate when they are distributed to your spouse or partner, and then again when they are distributed according to their will.

- In many cases, when leaving an estate to a spouse or a common-law partner, it is recommended that assets be left to a spousal or common-law partner trust (see section 5.5.2 of Chapter 5, "Married", for more information on these types of trusts). If you leave your estate to your spouse or partner in trust, then the assets in the trust will not need to be probated again when your spouse or partner passes away.

## 22.3.12 Universal Life Insurance

Assets that accumulate in an insurance policy, and are then distributed via a direct beneficiary designation, or an insurance trust, will not pass through probate. As discussed in section 25.2.3 of Chapter 25, "Insurance", it is possible to purchase insurance policies that have not only an insurance component, but also serve as a method of investment. Although these types of policies are generally not recommended unless there is an insurance need, the ability to invest within the policy may bring with it both income tax and probate fee advantages. Not only will the investments grow on a tax-deferred basis within the policy, but they can be paid out to a direct beneficiary or insurance trust without paying probate fees at the time of death. Note from the discussion in section 22.3.6 that direct beneficiary designations should be used sparingly — in most cases, as discussed in section 22.3.7, an insurance trust would be the recommended strategy for distributing the proceeds of an insurance policy.

# 22.4 JURISDICTION DIFFERENCES

## 22.4.1 Alberta

Probate fees in Alberta are extremely low. They are as follows:

- $25 for estates worth $10,000 or less;
- $100 for estates worth more than $10,000, but less than $25,000;
- $200 for estates worth more than $25,000, but less than $125,000;
- $300 for estates worth more than $125,000, but less than $250,000; and
- $400 for estates worth more than $250,000.

Probate fees in Alberta are calculated based on the value of the net estate, not the gross estate. If the deceased was resident in Alberta, then probate will be charged on all real property located in Alberta as well as the deceased's personal property.

## 22.4.2 British Columbia

In British Columbia, no probate fees are charged for estates with a gross value of less than $25,000. A percentage of .6% is charged for estates with a gross value of between $25,000 and $50,000. For estates with a gross value of more than $50,000, a fee of $150 is charged plus a percentage rate of 1.4% on the portion in excess of $50,000. If the deceased was resident in British Columbia at the time of death, then probate will be charged on all real property located in British Columbia as well as all of the deceased's personal property, wherever located.

## 22.4.3 Manitoba

In Manitoba, if the estate has a gross value of less than $10,000, it will be charged $70. If the gross value is equal to or more than $10,000, a fee of $70 plus a percentage rate of .7% on the portion of the estate worth more than $10,000 will be charged against the gross value. In Manitoba, all real estate is subject to probate, whether or not it is located in Manitoba, as well as all personal property owned by the deceased.

### 22.4.4 New Brunswick

In New Brunswick, a percentage rate of .5% is charged on estates with a gross value over $20,000. For smaller estates, a flat fee is charged as follows:

- $25 for estates worth less than $5000;
- $50 for estates worth less than $10,000;
- $75 for estates worth less than $15,000; and
- $100 for estates worth less than $20,000.

Fees are payable on the value of the whole estate, less the value of any encumbrance on real property.

### 22.4.5 Newfoundland

Probate fees are $60 where the value of the estate does not exceed $1000. Where the value of an estate exceeds $1000, the probate fees are $60 plus $0.50 for each additional $100 in the value of the estate. Only the value of assets located within the province is included in the calculation.

### 22.4.6 Northwest Territories

The probate fees assessed against the value of all property, real and personal, within the Northwest Territories, after deducting all debts and liabilities against that property are:

- $25 for estates worth $10,000 or less;
- $100 for estates worth more than $10,000 but not more than $25,000;
- $200 for estates worth more than $25,000 but not more than $125,000;
- $300 for estates worth more than $125,000 but not more than $250,000; and

- $400 for estates worth more than $250,000.

### 22.4.7 Nova Scotia

In Nova Scotia, probate fees are charged as follows:

- for estates not exceeding $10,000, $77;
- for estates exceeding $10,000 but not exceeding $25,000, $193.61;
- for estates exceeding $25,000 but not exceeding $50,000, $322.21;
- for estates exceeding $50,000 but not exceeding $100,000, $902.03; and
- for estates exceeding $100,000, $902.03 plus an additional $15.23 for every $1,000 or fraction thereof in excess of $100,000.

The value of the estate is the gross value of the assets, less the value of any encumbrances registered against real property.

### 22.4.8 Nunavut

The probate fees assessed against the value of all property, real and personal, within Nunavut, after deducting all debts and liabilities against that property are:

- $25 for estates worth $10,000 or less;
- $100 for estates worth more than $10,000 but not more than $25,000;
- $200 for estates worth more than $25,000 but not more than $125,000;
- $300 for estates worth more than $125,000 but not more than $250,000; and
- $400 for estates worth more than $250,000.

### 22.4.9 Ontario

In Ontario, probate fees are known as "estate administration taxes". The estate administration taxes are $5 per thousand for the first $50,000 and $15 per thousand on the value over $50,000. For the purposes of calculating the gross value of the estate, the value of all personal property plus all real property located in Ontario (less the actual value of any encumbrance on that real property) is included.

### 22.4.10 Prince Edward Island

Probate fees are payable as follows:

- $50 for estates with a gross value of less than $10,000;
- $100 for estates with a gross value of less than $25,000;
- $200 for estates with a gross value of less than $50,000;
- $400 for estates with a gross value of less than $100,000; and
- $4 per $1000 for estates with a gross value of $100,000 or more.

### 22.4.11 Quebec

There are no probate fees as in the rest of Canada. There is a nominal fee for proving a will to be the last will of the deceased if the will is not a notarial will.

### 22.4.12 Saskatchewan

Probate is payable in an amount equal to $7 on each $1000 of the estate (or fraction of $1000). The value of the estate does not include jointly held real property, joint deposit accounts, real property located outside of Saskatchewan, or registered assets or insurance proceeds with a direct beneficiary. A grant of probate is not required where the estate is worth less than $5000 and there is no real property involved.

### 22.4.13 Yukon

For every grant or ancillary grant of probate and administration, and on every resealing of an extra-territorial grant of probate or administration, the fee is $140. No fee is payable to obtain a grant of letters probate and administration where a person dies leaving an estate not exceeding $25,000 in value.

## 22.5 CASE STUDIES

### 22.5.1 Adding a Joint Owner

See section 22.3.1 above. Note that there are several parts to the case study in that section, including sections 22.3.1.1, 22.3.1.3 and 22.3.1.5.

### 22.5.2 Gifting a Property

See section 22.3.2 above. This case study is an extension from the facts in section 22.3.1.1.

### 22.5.3 Selling a Property for Less Than Fair Market Value

See section 22.3.3 above. This case study is an extension from the facts in section 22.3.1.1.

### 22.5.4 Selling a Property for More Than Fair Market Value

See section 22.3.4 above. This case study is an extension from the facts in section 22.3.1.1.

# CHAPTER 23

# TRUSTS

Trusts are a frequently used tool when structuring a wealth plan. Their uses are varied and broad, and not limited to the wealth plans of affluent individuals. However, due to a lack of understanding regarding their structure and purpose, many individuals who should use trusts, fail to. The following discussion is meant to provide a broad description of why and how you can use a trust in your estate plan.

## 23.1 WHAT IS A TRUST?

A trust is simply a mechanism by which assets can be left for the benefit of another person. Instead of transferring ownership of the property to another individual with no conditions attached, you can arrange to give it to them "in trust", meaning that the recipient will only receive the funds at a certain time, and/or under certain conditions. The person who creates the trust is referred to as the "settlor" and the person who holds legal title to the assets is referred to as the "trustee". The person for whom the assets are being held is referred to as the "beneficiary".

Unlike a corporation, a trust is not a legal entity. It is simply a relationship between the trustee, who holds legal title to the asset, and the beneficiary, who holds beneficial ownership of the asset. The trustee must always act in the best interests of the beneficiary, since they are acting as a "fiduciary". Although a trust generally does not have to be in writing, it is recommended that a trust agreement be signed indicating the terms of the trust and the powers of the trustee to avoid disputes in the future. Trusts that involve land or those governed by the laws of Quebec must be in writing.

Trusts were originally created primarily for control reasons, although recently they have become more popular due to their tax attributes. Here are some examples of when using a trust may be appropriate:

- when you want to leave money to a child, but you do not want them to receive the money until they are mature enough to manage it properly;

- when you want to leave money to a spouse, but you want to ensure, to the extent possible, that the capital is preserved for your children, and not passed on to a new spouse after you are gone;
- when you are in a blended family situation, and you want to ensure that you fulfill any obligations you may have to your new spouse or common-law partner, but still leave something to your children from a previous relationship; and
- when you have a disabled child to whom you would like to leave a portion of your estate, but you are concerned about their ability to continue to receive social assistance.

As you can see, there are many instances where a trust may be used for control purposes. If you want to leave money to someone else, but only upon certain conditions, then a trust is usually the best mechanism to use. If you want to leave funds to beneficiaries at the time of your death, when you will no longer be able to control when and how the money will be used, a trust is generally the only option. Speak to your lawyer when you are re-writing your will to ensure that the proper conditions are attached to the gifts you are leaving to your heirs.



If the trust is created during the lifetime of the person who has created the trust, it will be referred to as an *inter vivos* trust. If the trust is created in a person's will, and therefore only takes effect at the time of their death, it is referred to as a *testamentary* trust.

## 23.2 TAXATION

### 23.2.1 Taxation of a Trust

Trusts are taxed in a unique manner, which gives them many purposes in wealth planning. The *Income Tax Act* treats a trust as a separate taxable entity, like an individual or a corporation. This means that any income earned within the trust is taxable to the trust as a separate taxpayer. Given our system of graduated tax rates in Canada, having income taxed in the trust, as opposed to having the beneficiary report the income, may result in less tax overall. Therefore, if one of your beneficiaries is already in a relatively high tax bracket, it may be best to leave them their inheritance in a trust, as opposed to giving it to them directly, since some of the income earned within the trust may be taxed at a lower rate (note that this is not true for *inter vivos* trusts).

However, unlike a corporation, a trust is also a flow-through entity. This means that if the terms of the trust are flexible enough to permit income earned by the trust to be paid to the beneficiaries (which is usually the case), then any income paid to the beneficiaries can be taxed in the hands of the beneficiaries. If the beneficiaries are in a low tax bracket, in some cases it may be more beneficial to have income taxed in the hands of the beneficiary instead of in the name of the trust, particularly because individuals are entitled to a personal tax exemption, whereas trusts are not.

If the income is taxed in the trust, the taxable income is generally calculated in the same manner as for an individual, with a few exceptions.

- *Inter vivos* and testamentary trusts are taxed differently. Every dollar of income earned in the name of an *inter vivos* trust (and not paid out to a beneficiary) is taxed at the highest marginal tax rate, whereas income earned by a testamentary trust is subject to graduated rates of tax.

- Trusts cannot take advantage of the personal tax exemption that is available to individuals. Approximately the first $10,382 of taxable income earned by an individual is earned tax free. This is not the case for trusts.

- When assets are held in the name of a trustee, there will be a "deemed disposition" of the assets every 21 years. This means that if a stock is owned by a trust, and after 21 years it has risen in value from $10 per share to $100 per share, the trustee must report a taxable capital gain of $45 (50% of $100 – $10), even though the trustee has not actually sold the stock. This is why many trusts are wound-up prior to their 21st anniversary. Certain types of trusts are not subject to this rule, particularly spousal trusts, alter ego trusts and joint partner trusts, which are discussed later in this chapter. Exempt life insurance policies are not subject to the 21-year deemed disposition rule since they are not considered "capital property". Therefore, where appropriate, a maximum-funded universal life insurance policy may be a good long-term investment within a trust.

- Testamentary trusts can choose any date as their fiscal year end, unlike *inter vivos* trusts which must use December 31st. However, the fiscal year end for a testamentary trust must be no later than one year from the date of death. From a practical perspective, it is generally easier to use December 31st as a fiscal year end, since most financial institutions provide tax slips based on income earned to December 31st, and the Canada

Revenue Agency usually only produces the most current tax returns late in the calendar year. However, from a tax perspective, there may be an advantage to using an off-calendar year end. This is because income received by a beneficiary from a trust is taxable in the beneficiary's taxation year in which the trust's year ended. For example, if a trust having a February 28th fiscal year-end pays income earned by the trust to a beneficiary in August of 2007, that income would not be required to be reported by the beneficiary until the 2008 taxation year (which would generally be filed by April 30, 2009) since the beneficiary is not considered to have earned that income until the February 28, 2008, year-end of the trust. If the trust reported income on a calendar-year basis, the beneficiary would report income in the calendar year when it became payable from the trust. Therefore, if the trust has a non-calendar year-end, the beneficiary may be able to defer the tax liability.

- Trusts must file their income tax returns within 90 days of the end of their fiscal year, unlike individuals, who must file a tax return by April 30th in respect of the previous calendar year. It is important to keep this in mind, as the filing date is earlier than many people anticipate, catching them off-guard and potentially subjecting them to interest and penalties.

You can see from the above description that trusts can provide quite a bit of flexibility from a taxation standpoint, but also have some unique attributes that can lead to unintended consequences.



## 23.2.2 Attribution of Trust Income

If you are creating an *inter vivos* trust (that is, creating the trust during your lifetime), as opposed to creating a testamentary trust (which is created only at the time of your death through your will), you must be careful of the "attribution rules". The attribution rules are a series of rules in the *Income Tax Act* that will attribute income back to you, even where you have transferred or loaned income to certain other individuals. Here are some of the situations where the attribution rules may apply.

- If you have transferred or loaned assets to a trust that includes your spouse or common-law partner as one of its beneficiaries, then any income or capital gains earned by the trust will be attributed back to you, even if the income or capital gains are paid out to your spouse or partner.

- If you have transferred or loaned assets to a trust that includes a related minor as one of its beneficiaries, then any income (but not capital gains) will be attributed back to you, even if the income is paid out to a related minor. For these purposes, the definition of "related minor" includes a child, grandchild, niece or nephew under the age of 18.

- All income and capital gains will be attributed to you if you transfer or loan assets to a trust, and:

  - your consent is required in order for any payments to be made to a beneficiary;
  - you can determine who will receive any part of the trust assets in the future; or
  - it is possible that the assets may revert back to you.

  This is the case regardless of the age or relationship of the beneficiary. This is most often the case with "informal trusts", which are discussed in section 23.3. This is a very punitive attribution rule, and must be kept in mind at all times when creating a trust for tax reasons.

You can see from the above list that it is relatively easy for the attribution rules to apply. It is for this reason that it is very important for the trust to be structured properly, with the assistance of a qualified lawyer.

## 23.3 INFORMAL TRUSTS

Some people put assets "in-trust" for their children or grandchildren simply by establishing what they refer to as an "in-trust" account at a financial institution. In many cases, there is in fact no trust agreement, so the terms of the trust are determined by provincial legislation. Generally speaking, informal "in-trust" accounts are not recommended. If there are no conditions attached to the trust, your child (or grandchild, or whomever is the beneficiary) will be entitled to the capital of the trust when they reach the age of majority (which is 18 or 19, depending upon your province of residence — see section 10.7 of Chapter 10, "Children").

Also, although some people are under the impression that informal trusts are a good way to transfer the taxation of capital gains on an asset from a parent to a child, the attribution rules will work to preclude any tax savings in the case of most informal trusts. As mentioned in section 23.2.2 above, the attribution rules regarding capital gains and income will apply if the trustee continues to have control in determining who will receive the assets and when they will be received. If the person who created the informal trust continues to treat the assets essentially as their own (e.g. they continue to manage the assets themselves, withdraw funds as and when they please, only make payments to beneficiaries when they feel the payments are appropriate, etc.), then they will be seen to still be in control of the funds, in which case all capital gains (as well as income) will be attributed back to them, regardless of the age of the beneficiary.

Most individuals find that the advantages of establishing these types of trusts (if in fact there are any) are not as great as the disadvantages of losing control over the assets when the beneficiaries are still relatively young. Consider the disadvantages carefully and speak to a financial advisor prior to establishing this type of account.

## 23.4 STRUCTURING A TRUST

You will need to speak to an advisor about the best way to structure a trust for your specific situation. However, here are a few things to keep in mind.

### 23.4.1 Trustees

You should choose a trustee who is extremely trustworthy, and will properly manage the assets. This is especially true where the trust is a testamentary trust (which will come into existence only once you are deceased, and therefore not able to monitor how the assets are being managed or distributed), so you must ensure that you choose your trustee wisely. In many cases, you may ask your personal representative to be the trustee of your trust if you are creating the trust in your will. See section 20.1 of Chapter 20, "Personal Representatives", for a list of attributes to look for in a personal representative — these are essentially the same attributes you should look for in a trustee.

The choice of trustee is also important because the residence of the trustee(s) will determine the residency of the trust. A trust is resident wherever its "mind and management" is resident, and this is usually determined by the residence of the trustee or a majority of the trustees. However, even if a majority of the trustees are resident in a particular province or country, it is possible that the trust will still be deemed to be resident in another jurisdiction if there is a trustee in that other jurisdiction who controls the decisions of the trust. If it is unclear as to where the "mind and management" of the trust resides, the Canada Revenue Agency has "tie-breaker" rules set out in its Interpretation Bulletin IT-447 that consider things such as where the assets of the trust are located in determining the residency of the trust.

You must also ensure that your choice of trustee does not cause the attribution rules to apply. See section 23.2.2, "Attribution of Trust Income", for further information on the attribution rules. In many cases, this means that you cannot be the sole trustee of a trust established for a related minor or your spouse or common-law partner. Although in some cases you may be one of the trustees, in order to avoid the attribution rules, there usually should be at least three trustees of the trust, all decisions should be made by majority vote as opposed to unanimous vote, you should not have a veto right, and there should be no possibility of receiving the trust property back in your own name.

Consider carefully whether the trustees must give unanimous consent to all decisions. Unless the trust agreement specifies to the contrary, all decisions will have to be made by unanimous vote (*Note*: this is not the rule in Quebec), which can be difficult to obtain in various circumstances. In many cases, majority vote is more appropriate, and if you created the trust and you are also one of the trustees, majority rule as opposed to unanimous consent may alleviate problems resulting from the attribution rules.

## 23.4.2 Trustee Powers

Unless you specify to the contrary, your trustees will be limited to the powers granted in the provincial Trustee Act. Although these powers may be sufficient in some cases, depending upon the purpose of the trust, they may not be appropriate in all cases.

For example, if appropriate, consider giving your trustees broad powers of investment. Although all of the provincial trustee acts now have fairly broad powers of investment, they are subject to change at any time. In many cases, you will not want to limit the powers of your trustees to the powers given to them by the provincial government. See section 23.6, "Jurisdiction Differences", for a description of the types of investments that trustees are authorized to make in your jurisdiction.

## 23.4.3 Beneficiaries

When listing the beneficiaries of a trust, you do not have to name the beneficiaries individually — you can instead define the beneficiaries by class. This means that you could leave the assets in trust for all of your "children" or "grandchildren" so that if a child or grandchild is born after the trust is established, they can still benefit from its provisions.

If you are establishing a trust for your children for income-splitting purposes, consider making both your child and their children (your grandchildren) the beneficiaries of the trust. By having more beneficiaries of the trust, this allows for more income-splitting opportunities. However, since most trusts are wound-up within 21 years in order to avoid the deemed disposition of any unrealized capital gains (as described in section 23.2.1), it is unlikely that the trust would extend further than a couple of generations.

### 23.4.4 Settlor

The settlor is the person who establishes the trust, by transferring legal title to property to a trustee or trustees, to be held "in trust" for the beneficiary or beneficiaries. Once the settlor has "settled" the trust with the trust property, they have no ongoing obligations to, nor will they receive any benefits from, the trust. A settlor will not be entitled to revoke a trust unless such power has been expressly reserved in the trust agreement.

The *Income Tax Act* defines the term "settlor" in specific ways. In the case of a testamentary trust, it is the person upon whose death the trust arose. However, in the case of an *inter vivos* trust, the settlor is the person who creates the trust, so long as the fair market value of the property contributed by the settlor exceeds the fair market value of property contributed by anyone else. If someone else makes a contribution to the trust whose fair market value exceeds that of the contribution made by the settlor, then the trust effectively has no settlor.



Although the settlor has no ongoing relationship with the trust, the choice of a settlor may be important for tax reasons. For example, if the settlor has any right to receive any of the property, or his or her consent is required in order to dispose of the property, the attribution rules could apply.

The choice of settlor is also important in the context of the preferred beneficiary election (as discussed in section 12.3 of Chapter 12, "Disabled Persons"). If one of the beneficiaries becomes mentally or physically disabled, the trust may be able to take advantage of the preferred beneficiary election. However, this election can only be made if the beneficiary is a lineal descendant of the settlor, making grandparents a preferable choice as settlor in many scenarios involving family trusts.

# 23.5 WEALTH PLANNING USING TRUSTS

## 23.5.1 *Inter Vivos* Trusts

The term *inter vivos* is a Latin term that refers to trusts created during the settlor's lifetime. There are many different types of *inter vivos* trusts — a trust can be an *inter vivos* spousal trust, an *inter vivos* family trust, an *inter vivos* alter ego trust, etc. However, because every dollar of income taxed within an *inter vivos* trust is taxed at the highest marginal rate, the use of *inter vivos* trusts is somewhat limited. The most popular form of *inter vivos* trust is a family trust, discussed in section 23.5.9 below. Family trusts are most frequently used in the context of business succession planning (see section 16.5.2.4 of Chapter 16, "Business Owners").

## 23.5.2 Testamentary Trusts

Testamentary trusts are created at the time of death of the settlor. They may be created in a will, or in a separate declaration that states that the trust is not to come into effect until the time of the settlor's death. However, a testamentary trust may only be created by an individual — it cannot be created by another trust.

Testamentary trusts are very popular, and are used for two main purposes — control of funds and tax savings (see section 23.2.1 for an explanation regarding the way in which they are taxed). Here are some examples of when a testamentary trust may form a part of your wealth plan:

- when you want to leave money to a child, but you do not want them to receive the money until they are mature enough to manage it properly (see section 10.5.3 of Chapter 10, "Children");

- when you want to leave money to adult children who are in a higher income tax bracket (or have the potential to be in a higher income tax bracket), since the use of a testamentary trust may allow the beneficiary to pay less tax on any income earned by the assets in the trust. A testamentary trust may also be useful for adult children where there is a concern about the division of an inheritance in the event of relationship breakdown (see sections 10.5.4 and 10.5.5 of Chapter 10, "Children");

- when you want to leave money to a spouse, or common-law partner but you want to ensure, to the extent possible, that the capital is preserved for your children, and not passed onto a new spouse after you are gone (see section 5.5.2 of Chapter 5, "Married");

- when you are in a blended family situation, and you want to ensure that you fulfill any obligations you may have to your new spouse or common-law partner, but still leave something to your children from a previous relationship (see section 8.5.2.1 of Chapter 8, "Blended Families"); and
- when you have a disabled child to whom you would like to leave a portion of your estate, but you are concerned about their ability to continue to receive social assistance (see section 12.3.1 of Chapter 12, "Disabled Persons").

### 23.5.3 Insurance Trusts

An insurance trust is a form of testamentary trust that is used in order to maintain control over an estate and take advantage of the income tax benefits afforded to testamentary trusts, while at the same time saving probate fees. See section 22.3.7 of Chapter 22, "Probate", for a further explanation about this type of trust.

### 23.5.4 Henson Trusts

Henson trusts are a form of testamentary trust that are used to maintain control over an estate that is intended for a disabled beneficiary, while at the same time preserving the beneficiary's right to receive social assistance payments. See section 12.3.1 of Chapter 12, "Disabled Persons", for a further explanation regarding these types of trusts.

### 23.5.5 Spousal Trusts

Spousal trusts are a form of trust that may, in fact, be established either for married spouses, or individuals who meet the definition of common-law partner under the *Income Tax Act*. These types of trusts provide income tax advantages, as well as provide for control in situations where there are blended families. See section 3.6.3 of Chapter 3, "Common-Law Couples", section 5.5.2 of Chapter 5, "Married", and section 8.5.2.1 of Chapter 8, "Blended Families", for further information regarding these types of trusts.

## 23.5.6 Inheritance Trusts

Inheritance trusts are trusts created by non-residents for inheritances intended for Canadian resident beneficiaries. Residents of Canada are generally taxed on their worldwide income, regardless of where the income was earned. However, if a non-resident leaves money in a trust for a resident of Canada, and it is managed by trustees who are not resident in Canada, then the income in the trust will not be taxable in Canada for up to the first 60 months during which the trust is in existence. If you believe that you may inherit money from a non-resident of Canada, see if it would be possible for them to change their will to ensure that they have left the money in a trust that would not be taxable in Canada for a period of time, and speak to a tax lawyer about the intricacies of establishing this type of trust.

## 23.5.7 Immigration Trusts

As mentioned above, residents of Canada are generally taxed on their worldwide income, regardless of where the income was earned. However, new immigrants to Canada can avoid tax for a period of time on assets held in trust in another jurisdiction. The income earned on these trusts is not taxable in Canada for up to the first 60 months after the immigrant has arrived in Canada (depending upon when in the year the immigrant arrives in Canada). If you have a relative who is considering immigrating to Canada, speak to them about the possibility of establishing this type of trust prior to their departure. Although it is possible to create this type of trust after arriving in Canada, the benefits will obviously decrease as time passes.

## 23.5.8 Age 40 Trusts

An "age 40" trust is simply a trust that is structured in a way that takes advantage of certain opportunities set out in the *Income Tax Act*. If a trust is created for a minor, and the assets are held on condition that they are not to be received by the beneficiary until some point in the future, but that date will be no later than their 40th birthday, then certain types of tax planning may be available. If the trust is non-discretionary in nature, meaning that the beneficiary is entitled to receive all of the income every year, but it is to be held in trust as mentioned above, then the income can be taxed in the hands of the beneficiary each year until they turn 21, even though it is not paid out to them. Assuming the beneficiary is in a low tax bracket, this may result in the income being taxed at a very low rate, even though the assets themselves will remain in the trust, so the trustees will retain control over them. These types of trusts may be appropriate if you are considering leaving assets to young beneficiaries, although they are not as frequently used as discretionary testamentary trusts, which allow the income and capital to be paid out at the trustees' discretion.

### 23.5.9 Family Trusts

The term "family trust" is applied to trusts that have been established for family members. The label "family trust" is not a legal term, but merely a manner of describing the beneficiaries of the trust. Family trusts are usually completely discretionary in nature, meaning that the trustees have the discretion to decide which beneficiaries will receive the income or capital from the trust, how much they will receive, and when they will receive it. Family trusts are most frequently used in the context of business succession planning. See section 16.5.2.4 of Chapter 16, "Business Owners", for a further discussion on when these types of trusts may be appropriate.



### 23.5.10 Alter Ego and Joint Partner Trusts

Alter ego and joint partner trusts are *inter vivos* trusts that are usually created for the purpose of saving probate fees. However, due to the low rate of probate fees across the country, and the many disadvantages that can be experienced due to probate planning, these trusts are generally not recommended, except in rare circumstances. See section 22.3.5 of Chapter 22, "Probate", particularly sections 22.3.5.2 and 22.3.5.3 for more information on these types of trusts.

## 23.6 JURISDICTION DIFFERENCES

### 23.6.1 Alberta

A trustee may invest trust funds in any kind of property if the investment is made in accordance with the *Trustee Act* of Alberta. A trustee must invest trust funds with a view to obtaining a reasonable return while avoiding undue risk, having regard to the circumstances of the trust, including:

- the purposes and probable duration of the trust, the total value of the trust's assets and the needs and circumstances of the beneficiaries;

- the duty to act impartially towards beneficiaries and between different classes of beneficiaries;

- the special relationship or value of an asset to the purpose of the trust or to one or more of the beneficiaries;

- the need to maintain the real value of the capital or income of the trust; and

- the need to maintain a balance that is appropriate to the circumstances of the trust between:

  - risk;
  - expected total return from income and the appreciation of capital;
  - liquidity, and regularity of income;
  - the importance of diversifying the investments to an extent that is appropriate to the circumstances of the trust;
  - the role of different investments or courses of action in the trust portfolio;
  - the costs, such as commissions and fees, of investment decisions or strategies; and
  - the expected tax consequences of investment decisions or strategies.

Investment in a mutual fund or segregated fund is authorized so long as the investment is in keeping with the above principles.

Since certain trusts created prior to the enactment of the current legislation are governed by a different set of rules, it is important to speak to your lawyer to understand if the current regime applies to the trust in question.

## 23.6.2 British Columbia

A trustee must use the judgment that a prudent person would exercise "in making investments", indicating that the trustee can use the same standard of care with respect to his or her personal investments as with the trust investments. When deciding whether or not an investment is prudent, a trustee can make the decision based on the overall portfolio, not just that investment in isolation. Buying mutual funds is acceptable so long as they are a prudent investment.

### 23.6.3 Manitoba

A trustee may invest in any kind of property, subject to the terms of the trust. Also subject to the terms of the trust, a trustee must exercise the judgment and care that a person of prudence, discretion and intelligence would exercise in administering the property, when investing the trust property. Buying mutual funds is acceptable so long as they are a prudent investment.

### 23.6.4 New Brunswick

A trustee may invest trust money in any kind of property, real, personal or mixed, but in so doing, he or she must exercise the judgment and care that a person of prudence, discretion and intelligence would exercise as a trustee of the property of others. Buying mutual funds is acceptable so long as they are a prudent investment.

### 23.6.5 Newfoundland

A trustee may invest trust funds in any property, and must exercise the care, diligence and skill that a reasonably prudent person would in comparable circumstances. A trustee must consider the following factors when investing trust funds, in addition to others that are relevant to the circumstances:

- general economic conditions;
- the possible effect of inflation and deflation;
- the expected tax consequences of investment decisions or strategies;
- the role of each investment within the trust portfolio;
- the expected total return from income and the appreciation of capital;
- other resources of the beneficiaries;
- the need for liquidity, regular income and preservation or appreciation of capital; and
- the special relationship or value of an asset to the purposes of the trust or to a beneficiary.

Buying mutual funds is acceptable so long as they are a prudent investment.

## 23.6.6 Northwest Territories

Subject to the terms of the trust document, a trustee is authorized to invest in every kind of property, real, personal or mixed, but in doing so, they must exercise the judgment and care that a person of prudence, discretion, and intelligence would exercise as a trustee of the property of others. Buying mutual funds is acceptable so long as they are a prudent investment.

## 23.6.7 Nova Scotia

A trustee must use the judgment that a prudent person would exercise "in making investments", indicating that the trustee can use the same standard of care with respect to his or her personal investments as with the trust investments. In addition to being "prudent", a trustee may also consider the following criteria, in addition to any others that are relevant to the circumstances:

- general economic conditions;
- the possible effects of inflation and deflation;
- the expected tax consequences of investment decisions or strategies;
- the role that each investment or course of action plays within the overall trust portfolio;
- the expected total return from income and appreciation of capital;
- needs for liquidity, regularity of income and preservation or appreciation of capital;
- an asset's special relationship or special value, if any, to the purposes of the trust or to one or more of the beneficiaries; and
- other resources of the beneficiaries.

The trustee can make decisions on an overall portfolio basis. Buying mutual fund units is acceptable so long as the above considerations have been taken into account. A trustee is also required to diversify the investments "to an extent that is appropriate", having regard to the terms on which the trust property is held and the general economic conditions.

## 23.6.8 Nunavut

The rules in Nunavut are essentially the same as those in the Northwest Territories. See section 25.6.6 for further information.

## 23.6.9 Ontario

When making investments, a trustee must exercise the care, skill, diligence and judgment that a prudent investor would exercise in making investments. The *Trustee Act* of Ontario does not specify that the degree of skill must be the same as when making investments for "others". Trustees are specifically authorized to invest in mutual funds. Trustees must consider the following criteria in planning the investment of trust property, in addition to any others that are relevant in the circumstances:

- general economic conditions;
- the possible effect of inflation or deflation;
- the expected tax consequences of investment decisions or strategies;
- the role that each investment or course of action plays within the overall trust portfolio;
- the expected total return from income and the appreciation of capital;
- needs for liquidity, regularity of income and preservation or appreciation of capital; and
- an asset's special relationship or special value, if any, to the purposes of the trust or to one or more of the beneficiaries.

A trustee must diversify the investment of trust property to an extent that is appropriate to:

- the requirements of the trust; and
- general economic and investment market conditions.

## 23.6.10 Prince Edward Island

A trustee may invest trust property in any form of property or security in which a prudent investor might invest, including a security issued by a mutual fund, so long as the investment is not inconsistent with the trust. A trustee may have regard to the following criteria in planning the investment of trust property, in addition to any others that are relevant to the circumstances:

- general economic conditions;
- the possible effect of inflation or deflation;
- the expected tax consequences of investment decisions or strategies;
- the role that each investment or course of action plays within the overall trust portfolio;
- the expected total return from income and the appreciation of capital;
- other resources of the beneficiaries;
- needs for liquidity, regularity of income and preservation or appreciation of capital; and
- an asset's special relationship or special value, if any, to the purposes of the trust or to one or more of the beneficiaries.

A trustee must diversify the investment of trust property to an extent that is appropriate having regard to:

- the requirements of the trust; and
- general economic and investment market conditions.

## 23.6.11 Quebec

In Quebec, there are different standards for trustees depending upon whether or not they have been granted "simple administration" and "full administration" in the trust agreement. With a simple administration, trustees are granted limited powers, so they are required to invest the trust money in presumed sound investments. Some types of mutual funds qualify in limited circumstances. When a trustee has powers of full administration, he or she will have broader powers and is not limited to presumed sound investments. Although they can select any type of investment, they are required to act with prudence and diligence in making the investments, and must act in the best interests of all of the beneficiaries.

## 23.6.12 Saskatchewan

A trustee may invest trust property in any form of property or security in which a reasonable, prudent investor would invest, including a security issued by a mutual fund. In making an investment of trust property, a trustee must have regard to the following factors in addition to any others that are relevant in the circumstances:

- general economic conditions;
- the possible effects of inflation or deflation;
- the expected tax consequences of investment decisions or strategies;
- the role that each investment or course of action plays within the overall portfolio of trust property;
- the expected total return from income and appreciation of capital;
- other resources of the beneficiaries;
- needs for liquidity, regularity of income and preservation or appreciation of capital; and
- an asset's special relationship or special value, if any, to the purposes of the trust or to one or more of the beneficiaries.

In investing trust property, a trustee must exercise the care, skill, diligence and judgment that a reasonable, prudent investor would exercise in making investments. A trustee must diversify the investment of trust property to an extent that is appropriate having regard to:

- the terms on which the trust property is held; and
- general economic and investment market conditions.

Buying mutual funds is acceptable so long as they are a prudent investment.

## 23.6.13 Yukon

Unless the trust document authorizes otherwise, the trustee may invest trust money in any kind of property, real, personal, or mixed, but in so doing, the trustee shall exercise the judgment and care that a person of prudence, discretion, and intelligence would exercise as a trustee of the property of others. Buying mutual funds is acceptable so long as they are a prudent investment.

## 23.7 CASE STUDIES

See the following case studies for examples of when a trust may be used as part of a wealth plan:


| | |
|---|---|
| 5.8.2 | Married, With a Spousal Trust |
| 8.8.1 | Blended Family, Living Common-Law, With Will |
| 10.8.1 | Married, With Minor Children |
| 10.8.2 | Married, With Adult Children |
| 12.6.1 | Disabled Child, Henson Trust |
| 13.8.1 | Elderly Parents with Adult Children |
| 16.8.1 | Estate Freeze |

# CHAPTER 24

# CHARITABLE GIVING





More and more Canadians are choosing to leave a legacy by making a charitable contribution either during their lifetime, or at the time of their death. Not only does this provide a social benefit, but it can also provide the donor with tax benefits. However, before you make a charitable donation, speak to your advisor to ensure that the gift is structured so that it will result in the maximum benefit both for you and the charity.

## 24.1 INCOME TAX IMPLICATIONS

If you make a donation to a registered charity, you will receive a federal tax credit equal to 15% of the first $200 in contributions, and 29% of any amount above that. Each province also provides additional provincial credits.

The charitable tax credit is a non-refundable tax credit that reduces the amount of income tax you are required to pay. This means that if you do not have any tax payable in the year, you will not receive a refund, but you can carry the tax credit forward for up to five years. The maximum contributions eligible for the tax credit generally cannot equal more than 75% of your net income in any year (as calculated for tax purposes), except in the year of death and the year before death, in which case the limit is 100% of your net income.[1] Generally, charitable receipts cannot be carried back to be used on the tax return of a prior year, but in the year of death, unused receipts can be carried back to the year prior to death.

When making a gift to a charity, be aware of the fact that making the gift could in fact create taxable income, although the tax credit should more than offset this amount.[2] For example, if you donate a piece of land that has an unrealized capital gain, the transfer of that land to the charity will trigger the capital gain, 50% of which must be included in your tax return in the year of transfer (although there is no capital gain when donating certain types of capital property, as discussed in section 24.2.4). However, the tax credit received for the donation should be sufficient to offset the amount of the taxable capital gain. In addition, the maximum amount that you may claim as a charitable donation will be increased as a result of the capital gain. However, if you have large capital gains in a year from other dispositions of property, gifts that trigger significant gains could result in a liability for alternative minimum tax. Before you

1 The maximum charitable donation allowed in any year prior to the time of death is equal to the sum of:

- 75% of the person's net income;
- 25% of the taxable capital gains incurred on donations of capital property;
- 25% of recaptured depreciation incurred on donations of depreciable property;
- 100% of the value of a gift of Canadian Cultural Property;
- 100% of the value of a gift of ecologically sensitive land; and
- 100% of the value of gifts to the Crown.

2 The capital gain on gifts of Canadian Cultural Property is exempt from tax (although losses may still be claimed). The capital gain on qualifying gifts of ecologically sensitive land is reduced from 50% of the capital gain to zero. In order to ensure maximum tax advantage, it may be best to obtain an advance certification from the Canada Revenue Agency that the property is in fact Canadian Cultural Property or ecologically sensitive property.

make such a donation, consult with your advisor to ensure that minimum tax will not result.

If you are trying to minimize your income in order to qualify for the Old Age Security benefit (or other social benefits), a charitable tax credit will not help to lower your income, since the taxable income figure used to determine whether or not you qualify for Old Age Security is not reduced by the amount of these types of credits. Although your tax payable may be reduced by the amount of the donation tax credit, the amount of your net income for the purposes of calculating your entitlement to Old Age Security will not be reduced by the amount of the credit. Also, if you are giving a gift that will trigger an unrealized capital gain and in fact increase your taxable income, you must understand the negative impact that the capital gain may have on your Old Age Security benefits.

If you have a corporation, it is often best to make all charitable contributions in your personal name, especially if you are in a low tax bracket, and your contribution is large enough to result in a tax credit at the high rate (i.e. 29% vs. 15% federally). This is because contributions made by corporations are treated as a tax deduction and do not result in a tax credit in the same manner as when made personally. However, if you are contributing to an organization that is not a registered charity (and therefore unable to issue a tax receipt), it may be best to make the contribution corporately if you can deduct the donation as a promotional cost.

## 24.2 PLANNED GIVING STRATEGIES



The following is a description of some of the strategies which may be appropriate for maximizing the use of the charitable tax credit.

### 24.2.1 Making a Gift in Your Will

One popular charitable giving strategy is to make a gift in your will. If your intent is to leave a gift in your will, you should ensure that your will properly sets out the names of the charitable organization or organizations you wish to benefit. There have been numerous cases where a gift has failed due to uncertainty as to which organization the gift was intended. The full legal name of the organization should be set out in the will, and if there are several branches of the organization, the branch that is to benefit should be specifically mentioned. Also, if you want the donation to qualify for a tax receipt, make sure in advance of signing your will that the donation is being made to a registered charity, not just a non-profit organization. There are many non-profit organizations that do not have a charitable registration, and are therefore not authorized to issue tax receipts.

When giving a gift in a will, it is especially important that the personal representatives have the ability to transfer assets to a beneficiary in kind. A personal representative should not rush to liquidate the assets of an estate where one of the beneficiaries is a charity — if the will allows assets to be distributed in kind, it may be better to give publicly traded securities or mutual funds to the charity and save money for the estate (since the capital gain on publicly traded securities and mutual funds is reduced from 50% to 0% — see section 24.2.4 for more information). The amount of the charitable receipt will be the fair market value of the property immediately before the donor's death.

It is usually desirable for a charitable gift given in a will to qualify for a charitable receipt issued in the year of death, in the deceased's name. This is because the taxable income of a deceased person can often be very high due to the de-registration of any registered funds (such as RRSPs and RRIFs) and the deemed disposition of capital property (see Chapter 21, "Taxation at Death", for a description as to how tax is calculated in the year of death). However, if the will leaves it to the personal representative to decide how much money to donate to the charity, then the receipt will instead be issued to the estate (as opposed to the deceased). In many cases an estate may not have enough income to take advantage of the tax receipt. It is for this reason that charitable gifts given in a will should be specific as to amount. Although there is some flexibility in this area (for example, the will may set out a formula for calculating the amount of the gift, as opposed to designating a specific amount), it is recommended that you speak with a qualified professional to ensure that the gift achieves the desired tax consequences.

## 24.2.2 Direct Beneficiary Designations

Another method by which to make a charitable donation is to designate the charity as the direct beneficiary of a registered asset such as an RRSP or RRIF or an insurance policy (note: direct beneficiary designations are not effective in all cases in Quebec with respect to registered assets). The asset will then be paid directly to the charity, and will not form a part of your estate, and will therefore not be subject to probate fees, or exposed to estate creditors (other than potentially the Canada Revenue Agency, or in some provinces, beneficiaries who were financially dependent upon the estate). Another advantage to making a direct beneficiary designation on the insurance contract, as opposed to through your will, is that you can change the beneficiary designation at any time simply by advising your insurer (or the plan administrator, in the case of registered investments). If you make the beneficiary designation in your will, and you decide that you would like to change it, you will need to either sign a new will or a codicil.

Keep in mind that if you designate a charity as the direct beneficiary of an asset such as an RRSP or RRIF, that your estate will remain liable for the taxation of that asset at the time of your death. For example, RRSPs are 100% taxable in the year of death (unless transferred to certain beneficiaries, such as a spouse or common-law partner). Therefore, if a charity is listed as the direct beneficiary of an RRSP, the estate will still have to report the taxable income resulting from the death of the owner of the RRSP, although it will have a corresponding charitable tax credit to offset the tax owing. If you want your estate to have a specific after tax value after the gift is given, consider purchasing insurance to fund the tax liability.

Please see section 24.3 for more information on whether to simply designate a charity as the beneficiary of an insurance policy, or make them the owner of the policy.

## 24.2.3 Maximizing Amounts Over $200

As mentioned above, the federal tax credit on the first $200 of donations is only 15%, whereas the tax credit on amounts above that is 29% (and the additional provincial credits are usually based on the same thresholds, except in Quebec – see section 24.5.1). Therefore, if possible, it is best to maximize the amount of the donation above $200. Here are a couple of possible strategies.

- If you donate only small amounts every year, consider carrying some donations forward (to a maximum of five years) in order to qualify for the higher tax credit on amounts over $200.

- If you are married or in a common-law relationship, and both spouses or partners have made charitable contributions during the year, consider transferring the charitable receipts to one spouse or common-law partner. For example, if each spouse or common-law partner contributed $150 during the year, the total federal tax credit that the couple would be entitled to would be $45 ($150 x 15% plus $150 x 15%) if they each claimed their donations separately. However, if all of the receipts were claimed by one spouse, the total federal tax credit would be $59 ($200 x 15% plus $100 x 29%).

## 24.2.4 Donating Capital Property

If you are planning to donate capital property (e.g. a piece of property with an unrealized capital gain), it may be better to donate the property itself to the charity, rather than selling the property first and then donating the cash proceeds. This is because a gift of capital property that results in a taxable capital gain will increase your annual donation limit by 25% of the taxable capital gain triggered by the donation.

Another advantage available where the gift is comprised of publicly traded securities or mutual funds is that the amount of the capital gain that must be reported for tax purposes is eliminated.[3] If you own assets of this nature, and you are contemplating giving a gift to charity, consider whether it would be best to give a publicly traded security or mutual fund, as opposed to cash. In fact, if you would like to retain your position in a particular stock, there is nothing to prevent you from re-purchasing the stock immediately, even though you have sheltered the gain on your previous position by donating the shares to a charity.

Note that the lower capital gains inclusion rate (from 50% to 0%) applies only where the securities or mutual funds are gifted to a charitable organization, or other types of "qualified donees", such as public and private foundations. Also keep in mind that gifts of shares in a small business to a private foundation, gifts of debt in a small business to a private foundation and gifts of debt in a small business to any charity will not qualify for a charitable credit unless the shares or debt is converted to cash within five years of receipt, so you may want to make this a condition of the gift if you are donating an asset of this nature. Also keep in mind that there are restrictions on what percentage of a company a private foundation can own, so the private foundation may have to divest itself of the shares if the gift makes it go offside.

Another form of property that receives special tax treatment is an employee stock option. If you donate stock that was purchased by virtue of an employee stock option, and the donation is made to a qualified charity in the year of acquisition and within 30 days of the acquisition, the amount of capital gain that is taxable will be reduced from 50% to 0% of the gain. Therefore, if you have the option between donating cash, and using the cash to exercise options on shares that you

3 The reduced inclusion rate from 50% to 0% applies to gifts of shares, bonds, warrants and options, if listed on a designated stock exchange. The Department of Finance considers a "designated stock exchange" to include the Toronto and Montreal exchanges, tiers 1 and 2 (but not 3) of the TSX Venture Exchange (formerly the Canadian Venture Exchange), the NYSE, NASDAQ (excluding the Over-the-Counter Bulletin Board) and most other major foreign exchanges.

intended to sell in any event, it may be more beneficial to donate the shares purchased by virtue of the stock option, than to donate the cash.

### 24.2.5 Donor Advised Funds

If you want to make relatively significant gifts to charity during your lifetime, you should consider establishing a donor advised fund. These types of funds are essentially endowment funds, where you make a donation to a financial institution or community charity that has registered as a charity with the Canada Revenue Agency for the purpose of receiving funds ear-marked for charitable purposes. In this way, you will receive an immediate tax receipt for the amount donated to the fund, but you will not have to decide immediately to which charity to give the funds. All the income and growth will accrue within the fund on a tax-free basis, and you will be able to give directions regarding which charity you would like the income paid to (subject to the restrictions regarding which entities are entitled to receive such donations). The advantages to using this type of fund include the ability to access professional money managers to manage the assets, the ability to include family members in making the decision as to where to allocate annual donations, and the immediate tax advantage of receiving a donation tax credit for the amount contributed to the fund. You can continue to make further donations to the fund, and designate where you would like the funds to go at the time of your death. Speak to your financial advisor to obtain more information about which donor advised funds may be available through your financial institution, or through local community organizations.

### 24.2.6 Annuities

Another strategy that may provide you with a tax advantage, while still allowing you to make a charitable gift, is the use of an annuity. This strategy may be appropriate for individuals who have a large investment that is producing an annual income stream for them. Here are a few examples of how an annuity could be used to make a charitable gift.

- If you have $200,000 invested in a GIC, and you are receiving $7000 in annual income, that amount is 100% taxable, resulting in a net after-tax return of a much lesser amount (let's assume $4000 for our purposes). It will cost you significantly less than $200,000 to purchase an annuity that provides you with a return of $4000 annually, since part of the annuity payment will include a return of capital, which is non-taxable. Therefore, if it only costs you $150,000 to purchase an annuity that produces an annual after-tax return of $4000, you can donate the remaining $50,000 to a charity in order to obtain a charitable tax receipt (which can reduce your taxable income even further).

- Alternatively, you could use the entire $200,000 to purchase an annuity, which would provide you with more than $4000 after-tax on an annual basis, since some of the payment is a tax-free return of capital. If you only need $4000 annually for your living expenses, you could donate the excess, and receive an annual tax receipt for that amount (which also allows you to decide each year which charity or charities will receive the gift). Alternatively, you could use the excess income to pay the premiums on an insurance policy that could be donated at the time of your death, so that your estate would receive one large tax receipt at that time.

However, there are some potential drawbacks to the use of an annuity.

- These strategies are somewhat inflexible, and should only be used by individuals who are confident that they will not need the capital for their own purposes. Although an annuity does provide for a secure income stream, you may prefer to invest the capital on your own, especially in a low interest rate environment.

- If you have to sell assets in order to purchase the annuity, be aware of any income tax consequences or penalties that may be incurred in order to do so. For example, if you have to sell investments that have an unrealized capital gain, selling the investment to purchase the annuity may result in a tax liability.

- Unless there is a guarantee feature to the annuity regarding the number of payments you are entitled to receive, generally speaking, the payments will cease at the time of your death, potentially leaving nothing for your estate. Therefore, you may wish to purchase an insurance policy in order to replenish the estate after the time of your death. This strategy is referred to as an "insured annuity" or "back-to-back" annuity, since the annuity and the insurance policy are purchased "back-to-back". If it is important for you to guarantee that your heirs will be entitled to the same amount of capital as if you had not purchased the annuity, then you should apply for the insurance policy before you purchase the annuity, to ensure that you are insurable, and for a reasonable price.

## 24.2.7 Charitable Remainder Trusts

Another option for making a charitable gift is to transfer an asset to a trust that names the charity as the capital beneficiary, and the donor as the income beneficiary. This will allow you and/or another designated beneficiary to receive the annual income from the trust, and ensure that the charity receives the capital of the trust upon the death of the income beneficiary.

If the trust is irrevocable, the charity can issue a receipt to the donor at the time the asset is transferred. The amount of the charitable receipt will be calculated based on the present value of the asset being transferred to the trust, which is determined using actuarial calculations based on the life expectancy of the income beneficiary. In many cases, a valuation will be required — if no valuation can be determined, no tax receipt can be issued. Assuming a tax receipt is issued, it can help to reduce your taxes in the year in which you make the donation, and the next five years as well, if the donation exceeds the maximum amount allowed and you need to carry part of the donation over to subsequent years. If you anticipate that your estate will not have much income in the year of death, then receiving a smaller tax receipt now may be more valuable than your estate receiving a larger tax receipt later (which would be the case if you donated the gift at the time of your death).

Some of the issues to consider with charitable remainder trusts include those listed below.

- Is there any possibility that you may need the funds in the future? If so, think twice about transferring the funds to the trust, as the transfer is irrevocable (in cases where you want a tax receipt issued immediately).
- If you do transfer the funds to the trust, they will pass outside of your estate, and will therefore not be subject to probate fees, or claims by your creditors (or disappointed beneficiaries), but you will also not be able to leave them to your beneficiaries. If leaving a specific amount for your beneficiaries is important to you, consider purchasing insurance to replenish your estate.

Charitable remainder trusts are sometimes used with assets such as art or real property. However, due to their complexity, you should confer with a qualified tax professional prior to implementing this type of planning.

# 24.3 PLANNED GIVING USING INSURANCE

Insurance is a popular way to fund a charitable gift. In many cases, it is the most economical and effective method available to ensure that all of the donor's estate planning objectives are achieved. Since there are many potential strategies for using insurance for charitable gifts, it is important to confer with an insurance professional prior to implementing any of these strategies.

## 24.3.1 Designating a Charity as Beneficiary

One possible method of making a charitable gift is to purchase an insurance policy and name the charity as the beneficiary of the policy. If the donor retains ownership of the policy, then the payment of the premiums will not be deductible, but the death benefit will result in a tax receipt issued in the name of the donor at the time of death. Here are some of the issues to consider when deciding whether or not it would be more advantageous to receive a tax credit personally for the premiums during your lifetime or to have your estate receive a tax credit for the death benefit.

- If the donor would like to receive tax receipts for each of the premium payments, then the charity must be the owner of the policy, and no tax receipt will be issued at the time of death upon payment of the death benefit to the charity. Although it may sound appealing to receive tax credits immediately for your premium payments, you will retain more control over the policy if you maintain ownership and simply designate the charity as beneficiary at the time of death. If you maintain ownership of the policy, you can decide at a later date to change the beneficiary. If you assign the policy to the charity and later change your mind, you can stop paying the premiums, but if you want to reapply for a new policy, the premiums may be more expensive, and it is possible that you may no longer be insurable.

- If you will not need a large tax credit in the year of death since you do not have many registered investments or unregistered investments with unrealized capital gains, then it may be better to receive the tax credit on an annual basis in respect of the premiums, rather than one large tax credit in the year of death, which may go partially (or completely) unused. The tax credit can be carried back to the year prior to death, but even then, it is possible that a portion of the tax credit will be lost.

## 24.3.2 Distributing the Insurance Proceeds Through Your Will

Another option is to make the estate the beneficiary of your insurance policy, and then make a bequest in your will to the charity. However, if you intend to leave the entire policy to the charity, then it may be best to simply designate the charity as the beneficiary of the policy, instead of making the gift through your will, as that will help to avoid probate taxes and a challenge to the gift. There have been cases where beneficiaries under a will have not been happy about the fact that a charity is to receive a large portion of the estate, and have challenged the will based on various grounds, including testamentary capacity, duress and undue influence. Another problem with making the gift in the will is that you will have to change your will every time you wish to make a change regarding the gift.

However, if you only want a portion of the policy to go to a charity, or you want to make gifts to several charities, it may be more practical to do that in your will. Another advantage to leaving an insurance policy to be distributed through your will is that it may provide your personal representative with more flexibility when determining the most tax advantageous way of making the donation. For example, as explained in section 24.2.4, it may be more advantageous to donate securities to the charity, leaving the insurance to be distributed to your other beneficiaries.

## 24.3.3 Purchasing an Insurance Policy

If you are applying for a new insurance policy for the purposes of making a charitable contribution, consider the issues below.

- It may be better to purchase a whole life policy, since the insurance need is permanent (assuming you will want to make the charitable donation regardless of how long you live). A paid-up or partially paid-up whole life policy has more value to a charity than a term life policy because it has value even if you discontinue paying the premiums. If you do choose to stop paying the premiums, the charity can continue paying the premiums with its own funds, cash in the policy for its cash surrender value or use the cash value to purchase a reduced paid-up policy with a smaller face amount. (See section 25.2.3 of Chapter 25, "Insurance", for a further discussion regarding the different types of insurance that are available.)

- If you want the charity to be able to issue a tax receipt to you, the policy must be in your name alone. No receipt can be issued where the policy is a first to die policy, which is owned by more than one person, since no one owns the policy absolutely.

- Depending upon the charity, it may be helpful to direct that the gift of the premium be held by the designated charity for a period of ten years. This direction would apply to each premium paid under the policy, as well as any death benefit. This is because charities are usually required to disburse a large portion of their receipts on an annual basis. If you are making a significant gift, and you want the charity to have the ability to retain the funds for a period of time so that they can be used for a major capital expenditure, for example, this type of direction may be useful, but you should confer with the charity first, since some charities may need to use the funds immediately for pressing needs.

### 24.3.4 Transferring Ownership of an Insurance Policy to a Charity

If you already own an insurance policy, and you want to transfer it to the charity so that all future premium payments will qualify for a tax receipt, you should speak with an advisor prior to transferring the policy if the policy is quite old. This is because the transfer could result in tax consequences if the cash surrender value exceeds your adjusted cost base for that policy. If you transfer a policy of this type to a charity, you will be considered to have cashed in the policy for the cash surrender value under the deemed disposition rules, which could result in taxable income. However, this may be offset by the tax credit for the donation. If you assign a policy to a qualified charity, you will receive a tax receipt for the value of the policy, which is the amount by which the cash surrender value at the time of the assignment exceeds any loans taken out against the insurance policy, plus any interest and accrued dividends which are also assigned.

### 24.3.5 Buying an Insurance Policy Through Your Corporation

If you own a corporation, you could purchase an insurance policy through your corporation, which will pay for the premiums with lower after-tax dollars, if the corporation is earning active business income. When the insurance proceeds are received by the corporation, they will be paid into the capital dividend account, which can pay out dividends to shareholders on a tax-free basis. These funds could then be used by the estate to fund charitable bequests made in your will.

However, if there are several shareholders, you will probably need a shareholders' agreement in place, in which the other shareholders agree to pay the insurance proceeds out to your estate. Also, if all of the dividends are to be paid to one shareholder only, it will be important for that shareholder to have a separate class of shares. Another potential problem may arise if the corporation wants to maintain its ability to use the $750,000 capital gains exemption — if the corporation is mainly comprised of active assets, be careful that the cash surrender value accumulated in the insurance policy does not put this exemption in jeopardy.

### 24.3.6 Other Insurance Strategies

Here are some other strategies using insurance that you may consider.

- You could donate funds to a charity and use the tax savings to purchase a life insurance policy that will replenish your estate at death for your beneficiaries.

- If you are making regular annual donations, consider redirecting these amounts into a charity-owned life insurance policy. The annual cost to you will remain the same, and you will continue to benefit from the tax credit, but it is possible that the total amount received by the charity will be much higher if the premium funds a large death benefit (although the charity will not receive the benefit until the time of your death).

- If you are required to withdraw minimum annual amounts from your RRIF, but you do not require the funds, consider using the funds to make the premium payments on a life insurance policy. If the charity is the owner of the policy, the charity will issue a tax receipt for the premiums to you, offsetting the income inclusion as a result of making the withdrawals from your RRIF.

## 24.4 STRUCTURING THE GIFT

There are issues other than just the tax benefits that should be considered when making a charitable gift, including those described below.

- If you are making a gift in your will or by designating a charity as a direct beneficiary of a registered asset or insurance policy, keep all potential beneficiaries of your estate in mind. If you financially support someone, it is possible that they will have a claim against your estate. In some provinces and territories, even assets that are given directly to a designated beneficiary can be clawed back to ensure these financially dependent individuals are cared for. If such a claim is made, it is possible that the charity may not receive as much as you intended them to receive. See section 19.6 of Chapter 19, "Distribution of an Estate", for more information on the dependants' relief legislation in your jurisdiction.

- Ensure that your beneficiary designations in your will, registered assets (such as RRSPs and RRIFs) and insurance policies are consistent — if there is an inconsistency, the last designation will prevail.

- Charities are normally required to disburse the majority of the funds they receive on an annual basis (generally 80% of the amounts for which charitable receipts were issued in the previous year). If you do not want the charity to have to disburse the funds immediately, then consider putting a restriction on the gift indicating that it is to be held for a minimum of ten years. Depending upon the size of the charity, this may or may not be a benefit — speak to the charity in advance as to the nature of their needs.

- Before giving the gift, be sure to speak with the charity to see if they are willing and capable of accepting the gift. Some charities are not properly equipped to receive real property or securities, or they may prefer that the money be given to a foundation that has been set up to receive gifts, as opposed to giving the gift to the operating arm of the charity.

- Verify in advance that the organization is capable of issuing a charitable receipt for tax purposes. Some individuals have made gifts to organizations on the assumption that they were registered charities, only to find out that they were non-profit corporations not able to issue tax receipts. If the donation is made after the time of your death, your personal representative will not have the discretion to simply give the funds to another organization, so this should be verified in advance. This issue may be particularly important if the organization is located outside of Canada — check in advance to ensure that the foreign organization is considered a qualifying charitable organization for Canadian tax purposes. The organizations qualified to issue tax receipts are listed in Information Circular 84-3R5 (which can be found on the Web site for the Canada Revenue Agency) and Schedule VIII to the *Income Tax Regulations*.

- As a result of some abusive strategies developed to take advantage of the charitable tax credit, be aware that there are some limitations regarding the amount that can be claimed as a charitable donation. For example, if property was acquired less than three years before it is donated, the fair market value of the gift will generally be the amount paid by the donor. If you are contemplating acquiring an item and then immediately donating it, or entering into an arrangement such as a charitable gift tax shelter, be sure to consult with your tax advisors to ensure you are aware of the limitations attached to these strategies.

## 24.5 JURISDICTION DIFFERENCES

### 24.5.1 Quebec

Unlike the federal tax credit, the provincial credit is 20% on the first $200 of charitable donations, and 24% on any amounts over that. Also, if you give art to a charity other than an accredited art gallery or cultural organization, you will not receive a tax credit until the charity sells the art, at which time you will get a credit for the amount received from the sale. Also, in order to receive a tax credit, the sale of the artwork must take place prior to the end of the fifth calendar year following the year of the gift.

## 24.6 CASE STUDIES

### 24.6.1 Insured Annuity

See section 24.2.6.

### 24.6.2 Using Insurance to Fund a Charitable Gift

Jack has a home with an unrealized capital gain of $400,000 and a cottage with an unrealized capital gain of $300,000. Since he will be using the principal residence exemption on his home, the capital gain on his cottage will be taxable, resulting in approximately $67,500 in tax ($300,000 x 50% taxable = $150,000 in taxable income x 45% tax rate = $67,500 in tax). Jack would like his beneficiaries to be able to keep the cottage and would also like to make a charitable donation. Jack decides to purchase $500,000 in insurance, naming his estate as beneficiary, but designating a charity as a beneficiary of part of his estate. This results in a tax credit for his estate, which more than offsets the tax owing as a result of the deemed disposition of his cottage at the time of death (for more information on how income tax is calculated at the time of death, see Chapter 21, "Taxation at Death"). Jack's estate is then large enough so that his children can keep his cottage and the charity will receive a significant gift.

# CHAPTER 25

# INSURANCE



Insurance can play many important roles in your wealth planning strategy. For example, when you are young, your goal may be to create an estate in the event you die while you still have dependants, or you may require disability insurance or critical illness insurance to fund the costs of an illness or disability at a time in your life when you have not built up significant assets. Later on in your life, you may want to insure a tax liability in order to preserve your estate for your family, or you may want to purchase insurance for the purpose of equalizing an estate if one of your children is to receive a vacation property or business, and the other child is to receive liquid funds. If you have philanthropic goals, you may also want to consider insurance to give a gift to your favourite charity. However, which type of insurance should you use, and when? This chapter will review some of the various types of insurance, and when you should consider using them as part of your wealth plan.

## 25.1 LIVING BENEFITS

### 25.1.1 Disability Insurance

Disability insurance is very important if you or your family depends on your ability to earn an income. If you become disabled, you may experience a significant reduction in your income, as well as a marked increase in your expenses. Most employed individuals have disability insurance through their group plan with their employer. However, the terms of these group plans are obviously not customized to your personal situation, and depending upon the circumstances, may or may not be sufficient to meet your needs. Also, these plans are generally not portable, meaning that if you change employers, your disability plan will change as well. If you choose to become self-employed, depending upon your health situation, you may not qualify for any disability insurance. For these reasons, it is particularly important that you review your disability insurance needs with your financial planner. If you do want to consider purchasing an individual disability policy, here are some of the terms or attributes for which you should look.

- In many cases, it will be important to ensure that the policy will pay out if you are prevented from carrying on your "own occupation", as opposed to "any occupation". If the policy is "own occupation", you will receive disability benefits if your disability prevents you from doing the occupation you were engaged in prior to the disability. If the policy is "any occupation" you will receive disability benefits only if you are not capable of doing any occupation within the same pay range. For highly trained professionals, it may be beneficial to obtain an "own occupation" policy so that you are not forced to take on unsatisfying types of work. Obviously, "own occupation" policies are more expensive than "any occupation". Some plans convert from an "own occupation" policy to an "any occupation" policy within two years of the commencement of payment, so read the policy carefully to ensure the terms are consistent with your needs.

- Review the "elimination period", which is the time you must wait prior to receiving payments. Since shorter waiting periods are more expensive, it may be more cost effective to choose an elimination period of six months, as long as you have an emergency fund that will cover your living expenses for that period of time.

- Some policies actually penalize you if you return to work for a short period of time or on a part-time basis. Review the policy to ensure that benefit payments will not be affected if you try to return to work, but are unable to do so, or are only able to work part-time.

- The definition of "disability" in the policy should include the more common forms of mental illness.

- Review the types of income that are covered. For example, group plans may not cover income earned while working overtime, bonuses, or profit sharing plans, so the replacement income may be well below what you were used to receiving on an annual basis. If you are a professional, and you have decided to incorporate your practice, you will want to ensure that all of your billings are insured, not just the portion you pay to yourself as a salary. With many professional corporations, professionals choose to pay only a portion of the corporation's income to themselves personally, leaving a portion of their earnings in the corporation so that they can defer some of the tax until a later date. If you are in this type of situation, you will want to review your disability insurance coverage at the time you incorporate.

- A guaranteed renewable, non-cancellable policy cannot be cancelled, and must be renewed without a medical exam. In addition, the premiums will remain constant throughout the policy.

- A future-earnings option allows you to purchase additional coverage if your income increases.

- A waiver of premiums option means that you do not have to pay premiums during any period of disability.

- A cost-of-living allowance provides that your benefits will increase with the rate of inflation.

- A refund of premiums option allows you to receive a refund of all of your premiums (without interest) if you do not make a claim against the policy by a certain time.

Not all of these issues or options may be of concern to you, but it is important to review your policy to ensure that it includes the terms you need.

Generally speaking, a disability policy will not cover 100% of your salary, to ensure there is some motivation for you to return to work. However, since disability payments are not generally taxable, and you will not have to incur the regular costs of going to work (e.g. transportation, work clothing, etc.), the policy payments should be sufficient for you to maintain your standard of living. In some cases though, a disability may bring with it other expenses, so you may want to consider a critical illness policy for additional costs related to a disability, such as home renovations or care services. Also, confirm with your advisor that the policy payments will be received tax-free. There are some instances where disability payments are wholly or partially taxable (for example, when your employer pays all or a part of your disability premium for you), so be sure you know how much you will receive on an after-tax basis.

Also be aware of the fact that if you purchase a private policy while you are a member of a group plan, the benefit you receive from the group policy may reduce the private policy benefit. However, in most cases it is still a good idea to have a private plan, since there may be situations where a private plan would pay a benefit, but a group plan will not (for example, where the private policy is "own occupation" whereas the group policy is "any occupation", and you are capable of doing some sort of work, just not the type of work for which you were trained). Group policies tend to be more restrictive, whereas private policies can be structured to meet your personal needs and are portable.

## 25.1.2 Critical Illness Insurance

Critical illness insurance is a type of insurance that pays out a lump-sum payment once you are diagnosed with one of a specific list of diseases. Most policies cover a variety of major illnesses, such as Alzheimer's, heart attack, stroke, cancer, multiple sclerosis, or Parkinson's, but you must usually survive 30 days in order to receive the funds. However, once you receive payment, there is usually no restriction on how the money may be used. Whereas disability insurance replaces your income (which you may need for ongoing expenses), a lump-sum critical illness payment may provide you with funds for other expenses that arise due to your illness, such as home renovations, medications or other services (e.g. physiotherapy, home care, out of country medical care, etc.).

Critical illness insurance may be particularly appropriate for people who are out of the workforce and therefore cannot obtain disability insurance (e.g. stay at home parents who are not earning a steady income). If you are not earning an income and therefore unable to obtain disability insurance, consider purchasing a critical illness policy in order to fund the additional costs that could arise if you were diagnosed with a serious illness or disease. Obviously, your ability to obtain this type of insurance may decrease over time (depending upon your health), and the premiums will be more expensive if you apply later in life, so be sure to consider this type of insurance while you are still young enough to qualify for it, and at a reasonable price.

## 25.1.3 Long-Term Care Insurance

Long-term care insurance is a form of insurance that usually pays out once you are no longer capable of performing two of the basic activities of daily living. These are usually defined as walking, bathing, feeding yourself, being able to use the washroom, dressing and transferring positions (e.g. moving from the chair to the bed). In some cases, payments are made once cognitive abilities are impaired, such as with Alzheimer's and dementia.

The form of policy may vary, and you can usually choose to either receive a pre-determined monthly benefit, or be reimbursed for expenses (which are evidenced with receipts). Although many nursing care costs are paid for by the provinces, in some provinces a long-term care policy will allow you to obtain private care, or supplement your care by paying for an attendant. Many individuals in nursing homes require part-time or full-time attendants to care for them, which can result in a serious erosion of the amount left in your estate for your beneficiaries.

You may also want to consider long-term care insurance in order to preserve the standard of living of the spouse who will not be going into long-term care. In many provinces, the rate charged by nursing homes is calculated based on a financial needs analysis. This calculation usually does not factor in the cost of the other spouse remaining in their current home. Therefore, the spouse who remains at home may suffer a setback in their standard of living in order to pay for the cost of placing the other spouse in a nursing home. Long-term care insurance can help defray these costs.

As with other types of insurance, your ability to obtain this type of insurance may deteriorate as you grower older (depending upon your health), and the premiums are generally higher if you apply later in life. Given the long life expectancies of many Canadians, and the rising costs of home care and other personal services, speak to your financial planner about whether or not this type of insurance would be appropriate for you.

# 25.2 LIFE INSURANCE

Life insurance is an integral part of many wealth planning strategies. However, it is important to ensure that you purchase the appropriate type of insurance for your needs.

## 25.2.1 General Considerations

There are usually three key reasons why individuals need life insurance.

1. *To Create an Estate.* If your children are quite young, or you have large amounts of debt, and you have not yet acquired significant assets, you may need insurance in order to leave a sufficient amount for your beneficiaries.

2. *To Preserve an Estate.* As your assets increase in value, so may the tax liability that your estate may have to pay at the time of your death (see Chapter 21, "Taxation at Death", for a discussion as to how you are taxed at the time of death). If you want your beneficiaries to be able to keep specific assets (such as a vacation property or business) instead of having to sell them to pay the tax liability, it may be important for you to have sufficient insurance.

3. *To Equalize an Estate.* If you have a large asset that is indivisible in nature (e.g. a vacation property or family business), you may want to purchase insurance to ensure there is sufficient liquidity for your estate. For example, if you have three children, and only one of them is interested in inheriting your vacation property or business, but they will not be able to afford to buy out their siblings, then an insurance policy may provide the estate with sufficient funds for the other beneficiaries.

Many people who have life insurance through a group policy do not pay much attention to the amount of coverage they have, and whether or not it is sufficient for their needs. However, with most group plans, the benefit is based on a multiple of your salary (e.g. at the time of death, your estate would receive a death benefit equal to twice your current salary). Depending upon the age of your dependants and the amount of debt you have, this death benefit may or may not be sufficient for your purposes. Group policies may also end or be reduced at the time of your retirement, by which time you may no longer be able to purchase a private policy, as your health may have deteriorated to the point where you are no longer insurable.

You should not assume that the arbitrary amount set in your group policy will be appropriate for you, and, if necessary, you should obtain some additional insurance through a private policy. When determining how much life insurance you will need, consider all of your debts, as well as the ongoing financial needs of your children, spouse, and any other dependants you may have (e.g. elderly parents). Also consider how much your dependants will need in the future for items such as post-secondary education. In many cases, the best approach is to speak with your financial planner to calculate the amount of coverage you think you will need.

If you do decide that your coverage is insufficient, you may be able to simply buy additional group insurance. However, it may be more appropriate to purchase a personal policy, since a personal policy is portable in the event you should choose to change employers or become self-employed. A personal policy may also allow you more flexibility in the types of provisions included in the policy. For example, when purchasing your policy, consider whether or not you want a "waiver of premium" rider, which means that the insurance company will waive your premiums during a period of disability, when your income may be reduced.

If the insurance need is in respect of a tax liability that will arise only at the time of death of the second spouse, consider a "second-to-die" policy, which may have lower premiums than a first-to-die policy, since the joint life expectancy of two people is generally longer than where there is only one person insured. However, individual policies are often easier to administer than joint last-to-die policies, since joint policies can be difficult to separate at the time of separation or divorce.

You may also wish to designate a direct beneficiary on your insurance policy, which will allow your policy to be paid directly to that beneficiary without going through your estate. This will prevent the insurance proceeds from being subject to probate fees or being exposed to creditors of the estate. In fact, if you designate one of a specified class of beneficiaries (referred to as the "protected class"), the cash surrender value of the policy may even be exempt from seizure by creditors while you are still alive (see section 25.4 of this chapter, "Jurisdiction Differences", for a discussion as to the types of beneficiary designations that may give you some creditor protection during your lifetime in your jurisdiction). However, there are many disadvantages to designating a direct beneficiary, as discussed in section 22.3.6 of Chapter 22, "Probate", so speak with your financial planner prior to designating any beneficiaries on any of your insurance policies. For example, if you list all of your children as beneficiaries, and one of them predeceases you, then their children may not receive any of the insurance proceeds. In most cases, if you are going to designate a beneficiary, it would be best to designate the trustee of an insurance trust, which is discussed in section 22.3.7 of Chapter 22, "Probate". Also, in some cases, even a direct beneficiary designation may not be sufficient to prevent a claim against the policy by the Canada Revenue Agency, or a dependant after the time of death.

## 25.2.2 Term Insurance

Term insurance is a type of "pure insurance" that simply pays a death benefit to your beneficiaries if you die during the term of the policy. The policy is only in force for a pre-determined period of time, or "term", at the end of which the insurance expires (unless you choose to renew the policy). Therefore, if you live longer than the specified term, and the policy expires, nothing is paid out to your estate. This type of insurance is used simply to protect your estate from risk, and has no investment component (unlike permanent insurance, which is discussed in section 25.2.3). Here are some of the issues to consider when making a determination as to whether or not term insurance is appropriate for you.

- Since term insurance is usually less expensive than permanent insurance, it may be appropriate for individuals with limited cash flow.

- Term insurance is usually used to cover temporary needs, such as providing an income while your children are still young, or to pay for an outstanding mortgage.

- The premiums will increase over time, so if the need is permanent (e.g. you will need insurance to fund a tax liability at the time of death), then this may not be a good option, as the premiums may become cost prohibitive over time.

If you do choose to purchase term insurance, consider the issues below.

- Ensure that the policy is guaranteed renewable, which means that you will be able to renew the policy at the end of the term without a medical exam (although the cost of the premiums may increase).

- Ensure that the policy is convertible, which means that the policy may be converted into a permanent policy in the future without a medical exam should you determine that you will have a permanent need for insurance. Conversion without a medical exam is generally only allowed within the same company, which is why it is important to determine in advance whether or not the policy is convertible. Sometimes the convertibility feature is expensive because the insurer feels that the insured is converting only because they are unable to obtain insurance elsewhere without a medical exam. If you are in fact still insurable when the term expires, investigate the cost of obtaining a new policy prior to converting.

### 25.2.3 Permanent Insurance

Permanent insurance differs from term insurance in that it provides insurance coverage not just for a defined term, but for your entire lifetime (or for as long as you continue the payments). Therefore, the premiums are usually more expensive, although they remain constant (in most cases). Examples of where you may need permanent insurance include situations where the purpose for the insurance is to fund an estate tax liability, funeral costs, or provide a source of income for a dependant who will never be financially independent (e.g. a dependent spouse, or a dependent child, such as a disabled child).

One of the advantages with permanent insurance versus term insurance is that your insurance will continue in force even if you become uninsurable. Although term insurance may be less expensive, you must renew it when the term has ended if you want it to continue, and this may not be possible if your health has deteriorated in the interim. For this reason, you may wish to apply for some permanent insurance while you are still young, and therefore insurable at a reasonable price. Individuals over the age of 80 are usually unable to obtain term insurance, at which point it may also be too late to obtain permanent insurance (either because you have health problems that make you uninsurable, or the insurance is only available at astronomical prices).

Some types of permanent insurance have an investment component as well as an insurance component. Part of your premium is invested inside the policy, and the growth on these policies accrues on a tax-deferred basis. It is the opportunity for tax-deferred growth on investments that has made permanent insurance a popular wealth planning strategy for many Canadians. Should you need the funds in the future, you may be able to take a loan against the policy for a percentage of the cash value, which will be repaid at the time of your death using the insurance proceeds (this is sometimes referred to as an "insured retirement plan"). Under current tax legislation, this strategy allows a tax-free withdrawal of a portion of the accrued cash value of such policies. Another alternative may be to cancel the policy and receive the cash surrender value, but this may have tax implications and you will obviously no longer have insurance coverage.

Although there are some tax advantages to using permanent insurance, you would generally only consider permanent life insurance if you in fact have a need for life insurance and you have exhausted all other tax shelters such as RRSPs, TFSAs and RESPs. It is also usually recommended that, to the extent possible, you should try to pay down your non-deductible debt before directing large amounts of cash into these types of policies. This is because there are costs involved with having an insurance policy, including the overhead of the insurance company, various taxes and commissions. However, if there is a genuine insurance need, and you have sufficient cash flow to pay the premiums, then the tax advantages of permanent life insurance should be considered.

### *25.2.3.1 Term to 100 Insurance*

Term to 100 insurance is a type of term insurance that never expires (generally even past age 100), so the coverage is in fact, permanent. Generally, the premiums do not rise (and neither does the coverage), but this type of insurance is for risk protection only — there is no investment component or cash value. Once the policy is in place, you will usually not need to take a medical exam again, unless you allow the policy to lapse. If you want to ensure that the policy will continue in force, consider using automatic pre-payments for the insurance premiums, so that a simple mistake does not lead to cancellation of the policy. For example, if the policy is inadvertently cancelled while you are in your 80s, you may not be able to obtain another policy.

### *25.2.3.2 Whole Life Insurance*

Whole life insurance is a type of permanent insurance that has an investment component inside the policy that grows on a tax-deferred basis up to certain limits. The death benefit as well as the investments and all growth on the investments are received tax free by your estate or your beneficiaries after the time of death, so if the investments are not withdrawn during your lifetime, the tax deferral is in fact a permanent tax savings.

As mentioned previously, the premiums for permanent insurance are level, which gives you certainty as to how much you will be paying in the future. In fact, the cost of the premiums actually decreases over time if inflation is factored in. However, some whole life policies can be paid off in full in advance of the end of the term. With whole life policies, you "own" the policy, and if the policy is "paid-up", you will continue to be insured even if you are no longer paying premiums. Sometimes the premiums are offset by cash generated within the policy, but this is not guaranteed. If you want premiums to cease at a specific point, you must choose an option that provides for that, for example, a policy where premiums cease at age 65, or after 20 years of payments. Some policies are "participating", meaning that the company will pay dividends to the policy holder, while others are "non-participating". Be sure to check the terms of your policy to determine whether or not it is participating.

You can choose to make payments to the insurance policy within a stated minimum and maximum range. If you contribute more than you are allowed to under the *Income Tax Act*, the tax advantages will be lost. The maximum amount you may contribute is referred to in the *Income Tax Act* as the maximum taxable actuarial reserve ("MTAR"), and any amount over the MTAR will be taxable in the same manner as any other investment. If you minimally fund the policy, you are essentially buying a term policy, but the premiums are guaranteed and the policy term is not for a fixed period of time. When you contribute more than the minimum, the additional amounts are invested in a tax-sheltered manner, up to the MTAR amount.

Be aware that if you simply minimally fund the policy for a long period of time, that you may lose the ability to contribute additional amounts to the policy to take advantage of the tax-deferral opportunities in the future. In order to ensure that the policy is used primarily as an insurance tool as opposed to a tax-deferral arrangement, the government has an "anti-dump-in rule" which provides that starting in the tenth year of the policy, the value of the policy cannot be more than 250% of the value three years earlier. If you want to preserve the ability to invest in the policy on a tax-deferred basis, it is important to contribute more than the minimum amount in the first seven years of the policy. Generally speaking, it is best to try to contribute at least 20 to 30% more than the minimum amount required by the policy each year.

If you want to access the funds accumulated within the policy while you are still alive, most financial institutions will allow you to borrow against the cash surrender value in the policy (depending upon the types of investments in the policy). The loan proceeds will be received tax free, although interest must be paid on the amount borrowed (and the interest will not be deductible unless you are using the loan proceeds for the purpose of earning income). However, in most cases it is still more advantageous to pay the interest cost than lose the tax-deferral, depending upon your tax rate. Keep in mind that the bank will then use the death benefit to discharge the loan outstanding, so there will be less left for your estate. Although the investment component (i.e. the cash surrender value) can usually be accessed by the insured during their lifetime, some companies require you to surrender the policy in order to do this, so check the policy and confer with your advisor before doing this.

Consider "split-dollar" arrangements where there are advantages to doing so. See section 16.6.2 of Chapter 16, "Business Owners", for a discussion of the advantages of split-dollar arrangements for executives.

### 25.2.3.3 Universal Life Insurance

Universal life insurance is another type of permanent insurance that includes an investment component with tax-deferred growth. However, with a whole life policy, the investment choices are quite limited and tend to be quite conservative. With a universal life policy, you will have increased choice, with the possibility of increased return. However, this can also mean increased risk, so you still want to ensure that the asset allocation within the policy is consistent with your risk tolerance. For instance, some insurance companies have indexes that are linked to Canadian equities, U.S. equities, international equities, balanced indexed accounts, or even guaranteed "GIC" rates. Although the management expense ratios can be higher in a universal life policy than in a similar index fund, the tax savings will outweigh the additional costs in many cases, particularly where the investments are held for a long period of time, as the monies inside such policies grow on a tax-free basis. This type of insurance may appeal to more sophisticated investors who are comfortable making ongoing decisions regarding the investments in the policy.

Again, it is generally not recommended that you buy this insurance simply for the tax advantages. Generally, it is only recommended that you buy insurance if you have a genuine insurance need, since the return on the investment will be eroded to some degree by provincial taxes that are levied on insurance premiums, as well as overhead costs and commission fees.

Unlike other forms of permanent insurance, where the premiums remain the same for the entire policy, with universal life insurance, you can either choose level premiums or yearly renewable term premiums. Although the amount of the minimum and maximum premiums remains the same, with yearly renewable term premiums, the cost of insurance will fluctuate with your age. Therefore, in the early years of the policy, more of the premiums will be devoted to investments, and in the later years, more of the premiums will be devoted to covering the increased cost of insurance. Therefore, if your objective is to shelter the maximum amount of income, it may be preferable to choose the yearly renewable term premium option since more of the premium will be devoted to investments in the early years, resulting in more tax-deferred compounding. The disadvantage is that the rising cost of insurance could reduce the value of your investments at some point in the future. It may be possible to start with yearly renewable term premiums and then switch to level premiums later in life. Universal life does give more flexibility, since you can decide to increase or decrease the payments within certain limits.

Some people prefer to "quick pay" a universal life policy for a period with which they are comfortable. It is possible to have a policy paid-up within five, ten or fifteen years, depending upon the amount deposited. In fact, it may be possible to buy a fully paid-up policy by paying in one lump sum.

## 25.3 PERSONAL INSURANCE POLICIES

When determining the amount and type of insurance you need, it is very important to speak to your financial planner to ensure that the insurance products you use are appropriate for your needs. Many individuals simply purchase group insurance offered by their employer, or mortgage insurance offered by their bank, without considering whether that is the most economical or appropriate choice. In many cases, it may be more beneficial to purchase an individual policy that you will retain control over. Here are a few things to consider when purchasing insurance.

- Many people assume that they have sufficient insurance through their group plan at work. However, the amount of insurance provided by a group plan is arbitrary, and may not be sufficient for your needs. Also, if you later decide to change employers or start your own business, you may find that you are no longer able to obtain insurance if the new employer does not have a group policy, or you are no longer insurable.

- If you purchase mortgage insurance as opposed to simply buying more term or permanent insurance individually, this may give you less flexibility in the future if you want to refinance with another financial institution, since you will need to re-qualify for insurance. If your health situation has deteriorated since you originally obtained insurance, you may not qualify, and you may be forced to refinance with the existing mortgagee.

- If you own your insurance personally, then you may have more control over the terms of the policy. If you purchase insurance through a lender, they will be the owner and beneficiary of the policy and coverage will expire when the mortgage is paid off. The total value of the coverage decreases with the mortgage balance, so that only the amount owing on the mortgage is paid out at the time of claim. In addition, premiums can be adjusted by the lender at any time and the lender can change or cancel the policy at any time. If you buy insurance personally, you own the policy and designate the beneficiary, and coverage can continue after the mortgage is paid. The total value of the coverage remains the same during the term of the policy and the premiums are guaranteed for the life of the plan. Only you can cancel or make changes to your plan.

When reviewing your insurance needs, ask your financial planner to review your group policies to determine if there are any "gaps" in your current coverage. If so, consider purchasing a personal policy to cover contingencies not included in your group coverage.

## 25.4 JURISDICTION DIFFERENCES

### 25.4.1 Alberta

While a beneficiary designation in favour of a spouse or adult interdependent partner, child, grandchild or parent of the life insured is in effect, the insurance policy will be exempt from seizure by creditors. For a definition of an adult interdependent partner, see section 3.9.1.1 of Chapter 3, "Common-law Couples".

### 25.4.2 British Columbia

While a beneficiary designation in favour of a spouse, child, grandchild or parent of the life insured is in effect, the insurance policy will be exempt from seizure by creditors. In British Columbia, common-law partners are not included in this list.

### 25.4.3 Manitoba

Where a beneficiary designation in favour of a spouse, common-law partner, child, grandchild or parent of the life insured is in effect, the insurance policy is exempt from seizure by creditors. For these purposes the "common-law partner" of the insured means a person who, with the insured, registered a common-law relationship under *The Vital Statistics Act* or a person who, not being married to the insured, cohabited with him or her in a conjugal relationship for a period of at least three years, or for a period of at least one year and they are together the parents of a child, except where either the dissolution of the common-law relationship has been registered under *The Vital Statistics Act*, or the insured has lived separate and apart from the other person for at least three years.

### 25.4.4 New Brunswick

While a beneficiary designation in favour of a spouse, child, grandchild or parent of the life insured is in effect, the insurance policy is exempt from seizure by creditors. In New Brunswick, common-law partners are not included in this list.

### 25.4.5 Newfoundland

Where a beneficiary designation in favour of a spouse, child, grandchild or parent of the life insured is in effect, the insurance policy is exempt from seizure by creditors. In Newfoundland, common-law partners are not included in this list.

### 25.4.6 Northwest Territories

Where a designation in favour of a spouse, child, grandchild or parent of the life insured is in effect, the insurance policy is exempt from seizure by creditors. The definition of spouse is the same as in the *Family Law Act*, so it includes common-law partners who have lived together for a period of at least two years, or who are in a relationship of some permanence where together they are the natural or adoptive parents of a child.

*The Dependant's Relief Act* may enable a court to "claw-back" life insurance proceeds paid to a direct beneficiary if a dependant makes an application for support from an estate.

### 25.4.7 Nova Scotia

Where a beneficiary designation in favour of a spouse or common-law partner, child, grandchild or parent of the life insured is in effect, the insurance policy is exempt from seizure by creditors. For these purposes, the definition of "common-law partner" means an individual who has cohabited with the insured in a conjugal relationship for a period of at least one year, neither of them being a spouse, and the definition of "spouse" includes a domestic partner. Please see section 3.9.7.1 of Chapter 3, "Common-law Couples, for a definition of the term "domestic partnership".

### 25.4.8 Nunavut

Where a designation in favour of a spouse, child, grandchild or parent of the life insured is in effect, the insurance policy is exempt from seizure by creditors.

### 25.4.9 Ontario

Where a beneficiary designation in favour of a spouse, child, grandchild or parent of the life insured is in effect, the insurance policy is exempt from seizure by creditors. The definition of "spouse" for these purposes includes two people who are not married to each other and live together in a conjugal relationship outside marriage. However, the dependant's relief provisions of the *Succession Law Reform Act* may allow a court to "claw back" insurance proceeds paid to a direct beneficiary if a dependant makes an application against an estate for support.

### 25.4.10 Prince Edward Island

Where a beneficiary designation in favour of a spouse, child, grandchild or parent of the life insured is in effect, the insurance policy is exempt from seizure by creditors. In Prince Edward Island, common-law partners are not included in this list. However, the *Dependants of Deceased Persons Relief Act* may enable a court to "claw-back" life insurance proceeds paid to a direct beneficiary if a dependant makes an application for support from an estate.

### 25.4.11 Quebec

The *Civil Code of Quebec* provides an exemption from seizure for insurance where a beneficiary designation is made in favour of the policyholder's "married or civil union spouse, descendant, or ascendant". Examples of descendants and ascendants would include a grandparent, parent, child, or grandchild.

The designation of a married or civil union spouse as a beneficiary in a written document other than a will is irrevocable unless otherwise stipulated. The designation of any person other than the above is revocable unless otherwise stipulated.

## 25.4.12 Saskatchewan

Where a beneficiary designation in favour of a spouse, child, grandchild, or parent of the life insured is in effect, the insurance policy is exempt from seizure by creditors. In Saskatchewan, common-law partners are not included in this list.

## 25.4.13 Yukon

Where a designation in favour of a spouse, child, grandchild, or parent of the life insured is in effect, the insurance policy is exempt from seizure by creditors. Common-law partners are not included in this list.

The *Dependant's Relief Act* may enable a court to "claw-back" life insurance proceeds paid to a direct beneficiary if a dependant makes an application for support from an estate.

# REFERENCES

## LEGISLATION

### Alberta

*Administration of Estates Act,* R.S.A. 2000, c. A-2
*Adult Interdependent Relationships Act,* S.A. 2002, c. A-4.5
*Age of Majority Act,* R.S.A. 2000, c. A-6
*Assured Income for the Severely Handicapped Act,* R.S.A. 2000, c. A-45
*Dependants' Relief Act,* R.S.A. 2000, c. D-10.5
*Dependent Adults Act,* R.S.A. 2000, c. D-11
*Dower Act,* R.S.A. 2000, c. D-15
*Employment Pension Plans Act,* R.S.A. 2000, c. E-8
*Family Law Act,* S.A. 2003, c. F-4.5
*Insurance Act,* R.S.A. 2000, c. I-3
*Intestate Succession Act,* R.S.A. 2000, c. I-10
*Matrimonial Property Act,* R.S.A. 2000, c. M-8
*Minors' Property Act,* S.A. 2004, c. M-18.1
*Personal Directives Act,* R.S.A. 2000, c. P-6
*Powers of Attorney Act,* R.S.A. 2000, c. P-20
*Surrogate Rules,* A.R. 130/95
*Survivorship Act,* R.S.A. 2000, c. S-28
*Trustee Act,* R.S.A. 2000, c. T-8
*Wills Act,* R.S.A. 2000, c. W-12

### British Columbia

*Adult Guardianship Act,* R.S.B.C. 1996, c. 6
*Age of Majority Act,* R.S.B.C. 1996, c. 7
*Conflict of Laws Rules for Trusts Act,* R.S.B.C. 1996, c. 65
*Continuing Care Act,* R.S.B.C. 1996, c. 70
*Employment and Assistance for Persons with Disabilities Regulations,* B.C. Reg. 265/2002
*Escheat Act,* R.S.B.C. 1996, c. 120

*Estate Administration Act*, R.S.B.C. 1996, c. 122
*Family Relations Act*, R.S.B.C. 1996, c. 128
*Infants Act*, R.S.B.C. 1996, c. 223
*Insurance Act*, R.S.B.C. 1996, c. 226
*International Trusts Act*, R.S.B.C. 1996, c. 237
*Land (Spouse Protection) Act*, R.S.B.C. 1996, c. 246
*Law and Equity Act*, R.S.B.C. 1996, c. 253
*Marriage Act*, R.S.B.C. 1996, c. 282
*Parental Responsibility Act*, S.B.C. 2001, c. 45
*Partition of Property Act*, R.S.B.C. 1996, c. 347
*Perpetuity Act*, R.S.B.C. 1996, c. 358
*Power of Appointment Act*, R.S.B.C. 1996, c. 369
*Power of Attorney Act*, R.S.B.C. 1996, c. 370
*Probate Fee Act*, S.B.C. 1999, c. 4
*Property Law Act*, R.S.B.C. 1996, c. 377
*Representation Agreement Act*, R.S.B.C. 1996, c. 405
*Survivorship and Presumption of Death Act*, R.S.B.C. 1996, c. 444
*Trust and Settlement Variation Act*, R.S.B.C. 1996, c. 463
*Trustee Act*, R.S.B.C. 1996, c. 464
*Wills Act*, R.S.B.C. 1996, c. 489
*Wills Variation Act*, R.S.B.C. 1996, c. 490

## Canada

*Canada Pension Plan*, R.S.C. 1985, c. C-8
*Divorce Act*, R.S.C. 1985, c. 3 (2nd Supp.)
*Income Tax Act*, R.S.C. 1985, c. 1 (5th Supp.)
*Income Tax Regulations*, C.R.C. c. 945
*Indian Act*, R.S.C. 1985, c. I-5
*Old Age Security Act*, R.S.C. 1985, c. O-9
*Pension Benefits Division Act*, S.C. 1992, c. 46, Sch. II
*Pension Benefits Standards Act, 1985*, R.S.C. 1985, c. 32 (2nd Supp.)

## Manitoba

*The Age of Majority Act*, C.C.S.M. c. A7
*The Court of Queen's Bench Surrogate Practice Act*, C.C.S.M. c. C280
*The Dependants' Relief Act*, C.C.S.M. c. D37
*The Employment and Income Assistance Act*, C.C.S.M. c. E98
*The Employment and Income Assistance Regulation*, M.R. 404/88 R
*The Family Maintenance Act*, C.C.S.M. c. F20
*The Family Property Act*, C.C.S.M. c. F25
*The Health Care Directives Act*, C.C.S.M. c. H27
*The Homesteads Act*, C.C.S.M. c. H80
*The Infants' Estates Act*, C.C.S.M. c. I35

*The Insurance Act*, C.C.S.M. c. I40
*The Intestate Succession Act*, C.C.S.M. c. I85
*The Law Fees and Probate Charge Act*, C.C.S.M. c. L80
*The Law of Property Act*, C.C.S.M. c. L90
*The Parental Responsibility Act*, C.C.S.M. c. P8
*The Parents' Maintenance Act*, C.C.S.M. c. P10
*The Pension Benefits Act*, C.C.S.M. c. P32
*The Pension Benefits Spousal or Common-law Partners Agreement Regulation*, M.R. 205/92
*The Perpetuities and Accumulations Act*, C.C.S.M. c. P33
*The Powers of Attorney Act*, C.C.S.M. c. P97
*The Retirement Plan Beneficiaries Act*, C.C.S.M. c. R138
*The Soldiers' Estates Act*, C.C.S.M. c. S170
*The Survivorship Act*, C.C.S.M. c. S250
*The Teachers' Pension Act*, C.C.S.M. c. T20
*The Trustee Act*, C.C.S.M. c. T160
*The Vital Statistics Act*, C.C.S.M. c. V60
*The Wills Act*, C.C.S.M. c. W150

## New Brunswick

*Age of Majority Act*, R.S.N.B. 1993, c. A-2
*Conflict of Laws Rules for Trusts Act*, R.S.N.B. 1993, c. C-16.2
*Devolution of Estates Act*, R.S.N.B. 1993, c. D-9
*Family Income Security Regulation*, N.B. Reg. 96-61
*Family Services Act*, R.S.N.B. 1993, c. F-2.2
*Guardianship of Children Act*, R.S.N.B. 1993, c. G-8
*Infirm Persons Act*, R.S.N.B. 1993, c. I-8
*Insurance Act*, R.S.N.B. 1993, c. I-12
*Marital Property Act*, R.S.N.B. 1993, c. M-1.1
*Probate Court Act*, R.S.N.B. 1993, c. P-17.1
*Property Act*, R.S.N.B. 1993, c. P-19
*Provision for Dependants Act*, R.S.N.B. 1993, c. P-22.3
*Registry Act*, R.S.N.B. 1993, c. R-6
*Retirement Plan Beneficiaries Act*, R.S.N.B. 1993, c. R-10.21
*Survivorship Act*, R.S.N.B. 1993, c. S-20
*Trustees Act*, R.S.N.B. 1993, c. T-15
*Wills Act*, R.S.N.B. 1993, c. W-9

## Newfoundland

*Accident and Sickness Insurance Act*, R.S.N.L. 1990, c. A-2
*Advance Health Care Directives Act*, S.N.L. 1995, c. A-4.1
*Age of Majority Act*, S.N.L. 1995, c. A-4.2
*Children's Law Act*, R.S.N.L. 1990, c. C-1

*Enduring Powers of Attorney Act*, R.S.N.L. 1990, c. E-11
*Family Law Act*, R.S.N.L. 1990, c. F-2
*Family Relief Act*, R.S.N.L. 1990, c. F-3
*Income and Employment Support Regulations*, C.N.L.R. 144/04
*Intestate Succession Act*, R.S.N.L. 1990, c. I-21
*Judicature Act*, R.S.N.L. 1990, c. J–4
*Life Insurance Act*, R.S.N.L. 1990, c. L-14
*Pension Plans Designation of Beneficiaries Act*, R.S.N.L. 1990, c. P-5
*Private Homes for Special Care Allowances Regulation*, C.N.L.R. 968/96
*Rules of the Supreme Court, 1986*, S.N.L. 1986, c. 42, Schedule D
*Services Charges Act*, S.N.L. 1998, c. S-13.2
*Survivorship Act*, R.S.N.L. 1990, c. S-33
*Trustee Act*, R.S.N.L. 1990, c. T-10
*Wills Act*, R.S.N.L. 1990, c. W-10

## Northwest Territories

*The Age of Majority Act, R.S.N.W.T. 1988, c. A-2*
*The Children's Law Act, S.N.W.T. 1997, c. 14*
*The Dependants Relief Act, R.S.N.W.T. 1988, c. D-4*
*The Family Law Act, S.N.W.T. 1997, c. 18*
*The Income Assistance Regulations*, R.R.N.W.T. 1990, c. S-16
*The Insurance Act, R.S.N.W.T. 1988, c. I-4*
*The Intestate Succession Act, R.S.N.W.T. 1988, c. I-10*
*The Powers of Attorney Act, S.N.W.T. 2001, c. 15*
*The Probate, Administration and Guardianship Fees Regulations, N.W.T. Reg. 005-2002*
*The Retirement Plan Beneficiaries Act, R.S.N.W.T. 1988, c. R-6*
*The Social Assistance Regulations, R.S.N.W.T. 1988, c. S-10*
*The Survivorship Act, R.S.N.W.T. 1988, c. S-16*
*The Trustee Act, R.S.N.W.T. 1988, c. T-8*
*The Wills Act, R.S.N.W.T. 1988, c. W-5*

## Nova Scotia

*Age of Majority Act*, R.S.N.S. 1989, c. 4
*Employment Support and Income Assistance Regulations*, N.S. Reg. 25/2001
*Insurance Act*, R.S.N.S. 1989, c. 231
*Intestate Succession Act*, R.S.N.S. 1989, c. 236
*Maintenance and Custody Act*, R.S.N.S. 1989, c. 160
*Matrimonial Property Act*, R.S.N.S. 1989, c. 275
*Medical Consent Act*, R.S.N.S. 1989, c. 279
*Powers of Attorney Act*, R.S.N.S. 1989, c. 352

*Probate Act*, S.N.S. 2000, c. 21
*Probate Court Practice, Procedure and Forms Regulations*, N.S. Reg. 119/2001
*Survivorship Act*, R.S.N.S. 1989, c. 454
*Testators' Family Maintenance Act*, R.S.N.S. 1989, c. 465
*Trustee Act*, R.S.N.S. 1989, c. 479
*Vital Statistics Act*, R.S.N.S. 1989, c. 494
*Wills Act*, R.S.N.S. 1989, c. 505

## Nunavut

*The Age of Majority Act, R.S.N.W.T. (Nu.) 1988, c. A-2*
*The Children's Law Act, S.N.W.T. (Nu.) 1997, c. 14*
*The Dependants Relief Act, R.S.N.W.T. (Nu.) 1988, c. D-4*
*The Family Law Act, S.N.W.T. (Nu.) 1997, c. 18*
*The Insurance Act, R.S.N.W.T. (Nu.) 1988, c. I-4*
*The Intestate Succession Act, R.S.N.W.T. (Nu.) 1988, c. I-10*
*The Powers of Attorney Act, S.Nu. 2005, c. 9*
*The Probate, Administration and Guardianship Fees Regulations*, N.W.T. Reg. 005-2002
*The Retirement Plan Beneficiaries Act, R.S.N.W.T. (Nu.) 1988, c. R-6*
*The Social Assistance Regulations, R.R.N.W.T. (Nu.) 1990 c. S-16*
*The Survivorship Act, R.S.N.W.T. (Nu.) 1988, c. S-16*
*The Trustee Act, R.S.N.W.T. (Nu.) 1988, c. T-8*
*The Wills Act, R.S.N.W.T. (Nu.) 1988, c. W-5*

## Ontario

*Age of Majority and Accountability Act*, R.S.O. 1990, c. A.7
*Business Corporations Act*, R.S.O. 1990, c. B.16
*Children's Law Reform Act*, R.S.O. 1990, c. C.12
*Estate Administration Tax Act*, S.O. 1998, c. 34
*Estates Act*, R.S.O. 1990, c. E.21
*Estates Administration Act*, R.S.O. 1990, c. E.22
*Family Law Act*, R.S.O. 1990, c. F.3
*Health Care Consent Act, 1996*, S.O. 1996, c. 2
*Insurance Act*, R.S.O. 1990, c. I.8
*Ontario Disability Support Program Act, 1997*, S.O. 1997, c. 25, Schedule B
    Administration and Cost Sharing, O. Reg. 225/98
    Assistance for Children with Severe Disabilities, O. Reg. 224/98
    Employment Supports, O. Reg. 223/98
    General, O. Reg. 222/98
    Prescribed Policy Statements, O. Reg. 562/05
*Pension Benefits Act*, R.S.O. 1990, c. P.8
*Perpetuities Act*, R.S.O. 1990, c. P.9

*Powers of Attorney Act*, R.S.O. 1990, c. P.20
*Substitute Decisions Act, 1992*, S.O. 1992, c. 30
*Succession Law Reform Act*, R.S.O. 1990, c. S.26
*Trustee Act*, R.S.O. 1990, c. T.23

## Prince Edward Island

*Age of Majority Act*, R.S.P.E.I. 1988, c. A-8
*Commorientes Act*, R.S.P.E.I. 1988, c. C-12
*Consent to Treatment and Health Care Directives Act*, R.S.P.E.I. 1988, c. C-17.2
*Dependants of Deceased Person Relief Act*, R.S.P.E.I. 1988, c. D-7
*Designation of Beneficiaries Under Benefit Plans Act*, R.S.P.E.I. 1988, c. D-9
*Family Law Act*, R.S.P.E.I. 1988, c. F-2.1
*Insurance Act*, R.S.P.E.I. 1988, c. I-4
*Perpetuities Act*, R.S.P.E.I. 1988, c. P-3
*Powers of Attorney Act*, R.S.P.E.I. 1988, c. P-16
*Probate Act*, R.S.P.E.I. 1988, c. P-21
*Social Assistance Regulations*, R.S.P.E.I. 1988, c. S-4.3
*Trustee Act*, R.S.P.E.I. 1988, c. T-8

## Quebec

*Civil Code of Quebec*, R.S.Q., c. C-1991
*An Act Respecting the Quebec Pension Plan*, R.S.Q., c. R-9

## Saskatchewan

*The Administration of Estates Act*, S.S. 1998, c. A-4.1
*The Age of Majority Act*, R.S.S. 1978, c. A-6
*The Children's Law Act, 1997*, S.S. 1997, c. C-8.2
*The Dependants' Relief Act, 1996*, S.S. 1996, c. D-25.01
*The Family Maintenance Act, 1997*, S.S. 1997, c. F-6.2
*The Family Property Act*, S.S. 1997, c.F-6.3
*The Health Care Directives and Substitute Health Care Decision Makers Act*, S.S. 1997, c. H-0.001
*The Homesteads Act, 1989*, S.S. 1989-90, c. H-5.1
*The Intestate Succession Act, 1996*, S.S. 1996, c. I-13.1
*The Parents' Maintenance Act*, R.S.S. 1978, c. P-1
*The Pension Benefits Act, 1992*, S.S. 1992, c. P-6.001
*The Powers of Attorney Act, 2002*, S.S. 2002, c. P-20.3
*The Public Guardian and Trustee Act*, S.S. 1983, c. P-36.3
*The Registered Plan (Retirement Income) Exemption Act*, S.S. 2002, c. R-13.01
*The Saskatchewan Assistance Regulations*, S.R. 78/66
*The Saskatchewan Insurance Act*, R.S.S. 1978, c. S-26

*The Survivorship Act, 1993*, S.S. 1993, c. S-67.1
*The Trustee Act*, R.S.S. 1978, c. T-23
*The Wills Act, 1996*, S.S. 1996, c. W-14.1

## Yukon Territory

*Age of Majority Act*, R.S.Y. 2002, c. 2
*Care Consent Act*, S.Y. 2003, c. 21, Sch. B
*Decision-Making Support and Protection to Adults Act*, S.Y. 2003, c. 21
*Dependant's Relief Act*, R.S.Y. 2002, c. 56
*Enduring Power of Attorney Act*, R.S.Y. 2002, c. 73
*Estate Administration Act*, R.S.Y. 2002, c. 77
*Family Property and Support Act*, R.S.Y. 2002, c. 83
*Insurance Act*, R.S.Y. 2002, c. 119
*Retirement Plan Beneficiaries Act*, R.S.Y. 2002, c. 197
*Social Assistance Act*, R.S.Y. 2002, c. 205
*Survivorship Act*, R.S.Y. 2002, c. 213
*Trustee Act*, R.S.Y. 2002, c. 223
*Wills Act*, R.S.Y. 2002, c. 230

# GOVERNMENT POLICIES

## Information Circulars

84-3R5 — Gifts to Certain Charitable Organizations Outside Canada
93-3R — Registered Education Savings Plans

## Interpretation Bulletins

IT-120R6 — Principal Residences
IT-447 — Residence of a Trust or Estate
IT-495R3 — Child Care Expenses
IT-513R — Personal Tax Credits
IT-519R2 — Medical Expense and Disability Tax Credits and Attendant Care Expense Deduction

# CASELAW

## British Columbia

*Einfield v. Bellrichard* (2001), 37 E.T.R. (2d) 34 (B.C. S.C.)
*George v. Else* (1958), 26 W.W.R. 229 (B.C. C.A.)
*Piskor v. Piskor* (1981), 27 BCLR 230 (C.A.)

## Manitoba

*Davids v. Balbon Estate,* [2001] M.J. No. 470 (Q.B.), upheld on appeal, [2002] M.J. No. 244 (C.A.)

## Ontario

*Albrecht v. Albrecht* (1989), 23 R.F.L. (3d) 8 (Ont. Dist. Ct.)
*Amherst Crane Rentals Ltd. v. Perring* (2005), 46 E.T.R. (2d) 1 (Ont. C.A.)
*Gaunt v. Woudenberg* (2005), 74 O.R. (3d) 665 (Ont. S.C.)
*Granovsky Estate v. Ontario* (1998), 156 D.L.R. (4th) 557 (Ont. Ct. Gen. Div.).
*Madsen Estate v. Saylor* [2007] 1 S.C.R. 838
*Pecore v. Pecore* [2007] 1 S.C.R. 795
*Radziwilko v. Seef Estate* (2003), 1 E.T.R. (3d) 81 (Ont. Div. Ct.)
*Stone v. Stone* (2001), 55 O.R. (3d) 491 (Ont. C.A.)

## Saskatchewan

*DeRoche Estate* (1964), 51 W.W.R. 120 (Sask. Q.B.).

# PUBLICATIONS

Aird & Berlis, LLP, *Shareholders' Agreements — A Tax and Legal Guide*, 2nd ed. (CCH Canadian Limited, 2004)

Biscott, Lynn, *Retirement Planning Through Life Stages* (CCH Canadian Limited, 2000)

Blacklock, Jean, with Judy Miyashiro, and Susan Murphy, *Food for Thought — Bringing Estate Planning to Life* (John Wiley & Sons Canada Limited, 2001)

Cardy, Sandy, with Michael Fitzgerald, *The Cottage, the Spider Brooch, and the Second Wife — How to Overcome the Challenges of Estate Planning* (ECW Press, 2003)

Cardy, Sandy, *Tax Strategies for Financial Advisors* (Thomson Canada Limited, 2002)

Carter, Tom, *So You've Been Appointed Executor* (Self-Counsel Press, 2002)

CCH Canadian Limited, *Canadian Estate Planning Guide*, loose leaf service

Cestnick, Tim, *The Tax Freedom Zone*, annual (Penguin Canada)

Cestnick, Tim, *Winning the Tax Game*, annual (John Wiley & Sons Canada Limited)

Cochrane, Michael, *For Better or For Worse, The Canadian Guide to Marriage Contracts and Cohabitation Agreements* (John Wiley & Sons Canada Limited, 1999)

Cochrane, Michael, *Surviving Your Divorce, A Guide to Canadian Family Law* (John Wiley & Sons Canada Limited, 2002)

Cohen, Bruce and Brian Fitzgerald, *The Pension Puzzle — Your Complete Guide to Government Benefits, RRSPs, and Employer Plans* (John Wiley & Sons Canada Limited, 2002)

Cole & Partners, *The Tax Principles of Family Law*, annual (self-published)

Cuperfain, Joel and Florence Marino, *Canadian Taxation of Life Insurance — 2004* (Thomson Canada Limited, 2004)

Department of Finance, *Technical Advisory Committee Recommendations on Disability Tax Measures*, December 2004

Epstein, Philip M., Stephen M. Grant, and Gerald P. Sadvari, *Separation Agreement Annotated* (The Law Society of Upper Canada, 2002)

Fish, Barry and Les Kotzer, *The Family Fight — Planning to Avoid It* (Continental Atlantic Publications Inc., 2002)

Fithian, Scott, *Values-Based Estate Planning, A Step-by-Step Approach to Wealth Transfer for Professional Advisors* (John Wiley & Sons Inc., 2000)

Foster, Sandra, *Estate Planning Workbook — A Companion to You Can't Take It With You —* 2002 (John Wiley & Sons Canada Limited, 2002)

Foster, Sandra, *You Can't Take It With You, The Common Sense Guide to Estate Planning,* 4th ed. (John Wiley & Sons Canada Limited, 2002)

Frostiak, Larry and John Poyser, *Practitioner's Guide to Trusts, Estates and Trust Returns* (Thomson Canada Limited, 2005)

Gray, Douglas and John Budd, *The Canadian Guide to Will & Estate Planning,* 2nd ed. (McGraw-Hill Ryerson Limited, 2002)

Greenan, Jennifer A., *The Executor's Handbook,* 2nd ed. (CCH Canadian Limited, 2003)

Grimes, Paul with Susan Goldberg, *The Facts of Life — how to build wealth and protect your assets with life insurance,* 2nd ed. (John Wiley & Sons Canada Limited, 2003)

Haisman, Robert J. and Francis E. De Sena, *The Canadian Estate Planning Organizer — 2003* (self-published)

Hanson, Suzanne and Sandra Bussey, *Death of a Taxpayer* (CCH Canada Limited, 2005)

Harvey, Cameron, *The Law of Dependants' Relief in Canada* (Thomson Canada Limited, 1999)

Howlett, David A., *Estate Matters in Atlantic Canada* (Thomson Canada Limited, 1999)

Hull, Ian M., *Advising Families on Succession Planning: The High Price of Not Talking* (LexisNexis Butterworths, 2005)

Jacks, Evelyn, *Essential Tax Facts* (Knowledge Bureau Inc., 2005)

KPMG, *Tax Facts,* annual (self-published)

KPMG, *Tax Planning for You and Your Family,* annual (Thomson Canada Limited)

Lovett-Reid, Patricia with Donna Green, *Surprise! You're Wealthy — Every Woman's Guide to Financial Independence* (Key Porter Books Ltd., 2004)

Mott, John, *Tax Guide for Investment Advisors,* annual (Thomson Canada Limited)

Neeleman, Stanley D., Carla B. Garrity, and Mitchell A. Baris, *Estate Planning for the Healthy Wealthy Family* (Allworth Press, 2003)

O'Donnell, Jill, Graham McWaters and John A. Page, *The Canadian Retirement Guide; A Comprehensive Handbook on Aging, Retirement, Caregiving & Health, How to Plan and Pay for It* (Insomniac Press, 2004)

Olkovich, Edward, *The Complete Idiot's Guide to Estate Planning in Six Simple Steps for Canadians* (Pearson Education Canada Inc., 2000)

Ouellete, Laurie L., *A Practical Guide to Estates and Trusts* (CCH Canadian Limited, 2005)

Payne, Julien and Marilyn Payne, *Canadian Family Law* (Irwin Law Inc., 2001)

Paziuk, Timothy, *Professional Corporations — The Secret to Success* (Penfold Publishing, 2004)

PricewaterhouseCoopers, *Tax Rules for Family Law Practitioners*, annual (self-published)

Seltzer, Barry, *No One Should Have an Unplanned Death* (Prism Publishing Inc., 2000)

Shotwell, Barbara and Nancy Randolph Greenway, *Pass It On — A Practical Approach to the Fears and Facts of Planning Your Estate* (Hyperion, 2000)

Spenceley, Robert, *The Estate Planner's Handbook — 2005* (CCH Canadian Limited, 2005)

Spenceley, Robert, *Probate Planning Through Will Substitutes* (CCH Canadian Limited, 2000)

Stephens, Glenn, *Estate Planning With Life Insurance*, 3rd ed. (CCH Canadian Limited, 2005)

Theriault, Carmen, *Widdifield on Executors and Trustees*, 6th ed. (Thomson Carswell Limited, 2004)

Wark, Kevin, *Everything You Need to Know About Estate Planning* (Key Porter Books Limited, 2001)

# Index

## C

## D

# E

## F



## G



## H

## I



## J



## L

## R

## S

## T

## U



## V



## W